Shaping the City

SHAPING THE CITY

NEW YORK AND THE MUNICIPAL ART SOCIETY

By Gregory F. Gilmartin

CLARKSON POTTER/PUBLISHERS
NEW YORK

Published by Clarkson N. Potter, Inc., 201 East 50th Street, New York, New York 10022. Member of the Crown Publishing Group.

Random House, Inc. New York, Toronto, London, Sydney, Auckland

CLARKSON N. POTTER, POTTER, and colophon are trademarks of Clarkson N. Potter, Inc.

Manufactured in the United States of America

Design by Howard Klein

Library of Congress Cataloging-in-Publication Data

Gilmartin, Gregory.
    Shaping the city: New York and the Municipal Art Society / by Gregory F. Gilmartin.—1st ed.
    Includes bibliographical references.
    1. Municipal Art Society of New York—History.   2. Urban beautification—New York (N.Y.)—History.   3. City planning—New York (N.Y.)—Citizen participation—History. 4. Historic sites—New York (N.Y.)—Conservation and restoration—History. 5. Historic buildings—New York (N.Y.)—Conservation and restoration—History. 6. Municipal government—New York (N.Y.)—History. 7. New York (N.Y.)—Buildings, structures, etc. I. Title.
NA9127.N5G56   1994
709′.747′1—dc20

94-19398
CIP

ISBN 0-517-58574-X

10 9 8 7 6 5 4 3 2 1

First Edition

Acknowledgments

THIS BOOK WAS commissioned by the Municipal Art Society, but MAS assumed no editorial control over its contents; this is certainly an authorized history, but not an official one. If readers wish to quarrel with it, they have only me to blame.

All the photographic research was done by Nora Prentice. The manuscript was largely typed by Cassandra Bowen O'Neal and Peter Durwood. I'm grateful to Paul Gunther for coming up with the idea of a book, to Brendan Gill for encouraging it, to Dee Kilmartin for her constant support, and to all the people who granted me interviews. I owe a special thanks to Barea Lamb Seeley, who gave me access to the archives of her grandfather, Charles Rollinson Lamb. My own family lent me a good deal of financial support, and Peter Pennoyer gave me the precious gift of free office space.

Finally, this book would never have appeared but for the heroic patience of my publisher. My thanks to Roy Finamore and to Shirley Wohl.

The Municipal Art Society would also like to thank the National Endowment for the Arts, the New York State Council for the Arts, and the Andy Warhol Foundation for their generous support of this book.

CONTENTS

FOREWORD

TURNABOUT IS FAIR but uncomfortable play. Civic groups like the Municipal Art Society are accustomed to raising questions, not having to answer them. The society—operating under a veil of piety, the protective cover of powerlessness, and the previously unrecognized advantage of an incomprehensible name—has generally been spared the critical scrutiny accorded political candidates, mega-developers, and rock stars. Such celebrities may sometimes be treated unfairly, but they have, after all, gotten what they bargained for by relentlessly seeking attention with press releases and photo opportunities. Now, the Municipal Art Society has gotten, I suppose, what it may deserve for having decided in the euphoria of a hundredth birthday to commission what it assumed would be a largely complimentary history by an independent author.

Gregory Gilmartin has done an admirable job of rifling through ancient files, uncovering heretofore unknown sources, and making coherent the complex and fascinating story of how modern New York was shaped. Unhappily, along the way, Mr. Gilmartin reveals that many civic-minded shapers are as capable of outsized ego, petty jealousy, and downright foolishness as the powerful villains they have thwarted. In one volume, MAS has been carried from the safe shadows of obscurity only to be denied sainthood.

Yet for all the book dismays, it does not disappoint. Its real value is to present, as it does so effectively, the unmistakable evidence gathered over many decades that the involvement of citizens—even in a city as tough as New York—makes a critical difference. Today, our cities, our towns, our rural landscapes are under assault as never before. We hope the examples set forth in these pages will encourage others to step in, for there is more at stake in the battles just ahead than in any we have won or lost.

Kent Barwick
January 1995

INTRODUCTION

IF YOU ASKED a cross section of New Yorkers about the Municipal Art Society, the vast majority would surely greet you with a blank stare of confusion. Some might grow peculiarly suspicious—hearing the words "municipal" and "art" has that effect on people—while others would hazard that the society must be some obscure city agency. Only a relative handful of New Yorkers could summon up a few stray facts about the organization: that it's a private civic group involved in historic preservation (among other things), or that it has waged this or that battle over the fate of Grand Central Terminal or the Penn Yards site or Columbus Circle. If your survey roped in historians, you might also hear some details of the Municipal Art Society's early days: it started out as a quaint group of Beaux Arts aesthetes, they would tell you, who erected a few monuments at the turn of the century and were foolish enough to dream that New York might one day be a City Beautiful.

There is much more to MAS's history, however, than these spotty memories suggest. It's true that the Municipal Art Society was founded in 1893 by a band of rather innocent artists, and at first its mission was simply to paint murals and carve monuments for New York's public spaces: hence the phrase "municipal art." But since the turn of the century, MAS has been a voice of civic conscience in the great public debates over the plan of the city, the design of its municipal buildings, parks and monuments, the preservation of its landmarks and historic districts, and the public responsibilities of private developers. MAS has struggled against political expediency, bureaucratic inertia, and corporate greed in an attempt to make New York a more livable city. Faced with such enemies, it has lost a great many battles; it has also made its share of disastrous mistakes.

Even if the Municipal Art Society had accomplished nothing concrete, a history of the society might well shed some fresh light on the politics and development of twentieth-century New York. But in fact, MAS has achieved a number of benefits for the public out of all proportion to its own size and resources. It managed to goad the city into drawing the first coherent scheme to link the five boroughs, it gave the early reform movement a constructive agenda for shaping a better city, it introduced the concept of setback zoning to New York, and it conceived and masterminded the campaign for a landmarks law. Three city agencies—the Art Commission, the City Planning Commission, and the Landmarks Preservation Commission—owe MAS at least a partial debt for their very existence. The fact that they do exist testifies to the Municipal Art Society's greatest achievement: it introduced the laissez-faire city to a new sense of civicism.

This book is meant in part to honor a long line of forgotten New Yorkers—artists, architects, planners, historians, lawyers, politicians, bureaucrats, reformers, gadflies, and eccentrics—who gave of their time and skills to make life in this city a richer, or at least a more tolerable, experience. There is an element of historical redress in this. We rightly credit our politicians for the laws they enact, the initiatives they proclaim, and the public works they dedicate, but such things rarely spring full-blown from a mayor's imagination. There are usually citizen advocates lurking somewhere in the background, and that is where this book will focus: on unfamiliar people like Albert Bard, the crotchety lawyer who spent fifty years laying the groundwork for the Landmarks Law of 1965; or on Charles Rollinson Lamb, the ecclesiastical decorator who started drawing setback skyscrapers nearly two decades before New York adopted the Zoning Resolution of 1916.

The Municipal Art Society's history is well populated with strange and brilliant figures—and with others far less scintillating as well—but perhaps the lesson to draw here is ultimately about the power and usefulness of civic groups in general. Too many New Yorkers still assume that the voting booth represents their only hope of effecting change, and that the choice of one candidate over another is the only available method of participating in the democratic process. A civic group like MAS, however, tries to shift the focus of political debate from candidates to specific issues. By reshaping the political landscape it can win concessions from candidates of any political stripe. Historically, MAS was often stymied by Tammany Hall and made real progress only when reform administrations took office. But when Tammany returned to power, that progress was never fully reversed; a Tammany mayor like George McClellan found that he had to build new parks simply because his predecessor, a reformer and a Municipalian, had already done so and the public now expected as much. The society's agenda slowly worked its way into Tammany's platforms, and the machine itself was, in a sense, reformed.

Finally, one hardly expects readers to approve of every position MAS has taken over the past hundred years, and some will surely object to the Society's basic premises. But critics might bear in mind the advice of Richard Welling, a Municipalian for more than thirty years. "You alone can do almost nothing," he wrote in his 1942 memoirs, "but if you ... belong to some group where you all have a common ideal there is almost nothing you cannot do."

ART OF THE PEOPLE, FOR THE PEOPLE

IN THE FALL of 1892 the best place to look for a New York artist was in Chicago. Taking shape on the shore of Lake Michigan was the "White City," the fairgrounds of the World's Columbian Exposition of 1893. It was unlike anything yet seen in America. At a time when the essence of American character was supposed to lie in "rugged individualism," when the economy was based on laissez-faire and Manhattan was turning into a ragged pincushion of towers, the artists and architects of New York had assembled in the Midwest to create a vision of Classical order.

The summons to Chicago was a source of deep satisfaction to them, for it seemed to recognize something they'd long believed. As Chauncey Depew, a New York politician, put it at the fair's opening, "New York stands to the rest of the continent as Florence did to Europe in the fifteenth century"—that is, as a beacon of enlightenment and the birthplace of a renaissance.[1] That theme kept resounding through the fair. It echoed in the dome of Richard Morris Hunt's Administration Building, the shape and silhouette of which echoed Brunelleschi's dome for the cathedral in Florence, the first great work of the Italian Renaissance. It was there in McKim, Mead & White's New York State Pavilion, a structure conspicuously unlike what any other state thought fitting. Its neighbors were the overgrown Colonial buildings of Massachusetts and Pennsylvania, but New York State was lodged in an immense structure patterned on the Villa Medici in Rome, a Florentine outpost in foreign territory and a building that had since become home to the French Academy, where artists and architects went to drink from the wellsprings of Western art.

"This is the greatest meeting of artists since the fifteenth century," exclaimed sculptor Augustus Saint-Gaudens after the first meeting held to plan the fairgrounds. He was thinking of figures like Frederick Law Olmsted, the designer of Central Park, who would lay out the White City's gardens and parks, its lagoon and Court of Honor; of Richard Morris Hunt, dean of American architects, who was charged with designing the fair's Administration Building; and of the younger architects whose buildings would line the lagoon: McKim, Mead & White, George Post, Carrère & Hastings, and Charles Atwood. Saint-Gaudens himself was recruiting the band of sculptors, led by Daniel Chester French, Frederick MacMonnies, and Karl Bitter, whose work would soften and animate the blazing white icebergs of architecture, and the painter F. D. Millet was sending telegrams to the muralists, among them Edwin Howland Blashfield, H. Siddons Mowbray, and Kenyon Cox, who would bring color, pattern, and symbolism to the vast lobbies and corridors of the fair's buildings.

Chicago, of course, had its own school of designers, but what set the New York artists apart was that they measured themselves by the academic standards of Paris or Rome. They were brought to Chicago to mark a defining moment in American history. By 1892 the frontier was closed, the railroads had knit the nation together for the first time, the natural resources of this immense body of land were feeding factories and blast furnaces on a scale never seen before. The White Fleet had put to sea, and its gleaming battleships hinted that the United States was ready to join in Europe's imperial games. America had come to see itself as the next world power in the march of history. Only in New York could one find a circle of artists who could translate that optimism into plaster and lath, who could lay claim to Europe's past, and who could present it to the public as something to be perfected on American shores. What they made was a Classical utopia of art and architecture, a cityscape more idealized than any of the Old World's imperial precincts. And they said to the public, "This is yours."

The public, by all accounts, was stunned. The Frenchman Paul Bourget described not only the "many merry faces" that poured through the fairgrounds but also the look of "that serious attention of minds imperfectly grasping new ideas." The critic Montgomery Schuyler dismissed the fair as the biggest magic show in history, but another, Mrs. Schuyler Van Rensselaer, gushed that "We have done it! . . . and without foreign help." Historian Henry Adams sank down on the steps of Hunt's Administration Building to ponder what it all meant and decided that, whatever the fair's message, it was "the first expression of American thought as a unity."[2] If the public was overwhelmed, the artists who made the fair were also transformed by the experience. The year 1892 marked the first time that they, as a class, had felt important. Few had ever worked for the public before, much less for the audience of two million that would pass through the fair's gates. Until now, the nation's greatest sculptors had lived by carving portraits of wealthy children, tombstones for the rich and famous, or the mantelpieces of Fifth Avenue châteaux. Muralists had prayed for the chance to paint cherubs on someone's breakfast room ceiling. Now they were working, in effect, for the federal government, charged with representing the nation in plaster, lath, and paint before the entire world. For the first time they were designing not just a building, a mural, or a sculpture but an entire environment, and they worked in a kind of dreamworld. The muralist Edwin Howland Blashfield remembered the fall of 1892 as one of "busy days and enchanted nights" when

The Fire Department allowed our ladies the privilege of setting off a false alarm and watching the splendid scramble of men and horses that ensued. . . . Wise professors from the Cosmos Club of Washington climbed our ladders and counseled us. . . . Visitors of every degree of distinction dropped in upon the workers. We messed with the Army and Navy; and it was decided mutually among the artists and the officers that there was a natural affinity between us, based upon the fact that "none of us expected ever to make any money!" Meantime, a bugle summoned us daily to our meals, and a barge calling at the foot of our ladders carried to their lunch architects, sculptors and painters, like so many Antonies and Cleopatras.[3]

In the winter, when their work was finished and the artists streamed home to New York, it must have struck them how barren of art were the city streets and how sickly the art scene. A very few sculptors—John Quincy Adams Ward, Augustus Saint-Gaudens, and Daniel Chester French—could count on a steady stream of public commissions, but no painter could say as much, for not one mural graced the halls of New York's public buildings. For most artists the question was, after Chicago, what? Go back to carving mantelpieces? To painting breakfast rooms? Or accept the notion that Chicago was, in Edwin Blashfield's words, "a colossal object lesson"?[4]

There were at least two lessons to be drawn from Chicago. For Daniel H. Burnham, the fair's architectural coordinator, the Columbian Exposition had opened the door to urban design: "Here a great truth, set forth by great artists was taught to all our people. This truth is the supreme one of the need of design and plan for whole cities." It took some years for Burnham's great truth to take hold of the arts community. For the moment, New York's artists drew a different conclusion: as the painter Will Low wrote, "Art of the people, for the people had come to us."[5]

PUBLIC ART had gotten off to a poor start in New York City. It took five days for the text of the Declaration of Independence to reach New York, but on July 9, 1776, New Yorkers celebrated the occasion by marching to Bowling Green, site of the city's first and only work of public art. It was an equestrian statue of George III imported from London six years earlier in a moment of "Tory pride and folly": four thousand pounds of gilded lead modeled by Joseph Wilton, the king's coachcarver, on the ancient Roman statue of Marcus Aurelius, the philosopher king. The crowd toppled the statue and, not yet satisfied, hacked it to bits. Some Tories rescued the head, grossly mutilated, and sent it to England as a symbol of Yankee savagery. The rest was melted down by patriots, and with grim efficiency *George III* was transformed into bullets.[6]

In the years to come, a people driven to revolution remained suspicious of anything that smacked of "official" art, and a city of merchants and seamen gloried in the practical, not the aesthetic. After the Revolution, New York produced great craftsmen, but few artists. It wasn't until 1856 that New York's second public sculpture finally appeared, at Union Square.

This was *George Washington,* a monumental bronze by Henry Kirke Brown and John Quincy Adams Ward. It was as if Brown and Ward were trying to lay the ghost of *George III* to rest: theirs was another equestrian statue, based again on Marcus Aurelius, and enclosed in a circular fence that suggested a miniature of Bowling Green. *George Washington* remained unique until after the Civil War.

In 1865 Richard Morris Hunt, the first American to study architecture at the École des Beaux Arts in Paris, published a set of designs for gateways to Central Park. They were pure examples of Beaux Arts taste, with great masses of allegorical sculpture—indeed the critic Russell Sturgis warned Hunt that there weren't enough sculptors in America to carve them all. In later years Hunt's gateways were hailed as the beginning of the municipal art movement, but at the time they were denounced by the critic Clarence Cook as "un-American." Cook wrote, "We don't like to be reminded of the existence of such riff-raff as the French emperor."[7] Hunt's designs opened the floodgates, however. In 1873 the Park Commission noted with some alarm that it had received requests to place more than twenty statues in Central Park.[8] The pace increased in the 1880s. The Victorians worshiped heroes and wanted to honor them; the immigrant communities, newly assertive, were eager to celebrate their homelands' contributions to Western culture; the Civil War dead cried out for commemoration.

Still, when the Chicago fair opened in 1893, New York could boast few great monuments. The Statue of Liberty rose from the harbor waters, a gift of the French people, and there was the Admiral Farragut memorial by Augustus Saint-Gaudens and Stanford White. White had just finished building the Washington Memorial Arch, but its sculpture wasn't installed until the 1910s. The Soldiers' and Sailors' Memorial Arch in Brooklyn's Grand Army Plaza was still equally bare of sculpture, though construction had begun in 1889.

The typical Victorian monument, however, was a lone figure standing on a tall pedestal, placed almost randomly somewhere in a city park. Most were the work of artists with little or no formal training. The most ambitious was Thomas Ball's colossal *Daniel Webster,* in Central Park; the worst, by common consent, was the Samuel Sullivan Cox Memorial in Astor Place. (It was later moved to a less conspicuous site in Tompkins Square.) Cox was a congressman whose most signal achievement was to obtain a pay raise for postal workers. The mailmen were grateful, but they did Cox no honor with this sculpture. Cox stands rigid on a pedestal, with one arm pointing straight up and the other straight down. Alas, the arms are of very different lengths.

In Chicago art had celebrated communal ideals, not the petty achievements of obscure congressmen. It had been entrusted to a select band of sculptors and painters trained in composition and design, and instead of being dropped helter-skelter in a verdant landscape, it had been conceived as part of a larger whole, an integral element of the cityscape. In 1893 New York's artists decided to bring this approach to public art to their hometown.

THE MURALIST Edwin Blashfield had just returned from Chicago when, early in 1893, the artist William Vanderbilt Allen paid him a visit. As Blashfield remembered, "Allen said to me, 'I have an idea.' We must form a society, the annual dues of which shall be devoted to buying each year a picture or piece of sculpture for the city; and I want Mrs. Blashfield and you to write a paper encouraging such a movement."[9] If the Municipal Art Society was Allen's idea, it was to be Mrs. Blashfield's achievement. Brilliant and beautiful, Evangeline Blashfield was a writer and a feminist, and her home was the closest thing New York had to a salon. She was one of the few people to get along with everyone in the New York art world, from the "dignified and sincere" survivors of the Hudson River School to the class of "young men fresh from the banks of Seine and Isar,"[10] and these antagonistic camps rubbed shoulders in the Blashfield apartment for the sake of meeting her friends from the stage—she was close to James Hackett and Ellen Terry. She also saw the potential in Allen's idea. As she put it in an 1895 speech:

> Our learning and our history and our art are shut up under glass, behind bolted doors, in private houses, in museums and libraries. They must be brought out into the open air, into the sunlit street, made living and dramatic and human pro bono publico. Above all, we want to increase the sum of our pleasures, to teach the ignorant through its direct appeal to the eye, to create and stimulate patriotism, to educate our masses, to ennoble our civic life.
>
> The strongest appeal that can be made for municipal art is that it is a municipal educator. And have we no greatness to celebrate? Ah! It is not the great men we lack; it is the country, which is ingrateful.[11]

Evangeline Blashfield convinced her husband that Allen's idea was "worth trying" and she became the Municipal Art Society's "most influential promoter." She provided it with a motto—"To make us love our city, we should make our city lovely"—and persuaded her friends to crowd into Allen's studio on the night of March 22, 1893.[12] There they heard Edwin Blashfield deliver his "Plea for Municipal Art." Chicago, Blashfield argued, was an inspiration to artists and the public alike.

> New York must wish that some buildings should be translated into enduring stone. . . . New York, more enterprising than any other city, rich, prosperous, generous and proud . . . of her greatness, is yet far behind not only Paris and London, but even tiny provincial towns of France, Italy, Germany, in the possession of an art which should dignify and illustrate the history of her past and present.

May not we, as a league for the promotion of municipal art, stand at the beginning of a movement in which architecture, sculpture, painting, crystallized together as one immense factor, may be enlisted in the City's service[?][13]

Blashfield called on his audience to join him in founding the Municipal Art Society, an organization dedicated to providing the public buildings and spaces of New York with "adequate sculptural and pictorial decoration." The idea was to find two thousand members, each paying $5 a year in dues, or $100 for a life membership. With $10,000 in income MAS could give the city an annual gift of a mural, a fountain, or a monument. The artists would be chosen by competition to ensure that the city received only the very best efforts of the art community. Most of those present signed up then and there, among them two of the most influential figures in the New York art world: Richard Watson Gilder, editor of *The Century* magazine, and Richard Morris Hunt, who agreed to become the society's first president. Within a month bylaws were drafted and a board of nineteen directors assembled. One ex officio place was reserved for the mayor. (None has ever participated, but the provision remains as a harmless way to compliment a new mayor, and it lends the society a certain fictitious authority.) Hunt reigned over the first board as president; William A. Coffin and Vanderbilt Allen as vice presidents; Hamilton Bell served as secretary; Cyrus Lawrence as treasurer; and J. H. Ward as counsel. The other seats were divided equally among sculptors, painters, architects, and "laymen": painters Edwin Blashfield, Will Low, and George W. Maynard; sculptors J.Q.A. Ward, Augustus Saint-Gaudens, and Olin Warner; architects E. H. Kendall, Henry J. Hardenbergh, and Edward Bigelow; and three "art amateurs," William T. Evans, J. Armstrong Chambers, and Perry Belmont. Two hundred members had already signed on, most of them artists, and the Municipal Art Society had embarked on a wider search for members from the ranks of connoisseurs and patrons of art.[14]

A certain tension inherent in the mingling of artists and laymen became obvious as soon as MAS first pondered exactly how it should operate. Who would judge its competitions? The board of directors suggested forming juries dominated by professional artists, but when this idea was first broached at a public meeting in the borrowed hall of the Architectural League, the members rebelled. Many had imagined MAS as a little model democracy, like a New England town meeting, or Act-Up, and demanded that the entire membership take part in awarding prizes. That meeting broke up in confusion, with no vote taken; a month later the artists won the day (they may have taken care to show up in full force), and established the principle that their work would be judged by fellow artists. This seemed eminently reasonable, but perhaps it was a mistake. MAS was soon plagued by complaints that it gave its members nothing to do aside from paying their dues and attending an annual meeting.

The Municipal Art Society realized that it had better introduce itself to Mayor Thomas F. Gilroy, so Will Low and E. H. Kendall, who was also the president of the American Institute of Architects, led a delegation to City Hall in April 1893. Theirs was a delicate task, since Gilroy was a scion of Tammany Hall, the most notorious political machine in the country and one whose power lay in the immigrant masses of the Lower East Side. Without a word being said, Gilroy would have known that the middle-class, mostly native-born and Protestant members of the Municipal Art Society had voted for someone else in the last election, yet here they were asking to plant sculpture and paint murals in public buildings. Will Low assured the mayor that he need fear no Trojan horses: the Municipal Art Society was a "wholly artistic body," he said. "It disclaims any political party spirit, and the subjects chosen by it for celebration will be of national or civic interest, without distinction of partisan, racial, or sectarian spirit."[15] Kendall added that MAS hoped to improve the aesthetic standards of the city's monuments, and the mayor admitted that he'd received many complaints about ugly statues in the city parks. Gilroy thanked the society for its public spirit, and promised his cooperation. It would have been churlish to refuse. As the *Times* put it, MAS was

> the first attempt to bring decorative art in painting to bear on the adornment of halls to which the public have access. . . . The difference between the New York movement and that which is going on in Europe is . . . material, and springs from the purer form which democracy assumes here. . . . The costs of such decoration are not to be charged to the taxpayers, but will be met by those citizens sufficiently alive to the honor of their town to combine and present their fellow-citizens outright with objects of the fine arts. Favoritism is thus reduced to a minimum; jobbery is excluded and taxpayers who care little for art are stopped from growling. The work is done by men and women who prove the sincerity of their love for the arts by that argument, irrefutable, which consists in putting their hands in their own pockets instead of in the City Treasury.[16]

A year passed before MAS was able to announce its first commission. The society didn't have much money on hand, but it had to do something to attract more members, and so decided to install a set of murals in the new Criminal Courts Building on Centre Street. Edward Simmons won the competition for three panels: *Justice* flanked by the *Fates* and *Liberty*. They are arrestings images, for Simmons chucked aside much of the stale iconography traditional to his themes. The Fates are usually three old crones spinning in the gloom, but Simmons's canvas is radiant, and there are four women—five, if one counts the skull. They trace an idealized cycle of life, from infancy to youth (rapturous, she puts away her spinning as if to suggest that nothing is preordained in the land of opportunity), maturity, wisdom, and death. *Justice* is no less remarkable. She stands before temple doors like the deus ex machina in a Greek play, come to resolve the tangled affairs of humankind, but she's draped in the Stars and Stripes. This is clearly *American* Justice, though her crystal orb suggests that democracy will eventually triumph over all, and Simmons took care to stress that point in a city of immigrants. Cupids flutter into the canvas bearing the seal of New York, and two boyish attendants offer Justice a sword and a dove, but she wears no blindfold. Instead, she confronts the viewer with a commanding, omniscient gaze which suggests that the guilty cannot hide and the innocent need not fear.

The *Times* wrote that Simmons's murals would "keep before the poorest and most indifferent citizens several things which cannot be too frequently presented to their eyes. One is that New York is a great city with an illustrious past, a city to be loved, taken pride in, and guarded from despoilers within and without. Another is that New York contains many thousands of people who are not blind to the higher needs of the mass of citizens less energetic or less fortunate than themselves. The bitterness of poverty and disappointment is sweetened a little by signs of interest in, signs of respect for, the great mass of toilers."[17] There's no proof that convicts ever felt that their lot was sweetened by these murals, nor can one guarantee that the justice dispensed below them lives up to Simmons's ideal figure. But the paintings, which were moved in 1941 to a new Criminal Courts Building at 100 Centre Street (the Art Deco "Tombs," designed by Harvey Wiley Corbett), still convey a certain solemnity: looming over the routine workings of the justice system, piercing the boredom, are these monumental reminders of the weightiness of the law. Perhaps the effect was stronger when *Justice* was new. Arnold Brunner, architect and Municipalian, once told an audience in Boston that "in our daily lives we have underestimated the influence that our backgrounds, our scenery, exert on us," and he offered this as an example:

> Some years ago I had occasion to visit a court room in New York. Men kept on their hats, whistled and laughed. Large brass spittoons were numerous, but though necessary, were copiously disregarded. A noisy lady who sold apples was garrulous and apparently very popular. The general atmosphere was most disorderly and the attendants had difficulty in securing silence at the entrance of the judge.
>
> A few years later I visited the same court room and was astonished to find all this changed. Men removed their hats when they entered, and talked in low tones. The apple lady remained in the corridor and an air of dignity and decency prevailed. The reason ... was that the eastern wall had been covered by a mural painting of great beauty.... The picture made its appeal and the appeal was instantly answered.[18]

Richard Morris Hunt died in 1895, and the Municipal Art Society decided to honor its first president with its second gift to the city. At first it hoped to erect one of Hunt's 1865 designs for gateways to Central Park, but since these were too elaborate for the society's bank account, it settled on a more modest memorial to the man himself. In a sense this was a regrettable choice, for the memorial was a tad parochial. Whereas *Justice* might speak to all the unfortunate souls—not a large segment of the population, but presumably a varied one—who had occasion to find themselves in that particular courtroom, the Hunt Memorial, infinitely more conspicuous, was at the same time more obscure in subject matter: even at the height of his fame, Hunt's name meant little to the average New Yorker. It meant a great deal, however, to members of the Municipal Art Society. Hunt had been more of a figurehead than a president to the society, and this was just as well, as he wasn't a pleasant person. Even Henry Marquand, who built two houses by Hunt and persuaded the trustees of the Metropolitan Museum to hire him as their architect, admitted that he disliked the man. But many Municipalians owed him a personal debt. He'd discovered Karl Bitter, for instance, and had taught George Post; he'd given commissions to Saint-Gaudens, Low, Maynard, La Farge, and many others. And he was, indisputably, the father of America's Classical Revival. Hunt, as noted earlier, had been the first American to study architecture at the École des Beaux Arts in Paris, and by the time he died almost every ambitious architecture student was following in his footsteps, if he could afford to. Hunt's role in American architecture was aptly symbolized at the Chicago fair, where his domed Administration Building lorded it over a Classical cityscape designed by a younger generation of followers. It was no less evident in New York, where the architect's châteaux, all of them vanished now, had transformed Fifth Avenue into "millionaire's row." The Ogden Mills house stood at Sixty-ninth Street; Henry Marquand's at Sixty-eighth; the double house of Mrs. William Astor and John Jacob Astor IV at Sixty-fifth; Mrs. Josephine Schmid's at Sixty-second; Elbridge Gerry's at Sixty-first. Facing the Plaza from Fifth Avenue and Fifty-eighth Street was the most famous mansion in New York, the Cornelius Vanderbilt II house, designed by Hunt and George Post and decorated by John La Farge, Augustus Saint-Gaudens, and Will Low. With these châteaux Hunt had taught America's rich a game of masquerade, of disguising themselves as European aristocrats, and designing the architectural costumes necessary for the sport had become the bread and butter of Beaux Arts architects and artists.

It was almost a given that the Hunt Memorial should be built on millionaire's row, and the Municipal Art Society chose a site on the edge of Central Park facing the only public structure Hunt had lived to build in New York: the Lenox Library, a neo-Grec design from 1870–1877. The commission for the memorial was awarded to architect Bruce Price, the designer of Tuxedo Park and the father of Emily Post, who succeeded Hunt as president of the society,[19] and to sculptor Daniel Chester French. Their design was meant as a model monument and was integrated into the streetscape. It grew out of the wall of Central Park, providing a welcome decorative accent to that monotonously long stretch of granite. Its bowed form answered the axis of the Lenox Library, in effect extending that building's courtyard across the avenue. Its architectural details were based on the library's neo-Grec vocabulary, though Price took care to give them a more delicate scale. And finally, with its two curved stone benches nestled in the shelter of a colonnade, the memorial even succeeded in contributing a touch of urban amenity to the streetscape.

French contributed a bust of the architect—looking, with his upturned mustache, every inch the stylish gentleman—and allegorical figures of Architecture and Painting and Sculpture. Architecture carries a model of Hunt's Administration Building at the Chicago fair; Painting and Sculpture clutches a mallet, a palette, brushes, and a little copy of one of the Elgin Marbles. In the floor of the monument French set a bas-relief, almost worn away now, with an allegory of Municipal Art: a woman enthroned, flanked by symbols of the arts—a bough of oak leaves (emblem of wisdom) and another of laurel (the mark of glory, distinction, and honor). This bas-relief became the Municipal Art Society's own symbol. To this day it adorns the society's letterhead, its newsletter, and the President's Medal, the society's highest award.

Just before his death, Richard Morris Hunt had produced a master plan for the Metropolitan Museum of Art, a vast scheme to encase the original Victorian buildings in Beaux Arts pomp.[20] In 1901 the Municipal Art Society turned its eyes toward the Great Hall of Hunt's museum, which was rising in Central Park under the supervision of Hunt & Hunt, his sons' firm, and George Post. Hunt had imagined a didactic museum: the building itself was supposed to provide a critical gloss on the collections. The Fifth Avenue facade was dominated by four pairs of immense columns, and these were meant to serve as the pedestals for sculptural groups representing the "four great periods of art": Egyptian, Greek, Renaissance, and Modern.[21] Between each pair of columns sat a niche where Hunt intended to set a copy of one great work of sculpture from each historical era. Hunt probably meant to carry on with this approach in the interior of the Great Hall. A cornice at the second-floor level was decorated with a series of plaques that were probably meant to bear the names of great artists, just as Beaux Arts libraries often sport a frieze listing the great authors. Rondels decorated the room's massive stone piers, and these were surely meant to receive decorative reliefs—portrait heads of great artists, perhaps. The Municipal Art Society assumed, probably correctly, that Hunt wanted to see the vaults, pendentives, and domes of the Great Hall painted, and probably the lunettes at either end of the room. Charles Barney, the society's new president, entered into negotiations with the museum's board, offering to organize a competition for these murals.[22] He must have had high hopes for the project; after all, two of the society's incorporators, sculptor J.Q.A. Ward and art collector Henry Marquand, sat on the Metropolitan's Board of Trustees—Marquand as its president. Marquand, however, was already enfeebled by age and illness, and would die within a year,[23] while Ward, as it turned out, had already persuaded the trustees to abandon, or at least postpone, carving the sculptures on the Fifth Avenue facade. As the president of the National Sculpture Society and a member of MAS, Ward should have been well disposed toward the idea, but as a trustee of the museum he was troubled by the idea of that fourth era of great art. "Modern Art," he complained, is "too undefined, too chaotic to be clearly represented in a group, or by any one great example."[24] With Marquand ill and Ward perplexed, MAS had to contend with General Louis P. di Cesnola, the museum's director. The general was openly contemptuous of American artists, complaining that they "have always considered our Museum to have been established for their own pecuniary benefit, a kind of market place where their works were to be sold at exorbitant prices and permanently exhibited as their professional advertisement."[25]

The Metropolitan Museum rejected the society's suggestion of murals. The trustees wouldn't risk the museum's reputation on a living artist, nor would they tie the building to a Beaux Arts interpretation of art history. What would people say in a hundred years? (One can imagine what Hilton Kramer would say.) So Hunt's masterpiece remained unfinished, and the Great Hall is but a ghost of Hunt's intentions. The domes and vaults, where one should find color, pattern, and scale, are rendered in an impersonal beige that mimics the cold stonework below. As if to make up for this sad defeat, the Municipal Art Society eventually found other ways to honor Hunt. His sons, Richard Howland Hunt and Joseph Howland Hunt, each in time became president of the Municipal Art Society. And Hunt's memory is still invoked at MAS: its annual meetings are called to order with the gentle rap of an ebony cane that belonged to Hunt and, long before him, to Benjamin Franklin. It would be nice to report that the cane had been passed down from president to president in an unbroken line, but in truth the practice dates only from the 1950s, when Whitney North Seymour became envious of the fact that the head of the Saint Nicholas Society got to wear a sporty tricorn hat that had belonged to Washington Irving. Seymour wanted something similar; Hunt's family came up with the cane, lending it to the society "until all of our type of buildings are replaced by glass skyscrapers."[26]

THE MUNICIPAL Art Society had no intention of actually paying for murals in the Metropolitan Museum. It had reorganized in 1898, once it became clear that the society didn't quite work as originally intended. The founders had hoped for a membership of two thousand, but only a few hundred people had joined, and their dues didn't provide enough income for MAS to fulfill its mission of annual commissions. For the Hunt Memorial, a much more ambitious project than Edward Simmons's courtroom murals, the society had resorted to dunning members of the city's other art societies, and their names are inscribed there along with that of MAS.* Part of the society's problem was internal. In 1893 Vanderbilt Allen and the Blashfields had imagined MAS as a society with dues, as if it were to be a club, but it resembled a club only in that candidates for membership were normally put up by board members. (Even later, when MAS resorted to mailings to drum up new members, the board composed the mailing list with some care.) Such exclusivity was

---

* They were the American Institute of Architects, the Architectural League, the National Sculpture Society, the Metropolitan Museum of Art, the Century Club, the Artist Artisans of New York, the National Academy of Design, the Society of American Artists, the American Water Color Society, and the Society of Beaux Arts Architects.

pointless, as no one was beating down the doors to join the society. Membership wasn't very enticing. There was no clubhouse, and no program of exhibits or social activities to keep people interested when MAS disappeared from public view, as it did between its rare unveiling ceremonies. There wasn't even a newsletter in those days. A more fundamental problem was that, outside the arts community, people had little interest in municipal art per se. Private patrons commemorated friends and family members, as in the melancholically beautiful Straus Fountain at 106th Street and Broadway, or left bequests to honor themselves, as in the Pulitzer Fountain at the Plaza. Ethnic and professional groups were eager to honor their particular heroes, and so New York has monuments to Beethoven, Thorvaldsen, Joan of Arc, Verdi . . . and Richard Morris Hunt. But there was a limited constituency for something as abstract as *Justice.*

In 1898, the year Greater New York was formed as the city of five boroughs, the Municipal Art Society elected its first lay president, Charles Barney, a banker and a client of Stanford White. The society incorporated and rewrote its bylaws in an attempt to save itself from withering away.* Its goal was still to supply "adequate sculptural and pictorial decoration" for the city's public buildings, and it still hoped to give the city new monuments whenever funds allowed, but now the society allowed itself another venue: it would hold competitions for artworks commissioned by and paid for by the city itself. Of course, this required the city's cooperation. The society was now an advocacy group trying to persuade the city to take a particular course of action, and with this shift Municipalians had to take on new, less pleasant tasks: begging the Board of Estimate for appropriations, and trying to justify the expense of public art to politicians who found here an easy and harmless way to demonstrate their fiscal probity. And there were more subtle difficulties. It was always hard, for example, to explain the difference between a mere stone-carver and an expensive artist, why competitive bidding was a poor way to choose an artist, and why a large sculptural program should be divided among several artists, so that each would have time to study his work.[27] The society managed to obtain just one appropriation: $10,000 for an allegorical painting on the ceiling of the Board of Aldermen's Chamber (now home to the City Council) in City Hall. But for some obscure reason the incoming Van Wyck administration never actually released the funds.

The Municipal Art Society was proving to be remarkably ineffective, but its members and officers were enjoying much more success by working through other organizations. When MAS was founded there was already a congeries of art societies in New York. The venerable National Academy of Design dated back to 1826. A new crop of art societies had been founded in the 1870s by the first generation of artists trained in Europe: the Society of American Artists (1877), the

---

* *The incorporation papers were signed by architects William Robert Ware, Henry Hardenbergh, Charles Barney, and Charles Lamb; the painters Edwin Blashfield, Walter Shirlaw, Kenyon Cox, George W. Maynard, and C. Y. Turner; sculptors Henry Adams and John Quincy Adams Ward; art collectors Henry Marquand and William T. Evans; and "first citizens" E. Hamilton Bell, A. W. Drake, Herbert Satterlee, and Thomas Tryon.*

Art Students League (1875), the Tile Club (1877), the New York Etching Club (1878), and the Society of Decorative Art (1877). The eighties brought the Architectural League (1881) and the Society of Painters in Pastel (1883). Columbia University opened its School of Architecture in 1883. The Society of Beaux Arts Architects sprang up in 1897, and the National Arts Club in 1899. The creation of MAS in 1893 had had its own ripple effect.* In May 1893, three months after it was founded, the sculptor Frederick Wellington Ruckstull and the art critic Charles de Kay summoned New York's sculptors to the Fencing Club and organized the National Sculpture Society. Ruckstull had long thought of forming such a group, but the founding of MAS acted as a catalyst: if MAS became a major patron of public art, the sculptors wanted to be sure that their interests were well represented.[28] Two years later Frederick Stymetz Lamb, a painter and stained-glass artist, organized the National Society of Mural Painters.

By the late 1890s, then, there was an elaborate network of art societies in New York. Working in concert, they could train artists and architects, exhibit their work, defend their legal and financial interests, help them find clients and, on occasion, public commissions. Most of these groups were identified with a particular medium, but they welcomed sympathetic laymen and artists of other persuasions. Their memberships overlapped to such a degree that the art societies resembled a single floating club of artists and architects who met one day at the National Sculpture Society, and the next at the Architectural League. Their board members and officers were drawn from a common pool of volunteers who moved from one organization to the next. Charles Rollinson Lamb, for instance, an original member of MAS and one of its incorporators, was at different points president of the Art Students League, vice president of the Architectural League and the National Sculpture Society, and president of the Municipal Art Society (from 1906 to 1908).

While MAS languished, the National Sculpture Society and the National Society of Mural Painters were thriving, as these two new groups proved to be the prime beneficiaries of the Municipal Art Society's propaganda. When city officials decided to incorporate public art into new buildings, as MAS demanded, they went to the professional societies for advice on how to proceed and whom to hire. The first triumph of the municipal art movement was the new Appellate Courthouse on Madison Square, at the corner of East Twenty-fifth Street. Bruce Price, president of MAS and a board member of the National Sculpture Society, convinced the judges in charge that the best way to convey the dignity of the law was through the medium of public art. Price also recommended an architect: James Brown Lord, the designer of Delmonico's. Lord returned the favor by inviting the Sculpture Society and the National Society of Mural Painters to collaborate with him, and it fell to these two organizations to create Blashfield's dream of a public building with "adequate sculptural and pictorial decoration." Like beauty, however, adequacy lies

---

* *This extended around the country. Cincinnati founded its own Municipal Art Society in 1894, and Cleveland, Chicago, and Baltimore followed suit in 1899.*

in the eye of the beholder, and Lord and his collaborators produced an excess of riches, overloading the courthouse with decorative sculpture. More than a quarter of the budget went to pay for sculpture, and the result was a building that looked exactly like a little piece of the 1893 Chicago fair, only with the original plaster and lath translated into glistening white marble. The entrance portico on Twenty-fifth Street was flanked by Ruckstull's *Wisdom* and *Force*; the pediment was filled with *The Triumph of the Law* by Charles Niehaus and crowned by *Justice, Power, and Study*, a group by Daniel Chester French. On the Madison Avenue facade were four caryatids by Thomas Shields Clarke representing the seasons and a group of three figures by Karl Bitter symbolizing peace. Single figures dotting the parapet honored historic law-givers: *Confucius* was carved by Philip Martiny; *Moses*, by William Couper; *Zoroaster*, by Edward C. Potter; *Alfred the Great*, by Jonathan Scott Hartley; *Lycurgus*, by George Bissell; *Solon*, by Herbert Adams; *Saint Louis* (Louis IX), by John Donoghue; *Manu* (the Indian lawgiver), by Augustus Lukeman; and *Justinian*, by Henry Kirke Bush-Brown.

The interior of the courthouse was the province of the mural painters H. Siddons Mowbray, Kenyon Cox, and Will Low, who provided yet more allegories. The symbolism of their paintings, like that of the sculpture outside, was much harder for the average citizen to puzzle out than was Edward Simmons's work in the Criminal Courts Building downtown. Today most people are probably satisfied to regard the murals as simply one element in an extraordinarily luxurious decor, more evocative of a robber baron's mansion, perhaps, than of a court of law.

The planning of the Appellate Courthouse was a unique situation. The state judges enjoyed a good deal of control over their own building, and since it was financed by the sale of bonds from the sinking fund, there were no bitter disputes before the Board of Estimate over the size of its budget or the necessity of public art. Everything happened behind the scenes. The city government refused to be so spendthrift with its own buildings, and the fact remained that public art in New York was almost always privately financed. The Municipal Art Society had hoped from the very beginning that its work would inspire private donors to come forth. But just as it wanted to encourage good art on the city streets, the society wanted to banish bad art, and MAS and its allies felt free to criticize the artworks private donors offered the city. They'd forgotten that nothing provokes bad feelings like looking a gift horse in the mouth. The National Sculpture Society discovered this in 1895, when it prevented the German American community from erecting a monument to Heinrich Heine in the Plaza at Fifth Avenue and Fifty-ninth Street.

The Heine Memorial was an emotionally charged issue for the city's German Americans. Many were refugees from the Revolution of 1848, and they looked upon the poet as a pillar of German liberalism, which had been so brutally suppressed by the Prussian military. They sprang into action when the Prussian government forbade erection of a Heinrich Heine memorial in Düsseldorf, his birthplace. Building one in New York would demonstrate that German liberalism still lived, at least in exile. So a committee was formed by the Arion Society, money was raised, a fountain commissioned from Ernst Herter, a fashionable Berlin sculptor, and the parks commissioner was asked to authorize its construction in the Plaza. Only then did the National Sculpture Society and its allies step forward to object.

The Sculpture Society saw no reason to consecrate the Plaza—"the most festal and decorative part of our mechanical and commonplace town"—to the memory of a German lyric poet whose work was barely known outside the immigrant community.[29] It also objected to the design of the monument itself. Not only was it wrong for the site, the sculptors argued, but it was bad in its own right: Herter's rococo style might suit the taste of Wilhelmine Germany, but it would never pass muster in the more enlightened artistic circles of Paris ... or New York. The sculptors thus succeeded in insulting German culture and German art. They were accused of ethnic prejudice, and at least one member—the architect and critic Russell Sturgis—was surely guilty; he suggested that the Arion Society place the fountain in Tompkins Square, where its "sauerkraut-eating countrymen lived."[30] Yet the sculptors could point to prominent Germans, like Karl Bitter, in their own ranks, while the founder of their society, Charles de Kay, was serving in Berlin at the moment as the American consul; de Kay had even translated a volume of Heine's letters. It was harder for the sculptors to answer the charge that they wanted to obtain the commission for one of their own—since, of course, they did. The parks commissioner was inclined to agree with the Sculpture Society, but before he could announce a final decision, the Arion Society withdrew its offer. The German Americans were clearly outraged, the situation had now become politically embarrassing, and the Board of Aldermen stepped in to offer a solution, which wasn't entirely satisfactory to anyone. The Heine Memorial was built over the sculptors' objections, but banished to a traffic circle at 167th Street and the Grand Concourse in the Bronx, where there was a substantial German American population. It has since been moved a few blocks away, to Joyce Kilmer Park.

With the Heine Memorial the art societies had made the mistake of waiting until a design was unveiled before getting involved, and it was inevitable that hard feelings would arise. They were more cunning when it came to the Soldiers' and Sailors' Memorial, authorized by the state legislature in 1892 as a belated tribute to the city's Civil War dead. Despite Albany's action, the city wasn't overly anxious to actually allocate its own funds for an expensive memorial, so no city agency acted on the law. Indeed none had clear-cut jurisdiction: there was neither a Cultural Affairs Department nor an Art Commission, and while the Park Commission was regarded as the city's "aesthetic department," that designation was purely unofficial. In 1893 the National Sculpture Society, an infant organization only a few months old, decided to raise a ruckus about the languishing project, which it naturally hoped would be a superb showcase for public sculpture. To protect the Sculpture Society from seeming opportunistic and greedy, the art societies assembled a committee of artists and architects to take up the cause. It was a sonorous group: Richard Morris Hunt, Daniel Chester French, Frederick Wellington Ruckstull,

John Quincy Adams Ward, Edwin Howland Blashfield, Charles de Kay, Charles Rollinson Lamb, Richard Watson Gilder, Bruce Price, and Montgomery Schuyler.[31] Though chosen by several art societies, they were all Municipalians. It was a small world.

The site this committee chose was none other than the Plaza. It failed to win an appropriation from the city, but in 1897, when another committee of private citizens began a fund-raising campaign, the artists staged a competition for the memorial. They chose a scheme by the architects Charles and Edward Stoughton, two brothers from a distinguished Bronx family, and the sculptor Frederick Mac-Monnies, a brilliantly facile student of Saint-Gaudens. They'd designed a tall column crowned by a figure of Victory and rising from a great pedestal crowded with sculpture. But the project was too expensive, and Karl Bitter objected that the column was ill suited to its site. The site was switched to Mount Tom, a beautiful outcrop in Riverside Park, but this choice encountered the stern opposition of Samuel Parsons, a great landscape architect and former associate of Calvert Vaux, who pointed out that the monument would obliterate the very landscape feature that made the place so attractive.[32] The artists were willing to fight Parsons, but plans were announced for an apartment building nearby, and it was feared that the monument would be less effective if it were dwarfed by a nearby building.[33] So the roving monument migrated again, settling at last at Riverside Drive and Eighty-ninth Street. The Stoughtons, now associated with architect Paul E. M. Duboy, redesigned their project for the new site, and what emerged from all this—no doubt to the intense disappointment of the Sculpture Society—was a superb monument with almost no sculpture at all. A tall circular shaft ringed by columns, it was patterned after antique tombs and the Monument of Lysicrates in Athens (though the Stoughtons were accused of plagiarizing the Temple of Vesta in Tivoli, and there was a brief investigation of the charge).[34] It commanded a series of terraces where commemorative ceremonies could be held, and at the southern end was a flagstaff that marked the axis of Eighty-ninth Street without blocking its vista.

The disputes over the Heine Memorial and the Soldiers' and Sailors' Memorial taught the art societies certain lessons. They'd formed an ad hoc committee of artists and architects to deal with the latter monument, and people paid attention to that group because it seemed to speak for the entire artistic community. It had also shielded the professional societies from charges of self-interest. In 1896 the Fine Arts Federation was founded to do "in a general way" what that committee had done "in a particular way."[35] It was a sort of congress of art societies, with each group electing delegates. It allowed the art societies to keep abreast of one another's activities, appeal to one another for help, debate policy (discreetly, which was important), and speak to the city authorities with a single voice.

The battle over the Heine Memorial remained troubling, however, especially because it was so typical of how works of public art came into being in New York: a private group went out and hired its own sculptor and then offered the work to the city; the art societies had no official standing in the matter, and their intervention was bitterly resented by the donors. The city, in turn, had no mechanism for judging the aesthetic merits of such works and handled the situation as a purely political problem. The Board of Aldermen had been faced with two contending groups—the donors and the critics—and there's no evidence that it ever tried to address the aesthetic or urban design issues that lay at the heart of the dispute. It merely wanted people to stop screaming at the city, and to satisfy both groups as best it could. Had the donors been more powerful, or Heine more popular, the Plaza would have been ruined; as it was, the Sculpture Society had to accept the fact that Herter's insipid creation was now on permanent display in the Bronx.

The only solution, as far as the art societies could see, was to infiltrate the city government.

THE AESTHETIC CENSOR: THE ART COMMISSION

"INSTEAD OF A Municipal Art Society without authority," asked the artist Candace Wheeler in 1895, "why should we not have a board of municipal art, composed, not of men whose early and respectable occupation was that of a hod-carrier, or whose later business is the sustainment of the grog-shops, but a board of men educated in all means of art—architects and painters and landscape gardeners, who should agree upon schemes of improvement, and be able to carry them out?" As Wheeler described it, the Board of Municipal Art would have powers of breathtaking scope, not just over public art and architecture but over private construction as well. "We are exerting ourselves separately and energetically for many different benefits which would be included in a board of municipal art. It would rightly touch the tenement house question," she told the Nineteenth Century Club, "and cooperate with the Board of Health and Department of Buildings. It would bring expert knowledge to bear upon public safety as well as artistic knowledge to bear upon improvements of public property, and it would put these interests in the hands of citizens sensitive to public obligations and to the reward of public honor."[1]

Wheeler was no stranger to ambitious projects. She was fifty years old when she took up a career in textile and wallpaper design, but this late start hadn't prevented her from becoming one of the great decorative artists of her day, and an associate of Louis Comfort Tiffany. (Her work survives in the Seventh Regiment Armory and in the Mark Twain House in Hartford, Connecticut.) She founded the Society of Decorative Artists and the Women's Exchange as part of a bold agenda: by fostering a craft revival among women, Wheeler hoped to offer them financial independence.[2] I doubt, however, that Wheeler understood just how ambitious an idea was her board of municipal art, or how many toes her proposal would step on. It would require politicians, of whom the art societies were openly contemptuous, to surrender a good deal of their power over shaping the city; force the political clubhouses to surrender one of their major sources of graft and empire building in the Buildings Department; threaten dozens upon dozens of patronage appointees; and enrage all those men who built and developed tenements, the everyday fabric of the city. The city wouldn't even entertain Wheeler's idea, and to this day no single city agency enjoys the powers she meant to invest in the board of municipal art. (Something like it was achieved in the 1940s and 1950s in the person of Robert Moses, but even he managed it only by holding a dozen jobs at once, and the experiment was disastrous.) But Wheeler had succeeded in outlining an agenda for turn-of-the-century New York, and the individual parts of her proposal were attacked one by one. The New Law on tenements was finally passed in 1901, the achievement not of the art societies but of groups like the Charity Organization Society and the journalist Jacob Riis. The city's insane building code would remain a matter of dispute for more than fifteen years. Creating a planning agency was a still more difficult task. In 1903 the Municipal Art Society succeeded in creating a temporary body, the New York City Improvement Commission, but New York didn't acquire a permanent City Planning Commission until Fiorello La Guardia revised the City Charter in 1938. For the moment, in the mid-1890s, the art societies concentrated on the easiest task, what Wheeler described as bringing "artistic knowledge to bear upon improvements of public property."

The members of the art societies saw themselves as the only group professionally and artistically qualified to assume control of shaping the city. Their preeminence had been recognized at the Chicago fair, and the federal government had turned the design of its public buildings over to the Beaux Artists; it now required that the architects of public buildings be chosen in competitions judged by architectural experts who were, naturally, Beaux Artists. Municipalians were transforming the interior of the Library of Congress in Washington, D.C., and even the nation's currency would be reshaped by Municipalians: Will Low designed a dollar note; Blashfield a two; Walter Shirlaw a five; and Kenyon Cox a one-hundred-dollar bill, while Augustus Saint-Gaudens designed ten- and twenty-dollar gold pieces and Adolph Weinman produced the Liberty dime.[3] Yet the municipal authorities of New York City remained blind to their achievements. Tammany Hall had a record of patronizing men with little or no formal training in design. They weren't really architects in the modern sense, but builders; they specialized in the construction of tenements and were often the developers of these buildings as well. The Beaux Arts architects found these men deeply offensive, partly because of the crude ethnic prejudice that casts such a pall over Wheeler's speech—the ugly resentment of the native-born toward uppity immigrants. But other issues came into play as well. The Beaux Artist insisted that architecture was a profession, building a trade, and that the two must never mix in the same person. At stake was an important social distinction (when calling on their clients, architects wanted to use the front door) and an ethical issue (part of an architect's job was to ensure that his client got good value from a builder, but if the designer and the contractor were one and the same person, there was nothing to stop him from cutting corners in construction).

The actual work of the architect-builders provoked an even more visceral disgust, however.

There was the matter of taste: the Beaux Artists lavished on their Tammany competitors all the contempt that old money typically heaps on nouveau-riche vulgarity. No Beaux Arts architect, for instance, could admire Thom, Wilson, and Schaarschmidt's Criminal Courts Building, where the Municipal Art Society had installed Edward Simmons's murals in 1894. If one wanted a symbol of the gulf between Tammany and Beaux Arts taste one had only to consider the decoration of the courthouse's atrium. With its tiers of arcades soaring up to a skylight, it was an undeniably dramatic space, but why was it decorated with all those big-busted sirens? A Municipalian would have been horrified by the meaninglessness of it all (he preferred turgid allegories that required a pamphlet to decipher, like the sculpture of the Appellate Courthouse), by the inartistic and mechanical repetition of this one motif over and over and over again, and especially, I suspect, by this more voluptuous canon of feminine beauty. Such details led the *Architectural Record* to describe the Criminal Courts Building as "upon the whole the most discreditable edifice the city has ever created. . . . The judges do not care about such things; the criminals dislike it, not because it is an ugly and vulgar building, but because it is a court of justice, and would dislike a better building quite as heartily; the criminal lawyers, if they be of the shyster class, doubtless like it from natural affinity."[4]

Taste, professional ethics, and the social standing of architects: these were essentially parochial matters, and had these represented the full extent of the dispute, the Beaux Arts architects would never have won much support outside the art societies. Political reformers took up their cause, however, because of questions about the technical competence and honesty of Tammany's protégés. These builders weren't just loyal Democrats: they had silent partners high up in the Tammany hierarchy. In return they received contracts for public works, and their private commissions were exempt from the usual levy of bribes paid to the Buildings Department. As the *Times* reported in 1901, "All sorts of companies have been incorporated to furnish building supplies or do work in connection with buildings, and have been put on the list as authorized to do work the approval of which was assured in advance. The revenues of these companies have come to the Tammany leaders, and those not favored, who offered better work at less price, have been unable to get authority to do it."[5]

New York paid a heavy price for this relationship. Costs were inflated to siphon off funds to Tammany, yet the city got little for its money. Tammany buildings had a reputation for not quite working in one way or another. The most notorious example was the old New York County Courthouse, built in the 1860s and known ever since as the Tweed Courthouse. Despite repeated renovations the building remained an environmental disaster: so poorly ventilated that it was always too hot or too cold, and it reeked of lavatories. The judges and clerks were convinced that they were being slowly poisoned. But the Criminal Courts Building, built thirty years later, proved that nothing had changed since Tweed's downfall; indeed, this new courthouse was an even more spectacular failure. It was built on sand, on what had once been the site of the Collect Pond, but the architects nevertheless used a bearing wall structure resting on wooden piles. This was effective only so long as the sand was undisturbed by any new excavations. When the subway was built through Lafayette Street in 1901 the sand shifted, the piles sank, and the massive walls of brick began to crack. By 1909 plaster was raining from courtroom ceilings while gas and water mains burst within the walls. Engineers pasted paper over cracks in the walls and watched as it was slowly torn in half; as the apertures widened they saw "the gleam of sunlight in the street outside."[6] Only fifteen years after it opened, the courthouse was evacuated as a threat to public safety.

The sordid history of New York's public works resulted, in 1898, in the creation of the Art Commission, a city agency whose apparently innocent task was to review the aesthetic merits of public art and architecture. The Art Commission owed its existence to John Merven Carrère, a Municipalian and a partner in the architectural firm of Carrère & Hastings, designers of the New York Public Library, the Frick mansion, the Manhattan Bridge, and dozens of other Beaux Arts masterpieces. These designs were still in the future, however. When Carrère brought the idea of an Art Commission to the Fine Arts Federation in 1896, he was still, at thirty-seven, a young architect poised on the brink of greatness. Carrère imagined a body that would issue design guidelines for municipal art and architecture and have the power to enforce these, if necessary, by issuing subpoenas to recalcitrant designers. The Fine Arts Federation gave Carrère its blessing and appointed a committee to help him see the Art Commission written into law.

Carrère had set himself a delicate political problem. By its very nature the Art Commission would sometimes have to be obstructionist. Sooner or later some mayor, annoyed that his plans had been thwarted or delayed, would seek to abolish the agency. Nor could the general public be trusted to rush to the Art Commission's defense: the very idea of an aesthetic tribunal might grate on the public's egalitarian instincts; cynics would ridicule any attempt to legislate beauty; others would question why the city should worry about aesthetics when it was so beset by crime and poverty and disease. When Carrère took up the cause of the Art Commission in 1896, New York City was still just Manhattan and part of the Bronx (the Annexed District, as it was called), but in two years' time Greater New York, the city of five boroughs, was scheduled to come into being, and a Charter Commission was already at work struggling to write the new city's municipal constitution. Carrère decided to take his idea not to the legislature but to the Charter Commission. Engrave the Art Commission in the city charter, and it would acquire a certain moral authority no piece of mere legislation could give it: the charter, after all, is supposed to describe the most basic functions and responsibilities of city government—never mind that this particular charter would turn out to be hundreds of pages long and full of contradictory passages. There was another advantage as well: amending a charter is a much more cumbersome and weighty matter than repealing a law. This in itself might be enough to protect the Art Commission from the pique of an angry mayor or the scalpel of a budget cutter. At the same time, the process is one where political insiders are more important than popular support, and as Carrère soon demonstrated, the art societies might not be popular, but they were certainly well connected.

Carrère credited two people with creating the Art Commission: Seth Low, a member of the Charter Commission who let Carrère present his case, and Elihu Root, for the eloquence of his testimony. What was said, however, may have been less important than who said it. Low and Root were both prominent good-government Republicans, as opposed to the machine Republicans who dominated the statehouse in Albany. Low was a former mayor of Brooklyn and hoped to become mayor of Greater New York in 1898 (he didn't succeed until 1902); Root, a famous corporation lawyer, was a major figure in the inner councils of the Republican national party.* Whether by design or accident, Carrère had succeeded in identifying the proposed Art Commission with a particular political faction. Normally this might have been disastrous, but the Charter Commission was intent on giving all factions at least some satisfaction, and the Republicans got an Art Commission—of sorts.

What emerged from the Charter Commission was but a mangled and sickly version of Carrère's original idea—"an instrument of more force for resisting evil than for doing good," as the *Times* put it.[7] There was no mention of design guidelines. The Art Commission was merely an "aesthetic tribunal,"[8] the *Times* said, charged with judging the aesthetic merits of any artwork commissioned by or donated to the city. These the Art Commission could accept or reject, but it couldn't look at designs for public buildings unless the mayor or the Board of Aldermen asked for its advice. If the Art Commission had little power, the art societies were nonetheless overjoyed with one detail: how its members were chosen. It had ten members, none of them paid. The mayor and the presidents of the Metropolitan Museum, the New York Public Library, and the Brooklyn Institute of Arts and Sciences all served ex officio; in practice few mayors have bothered to attend meetings, however, and some of the other ex officio members have designated proxies. Of the other six places, three were reserved for artists—a painter, a sculptor, and an architect—and three for laymen. These six were appointed by the mayor from a list submitted by the Fine Arts Federation. Three candidates had to be submitted for each vacancy, but even so, the federation effectively controlled the makeup of the commission. This was a boon to the prestige of the Fine Arts Federation. It also guaranteed that public art, at least, would have to conform to Beaux Arts standards, and given the social and political complexion of the

---

* Root figures in architectural history for building a mansion by Carrère at Park Avenue and Seventy-first Street in 1903 and for abandoning that house in 1912 to take an apartment, at cut-rate rent, in 998 Fifth Avenue, the majestic Italian Renaissance apartment building by McKim, Mead & White. Root's example is said to have broken the old New York prejudice that the rich shouldn't live in apartments. He helped doom the palazzi and châteaux of Fifth Avenue, most of which were soon replaced by extravagantly appointed apartment buildings.

art societies, it ensured that the Art Commission would, for the time being, be a reform body.

The honor of appointing the first Art Commission fell to Tammany Mayor Robert Van Wyck, who was described by one Municipalian as "arrogant, inefficient, having done the city absolutely not a particle of good, and having a natural tendency to pervert the purposes of the administration and debase the morals of the community."[9] Nevertheless, it was "a very good commission," the *Times* wrote, "an achievement which may be attenuated by the fact that according to the charter . . . [the mayor] could not have appointed a very bad one."[10] Yet the mayor wasn't eager to hear the Art Commission's advice. Not once in four years of office did Van Wyck refer a building's design to the Art Commission. Its members were left to deal with purely artistic works, and these numbered no more than six a year.

The Art Commission's powers were picayune, but it was a toehold that the art societies would widen and deepen over the years. The Fine Arts Federation mounted a campaign to broaden the commission's power as early as 1898, and Mayor Van Wyck seemed determined to prove the art societies' point that the Art Commission should monitor the designs of city buildings and the proposed East River bridges. Van Wyck created a new position in city government, that of city architect, and appointed the partnership of Horgan & Slattery. The *Times* described the two architects as "a pair of obscure insolvents." At the time, they were defending themselves in a lawsuit that charged them with "something like fraudulent bankruptcy."[11] They lost the suit.

Horgan & Slattery's architectural practice had been limited to Old Law tenements, hardly a good training ground for dealing with all the programmatic, technical, and iconographic complexities of great public structures. Yet Van Wyck gave them the chance to design almost everything the city built: courthouses, prisons, fire stations, armories—even garbage scows. In a way, they did their best. They tried hard to ape the new Beaux Arts fashions,[12] but the real Beaux Artists merely jeered at their solecisms, and the *Times* bitterly complained that the firm inflated costs and funneled kickbacks to one John F. Carroll, a figure in Tammany Hall and a close friend of Boss Richard Croker.

While Horgan & Slattery reigned over municipal architecture, Van Wyck's Bridge Department drafted plans for the Williamsburg, Manhattan, and Queensboro bridges. This was an immensely ambitious campaign to link the new boroughs, but the art societies were appalled by the designs. They were the work of Leffert Buck, chief engineer of the Bridge Department and an erstwhile assistant to the Roeblings during construction of the Brooklyn Bridge. None of the Roeblings' aesthetic sense had rubbed off on Buck, however. His designs were utterly utilitarian—"A surrender," John De Witt Warner wrote, "of the City Beautiful to the City Vulgar."[13] The Fine Arts Federation pleaded with the city to use "only the best architectural talent" on the Williamsburg.[14]

Luckily the city charter had proved so unworkable by 1901 that a Charter Reform Commission was appointed, and the art societies managed to insert a clause granting the Art Commission the right to veto the design of any public work costing more than a million dollars. This was more limited than it sounds: a public bath, a recreation pier, a park shelter, a police station—all cost much less than a million dollars in those days. The new bridges, however, would cost many millions. This new clause took effect in 1902, when, by coincidence, Seth Low took his oath of office as mayor of New York. Low had been the Art Commission's original champion in 1896, and he'd been so touched then by Carrère's arguments for public art that he joined the Municipal Art Society. On taking office, Low promised to refer all public works, no matter how utilitarian or trivial, to the Art Commission. In so doing, he ushered in the golden age of municipal architecture in New York. It would be burnished by Low's paradoxical successor, George McClellan. A product of the Tammany machine but a true aesthete, McClellan was the only mayor in New York's history to describe the Art Commission as "one of the most important" of city agencies.[15] He actually attended its meetings, and in 1907 he ensured that the new, or newest, charter (its revisions never ceased) gave the Art Commission as a matter of law what it had enjoyed at the mayors' discretion for the past five years: aesthetic control of all city projects, regardless of cost.

In its infancy the Art Commission was intimately linked to the Municipal Art Society. Each of the commission's first two presidents, the banker Charles Barney and former congressman John De Witt Warner, served simultaneously as president of MAS. (Warner eventually decided that this was an unseemly conflict of interest, and stepped down from the Art Commission in 1904.) This wasn't entirely coincidental. The Municipal Art Society enjoyed a disproportionate influence on the makeup of the Art Commission. There was a sense at the Art Commission that laymen made better, or more disinterested, presidents, and for many years there was an informal understanding within the Fine Arts Federation that MAS would nominate the Art Commission's lay members. This arrangement strengthened over the years as groups like the National Sculpture Society gradually turned to narrow professional interests and their lay members dropped away. As the Art Commission's powers grew under Low and McClellan, so too did the Municipal Art Society's influence on public art and architecture. In 1906 Frederick Lamb boasted of the society's power: "The beautifying of the city is almost exclusively under its control, it is the artistic censor of public monuments, passes on the arrangement of streets and squares and other matters which effect [sic] the city's general appearance. . . . It is, in a word, the clearing house of suggestions for municipal betterment which are then passed for authorization and a general O.K. to the Art Commission of the City of New York."[16]

The Art Commission's role in public architecture will come up later—repeatedly—but for now one should note that the commission served the cause of public art in several ways. It removed the delicate issue of taste from the hands of bureaucrats and politicians, and while they lost a certain amount of power they were also relieved of much embarrassment. If a sculpture proved to be controversial, the mayor, the parks commissioner, and the borough president could all lay the blame squarely at the Art Commission's door. They could even score some political points at the same time: by ridiculing the commission as a bunch of empty-headed elitist aesthetes, a politician could reassert his own credentials as a man of the people. The Art Commission also served the interests of artists; they were still badly paid, but at least they were now judged by their peers. The artists were also exempt from some of the standard methods used to combat graft in public works, like competitive bidding. This was no way to pick an artist, but some mechanism was needed to ensure that the city wasn't wasting its money, and this was provided by the Art Commission's stamp of approval.

Of course the Art Commission could also make life difficult for an artist, and it could exasperate even its closest friends. In 1902 a member of the Municipal Art Society, Jacob Cantor, became borough president of Manhattan and revived the art society's four-year-old scheme for an allegorical painting on the ceiling of the Board of Aldermen's Chamber in City Hall. The chamber was created in 1898 to accommodate the new, expanded municipal assembly. It was designed by John Duncan, the architect of Grant's Tomb, and its ceiling was adorned with a huge oval panel in a gilt frame, some twenty by forty feet, which fairly cried out for a painting to fill it. Cantor could find only $2,000 for the project, not the $10,000 MAS had hoped for, and most established artists shunned the competition. It was won by Taber Sears, a young and little known painter who went on to become president of MAS in 1923. Sears produced a classic piece of allegorical folly.[17] The *Times* reported that its title was *New York Received by Europe at the Eastern Gateway of the Americas*, which must have left readers wondering. (How did Europe get here?) The real title was *New York and the Nations.* In the painting, Europe, the enthroned central figure, welcomes New York and the Future of New York—the proud woman and young boy in the foreground—into the ranks of civilized societies. Nothing could be more emblematic of Beaux Arts New York, with its mixed feelings of civic pride and cultural insecurity.

Sears must have found painting his mural a bitter experience. He was given a two-month deadline, and his fee didn't even cover his costs. Nevertheless, he plunged valiantly into the work, and as the painting took shape in a studio he received, at each stage, the required approvals by the Art Commission. When Sears mounted the canvas on the chamber's ceiling, however, the Art Commission refused to grant final approval. It found the figure of Agriculture too effeminate, the boy who represented the Future of New York too thin, and the red robe of Europe too prominent.[18] Having lost money already, Sears gave up in disgust, refused to make any changes, and forfeited his payment. Even the *Times*, normally so supportive of the Art Commission, was appalled at its treatment of Sears. "Already," it noted, "it is common studio talk that municipal work is not desirable. If that spirit should spread among the artists we shall have to suffer from the refusal of our best sculptors and painters to design and execute municipal decorations, though it is exactly in public structures that the very finest and highest order of art work is most needed."[19]

The monuments of New York display the work of the Art Commission to better advantage, for the agency changed the nature of public sculpture in New York. One can see the transformation by contrasting the Victorian sculpture in Central Park with the twentieth-century monuments along Riverside Drive. The older monuments, like Thomas Ball's *Daniel Webster* (1876) and Albert Thorvaldsen's *Self-Portrait* (a copy, erected in 1892), are nothing more than figures on pedestals scattered randomly about the park. The Riverside memorials, however, are woven into the design of the city at large. The best are by Municipalians: *Franz Sigel*, by Karl Bitter on West 106th Street (1907); the *Firemen's Memorial*, by H. Van Buren Magonigle and Attilio Piccirilli on One Hundredth Street (1913); *Joan of Arc* at Ninety-third Street, by Anna Hyatt Huntington and John Van Pelt (1915).[20] Each stands on the axis of a street, a focal point against the wall of greenery behind it, and as one approaches, one discovers that it commands a flight of steps leading downward into the park. (Bitter even made a joke of the Sigel monument's position: the general's horse pulls its head back, as if it just had noticed that the ground falls away in front. To study the motion, Bitter tied an apple around a horse's neck, just out of reach of its mouth.[21]) On Riverside Drive, sculpture celebrates heroes and heroines, but it also celebrates that moment of transition as one steps from the asphalt gridiron into Olmsted's vision of nature perfected.

This sampling of artists also suggests another aspect of the Art Commission: that its domination by the Fine Arts Federation inevitably meant that members of the art societies would nearly monopolize the field of public art. Given the intimate relationship between the art societies and the Art Commission, they functioned as a kind of old boy network, and the classic instance of this was Karl Bitter's involvement in the design of the Plaza at Fifth Avenue and Fifty-ninth Street.[22] Bitter, one of the Municipal Art Society's original members, was trained as an architectural sculptor in Vienna at a moment in Austrian history when no building was complete until it had been slathered with carved cupids and writhing giants. He arrived in New York in 1889 as a penniless fugitive, a deserter from his compulsory service in the Austrian army, where he'd been the victim of an unusually sadistic sergeant.[23] Richard Morris Hunt found him working as a stone-carver and barely able to speak a few words of English. Hunt saw that he was facile and talented: a true sculptor, not a carver. The architect set Bitter up in his own studio and fed him a steady stream of commissions. The most prominent was the Administration Building at the Chicago fair, which was "fairly swathed, one may say, in sculpture."[24] Bitter was eventually able to give up architectural sculpture altogether and devote himself to public art.

Bitter's training in Vienna had left him with a profound sense that monumental art wasn't an end in itself but rather an aspect of urban design, and the Plaza was too tempting a site for him to ignore. It was one of the rare events in New York's grid, an open space at the corner of Central Park, and for anyone heading up Fifth Avenue, as every tourist was sure to do, it was the introduction to "millionaire's row." The Plaza didn't yet live up to its potential, however. Olmsted and Vaux weren't adept at designing urban spaces, and their plaza was a strange beast: a stand of trees in an oddly shaped traffic island. In the 1890s Bitter was one of the leading figures in the campaign to block construction of both the Heine monument and the Soldiers' and Sailors' Memorial in the Plaza. His argument was that the Plaza didn't need a fountain or a column sitting in its middle; it needed to be defined as an architectural room. In 1899 Bitter published an article on public sculpture in *Municipal Affairs*, singling out points in the city where monuments seemed necessary, and putting forward his own design for the Plaza. Bitter imagined the Plaza as a forecourt to the park, half embedded in the urban grid, half in greenery. He designed two symmetrical plazas, one on either side of Fifty-ninth Street, each ending in a fountain of shallow basins modeled on those in the Place de la Concorde in Paris.[25]

In 1902 the statue of General Sherman by Augustus Saint-Gaudens was installed just off Fifth Avenue, between Fifty-ninth and Sixtieth streets. Otherwise, nothing happened until 1911, when Joseph Pulitzer died and left $50,000 for a fountain in the Plaza. In choosing the Plaza, Pulitzer threw down one last challenge to his bitter rival, William Randolph Hearst, who'd just erected the unfortunate *Maine* Memorial on Columbus Circle. Pulitzer must have seen Bitter's 1899 scheme, since he asked that his fountain resemble those in the Place de la Concorde. Knowing the National Sculpture Society's fierce interest in the site, and wondering how to proceed, Pulitzer's son decided to sound out the sculpture society. It agreed to hold a limited competition to choose a sculptor. When the members were polled, they remembered Bitter's scheme, and gave him more votes than anyone else. But Bitter wasn't happy with the idea and warned Pulitzer that he would oppose any move to erect a memorial unless the entire space was taken into consideration. "With $50,000," he complained, "we can only succeed in ruining the place and the hope of its future and proper development."[26]

Shortly afterward Bitter was appointed to the Art Commission, where he was perfectly positioned to thwart any scheme that didn't satisfy him. It seemed that he'd reached a stalemate with the Pulitzer estate, but the new parks commissioner was Charles Stover, a former Municipalian and a longtime ally; the society had tried to get him the parks appointment for years. Stover agreed to hold an invited competition to choose an architect rather than a sculptor to design the entire Plaza, as Bitter wished. The Pulitzer Fountain would be just one component of the scheme, and Stover would undertake the rest with city funds. The prize went to Thomas Hastings, whose scheme was modeled on Bitter's 1899 project, though the Sherman monument, relocated slightly, replaced the northern fountain. Hastings then chose Bitter as his sculptor. Bitter created *Abundance*, the graceful nude that rises above Hastings's fountain, pouring wealth from a cornucopia. He never saw it cast or installed, however. The day he finished the clay model, Bitter was run over and killed by a car outside the Metropolitan Opera House. Bitter had kept a watchful eye over the Plaza for some fifteen years, warding off halfway solutions and finally arranging for the erection of New York's most beautiful piazza. It might have been better, though, if he'd left *Abundance* to some other sculptor. Had Bitter been a Tammany official, reformers would have concluded that he used a government position to win himself a contract.

Despite such conflicts of interest, the Art Commission worked splendidly until at least the First World War, and then it entered a long period of decline. As long as there was a consensus that public art was to be Classical art, the Art Commission served to maintain a high aesthetic standard, but the seeds of its decay were planted in the Charter of 1898 when Carrère and Low ensured that the Fine Arts Federation would choose the commission's members. They didn't take into account the fact that institutions age. The federation and its member societies were created by a particular generation of artists, tied to a particular style and a particular moment in history. The next generation of artists formed its own societies and clubs free of the conservative influence of the Beaux Arts, and these new voices were excluded from both the Fine Arts Federation and the Art Commission. By the time of the Great Depression, the Art Commission had become a reactionary force that preferred bad Beaux Arts work to good Modernism, and the irony was that its senility coincided with the creation of the Works Progress Administration, the WPA, when the federal government put artists to work on the greatest campaign of municipal art the nation has ever seen.

An Unofficial Government

THE ART COMMISSION was one of the Municipal Art Society's great triumphs, but once it was established, Municipalians began wondering if the society itself still had a purpose in life. Its Beaux Arts monuments and murals were supposed to wean private donors away from the aesthetic crudities of the Victorian past and the clumsiness of stone-carvers, but there was less point to this once the Art Commission had the power to reject an ugly statue. In April 1901 the Municipal Art Society summoned its members to decide if the society should be dissolved. Of 350 members, only 30 bothered to attend. The directors put forward the case for dissolution. In the beginning, they admitted, MAS had "set a pace," but since then, the National Society of Mural Painters and the National Sculpture Society had become far more successful advocates for public art. With the Art Commission in place, there was no need for MAS to advise the city fathers on aesthetic matters. The board complained of the indifference of the public and the city authorities, of the difficulty of commissioning artworks with so few members and no endowment. It had taken three years to raise the money for Simmons's murals, they noted, and after six years Daniel Chester French still hadn't been paid in full for the Hunt Memorial. The directors voted to pay him $3,400 and prayed that this would satisfy him. It did; apparently it was all the money that MAS had in the bank.[1]

There was, however, a small group of optimists at that meeting, led by a young muralist and stained-glass artist named Frederick Stymetz Lamb. They forced a delay in the vote, if only to consider what MAS's dissolution would mean to the other municipal art societies that had sprung up around the country.[2] A week later they returned, ready to take over the society themselves, and as Charles de Kay reported in the *Times*, MAS was handed over "to a band of artists and men of affairs who have more confidence in the public and perhaps more practical views of the kind of propaganda suited to a community like ours." These men had a different explanation of why MAS had failed. As de Kay put it:

The Municipal Art Society . . . was managed in a way exactly right for a much smaller city than New York, where the strain of daily life is not so fierce as it is here and everyone knows pretty much everyone. But for New York, so big, so hurried, so mean and at the same time generous, so lacking in civic pride— subject to constant changes in population as the different waves of immigration break over it—there seems needed a different management. . . .

There has been a disposition to ignore the city officials on the part of the society. The reason whereof is not far to seek. The artist, architects and others who have given their time so generously to the society's work . . . feared to dis- cover in those officials persons who would not only be absolutely indifferent to the aims and purposes of the society, but suspect its offices of ulterior purposes not so altruistic and public-spirited as appeared on the surface. . . . The former managers of the Municipal Art Society were too retiring or not optimistic enough to beard these political lions, our municipal leaders, in their dens and thus dis- cover whether really they were the wild beasts they imagined them.[3]

The new board of directors swore to transform the Municipal Art Society into a true advocacy group, skilled in the ways of politicians and unafraid of bruising its own sensibilities, and as if to prove the point, they chose John De Witt Warner, a former Democratic congressman, as their new president. Just what the society would ad- vocate proved more difficult to define. Warner announced a break with the past, declaring that "the aim of such a society should not be to raise money for monuments and mural paintings to be presented to the city, but to try to advise citizens how the city may be embellished." In the *Times*, de Kay wrote that the society's "aim should be to present to the artists, manufacturers, artisans, art amateurs, and those interested in civic affairs some idea of what has been done and is being carried out elsewhere, and what ingenious minds can suggest in the way of original ideas to meet the special requirements of a city like ours."[4] Calvin Tomkins, a businessman new to MAS, described the society's purpose as "the stimulation of artistic interest in the city's public works," and in the "embellishment" of New York. The word "embellish- ment," however, was used quite promiscuously at the time to mean anything from a monument to a bridge, and as Tomkins wrote in 1905, "The membership and in- fluence of the society continued rapidly to increase, and its experience tended to broaden its views, so that it became more and more apparent that municipal em- bellishment also included the establishment of a comprehensive structural plan for the entire city."[5] By 1907, when MAS was trying to establish height regulations for skyscrapers and had wandered into the politically explosive issue of who should con- trol the subways, the city or private enterprise, Tomkins and his allies were forced to come up with a more explicit statement of the society's goals:

The object of the Society is to promote in every practical way the development of the City of New York along the lines of embellishment and greater benefit to its citizens.

To aid in planning and beautifying its streets, its parks and public spaces, its public buildings and other structures, and in providing adequate sculpture and decoration for these through appropriations, public subscriptions, or private benefactors.

To collaborate with other bodies aiming to secure similar results. To aid by exhibitions the presentation of all such work to the citizens of New York and to assist in every possible way the Municipal and State authorities, the Art Commission of the City and the heads of the Municipal Departments in securing such embellishments and benefits.[6]

NEW YORK was a very different city in 1901. Its economic life was dominated by the port and industry, by factories and wharves, freighters and railroads. Phrases like the "post-industrial city" or a "service economy" would have sounded like the rankest sort of science fiction. New Yorkers joked that the city would be "a nice place if they ever finished it." In 1901 the first subway line, zigzagging from City Hall to Bronx Park, had been in construction less than a year. Plans were in preparation for a tunnel beneath the East River to extend the subway to the Long Island Railroad depot in Brooklyn. Elevated lines still darkened the avenues; some, not yet electrified, rained sparks and cinders down on the streets and set afire the awnings and window shades of tenements. North of Grand Central Terminal, the train tracks still lay open to the sky: between Forty-second and Fifty-sixth streets, there was no Park Avenue. Freight trains enjoyed the waterfront of Riverside Park. Their tracks continued down Eleventh Avenue—Death Avenue, as it was known, because the trains had killed so many neighborhood children. Pennsylvania Station did not exist. No bridge or tunnel linked Manhattan to New Jersey. Barges and ferries crisscrossed the Hudson, laden with the freight and passengers from half a dozen railroads with terminals on the Jersey shore. West Street, clogged with cargo and travelers from the New Jersey railroads and the transatlantic liners, was nearly impassable.

Macy's had just announced plans for a new store at Herald Square. Times Square was still known as Longacre Square, and was still the northern fringe rather than the center of the theater district. The Astor estate had plans for a hotel there, but the *Times* wouldn't follow until 1903. John Jacob Astor was thinking of building the St. Regis Hotel on Fifth Avenue, the first skyscraper in the district. Midtown was still low-rise, and the Flatiron Building was a hole in the ground. Downtown, twenty skyscrapers were in various phases of construction in the financial district, the Stock Exchange was building its new home, and the Customs House was rising above Battery Park. Sailing ships and steamships mingled in the harbor.[7]

A new tenement house law was due to take effect in January 1901, ensuring for the first time that new apartments would enjoy more than symbolic amounts of light and fresh air, and that each would have a toilet. For the moment, however, it was still legal to build tenements with wooden staircases and with air shafts only three feet wide, and in fact builders were rushing to do so. Their handiwork was evident in the fact that one in ten New Yorkers could expect to die of tuberculosis, while 65 percent had no access to a bath. The Lower East Side was the most densely populated quarter on earth, more crowded than the slums of London, Budapest, or Calcutta. Yet maps of the city showed great white patches in the outer boroughs where streets were not yet even contemplated. The Brooklyn Bridge was still the only dry route to Long Island. Work had just begun on stringing the cables of the Williamsburg Bridge. The city was about to lay foundations for the Manhattan Bridge, while engineers studied soil conditions at the site of the Blackwells Island Bridge. Harlem was, in effect, a suburban town. Morningside Heights and Hamilton Heights were mostly open fields. Estates dotted Inwood. Queens was a district of villages and farms, a source of fresh vegetables. Manhattanites told stories of the rustic types they met on excursions to Staten Island.

A pall of soft coal smoke stung the eyes. Traffic regulations did not exist. Traffic lights were unheard of. Campaigning politicians had taken to driving automobiles through the crowded streets of the tenement districts, confident that crowds would materialize, curious to see an automobile. They knew better there the deafening clatter of wagon wheels and horseshoes on hard pavement, and the acrid smell of horse manure, which was everywhere.

T H E C I T Y was only three years old in 1901. On January 1, 1898, fireworks had exploded over City Hall to mark the birth of Greater New York, the city of five boroughs. The campaign for consolidation had lasted more than ten years. In 1887 a delegation from the Chamber of Commerce called on Mayor Abram S. Hewitt to warn that New York was strangling itself. Its streets were so congested with the press of people and vehicles as to slow movement to a crawl. The future of New York was at stake, they warned: the transportation of goods had become so difficult that it was more expensive to conduct business in New York than in other cities, and New York would lose its competitive edge unless it reformed. The only answer was expansion. The docks along the Hudson were bursting while those on the East River at South Street were useless for steamships, the river being too narrow. Yet New York Harbor had some four hundred miles of waterfront: plenty of room for new docks, new zones of factories, warehouses, and cheap housing for the working class. There were two problems: the waterfront was controlled by dozens of municipalities in several counties, and no system of bridges, roads, and trains existed to carry workers and goods out of Manhattan. The Chamber of Commerce asked "if it not be the true policy to unite New York and all its environs under one general scheme of municipal rule."[8] The boundaries of this greater city were drawn up by Andrew Haswell Green, who'd pondered the subject since the 1860s. Green had been parks commissioner when Central Park was built and when Riverside Park was first planned. The harbor, and only the harbor, determined the shape of his plan for Greater New York; he drew dozens of municipalities together in order to bring all the available shoreline under the rule of a single city government.

"Upon us is the responsibility never before laid on a people," John De Witt

Warner wrote of Greater New York, that of "building the world's capital for all time to come. What we do well will serve mankind forever; what we do ill will be a stumbling block until it is remedied. To none before us have been given such opportunities—to be used or wasted."[9] Yet New York was ill equipped to make anything of its opportunities. Property rights were sacred, and it was almost impossible to restrict builders unless one could prove that life and limb were at stake or that a proposed land use, like a slaughterhouse, was literally nauseating. There was no zoning law, and if asked, most Americans would have considered the very idea unconstitutional. There was no landmarks law, no system of tax abatements, no public housing, no complex of public authorities. Mass transit—the Els, the streetcars, and the nascent subway—was controlled by private monopolies over which the city had little control. The city could neither preserve old neighborhoods nor easily encourage the creation of new ones.

Greater New York had been imagined as a great experiment in planning a metropolis, but after years of debates and political jockeying, that vision had largely disappeared in the Charter of 1898. The Charter Commission had been concerned less with planning than with satisfying the conflicting patronage demands of all the different political clubhouses, and with reassuring the outer boroughs that they would continue to enjoy a good deal of autonomy. The city did acquire new powers over waterfront developments, and the right to grant franchises to street railways, yet the charter's effect was to so decentralize power as to render the city incapable of planning. Borough presidents were given the power to survey their domains, and once these surveys were completed, they became the official city map, yet the borough presidents couldn't change this map. That power was reserved for the Board of Aldermen, a body intended to give voice to neighborhood concerns but inherently ill-suited to considering the problems of the city as a whole.

In an attempt to counterbalance the pettiness of the aldermen, Seth Low had succeeded in fitting a Board of Public Improvements into the Charter of 1898. It consisted of the commissioners of all the city agencies involved in public improvements. Low hoped that the commissioners would be professionals—technocrats rather than politicians—and he imagined that the board would work as a policy-making body, at once setting a broad planning agenda for the consideration of the aldermen and coordinating the public works of the different city departments.[10] But the board had no strong director, and the charter did not require any professional qualifications for its individual members. The *Times* remembered that when Mayor Robert Van Wyck came to power in 1898, "the first actual board was composed of common Tammany politicians whose views extended only to the amount of available money in the City Treasury and the available means of getting it out."[11]

In even the best-intentioned administration the Board of Public Improvements might have devolved into nothing more than a debating club where commissioners argued over their respective shares of the capital budget. But Tammany wasn't well intentioned. The use of inside information on public improvements had long been a classic source of income for clubhouse politicians. According to George McClellan, that was how his mentor, Richard Croker, boss of Tammany during the Van Wyck years, had made his fortune: "He had become the silent partner of Peter F. Meyer, one of the shrewdest real estate operators in the city.... With advance information as to what new streets were to be opened and what old streets were to be improved, it was a simple matter for Meyer to buy options on real estate contiguous to the improvement and to sell at a great profit when the improvements were officially announced.... As he held no public office, what he did was, at least technically, perfectly legal."[12] With his share of these profits Croker was able, when things got tough in New York, to retire to a life of horse breeding in England—to the dismay of his Irish constituents. Tammany Hall was also determined to exploit, rather than remedy, the shortage in dock facilities. While Croker was amassing a fortune in real estate, his successor, Charles Francis Murphy, was making his own fortune on the waterfront. As Van Wyck's dock commissioner, Murphy happily took bribes in return for leases to the precious few Hudson River berths. The mayor himself made a killing. The demand for piers gave the city an excuse to declare that only one company could land ice at the city docks, and that happened to be a firm in which Van Wyck had received hundreds of thousands of dollars' worth of free stock.[13]

As it turned out, the Board of Public Improvements, created at the behest of reformers in 1898, was abolished in the revised charter that was due to take effect in 1902—this at the behest of the borough presidents, who demanded still more autonomy. Given the board's sorry track record, its disappearance was viewed at the time "with entire equanimity by everybody," the Times wrote.[14] It took a while for people to realize that this left no one in charge of making a planning policy for the city as a whole. "What is the business of all is the business of none,"[15] the Times soon lamented. "It is a pity, and not a credit, that the Charter should have made no provision for municipal embellishment. We do not forget the Art Commission. But the functions of that body are purely negative.... For any project of 'public improvement' in the sense of public embellishment we must rely upon individual initiative and private public spirit."[16]

The Times was speaking of the new Municipal Art Society, the only organization in the city that seemed capable of filling this vacuum. "The Society is merely an association of citizens without official status," the paper admitted, "but for that very reason ... has complete freedom to suggest, criticize, and memorialize when and where it sees fit.... An organization that studies the requirements of the city and indicates the way to meet them so plainly that no one can mistake is worthy of the metropolis. It should be supported by every citizen who cares for the place in which he lives and where his children are growing up; it would have a membership of thousands if people in general only fully realized what it is doing for New York and what it might do if made more popular and powerful."[17]

A HUGE array of advocacy groups already existed in New York. As activist Lawrence Veiller put it, "We have learned ... that without the aid of a group of citizens exercising what might be called 'the unofficial government by citizens' along with the official government of public officials, little improvement could be expected in municipal affairs. It was obvious ... that most public officials were content with executing the daily tasks and that few of them had either the time or vision to study their work or urge reform when reforms were needed."[18] Veiller's own field was housing reform, and the great triumph of his life was passage of the Tenement House Law of 1901, but the same tack was taken by groups with a bewildering variety of demands, from banning what they considered smutty books and closing saloons on Sunday to teaching schoolchildren the pleasures of gardening.[19] New Yorkers could choose to join the Reform Club, the Social Reform Club, the East Side Civic Club, the Women's Municipal League, the Good Government Clubs, the Outdoor Recreation League, the Kindergarten Association, the Public Education Association, the City Improvement Society, the Ladies' Health Protection Association, the New York Tax Reform Association, the Civil Service Reform Association, the City Vigilance League, the Society for the Prevention of Crime, the Anti-Spoils League, the Transit Reform Committee of 100, the Legal Aid Society, the Charity Organization Society, the Association for Improving the Condition of the Poor, the Ethical Culture Society, the City History Club, the American Scenic and Historic Preservation Society, the Merchants Association, and the Board of Trade and Transportation. Merely reciting these names suggests that the reform movement was terribly fragmented, but in fact such groups were often able to patch together a coalition to fight for a particular issue, and one cause succeeded another at the top of the reformers' agenda. In the mid 1890s it was educational reform, as the Public Education Association spearheaded the drive to create a centralized school system; in the late 1890s it was tenement reform, as the Charity Organization Society led the fight for the New Law of 1901; and as the new century began, the Municipal Art Society was determined that the next great reform cause would be the City Beautiful.

As Calvin Tomkins observed, "public charities in New York have always been liberally supported and other interests carefully guarded by a liberal, critical and intelligent supervision, but the embellishment of the city itself has not received the popular attention which it merits."[20] When the Municipal Art Society announced its intention to fill that gap, it immediately attracted a broad range of experienced advocates. There were four main camps, each with its own interest in "embellishing" New York. Political reformers like Richard Welling saw in the City Beautiful a way to forge "a genuine civic spirit in our overwhelming big town,"[21] and a way to counter the graft-driven public works policy of Tammany Hall. Charity groups and settlement houses were desperate to ameliorate living conditions in the slums by erecting parks and public baths in their midst. Merchants and manufacturers wanted to make New York a more efficient place to do business. They cried aloud for the new infrastructure, docks, and rapid transit that would let them expand, and which had been the whole point of creating Greater New York in the first place. Finally, the art societies wanted to bring to New York the urbanism of Paris, with its imposing Classical architecture and its noble public spaces. At the Municipal Art Society these groups found that their interests overlapped. Opening up new land for business would also provide an escape route from the Old Law and pre-law tenements of the Lower East Side. Creating a more efficient city would provide opportunities for Beaux Arts architects and artists to redesign the great nodes of the transportation system. Improving the lives of Lower East Siders would have advantages for political reformers: the immigrant might stop exchanging his vote for Tammany's favors if a reform administration gave him new municipal services as a matter of right.

These overlapping agendas would draw more than a thousand members to MAS. More important was the fact that the membership list, which the society enjoyed publishing, was so stellar, so well connected. It contained few members of "Society" as defined by Ward McAllister or Mrs. Astor, though one can find James Hyde of the Equitable Life Assurance Company, who threw a ball so lavish that Congress began an investigation of the insurance industry; George W. Vanderbilt, who commissioned Biltmore in Asheville, North Carolina, the most amazing of Richard Morris Hunt's Gothic châteaux; and George Post, designer of City College and the Stock Exchange, and the only architect to make it into McAllister's list of "The 400." Among MAS's other members were the most celebrated architects of the city: Bruce Price; the partners of McKim, Mead & White and Carrère & Hastings; Charles Coolidge Haight, designer of the old Columbia University campus in Midtown; Henry Hardenbergh, author of the Dakota, the original Waldorf-Astoria, and the Plaza Hotel; John Duncan, designer of Grant's Tomb; and William Robert Ware, founder of Columbia University's School of Architecture and author of *The American Vignola*, which is still popular in paperback. There were artists: Edwin Blashfield; Louis Tiffany; John La Farge; Lockwood De Forest, the great wood-carver whose work still graces Frederick Church's home, Olana, and his own row house at 7 East Tenth Street; and sculptors John Quincy Adams Ward, Augustus Saint-Gaudens, Karl Bitter, Henry Kirke Bush-Brown, and Frederick Wellington Ruckstull.

There was also a contingent of Wall Street bankers: J. P. Morgan and his son; Jacob Schiff, a trustee of Teachers College and the treasurer of the University Settlement; James Speyer; Henry Clews, a member of the Committee of Seventy that brought down Boss Tweed, treasurer of the ASPCA, and the father of a sculptor; Spencer Trask, president of the Broadway and Morningside realty companies and the man who reorganized the *Times* in 1897 and later founded Yaddo, the artists' retreat in Saratoga Springs[22]; Isaac Seligman, a trustee of the National Arts Club and the City and Suburban Homes Company, which built model tenements, and the treasurer of the City Club; and Otto Kahn, who went on to become the angel of the Metropolitan Opera Company. There were retailers like Isidor Strauss, of R. H. Macy and Abraham and Strauss, who was also president of the board of Teachers College and a trustee of General Theological Seminary; and there were people active in tenement reform: Alfred T. White, who built model tenements on the principle of "philanthropy plus five percent"; Mrs. Alfred Corning Clark, who financed model tenements on the Upper West Side; Caroline Phelps Stokes, active in the Charity Organization Society and the founder of the Phelps Stokes Fund, which still fights for better education in Africa and among American minorities; her nephew J. G. Phelps Stokes, a millionaire settlement house worker who married the celebrated Communist Rose Pastor; and Charles Stover, head-worker of the East Side Civic Club and a leading advocate of building small parks in the tenement districts. There were figures active in the good government move-ment, like Samuel Ordway of the Civil Service Reform Association, and George McAneny, who went on to become borough president of Manhattan and to give New York the Zoning Resolution of 1916.

It was an elite group, with all the advantages and disadvantages that implies. It could never hope to impress a politician with the length of its membership roll, nor could it present itself to Tammany Hall as a loyal constituency that deserved a reward. It had access to the newspapers, however; it could criticize, praise, or recommend, and know that its words would find their way into print. Jacob Cantor, an MAS life member, had ties to the *World*, and Spencer Trask, to the *Times*. Charles de Kay, that paper's art critic, was active in MAS and an intimate of many of its directors; Charles Israels had family ties to the *Real Estate Record and Guide*; Frederick Lamb was a friend of Gustav Stickley, editor of the famous Arts and Crafts journal *The Craftsman*, and often wrote in its pages on the subject of public art (Stickley, in turn, joined MAS). Aside from these direct ties, MAS could count on the boos-terism of the New York press, which was hungry for drawings of great public improvement projects to prove its point that New York was becoming a better place to live. The Municipal Art Society soon discovered that in a place like New York, where power over the cityscape was fragmented or evanescent, an articulate voice would carry far.

FOUR MEN came to dominate the Municipal Art Society, and some personal introductions are required. Two, John De Witt Warner and Calvin Tomkins, were laymen, and they were joined by a pair of artists, the brothers Frederick Stymetz Lamb and Charles Rollinson Lamb.

Warner was a politician turned citizen advocate. He was born upstate and went to Cornell, then edited a paper in Ithaca, taught German, Latin, and elocution, entered the bar, and moved to New York. In 1888 he secured his future by becoming known as a spokesman for free trade. New York's merchant class decided that it had found a voice for its fight against the high tariffs, so beloved by the Republican Party, that protected American industry at the expense of its foreign trade. Warner was sent to Congress for two terms in the 1890s as the representative of "the wealthiest parliamentary district in the world."[23] Merchants like W. R. Grace continued to support Warner after his years in Congress by patronizing his law firm, and he continued to fight for their agenda on the local scene: cheap transportation, a more orderly railroad system, a city planned like a machine to ferry goods and workers as efficiently as possible. Advocacy must have offered Warner certain rewards not available to him as an elected official. His support had always come from a coalition of Independent Democrats and Republicans; he no longer had to bargain with Tammany Hall for a place on the ticket, and could concentrate on his favorite issues while escaping the odious tasks of campaigning and constituent service. He enjoyed the pleasures of a political life—the intellectual challenge, the heady feeling of being an insider—without the messy compromises of a political career. He had more time to write pamphlets on topics that interested him—they ranged from "Sugar, Sugar Tariff, Sugar Trust" to "Sound Sequence in Shakespeare"—and to indulge his taste for art by joining the boards of the National Sculpture Society, the National Arts Club, and finally, MAS.

Warner's political base remained the Greater Democracy—the political club of W. R. Grace, the wealthy merchant and former mayor of New York—and he was active in the West Side Independent Club, but his pulpit was the Reform Club, organized in 1887 to foster "honest and efficient government." Its dominant figures were now Warner and Calvin Tomkins, and the latter especially gave the Reform Club, and MAS, a more specific cast. Tomkins had inherited a chain of family businesses that specialized in building materials, and he owned plants and quarries in the Hudson Highlands, Newark, Nova Scotia, and New Brunswick.[24] Such an empire was sensitive to the fact that Tammany Hall skewed the New York market by favoring its own loose empire of loyal companies, and its profit margins might well hinge on any inefficiencies in the Port of New York. Tomkins became a legendary authority on the problems of transporting goods through New York, an aspect of his business that was more challenging than baking bricks or ripping granite from the majestic bluffs of the Catskills. The Chamber of Commerce, the Merchants' Association, the Board of Trade and Transportation, and successive governors came to rely on his expertise. Tomkins had two major agendas. He thought of government as a vast public development agency whose role was to build the urban infrastructure that made it possible to do business in New York: the rapid transit, the docks, and the bridges that would ease congestion in the city and open up new land to development. This would put Tomkins—and MAS—in conflict with the private companies that operated the city's rapid transit system and the railroads that connected New York to the rest of the nation. Most of those railroads—six of them—had terminals on the Jersey shore and were forced to barge their cargoes and passengers into Manhattan, and that brings us to the second item on Tomkins's agenda: he was one of the first to demand the creation of a Port Authority that would allow development of the harbor irrespective of state lines. His "vigorous and tactful propaganda" didn't bear fruit, however, until shortly after his death in 1921.[25]

The Reform Club included in its ranks a number of artists: George Post, Karl Bitter, and those two brothers, Charles and Frederick Lamb, who joined Warner in remaking the Municipal Art Society. The Lambs ran a commercial decorating firm, the J. & R. Lamb Studios, which specialized in ecclesiastical work.[26] It had been founded in 1857 by the brothers' father and uncle, just arrived from England. Charles and Frederick were born into an atmosphere steeped in the philosophy of the Arts and Crafts movement, and they grew up among people who felt that the artist's mission was to design a whole environment. They designed the interiors of churches and mausoleums—stained glass, mosaics, murals, candlesticks, lecterns, pews, vestments, and so forth. They saw their studio as a kind of modern-day medieval guild, a place where artists joined craftsmen at the worktable, wives worked with their husbands, and children became their fathers' apprentices.

Of the two brothers, Frederick was the more intellectual and the more delicate, with a finely modeled face that looks a little neurasthenic in the surviving photographs. He was trained in Paris as a muralist, and founded the National Society of Mural Painters in 1895, but found his true métier when he returned to New York in 1885 and watched his friend John La Farge's experiments with opalescent glass. Lamb was one of the first of La Farge's colleagues to pick up the technique; his masterpiece is the window *Religion Enthroned*, an astonishing study in deep blues and purples, now in the Brooklyn Museum (a gift of Municipalian Irving Bush).

It was Frederick Lamb who articulated a social mission for the artists and architects of the Municipal Art Society. He yearned for "an art broader than the one we have today—an art that touches the lives of the people; an art that will be in their streets, in their parks, in their homes." This wasn't a utopian dream, he insisted, but a return to a healthier past. In the Middle Ages, "art sprang from the merchant, the magistrate, the artisan," Lamb wrote, and "then art was 'of the people, for the people, by the people.' " Even during the Renaissance there had been no distinction between "high art, municipal art, or applied art," but in turn-of-the-century America: "How art has drifted from the realization that it is in any way an integral part of our city!"[27]

According to Lamb, "Commercialism set in when art lost touch with commerce; when art ceased to answer the legitimate demands of the age in which it existed, decadence set in. Art degenerated into an aristocratic adjunct and was viewed with distrust by the people. Art, instead of answering the healthy demands of the masses, pandered to the wants of the luxurious few. 'Art for art's sake' became the cry."[28]

Charles Lamb was described as an "artist-architect" by the Municipal Art Society, but newspapers had more various labels: he was "one of the brainiest men in the New York art world," a "sociologist," an "expert in social matters" (not the same thing), or "the Evangelist of the City Beautiful movement."[29] He certainly looked the part of an evangelist, with a "classic profile disturbingly like one of his saints in stained glass,"[30] and the resemblance was all the more striking if one called on the Lambs at work. Their studio was the former Reformed Church at Sixth Avenue and West Fourth Street, and its nave was dappled with the glowing colors of opalescent glass and cluttered with Byzantine mosaics and Gothic lecterns. As for the confusion about Charles Lamb's profession, he'd trained as an artist at the Art

Students League, and later became the league's president. He had no formal education in architecture outside his father's studio, and aside from interiors his only built works were the Dewey Arch, his own home in Tenafly, New Jersey, and the Court of Honor for the Hudson-Fulton Celebration of 1909. One is tempted to call him an amateur, but with the proviso that so was Olmsted when he designed Central Park, and so was Holly Whyte when he set out to study the sociology of urban places.

Charles Lamb trained his intelligence on an amazing variety of urban issues: from skyscrapers and street signs to a proposal for communal kitchens that would, he hoped, save women from the drudgery of housework and free them to join in the city's public life. Few people have had such an effect on the shape of New York and yet been so thoroughly forgotten. In the early 1930s, when Lamb was already an obscure figure, the *New York Telegram* tried to sum up his accomplishments: "The new Sixth Avenue extension that funnels you into the Holland Tunnel today for your weekend jaunt in Jersey; 'step-on-it' boulevard, the new west side highway that will take the red out of traffic lights to Riverside Drive; the proposed development of City Hall Plaza; the Municipal Building that straddles Chambers Street—all had their origin in the churchly studios of Charles R. Lamb."[31]

None of these, one should add, was executed with anything like the intelligence or public spirit of Lamb's original conception. Nor did the *Telegram* exhaust the catalog of Lamb's achievements. He was the father of setback zoning in New York, and his ideas for "streets in the sky" and arcaded sidewalks, dismissed at the turn of the century, inspired the 1920s Art Deco visions of the skyscraper city. By then Lamb had withdrawn from the public eye, but he was still pondering the future. He assured the *Telegram* that "streets as we know them" were on their way out: the day was coming when people would get about by airplane and helicopter, and soon "we'll be tearing off our roofs for entrances." The paper hardly knew what to make of him: "An old-timer of the first water, a leader of the crowd in tall hat times . . . a curious mixture of tradition and progress is Lamb—a composite town pump and filling station."[32]

CHARLES LAMB was something of a celebrity at the turn of the century, and as one of the best known figures in the New York art world, he brought an immense amount of public goodwill to the Municipal Art Society. Lamb and Warner had long been colleagues on the board of the National Sculpture Society, and between Lamb's imagination and Warner's political acumen, they'd made that organization the most effective public art organization in the city. It was Lamb who realized that the way to make public art popular was to hitch it to a popular cause, and in 1899 he dreamed up the Dewey Arch, the greatest publicity coup in the history of public art in this city.

When the Spanish-American War broke out, Admiral George Dewey sailed from Hong Kong into Manila Bay, slipped past the harbor defenses, and sank the Spanish fleet without losing a single American life. It seemed miraculous, and Dewey was suddenly catapulted into the ranks of great naval geniuses. His personal achievement was untainted by what happened next: President McKinley decided not to liberate the Philippines but to colonize them. Imperialism deeply divided New Yorkers. Elihu Root, the Municipalian (and Republican) whose eloquence and influence had won the society an Art Commission, went to Washington as secretary of war and was responsible for suppressing Filipino resistance. John De Witt Warner, a Democrat, emerged as one of McKinley's most outspoken opponents. One of his speeches made the front page of the *Times*: "Mr. McKinley tore our own Declaration of Independence to shreds and flung them in the face of a friendly people fighting for freedom, who had welcomed us as allies, only, after victory, to be ordered to accept us as new masters. . . . Since then we have had . . . six months of deepening disgrace for the United States,"[33] and here Warner went on to note that reports of American atrocities, stories of rape and massacre, had filtered out of the Philippines despite the army censors. What other crimes, he asked, had been concealed? Republicans accused Warner of slandering American troops, and Warner was soon on the defensive, denying that he had ever said that American soldiers were rapists. He was already negotiating with the city government to let the National Sculpture Society build a triumphal arch at Madison Square to welcome Dewey home. It was Warner's way of showing support for the troops.

The city planned a great parade to mark the occasion of Dewey's return, and a reviewing stand would be built on Madison Square so Mayor Van Wyck and the sachems of Tammany Hall could bask in the admiral's reflected glory. In those days such a parade seemed to require a piece of festal decoration. In 1889 Stanford White had designed a wooden arch at the foot of Fifth Avenue to celebrate the hundredth anniversary of Washington's inauguration in New York, and a popular subscription campaign had succeeded in building a permanent version in Washington Square. Columbus Day 1892 had seen another arch, this one by the architects Herts & Tallant, at the Plaza on Fifth Avenue. So now the National Sculpture Society offered to design a triumphal arch for Dewey. The sculptors would donate their time and talent; they asked only that the city pay for materials and the cost of erecting the arch.[34] Tammany was suspicious, but a meeting was arranged on the yacht of Lewis Nixon, a shipbuilder serving as the interim boss of Tammany Hall, and Nixon was assured that the sculptors meant no criticism and that there were no partisan overtones to the proposal. It occurred to Nixon that Tammany Hall would look ungrateful—and philistine—if it turned down such a generous offer from the nation's most celebrated artists. The sculptors were granted $26,000 for their arch. They had six weeks' time to finish it.

At the Chicago fair, Blashfield had reveled in the stream of distinguished visitors who came to watch his work. For the sculptors of the Dewey Arch the experience was even headier, for they worked in full view of the public. Oblivious to traffic and trolleys, crowds filled the street to watch the sculptors. Most New Yorkers had never seen an artist at work before; none had ever witnessed a spectacle such as the *Times* described:

To see a huddle of four or five sculptor's assistants, employed at five or ten or whatever it may be dollars a day, working at the enlargement of a sculptor's model on the arch, and to see in the midst of them the actual author of the model, in what resembles a suit of pajamas, working away cheerily, and regardless of the fact that several thousand people are looking at him, for nothing at all a day, and working harder than any of the rest, for his own credit among his fellow-craftsmen, and for the honor of his city and the glory of his country, this is a sight which could not be seen in one of the "aesthetic" capitals, could not be seen in Paris or Vienna, has not, we believe, been seen on such a scale since the decay of the medieval guilds, the spirit of which the associated sculptors of New York have suddenly and of their own initiative revived.[35]

The Dewey Arch was "decoration for a pageant, showy, cultivated, but not very serious"—like the Chicago fair, the *Times* noted—and like the fair buildings it was concocted of plaster and lath.[36] Charles Lamb produced a loose copy of the Arch of Titus in the Roman Forum. It was just a sketch, he admitted, apologizing for the fact that he had no time for a more studied design, but that hardly mattered: Lamb's architecture was conceived as a mere frame for the work of twenty-five sculptors.[37] J.Q.A. Ward's *Victory at Sea* crowned the arch. Its piers were decorated with *Peace*, by Daniel Chester French; *Departure for War*, by Philip Martiny; *The Combat*, by Karl Bitter; and *Triumphant Return*, by Charles Niehaus. Portraits of historic naval commanders stood in the attic; reliefs graced the spandrels and sides of the arch. And there was more: Lamb added a forecourt of lofty columns with Winged Victories poised on their pedestals, and two more groups, George Bissell's *The Navy* and Frederick Ruckstull's *The Army*, stood at the entrance to the court.

On September 29, 1899, Dewey stepped ashore at Grant's Tomb and paraded to Madison Square. The rich had left town, shuttering their windows and fencing off their stoops as if they expected a revolutionary mob to roam the streets. Those who remained, however, greeted Dewey with a delirium not seen again in New York until Charles Lindbergh's return from Paris. The city was awash in bunting; crowds packed the sidewalks and fire escapes and threw candy to the soldiers and sailors. The public was enthralled by the beauty of the Dewey Arch, critics declared its sculpture an epoch-making triumph, and Russell Sturgis, infected by an imperialist mood, hailed it as the final proof that American artists had surpassed the French. As soon as the parade was over, a clamor arose to translate the arch into permanent materials as a monument to the navy. It began with Louis Stern, owner of Stern's Department Store on Twenty-third Street, who was thrilled at the idea of tourists streaming to the neighborhood. His ardor cooled when it was decided that the Battery would be a better location for a Naval Arch. Yet there was a great deal of popular support for the idea, and Charles Nicoll, a publisher, formed a committee to raise funds. He recruited one Colonel Church, editor of the *Army and Navy Journal*, former governor Levi Morton, J. P. Morgan, and former mayor Brody. Morgan offered $50,000 and hinted that he'd give more if needed, but it was agreed that most of the funds should be raised by public subscription. The *Times* came around to the project once Lamb promised to restudy his design.[38] But the sculptors themselves "seemed to think it would be more becoming to stay in the background."[39] They'd presented the temporary arch as a selfless contribution to the nation, and now they feared that if they pressed for a permanent arch they would seem less patriotic than opportunistic.

Even with the sculptors condemned to silence, the campaign should have succeeded, but things began to go awry. Dewey declared himself a presidential candidate, and the Naval Arch suddenly became a partisan issue. Then Dewey proved to be a singularly inept politician, outraging his own supporters, and finally the navy was racked by "bickering and division" as officers squabbled over the role they had played in defeating Spain. The fund-raising committee finally disbanded in 1901, complaining that it could do nothing due to "the disgust now prevailing in the minds of the American people with the nation's navy."[40]

THE SCULPTORS were naturally disappointed when the proposed Naval Arch fell through, but Charles Lamb and John De Witt Warner used the Dewey Arch as a stepping stone. The public now thought of Lamb as a brilliant and public-spirited patriot, and he realized that "people just now are in a mood to listen with particular complaisance to any projects brought forward by the Sculpture Society." Lamb decided that the opportunity was ripe to expand the boundaries of municipal art to focus not on the decoration of public buildings but on the city itself. This was "highly considerate and commendable" of him, the *Times* thought.[41]

In 1899 Lamb urged his colleagues at the National Sculpture Society to sketch "ideas for city improvements," and these, transferred to lantern slides, made the rounds of the various societies, where "arguments and discussions followed from month to month."[42] Some of their ideas were prophetic, some unconvincing, and some risible. The Sculpture Society, for instance, published a drawing of a reading room at an elevated railway station. New York didn't yet have a public library system—Andrew Carnegie would announce his gift in 1901—and there's an undeniable charm to the idea of whiling away one's wait for a train with a good selection of books, but this hardly excuses the ghastly, naive surrealism of the drawing, which showed a decapitated dome propped up on the iron skeleton of the El. In January 1899 the Architectural League showed its members stereopticon views of proposed improvements, gathered together under the rubric "The Plan of the City." George Post presented a proposal for a civic amphitheater on the blocks north of City Hall and for the Manhattan approach to the new Williamsburg Bridge; this called for a circular plaza with radiating streets, one running to Union Square, the others through Spring and Chatham streets. Milton See unveiled his scheme for extending Riverside Park over the railroad tracks; A. J. Thorpe presented a project for new docks and a double-decked elevated railway on West Street; Charles Stoughton offered a plan for the Bronx "showing the use of diagonal avenues."[43] In February the league devoted an evening to the waterfront.[44] In May the National Sculpture Society and the National Society of Mural Painters discussed "The Beautification of Our Public and Civic Buildings."[45] Karl Bitter published his plans for the Plaza; Charles Lamb prepared a series of sketches for beautifying intersections in the tenement districts.

The artists' starting point was an aesthetic critique of the gridiron plan, which was so lacking in public amenities and spatial variety. One should note that the gridiron seemed much more oppressive at the turn of the century, when there were few tall buildings outside of the financial district. There were no landmarks on the skyline, like the Empire State Building or the Chrysler Building, to help people orient themselves. The spatial hierarchy of neighborhoods like the Upper West Side, where densely built avenues now contrast with the intimate scale of side streets, had not yet evolved. To the Beaux Arts community New York seemed placeless, a giant checkerboard on which public and private buildings were randomly placed, and where every street and avenue ended in an identical vista of open sky. Their response was to single out the exceptional places in the gridiron—the parks, the odd intersections where Broadway sliced across the avenues, the great nodes of the mass transit system—and to try to make privileged spaces of them, focal points for public life and public buildings.

At the Reform Club the Beaux Artists began to learn of some of the more difficult issues facing New York. John De Witt Warner started publishing the magazine *Municipal Affairs* as the club's house organ (its editor, Milo Maltbie, later joined the board of MAS and served as secretary of the Art Commission). *Municipal Affairs* published many of the art societies' schemes for beautifying New York, but it placed them in a larger context of the city's political and economic life, and amid calls for the city's elite to awaken to its civic duty. In 1899 it also published a plan for New York by the architect Julius Harder, the first attempt at a comprehensive plan since 1811.[46] Harder's argument was that business would eventually devour all of Manhattan south of Central Park, and that the island's center of gravity would shift from the financial district to Union Square. Harder would have enlarged the square to create a new civic center and made it the focus of four new diagonal avenues heading northwest to Eleventh Avenue; southwest (really an extension of Christopher Street) to the West Street piers and ferries; southeast to the foot of the Williamsburg Bridge; and northeast to First Avenue. Broadway and Fourth Avenue served as additional rays in this sunburst.

New York didn't develop in quite the fashion Harder expected, but his plan deserves credit as the first acknowledgment of the scale of the problem. In the meantime Warner and Lamb would move their partnership to the Municipal Art Society. The Reform Club was so closely identified with political reform that it couldn't serve as an effective advocate while Tammany controlled City Hall, and the National Sculpture Society turned out to be a terrible place for Charles Lamb to consider planning issues. Entrusting the city plan to a sculpture society sounded incongruous, and the sculptors resented Lamb's effort. They had a reputation for backstabbing, but in the sculptors' defense one should note that they were vastly outnumbered in their own society—of three or four hundred members, only sixty had ever set their hands in modeling clay—and they felt put upon. Lamb's role in dreaming up the Dewey Arch, the National Sculpture Society's moment of glory, didn't help matters at all. The press had showered attention on Lamb as the architect of the arch, perhaps because it was easier to focus on one architect than on a dozen sculptors, and as the critic Barr Ferree sadly observed, "Mr. Lamb's well-nigh superhuman activity for artists created petty jealousies." Eventually the sculptors would force him off the board. "They threw mud at him," Ferree wrote, "and swept him out of office, with mental if not audible hurrahs."[47] Lamb's departure marked the beginning of the sculpture society's decline; it turned to narrow professional issues, like trying to enforce standards for impartial competitions and raising sculptors' pay, and the lay members, whose dues financed the group, drifted away. Something similar soon transpired at the Architectural League, where Julius Harder complained that "a distinct effort is being made to minimize its influence for public and professional good and to confine its activity to but one of its functions—namely, its exhibitions."[48]

A good many artists and architects resisted Lamb's call for a broader, more socially engaged conception of municipal art. Many thought it was a terrible idea for artists to waste their efforts on the mundane world. Charles Follen McKim, who served on the McMillan Commission to plan Washington, D.C., would refuse to join a similar planning effort in New York. He would only participate in "an ideal proposition," he explained to a friend, "which is not very like to be made. The difficulties to be overcome here are, so far as the Borough of Manhattan [is] concerned, insuperable, and with but a few years of breath left to hope for, there are several ways in which I could put in my time more effectively."[49] Charles Lamb was no more successful in interesting Russell Sturgis, a great figure of an older generation. Sturgis's career as a (not very good) Ruskinian Gothic architect was in eclipse, but he was still a lordly critic of art and architecture, and he edited "The Field of Art" column in *The Century* magazine. Lamb hoped to use Sturgis's column to introduce the City Beautiful to a vast national audience, but Sturgis wouldn't bite. Fine art in America, he argued, was too fragile an enterprise to risk diluting it in the hurly-burly of this new municipal art. "It is . . . not worth while," he wrote Lamb, "for a society of artists to concern itself with wide streets and clean streets, for the laymen can do that."

"I must disagree with you," Lamb answered. "It is the unfortunate divorcement of art from daily life, which in my opinion, is the cause of our inartistic general living. If art does not make for better living, it has no right to exist. I believe it does: that it always has, and that, therefore, it needs not only the producer, but the public for whom the art is produced, and the closer in sympathy these two parts are united, the better the result secured."[50]

As the other members of the Fine Arts Federation narrowed their focus, it occurred to people like the Lambs and Warner that the Municipal Art Society wasn't the redundant organization it seemed. It was tied to no professional group, and its bylaws invited laymen to join. It was an empty vessel, ready for a new crew and a new course. They took it over, brought in their allies, and set out to forge a true "society." MAS had always led a nomadic existence, living out of the offices of board members, but the Lambs found it a home in the National Arts Club. In a sense these were borrowed quarters, but they were borrowed from Municipalians. George Post, the Lamb brothers, Spencer Trask, Richard Watson Gilder, John La Farge, Henry Kirke Bush-Brown, and J.Q.A. Ward were all charter members of the National Arts Club, and when the club moved to its permanent home at 15 Gramercy Park South—the old Tilden mansion, with a superb Gothic Revival facade by Calvert Vaux—it was Charles Lamb who adapted the interiors and Post who built the crenellated twelve-story studio building in its garden.[51] In effect, the Municipal Art Society had acquired a clubhouse without the expense of building one.

Life at the National Arts Club offered the Municipal Art Society peculiar advantages. Charles de Kay had founded the National Arts Club to foster "the art side of American manufacturers" (founding clubs was almost a hobby of de Kay's; he also fathered the National Sculpture Society, the Authors' Club, the Fencing Club, and the Berliner Fecht Club), so it was open to businessmen, bankers, importers, and exporters—who soon communicated to the artists their own concerns about the city. It was also the first club in New York to admit women as equal members. Charles Lamb, a feminist and the husband of an artist, had insisted on this, and though no women ascended to the Municipal Art Society's board until the 1920s, they came to staff and sometimes to chair its committees.[52]

MAS now had an office, with a single secretary to staff it, a room for its board meetings, and a gallery where it could hold annual exhibitions. These would give the society a public face for the first time. No less important, the board and committee members now had a bar and a dining room at their disposal—the new board understood that if they expected people to volunteer their services they had to sweeten the pill. They were expected to work hard, as the society's board now met monthly, and sometimes weekly. It organized an elaborate network of committees that gave members an opportunity to work on the issues that most concerned them. They could choose from committees devoted to thoroughfares; the city plan; civic centers; parks; conference (to coordinate the society's activities with those of other advocacy groups); publicity; membership; the decoration of public buildings; the decoration of schools; private advertising signs; the law; and trees, plants, vines, and areaways.

The Municipal Art Society was ready to attack the problems of New York from a great many angles.

4

INGENIOUS MINDS:
BLOCKS BEAUTIFUL
AND USEFUL ART

IN 1901 THE *New York Times* announced the rebirth of the Municipal Art Society and hailed its "earnest spirit of civic pride, the same spirit that formed the City Club and the Reform Club and keeps them at work combating that apathy regarding New York affairs which is the chief sign of New Yorkers."[1] Such comments were flattering and obviously helpful, but the fact remained that MAS was still a group of just a few hundred people, and that for years it had been "vegetating in a corner, appearing only from time to time to unveil a monument."[2]

The society desperately needed to establish a record of public service, but the political climate was terrible. Tammany still reigned over City Hall. Its bureaucrats regularly commended MAS for its public spirit and expressed "interest" in its ideas, but beneath the surface there was "an antagonism hard to quell," as the *Times* put it, "between citizens who propose apparently harmless improvements and the average holder of office. Ignorance, conceit, and sometimes dread that the society may interfere with contracts and profitable arrangements of various kinds are factors of importance, any one of which may be a stumbling block."[3]

The mayor, Robert Van Wyck, did not even pretend to be polite. A sarcastic, surly, unhappy man, Van Wyck tongue-lashed anyone bold enough to appear in his presence to demand municipal art. Municipalians held it against Van Wyck that he "abused" the trustees of the New York Public Library when they came to him asking for money to build their $10 million building at Forty-second Street, and that he cut the budget for decorating the Hall of Records by $1 million. This was proof, Municipalians thought, of Tammany's philistinism. But what else could the mayor have done? The single most notorious act in Tammany Hall's history was the construction of the Tweed Courthouse behind City Hall, a building that cost four times as much as Great Britain's Houses of Parliament, Big Ben and all. In 1871 the *Times* had printed the scandalous details: $675,534.44 spent for carpets, window shades, and curtains; $531,594.22 for plasterwork; $1,294,684.13 for "repairs" to the plaster; $750,071.92 for repairs to the woodwork; $41,746.83 for "brooms, etc."[4] With this legacy still fresh in the public's mind, Tammany found it wise to preach a gospel of frugality—at least in public.

And so we had a curious spectacle at the turn of the century: reformers demanding that Tammany Hall, author of the Tweed Courthouse, spend large sums of money on public works and the lavish decoration of public buildings. Van Wyck must have found the situation deliciously ironic. He was too cynical to believe, as the art societies did, in the uplifting effects of a historical mural. Nor did he have a keen perception of the distinction between artists and craftsmen—a distinction fairly new to America and as yet only tenuously established. In Tammany's eyes the difference must have seemed to be a conflict, not of art versus craft, but of class, and Tammany sided with the working class, not the so-called best men. Moreover, as A.D.F. Hamlin admitted, Tammany officials were quite genuinely suspicious of the Municipal Art Society and its allies in the Fine Arts Federation. "The average official can see no motive," he wrote, "other than the selfish motive. They conceive of these societies as organized solely for the purpose of securing 'jobs' and 'plans' for their members, and turn down their recommendations with the feeling of virtue triumphant over selfishness and graft."[5]

The Municipal Art Society began looking for ways to overcome or circumvent Tammany's hostility, to provoke such a groundswell of support for the City Beautiful that politicians would have to pay attention. In 1901 the society laid plans for one project that it hoped would bear fruit in a few years' time. Since the Chicago fair of 1893 had awakened an interest in public art and Beaux Arts architecture, it occurred to Municipalians that the Louisiana Purchase Exposition, scheduled for Saint Louis in 1904, might be made to do the same for city planning. When Charles Coolidge Haight was dispatched to Saint Louis to meet with the fair's commissioners, he took with him the society's proposal that the fair include, in addition to the usual state and national pavilions, a Model City. It would serve as an object lesson in the "treatment of parks and plaza spaces, street crossings and other vistas, grouping and architecture of other structures" and of even the minutest details of municipal art, like mailboxes, streetlamps, and garbage cans.[6]

The result of this was a little disappointing. When the American League for Civic Improvement issued a statement endorsing the proposal, the press gave the league, not MAS, credit for the idea, and the league ended up as the idea's major sponsor and publicist. Moreover, the fair commissioners, faced with a tight budget, shrank the Model City to a Model Street. What emerged was more appropriate to the scale of a large town than to Manhattan, and it said more about street furniture than street layouts. Nevertheless, the Model Street was one of the hits of the Saint Louis fair, and visitors flocked to its buildings to see an exhibition of "municipal art *and* municipal service."[7] One could watch actors pretending to work in a Bureau of Municipal Statistics (at the time no city in America had such a department, or even a budget in the modern sense of the term) or admire a corps of mock firemen, as well drilled as a military honor guard, operating the latest in fire equipment. It was all meant to fire people up with the idea of progressive municipal government:

"scientific," impartial, devoted to providing services rather than dividing spoils, and run by a professional bureaucracy rather than patronage appointees. Most people probably took home with them the image of a pretty new town hall overlooking a pretty little park, or of the sparkling new fire engines.

In New York the Municipal Art Society had begun by pursuing a more modest course with a campaign for "useful art." Plans were laid for an exhibit of "lamp-posts, telegraph and telephone boxes, letter boxes, signs and placards which may prove suggestive for the city street . . . the right kind of fountain for public square or blank wall, the best sort of window box for flowers in a house front, the proper treatment of areaways, the way in which recreation piers might be made more attractive, shelters for the public at exposed places where transfers are made from one line of trolley to another, shelters for cabmen, etc." These were all items "close to popular needs," Charles de Kay wrote, and many could be achieved by private citizens or local women's clubs.[8] In part this was a bid for popularity, but the Useful Art and tree-planting campaigns also recognized that turn-of-the-century New York was an urban failure on even the most rudimentary level. It offered pedestrians no refuge as they crossed a busy street, nor, in many neighborhoods, were people given the faintest clue as to their whereabouts. They found no respite from the sun, and no place to slake their thirst (and if anything, New York has since moved backward in the area of drinking fountains). The Useful Art campaign was meant to make the city less confounding, the streets safer, and the sidewalks less cluttered, but behind this lay a larger agenda. The society was trying to demonstrate to the public that the city streets were not a no-man's-land but rather public spaces—our communal front yards and promenades.

''THE TIME will come when a city vista will always be terminated by a park, lined by a boulevard, or by a tree-shaded and vine-clad street"—this, at any rate, was the promise of Irene Hagamon Hall, for a decade the chairwoman of the Municipal Art Society's Committee on Flowers, Vines and Area Planting. If the small parks were "oases" in the city streets, as they were often called, then one could conclude only that much of New York was a wasteland. Hall's mission was to persuade the public to green this desert, to think of the typical city street as nothing less than "the logical extension of the system of parks and boulevards."

In 1902 she inaugurated the Municipal Art Society's Block Beautiful program, "the most practical and the simplest method for the civic embellishment of the city."[9] Hall persuaded the residents of a street in Brooklyn Heights to set potted plants on their stoops and to plant shade trees on their sidewalks, shrubs and vines in their areaways, and flowers in new window boxes. The program was lauded by the Brooklyn papers and by *House and Garden* magazine, and proved so popular that it was extended the next year to cover the whole of Brooklyn Heights.

Hall was able to turn this Brooklyn Beautiful campaign over to the Women's Municipal League; in the meantime her committee decided to bring the Block Beautiful movement to the city at large. It was still conceived as "an entirely private matter"; all that was needed to beautify the city, Hall thought, was "public enthusiasm." To drum this up, she became a fixture of the local lecture circuit. Women's clubs, church groups, and neighborhood associations watched her slide shows of embowered streets and heard her tell of the good works of the Municipal Art Society. She would recruit a few women on a given street and then rely on these converts to cajole, shame, or inspire their neighbors into joining the campaign. Hall soon discovered, however, that the Block Beautiful approach worked only in areas like Brooklyn Heights, a prosperous neighborhood of privately owned row houses, where each family felt responsible for its own patch of sidewalk and front yard. The support Hall received in such areas was gratifying, but these were the people who least needed to beautify their neighborhoods. What of the tenement dwellers? They had no yards in which their children might play; their apartments were small, dark, crowded, and noisy; and they conducted much of their social life, and perhaps their business, on the street. Hall was at a loss in these neighborhoods. Landlords were impervious to her propaganda, tenants had a less personal stake in their streets, and trees were beyond their means in any case. The only answer, she concluded, was for the Parks Department to take responsibility for the propagation, planting, and care of shade trees. Washington and Paris, Hall pointed out, each had some 80,000 shade trees—all grown in municipal nurseries and tended by municipal park departments—while another 7,000 grew on the grounds of Paris's public schools. There were just 4,000 trees on New York's sidewalks, and by the Park Department's own admission, they'd been "sadly neglected in recent years."[10]

Shade trees had long been a controversial subject in New York. In 1894 no less a figure than Frederick Law Olmsted advised the City Improvement Society, a short-lived advocacy group, to abandon its plan to plant trees on Madison Avenue. They wouldn't survive, he said. When the Municipal Art Society took up the subject there was already a Tree Planting Association, but it had found life difficult and frustrating. In the 1890s this association drafted legislation giving the Parks Department responsibility for planting and tending trees on the sidewalks. The bill passed the Municipal Assembly several times but was vetoed just as regularly by Mayor Van Wyck. At last Van Wyck signed a compromise bill that "allowed" the Parks Department to plant shade trees, but to the dismay of the Tree Planting Association, the department never lifted a finger to do so. True, the Parks Department was perennially underfunded, but it seemed remarkably uninterested in any attempts to obtain a larger appropriation for the new task it was now allowed to undertake. The Tree Planting Association was so disillusioned that it became, for the moment, unduly retiring. It had been shocked, too, by the outright hostility that greeted its efforts. In 1901, for instance, one gentleman wrote the *Times*:

> Anyone who lived in this city forty years ago can perhaps remember that there were a great many trees; that there was also a plague of worms, that fell on pedestrians and were crushed on the sidewalks. They crawled into houses and were a nuisance. To remedy this evil English sparrows were imported, suppos-

ing that they would eat the worms. This they refused to do, and instead drove our beautiful birds away and remained themselves, almost as much of a nuisance as the worms. Then ailanthus trees were planted and the others cut down. The odor from the ailanthus caused headache and symptoms of malaria, and they were cut down, but have never been gotten rid of. Let the Tree-Planting Association acquaint themselves with facts. There are only three months in the year when we have much sun in our streets. With more trees we would have more dirt and insects.[11]

The writer was apparently referring to cicadas, which are indeed obnoxious creatures, but they appear only in sixteen-year cycles. What seems remarkable, though, is that he wrote his letter in springtime, when the city parks were presumably full of gorgeous budding trees. He did sign his letter, "An Old Fogy," but he was less eccentric than one might think. In 1903, in the midst of Irene Hall's campaign for shade trees, the *Times* printed an astonishing editorial. Trees could not possibly survive on the sidewalks of New York, it argued, and in any case, "sunlight is best and cheapest of the disinfectants." Plant trees in the crowded tenement districts, the paper warned, and "the already large infant mortality rate might be alarmingly increased."[12]

Municipalians and members of the Tree Planting Association refused to believe that trees killed babies. It was true that some people, innocent of common sense, had attempted to grow trees in sidewalk openings no wider than their trunks; true that trees had to cope with an atmosphere fouled by the burning of soft coal; true that turn-of-the-century gas mains leaked like sieves and poisoned any nearby trees. The Municipal Art Society could do little about gas leaks for the moment, but Irene Hall's committee and the Tree Planting Association undertook a public education campaign to resolve the other issues; they told homeowners and neighborhood associations what species to plant and how to do so.

The city was unmoved, however. "The Park Department frankly confesses . . . its utter inability to care for the few trees that now do exist. It is useless to set out trees that cannot be cared for," Hall complained. "It is useless for private societies to attempt to aid the City in doing what only the City itself can do. It is useless for the City to attempt, under the present circumstances, to do anything itself. Supplying the streets of New York with the full number of shade trees is not only useless, but harmful; for inasmuch as the private societies will never accomplish work that amounts to serious consideration, and inasmuch as the existence of these societies apparently removes the responsibility from the Park Department, and hence saves the Park Department from the odium which it deserves for not taking an intelligent and up-to-date interest in such an important matter, the problem will either remain unsolved, or the responsibility must be positively shouldered by the City."[13]

Hall's despair was short-lived, however. The shade tree campaign resumed and made slow but steady progress. Caroline Phelps Stokes, a member of Hall's committee, organized a fund to plant trees on the grounds of charitable institutions; the Board of Education reported that it would be delighted to plant trees around its schools and to landscape their grounds, but pointed out that the Municipal Art Society would have to help it obtain an appropriation. And the Block Beautiful campaign continued. Hall went on showing her slides of beautiful, lushly planted side streets, slowly building a constituency for shade trees. Shortly before World War I, Brooklyn's parks commissioner finally bowed to the pressure and began planting shade trees. The other boroughs had to wait until the 1930s when Robert Moses became the city's parks commissioner.

THE MUNICIPAL Art Society had far better luck persuading the city to move forward with street furniture. Again it started out by taking advantage of the existing network of private groups. Temperance activists were trying to provide thirsty workmen with an alternative to the corner saloon, and animal rights groups were campaigning for better treatment of horses, so the Municipal Art Society organized competitions for the design of standardized public drinking fountains and horse troughs. These made life easier and cheaper for private donors, who no longer had to hire a designer for each fountain or win the Art Commission's approval for their work; the competitions also spared the Art Commission the unpleasant and unpopular task of constantly rejecting submissions. A number of these new drinking fountains were actually erected, but the public's "interest did not long survive the rivalry of more absorbing questions."[14] The dangerous conditions at crosswalks and the absence of street signs seemed much more pressing issues.

Entire neighborhoods, among them the Upper West Side, were without street signs. For years the city had been tearing down its old gas lampposts and replacing them with new electrical models, but at some point in this conversion, for reasons never explained, it stopped hanging street signs on the new lampposts. Even if one found the correct street, it took a still more intimate knowledge of the city to locate one's precise destination, for no law required that a building display its street number. All of this was annoying to those New Yorkers who dared stray out of their own neighborhood, but it was even worse for tourists. As the *Times* wrote in 1902, each day Manhattan was host to enough visitors to form "a city of the second class," and these poor souls had no alternative but to wander the streets begging passersby for directions.[15]

Mayor Van Wyck's administration was unwilling to touch the subject of new street signs, perhaps because it was still embarrassed by the fact that in 1899 it had embarked on an "absurd, annoying and useless" experiment with the old signs.[16] In that year Henry S. Kearny, Commissioner of the Department of Public Buildings, Lighting and Supplies, ordered that all street signs be hung in a new way: "the name of any given street shall be at right angles to the street, instead of reading along the street as heretofore."[17] This reversed traditional (and contemporary) practice. It took the public a while to discover what was going on, for Kearny made no advance announcement of his new policy, and to save money he decided to institute the change gradually, as the signs were cleaned. At first people assumed that the workers were confused, careless, or illiterate, but as bafflement spread through the entire city, the newspapers made inquiries. Kearny admitted what he was doing, and he explained that his innovation made the street signs easier to see. "A most convincing reason," one citizen wrote the Times in 1899, "but it has this drawback—it is not true."[18] Kearny dug in his heels, however, and two years later people were still complaining. "When a man has found a street and is walking on it," one wrote in 1901, "he certainly knows what street it is, and it is annoying to find every lamp post as far as he can see declaring to him what he already knows."[19]

Here, then, was a problem the city seemed unable to solve despite its embarrassment—a perfect opportunity for the "ingenious minds" of the Municipal Art Society.[20] In 1901 John De Witt Warner offered the society's assistance to the Board of Aldermen. He asked what the city required in the way of street signs, and what it was willing to spend. He offered in turn to sponsor a competition at the society's expense for a design that would meet the city's specifications. Warner suggested that the street signs also function as lampposts, letterboxes, fire alarms, and possibly fire hydrants; this would reduce clutter on the sidewalks and, it was hoped, ultimately cut the city's costs. In return he made only one request of the city: that this fixture "should be considered a work of art, and as such subject to the approval of the Municipal Art Commission."[21]

"The chances are that the offer will be rejected with scorn," the Times wrote, "as an impertinent hint that the City Fathers are not as competent to settle aesthetic questions as they are—in their own estimation—to decide all other matters."[22] In fact the aldermen simply asked MAS to forward specific ideas. The society discovered that combining lampposts with other functions was unworkable. Mailboxes were under federal jurisdiction, for instance. Fire alarms and hydrants were already in place in much of the city, and the fire department was unwilling to switch to new designs in newly settled districts.

As for street signs, MAS wondered whether it was possible to adopt the European system of compelling those who owned corner property to mount street signs on their buildings. The city's corporation counsel explained that this was illegal, and his reasons are worth noting as an illustration of just how little control the city thought it could exercise over private property. First, he argued, this would benefit the entire community, so the city had no right to shift the expense to particular property owners. Second, he wrote, "if there is any doubt as to the existence of such a power it should be resolved against the municipality."[23] And third, even if the city were to pay for the erection of these signs, it would still have to obtain the property owners' consent. By the same token, the city could not force its citizens to display their street numbers.

Nothing more was heard from the city until 1902, when a new reform administration came into office, and a member of the Municipal Art Society, Jacob Cantor, became Manhattan borough president. Charles Rollinson Lamb designed two types of street signs, and the Municipal Art Society erected several examples on existing lampposts. One type was square, lit from behind at night for better visibility, and elaborately crested. The other was similar, but triangular in plan. It was used on streets with trolley lines, so the signs were easier to read from inside the trolleys. Cantor adopted these designs, and the Municipal Art Society began to learn the hazards of dealing even with a friendly political administration. It took Cantor five months of arguing with Comptroller Edward Grout to get half the appropriation he needed, and then the Art Commission rejected Lamb's designs. A simpler design had to be provided, and in 1903 these at last began to appear on Manhattan streets and, shortly afterward, in Brooklyn. Grout's frugality told, however: by 1906 MAS and a coalition of civic and trade groups were holding public meetings to demand more street signs.[24]

There were no traffic regulations in turn-of-the-century New York: no red lights, no lane markings, no keeping to the right, no one-way streets. "The driver of every truck, trolley car, horse-drawn vehicle and motor was an absolute law to himself," George McClellan wrote in his memoirs, "and moved through the streets as best he could, relying on his nerve, his agility, and his bullying to get through."[25] When horses ruled the streets, moving at a stately average pace of eleven miles an hour, a pedestrian could still hope to survive such anarchy. Trolleys, though, were responsible for five times as many deaths in New York as in London or Paris, and the automobile was a source of growing alarm. The car was faster than a horse, harder to handle, and surely less intelligent, and if it didn't kill you itself, its backfiring engine might startle any nearby horse into a panic. In some neighborhoods autos were still a rare sight, but they were becoming common on the great north-south axes of prosperity, along Broadway and Fifth Avenue.

The most dangerous intersections in the city were the eccentric ones at Columbus Circle and at Fourteenth, Twenty-third, Thirty-fourth, and Forty-second streets where Broadway happened upon an intersection and the roadways merged in great deltas of asphalt. Here traffic moved in six directions and trolleys in four, yet no special provisions had been made for pedestrians' safety or peace of mind.

The most tantalizing of these sites was Columbus Circle, one of the very few exceptions to the gridiron plan. It wasn't yet marred by the hideous system of lane dividers and traffic islands (those were installed in the 1950s when, over MAS's strenuous objections, Robert Moses closed Fifty-ninth Street to build his atrocious Coliseum). At the turn of the century the area was merely a pool of asphalt crisscrossed by traffic and the broad arcs of trolley tracks. The traffic didn't have to bear right (that innovation arrived in 1906), and the trolleys discharged bewildered passengers in the middle of the asphalt. In the center of Columbus Circle stood the Christopher Columbus Memorial, erected in 1892 by the Italian American community, one of the city's most oppressed immigrant groups. It was a point of ethnic pride that the monument was designed by an Italian, Gaetano Russo, but the fin de siècle was no high point in Italian architectural history. There was a certain coarseness to Russo's design, and he had disastrously miscalculated its scale. The monument might have been effective in some narrow Roman street or piazza, but the circle was huge by Old World standards, and Columbus failed to command the space at his disposal.

In 1901 Charles Lamb saw an opportunity to make the Columbus monument an object lesson in the usefulness of municipal art. He suggested placing it atop a two-level arcade. The arcade would boost the monument's scale, provide for pedestrians, and serve, Lamb suggested, as a public forum. (It would also, unfortunately, have made the memorial look like a wedding cake.) At the same time, the trolley tracks would be rerouted to run just inside the circle's outer rim. "Isles of safety"—patches of pavement raised above the asphalt and equipped with large lamps known as electroliers—would be built between the tracks, so passengers would have a safe place to wait when they transferred from one line to another.

"So inconvenient is the Circle in its present state," wrote the *Times*, "so uncomfortable are the crowds that assemble and dissolve in successive waves without protection from the burning sun in Summer and the cold in Winter, so dangerous is the present arrangement for the crossing of the trolley tracks, that the man who proposes to make the Circle convenient, protected from the elements, and safe, without undue expense to the city, should be hailed as a benefactor."[26] The *Real Estate Record and Guide*, the *Mail and Express*, the West End Association, and the Municipal League joined in the praise for Lamb's scheme, yet the plan foundered on the question of who should pay for it. "Why should the city make the improvement?" wrote the *Times*.

> Why not the Metropolitan Company itself, which has made what so many bewildered passengers find a nuisance? The company hopes to "stick" the municipality with the expense, while it itself reaps the benefit. And, we regret to say, the Municipal Art Society fosters the delusion by admitting that the expense is properly chargeable upon the city. . . . We should suggest that the Mayor and the appropriate head of departments take counsel whether the city has not the power to compel the Metropolitan to this decent and civilized step, at the Metropolitan's own expense. . . . At any rate, let us not hear any more of this improvement in facilities transit at the expense of the city until it is made quite clear that it cannot be effected at the expense of the benefited corporation.[27]

The city found it had no power over the trolleys—the Metropolitan Company's franchise was ironclad—and Lamb gave up all hope of building his odd arcade. And so the project died, but not the idea of isles of safety. For some years the city had wondered whether to erect these in the middle of busy crosswalks so that, as the *Times* wrote, "people can be safe from the automobile when it crieth 'tuff-tuff,' champeth the bit, and smelleth the battle afar off."[28] The Municipal Art Society decided to give the city a push, and in 1901 it made an offer: if the city would put an isle of safety at the southwest corner of Madison Square, where Fifth Avenue, Broadway, and Twenty-third Street intersected, MAS would contribute a magnificent bronze electrolier. The society had chosen a glamorous location amid hotels and theaters and just north of the Flatiron Building. The city accepted, and in June 1902 the society held a competition for the electrolier. Victor Ciani won the commission and a prize of $500; Henrik Wallin won second place and $100; and Wilkinson & Magonigle, coming in third, received $50. There was a certain logic to the awards: Ciani's design was the most ornate, and Magonigle's the least. Indeed what Ciani produced was absolutely bizarre. Stacked atop one another were an altar draped with garlands and rams' heads; a collection of lions' paws; a group of children gamboling in the nude around a circular drum; a ring of acanthus leaves; a tall, tapering shaft, more like an onion stalk than a column; a quartet of dolphins clutching light bulbs in their mouths; and finally a big globe of frosted glass. The *Times* decided that it was "particularly jolly,"[29] and surely it was chosen precisely because it was so elaborate and festal. It made a splashy gift to the city, one that passersby could not help but notice. By the same token, however, it was probably a tactical mistake, for it was too expensive to serve as a prototype for other isles of safety.

Its inertia overcome, the city moved forward in 1902 with isles of safety at Broadway at Fourteenth and Thirty-fourth streets and at Fourteenth Street and Fourth Avenue, at Union Square.[30] Once Ciani's electrolier was unveiled and applauded, William Muschenheim approached the Municipal Art Society with an offer to pay for electroliers and isles of safety in Longacre Square (its name was changed to Times Square in 1904, when the paper moved into its new headquarters). Muschenheim was the manager of the Astor Hotel. Financed by the Astor estate and designed by Clinton & Russell in 1901, the hotel was nearing completion at Broadway between Forty-fourth and Forty-fifth streets. It was less a building than an act of colonization: its ballrooms, bars, grills, tearooms, and roof garden were meant to provide all the services needed to transform Times Square into the city's new entertainment district. The Astors owned the land stretching westward from the square all the way to the Hudson River, and it was on these blocks that the heart of the theater district was eventually built.

In the meantime, though, Longacre Square was still a seedy place battling an old reputation as Thieves' Lair, a haunt of pickpockets. Clinton & Russell had therefore taken care that the Astor Hotel would be one of New York's most brilliantly lit buildings. A picket of handsome bronze lamp standards surrounded the building at sidewalk level, and another crowned its mansard roof, where there was a famous roof garden. The new isles of safety would extend some of this brilliance—and presumably, security—into the square itself. This public improvement, then, benefited the Astor estate—a very unpopular organization, since the Astors were at once the most arrogant leaders of New York society and the city's richest slumlords. So it was that the estate approached the Municipal Art Society, rather than the city, with its offer of electroliers. The Astor name was to remain unspoken, and MAS was to obtain all the necessary city approvals in its own name. At Muschenheim's request, the society also agreed to use Henrik Wallin's design instead of Ciani's. Ciani's grotesquerie, it seems, didn't wear well.

The isles of safety were dedicated in March 1905. Times Square was draped in bunting for the occasion, and an audience of "persons prominent in the artistic and municipal affairs of New York" was on hand. The *Times*, which had just moved into its new Italian Gothic skyscraper at the south end of the square, was predictably boosterish, hailing the isles of safety as "isles of beauty."[31] And again the city was prompted to further action. In May it announced that Times Square would be the scene of "the biggest scheme of traffic regulation ever tried in this city,"[32] and for the first time triangular isles of safety were roped off in both halves of that strange bow tie–shaped "square."

These triangles were made permanent, but most isles of safety were removed before the First World War. They failed because there was still no system of lane dividers or medians, and drivers ran right over them. The city tried ringing them with low stone posts, but these wreaked havoc on careless drivers and failed to ensure that the isles of safety were, in fact, safe—Victor Ciani's electrolier was flattened by a fire truck in 1909.[33] The city concluded that isles of safety were a failed experiment. They returned to New York after World War II, but by then the Municipal Art Society had long since moved on to other subjects.

ALL THE CIVIC VIRTUES: SETH LOW AND THE MUNICIPAL ART SOCIETY

EXERCISES LIKE THE Useful Art and Block Beautiful campaigns won the Municipal Art Society a good name and a broader base of support, credentials it sorely needed if it was ever to address more complex issues like the city plan and the skyscrapers. Even so, there was no guarantee that the city would listen to MAS. Advocacy had its limits, especially when one was dealing with an organization as venal as Tammany Hall in the Van Wyck years. It seemed at first that the reformed Municipal Art Society would be more vigorous than in the past, but only a little more effective.

As Municipalians looked back on the city's history the current political scene seemed grim indeed. The nineteenth century had been an era of great public improvements. The Erie Canal and the improvement of the harbor had been carried out with government funds, and these had transformed New York into the mercantile capital of the nation. The construction of Central Park had been carried out through the years of Tammany control. Brooklyn had built Prospect Park. Broadway had been straightened (the original road, which the commissioners of 1807 wanted to eliminate, was far more meandering than the street we know today), and Andrew Haswell Green's Park Commission had widened the West Side's avenues, transformed Broadway into an embowered boulevard, and created Riverside and Morningside parks.

The exposure of the Tweed Ring, however, had put an end to this tradition. The Bronx had acquired its park system in the 1880s, but that was handled through the state, not the city. Since the 1870s, control of City Hall had seesawed between Tammany Hall and reformers while the city's problems grew more desperate and the public became more cynical about the political process. Tammany Hall could no longer afford to be so bold with its public improvements, and the reformers had done no better. New York's "cultured and well-to-do classes," John De Witt Warner complained, had sunk into "ignorance and narrowness."[1] Their notion of a reform mayor was someone who promised "honest government" conducted along "business principles," who pledged to root out waste and fraud and, especially, to lower taxes. Such reformers did little for the city or its people, for they believed in minimal government: just the basic services, efficiently delivered. It was enough to make Charles Lamb miss Boss Tweed. "I would rather have a man with imagination coupled with dishonesty than a man with rectitude coupled with stupidity," he declared in a 1903 speech.[2] "Faugh!" the *Times* replied, adding that "happily for himself" Lamb was too young to remember much of Tweed, whose "notion of public improvement was simply that of a basis for stealing."[3]

Lamb, however, kept returning to his theme. "Who has the imagination needed for our great city?" he asked a group of civil engineers in 1908. "Who had it in the past? The man who had more belief in what New York was going to be was that man who died in prison; he was a politician. You know his name—Bill Tweed. Riverside Drive, all the parks of the Bronx, these improvements of which we are so proud, and to which the 'Seeing New York' buses go driving and showing to the visitors, were believed in by him. Politician though he was, dishonest man as he was, he still believed in his city. How many of you do the same thing?"[4]

Tweed was long gone, and Municipalians despaired of finding such imagination in Boss Croker. In 1901 they shed their roles as citizen advocates and threw themselves into the mayoral campaign. Their venue was the Citizens Union, which had been cobbled together in 1897 as a Fusion Party—an uneasy, "nonpartisan" coalition of Independent Democrats and Republicans running on a good-government plank. It lost that election, but was back in 1901 with Seth Low as its mayoral candidate.

The Municipal Art Society claimed to be a nonpolitical group, of course, but Tammany Hall can be forgiven for doubting its word. The Citizens Union was financed by the same wealthy bankers and businessmen whose names now graced the membership rolls of the Municipal Art Society. Lacking a political machine, the union relied on the informal network of good-government clubs and charity organizations in which Municipalians were so prominent. Seth Low was a member of the Municipal Art Society, and so was Robert Fulton Cutting, president of the Citizens Union, and Jacob Cantor, its candidate for Manhattan borough president. But the society was much more deeply involved in Fusion's campaign. Seth Low's campaign posters were unique in the history of New York: classical allegories, with images of enthroned, idealized women and legends like "Our City" inscribed beneath. They were designed by Charles Lamb, who later explained that "artistic" advertisements were themselves examples of Municipal Art, and they were very much in the same genre as the seal Daniel Chester French had designed for the Municipal Art Society.[5] Frederick Lamb sat on the executive committee of the Citizens Union, and Calvin Tomkins chaired its County Convention in 1901. Samuel Ordway and Milo Maltbie were both prominent in civil service reform and were both critics of Tammany. John De Witt Warner campaigned for Low and helped convince the reformers that they should aim their strategy not at the Silk Stocking district but at the Lower East Side. He'd nearly received the mayoral nomination himself, but Thomas Platt, the boss of the state Republican Party, refused to support "a simon-pure Democrat."[6] Warner's crime, as far as Platt was concerned, was that in 1898 he had tried to persuade Theodore Roosevelt to break with the corrupt Republican machine and run for governor on the Independent line.[7]

This time the Citizens Union had the advantage of a great civic scandal. Under Boss Tweed corruption had been practiced on a grand scale, but it was tightly controlled by a relatively small band of people. Under Richard Croker, a more democratic boss, graft had become available to everyone. When the Mazet Committee conducted an investigation of the city government it left little doubt that the police department had become an association of pimps. The revelations were incredibly sordid: policemen didn't just sell protection to bordellos, they associated with a class of professional seducers who recruited young women from the tenement districts by "ruining" them first. Officers fleshed out their salaries by accusing innocent women of prostitution, and demanding a bribe to drop the charges. This meant that the Citizens Union could run its campaign on an exquisitely simple theme: "Are you for vice or against it?" This was at least as effective in the immigrant communities as anywhere else, for it was the poor who feared that their daughters would fall into the hands of "white slavers," and the Fusion ticket swept to victory.

A campaign against vice said nothing about what the Citizens Union intended to do once it was in office, nor did it provide any guarantee that the reformers would be able to stay in power. Seth Low had been elected on a wave of outrage, but "This is nothing but revolt," Lincoln Steffens wrote, and "Revolt is not reform." If the past was any indication, Lower East Siders would soon drift back to Tammany Hall. Their "sovereign power, in the form of votes, is bought up by kindness and petty privileges," Steffens wrote. "They are forced to surrender, when necessary, by intimidation, but the leader and his captains have their hold because they take care of their own. They speak pleasant words, smile friendly smiles, notice the baby, give picnics up the River or the Sound, or a slap on the back; find jobs, most of them at the city's expense, but they have also newsstands, peddling privileges, railroad and other business places to dispense; they permit violations of the law, and, if a man has broken the law without permission, see him through the court. Though a blow in the face is as readily given as a shake of the hand, Tammany kindness is real kindness, and will go far, remember long, and take infinite trouble for a friend."[8]

For years reformers had offered, in place of kindness, the cold comfort of an honest but minimal government. That might have been enough when this was a nation of farmers and tradesmen, but it didn't begin to answer the needs of a city in the industrial age, when workers had lost control of their destiny to factory owners and landlords. To keep the poor on his side, Low had to prove that a reform government could improve people's lives even as it shunned the traditional system of exchanging favors for votes. Perhaps the most important thing he did was to enforce the new tenement law, which took effect just as he stepped into office and which set minimum standards of sanitation, light, air, and fire safety. The law was at its most vulnerable moment: landlords were holding public meetings, demanding its repeal, and predicting economic disaster. Low threw the full weight of his administration behind the new Tenement House Department and its first director, Robert W. De Forest, a Municipalian and one of the law's authors. By the time Low left office, the campaign to repeal the law had almost evaporated: he had given it the chance to demonstrate its benefits.

Tenement reform was only part of the Citizens Union's agenda. It came to power determined to reshape New York, to transform it into the City Beautiful. When Robert Fulton Cutting, president of the Citizens Union, spoke at the Municipal Art Society's annual meeting in 1903, he admitted that

> Our fellow citizens . . . are not unnaturally languid when they are offered the stale and wearisome battle cries of the politicians, the iniquities of Tammany, the hypocrisy of the ins and the promises of the outs, the liquor question, Sunday closing [of saloons], and corruption of the police. These are old and are negative; they are not constructive; and more than all, they do not rouse [the public] to battle for an ideal.
>
> But the City Beautiful is constructive, is new and stimulating, is an ideal toward which to strive, without the taint of National or municipal politics, which all citizens can join as champions. It is something for the outs as well as the ins, which cannot be ignored by the distributors of patronage in either National party, and, what is of far greater importance, a cause which will start from their apathy the vast company of citizens who have looked on with loathing while the crapulous politician has been following his natural instincts of bargain and charade.[9]

Seth Low, "the placid container of all the civic virtues," seemed to be the Municipal Art Society's ideal mayor.[10] He was "bred to business," as Steffens wrote, but "rose above it."[11] Low's family fortune had been made in the China trade, and he shared with MAS and the merchants a basic conception of city planning as a means to ensure the free flow of goods and workers. When he ran for mayor in 1897, he spoke out against the private railway companies' stranglehold on city growth. He'd wheedled an Art Commission, however compromised, out of the Charter Commission of 1896, and in the course of those deliberations was so touched by John Carrère's description of the nobility of public art that he had joined the Municipal Art Society. Even earlier, when he was mayor of Brooklyn, Low had launched the campaign to build the Soldiers' and Sailors' Memorial Arch in Grand Army Plaza, at the entrance to Prospect Park, and so began the transformation of Olmsted's bucolic landscape into an Arcadian vision of the City Beautiful. As president of Columbia College, Low had chosen McKim, Mead & White to design its new Morningside Heights campus, and he had contributed a million dollars of his own fortune—a truly staggering sum at the time—to erect the centerpiece of McKim's design, the great domed library named for Seth Low's father. The Columbia campus, though never finished and much abused by later generations, ranks as one of the great achievements of the City Beautiful movement in New York. Surely, MAS thought, if Low saw this as the appropriate way to house a university, he'd want to do no less for New York's public buildings.

Yet the Municipal Art Society's relations with Seth Low grew tense as his term wore on. Part of the problem lay in the mayor's character. Low was a politician so lacking in charm and humor that his own supporters grew to dislike him, and even his running mate, District Attorney William Jerome, lamented "the unlovable personality of the man himself."[12] Low had a deep need to be *seen* acting righteously. It came out in his reliance on special commissions and expert advice—a quirk that the Municipal Art Society was often able to manipulate to its own ends, but one that also wasted precious time. Time was something Seth Low and the Citizens Union didn't have. Thanks to the Charter of 1902, his term of office was a mere two years. "In action," Steffens wrote, Low's conscientiousness was "often an irritation."[13] The true source of tension was that MAS kept pushing Low to go further than he wished or dared. Like the merchants, MAS wanted a new infrastructure; like the charity societies, it wanted new municipal services for the tenement dweller; and to these it added its own agenda for great and costly public buildings, like a new civic center at City Hall Park. Low was sympathetic to all of this, but he also had to guard his right wing—all those businessmen and property owners who demanded he keep a tight rein on city spending, and who thought that honest government and cheap government were one and the same. So when the Municipal Art Society demanded public improvements or a planning commission, Low tended either to stall for time or to grant the society only part of what it wanted.

This balancing act had long-term repercussions for the city, effects no one could have predicted at the time. Low was committed to a big campaign of public works, but raising taxes was politically dangerous. The city could float bonds, but it could borrow no more than 10 percent of the value of assessed real estate in New York. That limit was engraved in the New York State Constitution and defended by powerful interests. There was no hope of changing the constitution, but in 1902 the executive committee of the Citizens Union—one of whose members was Frederick Stymetz Lamb, secretary of the Municipal Art Society—pointed out that the city could borrow more money if it simply changed the way property was assessed. The city's assessors had always been told to estimate the size of the mortgage a given property could carry. The Citizens Union suggested that the assessors ask a different question: what would it sell for on the open market? Until the late nineteenth century there might not have been much difference between the two formulas, but the onset of steel construction had revolutionized the real estate market. Now a row house could give way to an apartment building; a sliver tower could spring from the site of a mom-and-pop store. Mortgages reflected the value of the old-fashioned building, but the market took into account the site's potential.

Changing the tax formula was the most controversial thing Low ever did. He explained that taxes wouldn't actually go up, that the city would *say* property was suddenly worth more and would borrow accordingly, but the city would simultaneously cut the property tax rate. People assumed, however, that the city would have to raise *some* taxes to pay off its growing debt, and businessmen and property owners grew disenchanted with Low and the Citizens Union. The immediate effect of the new assessment policy was a huge windfall in borrowing capacity—money needed for the East River bridges, schools, libraries, parks, public baths, and other projects. The long-term effect, however, was to wed the city's interests to those of the real estate speculator: rising land values became the engine of municipal government, and any move to produce a more humanely scaled city would run up against this basic conflict of interest.

WHEN SETH LOW came to power, so did the Municipal Art Society. By 1903, Frederick Lamb could tell his fellow Municipalians that, thanks to "the generous support of the Press and the considerate cooperation of our city officials, it looks at the present time as if the Society might not only pursue a prosperous existence, but might hope in time to equal the success of such societies as the Metropolitan Museum of Art, the American Museum of Natural History, the New York Zoological Society, the Botanical Gardens, and other public-spirited organizations of a kindred nature."[14] This sounds peculiar, but Lamb's point was that those organizations were all examples of public-private partnerships. The city, having decided that its citizens deserved to be exposed to great works of art and the glories of nature, had provided buildings and parks for this purpose, but it had also recognized that the vision and expertise necessary to run these institutions wasn't to be found among civil servants or patronage employees. Control of these cultural institutions had, in effect, been delegated by the city to private boards of directors, and in Seth Low's term of office municipal art, in its broadest sense, was effectively delegated to the Municipal Art Society.

The society took hold of the Art Commission, which finally began to live up to its founders' intentions. The new Charter of 1902 gave the Art Commission the power to review designs for any public work that cost more than a million dollars, thus dooming Leffert Buck's designs for the Manhattan and Queensboro bridges. But Low chose to go further, referring all public works, no matter how small the budget or utilitarian the program, to the Art Commission's experts. At the same time he made John De Witt Warner, the society's president, head of the Art Commission as well; Milo Maltbie, an MAS board member, became the commission's secretary; and Professor A.D.F. Hamlin of Columbia University did double duty as chairman of the society's Committee on the Decoration of Public Buildings and the Art Commission's dominant voice on all matters architectural.

The East River bridges would now have to be redesigned, and Low chose Gustav Lindenthal, "the most eminent bridge designer of his time," to serve as bridge commissioner.[15] The Art Commission was allowed to pick an architect to work with Lindenthal, and it chose the brilliant young designer Henry F. Hornbostel, Hamlin's colleague on the Columbia faculty. In turn, Lindenthal and Hornbostel joined the Municipal Art Society; so did Samuel Parsons, the Parks Department's new landscape architect, and George Rives, Low's corporation counsel. In the meantime Low launched a campaign against Horgan & Slattery, Van Wyck's city architects. They had contracts to design five new public buildings, including the Sixty-ninth Regiment Armory on Lexington Avenue between Twenty-fifth and Twenty-sixth streets and a two-million-dollar addition to the Tweed Courthouse. The *Times* demanded that Low cancel all of the contracts. Let Horgan & Slattery sue, the paper declared, and learn that "fraud vitiates every contract." Low held hearings on the courthouse project at which the Municipal Art Society argued successfully that the project was an intolerable encroachment on City Hall Park, and the mayor submitted Horgan & Slattery's armory plans to the Art Commission. John De Witt Warner referred them to Hamlin, who wrote a savagely critical report, and Low used this as an excuse to cancel all five contracts.

That was an expensive decision: the architects brought five separate lawsuits against the city, won them all (despite the *Times*), and collected some $600,000.[16] Low had expected as much, but argued that sparing the city five works by Horgan & Slattery was well worth the price.[17] (One contract remained that Low could not legally cancel: Horgan & Slattery continued as supervising architects of the Hall of Records.)

With the slate clear, Low inaugurated in New York's great age of municipal architecture, turning the city's public works over to the small band of Beaux Arts architects. He was determined to fulfill the *Times*'s prediction that, "if the reform administration succeeds in giving the people of New York object lessons in the value of municipal embellishment, such a success will be of distinct advantage to it when the next municipal election comes around."[18]

"Embellishment" didn't mean sheer aestheticism either to the *Times* or to the Municipal Art Society; it meant beautiful buildings serving the public and ameliorating the hellish living conditions of the poor. The most conspicuous of these structures were the sixteen public baths planned by the reform administration. It was a measure of how primitive New York was that in 1902 almost two-thirds of New Yorkers had no access to a bathroom, and given the "narrow space in which most families are compelled to live" it was difficult to arrange even "provisional bathing arrangements."[19] The city had created riverfront bathing tanks, open alternately to either sex, and five or six million people crowded into them each summer. Obviously these were useless in cold weather, and the rivers were already so polluted that bathing in them introduced an entirely new set of health risks. In 1894 the Association for Improving the Condition of the Poor opened a small indoor bath facility designed by Josiah Cleveland Cady, and a number of other private groups followed suit, charging five cents a visit. Their success inspired Seth Low to lay out "a great system of municipal baths" provided "as the people's right, not as a favor to anyone."[20] The first to open was the Rivington Street Bath.

Designed by York & Sawyer, it boasted a monumental screen of Ionic columns and a very large plaque declaring that its existence was due to the munificence of Mayor Seth Low and Borough President Jacob Cantor. In its first five months of operation the building served a quarter of a million people, and plans were laid for fifteen more facilities.

Embellishment also meant parks. It was relatively easy to buy parkland in outlying districts, where no demolition was required, only money and political will. In 1903 the Daughters of the American Revolution and the American Scenic and Historic Preservation Society persuaded Low to buy the historic Morris-Jumel mansion and its grounds for the Parks Department.[21] In turn, the Municipal Art Society took credit for persuading the city to improve Brooklyn's Ocean Parkway and to expand Coney Island Park. The parkway had been laid out by Frederick Law Olmsted to connect Prospect Park South with the Concourse Lands, a stretch of Coney Island beachfront purchased by the city of Brooklyn in 1876. East of the concourse was a colony of luxury hotels; to the west, the midway of West Brighton, where a collection of sideshows, dance halls, bathing establishments, and kinetoscope booths (where one could see "disgusting photographs") sprang up.[22] The idea of expanding this park had been broached in 1899 by Comptroller Bird Coler, whose department was "a sort of oasis in the savage Tammany desert."[23] Coney Island was the "only seaside pleasure ground in easy reach," Coler explained, but it was designed for only "two classes ... for those who can afford the relative seclusion and the good order to be obtained at the larger hotels east of the concourse, and for those who do not object to the vicious and vulgar features that prevail more or less between the concourse and the more or less exclusive little residence park known as Sea Gate at the extreme west end." Coler sought to make Coney Island "beautiful and enticing for the most fastidious and orderly, quiet and safe for all,"[24] and the Municipal Art Society took up the project in 1901, pointing out that very little of Coney Island's beach was accessible to the public unless they paid a fee to one of the private bathing establishments. The park's enlargement proved to be so popular that the public demanded more of it: in 1912 another reform administration would expand the park yet again and begin work on the boardwalk.

Small parks had long been a sacred cause among reformers. It wasn't just that they were keen to provide recreation to the tenement dwellers who most needed it. One camp of reformers stressed the need for organized play, supplanting the anarchic and amoral games of children with group activities that were supposed to teach cooperation and good citizenship. There was a broader belief, in the age before penicillin, that disease was caused not by germs but by a fetid, stagnant atmosphere. Many people regarded parks as the "lungs of the city," allowing the slums to exhale corruption and drink in fresh air. Reformers steered the parks program to "lung blocks," a more poignant phrase indicating blocks of tenements with a concentration of respiratory disease, hot spots of tuberculosis or whooping cough.

What the Municipal Art Society, the Outdoor Recreation League, and the settlement houses saw as improvements, local aldermen and their constituents often saw as devastating blows to their communities. In 1903, for instance, when the Low administration was planning to demolish a lung block on Catherine and Hamilton streets to replace it with Hamilton Park, the local alderman was outraged. The parish priest arrived at the Board of Estimate to complain that "A few idealists, who live in palatial homes, came into our district to tell the poor how to live," and enlisted the aid of reporters who "could be bought for a price ranging from a glass of beer to a dollar." The press painted a scandalous picture of disease and crime on the park site, but tuberculosis, he claimed, "is no more prevalent in this block than in other parts of the city"—an ambiguous boast—"and vice in Cherry Hill is no stronger than it is in Murray Hill."[25]

Low bought new parks and improved old ones. Since 1887 the Small Parks Law had allowed the city to pay a million dollars for parks in any given year (unspent money couldn't be carried over to the next year). Yet Jacob Riis remembered that in 1901 "the neighborhood parks, acquired at such huge sacrifice, lay waste. Tammany took no step toward improving them. In the Seward Park, where the need of relief was greatest, Tammany election district captains built booths, rent free, for the sale of dry goods and fish."[26]

One park was created by Tammany—Hudson Park, at Hudson and Le Roy streets, where the entrance to the Holland Tunnel now stands—but this was strangely inappropriate to its situation. It was designed by Carrère & Hastings, Beaux Arts architects who must have been dreaming of Paris. They built a rusticated pavilion presiding over a sunken formal garden and reflecting pool. It was all very beautiful, but with its sloping banks of earth and with fences ringing every patch of grass, Hudson Park was something to look at rather than play in. It may have seen more use in its previous incarnation as a graveyard, when little Jimmy Walker, the future mayor, used to play among the headstones. His father was the commissioner of public works, and the fact that the Walkers lived across the street no doubt explains why Tammany decided this once to build an urban park, and to do it so lavishly.[27]

According to Jacob Riis, when Mayor Van Wyck was asked for a $5,000 appropriation to equip a playground, he "replied with a sneer that 'Vaudeville destroyed Rome.' "[28] Playgrounds and playing fields, however, became the hallmark of Low's parks. Samuel Parsons and Arnold Brunner redesigned the empty wastes of Seward, Hamilton Fish, Thomas Jefferson, and DeWitt Clinton parks, though only the first two opened during Low's term of office. They were carefully crafted, designed to accommodate a variety of uses and age groups. They had looping paths, playing fields, playgrounds, and gymnasiums, and each park had a shelter, a Florentine loggia that provided shade and served as a bandstand or a speaker's platform. In their half-submerged basements were shower baths.

With the construction of Seward Park and the public baths, the city accepted the notion that the recreation and hygiene of the poor numbered among its pressing concerns, but the Municipal Art Society had less success convincing the city that it should encourage political debate. In 1901 Charles Rollinson Lamb proposed a new design for Union Square. The park had once been New York's most famous public garden, celebrated for its beds of exotic tulips, but that was when the square sat on the northern edge of the city and served as the centerpiece of New York's most expensive residential district. Since then fashionable stores and hotels had arrived, but by 1901 they were already beginning to leave. Loft buildings were beginning to appear in the area, and Fourteenth Street was evolving into a cheap amusement district. The city had grown up around the park, and the park had begun to acquire a new role as a center for political dissent. Labor Day had been celebrated in Union Square since 1887; May Day since 1890. Soapbox orators were now beginning to appear, and by the 1920s the square would be famous as a locus of radical politics.[29]

Lamb wanted to declare the northern end of Union Square a public forum, a place dedicated to civic pageantry and political rallies but especially to the spontaneous exercise of free speech. "In London," Lamb wrote, "it is possible to go to Trafalgar Square and to stand at the foot of the Nelson monument and say what you please. Also in Hyde Park, you may stand and speak at will, without being interrupted by the police or anyone else. Freedom of speech should have its possibilities." In New York, however, free speech was sometimes allowed, and sometimes not. Policemen felt free to judge the content of speeches and decide whether to tolerate or terrorize rallies. Nor was it just radical speech that was endangered. Lamb remembered the indignities of campaigning for a reform mayor: "standing on cart-tails and . . . speaking on a side street, backed up to the corner, facing out on an avenue, by the permission of the police and not by right."[30] Even if the police gave their consent, the public might not. Henry Curran, an eccentric Republican active in MAS in the 1920s, remembered his first taste of municipal politics, when he volunteered for Seth Low's speakers' bureau in 1903. Its director was Richard Welling, another Municipalian, who gave Curran an old horse cart and sent him to Tenth Avenue:

"The only thing I couldn't understand," Curran later wrote, "was the way the citizenry seemed to be reaching down and picking up things. The arms kept going down. Some of the citizens went across the street to pick up things. It was all very quiet. As I stood, trying desperately to remember the electric opening words I had known so well only a minute ago, something resembling a turnip whizzed past my ear. A portion of cabbage followed, then an old tomato. More seriously a cobblestone described a slow arc and landed at my feet. When a handful of moist Manhattan real estate made its appearance, I knew there was only one thing to do."[31]

Curran fled. Lamb hoped that people like him might find refuge in Union Square, and he rethought the park in terms of the pageantry of political rallies. Marchers heading up Broadway would no longer have to detour around the park. At its southern tip they would find Henry Kirke Brown's heroic equestrian statue of Washington, erected in 1856 and one of the city's finest works of public art. In 1901 it still stood outside the park, marooned on a circular traffic island in the triangular intersection of Fourth Avenue and Fourteenth Street. According to Lamb's plan, two new diagonal paths would open on either side of *Washington*, each broad enough for a procession. One would continue the visual axis of Broadway, while the other would head for Madison Avenue. As the marchers continued through the park they'd pass by Henry Kirke Brown's statue of Abraham Lincoln, relocated to the center of the park, and at its northern edge they would come upon the forum, a paved area designed to accommodate crowds and equipped with a monumental speaker's platform.

Lamb's design for Union Square was accepted by Parks Commissioner Wilcox in 1903, and another of Brunner's columned bandstands was erected at the northern end of the park. It made for a very handsome rostrum. Yet George Washington remained trapped on his traffic island until the 1930s, and the diagonal paths were never cut through the park. The project was probably vetoed by Samuel Parsons, a great landscape architect and a member of MAS, but a man who was fundamentally hostile to Lamb's intentions. He was willing to lay out playgrounds in the new small parks, but he saw himself as the curator of the old ones, the guardian both of their old trees and of their character as antidotes to urban culture. In 1902 Augustus Saint-Gaudens found it impossible to persuade Parsons to remove some trees that hid the Sherman Monument at Fifty-ninth Street. When some workmen were finally dispatched to trim them, one of Saint-Gaudens's assistants "plied them with whiskey" until they became "enthusiastic."[32] Parson's attitude brought him into a more and more bitter conflict with the Beaux Arts generation and eventually, in 1911, cost him his job.

In any case, the city proved to be no friend of free speech. The new rostrum in Union Square was rarely allowed to function as Lamb intended. In 1908 Lamb mourned that it was "in this Square, that not so many months ago a mob was dispersed by the police, and an individual killed in his illegal dynamitic protest against their way of handling the mob."[33] When Tammany Hall erected a new clubhouse in 1928 it chose a site at the park's northeast corner, overlooking the forum, and it must have had in mind the opportunity for staging great outdoor rallies before its very door. But Tammany was about to enter its decline by then, buffeted in turn by the Jimmy Walker scandals, by the city's bankruptcy in the early 1930s, and finally by twelve long years of reform under Fiorello La Guardia. The city continued to use the forum as it had almost from the beginning—as a parking lot. Only recently has it found an appropriate use as a farmers' market.

I T   H A S always been a somewhat delicate matter for the city to spend money to house its own offices. The public never approves; the papers make hay of any trace of self-indulgence.

City Hall Park was a vivid demonstration of the city's incompetence at planning facilities for its own use. Very little of this park remained by the turn of the century.

Since the end of the Civil War one building after another had sprung up amid the greenery. City Hall, the exquisite masterpiece of Joseph F. Mangin and John McComb, Jr., had been built in 1802–1811, when New York was a mere town at the foot of Manhattan Island. Famously, its rear facade was clad not in marble like the rest of the building but in brownstone, because it seemed unlikely to the city fathers that anyone would ever see the building from the north. As New York grew, however, so did its government, and City Hall threatened to burst at its seams. The courtrooms were moved out, and the notorious Tweed Courthouse rose in the park behind City Hall. The park suffered another grievous blow in 1875 when the city sold its southern tip to the federal government for one penny as a site for a new post office. That structure was designed by A. B. Mullet, the architect of the Treasury Department, in the heyday of the French Empire style. At the turn of the century the post office building was universally regarded as an eyesore, and not only because its loading docks faced City Hall. By 1902, however, the post office was looking for a larger and more central site. The Municipal Art Society prayed that the old building could soon be demolished, and it began trying to convince the federal government that a new post office could be an ornament to the city.

In the meantime another building in the park had been pressed into service to store the city's records. Built before the Revolution as a debtors' prison, the Hall of Records was an ancient building, older than City Hall itself. The British occupying forces filled it with captured revolutionaries (among them Ethan Allen), many of whom died in atrocious conditions. In the 1870s, when the Tweed Ring began to crumble under the pressure of exposés in the city's newspapers, it dawned on reformers that Tweed and his cronies might decide to destroy all evidence of their crimes by torching the Hall of Records. Citizens were dispatched to keep the building under guard, and what they discovered was appalling: a dilapidated firetrap bursting with paper documents, some of which had already fallen victim to rot. A single match would have destroyed the evidence of Tweed's crimes; it would also have destroyed the city's tax and property records, its birth and marriage and death certificates. Commerce would have been paralyzed for years.

When Tweed fell, the threat of sabotage subsided, but not that of an accidental fire. Yet years of austerity followed Tweed, and then years of municipal apathy. In 1888 Albany authorized construction of a new Hall of Records, but the city couldn't decide on a site. Should it be *in* City Hall Park or *near* the park? Each year the authorizing legislation was amended, until in 1893 the city decided to build itself a new City Hall, housing not only its records but also its bureaucracies, courts, and council chambers.[34] The building would virtually fill City Hall Park, and its construction would require the demolition of City Hall—but not of the Tweed Courthouse. Tammany Mayor Hugh Grant, "a callow youth of defective education,"[35] explained with a straight face that City Hall was old and outmoded, but that the Tweed Courthouse must remain because it had cost so much money. (The *Times* observed tartly that the money had gone into Tammany's pockets, not into the building.) At this point the Architectural League stepped in—not, to its shame, to protest the planned destruction of City Hall, but to offer its services. Architects were struggling at the time to ensure that competitions were impartially judged, and in pursuit of this worthy agenda the Architectural League effectively endorsed this very unworthy project. It provided Mayor Grant with a committee of architectural experts led by Richard Morris Hunt, the new president of the infant Municipal Art Society, to draw up the program for a competition and appoint a jury to judge the entries.

Luckily, the competition dissolved into a farce. None of the entries was deemed worthy of the prize, although six were singled out as the "least unsatisfactory," and of these one was thought to be a shade better than the others. The competitors demanded that the prize money be awarded to one of these faintly praised schemes, but a problem arose. To ensure the competitors' anonymity and the judges' impartiality, the competitors had been told to mark their drawings with a graphic symbol; each symbol was keyed to a sealed envelope containing the author's name. The competition rules, however, stipulated that these envelopes couldn't be opened until a winner had been chosen, and since the jury had refused to name a winner, it refused to open the envelopes. The identity of the six near-winners remained a mystery, the city kept the prize money, and the competitors cried fraud.

Three years later, in 1896, a Hall of Records Association was formed, and "this association," one member recalled, "adopted resolutions, then collected several thousand signatures favoring the plan, and thus caused a bill to be drawn by the city officials. Later the bill was passed at Albany."[36] Mayor Josiah Strong chose the site at Chambers and Centre streets north of City Hall Park. Leery of another competition and eager to quiet the angry competitors of 1893, Strong decided to give the commission to the man who had produced the best of the bad schemes for City Hall. When he asked who this was, the competition drawings were located—except, oddly, those of the "least unsatisfactory" scheme, which have never been found— but the famous sealed envelopes had disappeared. A search was ordered of all city offices. Some weeks later it was announced that the envelopes had materialized and that John R. Thomas would design the new Hall of Records.

Thomas was a famously honest and hardworking man, yet he was neither a first-rate talent nor a member of the Beaux Arts generation, and through no fault of his own the circumstances of his appointment were decidedly peculiar. The art societies had wanted a competition, preferably limited to a small group of the best architects in the city, whose names the art societies would have gladly forwarded to the city. In fact, Thomas was so ill at ease with the vocabulary of Classical architecture that he turned the design of the facades over to a young man in his office, Charles Israels. Israels had been trained in Paris, but as a painter, not an architect (his uncle, Jozef Israels, was a famous Dutch genre painter), and his inexperience told in the fussiness of the facades and their awkward proportions. Thomas also irked the art societies by hiring Henry Kirke Bush-Brown to carve all the sculpture on the building's dormers. Bush-Brown was well respected, but this was too much work for a single sculptor to do his best, and the Sculpture Society had hoped to have a say in the matter. That Thomas became a hero to the Municipal Art Society and the other art societies was due to two things. First, Thomas agreed to work with the Fine Arts Federation to make the Hall of Records a showcase of public art, with the federation developing a program for the building's sculpture and murals and staging competitions to choose the artists involved; second, Tammany tried to seize control of his building.

Thomas was appointed shortly before Strong, a reform mayor, left office. His Tammany successor, Robert Van Wyck, was left with the task of actually building the structure, and he liked to say that "the plans for the new Hall of Records were conceived in crime." He was powerless to oust John R. Thomas from the commission—the man had a contract—but the mayor charged that the cost of interior decoration, estimated at $2,500,000, was exorbitant, and he asked Horgan & Slattery, Tammany's new city architects, to prepare a report on Thomas's design. The city comptroller had already investigated, and commended, the scheme, but Horgan & Slattery's report "declared that the marble decorations were too elaborate for a municipal building, though they would not be out of place in an opera house." They recommended the elimination of some twenty-four statues, of mosaic floors, and of solid marble staircases, which would be veneered in marble instead. "As a whole," the *Times* reported, "the report was in favor of a general cheapening of the structure," and it asserted that the building's cost could be cut by about a million dollars. The report was made public at a Board of Estimate hearing, with poor Thomas listening "in evident distress" and "apparent despair." He had been, he said afterward, "as economical as [was] consistent with his desire to make the building an artistic success and a credit to the city," and he added that some of the proposed changes, such as the use of wood floors instead of mosaic, rendered the building less fireproof.[37]

Thomas died in early 1901. He'd finished the drawings for the Hall of Records, and he left behind him a competent staff that could have supervised the final stages of construction. Van Wyck seized the opportunity, however, to cancel the contract, which was with Thomas's firm, not with Thomas personally, and to appoint Horgan & Slattery to finish the building. It was a tasteless thing to do, for it stripped Thomas's widow of one of her major assets. Van Wyck, the *Times* wrote, "is perhaps incapable of appreciating the disgust felt by decent people at the violation of unwritten laws which forbid such open and flagrant spoliation of the orphan before the tomb has closed on the body of the father."[38] Nine months later, when Seth Low took office, he found that he couldn't remove Horgan & Slattery from the job. He summoned them to his office, however, to demand the "highest grade" of public art that money and taste could obtain. Low provided the money, allocating an extra quarter of a million dollars to ensure that the building's decoration would "cause the artistic soul of Father Knickerbocker to rejoice," but Horgan & Slattery were unable to provide the taste.[39]

It seems that Horgan & Slattery had already rewritten Thomas's specifications to delete any mention of competitions: they alone would choose the artists involved and direct their work. Thomas had planned an elaborate program of sculpture: at ground level, sculptures of New York in Dutch times and New York in Revolutionary times; above the colonnade, heroically scaled portraits of great mayors of New York; and crowning the dormers, more abstract themes like Heritage and Maternity. (Bush-Brown was already at work on these.)

The Municipal Art Society was allowed to choose which historic mayors would be immortalized. Most were safely selected from the city's early history. The only divisive choice was Abram S. Hewitt, Peter Cooper's son-in-law, who was mayor of New York from 1887 to 1888. Hewitt was a hero in MAS circles as the first mayor to sketch a vision of a new, comprehensively planned New York and as the father of the Rapid Transit Act. But if he was a great man, he came complete with a tragic flaw: the Irish aroused in him such brazen bigotry that even his admirers admitted that "Hewitt entertained prejudices which were unworthy of him."[40] Perhaps the Irish took their revenge on Hewitt's statue: when it was being installed on the facade high above Chambers Street, the crane suddenly collapsed, and Hewitt's effigy was smashed to pieces.

When Horgan & Slattery took over the Hall of Records they assigned all the remaining sculpture to one man, Philip Martiny. Martiny, a Frenchman, was a member of the National Sculpture Society and the Municipal Art Society, but his colleagues knew full well that he wasn't the most talented sculptor in New York; he churned out statues, according to Karl Bitter, "with incredible rapidity and apparently with little reflection."[41] The Art Commission, dominated by Municipalians, proceeded to make life sheer hell for both Bush-Brown and Martiny, rejecting their models one after another. Some of Bush-Brown's submissions were rejected four times by the Art Commission, and Martiny fared no better. The *Times* explained that the problem was "not that the sculptors selected are inferior, but that sculpture ordered wholesale cannot, in the nature of things, be the best that a good sculptor can supply."[42] Horgan & Slattery offered a different explanation, charging that the commissioners "either consciously or unconsciously . . . are injecting politics into the situation with the intention of 'pounding' the firm."[43]

"Messrs. Horgan and Slattery," the *Times* reported in March 1903, "have been for months in the depths of despondency because of the attacks of Mayor Low and his officials. Last week a change took place in the personal appearance of the architects." They were seen to "chuckle with glee," and Vincent Slattery was overheard telling a friend, "I have eaten the canary." The *Times* was so intrigued by this sudden mood swing that it made inquiries. The architects themselves refused to speak, but the paper located "a friend of John F. Carroll," the Tammany official believed to be the architects' silent partner, who explained:

> It's a great joke. . . . You see, the reform officials, under the lead of Mayor Low, have been camping on the trail of Horgan and Slattery. A heartbroken sculptor who has a reputation to sustain found a lot of his best work declared inartistic and immature by the Municipal Art Commission. He went to Horgan and said,

"I'm an artist and my work's all right, but the Art Commission rejects it. What's the matter?" Horgan told the artist that the Art Commission was aiming its shots, not at the artist, but at the architects. . . . Slattery said to his partner, "Let's put up a scheme." The next order the artist and sculptor got was to make careful copies of the gargoyles and some of the decorations of Michael Angelo [*sic*] and Leonardo da Vinci in Saint Peter's at Rome. "Make them careful copies," admonished Slattery. A batch of the drawings and some casts were submitted to the Art Commission.

Say, those drawings and other things were rejected by the Municipal Art Commission as immature and inartistic. Our reform officials have decided that the work of Michael Angelo [*sic*, again] and Leonardo da Vinci in the decorative line is not good enough to go in the Hall of Records. Now you know why Horgan and Slattery are laughing. That's the whole story.[44]

Not quite. No doubt the typical *Times* reporter today is better educated and would point out that no gargoyles adorn Saint Peter's, that Da Vinci had nothing to do with the building, and that the church contains just one sculpture by Michelangelo—the *Pièta*. (Surely Horgan & Slattery didn't try to run a copy of *that* past the Art Commission.) But these are details. It was all a hoax, a tall tale that Horgan & Slattery told their friends to buck up their own spirits and win some beery sympathy. They never intended it to reach the newspapers. When it did, they gave an evasive statement to the press, affirming that the Art Commission had indeed rejected a good many submissions, and leaving the impression that it would be indiscreet to say more. John De Witt Warner, as president of the Art Commission, denied the story; so did Bush-Brown, the "heartbroken" sculptor, and Horgan & Slattery eventually wrote to Warner, claiming they had never said such things. Yet the story didn't die; it only grew more elaborate with the passing years. By the time Mayor McClellan wrote his autobiography in the 1940s it had become the tale of a frieze of figures "copied bodily" from the Parthenon and from Donatello, Michelangelo, and "Bernini and his school."[45]

What's telling in all this is that it never occurred to Horgan & Slattery—or to McClellan, who was something of a connoisseur and should have known better—that an ecstatic saint from the school of Bernini, a cherub from the hand of Donatello, or a writhing slave à la Michelangelo might not be an appropriate decoration for New York's Hall of Records. The Art Commission took the sculptural program seriously; it believed in the power of allegory to speak to people of municipal ideals, and it wanted art, not decorative sculpture. One can still see in the files of the Art Commission plenty of evidence that they were right to reject Martiny's and Bush-Brown's first efforts. Each time a submission was disapproved, it came back better: simpler, less overloaded with details, and more powerfully composed.

As the reformers on the Art Commission tortured Horgan & Slattery, so Tammany eventually found a way to torture the art societies. When Tammany returned to power in 1903, the city decided that the Hall of Records, which was almost finished, needed to be altered. Every floor was affected, from the basement to the attic. The result, according to the *Times*, "promises to destroy much of the artistic effect of the interior work. . . . More fat fees for the architects is said to be the only motive in sight."[46] The *Times* grimly predicted that the work would cost $500,000; in fact the lowest bid would come in at $1.3 million. Yet there was no money to complete Thomas's scheme of decorative art. In 1904 the Fine Arts Federation and the Society of Mural Painters presented their project for murals in the Hall of Records. (Frederick Lamb, the Municipal Art Society's secretary, was also the chairman of the Fine Arts Federation's Committee on Murals.) It was championed by A.D.F. Hamlin, head of MAS's Committee on the Decoration of Public Buildings and the author, two years earlier, of the Art Commission's damning report on Horgan & Slattery's architectural competence. The paintings would have decorated the stair hall, one of New York's wonders: a soaring, vaulted room ringed by arcades. The room seemed to demand murals. Thomas had left empty panels for them in the upper gallery, and huge expanses of blank wall cried out for decoration at either end of the stair hall itself, just below the vault. The art societies asked to paint allegorical scenes in the stair hall and, in the arcades, a cycle of paintings tracing the city's history from Dutch days. Their proposal was rejected by the Board of Estimate, prompting Hamlin to a fit of rage: "Instead of adorning the walls of this fine building with the noblest and most interesting of all possible decorations, by employing our greatest artists to execute upon her walls and ceilings allegorical and historic paintings worthy of our wealth and civic greatness, our artistic progress and history, this Board resolves and decrees to cover those walls with the unmeaning ostentation of showy marble slabs, at a cost greater than would have sufficed to carry out the complete scheme of mural paintings."[47]

Those marble slabs had only one compelling advantage: they were supplied by a quarry controlled by Tammany loyalists who may or may not have passed some of their profits back to the clubhouse. Unfortunately, they also exacerbated a certain elephantine quality in Thomas's architecture. Upstairs, things got stranger. When the Hall of Records finally opened in 1906, a *Times* reporter noticed that "from the third floor up, the door heads and other fancy 'marble' embellishments shine beautifully—with the shine peculiar to enamel paint." They turned out to be "plaster enrichment," and no one could explain why.[48] "New York," Hamlin fumed, "utterly refuses to follow in the path of artistic civilization, and fastens upon herself the opprobrium of utter commercialism and philistine barbarism by her indifference to the function of art in civic life."[49]

THE CONSTRUCTION of the Hall of Records didn't solve the problem of housing the city agencies and courts. In 1899 Charles Lamb had published a scheme for a great skyscraper City Hall rising on the two-block-square site west of the Hall of Records and north of City Hall, a project that appalled Lamb's own colleagues in the art societies. In June of 1902 a special committee of the Municipal Art

Society, composed of Calvin Tomkins, Charles Coolidge Haight, and Charles Lamb, concluded that the city should erect a municipal complex on the north side of Chambers Street, west of the Hall of Records, and in July a *Times* editorial introduced the idea to the public:

> It is manifest destiny ... that the city is to build its municipal buildings on Chambers Street, fronting City Hall Park. That was the idea of the late John R. Thomas. He felt quite sure that the new Hall of Records was simply the first of these buildings, the other two of which he hoped to live to design, occupying the whole space from Centre Street to Broadway and from Chambers Street to Reade. That on Broadway he imagined as the counterpart to the Hall of Records, to be devoted, presumably, to courtrooms, while the central building, more extensive and conspicuous than either of the others, was to be the real City Hall of Greater New York, leaving the old City Hall as a relic, to be occupied as a municipal museum, excepting for the state apartments which we shall always, so long as the building lasts, doubtless avail ourselves of, in order to show distinguished foreigners that even New York was not "born yesterday."[50]

Two months later the Municipal Art Society's special committee dispatched a position paper to the Board of Estimate. It set forth a more persuasive and politically useful argument for the civic center scheme proposed by the *Times* (and by Thomas). MAS had discovered that the city was paying $175,000 a year to rent office space on the north side of City Hall Park, much of it in the old A. T. Stewart building on the corner of Broadway and Chambers Street. Other rented offices were scattered nearby. Obviously New York would soon need much more space for its agencies—population growth alone would cause the bureaucracy to expand rapidly. It was also faced with the necessity of building a new courthouse. (This was all the more pressing, since the Municipal Art Society had successfully campaigned to stop Horgan & Slattery from building an addition to the Tweed Courthouse.) The city could continue paying rent or, MAS suggested, it could make an investment in its future. The interest (at 4 percent) on $4,375,000 was $175,000, and for that sum the city could condemn the entire Chambers Street site from Broadway to the Hall of Records. Once that was done, the city could erect the pieces of the civic center as funds became available, and it could clear the park of all buildings other than City Hall: the Tweed Courthouse, despised by reformers; the old Hall of Records, which wouldn't be needed once Thomas's building was finished; and the post office. "The problems here presented can be faced in two ways," Tomkins and his colleagues wrote. "One is to potter separately with each detail, and this has been the course so far followed in regard to City Hall Park since 1865, the result being an expensive and incongruous medley of buildings which the City has outgrown.... The other is to anticipate needs, to lay out comprehensive plans, and then systematically to carry them out."[51]

The Board of Estimate mulled this over, but at the moment city officials were more concerned with another problem at City Hall Park: the congestion at the Brooklyn Bridge Terminal, where trolley cars—the so-called bridge cars—couldn't move fast enough to whisk the crowds of passengers away. The Municipal Art Society soon transferred its lobbying from the corridors of City Hall to the drafting room of the Bridge Department.

I N 1 9 0 2 the Fine Arts Federation's campaign against the ugly designs for the East River bridges had come to a triumphant conclusion. The Art Commission now had the power to review them, courtesy of the new charter, and Seth Low appointed the great engineer Gustav Lindenthal to head the Bridge Department. Lindenthal, born in Austria, had practiced in Pittsburgh, where he became the nation's leading expert in designing railroad bridges. New Yorkers knew him for his design for the North River Bridge, a vast, privately financed project meant to carry the New Jersey railroads across the Hudson River. (It was doomed when one of its sponsors, the Pennsylvania Railroad, abandoned the consortium and decided to build its own tunnels instead, but Lindenthal was still determined to see the bridge built.) Henry Hornbostel became the Bridge Department's consulting architect. Hornbostel is too little known, no doubt because he later moved his practice to Pittsburgh, far from the gaze of the architectural press. Yet he was one of the most brilliant and progressive Beaux Arts architects in America, a man fascinated by the task of reinterpreting traditional forms in new technologies. At the time of his appointment he was teaching at Columbia University, and it seems that he was recommended for the job by the Art Commission—probably by A.D.F. Hamlin, Hornbostel's former teacher, and now his colleague on the Columbia faculty.[52]

Hornbostel and Lindenthal were too late to save the Williamsburg Bridge, whose cables were already being strung across the East River when they took up their new positions. Hornbostel could only decorate what Leffert Buck had wrought, "adding architectural grace," as Lindenthal put it, "to a work hitherto directed by the minds of engineers alone."[53] Hornbostel's decorative plaques and comfort stations were handsome, but Buck's gross steelwork gave the bridge an "uncouth and bandy-legged aspect which no cleverness in detail could redeem."[54] Lindenthal and Hornbostel's designs for the Manhattan and Queensboro bridges were the epitome of "useful art," however, and among the most remarkable designs of their era. In the midst of their hectic work on the new bridges, Lindenthal and Hornbostel were asked to confront the congestion at the Brooklyn Bridge Terminal, a problem that had defied solution for twenty years.

As Calvin Tomkins wrote in 1904, "When the Brooklyn Bridge was first opened, our City officials standing upon it saw beyond neither end of it, and we had bridge cars—without connections at either end."[55] These were trolleys that shuttled back and forth across the bridge. Eventually the Brooklyn Rapid Transit Company acquired the franchise for the bridge cars, and naturally connected the bridge's rail lines to its own elevated system in Brooklyn. Since the company possessed no such system in Manhattan, a bridge terminal still stood at the Manhattan end of the bridge, just east of City Hall Park.

Every railroad car that crossed the bridge began or ended its journey in this building, an ugly structure of glass and iron raised above Park Row. Not only was it ugly; it was utterly inadequate to the task. The Madison, Third, and Second avenue trolleys converged here. Above ground were the Third Avenue and Second Avenue Els, and the Rapid Transit Commission was planning a new subway line linking the Brooklyn, Manhattan, and Williamsburg bridges. All of the passengers from these conveyances had to fight their way up the staircases and along the narrow platforms of the bridge terminal.[56]

In those days the index of the *New York Times* carried a separate heading, with a very long list of entries, called "Bridge Crush." The name was charmingly accurate, for in the early years of this century half a million people a day crossed the Brooklyn Bridge (roughly five times the current number), and twice a day, at the rush hours, there was pandemonium. So dense and vast were the crowds that they became, if not quite a tourist attraction, something foreign visitors found emblematic of the rude power of industrialized America. When the Lumière brothers, the pioneering film-makers, brought their cameras to New York at the turn of the century, they were careful to record the scene, and it provoked one of the more ecstatic passages in H. G. Wells's *The Future in America*. Wells wrote of the "convergent stream of clerks and workers" that approached the bridge every night:

> They arrive marching afoot by every street in endless processions; crammed trolley-cars disgorge them, the subway pours them out. . . . The individuals count for nothing, they are clerks and stenographers, shopmen, shop-girls, workers of innumerable types, black-coated men, hat and blouse girls, shabby and cheaply-clad persons, such as one sees in London, in Berlin, anywhere. Perhaps they hurry more, perhaps they seem more eager. But the distinctive effect is the mass, the black torrent, rippled with unmeaning faces, the great, the unprecedented multitudinousness of the thing, the inhuman force of it all.[57]

In 1901 a grand jury called the bridge crush "at certain hours hazardous to the health as well as the moral sensibilities of women," and questioned, since the terminal was "so much a public thoroughfare," whether the Board of Public Improvements couldn't claim jurisdiction over it.[58] In 1902 the Brooklyn chapter of the Manufacturers' Association issued a damning report on the bridge crush, and Seth Low, who had a passion for committees of experts, asked J. E. Breckenridge of the Brooklyn Rapid Transit Company, William Barclay Parsons of the Rapid Transit Board, and George Post to find a solution. (Post was representing the Manufacturers' Association, but he was also active in the Municipal Art Society.) The experts recommended some renovations to the terminal to ease crowding, but these, they insisted, were merely an expedient. The only true solution would be for the city "to take charge of the terminal and completely rebuild it."[59]

The Brooklyn Rapid Transit Company had once suggested solving the problem with a massive elevated platform that would extend the terminal westward over Park Row and into City Hall Park. The *Staats-Zeitung*, the leading German daily in New York, had stopped that project with a court injunction. The paper's headquarters overlooked the terminal, and it demanded compensation if its quarters were to suffer from such an onslaught of noise and shadow. The paper was willing, however, to let the city condemn its property, as long as it was treated fairly. It had already fought off one improper assault: the paper was such a thorn in the side of Tammany Hall that in 1892 Mayor Hugh Grant threatened not only to condemn the *Staats-Zeitung* building as the site of the Hall of Records but to "do up" the paper by evicting it immediately, before a condemnation award had been decided, much less paid.[60] A later Tammany mayor, George McClellan, was almost as unfriendly: in 1905, after years of discussion, the city suddenly voted to condemn the paper's headquarters for improvements at the base of the Brooklyn Bridge, and McClellan ordered the paper out within thirty days. The *Staats-Zeitung* managed to stall. The paper counted on better treatment from the Fusion administration. Its editor was Herman Ridder, founder of the Knight-Ridder newspaper chain, a prominent supporter of Low, and a close friend of Lindenthal; he'd persuaded Low to give Lindenthal his job as bridge commissioner.[61]

Low ordered the Bridge Department to prepare plans for a new municipal bridge terminal. In order to recoup the city's massive investment he asked Lindenthal to prop a city office building above the terminal. Lindenthal and Hornbostel chose George Post as an associate architect, perhaps because of his study of the terminal, but also because he had experience in designing office buildings. (Post had also joined the board of MAS by this time.) In July 1903, when the three unveiled their plans, Seth Low was surprised and dismayed to see that these three Municipalians had vastly expanded the scope of their assignment by grafting onto it the Municipal Art Society's proposal for the civic center on the north side of Chambers Street.[62] East of the park was a new bridge terminal, and at the corner of Centre and Chamber streets rose a skyscraper marking the park's northwest corner and housing the municipal agencies. This much represented what Low had asked for, but Lindenthal, Post, and Hornbostel went on to show City Hall Park cleared of all buildings except old City Hall, now meant to be a museum and reception building. Gone were the Tweed Courthouse, the post office, and the old Hall of Records; in their stead was a garden laid out in a stiff pattern of walks. On the corner of Broadway and Chambers Street rose a new courthouse, looking like a twin of Thomas's Hall of Records, and between the court and the hall stood a new City Hall. Its doors opened onto a terrace that bridged Chambers Street and linked the building, with a cascade of steps, to City Hall Park.

What attracted the most comment was the so-called campanile, the 650-foot skyscraper marking the park's northeast corner. Its reception was curious. The *Real Estate Record and Guide* wondered at first whether the city should encourage the phenomenon of skyscrapers by building one for itself. On reflection, however, the magazine decided that this particular design was worth building as a model for private developers, for it was a freestanding tower treated in the round, not at all like the ghastly sliver towers that reared bare party walls above lower Broadway.[63]

The Lindenthal-Post-Hornbostel plan threatened to drive a wedge between MAS and Low. The *Times* detected in Low a distinct antagonism toward the society that had sprung this project on him unawares—and used his own bridge commissioner to do it. Low wanted to build the terminal because the current bridge crush was so scandalous that it had become a political liability. The civic center seemed to him a lovely idea, but Low was appalled at the massive scale of investment involved, especially when many of his own supporters were bitterly complaining that the new tax assessment system heralded a gigantic capital budget. That the civic center was beautiful, that it might make for a more efficient government, or that it might save money in the long run—these were not issues likely to stir the hearts of voters.

Since the civic center was "the vital part of the Society's recommendations," the Municipal Art Society dispatched a second paper to the Board of Estimate. It was a very careful reply to Low, a piece of "friendly criticism," Tomkins insisted, in response to the equally "friendly criticism of the Mayor. . . . We are . . . convinced that he is actuated by the same consideration for the City's welfare which actuates the members of the Municipal Art Society. We are also alive to the fact that there is little responsibility on our shoulders for the expenditure of the City's great but inadequate annual fund."[64] Tomkins admitted that some details of the civic center scheme might be questionable, but he urged that the plan be accepted at once as the city's basic strategy, and this meant that the block north of City Hall Park should be acquired "before it shall fall into the hands of nimble speculators." The buildings there could be left standing, "if necessary . . . until such time as the city can, without straining its resources, afford to construct . . . monumental buildings."[65]

Low had pointed out that the bridge terminal site was vastly cheaper, and that the city could build offices for itself above the new terminal. MAS responded that the low asking price was itself evidence of the site's problem: if the noise and congestion of the bridge terminal rendered the area unsuitable for private offices, it would prove even more so for public facilities. Tomkins suggested that Low's priorities were misplaced: if the city couldn't afford both to build a terminal and to condemn the block north of City Hall, "then let the [Brooklyn Rapid Transit] do as the trunk lines have already done—purchase for themselves land they need, and by so doing leave the City free to provide the best site for its capital."[66]

MAS wanted Low to accept the civic center as a master plan, to go ahead and condemn all the property required before prices rose to impossible levels, and to effectively commit the city to building the complex piece by piece as funds became available. Through the summer and fall of 1903 the Municipal Art Society worked to win votes for the civic center on the Board of Estimate. The mayor seems to have softened, and it was a great coup when Comptroller Edward Grout endorsed the project as a wise use of the city's funds. Grout revealed that the city was paying more than $800,000 a year in rent, $250,000 of it for quarters south of Canal Street. Many of these offices could move to Chambers Street, he insisted, and once the city began capitalizing these larger sums it could well afford to build magnificent, commodious, and efficient quarters.

The project never came to a vote, however. It fell victim to the crossfire in the mayoral campaign of 1903 and to what George McClellan called "the cleverest political coup" of Charles Murphy's career as boss of Tammany Hall: "the kidnapping of Low's running mates." Murphy was looking for ways to demonstrate that Tammany "was not trying to 'grab everything in sight.' " To that end, he chose George McClellan—conspicuously a gentleman—as his mayoral candidate and offered places on the Tammany ticket to two members of Low's Fusion administration: Comptroller Grout and Charles Fornes, president of the Board of Aldermen. "They were both of the brand," McClellan wrote in his memoirs, "which is known as 'independent Democrats,' a euphemism for opportunist."[67] Grout and Fornes, scenting a Democratic victory in the air, accepted Tammany backing for their reelection. The *Times* labeled Grout "the most audacious turncoat that ever troubled the councils of reform politics in this city."[68] The Citizens Union immediately removed the two men from the Fusion party line. The result, as McClellan gloated, was that Grout and Fornes "were obliged to throw themselves wholeheartedly" into Tammany's embrace.[69]

Grout and Fornes were reelected; Seth Low was not. Most mayors who lose their reelection campaigns devote their last two months in office to pushing through as many pet projects as they can (Van Wyck, for instance, showered a flurry of city contracts on Horgan & Slattery in the final days of his term), but not Seth Low. He had at his disposal $140 million in borrowing capacity, largely the result of the new tax assessment policy, which had taken effect only in July. Pending before the Board of Estimate was the civic center complex, with its $50 million price tag; the Chelsea piers, at $12 million; the Staten Island Ferry, $2 million; the new police headquarters, $1 million; Manhattan Bridge contracts, $6.5 million; water tunnels, $50 million; and five mass transit projects, some endorsed by MAS, for another $62 million. The total bill would have come to $183.5 million.[70] Low didn't bring any of these to a vote. Some took this as making a virtue of necessity, since with Grout and Fornes's defection to Tammany, Fusion had lost control of the Board of Estimate. The *Times* admitted that "it is not at all certain that each of these officials would refuse to act with the present administration on the plans already outlined, and in which they have had their share," but the *Times* approved of Low's decision nonetheless: the campaign had been fought largely on "the conduct of Mayor Low and his associates as to the expenditure of money and as to the increased assessment which made great public works possible." A "pretty portentous majority" had voted against Low, and the *Times* concluded that "it is but right that the whole issue of these [public] works should be left to the new administration."[71]

For all his fondness for the City Beautiful, Mayor McClellan didn't build this civic center.[72] It would have cost a great deal of money, of course, and that in itself would have been a perfectly reasonable excuse to cancel the project. But one must also add other considerations that might have crossed McClellan's mind. The project was closely identified with Low's administration, and politicians are, quite humanly, reluctant to spend money on projects for which their political opponents could claim credit. Moreover, Tammany Hall could ill afford, in a political sense, to build itself a series of monumental structures. Baths, parks, and schools directly served the people, but municipal offices and courts conceived on a splendid scale were another matter. With the Tweed Courthouse still standing just across the street, McClellan was hardly likely to spend great sums of money on something so . . . well, self-indulgent.

THE CITY BEAUTIFUL

WHEN GEORGE MCCLELLAN took his oath of office in January 1904, an issue much weightier than the civic center hung in the balance: the New York City Improvement Commission, the Municipal Art Society's attempt to create the first true master plan for Greater New York. This plan had been the focus of the society's hopes for the past two years, since the moment Fusion swept into power in 1902.

In a general way everyone knew what shape Greater New York should take. The *Times* foresaw a day when subways, bridges, and tunnels would span the rivers that girdled Manhattan so that the teeming population would no longer be trapped on a long narrow island:

> The lower end of Manhattan is to be no longer, as it has been so long, a terminal merely. It is to become a center. The daily and nightly movement of its business population will no more be, by a huge majority, southward and northward. It will be centripetal and centrifugal. In other words, the business center of Greater New York will be a "hub" like Boston with spokes leading to a periphery of what the facetious Bostonians describe as "sub-hubs."
>
> How immensely the radiation of New York, as compared with its longitudinal extension, will simplify all our municipal problems and facilitate the solution of them we have to invoke the aid of the imagination to apprehend, in default of any satisfactory experience. But to begin to imagine . . . is to see that the tenement-house problem, the transportation problem, all our urgent problems, are at last on the way to a good solution.[1]

The question was how to make all this come true. Greater New York had just begun to evolve in 1902. Political union had been accomplished four years earlier, but physically the five boroughs were just as independent as in the past. In Manhattan there was hellish overcrowding; Long Island's empty space—fields and meadows, farms and villages—lay tantalizingly beyond reach. The city was building bridges, but had no plans for bridge approaches; it talked of new piers, but not of relieving the congestion on West Street or reforming the rail system. It was building one subway, but had no scheme for more; it saw the need for new parks, but had no clear idea where to put them. People were beginning to realize that the new bridges weren't even in the right places. Lower Manhattan would soon have three bridges, but the business district was expanding northward, propelled by rising land values at the foot of the island. It was still uncertain where it would come to a halt: the Midtown district around Grand Central Terminal was still a low-rise neighborhood and gave few signs of its future density; the investors in the Flatiron Building were betting that Madison Square would soon be the very heart of the business district and that their lonesome skyscraper would soon have company. At the same time, factories were beginning to move, sorting themselves out of the tenements on the Lower East Side. In the 1890s Jacob Riis had depicted the horrors of sweatshops in Old Law tenements, but now the Tenement House Department limited how many people could work in an apartment. Also, manufacturers wanted to follow their customers as the retail district moved northward, and labor demanded better working conditions.

Municipalians like Charles Lamb predicted the development of a dense new neighborhood of business and loft buildings around and north of Union Square, but Union Square, Madison Square, and Midtown were all far from the bridges of the Lower East Side—the bridges that were supposed to ferry New Yorkers to new, safer, healthier homes in the outer boroughs. They were also far from the financial center downtown and from the bustling factories and warehouses along West Street, and traffic between all these different destinations was thwarted by a very old mistake. The street commissioners who had laid out Manhattan's gridiron plan in 1807–1811 hadn't realized that the bulk of traffic would want to flow north-south, rather than east-west, and they had provided New York with few avenues. If the city didn't step in and create new avenues to link the different transportation nodes to the business and factory districts, Municipalians feared that all the spacious, empty land in the outer boroughs would go to waste. Businesses and workers would remain trapped where they were, and congestion would pile atop congestion.

The city had no way of even studying these problems. The Charter of 1902 had abolished the Board of Public Improvements, leaving the borough presidents in control of public works and the Board of Aldermen guarding the city map, but there was no agency to forge a citywide planning policy. The aldermen's role was especially troubling to the Municipal Art Society. Henry Curran, who served for a time as the board's lone Republican, described the aldermen as "the human face of government." Most reformers pictured them as Mephistophelian figures who purchased votes with petty favors, but those favors weren't petty to the poor. Aldermen distributed newsstand and street vendor licenses, which might save a family from starving, and handed out free tickets to sporting events (Tammany's unofficial tax on sports promoters). An alderman could give a license for just about anything that stood on the city streets, from building encroachments to the wooden Indians in front of cigar stores. Even a man with a sandwich board required a license—he was considered, legally speaking, a "parade."[2]

Reformers were always suspicious of the aldermen, but there was another problem. Aldermen were prepared to fight for the quality of life in their own wards, but it was difficult to convince them that the city should, for instance, buy large tracts of parkland in the Bronx and Queens—areas as yet undeveloped and barely accessible to their constituents. The Municipal Art Society saw such park purchases as an essential investment in the future: these areas were sure to be engulfed by development in the foreseeable future, and the city could only guarantee that these new neighborhoods would enjoy urban amenities if it reserved parkland well in advance, when the land was cheap. One other issue was even more painful to the aldermen, however, than the idea of spending large sums of money for distant wilderness, and it was even more central to the Municipal Art Society's intentions. That was the reconstruction of large swaths of lower New York, which the aldermen saw as the devastation of their neighborhoods and the dispersal of their constituents.

The reformers were determined to set up some sort of planning agency to supplant the aldermen, and they wanted to make sure that the new commission was incorruptible. Simply setting up a new city department was obviously dangerous, because Tammany might return to power. The Municipal Art Society decided that the answer was "to go outside the Municipal Government altogether and to appoint a commission of unofficial experts."[3] If the unpaid experts of the Art Commission could deal with the aesthetic side of public art and architecture, MAS saw no reason why a similar "Improvement Commission" couldn't deal with the more constructive task of designing a master plan. This arrangement seemed to have certain advantages. The society thought that it would be able to stack the new commission with its allies from the art and business communities, much as the Fine Arts Federation staffed the Art Commission. If the improvement commissioners were acknowledged experts, then MAS could dismiss any opposition as the ignorance or self-interest of local politicians. And if the experts weren't paid, it would underline the idea that the improvement commission was not a patronage mill but rather a group of citizens sacrificing their time for the noble cause of civic duty.

A model for this agency existed in Washington, D.C. In 1901 the American Institute of Architects had persuaded Senator James McMillan, chairman of the Senate Committee on the District of Columbia, to create just such a planning commission of unpaid experts for the nation's capital. The McMillan Commission included the senator himself, the architects Charles Follen McKim and Daniel Burnham, the landscape architect Frederick Law Olmsted, Jr., and the sculptor Augustus Saint-Gaudens. In 1902 the group produced a series of famously seductive perspectives that formed the cornerstone of the Municipal Art Society's city planning exhibit in 1903. Not all of the plan was carried out, but it inspired much of Washington as we know it now: the Federal Triangle, the Jefferson and Lincoln memorials, the great double file of Classical buildings that march down the tree-lined Mall. The American Institute of Architects had a fairly easy job of it, however. The power to shape Washington was centralized in McMillan's committee; the senator, in the custom of the day, ruled his committee like a personal fiefdom, and the architects had to convert only one man to their cause. New York presented a much more difficult situation. The Board of Aldermen would clearly not be pleased, and Seth Low proved to be extremely hesitant. The idea would have gone nowhere without Jacob Cantor, the new borough president of Manhattan and a life member of MAS.

Cantor had long been the Democratic leader of the state senate and chairman of the Senate Finance Committee, and he was "always standing for the commercial supremacy of New York."[4] He championed port, dock, and canal improvements, and he had pushed the Rapid Transit Act, which authorized construction of the first subway, through the legislature despite Tammany Hall's opposition. In 1898, when Greater New York came into being, Cantor stepped down from state office and entered city politics determined to shepherd into being the great planning enterprise implicit in consolidation. Cantor became the Municipal Art Society's most ardent ally in the reform administration—providing far more support than Seth Low did. Cantor erected Charles Lamb's street signs, he fought before the Board of Aldermen for Carrère & Hastings's proposed bridge at Fifth Avenue and Forty-second Street and for another at Broadway and Thirty-fourth Street; he hired William Martin Aiken, an excellent Classical architect, to coordinate and supervise all the architectural projects for which a borough president was responsible; he revived the Municipal Art Society's old project to paint the ceiling of the Board of Aldermen's chamber in City Hall; and he pressured a reluctant and overly cautious mayor to let the society take up the plan of New York. This was a pattern that would be repeated time and again in the art society's history: the borough president focused on the quality of life while the mayor nervously eyed the budget.

The campaign to create an Improvement Commission began in January 1902, when MAS held a dinner and symposium to discuss the need for a city plan. "One of the most hopeful signs of the occasion," the Times reported, "was the attendance of Mr. Cantor and the interest he took in the subject."[5] In February the Fine Arts Federation followed up by asking Seth Low to consult with the Art Commission, the federation's own little piece of the city government, on how to go about producing a city plan. In March, Cantor told the mayor, "I have noticed a lack of harmony as to the architecture, location, and other features of public improvements, and I believe that if a commission of architects, sculptors, civil engineers and others be appointed, as has been done in the City of Washington, the result would be very apparent in the general appearance of this city."[6] In April the Municipal Art Society opened an exhibit on city planning at the National Arts Club. It had originally planned an exhibit on street furniture and the Block Beautiful, but when Low was elected it threw together a more ambitious show devoted to the City Beautiful. There were samples of municipal art in the original narrow sense: a huge copy of

Raphael's *School of Athens*, painted by Municipalian George Breck for the University of Virginia; models of Daniel Chester French's figures for the Hunt Memorial; and models of Karl Bitter's caryatids for the facade of the Metropolitan Museum. There was a display of model tenement designs by James Ware, I. N. Phelps Stokes, and Ernest Flagg that plumbed the possibilities of the New Tenement Law, and the implication was that these buildings, limited by law to six stories, were to be the basic fabric of the City Beautiful. There were samples of the new Beaux Arts urbanism of *ensemble*: George Post's City College; McKim, Mead & White's Columbia University; and Arnold Brunner's plan for a monumental Civic Center in Cleveland. One section of the exhibit was devoted to waterfronts, and Milton See's project for covering the train tracks in Riverside Park hung by the plans for the Pan American Exposition on the Lake Erie shore of Buffalo. Another section was devoted to Boston's metropolitan park system, the most comprehensive in the nation. And in the place of honor hung the original drawings by Calvert Vaux and Frederick Law Olmsted for Central Park: a reminder of what had already been achieved in New York and, by implication, a challenge to the turn-of-the-century city.

In August, Joseph Cantor repeated his pleas for a planning commission; by now he'd begun wondering if he should simply appoint his own planning commission, but it would have been unseemly and impolitic for a mere borough president to suggest remodeling the entire city.

The *Times*, meanwhile, had been keeping up a steady drumbeat on behalf of the City Beautiful. "Any feature that tends to relieve the dreary monotony of the gridiron," it wrote in July, "whether it be Mr. Lamb's suggestion for a circular colonnade at the Eighth Avenue Plaza of the Central Park or Mr. Hastings's for a decorative bridge at Fifth Avenue and Forty-second Street, should be most hospitably and indulgently considered. The more such interruptions and reliefs of our street plan we have the better will life be worth living in Manhattan."[7]

Low still hesitated to appoint an Improvement Commission. It would surely call for vast expenditures stretching into the distant future, and he was trying to reassure people that the new tax assessment system wouldn't raise the individual tax burden. The new commission offered no prospect of an immediate political payoff, only of terrifying property owners, and Low might have preferred to wait for a second term of office before taking up the city plan. He was forced into action, however, by the fact that the issue of bridge approaches simply wouldn't wait. The Williamsburg Bridge was in the last stages of construction, and new designs for the Manhattan and Queensboro were taking shape on Lindenthal's drafting boards, but through the four cantankerous years of the Van Wyck administration Tammany had laid no plans for bridge approaches. The Manhattan and Williamsburg bridges threatened to simply dump more people into what was already the most crowded quarter on earth, exacerbating the very congestion they were meant to relieve, and property owners near the foot of the Queensboro were demanding that something be done to ensure that the narrow streets of their neighborhood wouldn't be choked with traffic once the bridge opened.

The Williamsburg approach was the most critical issue, and in July 1902 Bridge Commissioner Lindenthal presented his plan for the Delancey Street Parkway to the Fusion Board of Estimate. He asked for the condemnation of a 200-foot-wide strip of land reaching from the bridge westward across the Bowery to Elm Street, where a subway station was planned. Lindenthal admitted that he didn't need all this land for a bridge approach, but he argued that "in that section of the city there was a lack of small parks and the city should lay out a large boulevard, which would form an admirable breathing place in the center of the tenement house district on the East Side."[8] The Board of Estimate unanimously approved, but the Municipal Art Society warned that Lindenthal's proposal was inadequate. Charles Lamb demanded "angle streets," which, he admitted, "seem to be my personal obsession."

> I am a believer in them, but never can accomplish their realization. . . . I desired to give pedestrians a chance to walk from northeast to northwest, or the reverse, without having to make right angles all the time.
>
> When the Williamsburg Bridge was being completed, and the widening of Delancey . . . was under discussion, we urged as a Society that instead of widening Delancey Street, [the approach] should be made of two diagonals, one running down to the Bowery and connecting with the end of the Manhattan Bridge. But diagonal streets, for some reason, never seem to be of interest to the city . . . and inevitably the straight line from the end of the bridge was carried westward merely to increase the difficulties at the point where the widening stops. Instead of swinging the traffic to the northwest and to the southwest, as it wants to go, it is carried at right angles a little further west.[9]

While Lamb's idea floated around, the issue of what to do about Fifty-ninth Street had become a matter of bitter dispute. The street was already overburdened: a narrow crosstown street, it was forced to carry an extra measure of the traffic that was diverted around Central Park, plus a flood of vehicles circling Grand Central's train yards.[10] Now it faced two new threats: the Queensboro Bridge was soon to rise at its eastern end, and on the West Side a private consortium planned to build Gustav Lindenthal's railroad bridge across the Hudson River. Fifty-ninth Street, it seemed, would soon become a great cross axis of traffic between New Jersey and Long Island, but even Lindenthal, the author of both bridge projects, seemed unable to come to terms with this. He laid out "a wide and beautiful boulevard" at the foot of the Queensboro. It would be planted with trees and surrounded, he hoped, by a restricted zone of residences—not the most natural land use amid all the traffic.[11] Yet it was to be a very *short* boulevard, extending only to Second Avenue, and Charles Lamb, Jacob Cantor, and local property owners realized that this would never work. Channeling traffic onto Second Avenue was a silly idea, especially when the Grand Central train tracks blocked so many crosstown streets to the south.

What was needed was some way of letting traffic continue west so it could filter into a whole series of avenues. In 1902 Charles Lamb suggested "arcading" Fifty-ninth Street, condemning fifteen or so feet from the lower floors of each building, so that the city could move the sidewalks under cover of arcades and open the full width of the street, from building line to building line, to traffic. "But this did not seem sufficient," Lamb admitted. Cantor later came up with his own solution, suggesting that Fifty-ninth Street be widened by forty feet on its north side, making it as wide as Forty-second and Thirty-fourth streets. Emmanuel Bloomingdale, whose store stood in the way, naturally preferred that the city take the land on the *south* side of the street, but declared that he'd rather lose part of his store than see nothing done. Seth Low blocked this proposal, however, insisting that the Second Avenue Plaza was sufficient to disperse traffic. Cantor tried to compromise, pleading for at least twenty feet of land, but Low still refused to budge. He allowed the sidewalks of Fifty-ninth Street to be narrowed slightly, but this, Cantor complained, left the situation "up goose creek."[12]

These arguments over bridge approaches must have convinced Low that he needed some assistance, whether to obtain a broader understanding of the problem or simply to provide himself with some political cover. In November 1902 he asked the Art Commission what to do about the Williamsburg and Manhattan bridges. In effect he was asking the Art Commission to play, this one time, the role of a planning commission, which it had no statutory right to do. John De Witt Warner, A. Augustus Healey, and Frederick W. Rhinelander formed a subcommittee to study the issue. (Healey, head of the Brooklyn Institute of Arts and Sciences, was a member and future president of MAS; Rhinelander represented the Metropolitan Museum of Art.) They endorsed widening Delancey Street, as Lindenthal planned, but they also submitted a scheme for diagonal avenues leading from the foot of the Williamsburg Bridge to Cooper Square and the Manhattan Bridge.[13]

This was the same proposal Charles Lamb had drawn up at the Municipal Art Society, and perhaps it occurred to Low that he might as well deal with the society directly rather than through the Art Commission, for in the same month he decided to compromise. He didn't appoint a commission, as MAS wished, but he did ask the society "to give such information as it could get or could obtain in reference to the re-planning and beautification of the City."[14]

"Information," in this context, could mean many things. Low may have expected, even hoped for, some dry and earnest report detailing, as everyone knew, the fact that New York didn't work. The Municipal Art Society decided to make the most of this opening and report, not on problems, but on solutions. It would present Low with at least the beginnings of a plan.

Frederick Lamb decided to demonstrate that there was broad support for a planning commission, so he organized the Conference Committee on the City Plan, inviting representatives of art societies and business groups to a meeting at the Merchants' Association. The gathering was chaired by Henry Towne of the Merchants' Association. Among the others present were William Barclay Parsons of the Board of Trade and Transportation, who was better known as the chief engineer of the Rapid Transit Commission; William McCarroll of the Manufacturers' Association of New York; J.J.R. Croes of the American Society of Civil Engineers; William Laurel Harris of the Architectural League; Charles Lamb of the National Sculpture Society; Joseph Lauber of the National Society of Mural Painters; John De Witt Warner of the Municipal Art Society; and A.D.F. Hamlin of both the Art Commission and Columbia University's School of Architecture. (Towne, Harris, and Charles Lamb all served on the Municipal Art Society's Thoroughfares Committee, and Hamlin chaired its Committee on the Decoration of Public Buildings.) The *Times* described the Conference Committee as representing "all, or most, of the interests in municipal improvement; so far as that improvement may demand reconstruction or modification of what exists. It is also fairly well divided between the organizations that urge reconstruction on practical grounds and those which urge it on aesthetic grounds."[15] In fact this list of delegates must strike anyone today as thoroughly bizarre. Before inviting representatives of the decorative arts one might, for instance, think of including representatives of organized labor, delegates from the settlement houses, and experts in housing. Where were Lawrence Veiller, Robert W. De Forest, I. N. Phelps Stokes, Ernest Flagg, and Jacob Riis? Where were the park and playground advocates?

The first meeting was meant to establish the basis for a joint plan, and the delegates merely agreed that "before any scheme for beautifying Greater New York can be successfully carried out the structural and transportation changes must first be determined."[16] A week later the group reassembled, equipped this time with the specific recommendations of each organization. After that meeting, the conference disbanded and the Municipal Art Society was left to collate the various ideas and to draw up a comprehensive report.

"No city can be really successful," Frederick Lamb wrote in the report's preface, "unless it is so planned as to give its commercial interests every advantage, both from the point of view of speed as well as that of economy and delivery."[17] The problem of New York was "first of all, an engineering one," and its most crucial aspect was the integration of the individual boroughs into one greater city. "An effort must be made to render them attractive in appearance, accessible to all points and from all points, and thoroughly supplied, each according to its needs, with water, light and transport, and with means of disposal of waste."[18] The plan focused on Manhattan, however: the hub of Greater New York, where the dense gridiron plan was to be penetrated by a new network of traffic arteries. On the lower West Side, where the docks were concentrated and the streets were clogged with freight, the Municipal Art Society proposed widening Varick Street and extending Seventh and Sixth avenues southward to meet it (both avenues still stopped north of Greenwich Village).[19] Christopher Street would also become a major thoroughfare, broadened and lengthened to reach from the waterfront all the way to Union Square. On the Lower East Side, new streets would distribute traffic from the East

River bridges, with two diagonal avenues springing from the foot of the Williamsburg, one headed northwest to Cooper Square, the other southwest toward the Manhattan Bridge and the financial center. For Midtown, MAS suggested a subway linking the new Pennsylvania Station with the rebuilt Grand Central Terminal—both projects were in the planning stages—and it demanded that the new Grand Central Terminal allow for both a subway tunnel heading north and a vehicular link between the upper and lower halves of Park Avenue. For Fifty-ninth Street, MAS recommended Charles Lamb's system of arcades.

The most visionary proposal was not for New York at all, but for New Jersey. If New York was ever to have an efficient port, it would have to "transcend the ordinary city limits," Frederick Lamb wrote, and the Conference Committee demanded the construction of a huge freight terminal at Communipaw. Modeled on the Liverpool docks, it would serve the six railroad companies whose tracks now ended at the New Jersey shore of the Hudson River and who were forced to ship their freight across the Hudson on barges. It would "compel the eventual reclamation of the Newark meadows," where there was "ample space for the necessary manufacturing interests of not only the Greater City, but of Newark and the surrounding sections."[20]

What Lamb left unsaid was that the art society's plan would mean an immense amount of demolition in the tenement districts, and especially on the Lower East Side. MAS, however, blithely ignored the human cost of its proposals—neighborhoods torn up and dispersed, families separated, small businesses obliterated, not to mention the terrible overcrowding that would have surely ensued. This seems heartless, but one should mention that the campaign to win the New Tenement Law of 1901 had depicted the pre-law and Old Law tenements as veritable death traps for their tenants. The Municipal Art Society saw the Lower East Side through Jacob Riis's camera lens, and had every reason to believe that it was doing the poor a kindness by destroying their homes. Moreover the bridge approaches seemed essential if the poor were to have an escape route from the old slums to Brooklyn or Queens—to their own houses or, at worst, to New Law tenements.

Seth Low at last gave his blessing to the planning movement, and in 1903 Jacob Cantor went to Albany and came back with a state law authorizing the creation of a New York City Improvement Commission. The law named the five current borough presidents and left ten slots open for mayoral appointees. It also specified a technical staff composed of the chief engineers of the Board of Estimate and the Dock and Bridge departments, plus the landscape architect of the Parks Department. He still needed to fund the commission, and for that he had to turn to the city.

In April 1903, with Taber Sears's mural *New York and the Nations* hovering overhead and the report of the Conference Committee in hand, Cantor stepped before the Board of Aldermen to plead for $10,000, a piddling sum meant to pay for the commission's clerical expenses. He was not well received.[21] Things went no better at a second hearing a few days later: "Some of the cavillers seem to have taken the ground that the proposed revision [of the plan] was merely aesthetic, a matter of meaningless embellishment; others that it was a 'job.'" Of course, sneered the *Times*, the pleasures of living in a beautiful city "could be expected to appeal only to a certain degree of enlightenment, and it would be perfectly futile to urge them upon Aldermen Sullivan and Stuart. But, as a matter of fact, it is not only, nor primarily, in the interest of beauty that the revision of the municipal plan is needed. It is in the interest of the expansion of New York, which is hampered at almost every point by the want of intelligence of the plan imposed upon Manhattan almost a hundred years ago. It is, in the first place, the public convenience and comfort that are to be consulted, and that demand the revision. Beauty is a 'by product,' though not less important on that account."[22]

"Injustice has been done to this project," the *Times* complained, "by representing it as primarily a plan for 'beautifying' the city."[23] If so, the injustice was committed with the inadvertent assistance of the Municipal Art Society, of the *Times*, and of other equally supportive newspapers that used the words "embellishment" and "public improvement" interchangeably, and so handed the aldermen a useful weapon. The real issue, though, was power. The aldermen saw no reason to surrender control of the city map to an elite group of unnamed and unelected "experts" who would surely wreak havoc on the aldermen's own communities—the report of the Conference Committee left no doubt that the Lower East Side would be devastated.

The aldermen paid a steep price for their intransigence, however. In May 1903, over their howls of protest, Seth Low rammed a bill through the state legislature that transferred control of the city map from the Board of Aldermen to the Board of Estimate. Low explained its purpose: "In the near future great streets will have to be cut through densely populated sections, in both Manhattan and Brooklyn, in order to provide suitable approaches to the East River Bridges now building, and generally to improve circulation in various parts of the city. Work like this, if done at all, must be carried out from the general point of view. If it must wait until it can also command local approval—such as the Board of Aldermen represents—years are likely to pass before anything can be done, and during all those years the city will suffer, while it may easily lose its opportunity altogether."[24]

Some sort of centralization of the planning process was undoubtedly necessary, but in its determination to break Tammany's hold on the neighborhoods, and the neighborhoods' stranglehold over planning, the reform movement left communities with no real voice in the planning process. The danger involved in this wouldn't become clear to the Municipal Art Society for years—not until after World War II, when it realized that nothing could stop Robert Moses.

ON ELECTION night in November 1903, as word spread through the city that Tammany was back in power, "boys and girls [went] running up and down the streets . . . crying between prodigious blasts on their tin horns: 'The lid is off! The lid is off!'"[25] Their cries sent shivers of horror down the spines of reformers. At the Municipal Art Society the board desperately hoped that Low would make the most of his last two months in office. Even if he couldn't muster enough Board of Estimate votes for public improvements, he could appoint the members of the New York City Improvement Commission. MAS was ready to finance the commission's work with private funds from the business community, and it already had pledges in hand. What mattered at the moment was that the right people be appointed.[26] Tammany might let the commission wither away or, worse, transform it into a machine for dividing the spoils. MAS and its allies handed Low a list of candidates, delegates of the groups that had formed the Conference Committee. Frederick Lamb headed the list, while the arts community would also have been represented by George Post, Daniel Chester French, the painter Frederick Dielman, and the landscape architect Charles Lowrie.[27]

Seth Low refused to heed the society's pleas. The aldermen had every legal right to refuse funds for a commission; to appoint one nonetheless would violate the spirit if not, perhaps, the letter of the city charter. All he could do, Low explained, was write to his successor and lay the responsibility of creating an Improvement Commission in the hands of George McClellan.[28]

"When I became Mayor of New York," George McClellan wrote, "I was very much in the position of a medieval podesta called from outside to the chief magistracy of an Italian city with which he was utterly unfamiliar."[29] McClellan had been nominated for two reasons. While Tammany fought over the succession to Richard Croker, McClellan had been in Congress—"the very pleasantest of clubs," he called it. Since Tammany had so little interest in national affairs (McClellan once had to remind Richard Croker that Democrats were *against* imperialism, not for it), he and the Hall had left one another alone, and none of the machine's squabbling factions had anything against him. Second, McClellan gave Tammany a veneer of respectability. The Democrats had come to realize the advantages of picking a respectable candidate for mayor—the sort of man who could associate with a notorious political machine and still retain a reputation for being "personally" honest. In 1901 it had been Edward Shepard, a respected Brooklyn lawyer (and a member, even, of the Municipal Art Society), and now it was McClellan. He was "one New York gentleman to the manner born," a New York paper wrote, "who has eaten of the tree of knowledge of Tammany Hall and has had no stomach ache."[30]

McClellan was a Princetonian, the author of several histories of Venice, and an aesthete. He cultivated the friendship of artists; his address at the memorial for Augustus Saint-Gaudens was "so fair, so finished," that the artist F. D. Millet left feeling that "the right thing had been said at last."[31] The arts community was charmed by a mayor who rejected, in another speech, the legacy of Puritan culture that "tried to convince mankind that beauty and righteousness were antipathetic," and who turned to Venetian history to justify his lavish program of Beaux Arts public works: "Venice lived a thousand years. During her last two centuries she was kept alive by the love and devotion of her children. Do you suppose that they would have felt for their mother as they did, had she been the architectural ancestress of Hoboken or Jersey City?"[32]

In 1908 New York's Beaux Arts architects (the Société des Architectes Diplômés par le Gouvernement de France) gave him their gold medal as a sincere token of gratitude and esteem. In 1909 McClellan returned the favor by quashing a bill that would have revived the post of city architect—something that raised memories of the philistinism and the political pull of Horgan & Slattery, and would have threatened to deprive a good many designers of city commissions.[33] In later life he was a professor at Princeton and a trustee of the American Academy in Rome.

The professional art societies regarded McClellan as the most sympathetic mayor they'd ever known, but the Municipal Art Society could make no such claim. Its relationship with the mayor began badly and ended in open warfare. The problem was that the society, despite its claims to be nonpartisan, was clearly a think tank for the Citizens Union, and McClellan, despite his virtues, was still a Tammany Democrat. In a way, he shouldn't have been. There was nothing of the corner saloon in McClellan, and he found Tammany's bosses vulgar, crude, dishonest, and ill educated. ("I had great difficulty," he complained of Charles Murphy, "in inducing him to refer to himself in writing as 'I' and not as 'i.' "[34]) McClellan was a Democrat because his father, the Civil War general, had been one. The mayor had watched the ruin of his father's life—dismissed by Lincoln, accused of treachery during his doomed presidential race in 1864, and never afterward able to find a position worthy of his talent—and his own political career was meant to vindicate the general's memory. His eyes were on the White House, and for a brief time it seemed he might one day reach his goal. But to be elected president in this era of smoke-filled rooms and rigged conventions he would need Tammany's support, and to win it, McClellan became, by his own description, "an organization man."[35]

The mayor had made a Faustian pact with Tammany Hall, and the tension in this misalliance eventually proved more than he could bear. In 1906, having narrowly won reelection against William Randolph Hearst (only by massive fraud, according to the Hearst papers), he severed his ties with Boss Murphy and tried to take the reins of Tammany Hall in his own hands. He failed, and would never again be nominated for political office, yet this brought him no closer to New York's reform camp. McClellan never forgave Seth Low's supporters for tarring him, personally, with the brush of Tammany's vices. During the campaign of 1903, Low's "supporters . . . said things about me that were, to say the least, quite beyond the ordinary rules of decency, even in a desperate political fight." He resented one slogan in particular: "A vote for Low is a vote for the home, a vote for McClellan is a vote for the brothel."[36] The mayor was not averse to citizen advocates per se, but he despised all those advocates—like Warner, Tomkins, and the Lambs— who'd strayed into reform politics. "That the wrong men only too often control our local politics is due to the fact that the right men refuse to do their duty," McClellan wrote in his memoirs. "If those who spasmodically take part in so-called reform or fusion movements would join the organizations of the parties to which they profess to owe allegiance and would devote the time they spend in their clubs to the practice of the profession of politics (in other words, were they public-spirited enough to act more and talk less), they could acquire control of the machinery of politics and bring forth works meet for repentance."[37]

IN MARCH 1904 McClellan appointed the members of the New York City Improvement Commission.[38] There were ten slots for the mayor to fill, and the most conspicuous fact about his choices was that none was active in the Municipal Art Society or in the wider community of reformers.

It wasn't quite as bad as MAS had feared. McClellan didn't appoint Boss Murphy's lackeys—they only wanted jobs that paid. Instead he chose his own friends, like the financier Harry Payne Whitney. The commission's chairman was Daniel Lamont, an intimate from the mayor's days in Washington, when Lamont was secretary of war. Its secretary was a young lawyer named Francis Pendleton, whose father had been General McClellan's running mate in 1864.[39] Another member was Egerton Winthrop, president of the Board of Education, who happened to be married to the mayor's sister-in-law. The painter James Alexander and the sculptor Daniel Chester French clearly had limited roles on the commission. The name of Whitney Warren stands out, for he was a brilliant Beaux Arts architect, revered now as one of the designers of Grand Central Terminal. But Warren was fundamentally a society architect, not active in any form of citizen advocacy, and not really interested in the sort of complex urban design that was required. The ingenious planning of Grand Central was the work of his associates, and Warren tried hard to eliminate its most brilliant features—to replace the terminal's ramps with stairs and do away with the viaduct altogether, forever cleaving Park Avenue in two. There were other reasons to be disturbed by the mayor's choices. Any serious city plan, for instance, would have to address the intolerable fact that the New York Central Railroad's freight tracks defaced the waterfront below Riverside Drive and continued down the middle of Eleventh Avenue. But the New York Central was controlled by the Vanderbilts, Warren's patrons and cousins. Nor was Daniel Lamont eager to find a radical solution to the rapid transit crisis, for he was vice president of the Crosstown Street Railway Company.

"The Mayor has appointed a number of respectable or eminent citizens," the Times wrote, "of whom none has given any public evidence of any intelligent interest in the project of replanning the city. . . . Meanwhile the only body which is making any practical suggestions to that end is an unofficial body with no power to do anything except make and promulgate suggestions at its own expense. The Municipal Art Society, to which the Merchants' Association might be added, is engaged in supplying ideas for the mayor's official commission. The question naturally arises why the men who have thought about the subject and who have ideas upon it should not have been chosen, or some of them, to furnish what may be called brains for the official commission as members of it, instead of being reduced to volunteering unofficial suggestions to it from the outside." The *Times* especially mourned the absence of Charles Lamb, "a man of more fecundity of practical or plausible and at any rate interesting notions of municipal development than any other New Yorker. The man who originated the notion of the Dewey Arch, and who also originated the obviously sensible project of reducing to order such a chaos as that of the Eighth Avenue Plaza [Columbus Circle] . . . is clearly a man to be taken into counsel when the question is of municipal improvement."[40]

Yes, but in 1903 Charles Lamb was once again credited with designing Seth Low's campaign posters. They boasted more idealized women, this time standing before views of Fusion's public works. (Three years later, when they figured prominently in the Municipal Art Society's exhibit of artistic advertisements, they were revealed to be the work of Lamb's wife, the painter Ella Condie Lamb.) Frederick Lamb and Calvin Tomkins were even more deeply involved in reform politics, and McClellan had no guarantee that John De Witt Warner wouldn't run for mayor himself someday. Warner had, after all, come close to doing so in 1901. Thanks to its board's involvement in reform politics, the Municipal Art Society had won a good deal of power under Seth Low, but it now had to pay the price. Instead of staffing the Improvement Commission, it could only send the commission its recommendations and testify at its hearings. It actually helped that most of the commissioners were novices at their task and thus had no ideas of their own. It also helped that Jacob Cantor was a member of the commission. This was a happy accident. The authorizing legislation, passed in 1903, had appointed the five *current* borough presidents, which meant that Cantor's place was secure despite the fact that he was no longer in office.*

The Improvement Commission was instructed to have a report ready by the end of 1904. Its task was to "improve and develop the parkways and park systems of the city, adequately equip and beautify the main thoroughfares, so as to provide the best means of communication with the outlying boroughs, and make the points of entrance to and departure from the city, such as docks, railroad stations and bridges, properly representative of the leading city of the Western Hemisphere."[41] The commission was soon bombarded with the Municipal Art Society's ideas: new parks for Staten Island, an elevated boulevard on West Street along the proposed Chelsea Piers (this will come up later), proposals for parks and public esplanades atop new piers, a seaside park in Rockaway.

The most elaborate and grandiose of these schemes was Charles Lamb's newest project for Fifty-ninth Street. As Lamb told the story, he was still mulling over his idea for arcades when George Neidlinger,

---

* Cantor announced in August 1903 that he wouldn't run for reelection. Thomas Platt, the boss of the state Republican Party, is said to have refused to have Cantor, a Democrat, on a second Fusion ticket; even if Platt came around, Cantor expected that Tammany would concentrate its efforts on recapturing the borough presidency "because of its large powers under the new charter, and because of the valuable patronage that goes with it." ("Cantor Will Retire," New York Times, August 8, 1903, p. 6, col. 3.)

one of my friends, who had been a resident in that quarter some years ago, came to me and proposed that we "Cut it right out." I asked his meaning and he replied: "Let us suggest a good general scheme and put it right through; cut out the whole block, from Fifty-ninth to Sixtieth Street. There is the so-called Millionaires' Club there; we will run it straight from Fifth Avenue to the east ... and put here all these City buildings, or some City buildings, as interesting features of the scheme." So we developed it and planned the big buildings on both sides, and proved to our own satisfaction [never to anyone else's] that it would be a paying investment, if the various interests would only cooperate intelligently. . . . We also endeavored to prove to the gentlemen living north on Fifth Avenue, in the Millionaires' Row, that unless they put in some such buffer between themselves and the march of progress north, it would not be very long before business would take Fifth Avenue in the upper part away from them, as it is taking it away from those like William H. Vanderbilt, who put their houses south of Fifty-ninth Street.

In this respect, Lamb noted, "A park is a most beautiful thing; a park will interrupt lines of traffic, will interrupt lines of business, when nothing else will, and a great wide parkway of this sort would do that."[42]

The published perspective shows this great boulevard lined by hotels and stores on the south, cultural institutions (and the Metropolitan Club) on the north. Fountains and reflecting pools command the central axis, and in the distance a tower marks the transfer station at the foot of the Queensboro Bridge. Lamb prepared, but never published, an even more delirious drawing showing what should go below ground: subways, naturally, but also a vast public swimming pool.[43] Lamb called his scheme the "Court of Honor," seemingly an allusion to the Chicago fair, but there was a more relevant model close to home. In 1903 the architects Reed & Stem had won a competition to design Grand Central Terminal, and north of the terminal, over the railroad tracks, they planned their own Court of Honor. Bordered by buildings with a common low cornice line, it would have transformed Grand Central into the climax of a Beaux Arts ensemble. If a mere railroad could build a Court of Honor—and build it as a moneymaking real estate development—why not the city? Of course the railroad didn't have to condemn any property, and when Terminal City was finally built it wasn't quite as Reed & Stem imagined. The buildings were harmonious, but not as strictly controlled as first imagined, and the cornice line was set much higher—at thirteen stories, a height determined by the 1916 zoning code.

The Improvement Commission finished its report in December 1904, and the entire set of twenty-two beautiful watercolors went on display as the centerpiece of the Municipal Art Society's 1905 annual exhibit. Charles Lamb boasted that "fully nine-tenths" of the report's suggestions were inspired by the society, and indeed one finds in its pages Carrère & Hastings's bridge at Fifth Avenue and Forty-second Street; the extensions of Christopher and Varick streets and Sixth and Seventh avenues; the Chelsea piers with an elevated boulevard; and new avenues to the East River bridges. There was a plan to redo Battery Park with a water gate, a naval arch, and a monumental new ferry terminal. Another plan called for extending Madison Avenue south to Broadway and for a reviewing stand on the edge of Madison Square (not quite the public forum Lamb had proposed for Union Square). There was a handsome view of the Delancey Street Parkway, with subways underneath, and an elaborate transfer station at the foot of the Queensboro Bridge. In Brooklyn an *étoile*, complete with an obelisk and a copy of the Trevi Fountain, would link the approaches of the Brooklyn and Manhattan bridges. The most interesting sugges-tions were plans to connect the park systems of Manhattan and the Bronx. Upper Fifth Avenue would become a parkway leading to the Grand Concourse; Riverside Park would be extended to Inwood Hill. A narrow ribbon of greenery would link the Speedway on the Harlem River to Morningside, Saint Nicholas, and Central parks, and 181st Street would become a parkway heading east to a vast sports arena in the Bronx and, beyond that, to Pelham Bay.

It was true that most of the ideas in the 1904 plan sprang from the Municipal Art Society, but the Improvement Commission left out a good deal. It shirked certain controversial projects. By now, for instance, MAS and the Bridge Depart-ment were locked in a dispute over the Civic Center, and though the Improvement Commission mentioned the need for a new terminal at the Brooklyn Bridge, it chose not to propose anything concrete. In the rush to finish its report on time, the commission slighted Brooklyn, ignored Queens, and paid no attention at all to the eastern half of the Bronx, where MAS was soon engaged in a fight with Bronx Borough President Haffen over how to plan Chester. McClellan decided to extend the commission's life until 1907 so it could draw a more comprehensive scheme. In the meantime little was done to carry out its proposals.

The Municipal Art Society was unable to get the Improvement Commission a large, paid technical staff, nor was it having much luck in working out a way for New York to pay for the City Beautiful. In the meantime something curious happened between 1904 and 1907: the Municipal Art Society outgrew the no-tion of planning embodied in the Improvement Commission. MAS didn't aban-don its interest in magnificent public plazas, parkways, and avenues, but it widened its field of vision. By 1905 it was at work on a series of schemes to solve the city's freight problem, an incredibly knotty and treacherous issue that involved relocating the West Side tracks of the New York Central railroad, and by 1906 it was trying to introduce setback regulations for skyscrapers. It had also realized that planning involved something more fundamental than the street pat-tern: the subway.

WEARING A top hat and white gloves, George McClellan had opened New York's first subway in 1904. It followed a strange route (on tracks that have since been divided up between the Times Square Shuttle and the Number 1 and Number 6 lines) from City Hall to Grand Central Terminal, across town to Times Square, and then up Broadway to 135th Street. Within a year 106 million passengers had traveled on the subway, and 18 million fares had been paid at the Brooklyn Bridge alone.[44] So many people piled in that soon the platforms had to be lengthened and more ventilators installed. The subway was quicker than the old Els and had none of their unpleasant side effects: it didn't blanket avenues in deep shadow or awaken residents with the sound of screeching brakes. It was clear to MAS that the city should stop building elevated lines and instead plan a comprehensive system of subways. The Improvement Commission, however, declined any responsibility for laying out subways. (It paid more attention to the crosstown trolleys: a testament to the chairman's business interests.) Planning new subways was the job of the Rapid Transit Commission, an independent agency set up by the state to keep the subway free of local politics and patronage. Unfortunately the transit commission was equally free of accountability. The Municipal Art Society decided to step in, and in 1905 Charles Lamb admitted that the society's Thoroughfare Committee had been neglecting city planning: "The work of the Society with reference to the underground problems confronting the City, have [sic] been so energetically pushed that it has been thought wise ... not to urge, during the year past, upon the city authorities the development of the comprehensive plans prepared during the preceding season, with reference to the diagonal streets and the extension of prominent avenues which were shown in the printed report."[45]

The first subway was really "two half subways," as Calvin Tomkins sneered, and the obvious thing to do was to extend it down Broadway and up Lexington Avenue to make two separate lines, with a shuttle at Forty-second Street connecting them like the crossbar of an enormous H. In the meantime the West Side line would be extended into the Bronx, and the East Side line would be lengthened to meet the Long Island Railroad in Flatbush. But what next? The Municipal Art Society's plan, as published, is a bit confusing. It doesn't show the existing transit system—either the newly finished subway or the elevated lines on Second, Third, Sixth, and Columbus avenues—that funneled people north and south in the center of the island. It shows only what MAS proposed to add in the way of subways. It was a remarkable plan. It boasted a far better system of crosstown connections than now exists, with subways crossing the island at the major crosstown streets. A belt line would have surrounded Manhattan. This line was placed close to the waterfront, serving the most crowded industrial and residential districts in the city. Within this overarching loop, two smaller loops served lower Manhattan to distribute passengers from the East River bridges. Finally a series of radiating lines stretched to the farthest reaches of the city and beyond, to Yonkers, Mount Vernon, Flushing, Jamaica, East New York, Flatlands, Coney Island, Fort Hamilton, and thence, it was implied, to Staten Island.

The current subway map of the outer boroughs looks something like the Municipal Art Society's proposal. This is not, I think, because MAS exerted any real influence, but because the society did the obvious thing. In slicing through the thinly settled fields, it aimed the subway at the old towns that had been drawn into the city's net in 1898. MAS may have been the first to state this policy in such a comprehensive way, but it was implemented as a result of pressure from local real estate agents and chambers of commerce who demanded that the urban hordes be sent their way.

The Municipal Art Society's recommendations for Manhattan subway lines were far more controversial. The Board of Trade and Transportation, normally one of the society's allies, came out against the crosstown links, which would have upset the established pattern of land values. In all, the society's plan would have produced a very different New York: high land values wouldn't have been so concentrated in the center of the island, and the pressure to build skyscrapers might have been less intense. The waterfront, especially on the West Side, would have been a very different place today: other uses would have gradually infiltrated the factories and warehouses once the port collapsed.

The subway would soon involve MAS in bitter disputes with the mayor and the *New York Times*, but the Improvement Commission remained untouched by all this fuss. In 1907 it reappeared with its final report, which was basically a more elaborate version of the first. After a good deal of debate, the Improvement Commission succumbed to the temptation of Charles Lamb's Court of Honor at Fifty-ninth Street. It wasn't really a court anymore, but a boulevard lined by trees, pedestrian paths, and truly extravagant topiaries. At the east end of the Queensboro Bridge another *étoile* would distribute traffic through Queens. An even more extensive system of avenues would be cut through downtown Manhattan. One finds new parks proposed for Staten Island, much as MAS and Borough President Cromwell had advocated, and in the Bronx, though MAS had never offered concrete suggestions for that borough. The East River islands would become parks as well. There was to be a network of new parkways in Brooklyn and Queens, some running along the waterfront in south Brooklyn and Jamaica Bay and others threading through the boroughs to link the major parks. Flushing Meadows and Kissena Park made their appearance in Queens.

It was all very beautiful; indeed it struck almost everyone as *too* beautiful. A great deal of attention was paid to large "metropolitan" parks but, MAS complained, none to creating small parks in the tenement districts.[46] There were a great many parkways and drives, but these were restricted to carriages and automobiles. It might be too strong to say that these were "segregated" sequences, but they would certainly have had the effect of sorting people by income so as to free the prosperous from the physical and social inconvenience of sharing the streets with the rest of the world. The report's aestheticism and its social ethos seemed to be summed up in its notorious proposal to tear down the wall surrounding Central Park. Pages and pages of illustrations were devoted to the subject—so many of them, devoted to so trivial a subject, as to discredit the entire report.[47] It might have been worse: the Improvement Commission wasted a good deal of time holding hearings on an even more obnoxious scheme. In 1905 Fifth Avenue residents— among them Henry Phipps, Isaac Brokaw, Mortimer Schiff, F. W. Woolworth,

Otto Kahn, and Charles Gould—signed a petition describing the wall as "an eyesore" that "has long since outlived its usefulness, having been originally erected to keep out the cows, goats, etc., of the neighborhood." They wanted in its place "a new Park Drive and bridle path" on a strip of Central Park some ninety feet in width—twenty-seven acres in all.[48] The Board of Trade denounced this as "the most insidious" proposal yet made to tamper with Olmsted's design—"insidious" because the group thought it would be a delightful amenity in itself and "a most attractive border" to the park.[49] The Times was more cynical: "The owners of houses on Central Park East would like to have a view of the Park from their first floors, and even from their basements, as well as from their second-story windows."[50]

No one was more disappointed with the Improvement Commission's final report than Frederick Stymetz Lamb, the very man who had organized the Municipal Art Society's original Conference Committee. By 1908, when Lamb wrote about the Improvement Commission in the magazine Charities, MAS was advocating the creation of a Port Authority to deal with the problems of the harbor, and it had come to endorse not just setback regulations for skyscrapers but land-use zoning as well. The Improvement Commission had produced a report that looked like something the art societies might have done in the late 1890s. "The greater city of the future—the city of twenty years to come—has not been adequately realized in imagination," Lamb wrote. What of the subway? The new bridges? The New Jersey shore? "This area is just as important . . . to Greater New York as if it were contained within its boundaries." The lack of vision in the report, Lamb suggested, was due to the desire to propose only projects that could possibly be financed in the near future. "The work of this commission proves conclusively the necessity of a permanent commission . . . adequately remunerated to enable it to carry on its important work with efficiency."[51] Undoubtedly this was the correct conclusion, but it was not easy for MAS to convince others that, since a temporary commission had produced a timid report, the answer was to appoint a permanent commission with a larger appropriation.

Mayor McClellan, however, seems to have been delighted with the Improvement Commission's report as it stood. He was eager to carry out its proposals, and some aspects of the plan, like the Whitehall Ferry Terminal, the Chelsea Piers, Kissena and Rockaway parks, were set in motion during his term. For the moment, however, any large-scale reconstruction of Manhattan was stymied because New York had neither the money nor the constitutional power to put the plan into effect.

Money was the obvious problem. Nelson Lewis, chief engineer of the Board of Estimate, told the board he thought the City Beautiful plans would cost $86 million. Many of its recommendations could be deferred, he pointed out, but he suggested that "some of the more important items, the extension south of Sixth, Seventh and Madison avenues, the widening of the Fifth Avenue roadway, the extension of Flatbush and Hamilton avenues, in Brooklyn, and a new park for the Bronx near Spuyten Duyvil," should be attended to at once. They would cost about $37 million.[52] At the same time the Times calculated the cost of all public works just finished, under way, or definitely planned: $98 million—"more than the taxable valuation of all the personal property in Brooklyn, and as large as the assessed valuation of all the taxable property in Albany and Binghamton combined."[53] Lewis's estimate of the full cost of the City Beautiful does seem incredibly low. In 1905, discussing the first report of the Improvement Commission, McClellan had warned New Yorkers that they should expect to pay $250 million over the next ten years to create, in his words, "Greatest New York."[54]

How was the city to pay for all this? Taxes were as bitterly resented in 1907 as they are today, and the Municipal Art Society was keenly aware that much of Seth Low's constituency had abandoned him when he changed the city's assessment formula. Besides, Municipalians didn't want just money in the city's coffers. They wanted the city to have more power in determining its own shape. Since 1903 they'd been working for an amendment to the state constitution, the so-called excess condemnation law, which they hoped would give the city a painless way to finance its public improvements and the power to create Classical public spaces.

If your urban ideal was Paris, with its great boulevards lined by harmonious buildings, then you wanted, ideally, to control a host of issues: the height of buildings, their materials, and even their architectural style. Given the courts' understanding of property rights at the turn of the century, there was only one conceivable way for New York to achieve such control over private property, and that was to take it away from its owners—to condemn it. Even here, however, the city's power was hemmed in by the state constitution: it could condemn no more land than was strictly necessary for a public improvement. If New York cut a new street, it could take whatever buildings stood directly in the way, but not those to either side. It was common for condemnation commissioners to shave off part of a building and leave the rest standing, reimbursing the owner for only a portion of the building's worth. This meant that if the city had actually undertaken the new boulevards proposed by the Improvement Commission, or by MAS, the result would have been an urbanistic disaster: not the gorgeous Parisian boulevards so lovingly rendered in the 1907 report, but a whole network of brutal gashes in the cityscape that might never have healed. Certainly Delancey Street never became the handsome boulevard imagined by Gustav Lindenthal or pictured by the Improvement Commission. The north side of the street was untouched by the city and has changed fairly little since the parkway was created, but the south side still shows scars that date back to 1904. There the condemnation process left behind a ragged edge of vacant lots—little slivers of land that were too narrow to be of much use to developers. The Improvement Commission had shown the parkway lined by New Law tenements; instead, garages and shops sprang up, squeezed into rude two-story structures.

If the city had been able to take more land on the south side of Delancey Street, it could have combined the lots to make bigger, more useful parcels. It could have placed whatever restrictions it wished on their development, stipulating what kinds of building were allowed, and even setting design guidelines. It could even have

rebuilt these properties itself, and the Municipal Art Society saw in this an opportunity for the city to do something it had never done before: build housing. Seth
Low's small parks program continued under McClellan, but MAS began to wonder
if this was the solution. Each new park "affects but indirectly" the squalid conditions in the tenements, an MAS committee concluded in 1908. "This being admitted, can we doubt but that we may attack the problem directly by insisting upon
and even providing for housing and living conditions as we now do for recreation
and education?"[55]

Another issue, no less important, had to do with financing public improvements.
Whenever the city cut a new street, built a park, or laid out a parkway, the land
around it increased in value. The city naturally slapped it with higher assessments
and eventually recouped its investment through local property taxes. But no businessman would use his money like this. The city's capital was effectively tied up for
years while local property owners enjoyed a sudden windfall. They could sell their
land at a steep profit they'd done nothing to earn. Since the capital budget was
severely limited by the state constitution, the Municipal Art Society turned its
attention to this windfall. In 1903 it began to argue that the profits should accrue
to the city, not to the private citizens who happened to live nearby or to the
politically connected speculators who had advance warning of impending improvements. In order to seize the windfall, however, the city had to lay its hands on more
land: it had to indulge in "excess condemnation."

This meant condemning a swath of land, building a road through the middle of
it, and then selling what was left over at its new, higher value. This was British
practice, as Charles Lamb pointed out. "Here is the point: the British Parliament
now holds that where a municipality makes an improvement it alone has the right
to the natural increase in value of the abutting property. In New York this profit
goes into the pockets of selfish citizens who stand in with the politicians. . . . In
England, by special act of Parliament, the 'excess condemnation law' sets the egg
upon its proper end." Lamb told how his friend William E. Reilly, architect to the
London County Council, was at that moment laying out the Kings Highway
between the Strand and High Holborn. Reilly was able "to close about twenty odd
streets . . . and practically rearrange the map of London with the area." The new
buildings would be subject to the council's design guidelines, "so as to secure a
reasonable amount of harmony, if not absolute uniformity." The result would be
"as handsome a concourse as there is in all Europe," and because it was financed
through the excess condemnation law, all this was achieved, Lamb insisted, "without
cost" to the city of London. "Don't look as if the English are slow, eh?"[56]

There was an ugly tone in some discussions of excess condemnation, especially
when Municipalians proposed using it in the tenement districts as a way to finance
the new urban parks. In 1908 Charles Lamb remembered how, two years earlier,
he'd helped some "dear lady friends . . . get a little park in Chelsea." The experience—though it was one of his rare victories—was deeply troubling. "When after
great effort, they secured a small City Park of a block square," he wrote, "the cost

practically increased the debt limit by $1,000,000. Perfectly preposterous! And everybody who has been on the inside and has acquired a piece of property is making a profit, whereas, if condemnation had been possible for the City Park to the center of the block north and south, and the property facing out on the park re-sold, the park would have been built for no cost and the tax rate would not have been increased."[57]

This paranoia about those "on the inside" wasn't entirely unjustified. In 1906 the Bureau of City Betterment had indeed charged that there were irregularities in the condemnation proceedings at Chelsea Park.[58] When Lamb spoke in 1908 there were reports that "lawyers who make a specialty of condemnation work are canvassing the territory in and around the Manhattan end of the Blackwell's Island Bridge."[59] They were inspired by the Improvement Commission's report, with its gorgeous rendering of a Court of Honor between Fifty-ninth and Sixtieth streets. At the same time, John Purroy Mitchel, the future mayor, was launching his political career with an investigation of the borough presidents' handling of public works; four of the five were disgraced by his findings. Yet what Lamb proposed for cases like Chelsea Park smacks of gentrification as official policy. The neighborhood parks were supposed to improve the lives of local residents, but each one displaced hundreds of people. Excess condemnation would only have made this worse, for each block-square park would now displace twice as many families, and the new greenery would come equipped with a colony of new, more prosperous residents.

John De Witt Warner formed an Excess Condemnation Committee at the Municipal Art Society in 1905. He drafted a bill for the state legislature, but by January 1906 concluded that it wasn't "practicable" at the moment.[60] The Reform Club and the City Improvement Commission soon joined in the fight, but Warner's bill encountered significant opposition "on the Lower East Side by the small Hebrew and Italian property owners."[61] Their opposition was understandable: their neighborhood would have been hard hit by the new bridge approaches, and condemnation awards would not have paid for the fixtures in their stores or the goodwill they'd built up with customers. They managed to delay passage of the excess condemnation law until 1912. That was far too late to be of any use to McClellan. By 1907 the mayor's relations with Tammany Hall had grown so bitter that the Board of Aldermen thwarted his pet projects, and by 1910 his political career was at an end.

Excess condemnation was supposed to be the key to a beautiful New York. It made its debut, however, at Foley Square, one of the great disasters of urban design in New York. And it soon became clear that the city was reluctant to actually use the awesome power it had acquired. In 1913, when Sixth Avenue was finally extended through Greenwich Village, as MAS had first demanded in 1902, the city didn't resort to excess condemnation. Too many people would have been displaced, or perhaps too large an initial investment was required. Even in the 1950s, when Houston Street was widened, the old model of condemnation prevailed. Houston Street's scars have yet to heal.

LIVING WITH THE ENEMY:
THE MUNICIPAL
ART SOCIETY AND
TAMMANY HALL

WHILE THE IMPROVEMENT Commission whiled away the years, the Municipal Art Society had been working to shape a city that still lacked a plan. Its members roamed the corridors of City Hall, stood before judges, and lurked in waiting rooms, ready with advice, testimony, pleas, and lawsuits as the occasion required. Despite McClellan's distrust, things were by no means as bad as they had been during the Van Wyck years. Fusion's two years in power had left a number of legacies. There was the new tax assessment policy, which let the city's budget grow by leaps and bounds in the years to come while the average burden on individual taxpayers declined.[1] There was the program of baths and small parks, new municipal services that had not, after all, kept Low in power, but which were popular enough that Tammany Hall now embraced them. There was the Art Commission's newfound power over all public works, voluntarily extended by McClellan and soon codified in the new Charter of 1907. Tammany Hall had won control of the Board of Aldermen, the Board of Estimate, the mayoralty, and four of the borough presidencies, but MAS still had friends in the city government. The Improvement Commission was receptive to the society's ideas, in part because it had so few of its own, and if the society was disappointed with the commission's timidity, it had few objections to what the commission actually proposed to do; MAS merely wanted more. The new dock commissioner was a member of MAS (though he proved a great disappointment); Borough President Cromwell of Staten Island managed to keep his office; Comptroller Grout, despite his defection to Tammany Hall, remained sympathetic and even assured the Municipal Art Society that he regarded it "almost as one of the departments of the City government."[2]

Grout used his influence to continue Low's small parks campaign, and it was now the Democrats' turn to encounter the ambivalence of local residents. When tenements were demolished to expand Thomas Jefferson Park (stretching from First Avenue to the East River, and from 111th to 114th streets), Park Commissioner Pallas had to assure the residents of Little Italy that, no, the park wasn't a plot by local landlords to crowd the district so that they could raise the rent, nor was it meant "to give the police a rallying spot in case of trouble."[3] Like DeWitt Clinton Park (between 52nd and 54th streets, Eleventh and Twelfth avenues), Thomas Jefferson Park had been designed by Samuel Parsons, a Municipalian and a hold-over from the Low administration (Low had placed him on the civil service lists). The plans had even been drawn while Low was in power, but the parks opened during McClellan's reelection campaign in 1905. The health commissioner gave speeches dwelling on the medicinal effects of the parks. The Parks Department provided as much pageantry as it could muster, and a blaring brass band "frequently returned from patriotic music to the strains of 'Tammany,' for the words were far more familiar to many [in the crowd] than those of 'The Star Spangled Banner' and 'America.' "[4]

Small parks had become a motherhood issue, unless your own apartment was threatened. Charles Lamb noted that "it is somewhat peculiar that progress can be made in this city of ours, and in most American cities, by proposing parks and parkways, when nothing can be done by discussing streets, or architecture on streets, or other details of civic construction."[5] There was a flip side to this emphasis on urban parks as the city almost stopped buying land in outlying regions. The Municipal Art Society wanted two policies to go hand in hand: parks in the slums to ameliorate the awful living conditions of the tenements, but also land reserves in areas not yet settled, as a guarantee that when development arrived, the outer boroughs would enjoy a better quality of life than was available in Manhattan. "What we need," Frederick Lamb told the Municipal Club in 1908, "are public expenditures at the proper time. Those in authority should buy parks and reser-vations now that may or may not be needed for many years to come. . . . If these purchases prove not to be needed years hence they can be sold at a profit, but if we should need them the city will own them and no large outlay will be necessary."[6] Of course the long-range nature of this strategy left MAS and other park activists vulnerable to derision. Even the *Times* was an uncertain ally. The paper applauded the preservation of the Palisades, but it derided the project for a Palisades Park: "there is no population to be accommodated by it and no chance for there ever to be a population."[7] Yet Palisades Park was just a ferry ride from Manhattan, and the Lamb brothers were among its most fervent advocates. MAS was also hampered by the aura of malfeasance that surrounded the city's land purchases. Between 1907 and 1909, for instance, the city spent more than $400,000 on land for Kissena Park in Queens, as recommended by the Improvement Commission. It turned out that a fifth of this sum was kicked back to an intimate friend of Joseph Bermel, the Queens borough president. Bermel resigned when this information became public and, as an extra precaution against prosecution, set sail for Europe.[8]

In the spring of 1904 Charles Stover, the Charity Organization Society, MAS, and a number of other groups launched a campaign to convince the city that it should buy Rockaway Park (now Jacob Riis Park), on the peninsula between Jamaica Bay and the Atlantic Ocean. (Stover couldn't persuade the railroad tycoon

E. H. Harriman to give the city his land at the tip of the peninsula. Harriman sold it before his death—a pity, since his widow was a generous woman who channeled some of her philanthropy through MAS.) Here was a rare opportunity for an ocean beach within New York itself, but the mayor and comptroller preferred to concentrate on the small urban parks. Changing the mayor's mind required the Charity Organization Society to open a privately funded clinic in Rockaway; it was so successful in treating tubercular patients that McClellan promised, in his State of the City address in 1906, to open a "seaside fresh-air . . . resort for convalescents, discharged from our city hospitals."[9] Charles Stover succeeded in marrying the two issues: Rockaway Park was supposed to be the site of the municipal resort.

Even with McClellan's support, however, the park remained controversial. It cost forty cents to get to Rockaway from Manhattan on the mass transit system—this at a time when the masses, living on subsistence wages, could pay no more than a nickel to get to work. Brooklynites could get there for much less, but this was rarely mentioned. MAS and its allies pointed out that *someday* it would be easier to get to Rockaway, and that excursion boats would surely begin calling at the new park, but many dismissed these arguments out of hand.[10]

In 1908 the Board of Estimate refused to pay $1 million for the site (cheap by Manhattan standards, but far above market value in Rockaway), but Robert Fulton Cutting, as head of the Charity Organization Society, revived the fight the next year. Cutting equipped himself with pathetic letters purportedly written by the children in Sea Breeze Hospital, begging the mayor to buy the park and build the hospital "so that more boys and girls can come and get well like Madeline and Joe and like the rest of us will soon be."[11] Cutting was defeated by the Allied Real Estate Interests until finally, in 1912, a reform administration ended up paying $1,450,000 for a somewhat smaller site, though it was assessed at less than half a million dollars.

That land purchase would come back to haunt John Purroy Mitchel, who was the president of the Board of Aldermen in 1911 and supported the project. It turned out that the gentleman who assessed the property had ties to the landowners, and this tightly knit group contributed heavily to Mitchel's mayoral campaign in 1913.[12] The owners were indicted in 1917, during Mitchel's unsuccessful reelection campaign. Riis Park was by no means the most clear-cut instance of Mitchel's ties to "land grafters," but it was an effective weapon against the mayor: Tammany painted a picture of Riis Park as a stretch of worthless, inaccessible sand dunes, twenty acres of which had washed into the ocean since the city's purchase, and noted that "few people have availed themselves of its recreative privileges."[13] Under the circumstances, it was hard to make the case that the park was a long-term investment, nor did many people see any value in the land in its "unimproved" state. People celebrated the romantic and dramatic landscape of the Hudson Highlands, but not the scrubby look of a seashore. The city's purchase of the land was not vindicated until the 1930s, when Robert Moses built access roads, parking lots, and splendid bathhouses on the beach.

During McClellan's term of office the Municipal Art Society was in the delicate position of trying to influence an administration that by and large it didn't—couldn't—trust. MAS had to be both an advocate and a watchdog, and since Tammany was inclined to be indifferent or hostile, the society offered both a carrot and a stick. It praised what the city did well, damned what it did badly, and decried all the things it didn't do at all. The society's annual exhibits continued to feature surveys of the city's recent or proposed public works, and MAS could count on Charles de Kay to cover these in the *Times*. One finds him in 1905, for instance, patting the Street Department on the back for erecting structures that were not "purely utilitarian," and urging his readers to visit the National Arts Club gallery and admire the plaster model of Hoppin & Koen's new police headquarters on Centre Street. "The haphazard method of conducting large public works for the city is near its end," de Kay announced. "Without [MAS] we might never know how great a step the city departments, some of them, have taken in the direction of better service."[14]

Of course the credit for all this progress accrued to the Municipal Art Society's political enemies in Tammany Hall; in a sense it was counterproductive for MAS to publicize Tammany's good deeds, but the society had to demonstrate that its program offered political rewards, and it genuinely admired the city's new public works. Thanks to McClellan's support of the Art Commission, they were exceptionally beautiful. McClellan built the Ferry Terminal at Whitehall Street, by Kenneth Murchison; Staten Island's Borough Hall and Saint George Ferry Terminal, by Carrère & Hastings; the Municipal Building, by McKim, Mead & White; the police headquarters, by Hoppin & Koen; the boathouse in Prospect Park, by Helme & Huberty; and a series of public baths: on West Sixtieth and East Fifty-fourth streets, by Werner & Windolph; in John Jay Park, by Stoughton & Stoughton; and, most spectacularly, on Avenue A between Twenty-third and Twenty-fourth streets, by Arnold Brunner & William Aiken.

When the Municipal Art Society advertised such works it was also, of course, advertising the Art Commission. In a pamphlet MAS published photographs both of designs rejected by the Art Commission and of the vastly superior designs that superseded them. The before and after shots of the Slocum Memorial Fountain in Tompkins Square were poignant in a way that escaped the members of the Municipal Art Society. The *General Slocum* was an excursion steamboat that burned and sank in the East River in 1904, killing more than a thousand passengers, most of them women and children from the neighborhood of Tompkins Square. The Slocum Survivors Association erected a memorial in Middle Village, Queens, over the mass grave of bodies too charred for identification, but the Sympathy Society of German Ladies, "composed of the prominent ladies of the district that suffered so awfully," decided to erect a fountain in Tompkins Square, close by their own homes.[15] The first project was a gross mishmash, but one wonders about its unnamed designer. By the look of it, he may well have been a neighborhood stone-carver and, in that case, someone directly touched by the tragedy. When the

Art Commission rejected his work he was replaced by Bruno Louis Zimm, who designed a stele of Grecian sobriety with a bas-relief in the manner of Saint-Gaudens.[16]

The Municipal Art Society's *Bulletin* also illustrated a more controversial case, the Staten Island Ferry Terminal at the southern tip of Manhattan. Herman Metz, who became the city's comptroller in 1906, made the ferry terminal the subject of a noisy campaign against waste. The terminal was supposed to cost $250,000, he said, but it ended up costing $1,250,000 "because we have an Art Commission."[17] Metz was a great disappointment to MAS, as he'd been a board member from 1903 to 1905. He didn't mention that the original plans had only two ferry slips whereas the final plan had five (two more slips were planned, but never built). Nor did Metz mention that the original design was an engineer's utilitarian solution of banal, ugly sheds with an exposed iron structure. When the Art Commission saw these drawings it wrote to the mayor, hinting gently that the Dock Department's proposal would serve perfectly well for garbage scows or freight barges, but that this "most important terminal station, the connecting link between two boroughs," demanded a building before which the city "will not have to blush."[18] McClellan must have agreed. The project was turned over to Kenneth Murchison, a young architect trained at Columbia and in Paris, who produced a superb, festal Beaux Arts building sheathed in molded sheet metal. Even the rivets that held the cladding together were set in decorative patterns. Murchison also extended the building's program. The Municipal Art Society had been arguing that, in a city with so few parks and with so little waterfront available for recreation, new docks should double as recreation piers, with public esplanades on their roofs. The city failed to do this at the Chelsea piers, to the society's chagrin, but Murchison transformed the roof of the ferry terminal into a great terrace shaded by pergolas and looking out over the harbor.

Some things the Art Commission couldn't do. When Fusion was turned out of office the *Times* tried to console its readers by pointing out that at least "The Municipal Art Commission, which passes on the plans of new structures, is now . . . strongly Fusion," and likely to remain so; the *Tribune* added that the commission would serve as "a stumbling block to the Tammany grafter."[19] The Art Commission proved to be a clumsy weapon against graft, however. It could do nothing about corruption in the Building Department, a major source of funds for Tammany; neither could it touch the politically connected contractors and suppliers who built the city's public works and perfected a system of "low bids and short deliveries." All it could do was shine a spotlight on the borough presidents' choice of designers. The case of the Bronx County Courthouse will come up shortly; in the meantime the Art Commission managed to embarrass the borough president of Queens, Joseph Bermel, by rejecting a crony's project for rebuilding the Queens County Courthouse. The designer was Peter M. Coco, a builder of tenements who was confronted with a tricky problem. The old courthouse was an ugly thing built in 1876 in the Second Empire style. It burned in 1904, and the new courthouse was to rise from its gutted shell. Coco meant to patch up the old Victorian ruins, add a Greek Revival portico, and set a Beaux Arts glass dome on top, but the drawings looked as if the architect had been sleepwalking through history. They were rejected, and the newspapers jeered at "Rococo Coco," but Bermel decided to tough it out, telling his constituents that the courthouse was "too beautiful" for the Art Commission. Coco went back to the drawing board and eventually convinced the Art Commission that he was not committing any aesthetic crimes—or perhaps he simply wore the commissioners out: the building turned out to be bizarre. One might, charitably, term its style "mannerist." Coco would soon regret ever having taken the job. Samuel Ordway, a former MAS board member who sat on the Civil Service Commission, investigated the courthouse contracts in 1910, and Coco was charged with being a member of the "light brigade," a circle of grafters who skimmed money off public works contracts. Tried in his own courthouse, he was convicted of grand larceny, served two years in prison, and never practiced architecture again.[20]

Something similar may have been happening in Manhattan: in 1905 the *Times* brought its readers' attention to the "singular and suspicious" fact that Borough President Ahearn and Parks Commissioner Pallas had been "curiously impressed with the professional merits of a firm of architects which can hardly be said to be known at all to the architectural profession. The style of the firm is Bernstein and Bernstein. It is a question which ought to interest his Honor the Mayor, both in his capacity of honest public servant and in his capacity of a friend of civilization."[21] Whatever their sins, if any, Bernstein and Bernstein were the architects of a public bath on Rutgers Place, and this proved to be a perfectly acceptable Italianate design with a handsome rooftop loggia.[22]

McClellan's devotion to Beaux Arts architecture may have represented the triumph of the municipal art movement, but it also co-opted it. In the 1890s the art societies had imagined that Classical monuments would awaken "the ethnic conscience," as architect Henry Rutgers Marshall put it,[23] but now Tammany Hall was the patron of the city's finest Beaux Arts architects. McClellan was delighted to use them, while the borough presidents were in effect forced by the Art Commission to embrace the Beaux Arts style. The Art Commission imposed a uniformity of style in public architecture and a high aesthetic standard, but these were superficial achievements. There was still no city plan in force, still no way to coordinate even the work of different city departments, and Tammany Hall's newfound classicism was no guarantee of civic virtue. Even as Charles de Kay praised the Streets Department for its new buildings, the Municipal Art Society was investigating how that department conducted its everyday work.

In 1905 Borough President Edward Ahearn announced that the Streets Department would begin paving Manhattan's streets and the Williamsburg Bridge with wood blocks—a practice that had been abandoned a generation earlier. Ahearn described this as a blow against the Asphalt Trust, a consortium of companies that had driven paving prices up; he also pointed out that wooden streets were much quieter than asphalt roads. The *Times* countered that wooden blocks absorbed "liquid or solid street filth" and that it seemed strange to stand on an anti-monopolistic principle when wood paving cost $2.30 a square yard and asphalt, despite the trust's best efforts, was still only $1.60 a yard.[24] In the spring of 1906 the Municipal Art Society decided to investigate, and when Charles Lamb interviewed the traffic cops on the Williamsburg Bridge he discovered something far more disturbing: the wood-block pavement became so slippery in wet weather that the number of accidents had skyrocketed. Twenty-five horses had been killed, and four or five men.[25] Ahearn must have been aware of this long before the Municipal Art Society published Lamb's findings. Inspecting the street paving was the job of a good, dedicated, naive fellow named William Dalton. Dalton would later explain, during a criminal investigation of Ahearn, why the dangers of wood paving had escaped his notice: "Shortly after I was appointed to the department I was sent for by Mr. Ahearn, and he said: 'You have been off on some work today?' 'Yes.' 'Well now, you don't want to go out on this work, you want to stay in the office; don't bother with this thing; you stay in the office; let somebody else attend to that business.' I felt, having a horse and wagon the city was paying for, I ought to use it; I ought to be out. . . . But I was ordered to stay in my office. I said: 'I have a horse and wagon.' He said: 'You use them as you go home at night, or as you come down in the morning, or something like that.' As I say, that happened on two or three occasions; that happened on Broadway, this woodblock."[26]

Such investigations were not the Municipal Art Society's forte, however. The society lacked the time, the staff, and the expertise to conduct a thorough study of how Ahearn was handling public works. In 1906 the Citizens Union founded the Bureau of Municipal Research, headed by Henry Bruère, William H. Allen, and Frederick A. Cleveland and funded by the union's wealthy backers. It was meant "to enable the citizen to understand his rights as a taxpayer and property holder, and to assist the heads of city departments to realize the needs of the citizen and the obligations of his office."[27] Its mission was to introduce modern accounting techniques to municipal government, an idea that had been floating around for some time. In 1903, when it issued the Conference Report on the City Plan, MAS called for the advice of experts in municipal statistics. A year later, at the Saint Louis fair, the Model Street featured the mock office of just such a bureau. Tammany's return to power and the shamelessness of Ahearn forced the Citizens Union into acting. Tammany Hall didn't want "assistance" from its enemies, and the Bureau of Municipal Research was denied access to Ahearn's books. Contracts for public works were a matter of public record, however: they were published when the city solicited bids from contractors, and they specified just what quantities of building materials a contractor would have to provide. Bruère dispatched investigators to construction sites around the city. They counted the bags of concrete that were delivered to the sites and proved that the city was paying for material it never received—material it never needed. The figures in the contracts were phony, designed to let favored builders underbid anyone foolish enough to believe the city's specifications.

When the bureau published its findings, Ahearn demanded an investigation to clear his name, confident that it would go nowhere. But he had not taken into account Mayor McClellan's quarrel with Boss Murphy. When Ahearn threw in his lot with Murphy, the mayor authorized a *real* investigation and assigned it to his young commissioner of accounts, John Purroy Mitchel. Mitchel was never able to prove that Ahearn was corrupt, but he convinced Governor Charles Evans Hughes that the borough president was at the very least incompetent, and Ahearn was removed from office in 1908.

As for the Bureau of Municipal Research, it went on to create a Training School for Public Service in 1911, the first such institution in the country, and to introduce modern accounting and line item budgets to municipal governments for the first time in American history. It became the cutting edge of municipal reform, its innovations serving to make graft more difficult whether the machine or reform was in power.

DURING SETH LOW'S term as mayor the Municipal Art Society had concerned itself almost exclusively with Manhattan. Now it began to broaden its scope. It acquired committees in the Bronx and Staten Island, which lobbied, with limited success, for more imaginative city plans for these boroughs, parts of which were still officially unmapped. Its Civic Centers Committee took up the subject of municipal buildings in all the boroughs.

The Civic Centers Committee tried to address a host of issues. John De Witt Warner wanted to thwart "local rings of real estate interests" that were determined to scatter public buildings in order to "divide the benefit of their presence."[28] It was true that Tammany liked to enrich as many loyalists as possible. Rather than build a complex of municipal offices at a convenient transportation node, it preferred several structures widely scattered. This meant that several landowners would receive lucrative condemnation awards, several contractors would go to work, several building supply companies would be flooded with orders, and several sets of neighborhood businesses would be grateful for an increase in foot traffic.

There was some wisdom in the Tammany method. It supported small businesses and spread the benefits of economic development across a wider field, but the Municipal Art Society saw only the graft and the inefficiency. Civic centers offered certain aesthetic opportunities. A school, a library, a police station, a court, a firehouse, municipal offices—any number of these could be grouped in ensembles that would relieve the dreariness of the cityscape in tenement neighborhoods or provide a communal focus in the sprawling outer boroughs. There was an obvious economy to consolidating municipal offices and services in neighborhood civic centers, and there was the issue of the public's convenience. If city agencies were grouped together, one wouldn't have to shuttle across the city in search of the one department that could answer one's complaint. There was also a subtler issue at work. The chairman of the society's Civic Centers Committee was J. G. Phelps Stokes—a millionaire, a socialist, and a resident of the University Settlement on the

Lower East Side—and it struck him how elusive the city government seemed in that neighborhood.[29] Its offices were dispersed through the area, and many of its facilities were barely identifiable as public structures. It was no wonder, Stokes realized, that residents brought their problems to the local ward heeler rather than to city agencies. They always knew what saloon to find him in.

People like Phelps Stokes and John De Witt Warner pointed to the example of Paris, where each arrondisement had its own town hall—a beautiful and convenient building that offered citizens a kind of one-stop shopping for municipal services. The Municipal Art Society, however, couldn't create civic centers without a planning commission to coordinate public works, and probably not without changing the way the bureaucracy worked. The society's bulletin on civic centers lamented that New York had nothing worthy of the name. The *Times* objected, correctly, that the city had *one*, at Jefferson Market, where in the 1870s Frederick Clarke Withers had combined a market, courthouse, and prison in a superb picturesque ensemble dominated by a bell tower.[30] Four different city agencies used Jefferson Market, but turn-of-the-century New York seemed unable to duplicate such an efficient arrangement: with no central planning agency, there was no way to coordinate the building activities of the city departments. The Board of Education, the Police, Fire, Health, and Parks departments, not to mention the library system, were all busily engaged in their own building programs with only the slightest knowledge of what the others were doing, and any attempt to coordinate their programs was hampered by the fact that each department had its own method of dividing the city into administrative units.

There was, however, one major success for the civic center campaign: the complex of public buildings at Saint George, Staten Island. In 1898, when Staten Island became part of Greater New York, it decided to abandon Richmondtown, its old county seat in the center of the island (now the site of the Richmondtown Restoration). The borough government moved to Saint George, to a site on a high bluff overlooking the harbor and the ferry slips. The Municipal Art Society had good relations with Richard Cromwell, the reform Republican who was Staten Island's borough president. He asked for the society's advice on the borough's park system, and its recommendations found their way into the Improvement Commission reports of 1904 and 1907. The Saint George civic center probably owed less to Phelps Stokes than to Cromwell's friendship with another Municipalian, John Merven Carrère, who had an estate on the island.

Carrère designed the Saint George Ferry Terminal (the most beautiful in New York until it burned in the 1940s) in 1905. On the hill above the terminal a huge retaining wall was built to raise Bay Street above the hideous morass of train yards at the water's edge. At one end, above the ferry, Carrère placed the new Borough Hall of brick and limestone, with a tall clock tower facing the bay. To the right, along the corniche, sites for public buildings were interspersed with gardens. Not all of these structures were built, but behind Borough Hall was a small town square, and on its far side Carrère built a Carnegie Library.

The Staten Island Committee began life as an arm of the island's Chamber of Commerce. When it asked MAS for help, Calvin Tomkins simply enrolled its members in the Municipal Art Society and declared it a joint venture of the two organizations.[31] Its chairman was the brilliant and eccentric architect Ernest Flagg, the designer of the Corcoran Gallery in Washington, D.C., and the Naval Academy in Annapolis. Some of his New York buildings rank among the most cherished landmarks of turn-of-the-century New York: the Little Singer Building with its filigree facade of iron, terra-cotta, and glass; the Scribner's Bookstore; and the Great Jones Street Firehouse. Flagg was more than just an especially felicitous master of Beaux Arts vocabulary. He came from a colorful family. His father was the rector of Grace Church until he retired to become a real estate speculator; his favorite brother and erstwhile business partner got into trouble with the law for mail fraud and for running a whorehouse.[32]

Flagg's particular disease was his rationalism. He was tortured by the sheer idiocy and negligence with which New York was being built, a situation that doomed the poor to live in dark hellholes simply because the standard twenty-five-foot lot was traditional to New York, that turned the city streets into dark canyons because no one dared restrict property rights, and that threatened to paralyze traffic because, as Flagg saw it, the city had surrendered its core to the sentimental nature-worship of Vaux and Olmsted. He was one of the very few architects of his generation to undertake a serious study of how to build decent low-cost housing for the poor, or to ponder the urban implications of the skyscraper city. He was also the author of a notorious 1904 plan (MAS had *nothing* to do with this) to solve New York's traffic problem by replacing Central Park with a narrower, park-lined boulevard stretching from one end of the island to the other. He devoted his retirement to a futile search for some underlying system of proportions—which didn't exist—that would explain why the Parthenon is so beautiful.

Flagg's recommendations for Staten Island were less a plan than a geometrical diagram. He laid a great deal of stress on the fact that the island was a triangle, arguing that its three corners would be "the natural points of departure" and "centers of population" in a borough destined to be a bedroom community.[33] A marginal road was needed along the waterfront, and a fanlike system of avenues radiating from each corner of the island. Flagg admitted that these avenues would have to take the island's topography into account, but he never specified how. The Parks Committee had identified sites for parks at Wolf's Pond and Great Kills Harbor (not purchased until the Great Depression), but two of its most attractive ideas were never realized: the plan to make parks of Grymes Hill and Todt Hill—beautiful, wooded areas with views of the sea and the harbor. These sites were well known to Flagg—he built his estate on Todt Hill, surrounding it with a brilliant series of small houses designed on a strange modular system and meant as a model for suburban developers. In the 1940s, just before his death, Flagg offered the site to the United Nations for its headquarters. Grymes Hill has since become the most expensive residential neighborhood in Staten Island.

"It is currently hoped," Flagg wrote in 1905, "that the Municipal Art Society will take the matter in hand and use its powerful influence to secure for Staten Island the kind of plan it ought to have." But MAS didn't give him much help. Staten Island was still so isolated that its population was growing very slowly. Its plan seemed to be something that could wait until a subway tube was built, as MAS hoped, beneath the Narrows. Even if the Municipal Art Society had launched a full-fledged crusade on Staten Island's behalf, it couldn't have overcome the fact that the borough had little political pull in the hallways of City Hall, especially with its Republican administration. So Staten Island slipped out of the society's consciousness until the 1960s, when the Verrazano Narrows Bridge opened the floodgates of settlement.

THE BRONX used to be known as the "annexed district," which sounds as if the region had been conquered by marauding Manhattanites, but in truth the Bronx threw itself into New York's reluctant arms. In the 1860s the citizens of West Farms, Kingsbridge, and Morrisania decided that their sleepy towns should become Manhattan's suburbs. First they tried a crude physical assault, demanding that the Harlem River—"a narrow, marshy, unnavigable stream, more of a nuisance than a utility"[34]—be filled in with earth, and the watercourse channeled into an underground sewer. Fernando Wood, one of New York's more infamous mayors, rejected this idea—a decision Bronxites attributed to "the manipulations of speculators in river fronts"[35]—and the Army Corps of Engineers went to work on the Harlem River Ship Canal. A decade later "some shrewd and influential citizens" of the Bronx (they were "former New Yorkers") took a different tack and began a campaign to annex themselves to Manhattan. Despite the opposition of Manhattan's political machines, they were successful both in Albany and in a popular referendum, and in 1874 that portion of the Bronx west of the Bronx River became part of New York City. Chester, the region east of the river, facing Long Island Sound, was added in 1895.[36]

Planning issues were at the heart of political life in the Bronx. Its whole purpose in annexing itself to Manhattan had been to unlock the coffers of New York and acquire an urban infrastructure that the area's villages couldn't afford to build themselves. In 1884 the Bronx acquired its magnificent park system when the New York Parks Association, inspired by the *New York Herald*'s campaign for parks in the outlying areas of the city, persuaded the state to create a chain of three large parks (Van Cortlandt, Bronx, and Pelham Bay), three small parks (Crotona, Claremont, and Saint Mary's), and three parkways (Mosholu, Pelham, and Crotona) to tie them together.

Through the 1870s and 1880s, however, Bronxites were furious at the slow pace of street openings and at the Parks Commission's plans for the "North Side." Frederick Law Olmsted imagined the Bronx as "a sort of rural-residence district . . . like a park, with winding streets and avenues," and accordingly designed a pattern of looping, curving streets to thwart through traffic.[37] When rapid transit arrived in the 1880s, Bronxites discovered that the demand was not for villas but for more modest row houses and apartment buildings. They obtained a law stripping the Parks Department of authority over the North Side's plan, and creating the new position of commissioner of street improvements in the annexed district. The first commissioner, Louis Heintz, elected in 1890, threw out Olmsted's plan and replaced it with a dense gridiron. The Bronx was to be, not a suburb, but an extension of the city.

At the turn of the century the Bronx was the province of Bronx Borough President Louis F. Haffen. The son of a brewer, he'd once worked in the Parks Department as an assistant engineer. In 1890 Tammany tapped him to run against Heintz for the office of commissioner of street improvements in the annexed district. According to one observer, his credentials as an engineer mattered less to Tammany than the opportunity "to divide the German vote by placing one representative German against the other, and also the brewery vote by putting up the son of a brewer against the nephew of a brewer." (Oh, for the days of a brewery vote!) Haffen, however, always stressed that he was a professional planner. His 1890 campaign posters showed him drawing plans for public improvements while Heintz busied himself with a beer keg. The posters carried this caption: "Funny, isn't it? The one draws maps, and the other draws beer."[38]

Haffen was the greatest builder among the turn-of-the-century borough presidents, dedicating his years in office to transforming the Bronx, a land of fields and small towns, into a dense urban settlement. His single most conspicuous achievement was the Grand Concourse. Its design called for "a speedway 54 feet wide, with a sidewalk of artificial stone 15 feet wide, an asphalt driveway 24 feet wide, a macadam bicycle path 7 feet wide, and a promenade 18 feet on either side of it. Nearly 5,000 trees will be required to provide the necessary shade."[39] The Concourse had been designed by engineer Louis Risse in 1892, under Heintz's administration, but it was Haffen's tenacity that saw it realized. He began fighting for the Grand Concourse in 1895, when he was still the lowly commissioner of street improvements. Elected borough president in 1898, he could never convince Van Wyck to appropriate money for the project. At one point Haffen tried to begin work without the approval of City Hall and had to be restrained by a court injunction. Van Wyck's inaction led to persistent complaints that Greater New York was neglecting the Bronx in favor of Brooklyn and Queens, and in 1902 Seth Low moved quickly to begin work on the project.[40] By now Haffen's ambition had taken on breathtaking proportions, and he envisioned the Concourse as just one link in a great parkway scheme of metropolitan scale. The parkway would begin at the northern end of Central Park, head up Seventh Avenue, and cross the Harlem River on the Central Bridge to the foot of the Grand Concourse. From the Concourse, carriages could continue along Mosholu Parkway to the Jerome Park Reservoir, along Aqueduct Avenue to Washington Bridge, then down Manhattan's Boulevard and Riverside Drive and back to Central Park: "a picturesque and fully diversified drive fully twenty-four miles in length, and for the greater part at an elevation commanding a beautiful view of the surrounding territory."[41]

This was the sort of thing to warm a Municipalian's heart, but Haffen and the Municipal Art Society's Bronx Committee rarely saw eye to eye on other issues. The committee's chairman was Albert E. Davis, an architect, developer, and at one point president of the Bronx Board of Trade. MAS considered him an enlightened developer; one could say that he was determined to focus on an upscale market. He was a foe, all his life, of apartment living. Even in 1921, when the urban character of the Bronx was long established, one finds him arguing for "homes": "And when I say homes, I mean real homes, and not multi-family 'packing boxes'; homes occupied by but one or at most two families; homes of the kind the poet immortalized as 'be it ever so humble, there's no place like home.' "[42] Davis concentrated on Chester, east of the Bronx River, which was still sparsely settled. In Manhattan MAS was trying desperately to correct past mistakes, but Chester was a blank slate on which one could draw a plan "worthy of a L'Enfant or a Haussmann."[43]

Louis Risse had drawn a plan for Chester in 1898: a checkerboard enlivened with traffic circles, sprinkled with small parks, and equipped with a system of diagonal boulevards that would serve as major traffic arteries. Risse also designed a "Sound Shore Drive" looping around the inlets on the waterfront. It was an intelligent scheme, designed to keep heavy traffic out of residential streets and to create a whole series of individual neighborhoods with their own parks and commercial districts. Yet Haffen discarded it in 1903, eliminating the boulevards and traffic circles, except for Hugh J. Grant Circle, which still functions as a major center in Parkchester. He was acting at the behest of the area's large landowners, who were eager to sell their land off to tenement builders, and wanted as few complications as possible.

Albert Davis was desperate to reverse this decision, and he used the Municipal Art Society to lobby Haffen and the Improvement Commission for a plan that would incorporate "the most improved ideas of City Planning." He wanted Chester to have "street vistas, combined with parkways, circles, plazas, and other forms of embellishment. . . . Civic centers where the various municipal buildings can be grouped, river bank reservations and driveways along the Hudson, Harlem and Sound, as well as a Sound to Hudson Boulevard along the northernly City border."[44]

Davis was hampered by the abstractness of his argument: he had a wish list, but Risse's old plan was growing more irrelevant with each new development. Davis asked the Municipal Art Society to prepare a new plan, but it never did, and he was unable to overcome the fact that Haffen and most local realtors preferred a more expedient extension of the grid system and a denser pattern of development. Davis failed even to save the Sound Shore Drive, which may have had something to do with the fact that Haffen was a secret investor in the Sound View Land Company.

Yet Davis could congratulate himself on some small victories. The Bronx Committee lobbied successfully for expanding a number of existing parks: Crotona Park gained ground at its northeast corner so it could connect to Crotona Parkway, and

Joseph Rodman Drake Park was enlarged to take in the gravesite of that now forgotten poet. (Drake was Charles de Kay's grandfather, and de Kay contributed to the campaign by threatening to move the poet's remains to Manhattan if the park plan fell through.[45]) Davis could also take pride in the handsome new train stations of the New Haven and Hartford Line, for when that railroad asked the city for a new franchise so it could upgrade and electrify its tracks, Davis persuaded the mayor to secure the railroad's promise that the new train stations would be "artistically" designed.[46] The stations were assigned to Cass Gilbert, architect of the Custom House and the Woolworth Building, and they were a pleasantly varied lot: the City Island Station was a rustic Richardsonian design; Westchester Avenue was Italianate; Baychester and Van Nest Avenue were Dutch; and the Morris Park Station, with its stucco facades outlined in colored tile, was a charming Arts and Crafts design.[47]

Davis also lobbied for the Bronx River Parkway Reservation, perhaps the most influential improvement scheme of its day. This was based on another old idea, an 1895 proposal by the engineer J. J. R. Croes. Charged with the utterly mundane task of designing a trunk sewer to drain the Bronx River valley, Croes suggested cleaning up the sluggish, polluted river to quicken its flow and create a park along its length. Croes sat on the Municipal Art Society's 1902 Conference Committee on the City Plan as a representative of the American Society of Civil Engineers, and the Bronx River Parkway was endorsed by the New York City Improvement Commission in 1904 and 1907. Fifteen miles long, it stretched far beyond the city's borders, creating a continuous ribbon of greenery from the south end of Bronx Park to the huge land reserve at Kensico in the Croton Watershed. From there, a traveler heading west could cross the Hudson to Palisades Interstate Park, and beyond that second green ribbon lay the enormous expanse of Harriman State Park. This was a gift of Mrs. E. H. Harriman, a life member of MAS. The society served as the liaison between Harriman and the state, and persuaded her to establish summer camps in the park for poor city kids.

This concept of a regional park system was in place by 1907, when the state created the Bronx River Parkway Commission.[48] Its work wasn't finished until 1923, but this slow pace allowed the concept of the parkway to mature under the supervision of Bronx lawyer William White Niles* and landscape architect Gilmore Clarke. Until this time, "parkway" had often meant nothing more than a street framed by banks of trees, but Clarke designed the first true parkway in the modern sense of the term: a limited-access drive, with cross traffic separated by a system of bridges. Clarke was inspired by Olmsted's transverse drives in Central Park, but the idea had never been carried out on this scale before, and his work was the inspiration for the early, carefully crafted parkways of Robert Moses, many of which were landscaped by Clarke. But it was Moses, too, who effectively destroyed the charm of the Bronx River Parkway in the 1930s by adding a highway next to it:

---

* Niles became a major figure in the Municipal Art Society, but only after the Bronx River Parkway was complete.

Niles and Clarke's work, or what survived of it, is now the Bronx River Parkway's service road.

One advantage of having a state commission superintend the Bronx River Parkway was that it limited the influence of Borough President Haffen. By the time Albert Davis began his campaign to save Chester from a gridiron plan, the Art Commission and the Municipal Art Society's Civic Centers Committee had locked horns with Haffen and his favorite architect, Michael J. Garvin, over the Bronx County Courthouse. Garvin, like Horgan & Slattery before him, was a tenement builder transformed, by the grace of Tammany Hall, into an architect of public buildings. The *Times* described him in 1905 as "Louis F. Haffen's most trusted lieutenant in Bronx politics and secretary of Borough President Haffen's political club in the Bronx."[49] He built tenements even while he served as an official in the Building Department. He resigned from that position just before Haffen awarded him the commission to design the Bronx County Courthouse. The Municipal Art Society immediately raised objections, not to Haffen's choice of architect (the Art Commission could handle him), but to his choice of site. J. G. Phelps Stokes, chairman of the society's Civic Centers Committee, prepared an absolutely damning report. The site was at 161st Street at the intersection of Brook and Third avenues, three-quarters of a mile from the Bronx Borough Hall, a fairly new building designed by Municipalian George Post in 1897, and difficult of access from the settled areas of the Bronx. The Third Avenue El ran past the building, which would make it hard to hear what was being said in the courtrooms, since ventilation was still a matter of opening windows, and amplification systems were not yet available. The site itself was small, irregular, and bounded by streets on every side, meaning it would be impossible to expand the building as the borough's population continued to grow. (It had increased by 75 percent in just the past five years.[50]) It was also set on steeply sloping ground, and rested on a stratum of quicksand left behind by the old Mill Brook. Foundations would be outrageously expensive.[51]

Haffen was unmoved by Phelps Stokes's report and pressed to begin construction. With MAS's good wishes, Phelps Stokes filed a taxpayer's suit in his own name in an attempt to stop the project. This was dismissed, but a new obstacle arose when the Art Commission rejected Garvin's designs for the courthouse. Garvin had submitted amateurish elevations and a dreadful, incompetent plan, with "courtrooms of an unfortunate shape," cells close to the El, "which would be a great discomfort to the prisoners," and no way to get inmates from the jail to a courtroom without bringing them, in manacles, through the main lobby and up the main stair.[52] In desperation, Garvin turned to one Oscar Bleumner, who'd studied architecture at the Royal Academy in Berlin. Bleumner had come to America in 1893, "a young man in a strange land," and briefly worked for Garvin as a designer before setting out for Chicago. By 1900 he had his own practice with offices in both Chicago and New York. Garvin was then working for the Buildings Department, where he was able to do the architect "some kindnesses," as Bleumner delicately put it. Bleumner told the *Times* what happened next. "One day [Garvin] told me that he was in a bad fix—that Haffen had given him assistance in the matter of the new Court House, but that his plans had been rejected by the Municipal Art Commission. He asked me if I would not propose plans which he might put in under his own name, and promised me as soon as they were approved to associate me with him before the world, and to share the commissions with me." Garvin soon sent the Art Commission a new set of handsome plans and elevations for the courthouse, quite unlike anything he had submitted before. The Art Commission approved them, but Garvin—predictably—"turned the cold shoulder" to Bleumner. Bleumner filed suit to obtain his share of the architect's fee. He had no written contract, but he was able to prove to a jury that he was the designer, and that "Garvin couldn't draw the plans for a big thing like the new courthouse to save his life."[53]

None of this stopped the Bronx County Courthouse from being built in the wrong place, and in the circumstances it was small comfort that the Art Commission had achieved a more handsome building than Garvin alone would have been capable of designing. The Municipal Art Society used the case to illustrate why the commissioners' powers should again be broadened, this time to cover the issue of where public works were built. The scandal of the Bronx County Courthouse did, however, help destroy the career of Borough President Haffen.

Rumors of corruption had hovered over Haffen's career. It was suspected that his public works were designed for the private gains of political insiders. In 1905 the Bronx Civic League demanded an investigation of Haffen (Charles Stoughton, president of MAS from 1914 to 1916 and the designer of the Soldiers' and Sailors' Monument in Riverside Park, was active in the league), but the city stonewalled until 1907. After Mayor McClellan quarreled with Boss Murphy, Haffen sided with Murphy, and the mayor retaliated by turning the investigation over to John Purroy Mitchel.[54] In 1908 the Municipal Art Society's allies in the City Club and the Metropolitan Parks Association decided to provide Mitchel with ammunition by releasing a joint report on "licensed poaching on public preserves." They detailed the existence of hotels, roadhouses, private clubs, and houses on city parklands, especially in the Bronx. "In Pelham Bay Park there are ten buildings used as private dwellings enclosed by walls or fences. One tenant raises chickens, one pastures cows, and one maintains kennels. There are five buildings used as transient hotels, or boarding houses, and six clubs, and six hotels and three clubs the title of which does not vest in the city, only a nominal rent being charged."[55] As the *Times* pointed out, "there is no reason . . . why the rents for these places should be 'nominal' and friends or relations of politicians should be tolerated as squatters."[56]

Mitchel's investigation revealed nothing about Haffen's choice of 161st Street as the site of the courthouse, but it did hold him accountable for the fact that "he has appointed and continued as architect not only of the Court House but of other public buildings one who is without adequate professional qualifications for such important work. He [Garvin] is described . . . as 'primarily a politician,' and in respect to these public buildings to be . . . substantially a middleman who got the work through his political influence, and employed others to supply the necessary qualifications."[57] Mitchel also discovered that the courthouse contracts specified a peculiarly expensive variety of granite whose source was controlled by a Bronx alderman. There were two other charges: that Haffen had ordered the construction of a road on Clasons Point because he was himself an investor in the Sound View Land Company, which owned a good deal of the nearby land; and that he'd conned the Board of Estimate into paying more than a quarter of a million dollars for a "beach" at Hunts Point. This last charge was rich. The site had been assessed at less than $4,300, and it would have been hard to find a place less suitable for swimming. Only an acre and a half of ground rose above the high water line. The rest was awash in shallow waters: as far as three hundred feet from shore, the water was just three feet deep at high tide. But few people ventured out so far, for next to the beach was the mouth of a gigantic sewer.

Mitchel concluded that the Bronx had been "administered primarily in the political interests of President Haffen, and to this are ascribed most of the deficiencies, waste, irregularities, and departures from the law discovered by us."[58] Governor Charles Evans Hughes removed Haffen from office in 1909. While Haffen's career crumbled, construction of the courthouse was turning into a nightmare—or "a standing joke," as the *Times* put it—just as Phelps Stokes had predicted.[59] Work dragged on for a decade, complicated by that quicksand, and its ultimate cost was double the estimate. Perhaps more: in 1934, just twenty years after it opened, the courthouse was rendered obsolete by the construction of a new borough hall and county court building some blocks away on East 161st Street and the Grand Concourse, convenient to the subway. With its abstracted Classical architecture by Joseph H. Freedlander and its heroic sculpture by Municipalian Charles Keck, the Bronx County Building was one of the last great statements of the municipal art movement.

THE CURSE OF THE CITY: "SPITE BRIDGE" AND THE SUBWAY CRISIS

BY 1909 FOUR of the city's borough presidents had turned out to be crooks, and George McClellan's role in their downfall has burnished his reputation in the eyes of historians. The Municipal Art Society had a more jaundiced view of the mayor. McClellan did a good deal for New York: he created the Improvement Commission, extended its life, and worked hard to obtain the means of financing its recommendations. It was a matter of great regret to McClellan that the power of excess condemnation eluded his grasp. He was no Seth Low: McClellan *wanted* to spend vast sums of money rebuilding New York. But he and his Improvement Commission shared the same flaw: a commitment to aesthetics rather than to planning. His administration was dedicated to building beautiful Beaux Arts structures, but just as diligently thwarted the reform and expansion of the rapid transit system. The Municipal Art Society pilloried him, and nearly destroyed itself in the process. The quarrel started with the society's project for a great Civic Center north of City Hall and soon came to engulf the actions of McClellan's Bridge Department, and the city's entire transit policy.

Gustav Lindenthal, a political appointee, lost his job as bridge commissioner when George McClellan won the mayoralty. Lindenthal "was a mercurial, impulsive genius, full of Wagnerian ambitions and vainglorious dreams," one of his assistants recalled; another, Othmar Ammann, who went on to design the George Washington, Triborough, and Verrazano-Narrows bridges, remembered Lindenthal's insistence that one look "ahead for 1,000 years."[1] It was hard for such a person to suffer fools. Early in Lindenthal's term as bridge commissioner the *Times* wrote that it was "unpleasantly evident that his infirmities of temper are capable of warping his professional judgement, and that when annoyed and angry he does not consider either his facts or the language in which he expresses them as carefully as he should."[2] Lindenthal learned to conceal his emotions in public, resorting to an icy silence whenever reporters were around, and his designs for the Manhattan and Queensboro bridges were such carefully conceived works of municipal art, and so palpably public-spirited, that the *Times* eventually forgave him his temperament. Not so the employees of the Bridge Department.

The new bridge commissioner, appointed at the request of Boss Murphy, was George Best, a man with "not the least" knowledge of engineering. "No sane person," the *Times* wrote, "would give twenty-five cents for his opinion on any engineering question."[3] Best relied on the department's engineering staff, most of which Lindenthal had inherited from Tammany Hall and which he'd bullied to distraction. Leffert Buck, originally chief engineer and the designer of the monstrous Williamsburg Bridge, had been demoted and suffered a pay cut. His son and assistant, Richard Buck, had been driven to resign.[4] The staff despised Lindenthal, and after Best took charge there arose, as the *Times* put it, "a well-founded suspicion that the main motive of [Best's] 'technical staff,' in all its performances and operations, was to spite and discredit his predecessor, who had discharged it; not to do anything that Commissioner Lindenthal had desired to be done, and to do whatever Commissioner Lindenthal desired not to have done."[5]

Lindenthal's Brooklyn Bridge Terminal project was abandoned, along with the whole MAS-Post-Hornbostel-Lindenthal Civic Center plan. This was a bitter blow to the Municipal Art Society, but the society could hardly have been surprised that McClellan would cancel a project so closely identified with the previous, reform administration. What was appalling was that McClellan developed no alternative master plan, though the city still needed a new county courthouse, a municipal building, and a bridge terminal.

The state appointed a new commission to find a site for the courthouse, and it came up with two options: a site near Mulberry Bend Park, where "the Court House would be wedged in between undesirable buildings,"[6] and the corner of Broadway and Chambers Street, where MAS had always wanted it. This was the site of the old A. T. Stewart store, which was already filled with municipal offices. Where would they go? MAS had hoped to build the campanile first, demolishing the Stewart building when its occupants had moved to new quarters down the street. Without that first step in the master plan, the city couldn't proceed to the second. The Courthouse Commission went to work looking for new sites, and the end result was that the new courthouse in Foley Square didn't open its doors until the Great Depression.

Lindenthal's successor still had to face the problem of the bridge crush, a problem too conspicuous and dangerous to ignore. His proposal was, for MAS, the nightmare of solutions: to enlarge the bridge terminal by extending it over Park Row and into City Hall Park itself. This was, as the *Times* put it, "baffled" by a public outcry in the spring of 1905, and MAS and the *Times* continued to demand action on the Civic Center.[7] The pressure for a new terminal didn't let up, however. In June a crowd at the terminal grew so dense that people were pushed onto the trolley tracks and into the path of an incoming train. Twenty were injured.[8] The Bridge Department now unveiled a terminal design by Carrère & Hastings: a handsome building in Italian Renaissance style, with open arcades at ground level.

It would stand where Lindenthal and his colleagues had planned to put the terminal and campanile. Though beautiful, Carrère & Hastings's design was flawed in several ways. It had nothing to do with the architecture of the Hall of Records. The opportunity for a coordinated ensemble was slipping away. It was also a poor investment: too small to subsidize the city's expense in building a terminal that would benefit the Brooklyn Rapid Transit Company more than anyone else.

In 1907 McClellan built a bridge terminal and revived the idea of a municipal office building just north of it. Yet, bizarrely, the projects had nothing to do with each other, even though they stood side by side and were both erected by the Bridge Department.* The new terminal was the same expansion of the old that had been rejected in 1905, an "unutterably ugly chaos of iron."[9] It reached over Park Row and into City Hall Park. The city described it as a temporary structure, and as such it seems to have eluded the Art Commission. Hoppin & Koen, architects of the new Police Headquarters farther up Centre Street, did design a monumental terminal in 1909 to replace this structure,[10] but it was never built, and the "temporary" structure would stand in all its ghastliness until Fiorello La Guardia demolished it thirty years later.

In the meantime McClellan held an invited competition to choose a different designer for the Municipal Building—a project inspired by the campanile in the old Lindenthal-Post-Hornbostel scheme. It was won by McKim, Mead & White. McKim had originally refused to enter, since he disliked skyscrapers, but McClellan personally begged him to reconsider, and the firm's younger members pleaded for the opportunity to show their stuff. Their scheme was selected because it packed so much well-lit office space onto a difficult, awkwardly shaped site. There was much to admire about the building: the way it vaulted over Chambers Street, the marvelous open-air arcades that lifted the building off the ground and let crowds pass downstairs into the subway, the screen of massive Corinthian columns. On another level, however, the building was an abject failure. It acknowledged the axis of Chambers Street, but not the site's pivotal role as the corner of City Hall Park, nor did it make a good neighbor to the Hall of Records across the street.

One could ascribe the sorry fate of the Civic Center to stupidity or shortsightedness, but the Manhattan Bridge offered a byzantine tale of personal revenge and corruption. The Manhattan Bridge was a perfect example of what could go wrong when a municipality undertook a public improvement. The city had originally granted a franchise to build the bridge to a private consortium, but when nothing was actually built, New York was forced, at great cost, to buy the franchise back. In Van Wyck's term as mayor a general plan for the bridge was approved by the Board of Public Improvements, and the Board of Aldermen and the mayor fixed its location and determined its capacity. Only a tiny amount of money was appropriated for construction: just enough to begin work on the piers. When Low took

---

* McClellan had to appeal to Albany for legislation to transfer control of the Municipal Building to the Bridge Department; otherwise its construction would have been the job of Borough President Ahearn, who was already under investigation.

office, the construction of the piers was well under way, but by then it was clear that the bridge would have to carry a far greater capacity than the Board of Aldermen had expected. Lindenthal had to redesign the bridge to find a way to carry more traffic on the old piers. In all of this, the *approaches* to the bridge—roads, pedestrian ramps, and connections to mass transit—had still not been considered.

Lindenthal and Hornbostel produced a masterful design, unlike any bridge in New York. There were no cables, as on the Brooklyn or Williamsburg bridges. Lindenthal thought cables ill-suited to the peculiar stresses of a railroad bridge, and he could back up his argument with his extensive experience with building railroad bridges in Pittsburgh, and with the fact that the Brooklyn Bridge was showing signs of severe stress. Leffert Buck had succeeded in making the Williamsburg more stable, but only by resorting to massive, hideous stiffening trusses. Instead of cables and trusses, Lindenthal planned to use chains and eyebars—girders with flat, wide tips pierced by a hole (an "eye"). A pin inserted through the hole attached one eyebar to another. Eyebars made for a rigid structure without ugly trusswork, and for a bridge that was cheap and quick to build. (Eyebars roll out of a steel mill; cables are composed of countless steel threads braided together, an agonizingly slow process, since it takes place on site while exposed to the elements hundreds of feet above a river.) The new design also required less weighty anchorages, and Lindenthal found room within them for "fine and imposing assembly halls, each larger than Carnegie Hall." These were intended to boost the cultural life of the communities at either end of the bridge; they would also generate enough rental income to pay for painting the bridge.[11] Lindenthal's plans for the Manhattan Bridge were widely published and much admired; he looked forward to exhibiting them at the Saint Louis fair in 1904 and had "every reason to feel confident that the Bridge Department of New York City would receive from an international jury honorable distinction for both designs."[12]

As soon as Lindenthal left office, the Bridge Department announced that his design was structurally unsound, despite the testimony of a board of eminent engineers, which Seth Low had asked to review the designs; that the specific nickel alloy Lindenthal had specified was unobtainable, though a number of manufacturers ridiculed that statement; and finally that it had been conceived in corruption inasmuch as the unusual eyebar design had been selected so that the contract would have to be awarded to a specific company in Pittsburgh, Lindenthal's former hometown. Yet once again, a number of other firms leaped forward to declare that they were able and eager to bid on the contracts.

As smear campaigns go, this one was cunning and carefully calculated. It played on Lindenthal's reputation as a difficult, visionary egomaniac—a genius, perhaps, but too radical and experimental to entrust with public funds—and it turned the reformers' standard accusations of rigged contracts back on one of their own. What his opponents never knew was that Lindenthal *did* have a secret. Had they done a little digging, they'd have discovered that Lindenthal was apparently self-taught. He'd lied on his résumé when he claimed to have studied engineering at the Polytechnic Institutes of Brno and Vienna. (His brother had.)[13]

The bridge was redesigned by the engineer Leon Morsieff. Hornbostel was told that he could remain as consulting architect on the new design but that, having been paid his fee for designing one Manhattan Bridge, he would receive no more money for designing a second. He resigned and was replaced by Carrère & Hastings, who were, of course, paid. In the meantime Lindenthal had appealed to the Municipal Art Society for help. Calvin Tomkins, Charles Lamb, and George Bissell formed a special committee to defend him.[14] When Best presented the new scheme to the Art Commission, MAS pointed out that the drawings showed only Carrère & Hastings's decorative details. The bridge itself—the engineer's work—was not presented. MAS demanded that the Art Commission reject the submission as incomplete, which it did, and withhold approval of the new design until an engineering study could be made of the two schemes. To bolster the society's case, Calvin Tomkins recruited two prominent engineers, J. Burkitt Webb of the Stevens Institute and William H. Baur of Columbia University, to carry out a preliminary examination of Morsieff's work. Both called for an independent commission of engineers to undertake a careful analysis. They also ridiculed the idea that "aesthetic features" could be studied apart from the engineering, and they mentioned that, on first examination, it looked as if the stiffening trusses might be inadequate to their task.[15] Lindenthal himself looked at the revised plans and predicted that the new bridge would cost more, take up to two years longer to build, sacrifice a good deal of rental income (its anchorages were solid), and prove less rigid.[16]

The Municipal Art Society sent all this testimony off to the Art Commission and threw the commission into a state of confusion. Was engineering, even if married to decoration in this instance, really within its purview? Was the commission obliged to insist on the best of all possible bridges or merely on an excellent appearance? Tomkins tried to buck up the commission's courage by testifying in person. "Beneath the question of artistic design and aesthetics lies the question, 'Will the new bridge do its work?'"[17] Tomkins argued that "In this case the design depends for its success upon the solution proposed for the engineering problem involved. . . . Approval of any such design as to its aesthetic features, without reference to its fitness for the public utility intended, would be misleading. Such approval would utterly fail to meet the confidence which, by the extensive powers given it, the legislature has bestowed upon the Art Commission."[18] Had John De Witt Warner still been president of the Art Commission, he'd surely have taken the activist position, but his successor, Robert De Forest, was another matter; and this Art Commission was particularly close to Mayor McClellan, who actually enjoyed attending its meetings. Moreover, Carrère and Hastings were pillars of the Beaux Arts community, and Carrère himself was responsible for the commission's very existence. When Best submitted a complete set of drawings, the Art Commission couldn't deny the scheme's beauty, and it gave its stamp of approval to the new Manhattan Bridge.

The issue didn't die, however. That Carrère and Hastings—both Municipalians—should choose to profit from the shabby treatment of Hornbostel was more than Frederick Lamb could bear. In 1905 he lashed into the new scheme before a big crowd in Cooper Union's Great Hall: "Since Mr. Lindenthal . . . left office a firm of architects has been employed to draw new plans for the next bridge to cross the East River. Is the bridge to be cheaper than the one planned during the last administration? No. . . . It costs $2 million more, but it will give an opportunity for valuable contracts. That's why the plans have been changed."[19]

Lamb's speech cost the Municipal Art Society some friends. It was rash of him to imply that the problem lay with the bridge's new "architects"—Carrère and Hastings were, perhaps, no more than shamelessly opportunistic in taking the job. Neither architect would have anything to do with MAS in the future.* Nor would Arnold W. Brunner, a former board member who'd since become president of the Architectural League. The *Times* had mistakenly described Lamb as the league's vice president, but its next edition carried a brusque correction from Brunner, who warned that "Mr. Lamb occupies no official position in the league" and that the group did not endorse his comments.[20] The next day brought a letter from Charles Shean, who noted that he'd just stepped down as the league's secretary. (He was active in the Municipal Art Society, and at some point in his life Shean worked for the J. & R. Lamb Studios.) Shean pointed out that Brunner's correction had been a tad too concise: Lamb was the *former* vice president of the league and, for that matter, the former president of its mother organization, the Architectural League of America. Shean wondered why Brunner sought to depict Lamb as "an outsider whose ideas on public and professional questions were not familiar to the membership." He didn't point out that Brunner had worked with Carrère and Hastings on City Beautiful schemes for civic centers in places like Cleveland, but Brunner's colleagues would have understood the insinuation. "To those of us who know the membership," Shean concluded, "it is debatable whether on a vote in the organization Mr. Lamb's point of view would not be endorsed by an overwhelming majority."[21]

Lamb was right to suggest that the contract for the Manhattan Bridge would be an interesting document. When Best attempted to begin construction in 1905, the State Supreme Court and the Appellate Court ruled that the contract was unenforceable and therefore illegal. "Its 'specifications' did not specify," the *Times* explained. They stipulated "that certain materials should be used and certain work done, provided it should not in the meantime occur to the engineer that other and uncertain materials should be used in preference, and other and uncertain work done."[22] The contract, in other words, virtually invited cost overruns.

The *Times* began calling the new design "Spite Bridge." But in accentuating the

---

* *Hastings received a number of plum jobs from Tammany mayors in later years, after Carrère's death, and was an increasingly unpopular figure at MAS. Carrère was revered, however, as the father of the Art Commission and for his campaign to ban the burning of soft coal in New York. The society made amends to him posthumously: in 1934, when Hastings's widow announced plans to place a bust of her late husband in the New York Public Library, Electus Litchfield, the president of MAS, arranged to balance it with a bust of Carrère. Litchfield had worked for the partnership as a young man.*

personal aspect of the scandal the paper tended to underplay another detail: that as far as Tammany was concerned, the problem with Lindenthal's design was that it couldn't be built by the Roebling Company. Roebling had been founded by the great John A. Roebling, designer and builder of the Brooklyn Bridge. The company was now a major bridge contractor, and politically well-connected—a necessary qualification for any firm that worked in the field of large-scale public improvements. The company's secretary, and a stockholder, was Frank Croker, son of Richard Croker of Tammany Hall.[23] (Testifying before the Mazet Committee in 1899, the senior Croker refused to say whether his son had actually paid for his stock.) Leffert Buck, author of the original designs for the Manhattan and Williamsburg bridges, was a former Roebling employee. The Roebling Company knew nothing of eyebar technology; it knew only standard cable construction. It was no accident that the Bridge Department resorted to a cable design as soon as Lindenthal was gone.

There seemed to be one last chance for the Manhattan Bridge. In 1906, when McClellan purged his second-term administration of Tammany loyalists, he replaced George Best with James W. Stevenson, who'd earned a good reputation as a deputy comptroller. With a new bridge commissioner in office, "an official indisputably disinterested and uncommitted,"[24] hopes rose that the issue could at last be solved objectively. The moment was a test of McClellan's honesty. Some of his supporters, like the *Times*, assumed that up to now the mayor's hands had been tied—that he'd had no choice but to let Tammany have its way with the Manhattan Bridge. Now that McClellan had broken with Murphy, his supporters expected him to reverse his policy of the last two years. The Merchants' Association and the *Times* joined MAS in its demand for a "showdown" between the Lindenthal and Morsieff designs: they begged the city to ask for bids on both sets of drawings so that the public could compare the results. The issue even reached the national press: *Scientific American* published an open editorial letter to Mayor McClellan, begging for the same. It argued that there was no doubt, after Low's independent commission of engineers had examined the design specifications, that Lindenthal's design was structurally sound, and it disputed the charges of Best's in-house engineers.[25]

McClellan failed his test.[26] He was still devoted to Richard Croker, his old mentor. There was no showdown, not even a board of independent engineers to examine the Bridge Department's work, and the Manhattan Bridge was built to the designs of Morsieff and Carrère & Hastings. The architects used Hornbostel's work as their starting point, and Montgomery Schuyler, the *Architectural Record*'s critic, thought that in some respects they improved on it.[27] Morsieff's role, however, remains problematic. The stiffening trusses that line the roadway were unfortunate in that they looked so heavy and they cluttered the view from the bridge; yet it seems that they were still inadequate, as MAS had tried to warn the city. The bridge's current problems aren't *entirely* due to its lack of maintenance in recent years.

✳   ✳   ✳

THE MUNICIPAL Art Society fought for Lindenthal because the Bridge Department was so blatantly corrupt, but especially because MAS was convinced that Lindenthal's design was better equipped to withstand the stress of countless trains passing across its span in the century to come. Trains were the reason for building the bridge, after all, and MAS saw the span as a crucial link in the citywide mass transit system. This may seem laughably obvious today, but the point seemed to escape Mayor McClellan and his Bridge Department.

The crux of the problem was that Manhattan and Brooklyn had developed their own separate transit empires in the years before consolidation. By 1905 August Belmont, Jr., the son of the Rothschilds' New York agent and the father of Perry Belmont, one of the Municipal Art Society's original board members, had a monopoly on mass transportation in Manhattan: the franchises for the Interborough Rapid Transit subway, the four elevated lines, and the streetcars were all his. Another monopoly existed in Brooklyn, where the Brooklyn Rapid Transit controlled the surface cars and elevated tracks. Belmont's priority was to build a subway up Lexington Avenue from Grand Central and another down Seventh Avenue from Times Square. He also wanted to keep the BRT out of Manhattan. The BRT's strategy was to penetrate Manhattan across the East River bridges, but since its existing equipment wasn't designed to operate underground (its trains were wood) it was determined to build new Els—not subways—in Manhattan. The Municipal Art Society was determined that no more Els be built, and equally determined that new subways run uninterrupted from Manhattan to the underdeveloped areas of Brooklyn and Queens, where the IRT had no interest in building.

The city needed a single transportation system, even if it was run by two different companies, but as the *Times* complained, "The truth is, it is easier and simpler to build a bridge or a tunnel than to link it up with the streets and car routes which alone make it useful."[28] Despite the "painful education" afforded by the Brooklyn Bridge, McClellan's Bridge Department still thought of each bridge as "a complete proposition" with only tenuous ties to the mass transit system.[29] MAS had proposed a subway loop at the foot of the Manhattan Bridge. It would have crossed the island, dropping off passengers at the subway and elevated lines or conducting them all the way to the waterfront and the Jersey ferries. In 1905, however, the city published Carrère & Hastings's plans for a Manhattan Bridge terminal. It would leave the passengers from Brooklyn stranded blocks away from the nearest connection to Manhattan's mass transit system. "It seems unfeeling to criticize such prettily drawn terminals," the *Times* wrote, but "it is not to the purpose that the drawings are sightly, or that pleasing park spaces are provided. . . . The fundamental objection is that the $10 million, more or less, will be worse than wasted if it is spent in obstructing instead of promoting traffic connections." Why not spend that money, asked the *Times*, on the subway loop proposed by MAS? The paper pointed out that twenty organizations, including the Municipal Art Society, had taken part in one protest meeting. "There has . . . been such a chorus of condemnation that it may be doubted whether more complete proof of rejection by public bodies and newspapers can be had."[30] The protests succeeded in stopping the terminal's construction, but they didn't persuade the city to come up with a better rapid transit plan. Three years later, in 1908, Bridge Commissioner Stevenson simply denied that transit connections were his responsibility: by law, he explained, his department was authorized to do nothing more "than to build and maintain bridges."[31]

The Bridge Department produced an even more obnoxious plan for downtown. When the Municipal Art Society drew its own subway plan, it realized that there was no need for a Brooklyn Bridge terminal: a transfer station was required for crowds pouring off the Els and the subway, but there was no good reason why the bridge cars should end their run at the foot of the bridge. MAS wanted the bridge cars to continue west in another subway loop, this one running from the Brooklyn Bridge to West Street, then heading north to Canal, east again to the Williamsburg Bridge, and across the river to Brooklyn. The BRT liked the idea of a link between the Brooklyn and Williamsburg bridges (it would be able to run its trains in one continuous circuit through Brooklyn and Manhattan, over the river on one bridge and back again on the other), but it didn't like this talk of subways: a new El would be far cheaper to build and equip. The Bridge Department sided with the BRT and unveiled plans for a double-deck elevated loop. The proposed route was disappointing too: the El would run along Park Row and the Bowery, missing every opportunity to connect with other transit lines.

As Calvin Tomkins pointed out, the elevated loop would better serve the BRT than the throngs of commuters. For one thing, it was "the best possible excuse" for extending the El all the way up the East Side and into the Bronx, "and this consideration," Tomkins charged, "doubtless has much, if not most, to do with the persistency" of the BRT's demands for an elevated loop. The elevated loop would also do nothing to increase the capacity of the Brooklyn Bridge. The minimum headway between trains was forty-five seconds, and that limit had nearly been reached already. On that basis only 54,000 people an hour could cross the bridge, half of them standing, and the trains were slowly wrecking the bridge. The problem was not that the trains weighed too much but that, as they rolled across the span, their weight was unevenly distributed. All this stretching and pulling was more than Roebling's design could bear, and engineers had warned the city that the bridge would have to be rebuilt. A better solution, Tomkins argued, was to replace the trains with a continuous "moving platform"—a huge conveyor belt for people. Tomkins was backing the recommendation of a group of eminent engineers, including George L. Morison, Gustav Lindenthal, John Bogart, and Theo C. Clarke, and just such platforms had been used at the world's fairs in Chicago in 1893 and in Paris in 1900. The bridge commissioner, under pressure, had appointed an independent group of engineers to determine whether a moving platform, "when installed on so large a scale and subjected to traffic so much greater, . . .

may reasonably be expected to meet the requirements of the situation." Tomkins wanted Stevenson's assurance that their report, whatever its conclusion, would be made public.[32]

The commission of engineers reported in due time that a moving platform was perfectly feasible, and that it could carry 70,000 passengers per hour.[33] (A moving platform was eventually built for the Forty-second Street Shuttle, and it worked perfectly well until a fire destroyed it in the 1950s.) It turned out that there was one problem with the Municipal Art Society's scheme: the IRT's City Hall subway station stood in the way of any underground extension of the Brooklyn Bridge's transit system, whether subway cars or a moving platform. That problem wasn't insuperable, however: MAS produced a report showing that, if the subway station were lowered by eight feet, trains could pass overhead, but that would mean shutting down the subway for a time, and no one was prepared to do this. It was a perfect illustration of what could go wrong when the city embarked on public works without a comprehensive plan, but Tomkins drew a darker conclusion and charged that Interborough's City Hall station had been put in the wrong place deliberately: "the neck of the bridge has been effectively corked in the interests of the Brooklyn Rapid Transit Company."[34]

The city brushed off all of Tomkins's arguments for a rational transit system. MAS had the advantage of a reasonable argument, but the railway companies owned franchises stretching far into the future, which limited the city's leverage over them. The railroads could also make sure that the city didn't test its powers: they could pay bribes, make lavish campaign contributions, and deliver bundles of their own stock into the hands of political insiders. The only way to counterbalance the railways' power was to convince Tammany Hall that it would pay a political price for indulging them, but MAS could never succeed in doing this. A subway plan was too abstract an issue to fire up voters. Few New Yorkers bothered to follow the debate on arcane points of transit connections, or whether it was possible to move the City Hall subway station. Only when the residents of the Lower East Side came to feel threatened by the BRT was the city forced to modify its position.

Thousands of people had been displaced to make room for the Williamsburg Bridge approach, but Lindenthal's scheme for the Delancey Street Parkway—based on the Broadway malls, with a pedestrian promenade shaded by trees—promised to make it up to the community. Now the city was threatening to abandon this scheme for an El. Charles Stover, an MAS member who was president of the East Side Civic Club and the headworker of the East Side Settlement House, organized a campaign of East Siders to stop the BRT. The sachems of Tammany Hall suddenly felt vulnerable in the heart of their own territory, and a compromise was reached: MAS didn't get its subway loop, but the BRT never got its El, either. Its trains were forced underground, into a subway beneath Delancey Street. From the Municipal Art Society's point of view this wasn't much of a victory. True, the neighborhood was spared the blight of an El, but the new subway would follow the BRT's preferred route: down the Lower East Side to City Hall Park, not across the island. The *Times*, however, described the sense of relief on Delancey Street in 1908, where people "are rejoicing because their neighborhood is to have perpetual light and air, with no sacrifice of their health and property to the demands of the rest of the city for transit accommodations."[35]

Having obtained a subway, Stover suggested something more: a monument at Delancey and Essex streets, where "the people of the east side, for decades the objects of outsiders' benevolence and civic propaganda, may find a telling opportunity of expressing local pride and self-reliance."[36] He recruited the architects Howells & Stokes to design the Delancey Street Gateway, a monumental arch and clock tower to crown the axis of the parkway's promenade. (Stokes was I. N. Phelps Stokes, the brother of Municipalian J. G. Phelps Stokes and one of the first architects in New York to get involved in tenement reform.) The arch would have been sheathed in gleaming terra-cotta, decorated with portraits of Old World and New World lawgivers (Moses *and* George Washington, etc.), and crowned by an American eagle, wings outstretched. Stover formed the Delancey Street Subway Celebration Committee from local settlement workers, businessmen, and residents, and they set about raising the $15,000 needed. The idea was that the community would pay for the monument as a model of what the city should be doing: it would serve as "a visible expression of our belief that tenement house streets, as well as residential boulevards and civic centers, are worthy of beautification; that especially where great open spaces are cut through tenement house blocks from public necessity, as for bridge and transportation purposes, the opportunity should be seized of obtaining improvements which will enhance the beauty of regions affected as well as serve mere utilitarian ends."[37] It was, however, a bad time to raise money. The papers were full of reports of community groups demanding that the city undertake public works to mitigate the depression; Stover was speaking to a population already beleaguered.

In 1908 a BRT train finally crossed the Williamsburg Bridge for the first time. The bridge—"a monument of ability of construction and inefficiency of city administration"—had been open for four years, and it had been operating all the while at a third of its capacity.[38] The first trains across the bridge from Brooklyn stopped at the Bowery; it took five years for the BRT to finish the short tunnel to City Hall Park. When the tunnel finally reached its destination in 1913, the BRT was still using the same old rickety wooden cars that ran along its Els, though New York had long since learned that wooden trains—fragile, flammable, and prone to splintering in a collision—had no business burrowing underground. Little else was being done in the way of new subways. In 1908 the subway tunnel beneath the East River finally opened, linking Manhattan to the Long Island Railroad station on Flatbush Avenue in Brooklyn. That same year the Queensboro Bridge was so close to completion that dignitaries could walk across it, yet there was still, incredibly, no plan for trains to cross it. "It is unsettled," the *Times* reported, "whether to have a terminal—a word that millions have learned to hate—or whether its railways are to run across Manhattan in a loop and intercept all lines of north and south travel. Nor is it settled whether any Manhattan lines are to cross to Long Island."[39]

Part of the problem lay, once again, with McClellan's Bridge Department. Lindenthal and Hornbostel's design for the Queensboro Bridge hadn't been discarded, but it had been altered—a sadder fate, perhaps. Once Lindenthal was out of office the Bridge Department allowed the Queensboro's contractor to use an inferior grade of steel. Since the material wasn't as strong, there had to be more of it, and the city compensated by making all the girders thicker. This made the bridge uglier and heavier. Then, while the Queensboro crept across the river, a bridge of similar design in Canada collapsed during a gale; the Canadian bridge hadn't been finished yet, and cantilever bridges aren't very stable during construction. The Bridge Department's response was to quicken the pace of the Queensboro's construction, and then, once the cantilevers were joined and the structure was secure, to add yet more steel. Perhaps the Bridge Department felt ill at ease about what it already had done to Lindenthal's specifications; perhaps, as some people charged, it merely seized an opportunity to let more contracts for steel. The result of all this tampering was a bridge less strong than Lindenthal's—so much so that in 1913 the city decided it couldn't risk using all the train tracks Lindenthal had planned. Instead it built, at great expense, a tunnel at Sixtieth Street.[40]

The Queensboro and Manhattan bridges opened in 1909, roughly a decade after the city first drew plans for their construction. The Manhattan Bridge alone had been designed four times in all: by the men who held the original franchise, by Buck, by Lindenthal, and finally by Morsieff. The Queensboro had first been proposed by private parties in the 1870s. More than a quarter century passed before the span was finished. It seemed that the subway system would suffer similar delays. The Rapid Transit Commission was proving to be an ineffective, lackadaisical body. Its members were nominated by the Chamber of Commerce, but McClellan complained that the chamber seemed to pick only its most aged and doddering cronies. Calvin Tomkins seems to have been influential in persuading Governor Charles Evans Hughes to abolish the RTC, and in 1907 it was replaced by the Public Service Commission, a body appointed by the governor and answerable to him. A number of Municipalians would serve on it, including Milo Maltbie, a protégé of John De Witt Warner (he'd been the editor of *Municipal Affairs*, an MAS board member, and the secretary of the Art Commission) and George McAneny, the future borough president of Manhattan. In 1907 the Public Service Commission unveiled its plans for the "Triborough Subway System," not a true master plan but a plan for the next stage in subway construction. It included MAS's Canal Street subway loop in a scheme to link West Street to the Manhattan Bridge and to Brooklyn's Fourth Avenue subway, with one branch leading to Bay Ridge and another, on elevated tracks, to Coney Island. Construction began on the Canal Street loop, but the Public Service Commission was hampered by a very basic problem. It could lay out new rapid transit routes, but could it persuade private enterprise to build and operate them? The city needed subway lines stretching far into the farmlands of

Brooklyn and Queens, thus opening them up to development, but private railroad companies saw these lines as highly speculative. In the short term they wouldn't be profitable: it would take years for new neighborhoods to be built along the rapid transit lines, and in the meantime the trains would carry few fares. The railway companies would build only where they were sure of earning profits from day one, and this meant only in areas that were already congested. Their argument was that the city needed to provide better service where conditions were already crowded; the Municipal Art Society's fear was that this policy would only result in still more overcrowding.

No one could force the railway companies to invest their money—not the city, not the speculators who yearned to build apartments in the meadows, not groups like MAS that saw decentralization as the cure for slums. One possible answer to the dilemma was municipal "ownership," which actually meant that the city would build *and run* the subways, and in 1905 William Randolph Hearst ran for mayor on his own party line, that of the Municipal Ownership League. He lost to McClellan, but only narrowly and amid much evidence of fraud. Conservatives regarded Hearst's party line as dangerously radical, even socialistic, and as a new Pandora's box of graft. They feared that a municipal railroad would turn into a black hole of patronage, so overstaffed with the party faithful that its operation would be fantastically costly, and they were certain that Tammany would never pass these costs on to riders. The fare would be kept low to win votes, and the city would have to subsidize the subways. Conservatives regarded subsidies as economic heresy—as shocking, say, as the idea that the tax system should redistribute wealth.

The other alternative was municipal "control," which really meant that the private companies would continue to operate the subways, but on a shorter leash. Franchises would be granted for shorter periods—twenty years instead of fifty—and the city would retain the right to build subways itself if private enterprise refused to do so, or to cancel franchises if the operators provided poor service. For a time, this was Calvin Tomkins's agenda, and it was embodied in the Ellsberg Bill, of which he was an influential supporter. Enacted by the state in 1906, it limited new franchises to a maximum of twenty years, with just one twenty-year renewal. It was meant to encourage competition, and the threat of losing a franchise was supposed to make the rail companies more malleable, yet the Ellsberg Bill backfired disastrously. Tomkins and his allies never took into account one detail of the Rapid Transit Law, which let the city pay a private operator to build the subway tunnels, but not for providing the rolling stock, rail yards, or power plants. All this fabulously expensive equipment was the operator's responsibility, and no one was willing to try to amortize its cost over a mere twenty years. August Belmont, of course, had already built rail yards and a power plant for the IRT—he didn't have to worry—and the Ellsberg Bill had the perverse effect of ensuring that no one would step forward to challenge his monopoly.

Soon, though, even Belmont's ability to raise capital evaporated. The Panic of 1907 saw the market for railroad securities collapse. Even in the best of times the franchise system hadn't delivered the subway system New York needed, and now the private sphere seemed incapable of building any subway at all. What to do?

Calvin Tomkins became a spokesman for what now seems like a thoroughly reasonable solution: that the city build subways wherever private enterprise would not. Tomkins argued that New York should treat the subway contracts not as franchises but as concessions. It would build and equip the subways itself, and private companies would simply provide the manpower. "Subways are the subway streets of the city and should be continuously made subject to the same degree of public control as the surface streets," he insisted. "They should be built by the city and should not be alienated under franchise grants. Operating leases should be for short terms only. . . . In no other way can the city hope to control its future transportation, upon which depends its successful development."[41]

If it was difficult for private enterprise to raise the money to build subways, it was hard for the city, too. The debt limit was still a problem, despite the new assessment policy, and no one was willing to suggest that excess condemnation be used along subway routes. So Tomkins concentrated on a new way to raise the city's borrowing capacity. When the city borrowed money for public works it promised, in effect, to pay it back from property taxes, but some public works actually generated a profit. Steamship companies, for instance, paid dearly for leases to the municipal docks—more than enough to pay off the city's initial investment. There was no need to back up such a project with property taxes, and in 1909 Calvin Tomkins was instrumental in having these self-sustaining investments removed from the city's debt limit.

Financing docks in this fashion was uncontroversial, but Tomkins also argued that subways were self-sustaining, and could be built by issuing city bonds outside the debt limit. The mayor and the governor both rebuffed him, and so did the editorial board of the *New York Times*. The *Times* argued that new subways would benefit only a fraction of the population: the riders who made use of them and a small segment of the city's real estate speculators. Since they wouldn't provide a "universal benefit" like the water tunnel, the city should leave them to private enterprise.[42] (Yet a few days later a *Times* editorial noted that Manhattan was losing population to the outer boroughs—a "beneficent process," the paper decided, predicting that in the end Manhattan would be, like the City of London, purely a business center.[43]) The paper was afraid of seeing the city jump into "a speculation" with public funds, but it especially dreaded the notion that government should step into something that had always been the realm of private enterprise. It was an ideological issue that had come to poison the paper's relationship with the Citizens Union. When Robert Fulton Cutting suggested that municipal utilities would cut costs and provide more efficient service, the *Times* was outraged and denounced him as a socialist (he *was* influenced by the Christian Socialism of municipal governments in Germany and Austria), and it was no happier when Tomkins argued for municipal subways.

The result of all this was sheer paralysis. The next great phase of subway construction had to wait until 1913, when George McAneny undid the Elsberg Bill and negotiated the so-called Dual Contracts. In the meantime the Municipal Art Society had lost its most useful ally, the *Times* editorial board, and it was losing many members. Perry Belmont's resignation was predictable, but many others followed suit in 1907 and 1908, and others wondered how MAS had strayed from public art into a field so politicized and ideologically explosive. Those Municipalians who cared about subways transferred their efforts to the Reform Club, whose Municipal Reform Committee was chaired by Calvin Tomkins and included Municipalians John De Witt Warner, Charles Lamb, Bert Hanson, and Harold A. Caparn. There they could address the political aspects of the subway question, and they could savage George McClellan. "Our difficulties are directly caused by the policy of the McClellan administration," Tomkins declared. Since taking office, McClellan had issued almost $300 million in stock, but less than $20 million of this was for subway construction, and all but a tiny fraction of that sum was to fulfill obligations from earlier administrations. "The exploitation of the needs of the city is the curse of the city," Calvin Tomkins wrote, "and advances in municipal civilization depend primarily upon preventing the unfair use of the many by the few."[44]

The failure of New York's "municipal civilization" was writ large on the Lower East Side, where the city's inability to build subways was exacting an immeasurable cost. In the spring of 1904, just months after the Improvement Commission issued its preliminary report, a wave of rent strikes swept through the Lower East Side, and no clearer demonstration could have been provided of how desperately New York needed to provide its tenement dwellers with an avenue of escape. Landlords had announced that rents would rise by 20 to 30 percent, and those who couldn't afford the increase were confronted with the grim fact that there was no place else for them to go: there was a housing shortage. Municipal improvements—the very schools and parks that reformers had so long demanded—had drastically reduced the area's stock of apartments. In building the Williamsburg Bridge alone the city had demolished 17,000 apartments, and the bridge, far from opening a new set of housing opportunities for East Side residents, would prove to be a calamitous example of the city's failure to plan.[45] While some residents were able to flee to Harlem or Brooklyn, the flood of new immigrants more than made up for their absence: within five years the area's population jumped by 14 percent.

Nor did conditions get better while the Improvement Commission worked on its final report. The depression that followed the Panic of 1907 revived calls for new subways. Some made an economic argument: real estate had done comparatively well in the panic while railroad securities had plummeted, and it was widely assumed that investors would gladly shift large amounts of money from Wall Street to construction if only the opportunity presented itself. "If the city should fail to provide this subway on the score of the economy," one real estate speculator wrote, "it would be the old story of saving at the spigot and losing at the bunghole."[46] Another, Frank Bailey, pointed to the growing housing shortage in the Lower East

Side. He may have confused the effect of the tenement house law with its intentions when he wrote that it "was fostered by those who wished to scatter the population so closely assembled in the congested sections and who believed that by making construction more expensive the people would be driven to the suburbs. You cannot drive a man to the suburbs unless he can get there."[47] As Bailey wrote, in January 1908, New York was in the midst of another rent strike, even more bitter than the last. Since 1904 the rent for an apartment of two and a half miserable rooms had climbed from eleven or twelve dollars a month to sixteen or seventeen, and new increases had just been announced—this at a time when perhaps a hundred thousand East Siders were out of work.[48] This strike was regarded by the press as infinitely more dangerous than the last, for it was closely identified with the Socialist Party. (Rose Pastor Stokes, the wife of Municipalian J. G. Phelps Stokes, was a prominent supporter.)

The turmoil on the Lower East Side shifted the city's attention away from the City Beautiful and focused it on the appalling overcrowding in the slums. In 1908 the Municipal Art Society joined with other advocates to mount an exhibit known as the "Congestion Show" at the Museum of Natural History, and it came away from that experience with a very different approach to planning. Dreams of civic centers would largely fade away, replaced by demands for land-use zoning and building-height regulations. It was a dramatic shift. MAS had always relied on the city's own public works to reshape New York. Now it came to realize that the city also had to control private property.

THE LAISSEZ-FAIRE CITY

IN 1895, WHEN Evangeline Blashfield addressed the Nineteenth Century Club on the subject of how to make New York a beautiful city, she offered a simple solution: "We should bear in mind that, no matter how fine an edifice may be per se, it must be in harmony with its surroundings; that in a town, as in a *toilette*, it is the *ensemble* that tells."[1] Toilette was a serious matter in Blashfield's day. A man could disgrace himself by wearing the wrong thing to dinner, and the characters in an Edith Wharton novel are likely to study a woman's clothes for signs of her moral character—in *The House of Mirth*, for example, the heroine's destiny seems to hang in the balance every time she dresses for a ball. Even so, clothes were ruled by social conventions, not sumptuary laws.

The wealthy had their own ways of building, as of dressing, and today one can walk the side streets of the Upper East Side Historic District and find something of the decorous architectural ensemble Blashfield wanted. The row houses are good neighbors: similar in form, varied in style but within a fairly narrow range of tastes. Some are cast in the mold of Richard Morris Hunt's châteaux, others in the Beaux Arts Baroque, a little flashy in their evocation of Parisian boulevards; but as time wore on, the sober propriety of McKim's Italian Renaissance became more common, and so did the old money rectitude of the Georgian Revival.

Such order prevailed only in the wealthy residential districts, of course. In some neighborhoods the situation was formalized with a system of restrictive covenants: when developers sold off lots in a large tract, they often included in the individual deeds a clause forbidding the construction of stores and stables or requiring buyers to put up row houses of a certain character. A few neighborhoods, like Murray Hill, which was dominated by the Morgan family, tried to make these covenants permanent, but they usually expired in twenty years or so—even homeowners in New York were alive to the possibility that their houses could be turned to speculation.

When it came to their homes, the rich built what society expected of them, but their business buildings and investments were governed by no such conventions.

"The typical American has no 'sense of the state,' " H. G. Wells wrote after a visit to turn-of-the-century New York:

> I do not mean that he is not passionately and vigorously patriotic. But I mean that he has no perception that his business activities, his private employments, are constituents in a larger collective process; that they affect other people and the world forever, and cannot, as he imagines, begin and end with him. He sees the world in fragments; it is to him a multitudinous collection of individual "stories," as the newspapers put it . . . all a matter of personal doings. . . . And these individualities are unfused. Not a touch of abstraction or generalization, no thinnest atmosphere of reflection, mitigates these harsh, isolated happenings. The American . . . has yet to achieve the conception of a whole world to which individual acts and happenings are subordinate and contributory.[2]

New Yorkers had no more sense of "the city" than of "the state." The idea of limiting what a person could do with his private property—that there was an overarching public interest in how the city was shaped by private enterprise—flew in the face of what New Yorkers understood about their constitutional rights. It was accepted that government had the right, the "police power," to restrict property for the sake of public health and safety, or to bar "nuisances," but that was all. New York could require, as it finally did in 1901, that every new apartment have a toilet. It could demand certain standards in construction so that buildings neither collapsed on their owners nor took their neighbors up in flames. It could banish foul-smelling tanneries, soap factories, and abattoirs to out-of-the-way places in order to preserve property values in the city center. It could forbid stables from locating next to schools—though this law was often ignored. It could bar saloons within a certain distance of schools and churches, but this was handled through the state's control of liquor licenses, and churches demanded its enforcement more avidly than did certain school districts.[3] Otherwise, as far as the law was concerned, people were free to do with their property as they pleased.

"We can never have an artistic city," the *Times* wrote in 1899, "until we recognize the necessity of lodging somewhere a power to constrain private builders to observe public decencies. . . . We are very far short of the point at which public opinion would sustain so drastic a measure as this. If we ever come round to it, it will be because we are convinced that it pays." Paris and Washington, the editors suggested, were examples that beauty did pay. "Paris lives on its attractiveness," and Washington was becoming a winter resort for the same reason. Yet, "when any radical and comprehensive scheme for the embellishment of New York is brought forward, when even an effort is made to preserve one street for the spectacle of the pleasure-driving to be seen there, the answer is always that this is a 'business city.'* All beauty,

---

* This was in reference to the campaign to restrict Fifth Avenue traffic, at least in the afternoon, to pleasure vehicles. See Editorial, "The Traffic of Fifth Avenue," New York Times, May 10, 1899, p. 6.

all seemliness, even public decency, are sacrificed to this Moloch. The only way in which this Moloch can be appeased is to convince his worshipers that municipal embellishment and an attractive city are also 'business,' and that it pays to have them."[4]

IT TOOK another fifteen years to convince New York that "an attractive city" would pay; that laissez-faire was a dangerous and destructive model on which to build a city, and that developers themselves would be among its victims. The Municipal Art Society discovered how little control it could exert on private property when, in 1902, it suggested that the city require all buildings to display their street numbers. This was an unconstitutional infringement on property rights, the city said, and in 1907 Mayor McClellan vetoed a similar bill with the same explanation. By then the Municipal Art Society had already had a painful time trying to limit billboards.

While Municipalians struggled to make the city blossom with examples of civic art, they watched in horror as billboards, that weed of art forms, ran rampant through the streets. There were only the barest restrictions on outdoor advertising at the turn of the century. Posters for patent medicines and quack doctors were illegal, but there was no Consumer Affairs Department to investigate such matters, and enforcement was very spotty. It was illegal to hang ads on the outside of a van or wagon, but this was a traffic-control measure, designed to prevent people from flooding the streets with fleets of four-wheeled billboards. It also was forbidden to place ads on city property, but the motives behind this regulation weren't aesthetic; the law ensured that the city didn't compete with private enterprise. Otherwise, New York was an open city. Billboards, placards, and posters sprang up wherever space could be rented. Office buildings generally restricted the signs of their own tenants, but the *Times* described the retail district, stretching up Broadway from City Hall Park to Union Square, as "a frightful spectacle, made so more by the wilderness of discordant and shrieking signs than even by the ordinary architecture of the thoroughfare—trying as that also is. New Yorkers are so hardened to the exhibition that they are offended by it only on returning from cities in this respect more civilized. But it shocks all foreign visitors."[5] New Yorkers were usually more upset by the fact that residential districts weren't immune: vacant lots were typically enclosed with placarded fences, and it was especially galling to the art societies that billboards were often erected overlooking public parks. "Why," asked John Martin, chairman of MAS's Committee on Advertising Signs, "should the municipality, after taking so much [sic] laudable pains to make a 'City Beautiful,' permit the whole effect to be marred by the creation nearby, without any regulation for appearance [sic] sake, of monster signs and posters?"[6]

Many New Yorkers shared these opinions with the Municipal Art Society. But the society's revulsion went deeper. Its artist members were deeply offended by the artwork of ads. They worried over it just as many people today decry the inanities of television. It was a conflict between academic and vernacular art: all of the society's efforts to elevate public taste, to school the masses in the lessons of high art, were clearly going to waste as long as advertisements—so ubiquitous, so colorful, so seductive and full of false promises—constantly reaffirmed the values and aesthetics of popular culture.

In 1902 the Municipal Art Society introduced, through Jacob Cantor, a revision of the city building code designed to regulate billboards for the first time. The new code had three parts. First, the superintendent of buildings would have to license signs, ensuring that they were securely attached to their host buildings, that they were constructed of fireproof materials, and that they didn't obliterate the windows of occupied buildings. Second, new billboards and "sign fences" couldn't be more than ten feet tall, and any existing signs exceeding this limit would have to be removed "within a reasonable time." Finally, sky signs—billboards on the roofs of buildings—would be forbidden altogether.[7]

The bill hardly seems like an onerous restraint on free enterprise or free speech, nor would it have achieved many of the Municipal Art Society's aims, such as banning outdoor ads from residential neighborhoods. Indeed today it seems ridiculously weak. The proposed regulations were a reluctant compromise on the society's part, but at the same time it represented a gigantic and daring step forward for the Municipal Art Society, for this was the first time the society had ever sought to restrict, in however limited a fashion, the use of private property. In turn-of-the-century New York this was a bit like trying to pass a gun control law in Texas. The attempt to ban sky signs was immediately shot down by Seth Low's corporation counsel, George L. Rives, who ruled that the Board of Aldermen could limit the height and construction materials of sky signs as a matter of public safety, but was powerless to ban them outright. Rives was not some Neanderthal exponent of laissez-faire economics. Like Mayor Low, he was a member of the Municipal Art Society. Yet he found that in banning sky signs, the city would be legislating for a purely aesthetic end. That would be an unconstitutional "taking" of property, and the city would have to compensate property owners for lost income.[8] Cantor was forced to settle for modest restrictions that held sky signs and billboards to a ten-foot height limit.

This compromise was so unsatisfactory that in 1903 MAS tried a different tack, suggesting that the city tax billboards by the square foot. This would sidestep any constitutional complaint, and MAS hoped that large billboards would become prohibitively expensive, while small ones were hardly worth building. It isn't clear why the Fusion administration failed to act on this. Perhaps Seth Low thought new taxes impolitic, or perhaps the reformers simply had no time to deal with the issue before they were voted out of office.

Tammany Hall was predictably less interested in restricting signs. Indeed its attitude soon became clear. In February 1904, when McClellan had been in office for just two months, Municipalians were horrified to see long lines of billboards rise in Bryant Park. The signs were mounted on a fence around the Public Library's construction site. "The lettering of the signs is large and often fantastical and displeasing to the eye," complained Barr Ferree, a Municipalian and a columnist for *Architects' and Builders' Magazine*, "and the pictures often poorly drawn and offensive to the taste."[9] More to the point, Bryant Park was city property, where placards were barred by law. John J. Pallas, the new Tammany parks commissioner, had issued a permit for the signs and, as the Municipal Art Society soon discovered, he hadn't even charged the advertising agency. MAS called for a criminal investigation: surely, if the city hadn't been paid for the use of its property, some individual in the city government, perhaps Pallas himself, must have received a bribe. What, MAS asked, did the mayor know about the situation?

The *Times* agreed that the ads must go, but denounced the Municipal Art Society's insinuations as rash and irresponsible. The paper, which had vilified McClellan during his campaign, was now his chief supporter—a shift McClellan attributed to his friendship with the paper's owner and managers and to the fact that he had renewed the paper's lucrative contract to carry municipal advertisements.[10] The Republican *Tribune* dug deeper, however, reporting that Boss Murphy was behind the contracts: "Mr. Murphy has told Mr. Pallas that the storm will blow over in a few days and said 'don't get nervous.' "[11] It did not blow over. When Pallas stood his ground and refused to remove the billboards, MAS filed suit against the city for the first time in its history. This forced the mayor to summon Pallas to his office and demand an explanation. McClellan remembered the incident as "the first serious difference that I had with a department head." He wrote that he "was as much outraged by the matter as were the newspapers." John J. Pallas was in fact one of Murphy's—not McClellan's—appointments, as the mayor later admitted. Pallas was the head of the American Federation of Labor in New York State, and he'd once called McClellan an "aristocratic pup." McClellan, in turn, despised his parks commissioner. "When Pallas reached my office," McClellan wrote, "I proceeded to reduce the proud labor leader to a condition of pulp. He pleaded that he had allowed the signs to be painted much against his will under the direct orders of 'the Commissioner,' which was the title by which Murphy was known to the faithful. He acknowledged that without consulting me he had granted the concession for a year, without compensation to the city, to Harry Hart," Tammany leader of the Thirtieth District. Murphy confirmed the story, McClellan reported: "He had given Hart the concession in lieu of an office, and . . . it would net Hart about $50,000 a year. I told Murphy that unless Hart voluntarily yielded his concession I should have the signs removed anyhow and let him sue the city. After a great deal of grumbling and considerable ill temper, Murphy finally consented to make Hart yield gracefully and the signs were painted out."[12]

The Bryant Park case was clear-cut: ads didn't belong on city property. In 1905 the Municipal Art Society assumed that ads in the subway were just as simple an issue. But it found, to its intense mortification, that even with the support of the mayor and the newspapers, it could not have them removed—and that the public liked them there.

When the first subway line opened in 1904 its stations were much admired as examples of municipal art (now that some have been cleaned and restored, one can finally see why). They were designed by Heins & La Farge, architects of the Cathedral of Saint John the Divine, though much of their work at the cathedral was later altered, none too happily, by Ralph Adams Cram. Heins & La Farge's masterpiece was the City Hall station, no longer in use, with its soaring domes and skylights, but even the typical stations had been outfitted with glass tile, decorative mosaics, and glittering terra-cotta placques that helped passengers determine what station they'd reached. Shortly after the subway began operating, the stations, built and decorated at such great expense to the city, disappeared beneath a layer of advertisements, while flower stands and vending machines sprouted on the platforms. The Municipal Art Society was astonished. It looked up the text of the Rapid Transit Law, which authorized the subway's construction, and discovered that the legislation clearly described the subway as a public thoroughfare. "Legally the subway is a highway of the city," explained John Martin, the chairman of MAS's Committee on Advertising Signs, "and it is no more lawful to put advertising signs in it than it would be to place frames along the curb of Broadway and fill them with posters. Doubtless a large revenue might be got if the gutters were so adorned; but . . . the law forbids such a misuse of the streets."[13]

The Rapid Transit Commission had nonetheless signed a contract with the Interborough Corporation that permitted advertisements so long as these didn't interfere with "easy identification of the stations." President Orr of the RTC explained that this clause was "an inducement to get bids for the building of the subway."[14] MAS, however, was convinced that, contract or no contract, the RTC had no legal right to permit advertising, and Martin was all the more annoyed when he discovered that Interborough had rejected a bid for advertising by the Lee Lash Company. This scheme was sensitive to Heins & La Farge's architecture. Lee Lash intended to place its ads carefully: one ad centered in each tile panel, and artfully framed. Interborough, however, let the contract to Ward and Gow, who treated Heins & La Farge's carefully crafted elevations as just so much space to be covered. "Those whom the gods would destroy, they first make mad," Martin wrote. "Notice how, occasionally, a corporation's sin finds it out. Had the enlightened policy been adapted no outcry would have been raised, the stringency of the law would not have been discovered, and the Municipal Art Society would, quite possibly, have commended the advance. Then the company would have obtained a reasonable revenue along with congratulations on the progress it was making. But it allowed its greed to dominate; it scorned the sentiment of citizens; it refused to put any brains into the advertising scheme; and in consequence, it will, we hope, be forced to cast its gaudy picture frames away."[15]

Orr admitted that so many signs had been installed that, in the ensuing clutter, passengers were having great difficulty locating the terra-cotta and mosaic plaques that announced the stations. The ads, Orr asserted, must be thinned, but if they were removed altogether the city would have to compensate Interborough. The Times was ready to support such a payment, so long as the signs were banished.[16]

Calvin Tomkins denied any payment was necessary, and he objected to Orr's attempt to ameliorate the situation. The point, Tomkins argued, was that Orr had no authority to permit *any* advertising. Aside from the long-established ban on ads on public property, the ads violated at least three provisions of Interborough's contract: they ignored the approved specifications for the stations; they flouted the requirement that "the stations must be finished in a decorative and attractive manner, as is consistent with and suitable to buildings of such character"; and they made nonsense of the clause that "all details of the stations must be so arranged as to facilitate cleaning and to permit if desired a thorough washing of all parts of the stations and their approaches by means of a hose."[17]

Orr went ahead and had some of the ads removed. Dissatisfied, the Municipal Art Society replied by filing suit against Interborough and Ward and Gow (twenty members agreed to cover its legal costs), and it soon won the mayor's support. McClellan was as sincerely disgusted by the subway ads as he'd been by John J. Pallas's decision to adorn Bryant Park with posters, and having been embarrassed once by illegal signage, he was eager to take a stand against the Interborough Company. Corporation Counsel Delaney obliged him with an opinion that advertisements, flower stands, and vending machines violated the stations' design specifications and interfered with the ready identification of stations. McClellan informed Interborough that it had forty-eight hours to remove the signs. Failing that, one Thomas E. McEntegart, the city's superintendent of incumbrances (!), would "send out his axe brigade."[18]

Interborough and Ward and Gow answered with an injunction. At stake was their contract, worth more than $15 million over ten years. They pointed to the Interborough lease for justification of their actions, and they insisted that the subway was no highway, since admission was by payment of a fare; since it was leased for fifty years to Interborough; and since it was maintained and policed by Interborough and not by the city. They pointed out that the flower stands had been designed by Heins & La Farge and that in at least one instance, at the Fourteenth Street Station, vending machines had been installed at the RTC's request. Set "between a supporting column and the newel post of the stairway to keep persons from forcing their way between," these machines "are therefore 'not for the purpose of obstructing the public but to protect it.' "[19]

McClellan ordered the corporation counsel to sue, and the counsel in turn invited Nelson Spencer, the Municipal Art Society's own lawyer, to argue the city's case. MAS was convinced that the public supported its position. Certainly the city's newspaper editors did, and MAS took heart from the example of the great private railroad companies, which banned ads from their stations because they too believed that the public disliked them. But convincing the court was another matter. It brushed aside the language of the Rapid Transit Act and its talk of "public thoroughfares" and demanded instead that the city prove that the advertisements were a public nuisance. John De Witt Warner gave a gloomy report at the Municipal Art Society's annual meeting in April 1905: "The final outcome of this suit will depend on whether it is possible to establish to the complete satisfaction of the court that the advertising in the Subway is really regarded as offensive by the public. This is necessary in order to secure the designation of that advertising as a public nuisance. It is more than doubtful whether this can be done."[20]

Perhaps the judge read the papers' Letters to the Editor columns and learned that, once the ads were thinned, the public was no longer outraged by the placards, however poorly placed. Indeed they were a welcome diversion. As one reader wrote to the *Times*, "A casual reader who has studied the newspapers for the last few months would imagine that the population of New York were of a soulful and artistic temperament and probably wore long hair. The ordinary citizen cannot help thinking the unadorned stations a little bit dingy, low-roofed and dark. The ads certainly brighten up the place—besides being an inducement to the Interborough to spend more on lighting and giving one something to look at in the long wait for an express."[21] The debate inevitably turned to class issues: a gentleman named Max Wineburgh, speaking to the Sphinx Club in 1905, argued that "the worthy and eminently respectable gentlemen who are making all of this outcry are simply out of touch with the times. The masses who struggle for existence, who produce the money upon which their leisurely critics live, get much of their information about what is going on in the business world through reading the signs arranged for their entertainment upon the walls of the subway."[22]

In 1906 the court finally decided in favor of the IRT, finding that "the Subway is not a street in the strict sense of the term, that the usual city authorities have no power of supervision over it, and that the contract made with the company, both directly and by inference, grants the right of subletting advertising, slot machines, and newsstand privileges."[23] The Fifth Avenue Coach Company, which ran buses up and down New York's most fashionable street, decided to test the limits of the court's generosity. In 1907 ads appeared on the sides of its buses, and MAS took the coach company to court. The coach company argued that the law spoke of barring ads from "wagons" and "vans," not buses, but in 1909 MAS convinced the court of appeals that any four-wheeled vehicle was a wagon, and the U.S. Supreme Court upheld the statute in 1911.[24] In the meantime the Board of Aldermen passed a bill in 1910 that permitted "advertising wagons," but Mayor Gaynor wouldn't play this game. "Let them advertise in the newspapers," he said. "Certainly good advice," wrote the *Times*,[25] and a year later a lower court ruled that streetcars must also be "wagons."[26] And so the city streets, at least, were still sacrosanct.

As for Ward and Gow, the company kept its franchise for subway ads until 1925, and then sold it to Barron G. Collier. Perhaps Municipalians found Collier's ads a little more edifying, since he had a reputation for giving starving young authors jobs as copywriters—F. Scott Fitzgerald and Ogden Nash both passed through his firm.[27] MAS was not pleased, however, when Collier decided to enlarge his empire in the 1930s by placing ads on a fleet of delivery vans. Albert Bard of the Municipal Art Society protested to the police department, demanding that it enforce the ban on ads on public streets. The police were nonplussed until Bard acquainted them with the Fifth Avenue Coach Company case. They promised to act, but didn't, and Bard eventually discovered that Collier was such a close pal of Jimmy Walker, the playboy mayor, that he carried on his person an official ID card naming him an "honorary" deputy police commissioner.

Bard then decided to take matters into his own hands—one evening, coming upon one of Collier's vans, he performed a citizen's arrest on the driver. When the police arrived, they had to protect Bard from his burly and enraged "prisoner," but they refused to take the man into custody. MAS realized that it had no recourse but to file a lawsuit against Collier. The magistrate, however, was a Tammany hack; ruling against MAS, he displayed such a flagrant disregard for the law that, years later, when Samuel Seabury was investigating Tammany's sale of public offices, Bard sent him a transcript.

Losing the subway-advertising battle of 1905 had left the Municipal Art Society a little leery of the public. John De Witt Warner was thoroughly depressed that New Yorkers had failed to see the society's case as he did—as a moral issue, a case of private interests shamelessly exploiting public space. He told his fellow Municipalians,

> I am afraid that in this city, not only the great mass of the people, but the educated classes as well, are not opposed to the disfigurement of public property and to the use of that property for private gain. While it has been a fad during the last few years to profess a feeling of opposition to such disfigurement, it is not actually offensive to the cultured and wealthy classes, many members of which are only too willing to turn a dirty penny by means of that very kind of business.
>
> A city where, as in New York, the public will stand for months the defacement of its property without doing anything about it but talk, deserves every bit of insult it gets. If the moral force of the city is weaker than the power of the corporation, then it must stand to see its property so defaced. . . . The public, in other words, has today all the right to which it is entitled.[28]

With the Bryant Park and the subway-advertising lawsuits, MAS won a reputation as the city's leading foe of outdoor advertisements. Many assumed that MAS wished to ban *all* billboards, even those on private property, and this threatened to drive a wedge between the Municipal Art Society and the vast number of property owners who rented out their land, vacant or otherwise, to advertising agencies. Quite a number of Municipalians were landowners themselves, and there's no reason to think that they abstained from collecting advertising income. The society was soon taking steps to shed its radical image. John Martin insisted that MAS had "simply fought (quite *con amore*, to be sure) for the enforcement of the law," and he admitted that "Advertising is so necessary to business and the crowded streets of a commercial metropolis are so profitable for advertising that it would be futile to try to abolish sign boards and posters, desirable as such a consummation might appear to some artistic souls. Regulation and improvement, not suppression, is our policy."[29]

MAS's attempts at regulation involved the society in some curious activities. In 1907, for instance, it formed a pact with the Public Health Defense League to ensure that legal action was taken against ads for quack medicines.[30] Improvement was meant to come about through a public education campaign, an attempt to uplift the taste of the public, and especially of art directors, by introducing them to examples of "tasteful" advertising art. In 1905 MAS sponsored an exhibit of advertising art, because, as the *Times* wrote, "posters and placards . . . in themselves are important objects of civic art, since they are the most clamorous and ubiquitous things that citizens have about them when they go abroad on pleasure or on business."[31] The exhibit championed the work of O. J. Gude & Company, an advertising agency that pioneered a more focused and sophisticated approach to billboards and placards. Martin lauded its design for a fence board "with very little lettering used and all the pictures in Dutch style." This was "more nearly an ornament than an eyesore," Martin wrote. "If the rented sign boards in and around Union Square were chiefly pictorial and all of them in Dutch style, and if those around Madison Square were in the style of Louis XIV, and those within sight of Columbus Circle in Old English style, and so on, the heaven of art lovers might not be reached, but a long flight toward it would have been taken."[32]

In 1906 MAS followed up with an exhibition of posters by Alphonse Mucha, the famous Czech-born Art Nouveau painter. In 1909 Frederick Lamb, as head of the Exhibition Committee of the National Arts Club, organized a show of the best recent American ads. The *Times* concluded that Lamb's exhibit showed "less promise than we could wish for in the development of this important field,"[33] and indeed, MAS's campaign was not terribly effective. It never dawned on Martin that O. J. Gude's "Dutch" billboard, designed specifically for the Municipal Art Society's exhibit, flouted the most basic laws of advertising. He didn't grasp that the style of an ad's artwork had to reinforce something about the product, or that a placard's job was to leap out of its context, not participate in some overarching scheme of decoration. If MAS had any impact on the art of advertisements it was confined to the ads in tony magazines; the mass-market billboard continued on its own merry, vulgar way.

In the meantime, Cantor's law limiting the size of billboards was proving to be of little use. The new Board of Aldermen loosened its restrictions, allowing double-decker billboards eighteen feet tall, and in any case Tammany wasn't overeager to enforce the law. Martin complained that this laxity had encouraged "willful lawlessness" in the advertising industry. "One hundred fifty signs exist . . . which violate the law," he told the Board of Aldermen, "and the advertising firms find it profitable to risk having the sign torn down by the city as they get enormous profits in the meanwhile."[34] In 1907 the *Herald* launched its own campaign against billboards and described the Municipal Art Society's earlier attempts to curb them. Charles Israels, an architect new to MAS's Board of Directors, convinced the society that this was the time to take up the issue again. The *Herald*'s campaign led to a revival of MAS's proposal, now four years old, to tax billboards by the square foot. MAS called on all its members to demonstrate their support, but the bill didn't pass.[35] Two years later, in 1909, the state courts declared that the city's limit on the size of sky signs was an aesthetic measure and not, in fact, related to public safety. This clause of the building code was judged to be unconstitutional, and sky signs began to proliferate across the city.[36]

Other cities, Boston among them, did begin taxing billboards by the foot, and Municipalians spread pamphlets around the country to alert civic groups to the trend. Much of this work was delegated to the National Council on Outdoor Advertising, which was run out of MAS's office in the National Arts Club. In New York the issue lay quiet until 1911, the year guerrilla warfare began against suburban billboards.

The Automobile Club of America had won passage of a state law making it a misdemeanor to place a sign on private property without the owner's written permission, or anywhere on a public highway. The "magic phrase" of this law, however, was a clause providing that any illegal sign "may be taken down, removed, or destroyed by anyone."[37] The law took effect at midnight, September 1, 1911; by dawn, the Good Roads Committee of the Automobile Club had fielded a band of "sign smashers" equipped with "the implements of war—shovels, axes, hatchets, fire hooks on poles and climbing spikes, to say nothing of a ladder and a pair of rubber boots."[38] The sign smashers set to work in Jamaica, Queens, concentrating on billboards that obscured the Automobile Club's own directional and mileage signs, while a women's club in New Rochelle took advantage of the opportunity to savage cigar and liquor ads. Smashing signs became a sort of popular sport, in part because it was the one legal form of vandalism, and therefore fun, but also because of a widespread revulsion at advertisers' defacement of the landscape.

In 1914, with a Fusion administration in power, another assault was launched on outdoor advertising in the city proper. Henry Curran was ready with legislation for the Board of Aldermen. Curran was backed up by the Citizens Union, the Real Estate Board, MAS, and the City Club, but his bill was "so drastic" that it raised, once again, "the legal difficulties in the way of regulations based solely on the preservation of public beauty." Mayor John Purroy Mitchel was persuaded to appoint a Billboard Commission to study the problem. Dominated by Municipalian Albert Bard, the commission concluded that the only solution was an amendment to the state constitution that would let the city regulate private property "upon aesthetic considerations, just as may now be done upon considerations of sanitation, good order and the like."[39]

Bard's proposal wasn't taken up—not until 1956, that is—but advertisers were alarmed nonetheless. They didn't enjoy being depicted as public enemies, and they worried that this constant agitation against billboards would cause their clients to shy away from outdoor advertisements. They struck a deal with the civic groups. The admen issued a statement acknowledging the widespread desire to beautify the city. "We are in full accord with sentiments of this kind," they announced, "providing, of course, that these efforts progress along lines not merely of pure aestheticism, but of aestheticism coupled with the essential needs of and rights of the large real estate, labor and business interests involved."[40] Curran agreed to support a billboard law drafted by the Edison Company, a weak measure that focused purely on fire safety, and the City Club agreed to stop pressing for "aesthetic" legislation, which the state courts would surely overturn in any case. In return, the advertisers agreed to the City Club's proposal for an Outdoor Advertising Commission. Its members would be the president of MAS and representatives of the Mural Painters of America, the Architectural League, and the Real Estate Board. The advertisers promised to work with the commission in "an earnest effort to improve conditions around our more important parks, drives and public places." Advertisers agreed that the Outdoor Advertising Commission could comment on "such questions as the copy of advertisements, the artistic make-up of the [billboard] structures, and the matter of location," but all it could do was advise; it was up to the advertising industry whether to pay attention to its criticism. Predictably, the arrangement didn't work. After the first few meetings the admen made clear that they had no intention of bowing to what they now termed "censorship." The art societies realized that they were being taken for a ride, and the commission dissolved in acrimony.

THE MUNICIPAL Art Society tried to limit billboards by banning sky signs (unconstitutional), by controlling their height (which didn't work out), by getting them taxed (which the city wouldn't do), and by shaming advertisers (who proved to be fairly shameless). Now, signs were a fairly minor issue, but they seemed to the Municipal Art Society to be a symptom of a basic flaw at the heart of American politics and economics. Private enterprise reigned unchecked and barely regulated in virtually every sphere of the city's life. One could see it in the subway debate, where the intransigence of railway monopolies doomed the masses to blighted lives in the slums, in the horrific conditions in sweatshops and tenements, and in the stooped shoulders of workers who were paid a pittance for an inhumanly long workday. There was little the state could do about such problems. American law had not yet caught up with the evolution of the American economy. An almost libertarian notion of the individual's property and economic rights still prevailed. When New York State, for instance, tried to limit the workday in bakeries to ten hours, the Supreme Court decided that this was an unconstitutional infringement on the liberty of employers.

In the atmosphere of the times, when the rhetoric of good-government groups stressed a simple conflict of private versus public interests, reformers stumbled into some disastrous decisions. For more than a century New York had possessed a fairly complicated method of delimiting the public streets.[41] There was the building line, which officially marked the boundary between public and private space, but beyond this were two other boundaries: the stoop line, within which a property owner could build a stoop on public land to gain access to his house; and the courtyard line, which marked the area citizens could enclose with a fence, either for an areaway or simply for shrubs and trees. (Even today, on a street from the brownstone era, the marvelous stoops and gardens sit, in fact, on city land. These are the most colorful and vibrant part of the streetscape, but legally speaking, this is a gray area, belonging to the city though used by private parties.)

This system was oddly appropriate: in surrendering use of part of its land, the city in effect created a zone devoted to the adornment of public space. But the legal ambiguity was bound to be troublesome. It was naturally exploited for both good and ill. Much of the architectural richness of the nineteenth- and early twentieth-century architecture in New York depended on the legal ambiguity surrounding the building line. All across the city, bay windows swelled from the flat facades of row houses. So did entrance porches and porticoes. Many a doorway to a Beaux Arts row house or office building was adorned with flanking columns that stood on city land. Reformers, however, were ill-disposed toward the system because in many commercial districts ground-floor shops expanded outward into the street, completely and illegally filling their courtyards. The reformers were disturbed by the sheer messiness of this, by the congestion on sidewalks, and by the fact that the practice had been long overlooked by city officials, whether through apathy or connivance. There were widespread rumors of payoffs to local aldermen and borough presidents to win their indulgence, and the city's Department of Incumbrances, charged with removing illegal encroachments, seemed to do so only when the proper person had not been paid.

The issue lay dormant until 1903, when the New Amsterdam Theater was in construction on West Forty-second Street. The New Amsterdam is New York's sole masterpiece of Art Nouveau architecture. It was designed by Herts & Tallant, a firm whose motto was *"Le beau c'est le vrai,"* but in this case, *le beau* had to consort with rather seedy neighbors. Forty-second Street's row houses had long since been converted to commercial uses and sported a miserable array of signs and illegal projecting shopfronts. Herts & Tallant had to fit the theater entrance onto a lot only twenty feet wide (the auditorium is actually on Forty-first Street) and yet somehow convey something of the public scale and festal character of their building. They came up with a superb frontispiece, a monumental arch resting on bizarre Ionic columns and crowned by the sculpture of George Gray Barnard—Drama enthroned beneath a canopy, with Pierrot and Cupid, a knight and a damsel, in her retinue.

The New Amsterdam's owners, the producers Marc Klaw and Abe Erlanger, had rejected a neighbor's suggestion that they buy his lot and add it to their parcel, and in classic New York fashion the neighbor retaliated by calling in the Building Department. He pointed out that the theater's frontispiece, with its massive, rusticated pedestals, would extend beyond the building line by almost four feet. This was within the courtyard line, and Forty-second Street was already cluttered with illegal shopfronts that projected just as far. If I am right in suspecting that the unnamed neighbor was the partnership of Samuel and Albert McMillan, contractors and real estate speculators, then the complaint was shameless, for their own shop-front was illegal. Yet the Building Department was convinced, somehow, that Klaw and Erlanger must be stopped. "A lot of policemen and some inspectors" showed up at the site to make sure the arch was not built, but at the end of the day they went home, the contractor unveiled a bright carbon lamp, and by the next morning the marble arch was in place.[42] This wasn't a very tactful thing to do. The Building Department was now as angry as it was embarrassed, and Klaw and Erlanger had to go to the Board of Aldermen for special legislation to protect their building.

This set the Municipal Art Society to thinking. All over the city bay windows, porches, frontispieces, colonnades, and doorframes rested on what was technically city property. Shouldn't these be reviewed by the Art Commission? And naturally, wouldn't the Art Commission have to look at a building's entire facade, not just the decorative bits that reached beyond the building line, before granting its approval? The Municipal Art Society suddenly saw a way to impose its own aesthetic stan-dards on private buildings. It demanded that any building that encroached on the building line go before the Art Commission before the Building Department could issue a permit. Strictly interpreted, almost every structure in the city would have been subject to aesthetic review. In Europe this wouldn't have seemed radical. Vienna's building department, for instance, could withhold a construction permit on aesthetic grounds, and this power was the bane of a number of celebrated modernist architects.[43] America, however, wasn't ready for this sort of regimenta-tion of private property. Had MAS succeeded in winning such power for the Art Commission, the commission's days would surely have been numbered.

The issue of encroachments died down, only to be revived in 1906 when Mayor McClellan decided to widen Fifth Avenue from Washington Square to Forty-second Street. The sidewalks were cut back to allow two new lanes of traffic, and the stoops and areaways were removed to recover some room for pedestrians. (Widening the avenues was something the Municipal Art Society had advocated for years, and it was endorsed by the Improvement Commission. MAS had hoped, however, that the mayor would use Charles Lamb's system of "indented curbs" for parked vehicles. This would have kept the crosswalks at their old length, a more comfortable distance for pedestrians.) At first the Bureau of Highways told local property owners that, "as the object of widening the highway was to beautify it as well as make it more commodious," projections of up to two and a half feet would be tolerated. This was later switched to "a few inches."[44] Even the two-and-a-half-foot limit would mean, however, the mutilation of the Knickerbocker Trust Build-ing on Fifth Avenue and Thirty-fourth Street, designed by Stanford White for none other than Charles Barney, former president of the Municipal Art Society. Only four stories tall, it was meant to serve as the base of a thirteen-story tower that was never built—Knickerbocker went bankrupt in the Panic of 1907—but it was one of White's greatest masterpieces. With a colossal Corinthian order framing a curtain wall of bronze and glass, the Knickerbocker Trust set the pattern for innumerable colonnaded bank branches all around the country. So common did this sort of bank become that the style had ramifications on other building types as well: it killed off the brief fad for Classical synagogues, for instance, because whenever the public saw a colonnade it thought, not of temples, but of moneychangers.

White's design had pilasters on the side street and four magnificent engaged columns on Fifth Avenue. White regarded this as a portico, but the city viewed these columns, nearly six feet in diameter, as encroachments. Like most of the encroachments and gardens on Fifth Avenue, they'd been authorized by a special permit granted by the Board of Aldermen, but the city decided to make a test case of the building and took Knickerbocker to court. For White, like Herts & Tallant before him, it must have seemed idiotic to suggest that he'd acted against the public interest. He hadn't usurped city land for habitable space, as shopowners did, but to adorn the streetscape. Those columns were themselves an example of municipal art, erected at great expense by a private client who received no appreciable return. But White's argument was to no avail. In 1907 the court ruled that the aldermen had no right to grant these special permits. White's columns, and all other encroachments anywhere in the city, were declared a public nuisance. The city took pity on the Knickerbocker Trust, however, perhaps to avoid an appeal or a suit for damages. Since "to tear out the front portico would indeed seriously mar the front of the structure and would, moreover, mean the loss of a great deal of money," the columns were allowed to stay, and only the building's steps were removed.[45] The rest of the avenue was not so lucky. The stoops all disappeared, and the clubs all lost their gardens. Martin's Restaurant and the Waldorf-Astoria Hotel bade farewell to their sidewalk cafés, and the churches were especially hard hit: the Marble Collegiate Church, at Twenty-ninth Street, was stripped of an especially beautiful garden, and the Church of Heavenly Rest, at Forty-sixth Street, was forced to remodel its entire facade.

Three years later it was Forty-second Street's turn to be widened, and this was the curious and unintended consequence of an old MAS project. In 1902 the Municipal Art Society adopted as its own a scheme by Carrère & Hastings for a grade separation bridge at Fifth Avenue and Forty-second Street, where the architects were building the New York Public Library. Forty-second Street, or the center lanes of it, would have been depressed below grade while Fifth Avenue was carried across this valley on a bridge. This project wasn't as bizarre as it seems today. Until 1909, when the New York Central Railroad built bridges over its train yards as part of its reconstruction of Grand Central Terminal, the train tracks interrupted every cross street from Forty-second to Fifty-sixth. Park Avenue was also interrupted (the viaduct at Forty-second Street didn't open until 1916). Crosstown traffic was funneled onto Forty-second Street, while uptown traffic spilled over to Fifth Avenue, and the intersection of the two was the most congested in the entire city; in fact, a 1916 traffic study proclaimed it the most crowded in the world.[46] Carrère & Hastings's bridge was meant to ease traffic flow and to funnel trucks and wagons away from Fifth Avenue. The Board of Aldermen rejected the bridge scheme when

Borough President Jacob Cantor proposed it in 1902, but it found its way nonetheless into the Improvement Commission reports of 1904 and 1907. In 1908, when the library was three-quarters finished, Carrère & Hastings revived the project and added a new decorative touch: the bridge would now boast statues of Samuel Tilden and Grover Cleveland. It had a new champion, too, in Mayor McClellan, who introduced traffic regulations in 1906 and imagined the scheme as a prototype for busy intersections all over the city.[47]

Jacob Cantor appeared in City Hall to endorse the project, but he was almost alone in doing so. According to the Forty-second Street Association, not a single local property owner wanted to see the bridge built. The association's members did not want traffic to speed past their shopfronts. "The people along Fifth Avenue like the congestion," testified Morgan O'Brien. "They ride out to meet their friends in much the same way that they go to the opera; not so much to hear the music, but to be a part of the grand spectacle."[48] The Forty-second Street Association pointed out that a traffic cop or two could just as effectively force trucks off Fifth Avenue, that conditions would ease within a year, when the New York Central extended the cross streets over its tracks, and that the tunnel would make it impossible to build a subway under Fifth Avenue (not true). They threatened to sue the city for damages. But the thrust of their campaign was to tarnish the project with its own aestheticism, and in choosing this line of attack, the association made clear the depth of a growing backlash against the City Beautiful movement. "We question the good faith of this movement . . . to do away with the congestion," its statement read. "The purpose of building this bridge is to enable the city to accept as a gift two statues, one of Tilden and one of Cleveland, which statues must necessarily be placed on some pedestal, and as the architects of the Public Library could think of no other scheme or plan to make use of said statues other than to build such a bridge, they have come forward, and in fact use the statues as a bait to have the matter opened again, and have tried to make it appear as if they want to better conditions at Fifth Avenue and Forty-second Street, when, as a matter of fact, their purposes are simply to set off the library."[49] The Citizens East Side Improvement Association seconded this statement and reported that "not one property holder or business man" near Fifth and Forty-second was in favor of the proposal.[50] William Salomon, owner of the Bristol Building on the northeast corner, managed to get an injunction preventing the Board of Estimate from even considering the issue, on the dubious grounds that "the debt limit might be exceeded."[51]

The Forty-second Street Association proposed its own plan. Its members owned 90 percent of the stoops, porticoes, areaways, and decorative flourishes that stood on the sidewalk of Forty-second Street, and they offered to remove these so the street could be widened. They demanded that the city at least try this as an experiment before proceeding with the bridge.[52] McClellan had no choice but to accept, and within the year Forty-second Street was stripped of its projecting shopfronts, but also of much of its architectural richness. Balustrades, areaways, and stoops were uprooted; doorframes were shorn away; the Knickerbocker Hotel surrendered its lovely colonnaded porch; and the New Amsterdam Theater finally lost its magnificent frontispiece. Forty-second Street became a grimmer place as a result, not just because of the newly wide flood of traffic but because the street wall lost some degree of the sculptural plasticity, the human scale, and the play of light and shadow that had made it a pleasant environment for the pedestrian. As for traffic, the street was soon more congested than it had ever been. In the 1920s the Police Department's Bureau of Public Safety put up signs at Fifth Avenue and Forty-second Street with a gruesome image of death shaking his bony finger at pedestrians. "You are mine, jaywalkers," read the text. "I will get you taking chances."[53]

Since stripping buildings of encroachments was messy, expensive, unpleasant, and time-consuming, it seemed to Nelson Lewis that a reform of the building code was required. Lewis was the chief engineer of the Board of Estimate and a distinguished public servant; he had been appointed by Seth Low and then retained by George McClellan, who had his position converted to civil service so as to free him from political pressure. In 1909 Lewis persuaded the Board of Estimate to pass a resolution requiring all buildings to keep within the building line. Stoop line privileges were abolished in all future construction, and all projections over the building line were banned unless they were more than ten feet above street level. Cornices, in other words, were still acceptable. Lewis described this as "merely an enforcement of the law and a reform of serious abuses in encroachments on city property, which . . . have acquired a certain amount of customary sanction." Few people disputed that encroachments in business districts needed to be eliminated, or that the avenues, so few in number, needed to be widened even at the expense of their architectural character. But Lewis's new regulation applied everywhere, and he never considered its architectural ramifications. Albert Bard revived the Municipal Art Society's demand that the city grant the Art Commission jurisdiction over encroachments, but when no one paid any attention, MAS fell silent and at least tacitly approved of Lewis's new regulation. The society simply shrugged off the warnings of William Rouse, an architect who specialized in apartment buildings (his partner, Lafayette Goldstone, was the father of Harmon Goldstone, who went on to become one of MAS's most celebrated presidents). Rouse predicted that the rule "will make impossible any architectural treatment of the lower part of our buildings. . . . All ornamental porches will have to be abolished, and even if a few architects have abused the privileges granted them by the city in the past, this seems a very drastic measure."[54]

Lewis's regulations were apparently lost in the debate over a new building code, but in 1910 Cyrus Miller, the Fusion Party's new borough president of the Bronx, ordered his superintendent of buildings to comply with them, and the other borough presidents followed suit.[55] The most avid was George McAneny, a Municipalian and the new borough president of Manhattan, who boasted that "No architect hereafter will plan a building that contemplates the taking of one foot of city property."[56] McAneny saw to it that Fourteenth, Twenty-third, and Thirty-fourth streets were the next to lose their encroachments. Lafayette Street followed, and the Astor Library, now home to the Public Theater, lost its gracious steps and terrace.[57] By 1912 New Yorkers had spent $9 million to remove their stoops and areaways; forty-two streets had been affected, although only eight were actually widened.[58]

It was more than porches that disappeared. Classical architecture insists that a building rest on a substantial base, and since this base must seem to support the upper floors of a building, it normally projects slightly beyond the building line. The new building regulations made this difficult to achieve in New York, and the campaign to defend the public streets has actually impoverished them ever since. One can still see Lewis's hand in the wan aspect of so many Classical facades built in the 1910s and 1920s, where the ornament was flattened against the wall, causing shadows to disappear and the sculptural quality of buildings to vanish into thin air. In the hands of good architects this led to a newfound delicacy of scale and detail—there was a Regency revival in New York—but more often the effect resembled too little butter spread over too much bread. Art Deco architects of the 1920s learned to take advantage of this enforced flatness, but even so, Art Deco buildings are usually weakest at the base. They slam straight into the ground, where earlier buildings had managed to create a richer effect at the pedestrians' eye level. Even today, anyone complaining of the bald, impoverished effect of so much contemporary architecture should bear in mind the fact that architects are forced to work in absurdly low relief.

SKYSCRAPERS AND SLUMS

IF ONE WERE going to credit—or blame—a single individual for the New York skyscraper, it might well be the architect George B. Post. In 1867, more than a quarter century before he participated in founding the Municipal Art Society, Post's skills as an engineer brought him to the attention of Gilman & Kendall, architects of the new Equitable Life Assurance Building at 120 Broadway. Like most buildings of its day, Equitable was only five stories tall, but these were very tall stories, and at 130 feet the building was more than twice the height of a typical commercial building. It was an architectural stunt, a standard office building in-flated in every dimension as a way of flaunting the corporation's wealth. (In this it resembled Philip Johnson's AT&T Building.) It might have remained a freak except for one thing: Post had included a passenger elevator in his plans—the first in a New York office building.[1]

Until now the height of buildings had been limited by the endurance of "the unassisted human leg," as critic Montgomery Schuyler put it.[2] New York was a city of 50- or 60-foot buildings, its skyline a fairly even plane of rooftops broken only by church spires. The pinnacles of Trinity Church and Saint Paul's Chapel offered proof that it was possible to build high into the sky for the love of God, but the mundane world offered few incentives to do so. No one was willing to pay much rent for the privilege of arriving at his doorstep with rubbery legs and wheezing lungs, and there was a kind of economic stratification within buildings. With each flight of steps a tenant climbed, his rent sank, and the rooftop garret reigned as a symbol of, at best, a bohemian existence. Equitable changed all this. Thanks to the elevator, its upper floors were able to command high rents, and suddenly it made economic sense to pile more and more stories atop each square foot of ground. Soon property values would spiral upward, height would become an index of power, and the garret would give way to the penthouse.

In 1872 Post designed the Western Union Building, eleven stories and 230 feet tall, at Broadway and Dey Street. In 1875 his mentor, Richard Morris Hunt, finished the New York Tribune Building on Park Row. It was 260 feet tall. These two buildings pushed masonry construction about as far as it could go: at ground level, their walls were as thick as those of a fortress, and they devoured interior space. As long as this was the case, skyscrapers made sense only on fairly large sites, but in 1881 Post experimented with a different system in the Produce Exchange at Bowling Green. It was a shell of massive masonry with an iron skeleton inside. In 1889 the architect Bradford Gilbert took the next step. For the Tower Building, at 50 Broadway, Gilbert imported the Chicago method of skyscraper construction: a steel skeleton actually supported the thin exterior walls, and Gilbert was able to stack eleven floors on a lot less than 22 feet wide. When people saw this strange beast rising from the ground they thought that Gilbert was deranged, and when a gale struck, crowds gathered nearby, waiting merrily for the building to topple in the wind. Instead they saw Gilbert climb a shaky scaffold to the very top of the tower. The building was as solid as a rock and, unlike Ibsen's Master Builder, Gilbert didn't fall. He produced a flag. The crowd cheered.

The steel skeleton meant that even small lots could support tall buildings, that scraping the sky would no longer be the prerogative of just a few corporate monuments, but the ambition of every builder. All that was needed was a little land, a lot of money, and tenants. Brokers would spring up to provide the first two; the supply of fresh tenants would always be a much more iffy proposition. In the meantime the skyline enjoyed yet another spurt of growth. In 1890 Post used a steel skeleton for the Pulitzer Building on Park Row and raised a gilded dome twenty-six floors above City Hall Park. For the first time the spire of Trinity Church had been overtopped.

BY AND LARGE these early skyscrapers were remarkably ugly. Most were built on deep, narrow lots. A lot of confused architectural rhetoric was pasted to their facades, but their sides were unadorned, and these scabrous sheets of raw brick, pockmarked with windows, towered above the low buildings of old New York. Such skyscrapers seemed to embody everything that the art societies found embarrassing about America. The thin veneer of culture on their facades could barely hope to conceal the grasping, greedy reality revealed in the "cheap, mean brickwork" of the party walls, and to architect Harvey Wiley Corbett the contrast seemed a "mirror of our national character," a symbol "of our naive bluff, our desire at all costs to put up a bold front."[3] And if these buildings were disappointing individually, their impact on the cityscape was far more alarming. The skyline became jagged, serrated, as ten- and soon twenty-story buildings sprang up among older structures of five floors. The new towers enjoyed sunlight, but only at the expense of their neighbors and the surrounding streets. Broadway was falling into deep shadow, and the city seemed, as it never had before, to be nothing more than an anarchic collection of real estate speculations.

Post must have been ill at ease at what he'd wrought. As president of the Architectural League, he organized a debate in 1894 on whether to seek a law limiting building heights. He invited two architects from Chicago, that other skyscraper city: Dankmar Adler, who was Louis Sullivan's partner, and Daniel Burnham, the architectural coordinator of the Chicago fair and, in seven years' time, designer of New York's Flatiron Building on Madison Square. The Architectural League's members were curiously torn. Upset by the impact of tall buildings on narrow streets, they generally endorsed the notion that there should be height limits. They knew that European cities regulated height, and they admired the results, yet they were unwilling to suggest similar legislation for their hometown. Instead they assured one another that the market would eventually regulate itself: that the inconvenience of congested streets, the impact of tall buildings on the urban environment, and certain technical difficulties with wind bracing and elevator speeds would somehow conspire to enforce a rational height limit without any government interference at all. The heartiest applause of the evening was reserved for a comment by Adler: "The less building legislation we have the better."[4] Considering the state of the building arts in 1894, it was a disgraceful remark.

Charles Lamb was at that meeting, and he had more faith than his colleagues in America's ability to solve technical problems. That was, after all, one of our great national talents. In 1898, Lamb wrote an article for *Municipal Affairs*, arguing that New York had to face the fact that the skyscraper was becoming the standard form of development in lower Manhattan and that architects had better consider what this would do to the city.[5] Streets laid out when New York was a mere village couldn't carry the crowds that thronged to work in skyscrapers. Nor had the city taken into account the environmental cost to be paid when entire neighborhoods were built to a height of twenty stories. Bigger buildings were yet to come, Lamb pointed out. Practice would teach engineers how to stretch buildings to still un-imagined heights, and as they did, another factor would come into play: construction sites would get bigger. The taller the building, the more elevators one had to build, until at some point they would take up so much space that it wasn't worth going any higher. Eventually, Lamb knew, builders would take care to assemble huge lots in order to mine every ounce of profit out of the land. Pushed to its logical extreme, this could only mean that someday developers would aim to control and develop entire blocks of the city.

Lamb liked skyscrapers. They were more efficient than the old buildings, safer and better built, and while they threw the streets and neighboring buildings into shadow, skyscrapers offered their occupants more light and air than the ground-hugging structures of gaslight New York. The problem was to harness the sky-scrapers, to find a way to keep tall buildings from suffocating one another. In 1899, Lamb published his project for a new City Hall on a two-block site north of the present building. It would be 750 feet tall—twice the height of any building then standing in New York—and it appalled Lamb's friends in the National Sculpture Society.[6] It *was* ugly, and in this one respect it was typical of its time. (The columnar model of skyscraper design, in which an architect provides the building with a decorative base and cap but leaves the many-storied shaft in between simple and undecorated, was not yet established in New York. Montgomery Schuyler called it the Sophoclean model, in that a skyscraper, like a good tragedy, should have a beginning, a middle, and an end.) Lamb had fallen into the same trap as most of his contemporaries, trying to humanize the skyscraper's unprecedented bulk by slathering it with small-scale ornament. The effect was to make the building look cancerous—a picture of uncontrolled cell growth. Even so, it was a breathtaking project and one of the first serious studies of what the skyscraper meant to urban design. Lamb's tower would vault over Reade Street, transforming it into a covered arcade like the Galleria in Milan; its vast lobbies would serve as extensions of the street system—quasi-public passages for the ambling pedestrian, shortcuts for the harried commuter. And though the building was immensely tall, the sun would still shine on its neighbors, for Lamb had shaped his skyscraper like an enormous stepped pyramid.

Louis Sullivan had drawn a "setback skyscraper city" in 1891,[7] but Lamb always claimed that his own inspiration was French. Paris enforced a strict height limit, but below this point its zoning code relied on the principle of an "angle of light"—an invisible, imaginary plane that tilted upward from the center of the street, and which no building was allowed to interrupt. In practice this meant that a building's cornice line, the angle of its mansard roof, and the crest of that roof were all set by law. It made for sunny streets, but just as compelling was the fact that these streets were so harmonious, for this sort of urban design began by defining the street as a regular, ordered space—an outdoor room—whose walls happened to be filled in over time by individual builders and architects. Lamb took the idea of an angle of light, but he discarded both the mansard roof and the ultimate height limit. Instead, angles of light would rise into the sky above each city block until they collided with one another. Each block would become a stepped pyramid.

Few of the people who recoiled from Lamb's project realized just how prophetic it was of the scale of the twentieth-century city. For the moment they dismissed it as an impossibility. Elevator cables couldn't stretch so far yet; sky lobbies were unthought of; engineers had no experience in constructing the sort of massive transfer trusses needed to prop a tower above a street; and the tallest buildings in the city were still just 300 feet high. Within a decade, however, Ernest Flagg's Singer Tower rose 612 feet above Broadway, and Napoleon Le Brun was building Metropolitan Life's 700-foot campanile on Madison Square. In 1907 McKim, Mead & White designed the Municipal Building, and one can detect in it the ghost of Lamb's City Hall project: the building hovers above a great open-air arcade and bridges Chambers Street. Today the technology is almost commonplace: the Citicorp tower struts on elephantine legs, a Times Square hotel is cantilevered over a landmark theater, and until recently the AT&T Building lifted its granite skirt above a public plaza. In 1908, looking back on his design, Lamb mused: "I wanted a building so tall that it represented the City of New York, not a Life Insurance Building, or a Sewing Machine Company.... It was ten years ago, and it was ridiculed."[8]

For years, Lamb's idea of setback towers lay dormant, waiting for the scale and technology of skyscrapers to catch up with his imagination. The skyscraper was increasingly accepted as something inevitable, a logical product of the fantastically high land values in the business district. Many blamed the long, narrow shape of Manhattan Island, claiming that there was no room for business to expand except up into the sky. But of course it was the skyscrapers themselves that so inflated the price of land. A couple of blocks east or west of the financial district sat "hundreds of properties that would bring no more in the open market today than they would have brought a hundred years ago."[9]

Architects concentrated on solving the skyscraper's aesthetic problems. Some, like Cass Gilbert, turned to Gothic to stress the soaring vertical lines of a tall building; others, like MAS's Bruce Price, stressed the need to treat towers in the round. The new, more lovely Beaux Arts skyscrapers assuaged a certain amount of public concern. New York began to take on a fairy-tale aspect, with temples and castles floating in the sky. In the meantime lower Broadway and Wall Street had become dark canyons, and the architectural community sometimes voiced regret at this, but there was no concerted movement to do anything about it. Few people worried about the quality of life in commercial districts: though sun and air and human scale were treasured where people lived, they seemed expendable where people worked. No law existed to keep skyscrapers penned up in the financial district, however, and soon enough it occurred to developers that a tower in a walk-up district, where land was still relatively cheap, might be very profitable. Ten-story apartment buildings had appeared as early as the 1880s, and skyscraper hotels arrived in the 1890s. When the Astors finished the Waldorf-Astoria in 1897, it rose sixteen stories at Fifth Avenue and Thirty-fourth Street. Still, it aroused no complaints from MAS, perhaps because it was designed by a Municipalian, Henry Hardenbergh, and its public rooms glowed with the murals of Edwin Blashfield, Kenyon Cox, and H. Siddons Mowbray. For the moment, the Astors seemed like modern Medici, but when John Jacob Astor built the St. Regis Hotel on Fifth Avenue and Fifty-fifth Street, the price seemed too high. Its eighteen stories towered above the avenue's mansions and churches, and its ugly rear wall ruined the vista north from Vanderbilt Row.

It dawned on the Municipal Art Society that skyscrapers threatened the scale and character of the most beautiful neighborhoods in New York, and in 1903 Charles Lamb focused his ire on Daniel Burnham's new Flatiron Building: "It stands there as an example of the greed of the corporation controlling it and owning it. Architecturally, it is unfit to be in the center of the city."[10] It was twice the height of the newest buildings on Broadway and three times as tall as the theaters and hotels on Madison Square, but Lamb focused on Flatiron because of its owner and builder. Flatiron was the headquarters of the Fuller Company, a Chicago contracting firm that had just entered the New York market. It had a reputation for ruthlessness—it was Fuller, for instance, that put up the New Amsterdam Theater's facade in the dead of night—and for shady stock manipulations, while *McClure's Magazine*, home of the muckrakers, explored its ties to the corrupt union boss Sam Parks.[11] *McClure's* charged that Fuller once bribed Parks to call a strike against its competitors, and that sometimes, if the company fell behind schedule and faced a penalty clause, it even arranged for its own workmen to walk off the job. What was most frightening about Fuller, however, was that it was a subsidiary of the United States Realty Company. As steel and the elevator revolutionized building, U.S. Realty was meant to transform the real estate business. It marked the first application of "the trust idea" to building. Its board included Henry Morgenthau, John "Betcha Million" Gates, Charles Schwab, James Stillman, Cornelius Vanderbilt, and former Tammany mayor Hugh Grant, and the idea behind the company was to funnel huge amounts of Wall Street capital into real estate speculation. The builder Paul Starrett explained that the firm specialized in "neglected opportunities": "If a man owned a piece of metropolitan real estate and had no money [U.S. Realty] would finance a building for him and take a mortgage on it. If a man had money and no land [the company] would show him how he might acquire a valuable corner and erect a profitable skyscraper."[12] To many, it seemed that speculation on such a massive scale threatened to divorce building from any actual human need, and that it opened the floodgates to massive overdevelopment.

WHEN CHARLES LAMB was elected president of MAS in 1906 the society announced that it would draw up "a bill to be presented at Albany with reference to tall buildings, *different heights to be established in different quarters of the city*, following somewhat the law of Paris."[13] But the scene of action soon shifted back to New York City, to the unexpected, unlikely forum of the Building Code Revision Commission. New York's building code had been written well before the days of steel frame or concrete construction, and it bore faint relation to how things were actually built in the early 1900s. The code still required, for example, that masonry walls thicken at the bottom—fine in the old days, when walls bore the weight of a building, but ludicrous in an age of skyscrapers, when the steel frame did all the work and a wall's sole function was to keep out the weather. Such standard techniques still required the special approval of the superintendent of buildings, and this didn't come cheap. In 1903 Lincoln Steffens estimated that Tammany Hall collected a "banker's commission" of one percent of the construction cost of all plans that passed through the Department of Buildings—a hefty sum, since in that year alone there was 100 million dollars' worth of construction in New York.[14] The *Times* gave more details of this "old and sordid story":

> The system has been worked in the familiar way. As a rule the department employees have been simply reticent and obstinate in their technical requirements, or have "hung up" applications and plans without explanation. When the parties interested became impatient and were unable to get any satisfaction from the office, a "mutual friend," not ostensibly connected with the department, has called and offered his services as mediator, promising to secure what

was wanted for a price as much more than it was worth as would leave a margin for shrinkage if the first demand was refused. This system of blackmail has been undiscriminating and merciless.[15]

People had talked of revising the building code since at least 1895. It was one of the many things Candace Wheeler's Board of Municipal Art was supposed to do. The Tenement Law of 1901 updated the building code for low-cost housing—banning wooden stairwells, for instance—and a separate agency was created to enforce this New Law, since the Building Department couldn't be trusted, but commercial buildings and workplaces were untouched by this. A commission was finally appointed in 1907. Tammany must have been asleep, as it was very unhappy with the commission's makeup.[16] The Municipal Art Society had a friend on the commission—Electus Litchfield, architect of the City Club's headquarters and a future president of MAS—and its chairman was a new MAS board member, Charles Israels. Israels was a well-known authority on the design of middle-class apartments. He'd designed the facade of the Hall of Records for John R. Thomas and now had a thriving, though not very prestigious, practice with Julius Harder.[17] Israels repeatedly asked his colleagues at the Municipal Art Society if they had any suggestions for the new building code, but the board ignored him, failing to see how purely technical issues of construction fell within the scope of MAS's activities. (It did help Israels fight off Tammany's attempt to take control of the commission by adding two plumbers, the five borough presidents, and the fire chief.[18]) Only when a draft of the new code was published did MAS finally understand that Israels was proposing to limit building heights.

Israels, however, was thinking about fire protection, not urban design. Three years earlier, in 1904, flames had consumed the central business district of Baltimore; in 1906 fire swept across San Francisco in the earthquake's wake. In both cases firemen were unable to reach the flames in tall buildings, and the public learned that the vaunted "fireproof" construction of skyscrapers simply meant they wouldn't fall down in a fire, not that they wouldn't burn. Insurance companies and underwriters totted up in their minds the cost of a conflagration in Manhattan's canyons; they demanded that something be done, and their calls were echoed from the opposite end of the economic spectrum, where labor leaders decried the appallingly unsafe conditions in the city's sweatshops, many of which were housed in converted Old Law tenements. The 1901 Tenement House Law already limited tenements to six stories; Israels wanted to set a sliding scale for other building types. Factories and mercantile buildings would be kept to 100 feet, or 150 if they were "fireproof" and equipped with sprinkler systems. There was a general height limit of 200 feet for first-class office buildings, but another clause ensured that it would still be possible to build soaring towers like the Singer Building. The catch was that the tower's square footage would be limited to 17.4 times the area of the lot. This sort of formula is now known as the floor area ratio, or FAR; it was apparently introduced here by Electus Litchfield. In most circumstances it would mean a seventeen-story building covering the entire lot, but if the site was so large that light courts were needed, one could add the equivalent volume to the top of the structure, and anyone determined to build an architectural monument—whether to himself, his corporation, or his architect—could build a thirty-four-story tower on half the site or a sixty-eight-story pinnacle on a quarter of the lot, and so on.

Only a few behemoths in the financial district exceeded these proposed height limits: the new Trust Company of America Building at 37–39 Wall Street, 321 feet tall and covering more than 80 percent of its lot, would have lost a third of its floor area if built according to Israels's specifications. In other areas of the city the code would have been extraordinarily permissive. "Half-baked and impracticable," one realtor called it, but he was objecting to the idea of *any* height limits.[19] From Charles Lamb's point of view, Israels's system had several disadvantages. Its sliding scale of height limits was based on a building's use, not its place in the city. An office building could rise to 200 feet no matter where it stood—on a broad avenue or a narrow side street, in the teeming financial district or on the Upper West Side. Lamb wanted an approach that would vary by neighborhood, where skyscrapers could rise in business districts, but not in residential or retail areas, and he wanted orderly streetscapes within each district, not 200-foot office buildings jostling 100-foot factories. The Municipal Art Society at last sent Israels its scheme for setback zoning, but it was rather late in the day, and Lamb's ideas were brushed aside.[20]

As it turned out, Israels's building code met a grisly fate. He presented it to the lame-duck Board of Aldermen in December 1907, but the *Times* reported that "the Tammany plan, as outlined in gossip heard yesterday, is to postpone action on the matter until after January 1. Then there will be in the Board of Aldermen a much stronger Tammany majority than at present, making it possible to reject definitely and finally the revised code now under consideration and to appoint a new commission which will frame a new set of building regulations more in harmony with the Tammany idea of what such regulations should be."[21] Eventually Tammany would have objected to Israels's height limits, but for the moment it had more immediate concerns. It disliked, for instance, the section of the code dealing with theaters. Many of the vaudeville houses near Union Square were owned by "Big Tim" Sullivan, a man as prominent in the gambling and prostitution rackets as he was in the councils of Tammany Hall,* and he was appalled by what Israels proposed—"not," the *Times* wrote, "because the new regulations afford less protection against fire, but because they would make the building of theaters more attractive financially, thus threatening some competition for the group of old playhouses."[22] Even worse, in Tammany's mind, was the fact that the new code was so detailed and specific that it left the superintendent of buildings few chances to

---

* He should also be remembered for one wonderful thing: the Sullivan Law, New York's first gun control measure, which barred people from carrying firearms without a license. His motives, however, may not have been humanitarian. According to M. R. Werner, a foe of gun control, Sullivan simply wanted to keep his own enforcers in line. For an account of Sullivan's career, see M. R. Werner, Tammany Hall (Garden City, N.Y.: Doubleday, Doran, 1928), 438–40, 498–510.

exercise his "discretion"—and few opportunities to withhold his stamp of approval until money changed hands. Of course new materials would be invented, and novel construction techniques would still require the superintendent's attention, but whenever he "interpreted" the code he would now have to publish all the pertinent facts in the City Record, and these decisions could be cited as precedents in future cases.[23] The superintendent's actions would finally be exposed to the clear light of day; he might be able to take a bribe the first time some innovation crossed his desk, but not the second.

Tammany had its way. In January 1908 Israels and his colleagues were discharged, their work was discarded, and a new commission was appointed to draft another code by the coming fall. Poor Israels wasn't even paid his fee. The only surprising thing was that he had gotten so far. MAS was relieved that he'd failed, but it noticed that at least some bankers and insurers had listened calmly to the suggestion that the city needed to control building heights. They weren't necessarily convinced of Israels's wisdom, but they didn't erupt in outrage or sputter about sacred property rights. They were receptive so long as the issue was framed in terms of public safety or property values and not of aesthetics. The Municipal Art Society saw an opening in this, a sign that even conservative financial interests could be persuaded that laissez-faire was a dangerous ideology for building cities. The society needed a way to demonstrate that its own more subtle approach to shaping the skyscraper was more than a purely aesthetic measure. And so in 1908 MAS abandoned its old buzzword, "embellishment," and took on a new one: "congestion."

AESTHETICISM WAS in ill repute at the moment. In January 1907 the Improvement Commission had released its final report, a document so disappointing that it set the planning movement back half a dozen years. Back in 1902, when the Municipal Art Society created the commission, it had hoped for an immense development scheme that would solve the city's transit and freight problems and provide amenities for the working class. Beauty would have been merely a byproduct of such a plan. But MAS had lost control of the commission, and the 1907 report was so exclusively focused on the pretty aspects of a new New York that the entire planning movement was effectively discredited. As the activist Benjamin Marsh wrote, "The grouping of public buildings, and the installation of speedways, parks and drives, which affect only moderately the daily lives of the city toilers, are important, but vastly more so is the securing of decent home conditions for the countless thousands who otherwise can but occasionally escape from their squalid, confining surroundings to view the architectural perfection and to experience the aesthetic delights of the remote improvements."[24]

In the Improvement Commission's wake, the very names of the City Beautiful and Municipal Art movements seemed to label them as useless luxuries, and they were disparaged by some of the most dedicated citizen activists in the city. Through the McClellan years, Municipalians found themselves sparring with social workers and public health advocates for a share of the city's scant resources. In 1905 Frederick Lamb debated Homer Folks at Cooper Union. Seth Low's commissioner of public charities, Folks had a long history of activism in behalf of neglected children and the insane.[25] At Cooper Union, he pleaded for more hospitals and ambulances; Lamb demanded art and city planning and called on the municipal government to create a network of craft schools that would offer students a future more rewarding than a place on the assembly line. "I don't want to criticize Mr. Homer Folks," Lamb told the crowd, "but I ask: what are you going to do with your son between the time he leaves school and the time he enters a hospital or a poorhouse? If we would pay more attention to giving opportunities to men and women there wouldn't be so much need for the hospitals and the ambulance and the poorhouse."

Lamb's audience was visibly unconvinced, and, as the *Times* reported, his self-control slipped: " 'Art is a joke in your eyes!' he exclaimed. 'It is a joke in the eyes of some of the city officials.' Here several persons in the audience burst into laughter. 'And by your applause and laughter,' continued Mr. Lamb, 'you only prove what I say—that it is all a huge joke, and the real significance of it is not apparent to you. Why, I would not give my knowledge of art, limited as it is, for all the wealth of the wealthiest men in America. I can get more pleasure out of a ten-cent print than Mr. Morgan can out of all his hundred-and-twenty-thousand-dollar paintings.' "[26]

No doubt most New Yorkers would have chosen a little wealth over art, and in 1908 the superintendent of schools even called for "baths before books," arguing that public baths were more important "from a moral and hygienic point of view" than the Carnegie Libraries.[27] That same year Charles Lamb was found arguing with Dr. Thomas Darlington, McClellan's health commissioner. Darlington declared that medical science had progressed to the point that, if only he had the money, he could cut the city's death rate in half. "The City Beautiful was needed," he said, "but . . . the city healthful should come first."[28] Lamb insisted that the two were one and the same, and he wasn't being cavalier. Folks and Darlington wanted to save the slum dwellers by treating their illnesses; the Lambs wanted to save the poor by getting them out of the slum and away from its infectious diseases. The City Beautiful, they insisted, was a kind of preventive medicine.

By 1907 some social workers and activists had come around to the Lambs' point of view. They'd realized that the sheer number and concentration of people on the Lower East Side made it almost impossible to create any significant improvements in their lives. The small parks movement had cost millions of dollars, and the metropolitan parks in the Bronx cost millions more, but as Municipalian Harold Caparn pointed out, this was still just a drop in the bucket. (Caparn, a landscape architect in great demand on Long Island's Gold Coast, chaired MAS's Playgrounds Committee.) There were still more than 460 New Yorkers for each acre of park in the city, and effectively the situation was much, much worse. Below Fourteenth Street lived a population equal to that of Buffalo and Pittsburgh combined: there were 11,000 people per acre of park in that neighborhood. The problem, Caparn concluded, was that "there is no city ordinance forbidding more than a certain number of people living in a certain space."[29]

In 1908 the whole raison d'être of the planning movement was recast. The new attitude was summed up in 1910 by John G. Agar, MAS's president at the time. Agar was a lawyer, a former U.S. district attorney, and a fiery political reformer. Speaking to the Republican Club, Agar "said that he himself was not an artist, but had been merely selected to keep together certain contending spirits, as artists do not do good team work under their own auspices. He said the object of municipal art was the promotion of the useful in terms of the beautiful." Agar's remarks were "somewhat different from what the members had expected, [but] were received with marked approval." They must indeed have been surprised to hear MAS's president argue that "improvement of the dwellings of the poor should be considered before the erection of monuments and statues and fine public buildings."[30] Agar pointed out as a model, not Haussmann's Paris, but the municipalities of Germany, whose improvements focused on "better housing for the people. 'It can't be done,' said he, 'under the limited powers of our governments. But we've got to do it somehow, and that's where good citizenship comes in.' "[31]

The idea wasn't Agar's or Caparn's or the Municipal Art Society's. It stemmed from the Committee on Congestion of Population, a group formed late in 1907 by Florence Kelley, a well-known social worker and secretary of the National Consumers' League (which used a carrot-and-stick approach to improve working conditions in the city, threatening bad factories with a consumer boycott and boosting good ones with an endorsement). Kelley wanted to focus the city's attention on the human misery and disease caused by overcrowding in the tenements. She was joined by Mary Simkovitch of Greenwich House; Lillian Wald, of the Nurses' Settlement; Herman Bumpus of the Museum of Natural History; and the Reverend Gaylord White of Union Theological Seminary and the Union Settlement. The dominant figure, however, was Benjamin Marsh, the Congestion Committee's executive secretary. He'd been recruited from the Pennsylvania Society to Protect Children from Cruelty, but he was an economist by training, a Fabian Socialist, and an ardent advocate of Henry George's single tax.* Marsh prepared for his new job by going to London for the International Housing Congress of 1907, and there he was deeply impressed by the IHC's conclusion that the solution to the housing problem lay not in the city center (the focus of MAS's interest), but in the open fields on the fringes of the city.

From 1908 to 1910, MAS and the Congestion Committee worked together in a kind of loose partnership. This marriage was arranged by Charles Israels. Israels was connected to the social work movement through his work at the Educational

---

* George, a candidate for mayor in 1897, died just before the election, to the relief of the city's moneyed class. His single tax was to be a high tax on land. On the one hand it was meant to capture the unearned income of rising land values; on the other, to solve the housing crisis by making it too expensive for people to simply sit on undeveloped property.

Alliance, one of the leading Jewish settlement houses, and the most virulently Americanist.* As chairman of MAS's Exhibit Committee he saw to it that the Municipal Art Society joined in the great Congestion Show of 1908 and that it cosponsored a city planning exhibit in 1909.

The Congestion Show enlisted the whole panoply of charity and reform groups in New York, and the *Times* seemed almost surprised by the "extent and variety of organized effort, of generally benevolent nature, that is here represented. There are nearly two score organizations taking part. They range from the departments of the State and City through the Charity Organization Society and kindred associations, to school garden associations and the Municipal Art Society. Every one of them has something to say. . . . Taken together their message is important and of the intensest interest."[32] With "a quaint fitness," the show was held at the Museum of Natural History. "There is a touch of unconscious sarcasm in the fact that the visitor to the exhibit passes a commodious Indian wigwam, which for ventilation at least far excels the white man's houses shown further on, and is indeed a sort of model for the device by which the city is trying to prevent and cure tuberculosis."[33] It was the first time in years that a spotlight had shone on the slums. The tenements had dominated the reform agenda in the late 1890s as the campaign for the New Tenement Law took shape, but one effect of that law was to lull people into assuming that the problem was on its way to a solution, while all the while it had been getting worse. Every year the city's population grew by 90,000 (as many people as lived in Atlanta), and the housing market hadn't kept up. How could it, when the city was so slow to build subways? True, some people managed to flee the Lower East Side for the Bronx or Brooklyn, but more immigrants arrived in the neighborhood than left it.[34] The New Tenement Law barely affected their lives; it may even have made them worse by raising the cost of new construction. The Congestion Committee tried to bring the effects of this home to its audience. It built "a typical tenement dwelling room which, even to the rickety bed, broken chair, and other details, had been brought out from the congested district to show how the 'other half' lives."[35] It also amassed great quantities of appalling information, comparing the death rates of different ethnic groups and neighborhoods, and these charts offered the most telling evidence possible of the inequities of life in New York City. The inescapable point was that the death rates correlated so closely with the density of neighborhoods. Some blocks in the Lower East Side had a population of more than eight hundred souls per acre; in Brooklyn the average was thirty-five to the acre; in the Bronx, twenty; in Queens, three; and in lonesome

---

* Its school produced David Sarnoff, Louis Lefkowitz, and Meyer Lansky. Something of its flavor was captured in 1906 by H. G. Wells, who visited "a big class of bright-eyed Jewish children, boys and girls, each waving two little American flags to the measure of the song they sang. They sang of America—'sweet land of liberty,' as they drilled with the little bright pretty flags, swish they crossed and swish they waved back, a waving froth it was of flags and flushed children's faces, and then they stood up and repeated the oath of allegiance, and at the end filed tramping by me and out of the hall." Wells, no friend to the immigrant and an anti-Semite to boot, adored the alliance: it was "practically the only organized attempt to Americanize the immigrant child," and quite "the most touching thing I had seen in America." H. G. Wells, The Future in America (London: Chapman and Hall, 1906; New York: St. Martin's Press, 1987), 110–11.

Staten Island, just two. To make this vivid, the Congestion Committee spread a big map of New York across a tabletop and used grains of shot to represent the population density in each district. Queens was lightly dusted, but on the Lower East Side great heaps of shot spilled across the map.

If nothing else, the exhibit succeeded in shocking the public out of its blithe assumption that New York had been making progress in recent years. As the *Times* wrote, "It is not yet even a question of remedies. It is first a question of preventing even worse things. These exhibits show that along with the marvelous increase in the area of the city, in means of transportation, in total wealth, there is a constant, in some places a progressive, tendency to congestion, so that the proportion of the population subjected to the evils of congestion cannot clearly be shown to lessen, while the volume and area of congestion necessarily affect each year largely increased numbers."[36]

When the Congestion Committee organized a series of lectures and symposia, one speaker after another suggested ways to force the poor into the suburbs. Dr. Henry Seager of Columbia University suggested busing their children to suburban schools on the theory that they would learn "to love life in the open"—as if slums were the result of mass agoraphobia.[37] More common was the demand that factories move to the fringes of New York, but the city had no power to bar them from Manhattan, and no manufacturer in his right mind would build and equip a plant in a place with no workers and no infrastructure. Others advocated unionism as a tool to battle the sweatshops. It was said that only labor—not legislation, interestingly—could force management to improve factory conditions, and that would mean abandoning the Lower East Side sweatshops for new buildings in other areas.

All these suggestions seemed to take for granted that the city itself was impotent. If it found the money and the political will, the city could, of course, build subways, and the organizers of the Congestion Show were desperate to spur the Public Service Commission to action. When the commissioners arrived for a tour, they were met by Henry Wright, Sr., secretary of the City Club and father of the great housing advocate and regionalist, who brought them straight to one particular exhibit. It was a little cube just a tenth of an inch square, and it represented the fabled purchase price of Manhattan: $24. Beside it stood another cube five feet square: *that* was the current taxable value of New York real estate. "Now, Mr. Commissioner," someone asked, "doesn't that look as if we ought to be able to borrow a little money for subways?"[38] One of the commissioners was the Municipal Art Society's own Milo Maltbie, who needed no convincing, and another was the lawyer Edward Bassett, who in the years to come would play a crucial role in the campaign to zone New York. After his tour Bassett admitted, "I am more deeply impressed than ever in my life by the pressing necessity of limiting the height of office buildings, and spreading the factories over a wider territory. I think manufactories should be segregated as much as possible, and the district below Fourteenth Street relieved."[39] Echoing one of Charles Lamb's favorite images, Bassett described his aims as the transformation of New York into "a round city."[40] The waterways of New York had trapped development in Manhattan, but the subway knew no such barriers. As Bassett pointed out, it hardly mattered to a subway whether it tunneled beneath a skyscraper or a flood.

THE CONGESTION Show did a splendid job of illustrating New York's problems—indeed, Mary Simkovitch complained that it made New York seem an utterly hopeless cause—but it hadn't done much in the way of advocating solutions. In 1909 MAS and the Congestion Committee cosponsored a huge City Planning Exhibit. It filled the enormous hall of the Twenty-second Regiment Armory at Broadway and Sixty-seventh Street, and it was the first time MAS had ever tried to present a vision of the city in its totality. It ranged from noble public buildings to skyscrapers to workers' housing and factories.[41] It included sculptures for the Brooklyn Museum by Daniel Chester French and Attilio Piccirilli, and paintings "suitable for schoolrooms," like Frederic Remington's *Hiawatha* and Winslow Homer's *All's Well.* There were schemes for neighborhood civic centers, bridge plazas, recreation piers, freight terminals, and even new letter boxes.

Charles Lamb offered a kind of summation of everything he'd done in the last decade. There was a scheme for communal kitchens in the tenement districts. They would stand in the center of each block and have their own staff of cooks, freeing working-class women to join the labor force.[42] There were drawings of setback skyscrapers, of the public forum in Union Square, and of the Court of Honor at Fifty-ninth Street; schemes to rearrange trolley tracks and crosswalks; a simplified version of his old Columbus Circle project; plans for an elevated highway ringing the lower half of Manhattan Island; and a perspective by Vernon Howe Bailey showing MAS's plan for lower Manhattan with new bridge approaches slicing across the island and with Varick and Christopher streets and Sixth and Seventh avenues lengthened or widened. The *Times,* introducing Lamb's plan, gloated that the bridge approaches would mean the end of Chinatown. It also observed that "several of the suggestions were embodied in the [improvement] commission's report, now before the Board of Estimate. But the present plans go further than the commission's recommendations in extent and utility as traffic and subway routes."[43]

Skyscrapers, municipal art, vast schemes for new avenues: all this was to be expected of the Municipal Art Society, but now it was joined to the Congestion Committee's proposals for the edges of the city. "Manhattan has sinned away its day of grace, so far as normal living conditions for the working people are concerned," Benjamin Marsh declared. "The real opportunity lies in the outer boroughs."[44] But so did great danger.

The Congestion Committee offered a look at what had been happening in Brooklyn since 1898, and at what would likely happen to Queens in the near future. The answer was clear enough, and it was the nightmare of all those Brooklynites who'd fought consolidation: Brooklyn was being Manhattanized. Greenpoint and Brownsville were already transformed into New Law tenement sections, "only a little less murderous," Marsh insisted, than the old slums of the Lower East Side.[45] He pointed to the double-edged nature of the tenement law: "drawn up to fit congested conditions in Manhattan," it endorsed a mode of housing that was "not necessary in Brooklyn or Queens. Six story tenements may be erected which are not needed to house the population outside of Manhattan, but which make profitable investments and so give a fictitious value to the land. In the last year one trust company gave out $126,000,000 to workingmen for the erection of two-, three-, and four-party houses, which are very suitable as housing for the working population of Brooklyn. The danger is, though, that the land is bought up by speculators who hold out for prices far beyond what the working [class] now could pay. This has given rise to tenements in Brooklyn."[46]

New York built roads and transit systems, opening up new land to development, but it placed almost no controls on how that land was developed. "American planning rewards speculation," Marsh said in a speech, "while foreign city planning protects workingmen."[47] The Congestion Committee explained how German cities used height limits and land-use laws to keep factories away from residential districts, and especially how they went about providing for low-cost housing. In Germany, cities bought large tracts of cheap land to keep them out of the hands of speculators; then they drew up master plans and zoning codes to give workers "abundant opportunity to obtain homes, some even surrounded with gardens, at far less rent than is possible in the more congested sections."[48]

"We have been like carpenters exceedingly busy at hammering and sawing without knowing what we were making"—so wrote Alan Benson of the *Times* after visiting the City Planning Exhibit. "Cities," he continued, "instead of merely accumulating like bits of driftwood above a fallen tree, are in fact made by man and can be made right."[49] Without a planning commission, however, New York could never be "made right." Charles Israels insisted that the commission mustn't be a temporary body like the old Improvement Commission, but a powerful full-time agency that could prevent "such mistakes as the building of the Queensboro Bridge, with no provision for a proper approach to it."[50]

Benjamin Marsh added that the planning commission would need a new set of legal tools as well. He demanded that the city finally obtain the power of excess condemnation so that it could build public works at "no net expenditure," that it secure "proper means of transportation" for both people and freight, and that it build streets, parks, and playgrounds in anticipation of the city's needs.

All this had long been a part of the Municipal Art Society's agenda, but Marsh also insisted that New York use height and area limits to ban tenements from Brooklyn and Queens, and land-use restrictions to create an industrial zone along the East River from Gowanus to Newtown Creek. Within this area would be a retail and office zone; then houses, carefully buffered from the waterfront factories.[51] This was far more subtle than anything MAS had come up with on its own, and far more ambitious in terms of extending the city's police power. Area restrictions, Marsh argued, were nothing more than an extension of what the Tenement

House Department already did when it set minimum standards of air and light for each person. The idea of special factory zones rested on a more delicate legal foundation. Unless factories were nuisances, the city was still powerless to act against them. In 1907 MAS had toyed with the idea of trying to restrict them, but John De Witt Warner had warned the board that "injurious structures could be prohibited, that such laws would be valid, and had been passed, but were generally not enforced, as they do not appeal to the general sentiment of the community."[52]

Marsh argued that enlarging the city's power was justified as a matter of social justice, a way to help the beleaguered wage earner to a decent life: the workingman had a right "to leisure, and to a home life during the time when he is not employed." He should be able to live near his job and not fritter away precious hours on a ratchety elevated train; and he shouldn't be a pawn in the real estate market, but rather have his own home, safe from the cycle of rent increases over which he had no control.

The city fathers were probably willing to acknowledge a moral right to leisure but not a legal one. In that case, Marsh argued, the city must make a bargain with factory owners. In exchange for confining themselves to distinct zones, "we stand ready to help you in securing the proper transportation facilities for your freight."[53]

By and large, harmony reigned in the planning community in 1909. MAS and the Congestion Committee seemed to complement each other, and reformers could rally around Marsh's agenda even if they didn't share his philosophy. There were some peculiar ironies. The idea of providing houses for the working class, for example, had been a dream of the consolidation movement, and it was still shared by both ends of the political spectrum, but for Marsh, the socialist, houses meant freeing workers from the tyranny of landlords; for conservatives, houses seemed the perfect way to inoculate workers against socialism.

There was also one genuine conflict, for Marsh and Lamb had very different views on skyscrapers. Lamb's talk of setbacks, sunny streets, and level cornice lines was meaningless aestheticism to Marsh. As far as Marsh was concerned, the only issue was reducing the number of people who worked in a given place; and to achieve this he wanted the city to tax buildings by the floor, or limit their volume, or else apply a height limit.[54] Despite such ripples of disagreement, the art societies and reformers banded together and demanded that the city create a planning commission.[55]

Tammany was unmoved. When President MacGowan of the Board of Aldermen addressed the city planners he promised to work hard for new playgrounds,[56] but no more, and when Comptroller Metz spoke, the audience heckled him. "Not hesitating to use the Brooklyn brand of slang and any other homely phrase which suited his purpose and carried the point," Metz derided every goal of the would-be city planners—even the eight-hour workday. "He declared that the best things of the city . . . went to those who made the biggest noise and had the biggest pull. 'Take the Bronx, for instance,' he said. 'The people up there are wanting more parks, though seventeen percent of their borough is already parks. But they probably have some vacant land which they can't build up and so want to sell it to the city.' " He rebutted Calvin Tomkins, who'd just spoken on mass transit as president of the Reform Club. " 'There was no justice,' Metz claimed, 'in requiring a railroad company to haul a passenger from Woodlawn Cemetery to Coney Island for five cents, as some would have the transit companies do.' . . . He declared that subways should be built in congested districts, where they were needed. . . . 'I am not in favor of building subways in the woods to boost some one's real estate.' "[57]

WHILE TAMMANY Hall stymied the planning movement, the only forum available to the Congestion Committee and MAS was the Building Code Revision Commission. In 1908 the civic groups had descended on City Hall to take a look at Tammany's idea of a building code, and this time the Municipal Art Society, the American Institute of Architects, and the Congestion Committee all came armed with their own schemes for height limits. Tammany's code was weaker in every way than that of Israels. It had its own system of height limits: buildings on streets less than 45 feet wide—there are some, dating back to Dutch times—would be held to 135 feet, but 300 feet would be the standard, and any building facing a park or plaza could rise to 350 feet.

The code's most effective critic was Electus Litchfield, who'd served on the 1907 commission. Why, he asked the commission, were high buildings a problem? One could say that they darkened the streets, that their shadows fell across neighboring structures, and that they produced intolerable congestion, but not one of these issues was addressed by an arbitrary 300-foot height limit. To serve a public purpose, the building code would have to require setbacks from the building line, light courts, or a limit of volume; it wouldn't necessarily have to limit height per se.[58] Litchfield pressed for the floor area ratio, or what he called "a limit of occupancy." His scheme was backed by the Congestion Committee, which wanted to control population density regardless of the architectural results, but the proposal won very little support in the architectural community. It would encourage "diversity and variegation," Montgomery Schuyler admitted in the *Architectural Record*, and in an ideal world, where every architect was talented and every client an aesthete, it might produce a wonderful city, but Schuyler argued that "the actual race of architectural practitioners" shouldn't be trusted so far.[59] (This sensible caution was finally thrown to the winds in 1961, when the floor area ratio became the basis of a new zoning code, and monolithic buildings on windswept plazas proliferated across Manhattan.)

Two proposals remained: Lamb's vision of a city of setback skyscrapers, and Ernest Flagg's of a city of towers. Flagg was no longer active in the Municipal Art Society. The Staten Island Committee he headed had produced few results, and he may well have felt that MAS, so centered in Manhattan, had given him little assistance beyond the use of its name. When he appeared before the building code commission on behalf of the Fine Arts Federation and the American Institute of Architects, he presented his own weirdly schizophrenic model for the skyscraper.

Like Lamb, he admired the sunlit boulevards of Paris with their unbroken cornice lines, so he proposed setting a height limit of one and one half times the width of the street, up to a maximum of one hundred feet. On a quarter of the lot, however, one could build a tower as tall as one wished or dared. It would have to be set back from the lot lines, so as not to interfere with a neighbor's windows; all four of its facades would have to be "treated architecturally" so that it wouldn't be an eyesore; and no wood would be allowed inside, so that it wouldn't burn like a torch.[60] The owner might build his tower over a larger area if he bought his neighbor's air rights, but in no case could more than one-fourth of a block rise above the cornice.

Flagg had one great advantage in making his arguments. He'd just finished the Singer Tower on Broadway and Liberty Street, a breathtakingly thin forty-seven-story tower rising out of a fourteen-story base. It was only a rough model of what Flagg wanted to write into law—its tower was even more slender while its base was taller—but the Singer Tower was a commanding advertisement for Flagg's idea. For the moment, it was the tallest building on earth, topped only by the Eiffel Tower, and every night thirty searchlights were trained on its shaft, and sixteen hundred light bulbs twinkled on its crest.

Since Charles Lamb had never built anything larger than his own house, he had to argue his case in the newspapers. The *Herald* carried a beautiful drawing by Vernon Howe Bailey, Lamb's favorite renderer, showing "How the Proposed Terrace Buildings Will Compare with the Present Tower Form." On the left sat Lamb's setback buildings, with an aerial street on the twelfth-floor setback. On the right were Flagg's towers—or what purport to be Flagg's towers. In fact, Lamb played with a stacked deck. He fairly suggested the unlimited height of Flagg's towers, but he lined them up shoulder to shoulder to create a continuous wall along the avenue, something Flagg wouldn't have allowed. It may have been this drawing that convinced H. Knickerbocker Boyd, head of the Philadelphia branch of the American Institute of Architects, to argue that Lamb's setbacks would make for sunnier streets than would Flagg's scheme. In fairness one should imagine shafts of light piercing that awful palisade on the right-hand side of the drawing.

Lamb had to convince people that setbacks represented more than an aesthetic interest in sunlight, so he kept harping on the danger of an apocalyptic firestorm in the financial district. If even one great skyscraper were suddenly evacuated, the streets couldn't handle the crowd, Lamb insisted. Think what would happen if fire swept from building to building.[61] The papers found this irresistibly romantic, like something out of *Quo Vadis?* or *The Last Days of Pompeii*. And then there were Lamb's other ideas. He realized that, as buildings grew larger, their lobbies would swell to grandiose proportions to accommodate the rush-hour crowds. Lamb saw that this opened up the potential for a new kind of public space: lobbies that would serve at once as covered pedestrian streets, as shopping concourses, and as multilevel circulation systems linking the building, the street, the subway, and the Els. Six layers of transportation sat one beneath the other at Park Avenue and Forty-second Street: the elevated railroad, the street itself, two layers of New York Central railroad tracks, the subway, and at the bottom of it all, the Belmont Tunnel.[62]

In the financial district, the Els, the bridge terminal, and the two-level ferry terminals kept pedestrians racing up and down stairs. "If you go up to the elevated platform," Lamb asked, "why not go along"?[63] He proposed a system of double-decked streets, the lower level reserved for vehicles, the upper one for pedestrians. These elevated sidewalks might be set within the building line as an arcade or cantilevered over the streets like balconies. Or one could roof entire streets with glass, as Lamb proposed for Nassau Street. This narrow, twisting road was a shortcut between the financial district and the bridge terminal, and it was lined with shops and restaurants serving workers. At rush hour and at lunchtime the sidewalks overflowed, and the crowd was forced into the roadway itself.[64] "Since the surface of the earth refuses us sufficient space," wrote M. H. Morgan of MAS, "it is necessary to go either higher or lower, and the elevated sidewalk offers many advantages over the subterranean one."[65] Lamb suggested turning Nassau Street into a pedestrian mall enclosed in a 100-foot-tall cage of glass and steel—the roof was set so high because Lamb expected that one day Nassau Street would be lined with tall buildings. This scheme could be repeated whenever needed, and as one newspaper wrote, Lamb "would practically convert lower New York into one vast building on either side of Broadway. These street corridors would be almost endless. A person might make a tour of the whole financial district without even going out from under a roof."[66]

Nor was this all. To the setback skyscraper, Lamb added the notion of aerial streets—pedestrian streets atop the twelfth-floor setback, vaulting over the inter-sections and continuing "as far as the congestion extended."[67] The idea may have sprung from a desire to win property owners over to the idea of setback zoning: they would lose some floor space, but they'd gain a second street frontage high in the sky. The *New York American*, a Hearst paper, was smitten with such ideas, and in 1908 it carried a breathless report on Lamb's work:

> He foresees that the greatest innovations in the immediate future will not be merely the height of the skyscrapers. Buildings of twenty to thirty stories have ceased to excite any wonder, and even the new Singer Building of forty-one stories has not aroused anything like the wonderment that the Park Row and St. Paul Buildings did a few years ago, with their twenty-nine stories.
>
> The things that will change the looks of the city most from now on, artist Lamb believes, will be arcaded streets, an elevated boulevard clear round Manhattan Island along the water-front, lofty monuments at places like the Circle at Fifty-ninth Street and Eighth Avenue, and broad approaches to the bridges spanning the East River.
>
> Many of these changes will doubtless be seen by many of the middle-aged residents of today, while most of the younger generation of the present can hopefully look forward to seeing New York at the 1933 period, when all the

improvements pictured herewith will doubtless all have been accomplished, and probably many other things which will be far more wonderful.

The *American* added some "wonderful" ideas of its own. "The era of the airship is about to dawn," the paper exclaimed. "Within the lifetime of this generation, we shall see lines of airships above the streets, just as we now see long lines of cabs and automobiles standing at the curb in the streets below." Deciding that Lamb's aerial streets would make perfect "airship landing stations," the *American* produced "What You May See before You Die," a picture of a fashionable party stepping from the umpteenth floor of a skyscraper into a taxicab of the future—a dirgible.[68]

Moses King, publisher of a popular guide to New York, picked up this theme in his 1908 edition. "King's Dream of New York," drawn by illustrator H. M. Petit, was an imaginary view of lower Broadway in what was then the near future. Multilevel sidewalks clog the street. In the distance, the 600-foot Singer Tower is dwarfed by imaginary neighbors. Only a few of the skyscrapers resemble Lamb's setback towers, but his aerial streets have taken on new life and randomly crisscross Broadway. Dirigibles fill the sky, careening among the skyscrapers on their way to every corner of the globe. From King's Dream it was only a short step to the film *Metropolis*, Fritz Lang's dystopian nightmare of New York.

IN 1908 skyscrapers were the talk of the town: the subject of sober discussions at the City Club, of heated testimony at City Hall, and of delirious renderings in the newspapers' Sunday supplements. Developers sniffed the air, decided that the city just might institute height limits, and sent their architects scurrying to the Building Department to file plans before the law could be changed. Some builders acted quickly because, once approved by the department, these structures could be erected no matter what the new regulations allowed. Thus Robert Goelet ordered his architects, Warren & Wetmore, to rush their plans for the sixteen-story Ritz-Carlton Hotel, on the west side of Madison Avenue between Forty-sixth and Forty-seventh streets.[69] Other developers may have been trying to lay the ground-work for damage suits against the city. More alarming was Daniel Burnham's design for a new building on the site of the Equitable Life Assurance Society Building, for here at last was a building of the size and scale Charles Lamb had predicted in 1898.

The old Equitable Building had grown since 1867. The original structure was only ninety feet wide, but it was "the life ambition" of Henry Hyde, the company's founder, to make of this something even more splendid.[70] Over the years he bought up the adjacent lots, and by 1888 Equitable had expanded southward to Cedar Street. Its mansard roof grew as well, with additional floors poking into the sky. In 1906, not long after Hyde's death, his company finally acquired the entire block, and two years later Burnham was called in to prepare designs for a new building. The site was roomy enough for enormous banks of elevators, and Burnham designed a sixty-two-story building, half again as tall as the Singer and Metropolitan Life towers. Its flagpole would have risen 1,059 feet above Broadway—higher, even, than the Eiffel Tower. It looked suspiciously like one of Charles Lamb's setback skyscrapers, except that it was far bulkier, climbing straight up from the surrounding streets for thirty-four stories before stepping back, twice, to a tower. (Lamb would have required a setback at the twelfth story.) Burnham's design, presented in the form of seventy separate sheets of drawings with plumbing diagrams showing 1,967 bathroom fixtures and 169 drinking fountains, was approved by Building Superintendent Murphy with astonishing, even suspicious, speed: "It took but a single day for the Chicago designers . . . to arrive at a complete agreement with the department's engineers."[71]

Developers shouldn't have worried, for once again the height limits never reached a vote. While the architects, the art societies, and the Congestion Committee argued with one another, the aldermen were hard-pressed from every direction. The concrete industry claimed that the new code was biased against it; contractors demanded a general cheapening of construction standards; and virtually every niche of the building industry sought to rewrite the code to its own advantage. So many people were pulling strings in so many different directions that the aldermen postponed any action while they sorted out all the political and financial ramifications. Satisfied that there was no rush anymore, Equitable decided to shelve its plans for the moment.

Then, in 1909, Boss Murphy drew up a *third* proposal, one designed to delight the seediest sort of builder. It "beggared description," Mayor McClellan wrote in his memoirs, adding that "among its worst features" was one that benefited "a small company in which Murphy was interested." What McClellan wouldn't admit, even thirty years after the fact, was that the existing building code had been written to enrich Richard Croker, the mayor's mentor. Croker and his associates in the Roebling Company had invested heavily in cinder block and had a near monopoly in the New York market. Naturally Croker had seen to it that the old building code required the use of cinder block, and only cinder block, in all fireproof partitions. Croker was now living the life of a gentleman farmer in England. He still kept in touch by cable with his cronies in New York, and he still had a loyal following, but his successor, Murphy, now saw the opportunity to create his own monopoly. Murphy had invested in hollow terra-cotta tiles, an eminently fireproof material. Any sane and just building code would have allowed the use of either terra-cotta or cinder block, but when Murphy introduced his building code he was careful to specify that terra-cotta would be the one fireproof material allowed in New York.[72]

Murphy made his move while McClellan, now his bitter enemy, vacationed in the Adirondacks. The mayor's fishing trip ended abruptly when Edward Cahill, "an old political friend of mine, who was a building contractor"—and one of Croker's business partners—appeared in the mountains with a draft of Murphy's building code. The aldermen planned to approve it the next day, and Patrick McGowan, president of the Board of Aldermen, would sign it as the city's acting mayor. McClellan rushed back to the city and arrived at City Hall just as McGowan was calling the aldermen to order. "I shall never forget McGowan's face as I entered the room," McClellan wrote. "He turned a pasty white and as I took the chair muttered, 'By butting in you've done me out of the mayoralty,' for Murphy had made the old man believe that he would nominate him in return for his signature of the proposed code."[73]

McClellan vetoed the code, and reformers rejoiced at Murphy's defeat, but nothing had actually been accomplished. Reformers, it's true, were confirmed in their opinion of the aldermen—"They are ignorant, supine rubber stamps or worse," cried the Citizens Union[74]—but cinder block retained its monopoly, and the hoary old building code remained in force. The issue had become such political "dynamite," as Henry Curran remembered, that the aldermen shied away from any new attempt to revise the code.[75] And the cost of this? New York remained a singularly dangerous city. Per capita, it spent five to six times as much as European cities to repair fire damage.[76] Given the aldermen's negligence and the perilous conditions in sweatshops, the labor movement was forced to take matters into its own hands. When the cloakmakers went on strike in 1910, one of their demands (aside from a fifty-hour workweek) was the creation of a Joint Board of Sanitary Control to police sweatshops for safety and fire violations. They won this point, but it was too little and too late to forestall the Triangle Shirtwaist Factory fire of March 1911. The Triangle company was housed in a modern "fireproof" structure built in 1908, a year after Tammany had discarded Charles Israels's building code. There were no sprinklers, as there would have been had Israels prevailed, and the fire escape was so shoddily built that it buckled as people tried to escape. The other escape routes were locked. More than 140 people died.

The fire sent shock waves through New York. A hundred thousand people marched with the funeral cortege of those scores of victims who were burned beyond recognition, and on April 2, 1911, thousands of reformers, social workers, clergymen, and labor leaders packed the Metropolitan Opera House for a protest meeting. They heard Henry Moskowitz of the Joint Board of Sanitary Control describe the true cause of the Triangle tragedy: the fact that New York had long known that even its most modern sweatshops were appallingly dangerous and yet had done nothing. And they hung on the words of one Rose Schneiderman, a garment worker and labor organizer. She blamed the reformers themselves, who had given organized labor such niggardly support. "We have tried you good people of the public and we have found you wanting," she said in a voice choked with tears. "The life of men and women is so cheap and property is so sacred. There are so many of us for one job it matters little if a hundred forty-three of us are burned to death."[77]

One of those present at the protest meeting was Belle Israels, Charles Israels's wife. Like many reformers she'd been more concerned with the morals of the poor than with their social welfare. She'd been active in the Educational Alliance, but her great cause had been the Committee on Amusements and Vacation Resources of Working Girls, a group that succeeded in having the city license dance halls. It also set up model dance halls, where no booze was served and no ragtime was played, and where the turkey trot, the bunny hug, and the grizzly bear were banished from the dance floor.[78]

Now Belle Israels went to work for the Committee of Safety, a new advocacy group financed by Robert Fulton Cutting. Henry Moskowitz sat on its board along with Mary Dreier of the Women's Trade Union League and Frances Perkins of the Consumers' League. The Committee of Safety was meant to keep up the pressure on the New York State Factory Investigation Commission, which had been created by State Senator Robert Wagner and Assemblyman Alfred E. Smith. Smith's work on the Factory Commission marked his first real encounter with the progressive camp of reformers. Until now he'd been just another Tammany loyalist, but his investigation of factory conditions and the plight of labor set him on a different course. In the next two years he sponsored more than thirty bills to tighten fire regulations, limit working hours, organize the Labor Department, and institute workmen's compensation. In the meantime Belle Israels had been widowed (Charles died of pneumonia in 1911), had married Henry Moskowitz, and become a labor arbitrator, and in the years to come Belle Moskowitz became the bridge between Smith and the progressives. She was the most brilliant of his advisers, and in the 1920s their alliance would finally produce Smith's "New Tammany."

But in 1911 Tammany's redemption was still far in the future. Seven months after the Triangle Fire, Fusion candidates won control of the Board of Aldermen. Before they could take office, Boss Murphy made one last try at revising the building code. The Tammany aldermen "fought desperately to the last ditch," the *Times* reported:

> They had their steam roller well oiled and . . . overrode all opposition until the final roll call. . . . For a time when the voting began, it looked as if the police would have to be called in to quell the disorder. The half-dozen sergeants-at-arms were powerless. . . . Even the pounding of the chairman's gavel was scarcely heard half of the time. . . . [Borough] President McAneny shouted that the question was not properly before the board and quoted sections of the Charter to prove it. . . . Chairman Bent ruled amid hisses and jeers that Mr. McAneny's point of order was not well taken. . . . At this point Alderman Callaghan, Republican, who possesses a booming voice, offered a motion to adjourn. It was greeted with hoots on one side and yells of approval on the other. . . . "You are out of order," shouted Bent, swinging the gavel with all his force. "Let him alone; he's all right," yelled the Fusionists and the gallery. Alderman Nicoll . . . said the proceedings reflected no credit upon the city or the board. . . . "Croker got his building code, and now Murphy wants his," he shouted.

In the end, fearing that Tammany would pay too high a price for Murphy's profits, four Democrats broke with their boss. The code was rejected, and "a cheer went up that startled the people on Broadway."[79]

✻   ✻   ✻

ALL THE scandals of the McClellan years took a toll on Tammany's popularity, and the time was ripe for another Fusion victory in 1910. The old Citizens Union coalition was fractured, however. It no longer had the energy to maintain a machine of volunteers, and it was split over fundamental ideological issues.* The "municipal socialists," like Calvin Tomkins, argued that the city government owed the public a host of municipal services: new subways and public utilities, and perhaps even public housing, as MAS had hinted in 1908. The conservative camp yearned for a "business administration"—an efficient and a frugal government. In 1909 the executive committee of the Citizens Union—which included Charles Stover, Frederick Lamb, and Charles Israels—had voted to transform the organization from a political party into an advocacy group. It would comment on legislation and candidates (it still does), but it would no longer put forward its own candidates.

This change at the Citizens Union would eventually have disastrous ramifications for the Municipal Art Society. The two groups had developed close ties over the years. As long as the Citizens Union served as New York's Fusion Party, and as long as Lamb, Stover, and Israels played a central role in it, MAS felt sure that the Fusion movement couldn't veer too far to the right. But when the Citizens Union disappeared from the ballot, some new organization had to step forward to field a slate of reform candidates, and the opportunity was seized by Eugenius Outerbridge, chairman of the Chamber of Commerce. He summoned New York's reformers, and their bankers, to Sherry's restaurant. During an opulent dinner, Outerbridge organized the Committee of One Hundred: a new ad hoc Fusion Party, and one with a distinctly more conservative cast. This committee soon announced its first nominations. For president of the Board of Aldermen it chose John Purroy Mitchel, fresh from his investigations of the borough presidents ("Young Torquemada," as Tammany called him). For Manhattan borough president it picked George McAneny, who was the president of the City Club and a Municipalian. Finding a mayoral candidate was harder.

The popular choice for mayor was Judge William J. Gaynor, a strange man from Brooklyn.[80] His hobby was raising pigs, and he was a connoisseur not of art but of the Stoic philosophers, astonishing reporters by quoting Epictetus off the top of his head. Yet when roused to anger his rages were legendary, uglier even than La Guardia's—at least the Little Flower never threw his wife out of the house in the middle of a blizzard. Gaynor had made his name as an activist lawyer practicing what one Municipalian called "popular government by lawsuit." His suits were aimed at exposing corruption in public works and the railroads' abuse of their franchises. His most celebrated achievement had come in 1893 when he ran for the

---

* At least one Municipalian had given up altogether on Fusion politics: In 1909, J. G. Phelps Stokes, former chairman of MAS's Civic Centers Committee, ran for Congress on Eugene Debs's Socialist line. He's remembered today, however, for his 1905 marriage to Rose Harriet Pastor. The union of a blue-blooded millionaire to a Jewish Marxist woman from Poland fascinated, and scandalized, the public. Rose Pastor Stokes's anti-war agitation led to her conviction on sedition charges in 1918, but she was acquitted on appeal. The couple divorced in 1925. See Stephen Birmingham, The Rest of Us: The Rise of America's Eastern European Jews (Boston: Little, Brown, 1984), 50–62, 114–31, 207.

State Supreme Court on the Republican line and confronted John Y. McKane, the Democratic boss of Gravesend. Gravesend wasn't a very populous town then, but it regularly cast four times as many votes as it had voters. McKane used to record the names of the guests at Coney Island's summer hotels and then kindly cast votes for them once the season was over. Nor was he shy about using his power: in 1888, unhappy with the state Democratic Party, McKane had retaliated by denying presidential candidate Grover Cleveland a single vote in his district. For want of Gravesend, Cleveland lost New York State, and for want of New York he lost the electoral college. Now Gaynor feared that without Gravesend, he'd lose his election. He demanded to see Gravesend's voting lists, but McKane ignored him. Gaynor answered with a court order and dispatched volunteers to copy the lists; they were beaten, jailed as vagrants, and denied bail. So Gaynor sent poll watchers armed with a court injunction forbidding any interference with their work, but McKane met them at the head of a mob and announced that "injunctions don't go here." The poll watchers, too, were beaten and carried off to jail. This was "civil war," wrote the *Brooklyn Eagle*. It was "treason triumphant," and McKane's shamelessness provoked such revulsion that Gaynor was swept into office. McKane was prosecuted on charges ranging from contempt of court to assault, and after four years of hard labor, he emerged from Sing Sing a pitifully broken man.[81]

Judge Gaynor exercised his gavel in Brooklyn, Staten Island, and Queens, and what strikes one today is his concern for civil liberties. He launched a one-man crusade against police brutality and arbitrary arrest. Alone among reformers, he spoke out against Seth Low's anti-vice campaign, which took the form of bursting into suspected brothels and gambling dens, arresting everyone in sight, and smashing the place up—all without a search warrant. For this, the *Times* would label him "anarchistic"—for this, and for his attitude toward the subways. "If the city is to build subways," said Gaynor, "it should own them absolutely, the day they are completed and opened, without anyone having any strings on them whatsoever, and then be free to lease them out at public competition for the highest rent obtainable for a reasonable term of years."

Calvin Tomkins was charmed; the more conservative reformers wrung their hands. Gaynor presented the Committee of One Hundred with another problem as well. Charles Murphy understood that Tammany's electoral prospects were grim, but he calculated that the machine could live with an incorruptible mayor as long as it kept control of the borough halls. And so, hoping Gaynor's popularity would save the rest of the Tammany ticket, Murphy offered him the Democratic nomination. The Committee of One Hundred told Gaynor that he could have the Fusion nomination, but only if he rejected Tammany's endorsement. Gaynor picked Tammany. He explained that, whatever was printed on the ballots, the public knew that Tammany couldn't boss *him*, and he wanted it understood that he wasn't beholden to Fusion's top-hatted bankers either.

Deprived of Gaynor, Fusion finally settled on Otto Bannard as its nominee. He was a Republican, a bank president, a political novice, and a clumsy campaigner.

Calvin Tomkins and Charles Lamb could forgive Bannard his amateurishness—that trait was still almost a badge of honor in reform circles—but not his stance on the subways. Bannard insisted that the city had no business building them, not even as a last resort, and this was simply unacceptable to the Municipalians. They knew William Gaynor, they trusted in his independence, and so they threw themselves behind him despite his Tammany tag.[82]

In the end, Gaynor was elected mayor, Fusion triumphed in the Board of Estimate, and Tammany held on to just the Board of Aldermen. Murphy's gamble hadn't paid off. The mayor rewarded Calvin Tomkins by naming him dock commissioner. In that post, Tomkins would draw up a vast master plan for the Port of New York—the very scheme that the city needed if industry and the working class were to find healthy new homes in the outer boroughs, as MAS and the Congestion Committee had been urging. At the same time, Gaynor appointed Charles Stover, MAS's friend and ally, to the Parks Commission. Stover would set in motion some of the Municipal Art Society's most cherished projects: public forums appeared in the parks, new monuments graced the gateways to Central Park, and work began on an immense scheme to cover the railroad tracks in Riverside Park. But both Stover and Tomkins found that the mayor's power was limited by his own independence; and both would see their careers in government come to a miserable end.

The real power in City Hall lay in the Fusion Board of Estimate, and its most brilliant figure was another Municipalian, the new borough president of Manhattan, George McAneny.

JUSTICE

Previous page: Justice, one of Edward Simmons's murals in the Criminal Court Building, 1894. **Right:** Daniel Chester French's portrait bust of Richard Morris Hunt. **Far right:** The Hunt Memorial by Bruce Price and French. **Below right:** A typical Victorian monument, Ferdinand von Miller's statue of Dr. James Marion Sims in Bryant Park. **Below:** The Appellate Courthouse on Madison Square by James Brown Lord and members of the National Sculpture Society.

C = Crack
H = Hair Crack
P = Pointed
O = Open
J = Joint
SP = Spalled

Left: New York and the Nations, *Taber Sears's painting on the ceiling of the City Council Chamber in City Hall.* **Far left:** *Tammany architecture. A 1909 view of Thom, Wilson & Schaarschmidt's Criminal Courts Building on Centre Street, with structural damage noted by a city engineer.* **Above:** *The Plaza at Fifth Avenue and Fifty-ninth Street, designed by Carrère and Hastings in 1913. Karl Bitter's* Abundance *crowns the fountain, and behind it stands the Cornelius Vanderbilt II house by George B. Post and Richard Morris Hunt.*

Left: Columbus Circle shortly before World War I with, in the center, Gaetano Russo's Christopher Columbus Memorial and, to the left, H. Van Buren Magonigle and Attilio Piccirilli's Maine Memorial. Note the trolley tracks and pedestrians. *Above:* The Dewey Arch, 1899, by Charles Rollinson Lamb and members of the National Sculpture Society. *Below:* An 1896 map of New York City. Note the absence of streets in the outer boroughs.

*Left: Victor Ciani's 1902 design for an electrolier, erected by MAS in Madison Square. **Above and right:** Two views of John R. Thomas's Hall of Records on Chambers Street. **Below:** A page from the* New York Times *of 1908 with Charles Rollinson Lamb's schemes for a West Side Boulevard, indented sidewalks, pedestrian malls, park shelters, and relocated trolley tracks.*

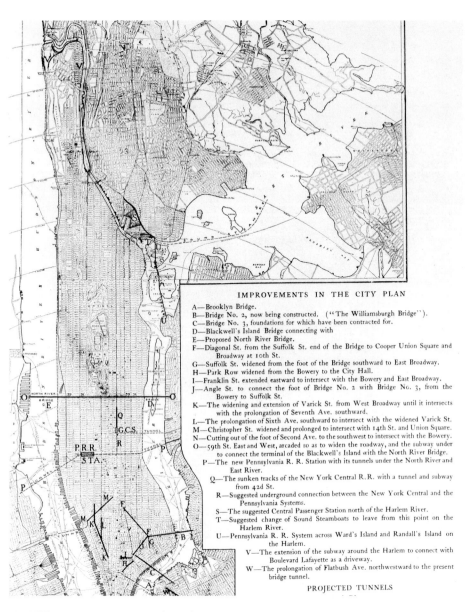

IMPROVEMENTS IN THE CITY PLAN

A—Brooklyn Bridge.

B—Bridge No. 2, now being constructed. ("The Williamsburgh Bridge").

C—Bridge No. 3, foundations for which have been contracted for.

D—Blackwell's Island Bridge connecting with

E—Proposed North River Bridge.

F—Diagonal St. from the Suffolk St. end of the Bridge to Cooper Union Square and Broadway at 10th St.

G—Suffolk St. widened from the foot of the Bridge southward to East Broadway.

H—Park Row widened from the Bowery to the City Hall.

I—Franklin St. extended eastward to intersect with the Bowery and East Broadway.

J—Angle St. to connect the foot of Bridge No. 2 with Bridge No. 3, from the Bowery to Suffolk St.

K—The widening and extension of Varick St. from West Broadway until it intersects with the prolongation of Seventh Ave. southward.

L—The prolongation of Sixth Ave. southward to intersect with the widened Varick St.

M—Christopher St. widened and prolonged to intersect with 14th St. and Union Square.

N—Cutting out of the foot of Second Ave. to the southwest to intersect with the Bowery.

O—59th St. East and West, arcaded so as to widen the roadway, and the subway under to connect the terminal of the Blackwell's Island with the North River Bridge.

P—The new Pennsylvania R. R. Station with its tunnels under the North River and East River.

Q—The sunken tracks of the New York Central R.R. with a tunnel and subway from 42d St.

R—Suggested underground connection between the New York Central and the Pennsylvania Systems.

S—The suggested Central Passenger Station north of the Harlem River.

T—Suggested change of Sound Steamboats to leave from this point on the Harlem River.

U—Pennsylvania R. R. System across Ward's Island and Randall's Island on the Harlem.

V—The extension of the subway around the Harlem to connect with Boulevard Lafayette as a driveway.

W—The prolongation of Flatbush Ave. northwestward to the present bridge tunnel.

PROJECTED TUNNELS

Left: The Conference Committee on the City Plan's 1902 scheme for Manhattan, with new bridges and avenues shown in heavy black. Below left and below: MAS's 1905 scheme for new subway lines. Right: The New York City Improvement Commission's 1907 project for an East Fifty-ninth Street Boulevard.

PROPOSED SUBWAY EXTENSI[ON]
IN OTHER BOROUGHS

Above left: A bird's-eye view of Manhattan from the *1907 Report of the Improvement Commission*. **Left:** Project for Brooklyn Bridge Terminal and Civic Center, by Gustav Lindenthal, George B. Post, and Henry Hornbostel. **Above:** Charles Rollinson Lamb's proposal for a Court of Honor at East Fifty-ninth Street.

Part Five
Magazine Section

The New York Times.

SUNDAY, JUNE 27, 1909.

Part F
Magazine

THE NEW FIFTH AVENUE

dditional Width of Fifteen
eet to Provide Space for
wo More Lines of Vehicles.

New York Cit
Greatest Drivewa

AN ENCROACHING TERRACE

THE STOOP

OVING
SS PLOTS AT
THE BRICK CHURCH

A RECONSTRUCTED HOUSE ENTRANCE

22½ FT.

7½ FT.

40 FT.

OLD CURB

NEW CURB

22½ FT.

7½ FT.

NEW CURB

OLD CURB LINE

Vernon Howe Bailey

VIEW NORTH FROM THIRTYE

**The Above Diagrammatic Picture
Shows the Transformation in Prog-
ress on Fifth Avenue. It Brings Out
Sharply the Increased Width of the
Famous Thoroughfare.**

ABLY no local improvement
te by the city at nominal cost
he municipal treasury was ever
lived by the people most di-
ected with so much regret as
ng of Fifth Avenue, now in
While it is generally admitted
usefulness and beauty of the
uth as a driveway and as a
general traffic, will be greatly
by adding fifteen feet to the
not appreciate the amount of
it is costing them to remove
chments outward from the
se on to the sidewalk.
we decided to cut seven and a
f the sidewalk on each side of
It was necessary, in order to
suitable width for the walks
these encroachments, and
cos, areaways, and flower gar-
ong the line, many of which
out on to the sidewalks many
were condemned. Many of the
ners maintained that if the city
elled to cut off these projec-
buildings would be spoiled, but
a obdurate, and with a few ex-
ey will all have to come down.
e work has already been com-
the unfinished part is being
ead rapidly, the city having
e property owners who have re-
e that if they do not remove
the city's size brigade will
ages.
two years ago that the city
consider measures for reliev-
ion of traffic on Fifth Avenue.
tine the problem had been rec-
a serious one. The avenue
out a 100-foot street, with
-foot sidewalks and a forty-
This allowed the accom-
of four lines of traffic, or ap-
ace at each curb for waiting
ractically only one line moving
ness.
This was about all that the
emen could handle during the

northwest corner of the avenue and Thirty-fourth Street, projected a series of
steps noticeably out onto the sidewalk.

Investigation revealed the fact that
besides these steps, the massive row of
pillars in the portico were also five feet
ten inches outside the building line.
The case was carried through the courts
and finally won by the city. In the
meantime Mark Cross, whose uptown
building is on the west side of the avenue,
between Twenty-fifth and Twenty-sixth
Streets, brought action against Martin's,
which adjoins Cross's on the north, alleg-
ing a nuisance from the Summer garden
of the restaurant, which ran out onto the
sidewalk nearly sixteen feet. Mr. Cross
won the case, and it was not appealed.
On the strength of these two suits the
widening of the avenue. The section from
Twenty-fifth Street north to Forty-seventh Street was selected for the com-
mencement of the work. Martin's Sum-
garden was one of the first en-

have had to be torn out and filled in. A
very bothersome problem has been the
many old brownstone houses along this
part of the avenue. But in removing the

front of the building will be ruined, and
the work has not been started. The city,
however, insists that it must come down.
The block of houses across the avenue,
between Thirtieth and Thirty-first
Streets, owned by the Marshall Field estate, has a stoop which offends to the
tune of sixteen feet. The residence of
Johnston Livingston, at No. 309, in the
next block, had a sixteen-foot courtyard
and area which have been removed

to stand, as to remove it it would be
necessary to tear down the entire avenue
frontage. A sixteen-foot stoop has been
removed from 361 in the next block on
the same side of the avenue, owned by
Adrian Iselin. Across the way at 362
there is a fifteen-foot stoop, area, and
steps which will have to be taken away.
Work is in progress on the removal of
a fourteen-foot stoop from the front of
the Astor Trust Company's building at

the avenue
second St
year ago.
The Br
corner of
canopy ov
ern corner
platform b
adjoining
and area
street a 10

Far left: Vernon Howe Bailey's rendering of the widening of Fifth Avenue. **Above**: Tammany architecture improved. The Bronx County Courthouse, designed by Oscar Bleumner. **Left**: A model of Gustav Lindenthal and Henry Hornbostel's design for the Manhattan Bridge.

What the elevator wrought. **Below:** *The old Equitable Building at 120 Broadway, designed by Gilman & Kendall with George B. Post.* **Left:** *The Flatiron building at Broadway and Twenty-third Street, designed by Daniel Burnham.*

George McAneny and the Zoning Resolution of 1916

GEORGE MCANENY WAS an unusual figure in the reform camp. He had no family fortune and not much formal education.[1] He was born poor in Jersey City, and began his working life as a barefoot boy selling newspapers. He left school at sixteen and became a reporter, first for the *Jersey City Journal* and later for the *New York World*. He was discovered in 1892 by Carl Schurz. Schurz, by then, had been a German revolutionary, an American abolitionist, a major general in the Union army, a Republican senator, secretary of the interior, and editor of the *Evening Post*. When McAneny met him, Schurz was head of the Civil Service Reform Association. He made McAneny the group's secretary and launched him on a career as citizen advocate and reform politician. It was McAneny who drafted the amendment to the state constitution that created a civil service in New York, who wrote the statute that put the amendment into effect, and who drew up the regulations that interpreted the statute. In 1902 he became Seth Low's civil service commissioner; afterward he apprenticed in the law firm of Edward Shepard, and he was one of the founders of the Bureau of Municipal Research.

McAneny joined the Municipal Art Society in 1903. He showed up at the annual meetings and exhibits, but he wasn't active in the society until he became its president in 1927. In the early 1900s, though, his work in civil service reform had already drawn him into the orbit of a number of MAS board members; he was very close to Karl Bitter (and one of the instigators of Bitter's masterful Carl Schurz Memorial at 116th Street and Morningside Drive); and he worked with MAS through the City Club. McAneny was the City Club's president from 1906 to 1909, when the congestion shows were being mounted and the club's City Plan Committee overlapped with that of MAS. He sat on its Public Improvements Committee with John Carrère and Arnold Brunner, who still hadn't forgiven MAS for Frederick Lamb's critical remarks about the Manhattan Bridge. Both MAS and the City Club were determined to create a city planning commission, some system of height limits, land-use regulations, and a new network of subways.

In 1910, when McAneny became Manhattan borough president, he brought this agenda with him to City Hall. "We have got to build a city fifty years or one hundred years ahead," he told the Saint Nicholas Society in 1910,[2] and he promised the City Club to have a planning commission appointed by the end of the year. It would design, he said, "a great city plan contemplating all future developments for our city, the laying out of new boulevards, subways, waterfronts, avenues, and streets, even into the distant future."[3]

The Board of Estimate didn't create such a commission after all. The other borough presidents valued their autonomy too much, and the Board of Aldermen, affecting a new seriousness of purpose, did the one thing no one wanted: it established another powerless temporary commission to study the problem. Jacob Cantor agreed to become the president of this Congestion Commission, and the architect Walter Parfitt joined as MAS's representative. Benjamin Marsh was its secretary, but he retained his post with the private Congestion Committee. In 1910 the Congestion *Committee* recommended that the city double its tax on land and halve its tax on buildings; the Congestion *Commission*—the official body—satisfied itself with a vague recommendation that the city study such a change. It didn't take much imagination to see what Marsh was after: the high land tax would make it too expensive to simply sit on undeveloped land and would force people either to develop their property or to sell it—quickly. Flooding the market would drive the price of land down—down far enough, Marsh hoped, to put it within the reach of wage earners.[4]

This was an explosive proposal. Marsh told the *Times* that "some real estate speculators have told me personally that they would spend hundreds of thousands to defeat legislation suggested by the Congestion Committee."[5] In fact they didn't need to spend a dime. Marsh's strategy was anathema to all those people in the planning and reform communities who were, after all, still capitalists, and, as one of Marsh's supporters told him, "We can't expect people to cut their own throats."[6] Some owned land; others were bankers. Lawyers and architects defended the financial interests of their patrons, and many others saw great danger in opening the door to a tax on unearned income. Robert W. De Forest, an estate manager active in the Metropolitan Museum, the Art Commission, and the Charity Organization Society—and for years a vice president of the Municipal Art Society—told his friends not to underestimate Marsh's radicalism. By the end of 1911 MAS had distanced itself from Marsh, and though it's difficult to reconstruct what happened—the minutes of board meetings can become very terse—it seems that Marsh asked for an endorsement of his tax scheme and was brusquely told that taxes weren't in the sphere of the Municipal Art Society's interests.[7]

The rift between MAS and Marsh wasn't a complete break, though. Albert Bard, MAS's secretary, remained in touch with one branch of the city's Congestion Commission—a committee studying how to implement height limits—and he took it upon himself to make the rounds of civic groups to win their support. Two bills emerged from these deliberations and were presented to the state legislature. One, the Colne Bill, endorsed by the Congestion Commission, MAS, and the Citizens Union, would have given New York the power to divide the city into districts with different height limits.[8] The other was the Municipal Planning Commission Bill, which would have allowed cities across the state to set up their own planning commissions.[9] But as long as these bills were tainted by their association with Benjamin Marsh and his agenda, they simply languished in Albany. The Colne Bill failed in 1912 and 1913.

The planning movement stalled again.

GEORGE MCANENY, in the meantime, had turned his attention to the subways. When William Gaynor ran for office he had promised that the city itself would build subways. That oath had endeared him to Calvin Tomkins, and it had convinced Tomkins and other leading Municipalians that they should break away from the Fusion Party. Yet the city's hands were still tied by its debt limit and by conservative opposition, while the construction of privately run subways was blocked by the Elsberg Law and the sheer scale of investment required. The impasse was broken by the so-called Dual Contracts, in which the city went into partnership with the Interborough Rapid Transit Company and the Brooklyn Rapid Transit Company. Given his tact and infinite patience, George McAneny was placed in charge of the tortuous negotiations between the city and the railroads. The Elsberg Law, which Calvin Tomkins had backed, was superseded; the state constitution was amended; legislation was passed; and lawsuits were fought off. The city's debt limit was enlarged so it could float bonds to cover part of the construction cost of new rail lines. The IRT and the BRT paid the rest and supplied the equipment in return for forty-nine-year leases. Fares were held to a nickel—inflation, which didn't arrive until World War I, was apparently beyond the railroads' imagination. Their revenues were governed by a complex formula: first they had to pay off the city's debt; then they were allowed to take a guaranteed profit, and anything left over was split with the city.[10]

The Dual System was an enormous project: 147 miles of track at a cost of more than $300 million—only a little less than the cost of the Panama Canal. The Interborough finally got to complete its H plan. Its West Side line was extended down Seventh Avenue to the Battery and up to 241st Street and White Plains Road in the Bronx; on the East Side it reached up Lexington Avenue from Grand Central Terminal, built an elevated line up Jerome Avenue and another reaching to Pelham Bay in the Bronx.

The new West Side line meant that one of MAS's old planning schemes was at last realized: Seventh Avenue was finally extended south through Greenwich Village, and Varick Street was widened. That part of the project alone cost $6 million a mile.[11] At the same time, Queens and Brooklyn were laced with a new network of subways and Els: Woodside, Corona, and Astoria were drawn into the net; Eastern Parkway and Nostrand Avenue got their subways; an El reached out to Jamaica; the West End, Sea Beach, and Culver lines were built; and the BRT built its Broadway line. Only Staten Island was ignored, and when residents learned in 1915 that it would be "at least" six or seven years before a subway tunneled under the Narrows, the island erupted in angry talk of secession.[12]

The financial arrangements behind the Dual System were a compromise between the city and the railroads, but so, unfortunately, was the layout of this subway. The Dual System plan was far less imaginative than what MAS had proposed some years earlier. The finely crafted system of crosstown connections, the subway loops that linked all the north-south transit lines, the belt-line subway servicing the East and West Side waterfronts—all these had disappeared. The IRT and the BRT managed to win routes through the congested spine of Manhattan, and the predictable result was to concentrate development.

The Dual Contracts were a contentious issue. The City Club was divided; it endorsed the contracts over the objections of its own Transit Committee, and when Benjamin Marsh protested, he was drummed out of the club.[13] Yet the Municipal Art Society didn't even dare to comment on the contracts. It was too closely tied to Mayor Gaynor to criticize the new routes; the membership had grown restive with the directors' "socialism"; and there seemed no viable alternative to McAneny's scheme.

McAneny would eventually pay a price for his role in the negotiations. He'd won the hatred of William Randolph Hearst, who could throw an election either to Tammany or to Fusion depending on whether his Municipal Ownership League presented a third ticket. In 1913 the Fusion leaders were convinced that McAneny was the best candidate for mayor, but they didn't dare nominate him. Instead they chose John Purroy Mitchel, who, as president of the Board of Aldermen, had voted against the Dual Contracts. McAneny gave up his post as borough president and ran instead for the Board of Aldermen.

In 1912, as soon as the outlines of the Dual Contracts were clear, McAneny decided to move on to the next step: the creation of a city planning commission. The Dual Subways would open up huge new tracts of land in Queens, and the Congestion Committee had made clear the danger of building mass transit without any control over developers. The result would be, as the *Times* wrote, "a repetition of the building chaos and economic injustice" that prevailed in Manhattan.[14] Manhattan, too, needed height limits for its skyscrapers.[15] In 1912 the excess condemnation law finally passed in Albany, and McAneny began experimenting with the city's new power. He laid plans for a new civic center northeast of City Hall Park, a foil for the much needed, much delayed county courthouse (decades later, this project yielded Foley Square, a very disappointing result), and he was trying to revive MAS's project for a diagonal avenue to the Manhattan Bridge.

New ideas were still cropping up at the Municipal Art Society. Both McAneny and the mayor were intrigued by Charles Lamb's scheme for a new street between Seventh and Eighth avenues, for example. This thoroughfare would carry traffic straight to the north door of Pennsylvania Station, which had just been finished in 1910. And at Fifty-third Street, where the new road would intersect Broadway, a circular plaza would make a fine home, Lamb suggested, for the Metropolitan Opera House.[16] E. P. Goodrich, the engineer of McAneny's Department of Public Works, was enthralled by another of Charles Lamb's schemes—the proposal for double-decked streets, which he presented to McAneny along with an elaborate plan for weaving pedestrian tunnels and second-story sidewalks through the financial district.[17]

Dozens of improvement projects were vying for City Hall's attention, and a planning commission was desperately needed to evaluate their merits and tie them into a comprehensive master plan. As McAneny wrote to Robert Fulton Cutting, the creation of such an agency "ought to have the vigorous support of those citizens who are interested in bringing municipal order out of the more or less chaotic conditions of the past."[18] Yet in 1912, when McAneny pressed forward with his campaign, he found that the older city planners were exhausted, defeated, or distracted. A decade earlier, the Lambs, Calvin Tomkins, and Jacob Cantor had launched the planning movement at the Municipal Art Society, but now they ignored McAneny's call for support. Frederick Lamb still chaired the MAS City Plan Committee, but he'd recently warned the society's directors that their emphasis on city planning rather than public art had alienated the average Municipalian.[19] Standing on such shaky ground, Lamb was of little help to McAneny. Nor did Charles Lamb rally to the cause. For years he had watched as his improvement schemes were praised by the city and then shelved for want of money. Don't bother with a planning commission, Lamb told the Board of Estimate: "It would be better to reform the method of issuing city bonds." Calvin Tomkins had his own reasons for withholding support. Now the dock commissioner, Tomkins was trying to push through his own vast scheme for new wharves and freight terminals, and, as we'll see later, McAneny was thwarting him at every turn. By 1912 the two men were barely on speaking terms. And finally there was Jacob Cantor, who had seen his work on the Improvement Commission and the Congestion Commission go to waste. When the Board of Estimate asked for his advice on a planning commission, Cantor "reminded the meeting that he had been a member of such a body and its results had gone for nothing."

> "I don't believe the present Board of Estimate even has a copy of our report," he said.
> "It lies on my desk," remarked McAneny.
> "But have you ever opened it?" asked Mr. Cantor, but the borough president did not answer.[20]

BENJAMIN MARSH had scandalized the financial and real estate community with his notion of pulling down land values as a route to social justice. A planning commission, a zoning code, and a high land tax were all tools to achieve that end, Marsh thought, and as long as these tools seemed to be linked to Marsh's goals, New York would remain a laissez-faire city. Unbridled competition has its dangers, however—there are always more losers than winners—and around 1912 it began to dawn on some real estate speculators that a zoning code, far from driving property values down, was needed to prop them up.

Legend has it that the Equitable Building at 120 Broadway was the immediate cause of zoning. Modern scholarship discredits that story,[21] but there is something to the folklore. The Equitable's site had been the subject of concern since 1908, when Daniel Burnham drew his plans for a sixty-two-story monster to replace George Post's old Equitable Building. Burnham's building, like the first Equitable headquarters, would have been a stunt: the tallest and probably the biggest building on earth. Equitable decided, however, "that the day of tall building for advertising has gone by."[22] Nothing happened for a time, but four years later the old Equitable burned in a spectacular fire. (Post's elevators were at fault. They were open to the public stair halls—as the building code still, unconscionably, allowed—and, like chimneys, they funneled flames to the upper floors.[23]) By then no one thought of Post's Equitable Building as a skyscraper; it had long since been surrounded by a palisade of office buildings twice as tall. When the blackened ruins were cleared away, the neighbors went into a panic. They remembered Burnham's project, and they knew what land cost in the financial district. A huge new structure would surely rise on the site, and when it did their own properties would lose, along with their sunlight and air, their ability to command prime rents. "These buildings," the *Times* wrote, "which had looked down with their thousands of eyes upon the roof of the old Equitable and up to the sky, did not relish having to look upon a mammoth and towering new Equitable and no sky at all."[24] "It would tower like an upas tree over all its immediate surroundings," one broker said, "casting a chilling, killing blight upon them, and sapping their vitality. No building in the vicinity would fail to suffer from it."[25]

The Equitable Company was worried by its neighbors' attitude. In 1905 James Hazen Hyde, a member of MAS and vice president of his family's insurance company, had thrown a ball at Sherry's. It was the first ball to be photographed, and the papers recorded a spectacle so extravagant that the public wondered whether such a spendthrift as Hyde could be trusted with the policyholders' hard-earned money.[26] New laws were passed to regulate the insurance industry, and one of these barred an insurance company from investing in "a building not needed for its own business."[27] The state normally waived this clause, but Equitable had reason to fear that its neighbors would bring pressure to bear on Albany. They might have forced a compromise (according to one realtor, a "moderately low building" of twenty stories would have given a decent return), so Equitable sold the site to Thomas Coleman Du Pont, heir to the chemical fortune.[28]

Du Pont was a vainglorious man, and when he put up a building he liked to boast that it was the biggest and best of its kind.[29] His neighbors appealed to the city to bail them out: condemn the site, they demanded, for a park. But it would have been a very expensive park—$15 million for the land, and another million each year in lost taxes—and for that matter few people understood that parks were of any use in business districts. (New York would have to wait for the example of the Seagram Building in 1956, for the vest pocket park movement of the 1960s, and for Holly Whyte's studies in the 1970s of how people use urban plazas.)

Next Equitable's neighbors did something remarkable: they offered to pay the city back over the sixty-year life of its bonds.[30] It wasn't clear that this was legal, so they tried a more modest proposal: extend New Street northward two blocks, they suggested, and thus cut the site in two, reduce the bulk of its replacement, and relieve congestion in the streets.[31] This too met with a stony response, and at this point the neighbors banded together. George Mortimer, manager of the United States Realty Building just across Broadway, organized a consortium with the Trinity Building, the Hanover Bank, the American Surety Company, the American Exchange National Bank, the Fourth National Bank, and the National Bank of Commerce. Together they meant to buy the block from Du Pont and erect an eight-story office building, an "underdevelopment" that would have meant an outright loss of $2.5 million. The consortium's members were prepared to split the loss among themselves, but Du Pont would not sell.

What Du Pont built was just two-thirds as tall as Burnham's 1908 project, but it was devastating nonetheless. Burnham had just died, and the new Equitable Building was designed by his successor firm, Graham, Anderson, Probst & White. It was finished in 1915, and in its own way it was a handsome building, with Roman detailing and a beautiful vaulted lobby, as wide as Trinity Street, running through the entire site. But the building rose straight from narrow streets for forty stories. It cast a shadow six times as large as the plot of land on which it stood. Buildings were darkened a fifth of a mile away, and those directly across Broadway reported that windows as high as the twenty-first floor no longer received any sunlight. The neighbors' worst nightmares were realized as their tenants fled in search of better lit office space, and the city was forced to reduce tax assessments in the area by a million dollars.[32]

Since the birth of the skyscraper, the standard theory of real estate development had maintained that each building should boast "as large an area of rentable space as the plot would carry," but in 1912 John Parish, a broker, had contemplated the Equitable site and seen the fatal flaw in this notion: "It takes no account of the effect on the ... neighboring property of other owners. The process is strictly individualistic and competitive; every man for himself and save himself who can."[33] The Equitable Building demonstrated that height limits were in the interest of realtors, and the wave of downward reassessments demonstrated that the unchecked skyscraper now threatened the city's own finances.

Meanwhile, Mortimer's consortium disbanded once Du Pont began to build. It had sprung up in response to a unique situation, and it died once it lost its battle. The campaign was carried on uptown by the Fifth Avenue Association, the wealthiest grassroots organization in the city.

WHEN THE Municipal Art Society was founded, Fifth Avenue was a street of mansions, churches, and clubs. Many still thought that Forty-second Street would always be the boundary between commercial and residential New York. By the turn of the century, however, the most chic shops in the city had begun to migrate to Fifth Avenue between Twenty-third Street and Central Park. The Gorham Company, Tiffany, Arnold Constable, W. & J. Sloane, Scribner's, and Duveen arrived, along with scores of smaller hatmakers, dressmakers, and jewelers. The Vanderbilts fought a rear guard action to protect their houses, and by 1904 they'd wasted $4 million in a futile effort to keep commerce away from that stretch of Fifth Avenue between Fifty-first and Fifty-third streets.[34] As shops, hotels, and restaurants took hold north and south of Vanderbilt Row, most families moved above Fifty-ninth Street. Some of them were driven north by the inroads of commerce and the new flood of traffic, while others were tempted away by a spectacular windfall: high rents in bigger buildings sparked a boom in Fifth Avenue real estate, and the value of their houses jumped two and a half times between 1900 and 1906.[35] In 1904 the *Real Estate Record and Guide* predicted that Fifth Avenue would soon be home to "nothing but hotels and shops—the most expensive in the city; and it will constitute the center of the distinctively metropolitan life of the metropolis—the life which is different from that which is to be found in any foreign capital or any other American city."[36]

That was the vision of the Fifth Avenue Association, a group formed in 1908 "for the purpose of standing together in all efforts to improve and beautify that street."[37] "Help Fifth Avenue and you help the whole city" was its slogan.[38] About a hundred firms joined, and the association's executive committee included jewelers, a purveyor of hair goods, a florist, the book dealer Simon Brentano, the piano manufacturer William Knabe, representatives of Lord & Taylor and the Gorham Company, and the architect William Kendall of McKim, Mead & White. Its president was Robert Grier Cooke, a publisher.

The Fifth Avenue Association resembled one of Irene Hall's Block Beautiful campaigns: it used peer pressure to urge property owners and retailers to fall into line. Its goal was to maintain and enhance the street's market niche as a shopping center for the rich, so the association wanted a clean street, a certain standard of personal service, goods that appealed to the highest end of the market, and the sort of discreet signage that whispers, "This is a very expensive store." It even hired its own security force and, until the city complained, dressed its men in uniforms remarkably like those of real policemen.[39] Finally the association gave awards each year to the best new buildings on the avenue. These awards always singled out designs whose refined detail and exquisite materials declared their own costliness and good taste.

When the Fifth Avenue Association held its first public dinner, Donn Barber, president of the Architectural League, toasted the group's program. This, he assured the audience, was the way to maintain Fifth Avenue's standards. When Charles

Lamb followed Barber to the dais, however, he told the same audience that it was naive.[40] Good taste was no defense against the avenue's real enemy: the inhuman scale of the skyscraper. The St. Regis Hotel, towering above the corner of Fifth Avenue and Fifty-fifth Street, had already breached the neighborhood's defenses, and if such buildings weren't checked they would turn the avenue into a canyon as sunless and scaleless—and plebeian—as lower Broadway. Lamb told the Fifth Avenue Association that if it wanted to save the retail district, it should fight for height limits and land-use restrictions.

But Lamb was the Municipal Art Society's own Cassandra; his warnings of approaching danger, or of opportunities about to slip away, were always dismissed until it was too late. The Fifth Avenue Association continued on its original course, and MAS was soon collaborating with it on a campaign against billboards and a competition for special mailboxes (it was won by Henry Bacon, who later designed the Lincoln Memorial in Washington, D.C., but that idea was apparently quashed by the post office bureaucracy[41]).

Charles Lamb joined the Fifth Avenue Association despite his dissatisfaction with the group, and, working through the Tree Planting Association, he produced a bizarre scheme for greening the avenue. Since there were many cellars under the avenue's sidewalks, Lamb meant to plant small trees in tall concrete planters along the curb with flower boxes and carriage blocks between them, while trees would sprout from isles of safety down the avenue's spine.[42]

In time, the Fifth Avenue Association did come to see Lamb's point about the skyscraper. The skyscraping loft district near Union and Madison squares began to spill over onto lower Fifth Avenue, and then the retail and garment industries began migrating northward. The two trades were closely intertwined—garment factories needed to be close to their markets—and as they journeyed up Fifth Avenue it was hard to tell at first whether the lofts were pushing the stores uptown or the stores were pulling the lofts along behind them. Perhaps both forces were operating at once, but one should also add into this equation the effects of Seth Low's tax assessment policy. The Congestion Committee was the first to observe that taxing property at its full market value had begun to spur the development of dense skyscraper neighborhoods: "A thirty- or forty-story building, we will say, is put up beside one that is not more than five. . . . The high building brings in revenue that is commensurate with its height, and its value for taxing purpose is placed accordingly—which is all right. But the land upon which the adjoining low building is situated is also assessed at a higher figure on the theory that it should pay taxes on the valuation which its best use would give it."[43] Obviously the low-rise building's days were numbered: its owner would replace it with a skyscraper, and that first tower would soon have neighbors just as tall. On the face of it, this seemed perfectly reasonable, and it often produced fairly coherent streetscapes, but in fact an economic disaster was in the making.

The problem was that most of Fifth Avenue's real estate was still held in small lots—the class of real estate speculator who patiently assembles large parcels of land over the years had only begun to evolve. A skyscraper on a 20-by-100-foot lot amounted to a long, narrow sliver tower. The first sliver tower on a block was a financial success only because it was surrounded by low buildings. Its party walls were riddled with windows in order to borrow light and air from the neighbors' air space, but this situation couldn't last. As soon as the neighbors saw their new tax bills, they ripped down their row houses and built their own skyscrapers—and all those party-wall windows were soon bricked up.[44] That first sliver tower still had windows on its narrow front and back facades, but between them stretched a hundred feet of dark space with no ventilation. The open office plan wasn't yet accepted in the business world, and before the invention of air conditioning it was impossible to divide up such a floor into windowless cubicles without their inhabitants suffocating in the heat or choking on cigar smoke. Only industry would rent such space; no one else would take it. "The high buildings" on Fifth Avenue "were not originally intended for sweatshops," wrote Robert Grier Cooke, "but in proportion as more and more of them were put up the owners could not get the high class of tenants that they used to have, the rents fell, and the garment manufacturers stepped in."[45]

Lofts rent for less than offices, so obviously this was an unfortunate outcome for the developers involved, but the ramifications were much wider than that. First, the loft buildings could no longer support the original high assessments that had, in part, spurred their construction. An alarming number of them went bankrupt. As they crept northward, land values collapsed in their wake. In the course of a few years the price of land on West Twenty-third Street plummeted from $13,000 to $3,000 a square foot.[46] Farther north, land was still costly, but the process was repeating itself: tall buildings were springing up in the lower reaches of the new retail district. As the *Times* wrote, "When the high buildings become dense the advantages enjoyed by those first constructed disappear, and they are abandoned for others which in turn ravage new districts. Individual fortunes have been created undeservedly in some cases, and at the cost of the wreck of other individual fortunes in still other cases. In the aggregate, millions of tax values have been disturbed and the city's finances disordered."[47]

By 1912 Fifth Avenue below Twenty-third Street was given over to garment factories. North of Twenty-third Street the avenue itself was still untouched, but a colony of lofts had sprung up in the side streets west of Fifth, just below Bryant Park. This had been a fashionable residential district in the 1890s, home to figures like Ward McAllister, but the rich had fled north and most of their town houses had been converted to commercial use or replaced by factories.[48]

The retailers began to panic. They couldn't continue moving north because a barrier loomed ahead in the form of Central Park. Nor could they coexist with lofts. The retail district was a world dominated by prosperous women shoppers, but at lunchtime the factory district was crowded with poor immigrant men, and retailers were desperate to keep the two crowds segregated. It was the custom for women in the garment trades to eat lunch at their sewing machines, but the men descended upon the streets and filled the sidewalks: a crowd of poor men in black suits, munching, chatting, and chewing and spitting tobacco. Women were reluctant to step into such a throng, rich women doubly so, and even if they did brave the sweaty masculine crowd, they found it impossible to window-shop when the sidewalk was packed with people.

THE PROPER tools with which to fight this battle were obvious to people like Charles Lamb: height limits and, especially, land-use restrictions. The power to enact such controls wasn't exactly in hand, but everyone knew of the Congestion Commission's work, and Albert Bard, MAS's secretary, was making the rounds of civic groups to drum up support for its zoning legislation. Yet the Fifth Avenue Association held back from endorsing zoning until it had exhausted every other remedy it could think of. Convinced that "something had to be done," the association first appealed to the police to arrest the lunching workers. The charge? Loitering.

"Arrests were made by the wholesale," Cooke remembered, and "the magistrates warned the prisoners, but the relief was only temporary. The crowd overran everything. Of course, we were criticized for attempting to interfere with the rights of American citizens"—not least by Mayor Gaynor, a great civil libertarian, who called the police off. "Then we started another plan," Cooke went on. "It was to educate the men themselves." The workers couldn't have been pleased with the grossly condescending placards that reminded them, in three languages, that "customers ... object to loitering, and to the sidewalks being littered with lunch, tobacco juice, etc." Labor leaders explained to Cooke that the men had no place else to go, and this gave him the idea of herding them into Union Square Park, but Charles Stover, the new parks commissioner, would have none of it: he believed in segregation, but only for African Americans. Thwarted again, Cooke suggested that the YMCA and the YMHA set up lunchrooms on the roofs of loft buildings, but "we were politely told that we couldn't dictate to the individual's enjoyment and we had to abandon this scheme.... We realized the problem was too big for the association and that the only solution lay in legislation."[49]

When Cooke approached the city, however, he found the mayor unsympathetic. Gaynor thought the Fifth Avenue Association's elitism distasteful. Anyway, in 1910 he'd floated a pet project of his own: a new avenue west of Fifth.[50] It would relieve traffic congestion, the mayor said, and correct an egregious flaw in the gridiron plan: the inordinate 900-foot length of the blocks between Fifth and Sixth avenues. Pedestrians found them wearisome, and because they were so barren of street life, their real estate was undervalued.*

The Fifth Avenue Association was appalled by Gaynor's scheme. Its nightmare

---

* Gaynor's point about the gridiron was well taken: the private street at Rockefeller Center was an attempt to do something about those long blocks; Jane Jacobs wrote about the problem in the 1960s, and the current zoning code is designed to create through-block pedestrian passages in the area.

scenario pictured Fifth Avenue devoured by garment workers while this upstart street became the new center of fashion. In his stoical way, Gaynor was saddened by their attitude, and when he addressed the association in 1912 he put on one of his strangest public performances. Fifth Avenue was "only one of my children," he told the group, "and I love them all just as much. . . . You don't like that, do you? Where is McAneny? As the Mussulman turns to the east when he thinks he wants to say his prayers, so I always turn to McAneny when I want to say something about Fifth Avenue."[51]

Cooke and his colleagues also turned to McAneny, and to stop the avenue from becoming "another and cheaper Broadway," the borough president created the Fifth Avenue Commission.[52] Cooke was a member, as was George Mortimer, fresh from his losing battle to head off Du Pont's Equitable Building. The new commission's chairman was Arnold W. Brunner, formerly of MAS and the Art Commission, McAneny's colleague from the City Club, and now head of the New York chapter of the American Institute of Architects. The commissioners were to advise McAneny "if the roadway needs further widening; . . . if 'isles of safety' should be set in the stream of traffic; if the traffic itself needs better regulation; if trees should be planted; if the height of factory buildings should be limited and their area restricted, and if the architecture of Fifth Avenue's buildings should be reconciled to a harmonious scheme."[53] Brunner and his colleagues answered yes to all of the above, but concluded sadly that the avenue "has been allowed to degenerate to such an extent that all thought of making it the counterpart of any of the splendid avenues of Paris or other great cities abroad must be abandoned, for the present at least."[54]

The idea of "harmonious" architecture was still a pipe dream; it would require an amendment to the state constitution to let the city concern itself with the aesthetics of private development (as Albert Bard had proposed in his battle against billboards). The Fifth Avenue Commission endorsed this as a distant goal. For the moment it called on the city to go ahead and impose height limits on Fifth Avenue, but there were already so many skyscrapers on the avenue—the St. Regis was 259 feet tall—that Brunner didn't dare propose a height limit stringent enough to ward off lofts. He ended up recommending a 125-foot cornice line—the height of the University Club—with a twenty-five-foot mansard above.[55] This wasn't ideal, the commission admitted; it would ensure Fifth Avenue's future as "a dignified street," but nothing more.

Nothing was said of actually banning factories, and this seems a strange oversight for a movement driven by the fear of immigrant hordes. In fact the Fifth Avenue Association was dealing with lofts separately and surreptitiously. After the Triangle fire the American Institute of Architects had launched an effort to draw up a new building code free of the baleful influence of the Board of Aldermen, and a joint committee of architects and builders was at work on this. Lofts were obviously of paramount concern, and the committee had a scheme to break up factory floors with fireproof partitions. These interior walls would have worked like watertight compartments in a ship: if disaster struck, workers could simply step through a door into safety.

The Fifth Avenue Association was in touch with Robert D. Kohn, a member of this committee. He was one of the most talented and progressive designers of his generation—the architect of the Ethical Culture Society Hall on Central Park West and the old Evening Post Building on Vesey Street—but he was also the son and heir of a Fifth Avenue jeweler. Kohn suggested that these new fireproof factory walls should extend down to the ground level of loft buildings. This sounded like an innocent technicality, but the point was that "these walls will interfere with the space which the large stores demand," and, if built, the ground floors "cannot be rented for store purposes."[56] Fifth Avenue's loft buildings were, at best, marginally profitable. Without the prime rents of a store, Kohn pointed out, no bank would dare lend money to a Fifth Avenue loft.

Neither Kohn nor the Fifth Avenue Association ever considered the danger concealed in this proposal. They might have succeeded in pushing lofts to some other, cheaper neighborhood, but they'd have made that area a blighted zone of factories with little commercial life on the streets: unpleasant by day; dangerous by night.

Fortunately the joint committee's building code was never passed by the aldermen, nor did the Board of Estimate appreciate a bill, introduced by McAneny, that incorporated the Fifth Avenue Commission's recommendations for a 150-foot height limit on the avenue. McAneny saw the bill as "the first step toward something definite" in the way of a broader citywide zoning law,[57] but Cyrus Miller, borough president of the Bronx, charged that it trampled on that "freedom which should be accorded property holders in the use of their property," and it was sent off to die in a committee.[58]

Arnold Brunner had boasted that "a finer civic responsibility" had awakened on Fifth Avenue, and he described it as "a fixed and unalterable determination on our part that every citizen shall, in what he may do for his personal advantage, consult and be subject to considerations which promote the general well being." Yet so far the Fifth Avenue Association had been remarkably selfish. Desperate to prop up its own real estate values, it never expressed an ounce of concern for any other neighborhood.

At the foot of the avenue, the Washington Square Association was also struggling to ward off lofts. It wanted to keep Greenwich Village residential, but the area was squeezed between lofts on Broadway and factories on the waterfront. The widening of Varick Street and the lengthening of Seventh Avenue threatened another industrial invasion, and lofts had already appeared on the south side of Washington Square itself. Meanwhile the residents of Murray Hill, just a few blocks east of Fifth Avenue, were waging their own battle to stave off commerce. Here, many town houses were protected by restrictive covenants, but these wouldn't last forever, and Madison Avenue was a tempting target for developers. Neither of these neighborhoods would have been helped by a special height district on Fifth

Avenue, nor would the neighbors of the Equitable Building; and plenty of other districts lacked the resources, the organization, or the skill to defend themselves.

In 1912 the Fifth Avenue Association saw its campaign for special treatment wither. McAneny's height limit bill died, and Tammany still had just enough strength on the Board of Aldermen to stall all progress on the building code. The Fifth Avenue Association had only one option left: to fight for a citywide zoning ordinance. The Colne Bill still hadn't passed the state legislature, but in 1913 McAneny convinced the Board of Estimate that it had the right to at least draw up a zoning scheme without any specific authorization from Albany. The board let him form the Heights of Buildings Commission. McAneny was its chairman, and he was joined by the borough presidents of the Bronx and Brooklyn and a whole raft of characters from the real estate and moneylending worlds, among them George Mortimer, who was now, ironically, the manager of the Equitable Building, and Walter Stabler of the Metropolitan Life Insurance Company, which had financed many Fifth Avenue lofts and was alarmed at how poorly they performed. But the commission's real work was largely done by two members of its own advisory committee: Edward Bassett, the advisers' chairman, who had been a devotee of height limits and land-use controls since his tour of the 1908 Congestion Show; and George Ford, the group's secretary, an architect who'd been active in Benjamin Marsh's old Congestion Committee.*

And so in 1913, as Bassett and Ford set up their advisory committee, the Municipal Art Society debated once again how to restrict heights. Electus Litchfield still wanted his floor area ratio system, which he demonstrated with little wooden blocks; Frederick Lamb argued for his brother's setback system; the architect Raymond Almirall thought up a new complication, demanding that the Art Commission take control over all buildings facing a public park or square; and finally, independent of MAS, there was Ernest Flagg, still arguing for his city of towers.

All of these contradictory notions were presented to George Ford and Edward Bassett's advisory committee. Ford and Bassett knew that "aesthetic" legislation wouldn't survive a court fight, and that they had to design a law that could pass muster as a defense of property values or public health, something whose benefits could be quantified in terms of light, air, rents, and tax assessments. A pure cap on heights seemed dangerous on this count. If sunlight was the point, the height limit would have to be very low indeed, and as Ernest Flagg had pointed out in 1908, "Our land values have been set on the basis of high buildings. To set a low limit of height now would ... bring about a great shrinkage of values."[59] Property owners would sue, and the courts would surely rule that the statute was confiscatory; moreover, the city's finances were inextricably tangled up with those high assessments. Eighty percent of the city's budget flowed from taxes on property or

---

* The other members of the advisory committee were C. Grant La Farge, Burt Fenner, Otto Eidlitz, Lawrence Veiller, and J. Monroe Hewlett. Veiller was a housing advocate; the rest were architects. Fenner worked for McKim, Mead & White; Eidlitz designed the Times Tower; Hewlett was Electus Litchfield's former boss, a muralist as well as an architect, and a future president of MAS.

buildings: the whole architecture of the municipal bond market rested on this foundation.

Charles Lamb's "angle of light" offered the sort of concrete public benefits the city could defend in court. It would result in even cornice lines, which was aesthetically pleasing, but setbacks could be built above those lines, which was financially attractive. Yet there were knotty problems with Lamb's idea. Lamb always liked to show his setback city with a single vast building covering each block, but in the real world each block was a mosaic of many lots. Simply imposing a pyramidal zoning envelope would affect the individual landowners in very different ways. Someone with property in the middle of a block could build a very tall building, but anyone with a corner plot would complain that he was being unfairly penalized, since two angles of light whittled away at his zoning envelope. Lamb's scheme was curiously blind to the traditional system of land values in New York, where avenue lots are more valuable than those on side streets, and corner lots are the most prized of all. His massive pyramids would also have blurred what we now regard as the quintessential urbanism of New York, in which avenues are densely developed and the narrow side streets retain a more intimate, human scale. And finally, people loved the latest crop of freestanding Beaux Arts towers. The Metropolitan Life, Singer, and Woolworth buildings were famous around the world. Since their towers were very thin and rose over only part of their lots, they didn't impinge on neighbors' sunlight the way the Equitable did.

George Ford and Edward Bassett decided to marry Charles Lamb's and Ernest Flagg's ideas: buildings would have setbacks *and* towers. Just as Flagg had proposed, the towers might be of unlimited height, but they could cover only a quarter of the lot. (His idea of transferring tower rights from one neighbor to another was not taken up.) The towers had their aesthetic attractions, but the issue of corner lots was perhaps just as important: a tower could make up for the disadvantage of having to follow setback lines on two sides of a building instead of one. The result was that both Flagg and Lamb were bitterly unhappy when the zoning resolution was finally adopted: Flagg because the setback system still allowed too much shadow in the streets; Lamb because those towers interrupted his angles of light.[60]

By 1913 George McAneny's Heights of Buildings Commission had agreed on the basic strategy of combining setbacks and towers, but it wasn't sure how to apply this system to the city at large. It didn't want all neighborhoods to be equally dense, but sorting out which neighborhoods should be dense and which shouldn't was well beyond the commission's portfolio. So Edward Bassett asked McAneny to create a second body, the Commission on Building Districts and Restrictions, which would divide the city into different zones, each with its own height, land-use, and area controls. Bassett drafted the necessary legislation, and to drum up support for it McAneny persuaded the Board of Estimate to cosponsor a city planning exhibit with the Merchants' Association. Charles Lamb was now the chairman of the Merchants' Association's Committee on City Planning,[61] and he and McAneny put together another advisory commission that included Municipalians Milo Maltbie,

Calvin Tomkins, and H. Van Buren Magonigle as well as George Ford. The planning exhibit was held in the New York Public Library; more than two hundred cities lent material, and it was so popular that it was sent on tour around the country. Yet there was still to be no City Planning Commission; instead the Board of Estimate created a mere standing Committee on the City Plan in 1914. Its members were the borough presidents plus the president of the Board of Aldermen, and McAneny became its chairman. It had none of the independence of a commission, but it did recognize that planning "should be a constant and not an occasional subject of study." It was the best he could do, McAneny told Frederick Lamb.[62]

In 1914 the New York State Legislature finally gave the Board of Estimate the right to impose zoning, and the new Commission on Building Districts and Restrictions set to work with Edward Bassett as its chairman. It took the system of setbacks and towers but played with the height of that first cornice line. In some places it would be only as tall as the street was wide, but this height was jacked up in four stages until, in the business districts, the cornice was set at two and a half times the street width. The commission also added a system of area limits—front, side, and rear yard requirements—whose most important repercussion was to create "villa zones" of single family houses in the outer boroughs. And finally, Bassett addressed land uses.

Three categories of land use were created—residential, business, and "unrestricted"—but these weren't as cut and dried as the later Modernist city planners would have liked. A residential zone might include churches, cultural institutions, clubs, and hotels. A business district might include all of the above as well as offices and stores, and a quarter of each commercial building could be used for manufacturing. Aside from that loophole, factories were confined to the unrestricted areas, but there they could continue to jostle tenements and businesses. Except along Riverside Drive, an unrestricted zone girdled Manhattan, and it engulfed most of the lower island, even the financial district. The old sweatshop district on the Lower East Side, however, was now zoned for business. The side streets of Greenwich Village and the Gramercy Park neighborhood were reserved for residents, but business zones ran up and down the avenues. Midtown was a business district except for a few residential pockets—Murray Hill, the side streets west of Fifth Avenue in the Fifties, and Park Avenue north of Fiftieth Street.

The Commission on Building Districts and Restrictions published its report in March 1916. It noted that "The social and economic desirability of limited height and minimum court and yard provisions has been clearly established by apartment house construction under the Tenement House Law. Had similar regulations been applied to office and loft buildings great loss would have been prevented."[63] The commission promised property owners that zoning would stabilize land values, but "the keynote of the report," addressed to a wider audience that included the vast array of apartment dwellers, was "the importance of proper home life. There is nothing more vital to the city than the housing of its people," it read. "There is nothing more essential to wholesome and comfortable housing than the exclusion of trade and industries from the residential streets."[64]

Through the spring of 1916 troops of New Yorkers descended on City Hall for public hearings on the zoning resolution. One witness insisted that zoning would be legal only if a single uniform rule were applied to the entire city: if skyscrapers were permitted in the financial district they ought to be allowed everywhere. " 'In Staten Island, for instance?' inquired Chairman Bassett. 'All over the city,' " the witness replied.[65] What was remarkable was that most of those who testified demanded more stringent limitations, not less. Many of the recommendations had to do with boundaries—whether residential zones should be expanded at the expense of business zones, or business zones should be expanded into unrestricted areas. The Board of Trade asked for a special district of one-family houses on the Upper West Side, where the mansions and row houses of West End Avenue and Riverside Drive were already falling victim to a wave of apartment construction, their restrictive covenants having expired. The Pennsylvania Railroad asked that factories be barred from the vicinity of Pennsylvania Station in order, it said, to prevent traffic congestion. Residents of quiet side streets who found themselves swallowed up in unrestricted areas petitioned for protection. The Murray Hill Association demanded that pockets of business be eliminated from Madison Avenue. Residents of Thirty-fifth Street complained that the treatment of Thirty-fourth Street, a wide crosstown street, was far too liberal.[66]

Certain aspects of the zoning resolution appalled even its most fervent advocates. Parks, for instance, were singularly ill treated. Since zoning was meant to protect light and air for residents, and parks were themselves reservoirs of these precious commodities, the 1916 Zoning Resolution allowed one to build much higher on streets facing a park. (Today the emphasis is often the reverse, and so the recent fight against the Coliseum Center centered on that project's impact on Central Park.) This was especially alarming because so many of the city's small parks— Thomas Jefferson, DeWitt Clinton, Chelsea, St. Gabriel's, Corlear's Hook, and the south side of St. John's—sat in areas that were scheduled to become manufacturing zones, while Hamilton Fish, Stuyvesant, Tompkins Square, and Gramercy parks would end up in business districts. In most cases, commercial or manufacturing establishments already existed on nearby streets, but the parks themselves were still lined with residences. The new zoning would serve to encourage the construction of commercial buildings in place of the homes, because of the higher cornice lines available.

The City Club wanted to preserve these neighborhoods as purely residential enclaves.[67] The cry was taken up by the Women's City Club, the Women's Municipal League, and Parks Commissioner Cabot Ward. "This is a matter of first importance," he testified, for the code "jeopardizes the small park, which has become a center in the life of the community. I have based my argument on the needs of the least fortunate elements of the community, but the expenditures of the city and its taxes fall upon the poor as well as the rich."

Ward also had more specific complaints that illustrated the cost of implementing zoning without a city plan. The city had just begun to purchase land for Inwood Hill Park in upper Manhattan, and the Isham family had given the city part of its tract for another park to the east.[68] Ward naturally intended to link the two parks one day, but the area between them was slated for unrestricted use. Factories had already begun to appear there, and the zoning code would allow others to be built. "It is not good business and it is not good policy for the city," Ward complained. "Someday the whole park system of the city will be connected, and if this section of the city is not restricted you can easily see how the city will suffer."[69]

There was another problem: zoning wasn't retroactive. Declaring Fifth Avenue a business district would not affect the garment factories already there. While hearings on the zoning resolution continued, a man named J. Howes Burton began a "Save New York Campaign." Burton summoned the avenue's retailers to lunch at Delmonico's and treated them to some unappetizing rhetoric:

> Gentlemen, you are like cattle in a pasture, and the needle trade workers are the flies that follow you from one pasture to another, nagging you into abandoning one great center after another and leaving a trail of ruin, devastation, and bankruptcy up and down the length of the city. The rich pasture of your predecessors was in Grand Street. The flies drove the trade to Fourteenth Street, where most of you took up the burden of trying to do business against these odds in a city that had no law and no plan to save itself from the spoliation of its choicest sections. Then you were driven to Twenty-third Street, and again, within a very few years, to Thirty-fourth and Forty-second Streets, and here, once more, the flies are threatening to swarm worse than ever.[70]

Burton suggested that the merchants take matters into their own hands and organize a boycott: unless garment factories moved out of the neighborhood by the end of 1916, shops and department stores would refuse to buy their goods. Fifth Avenue shops, department stores, hotels, and clubs all endorsed the campaign, and soon merchants in Chicago, Philadelphia, and Rochester pledged that they too would observe the boycott. More important was the participation of banks, trust companies, and real estate owners. As Burton put it, "the remedy lay with the money lender."[71] Walter Stabler was one of the first to endorse the Save New York Campaign, and by the time it went public, with full-page ads in the Sunday morning papers on March 6, 1916, it had won the support of Vincent Astor, the Astor Estate, the Astor Trust Company, the Columbia Trust Company, the Fifth Avenue Bank, the Guaranty Trust Company, and the Harriman National Bank. The Title Guarantee and Trust Company joined later. The banks soon adopted resolutions that they would make no loans for factories in "the forbidden zone."[72]

To preserve New York's premier retail district was a noble aim, and as Mayor John Purroy Mitchel said when he endorsed the Save New York Campaign, Burton succeeded in "calling attention . . . to a primary need of the entire city—a comprehensive, well considered plan for the control of city growth."[73] But Burton also injected ugly notes of ethnic and class bigotry into the campaign. The photograph in his newspaper advertisements managed to make a lunch hour crowd of garment workers look like a sinister mob, and Burton published an incendiary photo montage in which that same crowd was seemingly transported north to Millionaires' Row. The montage looked like the Upper East Side's nightmare—an immigrant horde seizing control of the streets—and this, Burton suggested, was precisely what lay in store if the Save New York Campaign failed.

Burton blamed Fifth Avenue's problems on an expansionist garment industry rather than on the miscalculations of local real estate developers, and it was probably a surprise to the Save New York Committee that the garment manufacturers themselves quickly endorsed the campaign. They asked only for a more flexible deadline so they wouldn't have to break their leases. But the garment trade, after all, relied more than any other on a thriving retail zone. For efficiency's sake it needed to be concentrated in one location, and for the sake of out-of-town buyers it had to be near the stores, hotels, train depots, and theaters, but that didn't necessarily mean on Fifth Avenue.[74] The garment industry saw the value of Burton's goal and feared his tactics at the same time. The Save New York Campaign had one singular advantage: it had nothing to do with the city government. As a result, "all red tape has been cut with one stroke," Burton boasted. "The zoning commission in the future will have no difficulty in carrying out its plans."[75]

THE ZONING RESOLUTION passed the Board of Estimate on July 25, 1916, but it would take years to make out its effects. The zoning code was passed in a depressed real estate market, and soon the United States was drawn into World War I. Even a bold investor found it hard to build when steel was diverted to munitions factories and shipbuilding plants. At first the new regulations simply brought a measure of calm and stability to the real estate market. Washington Square had actually begun to rebound in 1915 when Sailors' Snug Harbor, convinced that the zoning resolution would soon be approved, decided "to remodel into livable and artistic shape the worn-out buildings on the south side of Eighth Street and the small stables on the north side of the mews between Fifth Avenue and University Place." This was something of a triumph for the Washington Square Association, which had fought any influx of trade north of the park—although the group was disturbed at the prospect of more bohemians and artists flooding into the area. In fact, "one of the members intimated that the association did not desire a Latin Quarter in its neighborhood."[76] Murray Hill stabilized as soon as the zoning resolution was adopted. The neighborhood's vacancy rate fell by 40 percent in 1916. "Families of the class called 'fashionable' " were moving back to the area, and by November seventy houses were being renovated.[77] Even Ladies Mile began to recover. Its fortunes were no longer glamorous or chic, but by the end of 1916 the old department stores were finding new lives as lofts for the wholesale trade.[78]

The garment district, however, remained an unsettled question. E. J. Wile, president of the Cloak, Suit, and Skirt Manufacturers' Protective Association, endorsed the Save New York Campaign in 1916, but "Where do you want us to move?" he asked. "What buildings have you for us? We are not going to move from our light, airy buildings into holes—dark, dingy buildings."[79] Most people agreed that the needle trades should move somewhere—anywhere—south of Twenty-third Street, and there was hope that a new generation of modern loft buildings would revive the desolated business and retail districts. One could already see, however, signs that something different would happen—that the garment industry would settle west of the retail district, not south of it. In September 1916 the *Times* reported that plans were afoot for six new loft buildings on Seventh Avenue, meant to house showrooms for the millinery trade. They would sit just north of Pennsylvania Station and the new Pennsylvania Hotel—an ideal hotel for out-of-town buyers—just west of the department stores and south of Times Square, and when the Seventh Avenue subway opened in 1917, they would be even more convenient.[80] By the early 1920s this area was becoming the heart of the garment district—and the first real neighborhood of setback buildings.

By the mid 1920s a building boom had really arrived. A new crop of skyscrapers soared above the financial district, and Midtown became New York's second business district. Only then did it become clear that the Heights of Buildings Commission hadn't really understood what would happen. The commission didn't realize, for instance, that its work would encourage builders to assemble larger lots. The reason for this was very simple: the new setback rules meant that it wasn't worth building a very tall structure on a small site, since the upper floors would be tiny. Developers discovered that bigger sites meant taller buildings. The cityscape took on a far more massive scale as a result, and the effect on the real estate industry was just as marked. As Cass Gilbert had predicted in 1908, these restrictions tended to "concentrate operations solely in the hands of large corporate interests combining many small properties. It may then be considered a question of public policy in so placing the advantages on the side of the larger holders of real estate."[81]

Towers, too, proved to be a surprise. George Ford knew that the Woolworth, Singer, and Metropolitan Life towers were so thin that there wasn't enough rental space inside to pay back the investment. Their value lay in the realm of publicity and advertising, not real estate. Ford assumed that few corporations would follow such an expensive route to fame and that towers would rise over just a few large sites. He had no way of knowing that in the 1920s architects would figure out more efficient ways to plan towers. They played with oblong rather than square plans, and they moved the elevators from the middle of the tower to one wall, and suddenly very thin towers became far more practical.

There was another development that the Zoning Commission couldn't predict. Its members thought in terms of traditional architecture—Parisian mansard roofs, palazzi, and towers—and they assumed that architects would merely try to fit these old schemes into the pyramidal zoning envelope. In the 1920s, however, architects began basing their designs on the envelope itself. In 1921 the architect Harvey Wiley Corbett (a friend of Charles Lamb) and the renderer Hugh Ferris issued a legendary set of drawings exploring the potential of the zoning envelope. They began by treating the envelope as if it were a solid block of clay; next, they translated it into orthogonal steps; then they simplified these steps to get a more efficient steel skeleton; and only then did they worry about what the building looked like. This method of design, widely adopted in the 1920s, produced weird buildings—jumbles of cubic setbacks and towers—that rang the death knell for academic classicism in New York. One simply couldn't make sense of these shapes with the old vocabulary of columns, pedestals, and cornices. So the Zoning Resolution ushered in, quite by accident, the great experiment of Art Deco architecture.

GEORGE MCANENY RESIGNED his post as president of the Board of Aldermen in 1916, as soon as the zoning resolution was secure. He had a growing family to support, and his path to higher office was blocked by William Randolph Hearst, but his resignation was "a piece of depressing news," the *Evening Post* wrote, which "seems to imply Mr. McAneny's definite retreat from public life."[82] It was the end of his career in elective office, but certainly not in public life. In the years to come McAneny would serve as the first president of the Regional Plan Association and as the city's comptroller in the dark days of the early 1930s, when New York teetered on the brink of bankruptcy. He went on to play a crucial role in organizing the World's Fair of 1939, and his fight to save Castle Clinton from Robert Moses's demolition crews would launch the Municipal Art Society on the path to writing the city's first landmarks law.

For the moment, however, the *New York Times* took McAneny on as its executive manager. Adolph Ochs wanted him on board to lend "a kind of moral background" to the paper.[83]

With McAneny gone from the political arena the miserly and xenophobic tendencies of John Purroy Mitchel's regime came to the foreground. Mayor Mitchel and his comptroller, William Prendergast, were the sort of small-minded reformers who slashed the budget, the public be damned. The mayor didn't help matters with his war preparations. His grandfather had been a great Irish nationalist, but Mitchel was an Anglophile, and his eagerness to join the Allies in World War I enraged Irish and German voters. Mitchel lost his reelection bid to John F. Hylan, a mediocre judge foisted on the city by William Randolph Hearst.

When Mayor Hylan came to power he abolished McAneny's City Plan Committee—as an economy measure, he explained—and reformers were terrified that he'd scrap the Zoning Commission as well. He didn't. No one was opposed to zoning anymore. Property owners were grateful that it had brought some stability to land values; tenants were happy that it had steered obnoxious land uses away from their homes. And zoning turned out to be useful to Tammany itself, for the Board of Standards and Appeals had the power to review requests for zoning variances, a wide discretionary power that was ideally suited to the practice of "honest graft." Bribes, in the strictest sense of the word, never needed to change hands. All Tammany had to do was to make sure that certain lawyers, closely connected to the Democratic machine, enjoyed astonishing success when representing clients before the board. Hylan cooperated by appointing a gaggle of Tammany hacks to the Board of Standards and Appeals, and this practice continued under his successor, Mayor Jimmy Walker. By the 1920s it was common knowledge, at least in real estate and architectural circles, that even the ban on manufacturing in business districts was highly porous. The 1916 Zoning Resolution declared that, in a business district, 25 percent of a building might be used for manufacturing. This loophole had been included for the sake of certain Fifth Avenue merchants— expensive dressmakers, hatmakers, and jewelers like Tiffany, who produced custom wares above their own elegant showrooms. By the 1920s, however, the Board of Standards and Appeals had effectively thrown the doors open to loft buildings in restricted neighborhoods. Builders were allowed to whittle away at the 25 percent limit by deducting the square footage of circulation areas, showrooms, reception areas, and storage rooms from the "manufacturing" area. In practice, factories could be built in any business district so long as the machinery itself occupied less than a quarter of the floor area.

The tragedy, however, was not that Tammany succeeded in corrupting zoning in this petty fashion, but that the 1916 Zoning Resolution itself was so laughably crude. Its creators had been concerned above all to establish the basic principle that the city could limit private development for the public good. They did so by making these first limits as painless as possible. In terms of land use the 1916 Zoning Resolution largely enforced the status quo, while its height limits were so liberal that only a few existing skyscrapers would have been affected. McAneny had always intended that, once zoning was established and its legality upheld by the courts, the real work of shaping the city would finally begin. A City Planning Commission—that long-held dream of McAneny's—would be able to use the zoning code to design a better future for New York, but with Tammany back in power in City Hall, McAneny's dream was deferred for more than two decades.

The Insular City: Calvin Tomkins and the Port of New York

GEORGE MCANENY GAVE New York a zoning code and a new subway system, and these were two critical elements in the Municipal Art Society's agenda for the city. They answered only part of the problem, however. A zoning commission could declare that certain neighborhoods were going to be industrial zones; it could say that factories would be confined to particular districts; but it couldn't make new lofts or wharves materialize. The Dual Contracts meant that new subways would carry workers to better homes in Brooklyn and Queens, but they didn't guarantee that industry would move to the outer boroughs. Factories needed an infrastructure of docks, freight terminals, and train yards if they were to receive materials or ship their finished goods away. And so, while McAneny tended to the zoning and subway issues, Calvin Tomkins was trying to build a freight system for the greater city.

In *Moby-Dick,* Herman Melville described the "insular city" of Manhattan,

> belted round by wharves as Indian isles by coral reefs—commerce surrounds it with her surf. . . . Circumambulate the city of a dreamy Sabbath afternoon. Go from Corlears Hook to Coenties Slip, and from there, by Whitehall, northward. What do you see?—Posted like silent sentinels all around the town, stand thousands of mortal men fixed in ocean reveries. Some leaning against the spiles; some seated upon the pier-heads; some looking over the bulwarks of ships from China; some high aloft in the rigging, as if striving to get a still better seaward peep. . . . These are all landsmen; of work pent up in lath and plaster—tied to counters, nailed to benches, clinched to desks. . . . And there they stand—miles of them—leagues. Inlanders all. . . .[1]

Sixty years later, when Tomkins took office as New York's dock commissioner, Melville's sailing ships had given way to vast leviathans of steel, and the coral reef of commerce had grown denser, taller, and craggier.[2] The East River slips were now neglected as steamships claimed the broader current of the Hudson River, and the water lay behind long lines of sheds and loading docks that stretched from pierhead to pierhead: a scabrous cliff of wood and sheet metal walling in the city, broken only by the occasional dumping board, where garbage was heaped on barges headed for the open sea. West Street was less a road than a continuous loading dock, its surface almost invisible beneath the lines of carts and trucks drawn up to the piers. Railroads had sprung up to carry New York's commerce to the farthest corners of the continent. Across the river, half a dozen terminals lined the Jersey shore, and the Hudson churned with barges as the railroads ferried freight and passengers to Manhattan. An iron barricade of train tracks stretched along Manhattan's waterfront as the New York Central railroad skirted Riverside Park and plunged down Twelfth, Eleventh, and Tenth avenues. The poor inlander had little chance of enjoying an ocean reverie.

Today, New York's dock commissioner occupies an obscure post far from the glare of public interest, but in the early years of the century the Port of New York was the city's economic engine; its tariffs balanced the federal budget, and its potential for development had prompted the great experiment of a consolidated city. And absent a city planning agency, a dock commissioner might properly concern himself with issues far removed from the wharves themselves. The docks, after all, were just one cog in a machine to move cargo: raw materials to the factories, finished goods to markets abroad or across the continent. A good deal of freight was merely passing through the city. Carried by steamer across the ocean, it was unloaded on a wharf, carted to an importer, sorted, repacked, driven back to the pier, carried by barge across the Hudson, and placed on a train bound for points west. If it landed in New Jersey, there were additional steps: it was unloaded in Hoboken, put on a barge, unloaded again on West Street, sent off to the importer, and then shipped back to Jersey and its railroads. In any case, docks had to be married to railroads, and Calvin Tomkins would spend his days as dock commissioner thinking of trains.

THE NEW YORK Central's West Side tracks had long been one of the city's sorest political issues. The railroad dated back to 1846, when Albany granted the Hudson River Railroad Company a fifty-year franchise. By 1853 its tracks stretched to Albany. In 1869 the franchise was extended to five hundred years, and eventually the company was absorbed into the Vanderbilts' railroad empire, the New York Central. The city fathers never took into account the fact that trains ran through the streets of Manhattan; south of Seventy-second Street, the city grew up around the railroad. Trains crawled at a snail's pace through busy streets lined with tenements, factories, and warehouses. Merchants decried the railroad's inefficiency and lamented its monopoly, while Chelsea mourned the death toll among its residents and coined a grim new nickname for Eleventh Avenue, where the slaughter reached its peak: Death Avenue.

In 1908 alone, seventeen people were injured or maimed beneath the wheels of New York Central trains, and eleven more died.* One was Seth Low Hancow, age seven, born in the campaign season of 1901. "It did not matter to his playmates when the lawyers called Seth a trespasser," the *Times* reported. They answered with "a protest unique in the history of American cities," pouring onto Eleventh Avenue and raising "five hundred treble voices . . . in cries and jeers against the tracks at grade."[3] On the West Side, the managers of the New York Central were regarded as little better than a bunch of murderers, and their intransigence was all the more shocking given the Vanderbilts' wealth, so ostentatiously flaunted on Fifth Avenue in mansions designed and decorated by Municipalians.

"At times, feeling ran so high," the *Times* observed, "that there has been talk of tearing up the tracks and leaving the railway to its legal remedy, if any. But that was no more possible than to leave the railway there."[4] No more possible because the state legislature was in the railroad's pocket; because the courts callously rebuffed all attempts to declare the tracks a public nuisance; because so many jobs and factories depended on the railroad; and because without it, New York would be at the mercy of the New Jersey railroads. The Jersey companies had to ferry freight across the river on barges, and they swallowed much of this extra cost in order to remain competitive with the New York Central. "Now they must meet our rates," a Vanderbilt minion crowed, but "If we did not run into the city by land, the New Jersey lines would be able to add to their freight charges."[5] If that ever happened, New York would face far higher freight costs. Manufacturers would have to cut their profit margins or watch their customers find cheaper goods from other cities. Its export trade would drift away.

And so New York tolerated Death Avenue even after the turn of the century, when the railroad system began faltering under the sheer volume of traffic. The grain trade was lost to other, cheaper ports, and the railroads began charging a premium on goods bound for New York. Even so, the railroads' barges claimed so many of West Street's wharves that the transatlantic shipping lines couldn't expand. Even the New York Central was sorely pressed. It had transferred all its import and export cargo to the Jersey shore, where it owned the Central West Shore Railroad, but the West Side tracks were still so crowded that even the New York Central began using barges to get goods up, down, and across the river.[6]

In 1907 the railroad magnate James J. Hill sent tremors through the business community when he announced that "New York has reached the climax of her commercial supremacy. No city can maintain its control when its chief claim is that it is the dearest place in the world to do business. The cost of everything relating to trade and commerce has increased here beyond the point of profit. Traffic will be forced to seek other outlets; business other locations."[7] This was no idle threat.

---

* The city did require that a cowboy ride ahead of each train waving a red flag to warn of its approach, but the trains moved so slowly that drivers were constantly tempted to risk dashing across the tracks, and no cowboy could stop a child from chasing a ball into the street or prevent a horse from bolting.

New York was still the world's busiest port and the nation's largest manufacturer, but its position was slipping. Business still grew every year, but the city's share of the market steadily declined.

The business community was slow to act on Hill's warning. In the meantime Chelsea had already mobilized to battle the New York Central. The campaign started when the Social Reform Club launched a "Committee of Fifty" to rid Death Avenue of train tracks. The committee's members included local businessmen; Samuel Moffet, the editor of *Collier's Weekly*; and Father Chidwick, chaplain of the *Maine* when it sank in Havana Harbor and now a local parish priest. Their hopes were lodged in the Saxe Bill, which gave the Rapid Transit Commission one year in which to draw up a plan for moving the tracks. If the railroad didn't accept it, the RTC was to condemn the franchise. The Municipal Art Society tried to stop the Saxe Bill before it reached Albany. According to one committee member, Charles Lamb "came to us . . . and wanted to sidetrack our movement." The danger, as Lamb saw it, was that the Saxe Bill would push the city and railroad into a hastily designed and expedient solution. The most likely outcome was that the railroad would simply elevate its tracks. But where? On Eleventh Avenue? That would stop the carnage, but it would plunge the avenue into darkness, and noise and pollution would continue to blight what was, in part, a residential street. Nor did an El make sense in terms of the railroad's cargo, much of which was headed for, or bound from, the docks on Twelfth Avenue and West Street.

Lamb proposed an alternative solution: a freight subway circling Manhattan. The Committee of Fifty heard him out, but feared that in pressing for such an ambitious solution they would only make it more difficult to solve their most pressing problem: the fact that people were being mangled on Eleventh Avenue. The Saxe Bill was passed into law in 1906, and at the time it seemed a triumph of citizen advocacy. Chelsea rejoiced. Within a year, it was thought, the neighborhood would see progress. The railroad appeared to be cooperative at first, and it may have meant to be. There were things the New York Central wanted from the city—the right to expand its rail yards and to add more tracks to its franchise—and these gave it an incentive to negotiate. There was talk of a deal: the railroad would build a freight subway from Riverside Park to Thirtieth Street; it would pay the city for the privilege of expanding its facilities north of Seventy-second Street; and the city would use this money to cover the tracks in Riverside Park.

But 1907 was a year of panic on Wall Street. The New York Central broke off its talks with the Rapid Transit Commission, announcing that it wouldn't even consider any plans presented to it. Taking the railroad at its word, the transit commission never formally submitted a plan. No one noticed at the time, but the commission had fallen into a trap. The year passed, but when Chelsea looked expectantly toward City Hall for news of condemnation proceedings, it was reminded that the city couldn't condemn what it couldn't pay for, and that New York was already on the verge of its debt limit.

Another year passed, and in 1908 the Public Service Commission succeeded the

RTC. It unveiled a cheaper plan to elevate the tracks.[8] The Committee of Fifty was disgusted, but the Public Service Commission moved ahead with condemnation proceedings. Now the trap was sprung. The railroad went to court: the one-year period specified in the Saxe Act had elapsed, it pointed out, without the Rapid Transit Commission submitting a plan. The courts agreed with the railroad, the Saxe Act was declared null and void, and Chelsea was back to square one.

At this point the Committee of Fifty turned back to Charles Lamb. "We are all pretty much behind him," one member told the *Times*.[9] It may seem strange that in this moment of defeat the organization became more ambitious, but it must have hoped that Lamb's scheme would draw support from wider and more influential circles. It seemed to balance the needs not only of Chelsea but also of the steamship companies, the merchant class, industry—of any business that had a stake in the cheap, efficient transportation of goods through New York. Yet there were already cracks in what seemed a natural coalition, and this was clear as soon as the city published the designs for the Chelsea piers.

The Chelsea piers had been discussed for years, but it took an ultimatum from the steamship lines to finally prod the city into action. By 1903 the *Lusitania* and the *Titanic* were in construction and, at 800 feet, they were longer than any dock in Manhattan. Unless New York updated its harbor facilities, the steamship companies threatened to go elsewhere: to New Jersey or to the 1,300-foot pier that Irving Bush was building in Brooklyn—or, worse still, to Boston. Faced with this threat, Seth Low laid plans for new docks. He picked Chelsea because its "squalid and ill smelling" piers were especially dilapidated and its berths were choked with raw sewage, which was piped directly to the docks. Moreover, these sorry conditions had long stood in the way of waterfront development. Since most of their docks were downtown, and the steamship companies didn't want to disperse their operations, they had always resisted the idea of relocating to a site farther north. The Chelsea location had one great disadvantage, however: it sat at the narrowest part of the Hudson River, and Seth Low couldn't persuade the War Department to extend the bulkhead line.[10]

So George McClellan, Low's successor, inherited the monumental task of creating the long piers by carving 400,000 square feet of earth and stone out of Manhattan Island.[11] He had a "sentimental" interest in the project: in the 1870s, his father had found a job as chief engineer of the brand-new Docks Department, and one of General McClellan's many disappointments was that the department never had enough money to rebuild Chelsea's waterfront. The new mayor was happy to complete his father's work, and he was in a particularly receptive mood when the Improvement Commission insisted that the new piers, "the nation's watergate," should be every bit as monumental as the great railroad stations.[12]

Alas, McClellan was less receptive to the Municipal Art Society's ideas. MAS had evolved a policy toward the municipal piers, where public money was spent largely for the benefit of private commerce. True, the piers were leased at a profit, and they were an important investment in the city's economy, but MAS hoped for more direct public benefits as well. "The tendency lately," Charles Lamb complained, "has been to shut off the river from the people," and yet "it is possible to make every pier free of access to the public."[13] It would cost nothing, MAS insisted, to place flat roofs on the piers, and very little to provide stairs so that the rooftops could double as recreation facilities for the teeming tenement neighborhoods. With another small outlay, the city could build small parks between the piers, little places open to the breezes, sunsets, and lapping waves. And at the same time, Lamb argued, one might build an elevated carriage roadway in front of the piers. For the moment it would filter passenger traffic from the carts and wagons on West Street, and in the future it could be extended from Seventy-second Street to the Battery and perhaps up the East Side as well. Lamb called his road a boulevard, and in those days of carriages and just a few autos, he pictured it as a pleasure drive. Readers, however, will recognize in his idea the germ of the West Side Highway and the East River Drive.

The 1904 Improvement Commission took up this proposal for an elevated roadway.[14] This thoroughfare, as Lamb had suggested, could be extended into a longer boulevard, but the commission didn't quite dare to advocate that scheme. Shortly thereafter, the Docks Department hired Whitney Warren, who sat on the Improvement Commission, as its architect. It seems that McClellan's dock commissioner gave MAS some private assurance that the rooftop and waterfront public spaces would be included in Warren's final design, while the elevated road and even a freight subway might be added later, once the city settled on a waterfront policy. MAS believed him—he was, after all, a gentleman and a member of the Municipal Art Society—but the steamship companies were also murmuring in the dock commissioner's ear, begging him to eliminate the whole package of public benefits. The notion of parks between the piers was vetoed; the shipping companies wanted more loading space. As for those flat rooftops, the steamship lines were apparently worried about security, though a few night watchmen could have handled the problem. MAS knew nothing of these conversations, and its board of directors was shocked when Warren published his final designs.[15] At first glance they looked like a triumph of the City Beautiful. The *Times* admired Warren's "masculine, simple" architecture, with great pedimented entrances and sculpted trophies depicting the spoils of commerce. For the first time, wrote the paper, a visitor would find "no tawdriness in the way of piers, no narrow, cluttered up thoroughfare across which he must perforce make his way to the arteries of town."[16] But the pierheads were linked by a continuous wall of loading docks that shut out all views of the water, the roofs were pitched and inaccessible, and three-quarters of a mile of waterfront had been sealed off from the public. In Charles Lamb's mind, it was "practically a crime against the public."[17]

Although Warren's plans for the Chelsea piers were a disappointment to the Municipal Art Society, the larger issue was that of establishing a direct link between New York and the New Jersey railroads. In 1901 MAS's Conference Committee on the City Plan suggested that the railroads build a new joint freight terminal in

Communipaw. That would have been more efficient than six separate facilities, but it didn't solve the problem.

Finally, in 1903, the Pennsylvania Railroad decided to build its own tunnel to Manhattan. Its New York Extension project was "one of the costliest privately financed construction projects of the industrial age."[18] And when the tunnel was finished, the Pennsylvania's trains crossed the Hackensack Meadows and burrowed beneath the Bergen Cliffs and the Hudson River before arriving at Pennsylvania Station. From there, tracks crossed Manhattan and continued in four tunnels beneath the East River. Two of them linked the Long Island Railroad, which the Pennsylvania owned, to Manhattan. The others carried trains through Long Island City and Astoria, Queens, then northeast across the Hell Gate Bridge to the New Haven railroad yard in the South Bronx, and finally to New England.

In 1908 William Wilgus, the brilliant engineer who oversaw the planning of Grand Central Terminal, set out to build on the Pennsylvania Railroad's example. He incorporated the New Amsterdam Company and meant to build a massive freight yard in New Jersey, a tunnel linking it to Manhattan, and a freight subway ringing the island. On the West Side, Wilgus's subway would connect to the New York Central tracks; on the East Side, it would meet the New York, New Haven and Hartford railroad.[19] As it happened, Wilgus's company never got off the ground, although his plan did serve as an inspiration to MAS, and especially to Calvin Tomkins.

CALVIN TOMKINS'S CAREER in city government is generally remembered in a few grisly footnotes, for he unwittingly set in motion a chain of events that led to the death of Mayor Gaynor. When Tomkins took over the Docks Department he found an agency riddled with corruption and cluttered with patronage jobs, and like the good businessman he was, he started by cleaning house. He fired some workers for corruption—the dockmasters had been pocketing landing fees; six were indicted, and three fled to Canada—and many others "for cause." One was a laborer named James J. Gallagher, dismissed for chronic lateness and "insolence."

Already a troubled man, Gallagher slipped into insanity. He knew that Mayor Gaynor was sometimes merciful—at least to strangers—so he began to haunt City Hall, demanding his job back. The guards kept shooing him away until Gallagher, grown bitter, read that Gaynor was about to sail to Europe for a vacation. Gallagher tracked Gaynor to the pier. "You have taken my bread and butter away from me!" he shouted, and he shot the mayor in the throat. A second bullet wounded the street cleaning commissioner.

Gaynor survived, and the next time he saw Tomkins he greeted him with a weak grin and a hoarse whisper as "the man who is responsible for all this." But the bullet was never removed, the mayor became even more peculiar, and when he died in 1913—while plotting his reelection campaign—it was widely assumed that Gallagher had finally succeeded in committing murder.[20]

When Tomkins first took office, however, no such dark clouds were visible on the horizon. In fact it seemed the perfect moment to finally address the port's development. The need was finally reaching crisis proportions—Tomkins actually had to turn shipping companies away for want of space on the wharves—and at the same time a great opportunity beckoned. The Panama Canal was nearing completion, and New York hoped for a share of its traffic. Tomkins himself had the mayor's trust and the energetic support of the Municipal Art Society, the Merchants' Association, and the Board of Trade. He was still, officially, chairman of MAS's Port and Terminal Committee, though that committee found it unnecessary to actually meet anymore, since Tomkins's agenda and that of MAS were one and the same. Even the society's City Plan Committee concentrated its efforts on supporting him. And finally Tomkins had something truly valuable: the prospect of a great deal of money.

In 1909, Tomkins had finally triumphed in his fight to free self-sustaining improvements from the city's debt limit, and municipal piers were the prime example of this type of investment. Now, in 1910, the city succeeded in floating $73 million in bonds backed up by leases on its docks. Tomkins meant to invest this tidy bundle in building freight railroads, terminals, and new docks—all of which would be self-sustaining and capable of generating yet more capital for the city. The Docks Department would serve as an engine for economic development, and the promise of consolidation might be realized at last.

"New York . . . is a big city of little ideas," Tomkins wrote in the *Times* in 1911. "Its opportunity is world-wide, but its interest in its own development problems is parochial rather than cosmopolitan."[21] "A perfect ferment of ideas" sprang from Tomkins's Docks Department.[22] Speaking to the New Jersey Harbor Commission that same year, Tomkins outlined a visionary plan, much of it beyond the capacity of any single municipal government. There would be an assembly yard for the Jersey railroads in the Newark meadows. A freight tunnel at Fifty-seventh Street, built jointly by New Jersey and New York State, would connect the yard to a new municipally operated elevated line on Manhattan's West Side waterfront. This would replace the old Death Avenue tracks, but it would be open to all the Jersey railroads as well as to the New York Central. A second tunnel would link New Jersey to the Baltimore & Ohio tracks on Staten Island; a third, beneath the Narrows, would do double duty, connecting Staten Island to the Fourth Avenue subway and linking the B&O freight lines to the Bush Terminal in Brooklyn—and, in the distant future, to a new deep-water harbor in Jamaica Bay, Queens. From Brooklyn, freight could continue, via the Hell Gate Bridge, all the way to New England.[23]

All this, Tomkins promised, would let the city sort out the different facets of its economic life. The new rail facilities on Twelfth Avenue would free lower Manhattan's waterfront for the steamships: they could cluster below the Chelsea piers, where the Hudson was wider and longer piers could be built. Manufacturing would be free to settle in the outer boroughs, and as the factories moved, so too would the tenement population—"to the advantage," wrote Tomkins, "both of Manhattan, which will be relieved of undesirable congestion, and of the outer boroughs, whose lands are not now intensively used."[24]

Tomkins's plan was a sketch for the distant future, and enormous obstacles stood in the way. New York and New Jersey had little history of cooperating with each other, and since the U.S. Constitution forbade states to make treaties with one another, it wasn't yet clear how they could work in concert. Tomkins could point to one model of interstate cooperation in the Palisades Park Commission, but technically there were still *two* Palisades Park Commissions, one for each state. The two governors simply agreed to appoint the same commissioners to each body. That sort of gentleman's agreement sufficed for the Palisades, a subject of little controversy, but some stronger bond would have to be forged if rival states were to develop a port together. They would need a body isolated from local politics, from the whims of successive governors, and from the budgetary shenanigans of legislators. Tomkins dreamed of a Port Authority, a joint venture of both states, that would be charged with developing the entire harbor, but not until 1921, shortly after Tomkins's death, would such an agency come into being.

In the meantime, New Jersey's fragmented government offered Tomkins a series of obstacles. In 1906 John Cotton Dana, head of the Newark Public Library, spoke at the Municipal Art Society's annual dinner and predicted that "Within a few years, the cities of Jersey will be working in harmony with Greater New York."[25] But the very mention of cities touched on the problem: while New York had consolidated in 1898, New Jersey's shore was still home to a string of small municipalities. None had the resources or the vision to participate in Tomkins's planning scheme, no state agency oversaw their development, and just to make things more difficult, these cities, unlike New York, had long since sold their precious waterfronts to the private railroads.

Even without New Jersey's help, however, there was much that Tomkins could do. By 1911 he had already set part of his master plan in motion, setting his sights on Brooklyn's Bush Terminal. This was the creation of Irving Bush, a member of MAS since 1901. Bush had spent sixteen years building his terminal, and it was a triumphant demonstration of the economy of scale. One hundred twenty-two warehouses were spread across a mile of waterfront. Bush offered his tenants the longest piers in the city, the most efficient service, the lowest water and electricity rates, and twenty-five miles of private railroad tracks.[26] Tomkins spent $10 million buying up land to the north and south of Bush's property, building two 1,600-foot piers and laying plans for more. Yet he still needed to link these new piers to a railway and a complex of warehouses. When Tomkins brought the mayor to Bush Terminal in 1911, Irving Bush assumed the two men were on a fact-finding tour designed to show Gaynor the sort of facilities the city still needed to build. But the reporters in Gaynor's party told him the trip's true purpose: Tomkins intended to condemn Bush's piers and railway.[27]

Shortly after his visit to Brooklyn, Tomkins unveiled his plan for West Street at the Municipal Art Society's City Plan Exhibit of 1911. "The suggested solution," wrote the *Times*, "is based on the ancient art of making two blades of grass grow where only one grew before. The Dock Department would make three streets run where formerly there was but one. On the top layer . . . there would be a street for carriages and automobiles," and a chain of parks would be constructed atop the piers. The freight trains would run on the second level, "and underneath, on original mother earth, the trucks would pass."[28] All this would stretch from Sixtieth to Fulton streets. At Sixtieth Street the freight lines would connect to the New York Central tracks in Riverside Park, which would stay under that railroad's exclusive control, but the elevated itself would be controlled by the city and accessible to all the railroads. Spurs would link it to a complex of new municipal warehouses between Twenty-fifth and Thirtieth streets. Between Twenty-fifth and Fortieth streets Tomkins would build a float barge on the river, where freight cars from Jersey would be received, placed on ramps, and transferred directly to the El.[29]

Tomkins persuaded the city to hire John De Witt Warner as a special counsel, and Warner then drafted three bills for Albany: an enabling act for construction of the West Side joint railway terminal; an incorporation act for the terminal companies; and a third act ordering the New York Central to get its tracks off grade and into the elevated terminal.[30] The last bill also stipulated that, if the railroad wanted to expand its facilities (as it desperately did), it would have to pay for the privilege by roofing over the tracks in Riverside Park and landscaping a new terrace above them.

This, Tomkins hoped, was a bargain the New York Central could live with, but the New Jersey railroads were another matter. If the Jersey railroads were to share a new terminal, let it be in New Jersey, they said—a sensible request on the face of it, but when they issued this demand they knew full well it spelled the project's doom, for no city in New Jersey could build such a project. In fact, the Jersey railroads dreaded Tomkins's entire scheme. On the Hudson shore they had to rub shoulders with their rivals, but once their tracks fanned out to the west and south these companies became local monopolies, and phrases like "joint operation" simply didn't figure in their corporate culture. What they feared most, however, was the New York Central. The Vanderbilts already had the only dry route into Manhattan, and now they seemed on the verge of widening that opening by adding new tracks to the old franchise. The Jersey railroads would benefit from Tomkins's plan, but the New York Central might benefit even more, and so they announced that they would have nothing to do with Tomkins. Let him build his El and his terminals, they said: we simply won't use them.

Of course, this was a bluff. If the freight system were built, the New Jersey railroads would have to use it or see the New York Central profit alone. But they had managed to place Tomkins in a terribly weak position. As the *Times* wrote some years later, he resembled a lawyer who "comes into court without any clients. Worse yet, they repudiate their counsel's arguments. . . . Tomkins continues to present his idealist views of the sort of West Side Improvement he would prepare if he had a clean sheet of paper and a free hand to make the improvement. But on the same day appears the repudiation of his plan by those for whom he would prepare it."[31]

Left to his own desires, Tomkins would have happily called the railroads' bluff, but no mere commissioner was free to be so bold, and Tomkins was thwarted by the peculiar politics of the time. The city was governed by a Fusion Board of Estimate and a fiercely independent mayor. The result might have been complete paralysis, but Mayor Gaynor and Borough President McAneny had patched up a working relationship by referring the great policy issues of the day to special committees of the Board of Estimate. Tomkins was a member of the Port and Terminal Committee, but McAneny was its chairman, and the other members were Comptroller Prendergast and John Purroy Mitchel, president of the Board of Aldermen.

This Fusion majority had its own agenda. The public would forgive the Fusion Party for failing to rebuild the port, even if New York's long-term health required it, but Fusion could expect no quarter if it failed to build subways. McAneny's days and nights were consumed in negotiating the Dual Contracts; he had neither the time nor the expertise to ponder the port, and what he understood of Tomkins's plan, he didn't like. The Committee of One Hundred had rejected Tomkins's brand of big government and all his talk of municipal subways, and McAneny had little patience with the idea of a city-run freight system. Since he had to come up with the city's share of the cost of the new subways, McAneny was also on the prowl for money. There was just one ready source—Tomkins's precious $73 million in bonds—and McAneny took it away. He diverted $50 million to the subways, and he seemed intent on spending the remainder on what Tomkins dismissed as "local conveniences"—among them, the scheme for a new county courthouse and the disastrous beginnings of Foley Square.[32]

Tomkins, meanwhile, couldn't even get an appropriation for the engineering studies of the West Side Improvement plan, and had to go begging to the Chamber of Commerce for a $10,000 donation. Poor Tomkins, so used to giving orders in his own commercial empire, had little experience with frustration. When his bond money disappeared, he acted as if he'd been personally swindled. His relations with McAneny grew acrimonious, and at one point Tomkins even demanded that some other committee take over the port issue:

> "Why do you ask for such action?" demanded President McAneny.
> "Because one half of my tour of office is up and nothing has yet been done."
> "Do you blame that upon the President of the Borough of Manhattan?"
> "Very largely, yes."
> "Do you want to criticize the board . . . ?"
> "Oh no," retorted the Dock Commissioner. "You are the Lord's anointed and I am only a poor appointed official."[33]

Step by step the Fusion majority undermined Tomkins. The Board of Estimate agreed to buy the Bush Terminal piers and the Brooklyn Marginal Railway, as

Tomkins asked, but it leased them back to Irving Bush on such generous terms—he would have absolute control over the docks and train tracks for fifty years, and he could sublet them as he wished—that there was little point to the purchase. "These great undertakings," Tomkins complained, "are becoming the mere political footballs of private promoters who plan to forestall any system of effective city control."[34]

And for the West Side, the Fusion members of the Port and Terminal Committee came up with a scheme very different from Tomkins's plan. They recommended that the city order the New York Central to get its trains off Death Avenue within six months. The railroad would have to rely on trucks and barges while it built its own subway from Sixtieth Street to Thirtieth. The railroad would stop there, and trucks would service all the docks below Thirtieth Street.

Tomkins warned that this would only confirm the New York Central's waterfront monopoly, that it would hamper the port's efficiency and virtually invite the railroad to file suit against the city. "The change," he insisted, "can be more easily, quickly and cheaply brought about by some cooperation with the Central than by relying exclusively upon coercion."[35] No doubt the Fusionists knew this; one suspects that the whole point of their majority report was that six-month deadline—so exquisitely timed to coincide with the upcoming elections.

Certainly that deadline warmed the heart of the League to End Death Avenue, a successor to the old Committee of Fifty, which now turned its fury on Tomkins. As the full Board of Estimate debated the merits of the Tomkins and Fusion proposals, a hundred members of the league descended on the hearing with grim little badges shaped like coffins pinned to their lapels. They didn't care about monopolies and didn't want to hear of the Port of New York. All they wanted was the promise that their children would be safe in six months' time, and they demanded action on the majority report. Tomkins told them the deadline was a chimera. " 'Whatever final action is taken, the road will have to obey the law, won't it?' asked Mr. Shearn, the league's counsel. 'Yes, but it can tie the matter up indefinitely in the courts,' replied Mr. Tomkins."[36] Edward Shearn, a famously cunning lawyer, surely knew this to be true, but he brushed aside the warning. "If Mr. Tomkins were not known to be personally honest," said Shearn, the League would regard him "with grave suspicion. Being an honest man, however, the only possible explanation of his indefensible position is that he has become so obsessed with his water-front terminal hobby, denounced as visionary and impractical by engineers and railroad men, that his point of view has become warped."[37] At the next hearing, "not a kind word" was said for Tomkins's plan.[38]

Tomkins lasted a while longer as docks commissioner, however. He used the post as a bully pulpit, churning out pamphlets and stomping the lecture circuit, always in the cause of his plan for the port—and always dwelling on the ineptitude and distraction that marked Fusion's port policy. Naturally his relations with the Board of Estimate did not improve.[39] Mayor Gaynor at last lost patience with the endless and unproductive quarrel, and Tomkins resigned in 1913, saluting the mayor in the process. "If the world loves a cheerful loser," the *Times* wrote, "it must hold in high esteem Mr. Calvin Tomkins, who has just lost in the most smiling and affable manner the Dock Commissionership." His plan for the port "merited more attention than it received," but "it was put forth at a time when the proposed system of subway extension was uppermost in the public mind and demanded so much that nobody was thinking very much about the waterfront and the docks."[40] But Tomkins's smiles were reserved for the mayor. Summing up his career, he told the *Times*,

> I have had to contend with the constant obstruction of the Terminal Committee of the Board of Estimate, virtually no appropriations for new construction having been made since I took office.
>
> The physical results obtained are slight, but a comprehensive port development plan has been evolved and generally accepted by the commercial organizations of the city.
>
> In one respect my experience has been most satisfactory. When I took office the lack of intelligent interest in port development, even in expert commercial circles, was disheartening.[41]

TOMKINS MANAGED to set New York's business community thinking about the port in more organic terms, and the ultimate result would be the establishment of the Port Authority of New York and New Jersey in 1921. His tenure also had a more concrete result on the Upper West Side, for Tomkins's West Side Improvement project spurred Charles Stover, the parks commissioner, to begin work on one of the Municipal Art Society's most cherished projects: a vast scheme to stretch Riverside Park over the railroad tracks and into the bed of the Hudson River.

In the 1860s the Upper West Side was known as the West End, in vain emulation of a fashionable district of London. The New York neighborhood was still bucolic rather than chic—it was covered with farms and sprinkled with shanties—but a group of landowners and speculators formed the West End Association and plotted a more lucrative future for the area. They were determined to transform their land into a middle-class neighborhood, perhaps even a rich one, and they knew that the railroad tracks along their shore threatened the whole enterprise. If factories sprang up along the rail route, the West End would become another Chelsea.

The landowners had a second complaint: the Commissioners Map of 1811 called for stretching the gridiron plan across the West Side's steep bluffs. Grading those streets would be astronomically expensive, however, and the West Enders begged for relief. So in 1868 the Parks Commission laid out Riverside Park on the bluffs between 72nd and 125th streets. The new park's name was another empty boast, since the railroad, not the park, still ran along the bank of the Hudson River, and in hiding this eyesore Olmsted's landscaping hid much of the river view as well.

A quarter of a century later, when a riverfront gasworks was proposed, the West End Association took a further precaution. It persuaded Albany to transfer the land west of the tracks to the Parks Department. Just a thin strip of earth was visible between the tracks and the river. The true treasure lay underwater, for the grant included the riverbed itself, out to the bulkhead line some hundreds of feet from the shore.

The West End Association had built a wall of greenery as a buffer between the neighborhood and the ugly railroad, and in the 1880s magnificent row houses and apartment buildings transformed the area. West Siders were still dissatisfied, though. There were still awkward gaps in the waterfront park: garbage scows still moored at Seventy-ninth Street, and the Docks Department had kept title to its old piers at Ninety-sixth Street. And all along Riverside Drive, residents complained of the smoke and noise of trains passing below their windows, of the awful smell of cattle cars headed south to the Twelfth Avenue abattoirs (designed by our friends Horgan & Slattery—their best work), and of the sheer unreasonableness of it all. Here was a beautiful park; there was a beautiful river—and in between lay an industrial landscape of train yards, coal bins, and garbage dumps.

In 1898, when Charles Lamb first called on New York's artists to come up with their best ideas for the new consolidated city, the architect Milton See—a partner in the firm of Cady, Berg & See, whose best-known work is the majestic Romanesque south wing of the Museum of Natural History—cast his eye on Riverside Park. He suggested burying the railroad tracks beneath banks of earth and extending the park into the Hudson River itself. A broad new terrace would be embroidered with parterres, grottoes, lagoons, bandstands, playgrounds, and landing stations. See described it as an "Italian Garden," and his drawing became a fixture of the Municipal Art Society's annual exhibits, displayed again and again to keep it before the public eye.

The city concentrated, however, on the easier task of extending Riverside Drive northward. It left the railroad tracks untouched. In 1906, Columbia University unveiled plans for a stadium at the foot of West 116th Street. It would bridge the train tracks and extend on landfill into the Hudson. Since this was public property, the university was careful to include a number of public amenities. To the north and south would be playing fields, one open to the public, the other reserved for the Public Schools Athletic League; the roof of the stands would serve as a public recreation pier, and the whole complex would double as the city's official water gate.* Columbia itself would raise $1 million to pay for the project from "a few men who are wealthy and interested in Columbia and in the Public Schools Athletic League."[42]

William Barclay Parsons, the engineer for the first subway; George L. Rives, a Municipalian; and D. LeRoy Dresser were in charge of the stadium project. The money, it seemed, was promised if not yet in hand; the city authorities were willing

---

* This might seem presumptuous, but the navy anchorage was in that part of the river, and the Columbia Yacht Club had long served as the unofficial greeters of distinguished foreign guests. (The Prince of Wales, in particular, preferred the company of Columbians to that of the Irish sachems of Tammany Hall.)

to turn over the land to a private corporation, as they'd done for the sites of the Metropolitan and Natural History museums; and the plans by Henry Hornbostel were complete.

Columbia had some legal issues to resolve in Albany,[43] however, and while the university dealt with them, the Robert Fulton Memorial Association—a private group whose members included Robert Fulton Cutting (the inventor's grandson) and Cornelius Vanderbilt—blithely laid plans for a second water gate on the very same site. In 1909 this group held a competition for the Fulton Memorial, and one of MAS's board members, H. Van Buren Magonigle, came away with first prize.* His design called for a great colonnade at the top of the park, with a pavilion in the middle marking Fulton's grave, and a museum and reception hall at either end. Below this, great flights of steps, hundreds of feet wide, would cover the railroad tracks and sweep down the slope to a waterfront plaza and an artificial cove framed by recreation piers.

When Charles Stover became the parks commissioner in 1910—to the cheers of the Municipal Art Society—these two projects for monumental water gates awaited his attention. Assuming that they weren't built atop each another, as the Fulton Memorial Association seemed to expect, they could transform much of the shoreline of Morningside Heights. But at the same time, Calvin Tomkins was laying his ill-fated plans for the West Side freight system, and this added a third element to the equation. A waterfront El would suffice for downtown, Tomkins thought, but above Seventy-second Street the problem was how to build train tracks and freight yards and still achieve something that looked like Milton See's Italian Garden. He started with the assumption that the park should reach out into the river. The tracks would be moved west to skirt the new shoreline, and an immense platform would cover them, making a broad, flat terrace much as See proposed in 1898, but with trains rumbling below. Tomkins added something else, however. He found his "ultimate ideal" in "Antwerp, Vienna, and other foreign cities that have sought both artistic and commercial use of the waterfront."[44] His plan for Riverside Park called for quays at the water's edge, so that freighters could pull up along the shore and disgorge their cargoes directly into the railroad system. This last detail was impolitic of Tomkins: the Upper West Side was adamantly opposed to any commerce along the shoreline, and Charles Lamb, despite his best efforts, could never convince the neighborhood that freighters were picturesque.

The engineers in Tomkins's Docks Department produced rude utilitarian drawings of his scheme; they were hardly examples of municipal art. When Charles

---

* He'd been plain Harry Magonigle when he worked for McKim, Mead & White, but he tacked on Van Buren when he entered private practice. This may have been an attempt to compensate for an exotic upbringing. His grandmother was Martin Van Buren's niece, but his father was Edwin Booth's manager, his aunt was an actress, and Magonigle grew up in a theatrical milieu when all things connected with the stage were held in suspicion. His architecture was perfectly suited to the task of creating architectural eulogies: it always said the right thing—or at least, the expected thing—and it was exquisitely phrased. He designed the Maine and Firemen's memorials in New York, the McKinley Memorial in Canton, Ohio, and the Liberty Memorial in Kansas City.

Stover took up the project he married it to the two water gate schemes. He persuaded Columbia to move its site north, to a spot between 116th and 120th streets, and he talked the Fulton group into moving its monument south, to the axis of 110th Street. Stover also demanded a broader program for the Fulton Memorial: he thought it should include busts of other great heroes, like "an American Westminster Abbey."[45] The *Times* thought this silly, since New York already had a Hall of Fame at NYU's Bronx campus, but the paper, so tenacious a guardian of Central Park, nonetheless endorsed the project. It will "not be an encroachment on the park," the *Times* promised. "It will be a historical monument of importance, and an ornament to that part of town."[46] Next, Stover hired Magonigle to design the rest of the new, expanded Riverside Park. Magonigle and Stover included a few of Milton See's formal gardens, but most of the terrace was to be given over to athletic fields. "It is my theory," Stover told the *Times*, "that provision ought to be made in all the parks for the poor."[47]

Stover and Tomkins presented their scheme for Riverside Park at the Municipal Art Society's annual exhibit in 1911. Milton See was there to discuss the project, which owed so much to his design, now more than a decade old.[48] Stover was eager to begin work on the project, but there was no money: the Fusion Board of Estimate rejected all of Tomkins's railroad plans, and all hope of extending Riverside Park over the train tracks seemed to die with them. Yet the Parks Department already controlled most of the underwater land between Seventy-second and 125th streets; the actual landfill would be a simple matter, Stover reasoned, since the streets crawled with trucks hauling away dirt and ashes; and once the landfill was in place, the idea of beautifying it would surely prove irresistible. The only stumbling block was the construction of a seawall. Stover couldn't simply dump dirt into the river, to be swept away by the tides; landfill had to be edged with a stone wall, and quarrying stone was expensive.

New York, however, was building a new water tunnel at this time. At first the tunnel project seemed like a nuisance to Stover: the Water Board insisted on building pumping stations and even dynamite magazines in Manhattan's parks— "They are going to blow us all up," Stover cried.[49] He called on the art societies to help him fight these encroachments, and MAS duly protested them, but the Water Board's charter gave it absolute right of way. Stover realized, however, that something good might come of all this construction. The tunnel was being carved through bedrock, and countless truckloads of broken stone were being hauled out of town at the contractor's expense. Stover paid the man a visit. There's a place nearby to dump your rock, he pointed out: in the river.

Stover thus succeeded in creating, at virtually no expense to the city, a strip of new land two miles long and roughly three hundred feet wide. It took years to finish the seawall and landfill, and Stover himself never had the chance to build all the playgrounds, gardens, and water gates he so happily sketched: his career ended in bitter controversy in 1913, as we'll see later.

CALVIN TOMKINS'S fall from power was a catastrophe for the Municipal Art Society. For two years MAS had spent most of its energy and influence supporting him, and now the society was as bloodied as its favorite commissioner. And what made the defeat all the more devastating was that it was inflicted, not by Tammany Hall, but by a reform administration composed of MAS's own allies. Tomkins's quarrel with George McAneny laid bare the divide between reform's progressive and conservative camps, and much of the society's membership sided with McAneny rather than with its own board of directors. The members clamored for MAS to remember its old mission of creating public art, and the society soon trained its focus on a program to paint murals in the public schools. MAS gave up its role as the reform movement's great think tank on planning issues, and a new delicacy settled on the society. In 1913, when John De Witt Warner organized a new Port of New York Committee at MAS, he promised that it would "take no definite stand in questions of general municipal business policy, engineering, finance and the like" but would focus on "civic art, including [the] city plan and the efficiency and mutual relations of the civic factors involved." That was contradictory enough to ensure that MAS would indeed take no "definite stand." One year later, in a particularly miserable moment, the Municipal Art Society temporarily disbanded its Committee on the City Plan, lest it arouse new "antagonisms."[50]

WHEN TOMKINS was forced out of office, his project to expand the Bush Terminal was abandoned. As for the West Side Improvement project, Fusion soon came to understand Tomkins's warning that the New York Central could tie up any plan it didn't like. William Gaynor's death cleared the way for Fusion's John Purroy Mitchel to become mayor in 1914, and Mitchel and his comptroller, William Prendergast, went back to the negotiating table. Three years passed before they were able to announce an agreement. (By then, McAneny had returned to private life.) Gone was all talk of six-month deadlines, of forcing the New York Central to build a subway, and of banning freight trains below Thirtieth Street. Instead, the Vanderbilts would build an El all the way to Canal Street. Part of it would run down Twelfth Avenue and latch on to new docks, but between Fifty-first and Forty-second streets, and again from Thirtieth to Canal streets, the El would sit on a private right-of-way that sliced through the city blocks between West and Washington streets. The Central would also build vaults over the train tracks in Riverside Park, and once these were piled high with earth, the park could stretch to the waterfront.[51]

The public immediately seized on one detail of this new West Side Improvement scheme: the railroad was getting permission to vastly expand its facilities, but in return it was going to pay the city a mere $300,000; even the cost of landscaping Riverside Park would fall almost entirely on the city. Others—Calvin Tomkins among them—pointed out that the New Jersey railroads would never be able to operate in Manhattan. Theoretically the city had retained the right to add two more tracks to the El for the Jersey railroads, but the new inland route meant that the El would be cut off from the Jersey railroads' docks, and much of the new right-of-way had already fallen into the hands of the New York Central. As the League for Municipal Ownership reported, the railroad had been "quietly acquiring property for some time . . . with the view of getting control over the industrial development of the West Side."[52] So even if the Jersey railroads were able to add tracks, as the city promised, they were already frozen out of the terminals. Of course the New Jersey railroads were aghast, but the new dock commissioner dismissed their complaints and reminded the *Times* that "they themselves had held back in the past, and had done nothing to aid in a matter which they are now reported to consider vital to their welfare."[53]

One might expect the Upper West Side to have welcomed a scheme that hid the railroad tracks in Riverside Park, but in 1916 the neighborhood was surely the project's arch foe. West Siders wanted a guarantee that there'd be no shipping on their shore; they wanted the docks removed from the foot of Seventy-ninth and Ninety-sixth streets; and they objected to that broad, flat, hard-edged terrace over the train tracks. (The terrace would be especially wide at the southern end of the park, where the tracks were supposed to fan out and enter the New York Central train yard.) The terrace presented New York with a tricky aesthetic issue: should the new parkland be "terraced and treated in the Italian garden fashion," as MAS had always expected, or should it look "as though it had always been a part of the present Riverside Park"?[54]

The landscape architect Samuel Parsons now entered the scene. He was an old associate of Vaux and Olmsted, a champion of their naturalistic landscapes, and a severe critic of the formal gardens so popular with the Beaux Artists. Because of that stance, Charles Stover had driven Parsons out of the Parks Department four years earlier. Stover had lost his own post since then, but Parsons may have still been seeking vengeance when he contacted the *Times* in 1916. "An Italian garden is a very beautiful thing in its place," Parsons admitted, "but it would be quite impossible to lay one out at the edge of a strip of natural woodland and get an artistic and harmonious result. It would be entirely out of keeping." Then Parsons dropped a bombshell. "With some satisfaction," he broke the news that the Parks Department "was now missing a topographical map of Riverside Park."[55] Its disappearance sounds decidedly suspicious (and it's not clear if the city ever had such a map) but the inescapable point was that the Parks Department was operating blind. It had overlooked something rather crucial, Parsons pointed out: the covered railroad tracks would, in places, rise above the level of Riverside Park like a great earthen berm, shutting out views of the water.

Meanwhile the Women's League for the Protection of Riverside Park had emerged as the railroad's nemesis. While Tomkins still spoke of railroad monopolies, the language of the Women's League was infinitely more vivid. "Don't let them tear up eighteen hundred trees and put a gravel area in their place," one member told a rally. "Just think of the sweethearting done there. It's a regular mother to its country."[56] And the league had the good luck to recruit the actress Amelia Bingham, who lived on Riverside Drive, and whose speeches always made good copy. "I have lived on the Thames, on the Seine, on the Rhine, but always come home to get drunk again on the glory of Riverside Park," she told the League in the fluted tones of a tragedienne. "Tell them to have mercy on our happiness!"[57]

Privately the Municipal Art Society thought that the West Side Improvement project was "calamitous," but it was more circumspect in public.[58] It quietly approved of Calvin Tomkins's efforts to drum up opposition to the project, but MAS's only significant contribution to the debate was to convince Comptroller Prendergast that a model of the scheme would help the public judge its merits. When the model was unveiled in July 1916 at Grand Central Terminal, it showed that the tracks were open to the sky north of 145th Street, as was the huge train yard at 135th Street, but otherwise the model was a handsome, even a seductive, thing. One West Side alderman was suddenly converted. "It is the most beautiful proposition you ever looked at," he told the startled and disgusted Women's League. "Our meetings in the future should be to see that these plans are carried out."[59] The women shooed him away.

Joseph Howland Hunt, MAS's president, noted that "the city has labored for several years with this important question," and he assured the public that the model was a faithful representation of the city's plan.[60] "We are at least entering upon the improvement with open eyes," added MAS's Charles Stoughton.[61]

Yet open eyes were no defense against a mirage, and less trusting souls soon noticed that the lovely architecture and landscaping of the model were far more elaborate than anything specified in the city's contract. Others detected a note of sheer fantasy: thirty-foot trees were shown sprouting from six inches of soil. The model, in short, was a fraud.

This farce convinced many that Mitchel and Prendergast would do anything to win approval of the West Side Improvement plan, even if it meant pulling the wool over the people's eyes. Nor were matters helped by Fusion's decision to schedule public hearings for the middle of July: a time of year, many noted, when the scheme's well-to-do opponents normally sought out cooler climates. If that was Prendergast's calculation, it backfired disastrously. The members of the Women's League canceled their vacations, and having to brave both the summer heat and a coincidental outbreak of infantile paralysis only whetted their indignation.

The civic groups were badly divided, however. At first, the Citizens Union denounced the West Side project as a "giveaway" that was inexplicable without reference to the fact that Mitchel was a friend of the railroad's owners, but then the union decided that the scheme was, all in all, an improvement. Benjamin Marsh, who was now working for Hearst's Municipal Ownership League, called it "one of the worst hold-up cases ever attempted."[62] The City Club approved of the physical plan, but demanded that the contracts be rewritten so that the Jersey railroads might, at some future date, have access to the El. The Merchants' Association and the Board of Trade and Transportation backed the plan as essential to the city's commerce; the Washington Heights Taxpayers Association fought it for aesthetic reasons; the Chamber of Commerce, acting on Irving Bush's advice, gave its whole-hearted endorsement.[63] Charles Craig, counsel for the West End Association and the husband of one of the most active members of the Women's League, demanded that the city go back to Tomkins's and Warner's 1911 legislation. That was a better deal for the city, he said, since it forced the railroad to barter expanded facilities for landscaping the park.[64]

In January 1917, Prendergast announced that he'd ironed out the last details of the project. The railroad had made one last "concession," he said, in agreeing to let the city cover the 145th Street train yard. This would cost New York $6 million, but Mayor Mitchel praised the railroad for accepting the "inconvenience" of an underground train yard. It is impossible to tell whether he was being cynical or foolish; the railroad was surely delighted that the city would pay for a nice dry roof.

The Society for Prevention of Municipal Waste obtained an injunction, however, and Charles Craig announced that the West End Association would follow up with an "indefinite" series of lawsuits. It would be a simple matter, he noted, to tie up the whole project for five years or more. What mattered most, though, was keeping the subject alive through the campaign season of 1917.

The election was crucial to the West Side, for William Randolph Hearst was once again muddying the political waters. For all his millions of dollars and readers, Hearst's political career had come to naught. George McClellan, he believed, had stolen the mayoral election from him in 1905. His 1906 campaign for governor had been sabotaged by the treacherously lukewarm support of Tammany and by the cunning innuendo of Elihu Root, the Republican secretary of state, who had hinted darkly at the complexity of Hearst's private life. Frustrations had mounted. The Municipal Ownership League failed to block McAneny's Dual Contracts, and though Hearst had the satisfaction of barring McAneny from the mayoralty, it was only to see Mitchel betray him by pushing the West Side "giveaway."

In 1917 Hearst's political ambitions were reawakened, and Boss Murphy agreed to nominate the publisher's puppet, John F. Hylan, for mayor. "Honest John," the Hearst forces called Hylan, but his popular nickname was "Red Mike," a tribute to his ruddy complexion, carrot-colored hair, and apoplectic temper. Nothing roused Hylan's anger like the subject of private railroads. He'd had the unpleasant experience of once working as a motorman for the Brooklyn Rapid Transit, and the even more annoying experience of getting fired for rounding a curve too quickly—a charge he hotly denied. He never forgot the injustice, but losing that job was the best thing that ever happened to Hylan, for it led him to study law and to enter politics. McClellan had made him a magistrate; Hearst had made him famous by printing his tirades against the transit companies; and now Hearst and Murphy joined forces to make him mayor.

Hearst set his newspapers loose on Mayor Mitchel and found the incumbent an easy mark.[65] The Municipal Ownership League looked at the generous condemnation award for Bush Terminal and concluded that Fusion's "business administration" was just that: a government of, by, and for big business. (The deal looked especially bad when Irving Bush took his profits and unveiled plans for another massive terminal—in Bayonne, New Jersey.) As for Mitchel himself, he had all the reformer's usual vices and a few new to the movement. He alienated the Irish and German communities with a premature embrace of the Allied cause overseas; he outraged the Catholic church by probing its charities with wiretaps; and he alarmed parents with a program of education reforms that spoke more of penury than of pedagogy. New York's class and ethnic politics had already destroyed many a reformer's career, but John Mitchel was also said to be a womanizer, and he was certainly a social butterfly who chose his friends carelessly. One was "Senator" William H. Reynolds, a speculator in real estate and Broadway musicals, and a major contributor to Mitchel's campaign fund. On a more personal note, he entertained Mayor Mitchel with raffish parties in the Bryant Park Studios, and on one memorable occasion he forgave the mayor for accidentally shooting him. Shortly before the 1917 election, Reynolds was indicted for defrauding the city in a land sale.

Even more damaging was Mitchel's friendship with William K. Vanderbilt, the very fellow whose railroad was the bane of Chelsea and the great eyesore of the Upper West Side. When Mitchel was negotiating with the New York Central, the public naturally expected him to play hardball. Yet a sinking feeling swept across the city as Mitchel kept popping up at the Vanderbilts' balls and dinner parties. Hearst's *Evening Journal* drew the obvious conclusion that Mitchel had been bribed, not with cash, but with the cheap condescension of the 400. The paper even imagined a happy moment in Mitchel's social life:

> We allow you to see John Purroy Mitchel on the great night when, breathless and with a bright pink spot on each cheek, he burst through his front door and cried, "My dear, Mr. Vanderbilt called me Jack."
> While back at her stately mansion, Mrs. Vanderbilt complains:
> "My dear Willie, how could you call that uncouth, long-nosed person Jack?"
> "My dear," replies Mr. Vanderbilt, "he is uncouth if you like, and I admit that it is going a little far to ask you to have him so often. But remember that this young gentleman . . . has the power and willingness to cut a slice off the whole side of Manhattan and give it to me and my New York Central Railroad. I'd call the devil himself 'Jack' for that."[66]

According to one observer, this was the single most damaging piece of propaganda in the campaign of 1917. "Mike" Hylan was elected mayor by a record majority, and Charles Craig, capitalizing on his popularity with the Women's League for the Protection of Riverside Park, was swept into office as Manhattan's new borough president. Their triumph ushered in sixteen years of Tammany rule.

AN ARMY OF CHILDREN: ART AND THE PUBLIC SCHOOLS

WHEN CITY PLANNING became too heated an issue for the Municipal Art Society, MAS turned back to its original mission as a patron of public art. In fact the society had never entirely abandoned this role, and we have to catch up with one of its old agendas: bringing art into the daily lives of New York's schoolchildren.

In 1906, while news of the latest Russian pogroms was still filtering into New York, the principal of a Lower East Side public school informed the Health Department that a number of her students were suffering from adenoids. A medical team was dispatched. There was no fuss; the children submitted to the scalpel with the usual amount of trepidation and heroism, and the adenoids were successfully vanquished. But several days later, streams of parents descended on every school between Mulberry Bend and the East River. Strangely distraught, they wanted to collect their children, but they wouldn't, or couldn't, say why. (Many spoke only Yiddish.) As the crowds swelled, the principals grew frightened and bolted the doors of their schools. The parents became hysterical and tried to storm the schools. Policemen battled their way through the crowds and ordered the children evacuated from the buildings. As soon as they filed out, the riots stopped. The next day, however, there were new disturbances in Brownsville, Brooklyn, and three more Manhattan schools were stormed, this time by Sicilians and Calabrians.

The *Times* traced the trouble to jackleg doctors, the Old World village medicine men who had followed their patients to America. They charged a quarter for removing adenoids, and since the Health Department was stealing their bread and butter, they had floated the rumor of a terrible conspiracy. The city's doctors, they said, meant to slaughter the schoolchildren, slitting their throats as if they were sacrificial lambs.[1]

A group like MAS, which regarded public art as a medium for political education, might have drawn a lesson from the school riots of 1906 and from the general climate that made them possible. The riots made the recent immigrants seem more unreachable than ever. If they could imagine that the city was capable of a new

Slaughter of the Innocents—and this during a Tammany administration—what hope was there for the good-government forces to win their trust? The *Times* provided an answer in one detail of its reports: there were no disturbances *in* the schools. Although the students were ostensibly candidates for butchering, they stayed calm while their parents rioted. If the parents seemed irredeemably lost to MAS, the children were fertile ground. When MAS decided to focus on this new audience, it knew that a different style of art was needed. "Monumental art in this democracy can never be a toy for the rich," Charles Shean had written in 1904. "It must have for its base the broad support of popular pride and appreciation."[2] In order to win over the public, especially the young public, the Municipal Art Society abandoned the abstract imagery of Edward Simmons's *Justice* and Taber Sears's *New York and the Nations*. It was time to forgo "over-used allegories and personifications, characterless figures of no particular age or clime," as Shean wrote. Artists should turn instead to "the golden records of the nation's history."[3]

MAS thought that the Carnegie Libraries offered the perfect opportunity to create a far-reaching program of decorative art. In 1901, Andrew Carnegie had given the city $5.2 million to build a system of branch libraries; the city was responsible for providing the sites. The program went smoothly until 1908, when Mayor George McClellan made a disastrous miscalculation, telling Carnegie that the city had to discontinue the program because it couldn't afford to buy any more land. The mayor fully expected Carnegie to relent and offer more money, but the self-made multimillionaire was far too canny for that.[4] By then forty-two libraries had been constructed around the city. The Manhattan, Staten Island, and Bronx branches were designed by McKim, Mead & White; Carrère & Hastings; and Babb, Cook & Willard. MAS's own A.D.F. Hamlin served as the architectural adviser to Brooklyn's library system, and he handed out jobs to J. Monroe Hewlett and J. T. Tubby, his former students.* (Tubby helped MAS with its street sign campaign, and Hewlett later became the society's president.)

The libraries' architecture was in good hands, then; their facades would epitomize good taste; but MAS wanted the buildings to speak to the public. It thought each branch should have murals illustrating great moments of local history, and it

---

* It was Hamlin who put aesthetics above convenience and persuaded the Brooklyn Public Library to locate its main building on Grand Army Plaza. In architectural terms, the site was a perfect place for a monumental ensemble of buildings, but it was hard to get to it from some quarters of Brooklyn. The commission was handed to architect Raymond Almirall, who was modestly active in MAS, but construction went slowly for lack of funds and was suspended altogether during World War I. After the war, Mayor Hylan chose to abandon the project, no doubt because Almirall was also the aggressive foreman of a runaway grand jury. It had been convened to investigate Hylan's accusation that the IRT conspired to have its own workers call a strike. The strike, according to the mayor, was meant to force the city to approve a fare increase so the workers could receive a decent wage. Almirall led the grand jury down a very different path, however. There was a conspiracy, he claimed, but the mayor himself and William Randolph Hearst were the conspirators and their aim was to ruin the IRT by driving its stock price into the ground. Almirall apparently had no real evidence for his claims (nor did the mayor), and his good faith was open to question. It came out that he'd once worked for a subsidiary of the IRT. Construction of the Brooklyn Public Library resumed in 1941, after Almirall's death, with a new design by Githens & Keally. (Keally was MAS's president from 1948 to 1950.) For a very hostile, partisan view of the Almirall grand jury, see Henry H. Klein, *My Last Fifty Years: An Autobiographical History of "Inside" New York* (New York: Henry H. Klein, 1935), 303–7.

imagined their interiors painted with inspirational anecdotes from the neighborhood's colonial or revolutionary days. When MAS did some research, it discovered that events of "special local interest" were depressingly "few and . . . unimportant," but the society persevered nonetheless. In 1903 it asked that 5 percent of the cost of each library be set aside for "suitable decorative work upon its walls." The Board of Estimate "cordially approved" of the scheme but declined to appropriate any funds; the library trustees explained that they had no money to spare; and when the trustees themselves approached the Board of Estimate they were brusquely sent away. And so the project, in A.D.F. Hamlin's words, "died of asphyxiation."[5] With their splendid facades but spartan interiors, the Carnegie Libraries remained a lingering disappointment for the Municipal Art Society.

The society had far more luck, though, with its Committee for the Decoration of Public Schools, founded in 1902. In the early years of the century, every reform group had its own agenda for the school system. The system had recently been centralized in a bruising battle led by figures like Nicholas Murray Butler, of Teachers College; Felix Adler, of the Ethical Culture Society; the crusading journalist Jacob Riis; and Mrs. Schuyler Van Rensselaer, of the Public Education Association.[6] They were determined to free the schools from "parties, sects and personal preferments," as one supporter put it, though one might as well read "Tammany, Catholicism and patronage."[7] This, however, was only one aspect of educational reform in New York. Some, like Municipalian Richard Welling, championed programs to teach children the mechanics of democratic government; the Public Education Association demanded night classes for workers (Welling joined this campaign as well and, despite his wealth, spent his nights as a teacher); still others demanded vocational training or school gardens.

The schools had become the focus of reformers' attempts to Americanize New York's immigrants. The parents might be unreachable—mired in Old World ways, isolated by language barriers, or dependent on Tammany's largesse—but reformers were convinced that the future of democracy lay in the immigrants' children. And there were a lot of them: in 1909 the federal government reported that 70 percent of New York's schoolchildren had been born abroad. Teachers might find their students speaking half a dozen languages. To fill the needs of these children, the schools had radically expanded their scope: they now offered baths and medical care, and they taught hygiene, good manners, and "the simple business of getting along in the classroom."[8]

And now the Municipal Art Society was determined that children should also have murals in their schools. This might seem an inappropriately rich item in the menu of school reforms, but teachers welcomed the idea: there were no glossy photos in turn-of-the-century textbooks, and educators were grateful for any sort of visual aid that might spark a student's imagination. MAS had a more soaring ambition, though, for if architecture is frozen music, as Goethe maintained, then murals must be frozen propaganda. "In our schools, as in the churches in Europe, children can be given a chance to grow up under the influence of art and the sentiments expressed by it," explained the painter George Bissell.[9] MAS could capture the attention of students at "the most impressionable age" and leave an "indelible" stamp upon their minds. Bissell pictured a "vast army of children" growing up beneath murals patriotic in theme and academic in taste; eventually they would "go out into the world with tastes formed on correct lines and high ideals. Civic pride, such an important factor in the success of a city, will then be the controlling spirit, and the era of ugliness, confusion and disorder with which the city has been cursed to date will give way to an era of good taste, convenience and personal comfort."[10]

The Committee for the Decoration of Public Schools, chaired by Bissell, included the sculptor F. Wellington Ruckstull, the architect and developer Albert E. Davis (head of MAS's Bronx Committee), and two people new to the Municipal Art Society: Mrs. Schuyler Van Rensselaer and William H. Maxwell.[11] Given the political cast of this committee, its program was the very antithesis of multiculturalism. Maxwell, a highly respected educator, had been active in Brooklyn's League of Loyal Citizens, a group that had fought consolidation in an attempt to save that very proper city from domination by Manhattan's immigrant masses. When he lost that battle, Maxwell became Greater New York's first superintendent of schools in 1898. Van Rensselaer is remembered as an architectural historian and critic—her classic biography of H. H. Richardson is still in print—but at the time she was better known as the president of the Public Education Association.[12] A true Knickerbocker, she was probably already working on her magisterial *History of the City of New York in the Seventeenth Century*; if anyone could conjure up edifying incidents from local history, it was surely Mariana Van Rensselaer.

It helped that the public schools were designed by a Municipalian. C.B.J. Snyder, architect to the Board of Education, was a remarkable civil servant. He first earned the public's gratitude by introducing drinking fountains to the schools. Classes would never again have to share a single battered tin cup; viruses would no longer spread like wildfire. Snyder's eighteen years in office were untainted by scandal, and in that time he built dozens of school buildings with amenities—auditoriums, gymnasiums, courtyards, and rooftop playgrounds—hitherto unknown to New York. Snyder did for schools "that which no other architect before his time ever did or tried," wrote Jacob Riis in 1902. "He 'builds them beautiful.' In him New York has one of those rare men who open windows for the soul of their time."[13]

One of Snyder's most beautiful designs was Morris High School at 166th Street and Boston Road in the Bronx, a romantic Gothic building that rose over its neighborhood like a castle. Its auditorium opened onto a public park and doubled as a community center. The soaring, crenellated tower, a local landmark, was typical of Snyder's work: it made the most of necessity, serving to disguise the flues that funneled noxious fumes from the school's science laboratories. MAS laid ambitious plans for the building. In the auditorium, a cycle of paintings would trace the city's history; the corridors would be lined with illustrations of historic buildings, reproductions of famous paintings, and portraits of national heroes; and the classrooms would become textbooks in paint. They'd teach art, architecture, biology, zoology—"all studies susceptible of pictorial treatment."[14] MAS organized a public subscription to begin work and started it off with a $500 donation. It hoped to paint a huge mural covering the back wall of the auditorium's stage, but by the time MAS had raised enough money, its example had inspired another donor to come forth with the offer of a pipe organ. The society settled on the wall panels flanking the proscenium. This time it managed to find some reasonably local history as the subject of the murals: *The First Treaty of Peace between the Settlers of the Bronx and the Indians*, signed, or otherwise sealed, at the home of Jonas Bronck in 1642, and *Gouverneur Morris Addressing the Constitutional Convention*. (Morris, who drafted the final text of the Constitution, had come up with his own theory of education, which might have inspired a more interesting painting. He ordered that his son should never be schooled in Connecticut, "lest he imbibe in his youth that low craft and cunning so incident to the people of that country . . . that all their art cannot disguise it from the world."[15])

E. Willard Deming won the competition, but his murals weren't very successful. Indeed they might serve as an illustration of Kenyon Cox's argument that the historical subject was the "most difficult to handle successfully" in America. "Unfortunately our history is short, our modern costume formless and ugly, and American historical subjects particularly unfitted for pictorial and, especially, decorative treatment."[16]

By the time Deming's work was unveiled, two murals had appeared at DeWitt Clinton High School on Tenth Avenue between Fifty-eighth and Fifty-ninth streets. It was the largest high school in the world, with seventy-eight classrooms and two gyms, and its namesake was a particular hero to Municipalians. In building the Erie Canal, Clinton had secured New York's preeminence as a trading center, and his example, MAS hoped, might advertise the benefits of an ambitious public works program. Snyder lavished special care on the building, with its Dutch Colonial elevations and charming entrance loggia (a model was exhibited at MAS in 1906). He also persuaded the Board of Education to commission murals by Charles Yardley Turner. Again they flanked the stage. To the left, Clinton began his triumphal first journey down the canal; to the right, he poured a libation of Lake Erie water into New York Harbor. Turner proved to be a much better artist than Deming: he found a certain visual rhythm in the patterns of bunting and spars. DeWitt Clinton High School was dedicated in 1906, in the presence of Nicholas Murray Butler, president of Columbia University and the éminence grise of educational reform in New York.[17] Turner's murals were a great success; the Board of Education was clearly proud of itself, and even the comptroller, Herman Metz, conceded that "If we go no further in artistic achievement than to make a beautiful place for our children to attend school, the money will be well expended."[18]

With Metz's words ringing in its ears, MAS hoped that murals would now become a regular feature of new schools. It wanted the city to take up the program, but making the leap from a private demonstration project to a full-fledged publicly financed program was always the hard part for advocates. MAS had already wasted several years trying to unlock "the $50,000 appropriation" referred to in a state law, passed in the 1890s at the art societies' behest, which "allowed" the city to spend that tidy sum each year on municipal art (not counting any art included in a building contract, like the sculpture on the Hall of Records). For a time MAS even had a committee charged with thinking up ways to spend this money. It hoped to start by filling in the gaps in the city's collection of mayoral portraits. Nothing came of this heartwarming idea. The sum of $50,000 was big enough to attract the scorn of budget cutters, and the whole arrangement meant that each prospective work of art was subject to bruising debates in the Board of Estimate. MAS soon realized that it needed a new strategy. If it could tuck the cost of art into building contracts, and if it could come up with a way to make the price *sound* small, then public patronage of the arts might finally become politically palatable. So in 1907 the society went to the mayor and the Board of Estimate and asked them to dedicate 1 percent of the cost of new schools for mural decorations. Its request was denied, however, and as the city slid into a depression, New York was soon slashing its whole public works program.

After this disappointment, MAS itself abandoned the mural project for a time. To the dismay of many members, it devoted almost all of its income to its city planning and congestion exhibits. To calm the membership, MAS decided in 1909 that it had better come up with another monument—a cheap one.

In 1908 Fire Chief Kruger died in the line of duty, and at his funeral Bishop Henry Codman Potter called on the city to create a monument to all the city's fallen firemen.[19] Potter was a life member of the Municipal Art Society; so was his wife, the former Mrs. Alfred Corning Clark. Potter knew firsthand what public art could do for a neighborhood: he lived in considerable splendor in an Ernest Flagg mansion at Riverside Drive and Eighty-ninth Street, and his windows looked out on the Soldiers' and Sailors' Memorial. (The late Mr. Clark was so famous that his name stuck to his widow, and the Riverside Drive tour buses used to scandalize innocent tourists by pointing out the house "where Bishop Potter lives with Mrs. Alfred Corning Clark."[20]) Potter's eulogy eventually bore fruit ten blocks up the drive. The Firemen's Memorial, by H. Van Buren Magonigle (an MAS board member) and the sculptor Attilio Piccirilli, was finally unveiled in 1912.

Potter also set MAS to thinking that policemen deserved a monument to *their* fallen heroes. The timing seemed apt, as the architects Hoppin & Koen were at work on the Police Department's new headquarters on Centre Street. A swaggering, domed pile of a building, it was one of the most striking monuments of the McClellan administration, and the architects' model had been one of the highlights of MAS's annual exhibit. Just as important, given the society's straitened finances, MAS saw the opportunity to create an inexpensive "architectural" memorial to the fallen policemen by flanking the main staircase with a Roll of Honor, consisting of two marble plaques. Their bronze frames were decorated with eagles, stars, garlands, the departmental shield, and the city seal, and they bore, in bronze letters, the names of slain officers. The names presented a problem, at first because the Police Department had never kept a record of its own heroes (MAS organized a Citizens Committee to search through archives and newspapers), and then because, as the Police Department submitted new names over the years, MAS noticed that some of the officers, while indisputably dead, had not in fact died heroically. At least MAS didn't think so. Perhaps policemen were better acquainted with the notion of stress-related illness—or perhaps, as MAS suspected, they simply wanted to honor their late friends. In any case, MAS cracked down and sternly demanded a stricter accounting from the commissioner.

The Roll of Honor was supposed to be inexpensive, but in fact MAS found it hard to pay for casting new names each year, especially during World War I, when bronze became a nearly precious metal. It was with some relief, then, that in 1923 MAS noticed the unhappy fact that the plaques were completely filled. When the police commissioner asked for another, the society begged off. Policemen had grown attached to the Roll of Honor, however—it wasn't the most expressive of memorials, but it was all they had—and the department eventually honored MAS's precedent by continuing the series itself.[21] When the department finally decamped for larger quarters in the 1970s, the rank and file insisted that the Honor Roll move with it, and the plaques were transferred to the lobby of One Police Plaza.

Meanwhile, the mural program languished. In 1911 the chairman of MAS's Permanent Work Committee, charged with giving new works of art to the city, angrily complained that his committee was a "joke"—it had no money.[22] Embarrassed, the society soon started all over again with the decoration of Washington Irving High School, on Irving Place. MAS was interested in the school for Irving's sake. Many Municipalians traced their family histories back to the Knickerbockers, and Irving was their great ethnic folklorist. (Not that they thought of themselves as just another ethnic group. In their own minds, the "old families" were the guardians of American culture per se.) Something else distinguished the school: it was a vocational high school for girls. The "refinements of daily life" also figured in the school's curriculum; students were instructed in deportment and table manners, sewing was taught as a vocational skill, and all this was meant to prepare young women "for college, for business and for matrimony." The whiff of feminism that clung to the school, however faint by today's standards, unnerved some at the time, and one member of the Board of Education "expressed the hope that this country would never witness the spectacle of the 'woman on horseback.' "[23] But the school's program also attracted the interest of Mrs. Edward H. Harriman, the philanthropic widow of a railroad magnate and the mother of a future governor of New York State, and she bankrolled much of the school's decoration.

MAS itself paid for the mural decoration of the stair hall and vestibule, which was undistinguished: a matter of decorative panels framing scenes of New Amsterdam. The scheme was designed by Charles Stoughton and carried out by painter Salvator Lascari. Interrupted first by the war and then by MAS's poverty, it was finally finished during the Depression by the Works Progress Administration. The glory of the school was the Great Hall: two stories high, vaguely Tudor in style, ringed with flag-draped balconies, and paneled in wood. The hall was more than a particularly grand lobby. The school held its dances and art exhibitions there, and it was dominated by a great hearth in an alcove, a rather monumental symbol of domesticity. MAS installed an overmantel by the sculptor Frances Grimes, a protégée of Saint-Gaudens. (Mrs. Harriman paid for it, anonymously.) A delicate bas-relief in tinted plaster, it showed three young girls reading from an open book, and it was inscribed with an excerpt from "The Legend of Sleepy Hollow": "There was enchantment in the very air that blew from that haunted place, breathing an atmosphere of dreams and fancies." (Dreams and fancies are a bit more difficult to sustain today, when Grimes's relief is almost invisible in the glare of an electronic message board. "ID required at all times," it flashes. "Don't break! Mediate!")

The Great Hall of Washington Irving High School was the masterpiece of MAS's mural program. For once the society succeeded in treating an entire room, and it found in Barry Faulkner an artist with an appropriately decorative style. Faulkner was a protégé of Mrs. Harriman, and he'd painted murals in her mansion, Arden House, a forbidding structure by Carrère & Hastings that sits atop a mountain in Harriman, New York. So for once there was no competition involved, and ironically, the results were far better than anything MAS had recently achieved. If Faulkner's ambitions were modest, at least he fulfilled them. His art was frankly decorative and eclectic, touched by Japan, Art Nouveau, and the Arts and Crafts movement. His murals traced the early history of the city as told in Irving's winsome *Knickerbocker History of New York*.*

Faulkner painted sixteen scenes ranging from Henry Hudson's discovery of New York Harbor to the dubious tale of the Kissing Bridge; from a decorative map of the fur trade to the arrival of the British fleet. A panel devoted to the Peach Tree War offered a hint of stylized violence; otherwise, all was calm, even idyllic, in old New Amsterdam. Since the twentieth-century city could make no such claims for itself, some New Yorkers had little patience with MAS's approach to public art. In 1916, while Faulkner was still painting the Great Hall, a labor group hung an oil painting in the school's auditorium. J. C. Dollman's *Am I My Brother's Keeper?* depicted a homeless family pathetically huddled on a park bench. The scene was meant to illustrate the need for vocational training, but Edward Zabriskie, the school's principal, complained that the scene was so "morbid" that it was "unfit for the eyes of the young girl students." Zabriskie ordered the painting removed. His action unleashed a torrent of criticism; even the president's daughter, Margaret Woodrow Wilson, entered the fray. "It seems to me that this picture would give the children . . . a realizing sense of certain of the conditions of life in their part of

---

* The St. Nicholas Society—founded by Washington Irving—contributed a bronze bas-relief portrait of the writer by Victor Brenner, and in 1914 the Society of Mural Painters and the Society of Beaux Arts Architects decided to take up the school's auditorium. Robert K. Ryland won a competition for the decorations, but he succeeded in painting only one lone panel on the back wall before the war diverted everyone's attention. MAS Bulletin 4 (October 1915): MAS Archives.

New York City," she wrote the principal, "and . . . would make them want to help change those conditions. Do the educational authorities in this school want to send the children away without any sense of responsibility to their fellow men? Do they think that ignorance of life is a good preparation for life, or indifference to misery a good preparation for service?"[24] These were questions that MAS itself preferred not to answer. Dollman's painting was not restored to the school.

Other groups took up the cause of murals in the schools. The Public Education Association founded an Art Committee to encourage murals. The Hebrew Technical School for Girls had unveiled a set of murals painted by Frederick Lincoln Stoddard as early as 1908.[25] In 1915 Frederick Lamb painted *The Conference of Washington and His Officers at the Battle of Long Island*, a monumental mural ten feet high and thirty feet long, in Brooklyn's Public School No. 5 (now the George Westinghouse Vocational and Technical High School), but the mural was apparently destroyed during a remodeling in 1963.[26] The art department of the city's high schools formed an alliance with the Society of Mural Painters—headed at the time by William Laurel Harris, MAS's former president—and in 1914 they commissioned murals in the stair hall of Brooklyn's Eastern District High School. The mural painters were apparently more fond of allegory than MAS was, for the painter Frederick Lincoln Stoddard took *The Birth and Development of Education* as his theme and worked it out in three panels: *The Gift of Fire*, *The Dawn of Civilization*, and *The Birth of the Alphabet*. MAS called them "dignified and striking" and lauded Stoddard's "great breadth of view and refinement of technique," but today they are more likely to call forth indulgent smiles, at best. In the central panel the Genius of Civilization smiles upon a happy pair of primitives who've acquired more pottery than common sense: they watch approvingly as their infant child drapes a garland around a lion. One can only hope that it's a "symbolic" beast.

In 1915 MAS again petitioned the city to start a "percent-for-art" program for the schools. This time the Municipal Art Society was addressing the Fusion administration of John Purroy Mitchel. The regime had many virtues, but a liberal attitude toward the schools was certainly not one of them, and MAS was rebuffed yet again.[27]

In the meantime, as the war overseas sparked inflation at home, Mitchel began setting up new municipal markets in an effort to cut consumer costs. In the same vein, MAS hosted a series of lectures on the public markets of Europe; perhaps it was the slides of Les Halles in Paris or of the Campo dei Fiore in Rome that led Evangeline Blashfield to visit the new city market beneath New York's Queensboro Bridge. (On the other hand, she might have shopped there.) The space itself, with Henry Hornbostel's rough granite walls and Guastavino vaults, was handsome enough, but Blashfield noticed that the vendors' water supply was drawn from a single rude spigot. She saw the opportunity for a fountain commanding the market's hundred-foot axis, and she agreed to pay for it herself. Told of the scheme, the vendors were at first nonplussed. "Why," she said to them, "painters have no pigment for making pictures that can compare with your lemons and oranges and bananas and grapes, your tomatoes, even your onions," and according to her husband, "the Italians, remembering Verona's Piazza del Erbe or Venice's fruit market behind the Rialto bridge, saw at once what she meant."[28] Charles Stoughton contributed the architectural design, a sober basin in smooth granite with water pouring from a bull's head. Above, also framed in granite, was a mosaic figure of Abundance, her cornucopia laden with the same fruits and vegetables sold in the market. The mosaic was designed by Edwin Blashfield.*

Given Mrs. Blashfield's generosity, MAS finally moved to correct an old injustice typical of the times. More than any other person, she had been responsible for creating the Municipal Art Society. Now, twenty-five years later and just a year before women won the vote, Mrs. Blashfield was finally elected to the society's board of directors, its first woman member. She died shortly afterward, before the fountain was unveiled; it became, quite by accident, her memorial. Albert Bard, dedicating the fountain in May 1919, described it as an illustration of MAS's "two-fold faith. We know that men must have useful things, and we know equally that their hearts desire them to be beautiful. . . . Grace of environment is a part of the patrimony of the citizen, and his right."[29]

MAS started handing out medals to the best art students in the public schools, and it began a series of semiannual competitions at the Society of Beaux-Arts Architects. Some of the programs were quite bizarre and hardly relevant to the beautification of New York City. In 1915 entrants were asked to address "The Treatment of the Banks of a River Flanking a Natural Fall."[30] The program described a rocky chasm, a mighty waterfall, and twin cities building a power station. It wasn't your everyday problem, but perhaps its authors were thinking of Niagara Falls, where MAS's friends in the American Scenic and Historic Preservation Society were buying up the adjoining land and fending off a power company to make sure that the cascades' natural beauty was preserved. The next program was more pertinent to New York City, though the result was pure comedy. It asked for "An Architectural Solution of the Intersection of an Avenue and a Street"— specifically Fifth Avenue and Forty-second Street, a place that had fascinated MAS since Carrère & Hastings first proposed to put a bridge there in 1901. The winning scheme interpreted "architectural solution" a bit literally: it planted an enormous tower smack in the middle of the intersection. The competitions were called off in 1931 when the Society of Beaux Arts Architects decided it couldn't cover the administrative costs. Ironically, the competitions had never been more popular: with construction at a standstill, students were desperate to be noticed, and even more desperate for a fifty-dollar prize. The last competition attracted four hundred and one designs for a "Zoological Laboratory."[31]

---

* The fountain is no longer in situ. It was supposed to be relocated to a more prominent position in the Bridgemarket, a 1980s scheme to develop the hall beneath the bridge. The fountain was removed for restoration, but when the project fell through in 1990 the fountain was stored on Randall's Island.

THE WAR years had left MAS adrift. By 1916 public works in New York had already come to a standstill; there was so little to show at MAS's annual exhibit that the members decided to feature their own work "in other than strictly civic fields." The *Times* didn't enjoy this innovation: it charged MAS with betraying "the public whose interest it serves and upon whose intelligent cooperation it depends for support in its understandings."[32] Things became even more difficult once America entered the war: there were no exhibits at all. MAS tried to use the war to advance old causes, vainly suggesting to the Treasury Department, for instance, that a billboard tax be included in the war revenue bill. The society protested when war bond posters were chained to the trees of Central Park, though no one listened; and it begged Herbert Hoover, who was trying to feed Europe's refugees, not to advertise his cause with *electric* signs. Hoover never answered MAS's letters, but the society soon found some grim satisfaction in the war: Time Square's gaudy electric signs were briefly switched off to save coal.[33]

MAS struggled on with dreary lunches at the Ritz-Carlton Hotel (always the same menu—someone liked stewed tomatoes), and it treated members to lectures on "The Re-education and Re-employment of Disabled Soldiers," or "Camouflage and Protective Coloration." This last subject perplexed even the board of directors, and Albert Bard had to explain that, as he saw it, the lecture concerned "Art in Relation to War."[34] (Indeed the Camouflage Corps was full of artists, including MAS's Barry Faulkner.) In the meantime MAS invested its puny bank account in war bonds and sat by quietly while the Architectural League launched a campaign to ban all "Hun materials" from the drafting room.[35] It kept its tongue when Albert Jaegers's statue of Germania, high on the Custom House facade, was altered. Some patriot had "boiled with indignation" when he noticed the beefy, phlegmatic figure while walking past Bowling Green. Jaegers was asked to transform her into *Belgium*—a simple process, he was told: just change the label and the coat of arms—but he refused, explaining that "to comply with a request so strange would mean an admission that the work in question is lacking in character." After the armistice, MAS congratulated Jaegers, but it mourned that someone else had done the job.[36]

The arts community went to war in its own fashion. A group of New York architects went to work for the U.S. Shipbuilding Corporation where they designed, not ships, but new communities for the war plants' burgeoning workforce. These communities marked the federal government's first, temporary, foray into the housing and planning fields. Some of those designers, like I. N. Phelps Stokes and Electus Litchfield, never forgot the experience, and they would form the core of MAS's future life. In New York the war also brought a little renaissance of old-fashioned municipal art. Parades and rallies flourished, to keep people's spirits up; a steady stream of Allied dignitaries passed through the city, and MAS's competitions at the Society of Beaux Arts Architects turned to things like reviewing stands and water gates. H. Van Buren Magonigle went to work for the Fourth Liberty Loan campaign; he decorated the terraces of the Public Library, where its bond rallies were held.[37] More rallies were held downtown, and Thomas Hastings designed the "Altar of Liberty" on the west edge of Madison Square Park. Municipalians recognized it as a child of the Improvement Commission, which had hoped to build a festal reviewing stand on this same site. Given the circumstances, Hastings's design was much more sober than the Improvement Commission had intended. With its stark Doric order, its trophies and monumental braziers, it did indeed look like a pagan altar of sacrifice. It only wanted an Iphigenia.

When the troops came marching home in 1919, Magonigle designed "Victory Way"—the name given to Park Avenue between Forty-fifth and Fiftieth streets. He lined the sidewalks with enormous Doric columns and, on the malls, built huge, somber pyramids of captured German helmets. A little gilt figure of Victory hovered atop each pyramid, and there was something apt in the fact that these figures were so small and rested on such vast and morbid pedestals. Hastings celebrated the war's end by designing the Arch of Freedom at Madison Square. It stood on the site of the Dewey Arch, and Hastings seemed to think his task was to correct Lamb's old design. (Lamb, who wasn't even invited to join the advisory committee, fell into a depression.[38]) Hastings's arch was a much more suave statement of the same architectural theme, but something was missing. Lamb's arch had erupted with sculpture; Hastings's was covered with delicate, almost invisible bas-reliefs. Lamb's had seemed exuberant; Hastings's seemed studied, pedantic, exhausted.

The Arch of Freedom wasn't *un*popular, but neither did it open up any new horizon in public art, as the Dewey Arch had two decades earlier, and the public didn't take it to heart. Among intellectuals it seemed an embarrassment. Leo Stein—Gertrude's brother, and a noted art critic—wrote in the *New Republic*, "Why should there be thrown on our returning soldiers the momentary shadow of an arch that means nothing, that is nowhere, that leads nowhere, and that only brains pickled in Greco-Roman-Gallic brine could ever have conceived? A Roman triumphal arch, the emblem of the Caesars . . . seems not the most appropriate monument to celebrate the fall of the Caesars. Something might have been found a little less tedious and a little more to the point."[39] Just what that something might be, however, no one seemed to know. Modernist architecture had made few inroads in America, and it still seemed a largely German phenomenon, which didn't make it any more popular at the moment. A malaise was settling over the architectural scene, however. Beaux Arts classicism had begun to seem pro forma, but Art Deco had not yet arrived on New York's horizon.

Art evolves more quickly than architecture, however, and the academic artists had already been challenged before the war. The Ashcan painters had held their famous exhibit in 1908, and the Armory Show had shocked the public in 1913. Both presaged a troubled future for municipal art. The Ashcan painters found a friendly reception at the National Arts Club, and Robert Henri was briefly active in MAS, but this school of painters reveled in the vernacular, not the heroic; it sought not to inspire but to show things as they were. The various Modernists of the Armory

Show were united in at least one thing: their scorn for the "official" art of the salons and academies.

The academic painters were very much in view during the war, but in retrospect their exposure did them little good. Edwin Blashfield, for instance, became an ardent propagandist, and his art turned to themes like *Red Cross Christmas Roll Call* and, his best-known work, *Carry On*. Widely reproduced, *Carry On* was purchased by the Metropolitan Museum with much fanfare. It has since been "lost," no doubt to the relief of latter-day curators. The painting showed an angel exhorting a weary soldier, and this celestial pep talk was all too typical of how New York's academic artists responded to the war: they "so discredited the use of the allegorical figure in art," one historian has written, "that one must consider it a casualty of the war."[40]

Such thoughts did not yet trouble MAS, however. It was concerned now with the fact that posters like *Carry On* had popped up everywhere during the war: in the parks and on subway kiosks, streetlamps, and both public and private buildings. The ink had barely dried on the armistice when MAS asked the Liberty Loans campaign to take down its signs.[41] "Now that the orgy of war advertising is over, of course there should be a clean-up at once," wrote Albert Bard:

> You have gladly seen Patriotism written all over the beautiful buildings and places of the city—even though this writing was a kind of scribbling, so incongruous have the papers and flimsiness been. Beauty was for the moment nothing—nothing unless it too served. But now!
>
> Are we to be equally content to see Piffle's Pickles emblazoned where we have testified to our intention to save food and thus win the war? Will not chewing-gum and chicle be more than ever an impertinence when inflated to the dimensions of our fatherland, the liberty of the world and the sacrifices of our sons?[42]

Once again Bard cranked up the machinery of the anti-billboard campaign, and after a year of lobbying and a public protest, Central Park was finally stripped of signs.[43] Propaganda posters disappeared from the subway kiosks but, to MAS's disgust, the Salvation Army rushed into the breach and hung its own ads on the kiosks. By now Bard had given up any hope of influencing advertising agencies, but through the 1920s he aimed letter-writing campaigns at their clients, and these had some effect. He rejoiced that an appeal to John D. Rockefeller was successful: in 1924 the haughty Standard Oil Company agreed to dismantle its empire of billboards.[44]

These were little victories, but in 1918 Bard had stumbled onto something big. He'd become something of a one-man clearinghouse for information on billboard legislation around the country, and he noticed a fascinating detail in Los Angeles's zoning code. Los Angeles didn't have height limits yet, but it did have a system of land-use controls just like New York's, with separate zones for residences, businesses, and factories. What struck Bard was that it defined billboards as a type of commercial land use, and this meant that they were banned from residential districts. The point was so obvious that Bard must have kicked himself for not having thought of it before. Gleefully he spread the news in MAS's *Bulletin*, and in 1918 New York's Zoning Commission ruled that billboards were indeed a "nonconforming" use in residential districts. Any such sign erected since July 25, 1916, was declared illegal, and no new signs would be allowed. The new ruling "frankly recognizes that there is no such thing as a billboard sufficiently respectable to rub elbows with churches, schools and private homes," crowed the *Evening Post*. "At one stroke, the zoning resolution has . . . done more to remedy the billboard evil in the residence districts of the city than all the laws and ordinances previously passed on this subject put together."[45]

FINDING A positive mission for MAS was more difficult.* The Lamb brothers, Calvin Tomkins, and John De Witt Warner had gradually withdrawn from MAS, only to be replaced by figures less bold and less inclined to politics. Although the new board members were as well intentioned as the old Municipalians, they were too polite, too *nice* to make terribly effective advocates. MAS's presidents were now people like Taber Sears, the sweet-tempered painter who created *New York and the Nations*, and Joseph Howland Hunt, Richard Morris Hunt's son, whom I. N. Phelps Stokes remembered as "completely unselfish . . . a delightful companion, always, but full of yearnings and doubts." Phelps Stokes considered him "absolutely unconventional," but that was the perspective of a man who might have wandered in from the pages of Henry James. ("I have seen him [Hunt] sit down on the floor in a ballroom," Phelps Stokes wrote by way of example, "at the feet of some girl whom he admired, apparently blissfully unconscious of the fact that those who did not know him must be thinking him demented."[46])

Perhaps Hunt outgrew his eccentricities; in any case the Municipal Art Society grew terribly dignified after the war. It even dashed Albert Bard's cherished scheme to present an annual booby prize to the most offensive billboard in the city. The society also grew ever more blue-blooded. There had always been a very high proportion of Knickerbockers at MAS, but now other groups dropped away. Jews became very rare. There was no policy of overt exclusion, so far as I can tell, but then again, they weren't invited to join.

It was a bad time for advocacy, after the war. Tammany was back in power in the bumbling form of Mayor John F. Hylan, and a more venal variety of politician controlled the Board of Estimate. Reform's reputation lay in tatters, a victim of

---

* There was a sense that America should encourage the industrial arts—Germany's forte before the war, and perhaps an answer to America's postwar unemployment problem. It was a subject of much discussion and many lectures at MAS, and the Metropolitan Museum did indeed found an Industrial Arts Department in 1918 in anticipation of "the era of progress, which this war will certainly usher into the world." Its exhibitions would play an important role in popularizing moderne and Art Deco design in the 1920s, but by then MAS had dropped the subject utterly. "New Department in Museum," MAS Bulletin 16 (fourth quarter, 1918).

Mitchel and Prendergast on the local scene and of Woodrow Wilson in the White House.

As the soldiers flooded home, the arms and shipbuilding plants shut down, and the economy was thrown into turmoil. America was suffering from the worst inflation since the Civil War, and the rapid transit monopolies, tied to the nickel fare by McAneny's Dual Contracts, began their long slide into bankruptcy. Private builders refused to pay the new, higher wartime wages, and New Yorkers suffered from both overcrowding and unemployment. Nearly a hundred thousand New Yorkers received eviction notices in 1919. In 1920 New York became the first city in the nation to pass a rent-control law; and in 1921 tax abatements were first introduced to spur apartment construction.[47] It would have been the perfect time for a great campaign of public works, but no plans had been laid, and Mayor Hylan had dissolved McAneny's City Planning Commission. The West Side Improvement project had collapsed in acrimony, and neither the railroad nor the city was eager to revive it. The trains still lumbered down Death Avenue, and "Riverside" Park was still a euphemism.

The individual components of MAS's old master plans would take on a wayward life of their own in the early 1920s. Borough President Miller, for instance, revived the idea of a West Side Highway, but without the railroad or public parks MAS had intended, and Mayor Hylan built the city's first municipal subway, the IND line. Calvin Tomkins would almost live to see the creation of the Port Authority in 1921. Also, a whole cadre of city planners had sprung up—a profession that didn't exist when MAS was founded, or when Charles Lamb first set out to knit the five boroughs into one city. Yet the Municipal Art Society had entered into its "negative history."[48] No more city plans sprang from its ranks; it abandoned any efforts to set the city's agenda. Its role now was critical, not creative; its posture, defensive.

There were just two last public art projects between the wars. The first, a scheme for newsstands, revived the old notion of "useful art." Newsstands were far more common in the 1920s than they are today, and they tended to be even uglier. In 1921 Gerald Kaufman designed a number of alternatives for MAS. They weren't terribly handsome designs—misshapen Doric temples with stubby little piers and a big frieze for displaying magazines—but they were far prettier than the rude tar-paper shacks New Yorkers had come to expect. Kaufman designed two types: one would latch on to the back of subway entrances, and the other would be tucked beneath the stairs to elevated stations. The Municipal Art Society offered to produce other designs for freestanding sites, and Charles Stoughton hoped to have them prefabricated in order to cut costs. MAS went to the New York Newsdealers' Protective and Benevolent Association, and at first its leaders were enthusiastic, but it seems that MAS had unwittingly opened a can of worms. The vendors explained that an onerous set of regulations governed the dimensions of newsstands. As a result, some vendors couldn't stand up in their workplaces and others couldn't turn around.

These regulations dated back to George McAneny's reign as borough president of Manhattan. They'd been adopted to make sure that the sidewalks were passable; they'd been retained for quite another purpose. Such intolerable working conditions drove newsdealers to flout the law: they built their stands bigger than McAneny had ordained, and to protect their investments they were forced to pay off their local aldermen every year. The head of the Newsdealers' Association saw MAS's efforts as an opportunity to press the city for more reasonable regulations, but the rank-and-file membership grew nervous. They knew that the aldermen had grown accustomed to the extra income from payoffs. Fix the law, and the aldermen would demand to be paid in some other fashion: if not a small yearly bribe, then perhaps a large lump-sum payment when a license was renewed. The newsdealers preferred to leave matters as they were.

So the newsstand campaign fizzled. Instead of dozens or hundreds of prefabricated newsstands, MAS produced just one: a "model," but not a prototype. It was erected in Greeley Square, and it was not a great success. The vendor found that Kaufman's temple of newsprint offered too little room to display a full range of merchandise, and soon the newsstand was cloaked in a thick carapace of placards and publications. This was enough to "ruin the appearance of any newsstand," MAS complained. Some years later, when Manhattan's borough president asked for the society's advice on the newsstand problem, MAS decided not to get involved.[49]

As for murals, statues, and monuments—with its shrinking membership, MAS was too broke to do much. In 1926, however, a number of women members seized on a unique example of public service, one that would appeal to children. A year earlier Nome, Alaska, was stricken with an epidemic of diphtheria. A dogsled started out for the town with a load of serum, but in a gale so blinding that the driver couldn't see his dogs, much less his way. It was Balto, the lead dog of the team, who brought the sled safely to Nome and then died of exhaustion. The story struck a sentimental chord; the nation was swept up in a frenzy of Balto worship; and the heroic husky was hailed as a sort of canine Pheidippides. Miss Cecilia Beaux, a Municipalian, formed the Balto Monument Committee and commissioned a bronze statue from Frederick G. R. Roth, a sculptor who specialized in animals. It was mounted on a boulder along the East Drive of Central Park, at Sixty-sixth Street. MAS's modest role in this was to serve as the committee's treasurer, but the Municipal Art Society seemed to miss the point. Taber Sears complained that Balto should have been placed on a high pedestal far out of the reach of children. They were "abusing" the statue, he said: rubbing Balto's snout, climbing on his back, petting him.[50]

AND SO, with a whimper, MAS's campaign to create public art ended for a time, not to be revived until the 1970s.

Central Park

After World War I, the Municipal Art Society became obsessed with a subject that had long been nagging at its conscience: the preservation of Central Park, New York's greatest work of public art. New Yorkers had been attempting to tamper with Olmsted and Vaux's design since the day the park opened. Richard Morris Hunt was among the first to try, with his 1868 project for monumental gateways, and in the years to come, people kept thinking of buildings or "features" to put in the park: an ecumenical cathedral, galleries for trade shows, an observatory, a parade ground. . . . "If half of these schemes had been successful," Olmsted wrote in 1890, "the park would have entirely lost its designed rural character. It would have been divided into a hundred sections, each appropriate to some special sport or amusement, with only decorative trimmings of foliage and flowers; lacking all unity; lacking any element of breadth, repose and sylvan composition."[1]

The gravest threat to the park arose in 1892, a year before MAS was founded. The "trotting interests" had always complained that there was no place in New York where they could let their horses go, and there was little point in keeping a stable of fast horses—their favorite form of conspicuous consumption—if one couldn't race them. The sporting set could have bought land for a speed track—its members were certainly rich enough, and much of upper Manhattan was still almost unpopulated—but instead the trotters decided to buy the state legislature and the governor, and simply to take the land. In 1892 the governor signed a law authorizing construction of a speedway on the west side of Central Park. "The thing had been done noiselessly," the *Times* remembered years later. "There had been no public outcry—the public generally, in fact, knew nothing about it." When the public found out, its outrage crossed all boundaries of class and ethnicity. Only the trotters saw the point of surrendering acres of the city's one great public park to the exclusive use of a little band of rich men. The City Reform Club sprang into action. It formed a Citizens Committee to repeal the law—a thousand of "the most prominent men in the city" lent their names to it—and one of its founders, Richard

Welling, personally filed a lawsuit. The suit would at least delay the project; better yet, it would provide Welling with a forum in which to explore the seedy history of the speedway law. The *Times* joined the fray: the paper raised $9,000 in forty-eight hours to fund Welling's campaign. The trotters expected the protests to blow over, but "Train after train load of indignant deputations went to Albany under the auspices of the Citizens Committee. . . . The labor unions threw themselves into the fight body and soul and sent a workingmen's delegation to Albany." At last Richard Croker called on the track's sponsors "and threw up his hands. He said frankly that if the bill were not repealed Tammany could not hope to carry the coming election. . . . Some of the men who had voted for it were reputed to have received considerations so strong as to make them willing to encounter even the wrath of Tammany," but Croker pulled all his strings, and the speedway law was repealed within a month of its passage.[2] No state law had ever enjoyed such a short life.*

For a time the memory of the speedway fight served as a warning not to interfere with Central Park. But in the years before World War I, a new threat arose. It was no longer a case of private groups stepping forward with bad ideas; now the danger came from the Arsenal itself—the Parks Department's own headquarters. As the *Times* wrote in 1911: "The idea seems to have penetrated the noodles of the men lately placed in control of the park, especially of Central Park, that the science of park-making has in some way developed, that they know much more about it than the old fogies in whose brains the park plan originated. Consequently they are tearing down what they cannot build up. . . . Changes in the original plan are made without publicity, and . . . the people have no voice in the matter."[3]

The *Times* was speaking of Charles Stover, parks commissioner of Manhattan and Staten Island,** MAS's dear friend and ally, and "the stormy petrel of Mayor Gaynor's official family."[4] Stover has already cropped up in our story, but he needs a little more introduction. Born in Pennsylvania, orphaned at a young age, Stover was left with a comfortable income. He came to New York in the 1880s to study at Union Theological Seminary. He arrived at the height of the great Protestant revival, when activist ministers thundered that it was a Christian's duty to transform a hellish town into an earthly City of God. Stover abandoned his studies and helped found the East Side Settlement. He lived there in small bachelor quarters for the next three decades. He founded the East Side's first boys' club, fought for small parks and public beaches, championed municipal subways, presided over the East Side Reform Club, and led the petition drives that persuaded the Metropolitan Museum and the Museum of Natural History to break the Christian Sabbath and open their doors on the workingman's sole day of rest.

MAS tried to win the Parks Department commissionership for Stover in 1907, and an anonymous letter to the *Times* seems to state the society's case: "Breathing

---

* *The speedway eventually found a home on the banks of the Harlem River, its construction providing sorely needed jobs in the depression of 1893. The speedway was later transformed into the Harlem River Drive.*

** *The Bronx, Brooklyn, and Queens still had their own parks commissioners, courtesy of the City Charter of 1898. That system lasted until 1934, when Robert Moses became the first citywide parks commissioner.*

spaces for the poor have been Mr. Stover's special study for years. The network of New York's park playgrounds and gymnasiums is largely his work." He was also, the letter went on, a man "possessed of high artistic judgment . . . broadened by residence and travel in the chief cities of Europe."[5] Mayor McClellan wouldn't listen, but Mayor Gaynor's election offered Stover, and MAS, another opportunity.[6] "Dreaming of what he could do if he were in charge of the city's parks department," Stover asked for an interview with the mayor-elect, whom he'd never met. They chatted briefly of parks and playgrounds and then, "for a couple of hours, . . . congenially discussed the Bible and Shakespeare. Gaynor checked with trustworthy acquaintances of Stover"—including, no doubt, Calvin Tomkins—and gave Stover the job. The *Times* hailed his appointment, describing him as "almost a pioneer in the movement for open-air playgrounds and gymnasiums for children," and crediting him with the establishment of ten parks. Politicians, however, were stunned. According to Lately Thomas, Gaynor's biographer, "Such methods of handing out political plums seemed, to men who had passed their lives in political jobbery, insane, if not wicked."[7]

"There never has been a Park Commissioner . . . in whose hands the city's park system is safer than mine," Stover told an audience of three hundred Municipalians in 1910. (Then, alarmingly, he suggested widening the transverse roads in Central Park.) "Popular recreation will be a big item in my program," he said, and he outlined his plans for open-air dancing pavilions in High Bridge Park and beneath the Queensboro Bridge, for band concerts in Central Park and in the armories, and for the appointment of the city's first superintendent of recreation.[8] Stover planted shrubs in the Broadway malls, as MAS had demanded for years,* and on Mayor Gaynor's orders he set out to make "an open meeting place where all sorts of people can gather and hold meetings as in Hyde Park." So Union Square briefly became

---

* The Broadway malls, laid out in the 1860s, had been one of the original glories of the Upper West Side. They were planted with elms and shrubs, with little fountains and a pedestrian path up the middle. The malls were ripped up when the IRT subway was built between 1901 and 1904. The contractor was supposed to restore them afterward, but his contract was vaguely worded. He planted trees, which promptly withered, and grass, which was soon pounded into dust by pedestrians—he had not restored the fences that once protected it. The West End Association and Women's Municipal League demanded that the Rapid Transit Commission do something, but most people assumed the cause was hopeless—that the trees died because there was too little soil above the tracks. MAS investigated, and discovered the real problem: the contractor had filled all but the top six inches of the planting beds not with soil but with broken stone from his excavation. At this point, Mrs. Henry Codman Potter stepped in. She was a life member of MAS who'd inherited great patches of West Side real estate. (As mentioned before, her first husband, Alfred Corning Clark, had built the Dakota; her second was the Episcopal bishop of New York.) She adopted the mall between Eighty-seventh and Eighty-eighth streets, brought in topsoil, and grew a beautiful grove of trees. Such a conspicuous success inspired, or forced, the RTC to crack down on the contractor, who was ordered to try again, this time under the watchful eye of the Tree Planting Association. At the same time, the city agreed to extend the malls north of 135th Street, where Hamilton Heights and Washington Heights were developing into beautiful neighborhoods of New Law tenements and apartments. There were still no shrubs or fences, however, and MAS discovered that no city agency was willing to maintain the malls. Confused as to who had jurisdiction, MAS appealed to the corporation counsel. He delivered the Solomonic opinion that both the parks and highways departments were responsible, and this gave each an excuse to wash its hands of the matter. MAS replied by dispatching Charles Israels to Albany, and in 1907 the state transferred the malls to the Parks Department. Times: "Trees in Upper Broadway," December 12, 1903, p. 2; "Foliage on Boulevard," December 11, 1903, p. 8; "Upper Broadway, Once the Boulevard, Little Better Than an Abandoned Highway," June 10, 1906, sec. 3, p. 6. MAS Minutes, February 12 and November 11, 1907.

the public forum Charles Lamb had proposed in 1902. There were no physical changes to the park, but soapbox orators were no longer molested and Arnold Brunner's loggia became a speakers' rostrum.[9] The police force was utterly baffled by its new orders to let free speech flower—so much so that the journalist Lincoln Steffens was asked to tell them about the First Amendment.[10]

Stover's career was curiously mixed. He's been labeled a manic depressive;[11] he was an aesthete *and* a social worker; he built playgrounds *and* monuments. He was the first commissioner to build a park in an African American neighborhood—San Juan Hill, where one block held the city's record for population density—but he tainted this legacy by setting aside separate visiting hours for blacks and whites.[12] So far as I know, it was the first time segregation reared its head in New York's park system.* The great pity of Stover's career was that, though responsible for many excellent new neighborhood parks, he was utterly indifferent to the splendors of New York's *historic* parks. And the great blot on his career was the sad affair of Samuel Parsons.

Parsons had begun his career as a nurseryman, supplying Central and Prospect parks with some of their original plantings, and he was famous for scattering specimen trees across his native Queens. (One still stands at the center of Flushing's Weeping Beach Park, and it was named the city's first "living landmark" in 1966.[13]) He became Calvert Vaux's younger partner, and when Vaux and Olmsted were driven out of the Parks Department, Parsons stayed on, first as superintendent of planting and then for twelve years as the superintendent of parks. All this time, wrote Olmsted's son, Parsons "maintained his incorruptible political independence and his avowed loyalty to the ideals of the Olmsted and Vaux design."[14] As a reward, Tammany drummed him out of office in 1898, but in 1902 Seth Low brought him back as the Parks Department's landscape architect. By the next year, the last of Central Park's authors was dead. Vaux had been found floating in Gravesend Bay in 1895, an apparent suicide; Olmsted died peacefully in August 1903, long after his memory had slipped away; and three months later their erstwhile boss, Andrew Haswell Green, was slaughtered on Park Avenue, the victim of an insane man who mistook him for someone else.

Their legacy was left in Parsons's hands. Part of Parsons's job as landscape architect was to check the enthusiasms of parks commissioners. The City Charter of 1898 gave him the power to veto any major change in the plan of New York's parks, much as the Art Commission could veto the designs of new buildings and monuments. Parsons was a jealous guardian of Olmsted's tradition. In 1899 he worked to save Mount Tom from the Soldiers' and Sailors' Memorial, and, though

---

* *Race relations were growing nastier at the time. Blacks had just begun moving up to Harlem, an area overbuilt with middle-class apartments. Landlords were faced with two options: either to lower their rents or to offer their apartments to blacks, who were so desperate for housing that they would pay premium rents. Blockbusting flourished, and the* Times *perversely concluded that "this is the way colored folk reap the rewards of . . . prejudice." The paper recommended that landowners sign restrictive covenants barring "any negro, mulatto, quadroon, or octaroon" from the premises, save for servants. Editorial, "Apartments to Let,"* Times, *August 25, 1911, p. 6.*

Parsons was a Municipalian himself, in 1903 he vetoed Charles Lamb's scheme for rebuilding Union Square. Parsons didn't try to freeze the parks, however, merely insisting that parks commissioners respect Vaux and Olmsted's original intentions. Before Parsons acquired his veto power, great changes had already been made to Prospect Park—John Duncan had built the arch in Grand Army Plaza, and Stanford White had designed a chain of exquisite gateways. But when Parsons came along, he approved other changes, and under Commissioner Kennedy, McClellan's appointee, the Vale of Cashmere acquired its Classical balustrades; McKim, Mead & White built the "Grecian" Shelter; and Helmle and Huberty designed the Palladian Boathouse on the Lullwater (and, later, the Shelter Pavilion in Greenpoint's Monsignor McGolrick Park).[15] Despite these changes, Prospect Park remained surprisingly faithful to Olmsted's vision. Much of its Victorian architecture was replaced by Classical temples, but the landscape still dominated, and if anything the park came to look more like the great English estates that had inspired Olmsted in the first place.

This was no longer a fashionable approach to landscape design, however. Artists of the Beaux Arts school were trained in the French tradition of axes and vistas, of limpid pools, clipped box, and Classical pavilions—a language that spoke of man's ability to create a geometrical order in the midst of nature. And a second movement had sprung up to challenge Vaux and Olmsted: the recreation advocates, who were determined to get kids off the streets and onto playgrounds and ball fields. Olmsted and Vaux had permitted only the most demure and upper-class recreations—riding, croquet, boating, and so forth—but now there were insistent demands to open up the park to playgrounds and working-class sports.

In Charles Stover, Parsons faced a parks commissioner who gloried in the Beaux Arts and public sports and who wanted to bring both to the sacred grounds of Central Park. Stover began, fairly innocently, with Central Park's gateways, which had tantalized the Beaux Artists for decades. A storm of public protest, orchestrated by Vaux and Olmsted, had prevented Richard Morris Hunt from building gateways in 1868, and since then the scheme had acquired a nostalgic glow in Beaux Arts circles, and the sense remained that Central Park was "a picture without a frame."[16]

Stover began by placing the *Maine* Memorial on Columbus Circle. The money had been raised long before by Hearst's papers, and in 1901 H. Van Buren Magonigle and Attilio Piccirilli had designed a monument for the north end of Times Square, on the little trapezoidal block where the TKTS booth stands today. At the back rose a tall, square, tapered shaft of marble—a pedestal for Piccirilli's *Columbia Triumphant*, cast in bronze salvaged from the guns of the sunken battleship.[17] In front, filling the traffic island, was a fountain shaped like the prow of an ancient galley. It was quite a reasonable solution for this site; today one might even call it "site specific." The Art Commission approved the initial sketch, and the two artists went to work developing their scheme, but by the time they were ready to proceed, the site was no longer theirs. The Art Commission's clerk had "failed to record the grant of the site," and a comfort station had been erected instead.[18]

It's not clear who first suggested moving the memorial to Columbus Circle, but Stover saw the opportunity for a handsome gateway to the park. Hearst was anxious to start building (his political foes were accusing him of absconding with the public subscription), and since he was speculating heavily in Columbus Circle real estate, he must have been enchanted with the idea of a fine monument enhancing its value. As for Magonigle and Piccirilli, they were desperate to save their work, even if it meant that the monument and its site would be grotesquely mismatched. Magonigle tried to adapt his design by adding gateways to either side, but in his heart of hearts he must have known that his monument was all wrong for Columbus Circle. The new scheme wasn't exhibited at the Municipal Art Society, though Magonigle now sat on the society's board of directors, and a hush-hush atmosphere settled over the work. "Practically no New York painter or sculptor of note outside of the Art Commission has ever seen or passed judgment upon the plans," the *Times* reported, and the paper found that no one—not the Art Commission, not the *Maine* Memorial Committee, and especially not Magonigle—wanted to submit a photograph for publication. Parsons tried to stop the scheme, but Stover was determined to plunge ahead, and the Art Commission—embarrassed, no doubt, by its clerk's negligence—merely asked Magonigle to shrink it a bit, so as not to overpower Gaetano Russo's Christopher Columbus monument. Once he did so, Magonigle and Stover "were released from all official restraint."[19] *Still* Parsons protested, this time on behalf of all the glorious trees Magonigle hoped to uproot, the better to display his work. There were some testy meetings at the site, and Parsons was badgered into approving the death of some trees, but far fewer than Magonigle wanted.

The *Maine* monument was but a minor skirmish in a bitter war between Parsons and Stover, and if the parks commissioner won this battle, he wasn't so lucky in others. Parsons, bless his soul, managed to stop Stover from replacing Central Park's graceful cast-iron Bow Bridge with a low-maintenance concrete "facsimile" (as if concrete could reproduce that bridge's delicate tracery). Parsons also vetoed Thomas Hastings's plan to transform Bryant Park into a garden every bit as French and formal as the adjacent library—a scheme MAS had backed as early as 1903 and which it proudly exhibited again in 1911. Nor would Parsons let Stover build a playground in Colonial Park (now Jackie Robinson Park), though here Parsons was on much shakier ground. He admitted that the playground wasn't a bad idea, but insisted that the city must hold to the principle that no alien use should encroach on the parks.

It seems that Parsons assumed this extreme position only when he realized the full scope of Stover's ambition to "popularize" the park system. While Parsons could veto changes in the parks' *plans*, Stover was still at liberty to change the parks' *use*. He could turn lawns into baseball fields, for instance, and began doing so with great vigor. Sports arrived in Morningside Park, to the horror of Columbia University faculty members and "prominent persons interested in the Cathedral of Saint John the Divine and the Union Theological Seminary." "The park has been practically ruined by its promiscuous use as a playground and ball park," they complained. "Half grown youths or adults ... and even gangs of hoodlums from a distance crowded in." Tellingly, the complaints didn't come from Harlem, much less from the "half grown." The civic groups didn't much care what happened in Morningside Park, but they *did* care that Stover might do much the same thing in Central Park. In 1911 he entertained plans for a huge complex of ball fields and playgrounds north of the Reservoir. Henry Moskowitz of the Citizens Union protested that the city should build playgrounds in new neighborhood parks rather than sully the "beautiful landscape features" of Central Park. This was not "a stupid conservatism," Moskowitz wrote.[20] Harold Caparn, a Municipalian and a landscape architect, weighed in as well. The park's best use, he wrote, "is the most intangible and least understood by many self-styled practical men; that of the solace of beautiful scenery in the midst of the roar and bustle of the city." Build ball fields and "there might appear ... to be more going on because there would be more noise and more violent action. Two teams of boys playing baseball will create more bustle and excitement than 10,000 resting, strolling, or engaged in the milder forms of play. ... This 'popularizing' would result in giving over the parks to one ... class of the community—the boys of, say, eight to eighteen years of age. Not that the boys are at fault ... it is merely that they are doing a perfectly proper thing in an improper place."[21]

Stover backed down on this playground complex. Such a large facility, he realized, built in the face of such opposition, would threaten his entire program. Instead he would take smaller steps to "popularize" Central Park. The result was still, as the *Times* reported in 1911, open warfare between Stover and Parsons. "Mr. Parsons was by no means in sympathy with all Commissioner Stover's plans for the 'popularization' of the parks, and ... the latter believes he would be able to go ahead with his ideas if Mr. Parsons was [sic] not in office." Despite such rumblings, no one was prepared when Stover accused Parsons of corruption. The circumstances surrounding his accusation are a bit murky. For years Parsons had recommended replenishing the exhausted soil of Central Park, and as far back as 1903 he'd written that "the Park was starving to death, and that unless it were forthwith supplied with fresh soil, not one green thing in Central Park would presently be left upon another."[22] In 1910 Parsons wrote a little book on the subject and specified the precise mix of loam and clay that was required. Stover discovered that one of Parsons's friends—a friend with ties to the New Jersey Company, which supplied just the sort of soil recommended—had encouraged him to write the book. Moreover, this same company—without Parsons's knowledge, it seems—had guaranteed the book's publisher against loss.* Having learned all of this, Stover accused Parsons of collusion and brought him up on charges before the commissioner of accounts.

The commissioner turned up only "vague, unsatisfactory" evidence, and con-

---

* *The company did win the contract to provide the soil, but Parsons played no role in that. One should note that Parsons drew up his specifications in consultation with the U.S. Department of Agriculture. Moreover, Parsons's first contract with the New Jersey Company came after the specifications were drawn up.*

cluded that Parsons had probably been an innocent dupe.[23] Stover, however, used the investigation to paint Parsons as an old man who'd outlived his times. He "is not constructive," Stover testified, "and is not capable of dealing with new problems. His whole position is one of antagonism. A younger man, and a man with a more elastic mind, would be desirable."[24] Thomas Hastings, thwarted in his plan to tear up Bryant Park, "attacked Mr. Parsons as lacking experience in architectural landscape work and described him as . . . a 'planter' and not a 'planner.'" On these grounds, the commissioner of accounts recommended that Parsons be removed from office. The City Club was so disturbed that it launched its own investigation. It found no evidence to incriminate Parsons in the matter of Central Park's soil, yet it too concluded that he lacked the "stamina and virile executive ability" that the position demanded. The club's evidence was "the almost entire absence on his part of any attempt at vigorous defense." Perhaps Parsons was too proud or hurt to defend himself, or perhaps the City Club gave itself away when it recommended that a "broader-minded man" should be appointed. Others, however, read the same testimony and came to a very different conclusion about Parsons: "He has done . . . all that was within his power to prevent the destruction of the parks," wrote the *Times*. "He has thwarted many of Mr. Stover's wild schemes."[25] In fact, "Mr. Parsons is precisely the right man in the right place. We could better afford to lose ninety and nine Stovers than one Parsons."[26] Mayor Gaynor nonetheless dismissed Parsons. The mayor was surprisingly candid: the city, he said, needed a landscape architect with a more "subordinate disposition."[27]

Stover had succeeded in ridding himself of Parsons, but in the end this proved to be a Pyrrhic victory. All those people who honored the memory of Olmsted and Vaux were now deeply suspicious. The *Times*, Central Park's most consistent defender, was now Stover's sworn enemy. It grimly reported that, with Parsons gone, "there has been no check but Commissioner Stover's upon the removal of trees" at Columbus Circle, and that Stover had far exceeded his original agreement.[28] The newspaper chafed at rumors that Stover was secretly planning to remodel the Plaza at Fifth Avenue and Fifty-ninth Street. Those rumors proved to be true, and the paper's headlines grew ominous: "Stover Insists He's a Good Park Head" was typical. In an effort to soothe tempers, Mayor Gaynor made a show of choosing Parsons's successor, Municipalian Charles Downing Lay, without consulting Stover. Lay managed to restore the North Meadow without bringing in new soil—he grew a crop of rye and plowed it under before reseeding—but he was in an impossible situation. Lay was no populist—he even had doubts about tennis in the park—and he was asked to restrain Parks Commissioner Stover, who was clearly willing to go to great lengths to free himself of restraint.[29]

By then a new controversy had arisen. In 1911 the National Academy of Design, convinced that it was every bit as important an institution as the Metropolitan Museum of Art, decided that it, too, deserved a splendid gallery in Central Park. This seemed like an especially shameful proposition to the *Times*. The academy's artists were, after all, "the very men who would be expected to urge most effectively the preservation of every foot of park land," and the paper reported that few academy members actually favored the idea, but that those who did were "unceasingly energetic and hopeful."[30] This outcry forced the Academy of Design to withdraw its proposal, but the academy's architect, Thomas Hastings, had another trick up his sleeve: if he couldn't have Central Park, how about Bryant Park? Hastings, who was well on his way to acquiring a reputation as the parks' nemesis, had long wanted to screen Bryant Park from the Sixth Avenue El with some sort of colonnaded shelter. Now he proposed something more elaborate: a long, narrow building with art galleries raised above an open arcade. No one was fooled. Clearly the Sixth Avenue El wouldn't last forever, but the National Academy of Design might. Just when Hastings seemed beaten, something odd happened: Henry Frick, the steel magnate, offered to disassemble the Lenox Library and move it, stone by stone, to Central Park.

The Lenox Library was a building close to MAS's heart. It was Richard Morris Hunt's most interesting work, and it was urbanistically inseparable from MAS's own Hunt Memorial. But the building was doomed when the Lenox, Astor, and Tilden foundations merged to form the New York Public Library. That library's Forty-second Street home, designed by Carrère & Hastings, was finally finished, and its acres of empty bookshelves nagged at the trustees' conscience: they'd promised to provide New Yorkers with "any book available anywhere in the world," and they desperately needed money for their acquisitions fund. Meanwhile, Frick wanted "to build a home which shall rival if not outclass the Carnegie home, situated a mile farther up Fifth Avenue. In this connection," the *Times* reported, "it is recalled that Mr. Frick and Mr. Carnegie have been rivals in many ways for some years."* And Thomas Hastings, who had dreamed up the scheme to move the Lenox Library, wanted several things: to save Hunt's masterpiece from destruction; to provide Central Park with a Beaux Arts "ornament"; and maybe even to provide a home for the National Academy of Design—in the renovated and relocated Lenox Library.[31]

The mayor officially accepted Frick's gift, and the search for a site began. Technically, Frick had left the new location of the building to the city's discretion, so Hastings and Stover steered the discussion toward Central Park: the Sheep Meadow, perhaps, or somewhere along one of the park's transverse roads. Mayor Gaynor asked for the Art Commission's advice, and although the commission was free to examine any site in the city, it made the fatal mistake of looking only at Central Park. Predictably, the park's defenders howled: here was another land grab by the National Academy, another encroachment into Central Park. In the hope of quieting them, Parks Commissioner Stover and Robert De Forest, president of the Art Commission, seem to have worked out a deal: they would trade one building for another. The

---

* Frick's motives for offering to move the library are more obscure. He wasn't known as a philanthropist, and his sudden generosity may have been inspired by the byzantine legal complications of his real estate deal. The site had been given to the city with the stipulation that it would revert to the Lenox Estate—not the Lenox Foundation—if the Astor Library ever closed. The foundation's trustees had to persuade all the heirs to surrender their claims; and the state also had to approve this transfer of public property.

reassembled Lenox Library would replace the Arsenal and would become the home not of the Academy of Design but of the Parks Department itself.

The Arsenal stands just inside Central Park at Fifth Avenue and Sixty-first Street. Older than the park itself, the structure was built as an armory and had eventually become the Parks Department's unlovely headquarters.* According to the mayor, the building was "unsanitary and unfit" and needed to be replaced. Hunt's library building would certainly house the agency "more agreeably," as De Forest argued, but many were convinced that the administration was actually playing an elaborate shell game with the public. Once the library was rebuilt, they charged, the Academy of Design would cast its covetous eye on the building. It was really too luxurious, after all, to serve as office space for civil servants, but its noble, high-ceilinged chambers would make a perfect art gallery. The park's defenders agreed that the Arsenal should go, but they wanted to landscape its site. It was "a crying extravagance," said Frederick Law Olmsted, Jr., to suffer any building in the park. The *Times* swore that "in spite of the Municipal Art Commission's defiance of public opinion, the new conspiracy against the preservation of Central Park will be fought vigorously. . . . The old Arsenal will be removed in due time, but no other building will be put in its place."[32] It seemed that few weapons were available, however. The mayor had accepted the gift of the library building, Frick was putting up the money for its reconstruction, the Art Commission had given its okay, and workmen were already prying apart the library's stones in preparation for the move. There was just one flaw in Stover's plan, one vulnerable point: he still needed an appropriation to tear down the Arsenal. At this point the park advocates, sworn to the Arsenal's eventual *destruction*, descended on the Board of Estimate and demanded the building's *preservation*. The appropriation was defeated, and Frick, annoyed at the public's ingratitude—or perhaps convinced that his philanthropy would be wasted on a less conspicuous site—withdrew his offer to reconstruct the Lenox Library. Hunt's greatest building was lost to posterity.[33]

This outcome made no one happy. Having lost their battle, Gaynor and Stover might have made peace with the park advocates, but for all Gaynor's vaunted reading of the Stoic philosophers, he was a remarkably thin-skinned mayor. Criticism made him bristle, and instead of putting the fight behind him, he stirred the embers anew. Frick's action was a pity, said the mayor, because now the city would have to rebuild the Arsenal at its own expense. And Stover fanned the flames: he had a new proposal for remodeling the heart of Central Park.

While all of this was going on, a new municipal water tunnel was under construction, and Stover realized that when it was finished, the city would be able to dispense with the old receiving reservoir in Central Park. This "lower reservoir" occupied the site where the Great Lawn is today—between the Museum of Natural History, west of the park, and the Metropolitan Museum of Art on the east side

---

* *The Arsenal is much prettier now. Robert Moses remodeled it in 1934, stripping off its stucco to reveal the red brick beneath, redoing the doorway, commissioning WPA murals for the Great Hall, and, in general, making it look more like a little toy castle.*

of the park. Commissioner Stover now came up with an idea for the reservoir site: Beaux Arts gardens, he decided, should replace the old water tanks.

> [That] area, including a portion of the reservoir, should be devoted to a boulevard, sunken gardens, or some other connecting link between the two great structures. "If that is done," the commissioner declared to a *Times* man, "New York can have the grandest setting for its museums of any city in the world. . . . I know that my plan will ruffle the feathers of all those who resist change. . . . We all have the sentiment of preservation of beautiful things, so when a suggestion is made . . . for connecting the museums by means of a plaza or boulevard, it is sure to outrage the feelings of conservatives."[34]

For now there was nothing Stover could do, but this idea, and various permutations on it, would torture New York for the next twenty years.

THROUGH ALL this controversy, the Municipal Art Society remained strangely silent. It had backed Stover's appointment to begin with, and in an abstract way it was entirely in sympathy with his vision of the parks as a place of monumental art, recreation, and nature. I doubt that the Municipalians had expected Stover to go so far, however, and his plans for Central Park provoked in them a deep sense of unease. MAS itself ducked the issue, but its members and trustees couldn't keep silent, and gradually people realized that Central Park needed an organized constituency to thwart "the desires of the architects anxious to 'adorn' the parks with buildings." Encroachment by the National Academy of Design and the Lenox Library had been successfully fought off, but many New Yorkers grimaced at the sight of trees being felled for the *Maine* Memorial. They hated the idea of formal esplanades cutting the park in two to make a "setting" for the museums, and they resented the secrecy that surrounded Stover's plans for the Plaza.

One thing that was not secret, though, was Stover's friendship with Thomas Hastings, the man who had dreamed up the idea of putting the Lenox Library in the park, who had schemed to dig up Bryant Park, and who was now at work redesigning the Plaza. And when Stover spoke of the "beautiful harmonies of landscape combined with architecture," he seemed to be announcing his intention to lay Central Park at Hastings's feet. "The architects of the French school are making the trouble," complained Rollin Saltus, a landscape architect. "Not that there is anything wrong with French school architects, but our parks came from English models and are wholly different in spirit." If the architects "have their own way," he warned, "it will be only a short time before the entire spirit of our parks is changed, and they will become formal parks, after the French manner, instead of landscape parks after the English manner." Frederick Law Olmsted, Jr., weighed in as well. "It is entirely timely to inaugurate a movement to protect the parks," he wrote, and Eugene Philbin, head of the Parks and Playgrounds Association, answered his plea by organizing a Central Executive Committee to work "for the preservation of existing park spaces." Samuel Parsons and Harold Caparn joined; so did Charles Lamb, Seth Low, Albert E. Davis, Jacob Riis, Belle Israels, and Edward Hagaman Hall, not to mention a selection of Fifth Avenue millionaires. The park advocates' first demand, now that the Lenox Library had been reduced to rubble, was that the city tear down the Arsenal and landscape its site.[35]

But Stover wouldn't back down. In 1911 he'd staged a folk dancing festival in Central Park for ten thousand schoolgirls; a year later came a pageant, "Around the World in Search of Fairyland," with a cast of five thousand kids. In 1913 he announced plans for an athletics exhibition. Ten thousand schoolchildren would compete in this event, bleachers would be built for spectators, and the *Times* shrieked that the lawn "will inevitably be destroyed." Tired of trying to repair the park's lawns after such events, Charles Downing Lay resigned from his post, blasting Stover for denying him the resources to maintain the park. Stover had now driven two successive landscape architects from office, a dubious accomplishment. He looked forward to the opportunity to appoint a more sympathetic man to the post, but he found that the parks commissioners of Brooklyn and Queens and the American Society of Landscape Architects were lined up against him, and they urged Mayor Gaynor to appoint Carl F. Pilat. Much was made—too much—of the fact that Pilat's uncle had worked for Olmsted and Vaux, and the *Times* begged Pilat to remember this "inheritance," warning that "What he needs, most of all, is backbone." But Pilat, it turned out, was another Beaux Artist, and New York learned that education *does* count more than genes.[36]

With just a few demurrals, Mayor Gaynor had stood by Stover through more than three years of controversy. Their friendship is commemorated to this day by the Shakespeare Garden, planted by Stover in honor of their favorite poet. When the mayor died in 1913, Stover took it "very much to heart," one friend remembered, and "never seemed to recover from the shock." Aside from the personal blow, Gaynor's death left Stover with no protector. Almost every civic group in New York was opposed to his plans for Central Park, and the *Times* kept firing one volley of criticism after another. The pressure proved to be too much for Stover. Telling a subordinate that he meant to take a vacation, his first in four years, the parks commissioner walked out of the Arsenal one day in the fall of 1913. He never came back. Two weeks stretched to three, then four, and there was still no word from him. None of his friends knew his whereabouts, but at first they didn't worry overmuch. It seems that Stover had a history of strange disappearances—in the very midst of his fight to save the Delancey Street Parkway, he'd dropped out of sight for weeks, and he'd vanished again just before becoming parks commissioner, explaining afterward that he'd gone away to study some books on Italian landscaping. Now that Stover was a public servant, such behavior was highly embarrassing, and since the city charter made no provision for appointing an acting commissioner, work in the Arsenal ground to a halt.[37]

Rumors began to fly. The Parks Department work crews insisted that Stover must have eloped, but his friends were skeptical. "Stover married?" one gasped.

"Well, I don't know. I suppose anything might happen these days." Others suspected suicide or foul play, but the Hudson River stubbornly refused to yield Stover's body. A coroner in Maryland reported the discovery of a drowned corpse that bore "a striking resemblance" to Stover, but as it turned out, he hadn't even gotten the hair color right.[38]

When Stover paid some bills by check, with no return address on the envelope and no word of explanation, his friends finally grew frightened. Some worried that Stover was settling up his personal accounts as a prelude to suicide; all agreed that his reticence was deeply troubling. "The one conclusion that can best be drawn," one source told the *Times*, "is that he is the victim of some mental malady, perhaps amnesia. That might result in his forgetting his official life of the past few years, and his looking at himself as a private citizen with the right to go and come as he pleases. A blow on the head or an excess of grief over the death of Mayor Gaynor might produce this." Another friend announced that nickelodeons around the country would project Stover's picture on Thanksgiving Day 1913. As that date approached, a man checked into a San Francisco hotel, signed the registry as Charles Stover, and then vanished. The police concluded that this was a publicity stunt: a local nickelodeon was trying to drum up a big holiday audience. At this point, realizing he'd soon have no place left to hide, Stover telegraphed his resignation from Cincinnati. "Now let there be no further concern about me," he wrote a colleague. "In my day I have travelled not a little, and am fully competent to make my way anywhere around the world in safety. I repeat, therefore, let there be no worry."[39]

"Mr. Stover is seemingly having a good time as he rambles about the country," the *Times* wrote, rather heartlessly. "At last we can say farewell. . . . Nevertheless, the retirement of Mr. Stover relieves the intelligent citizens of New York of no responsibility. The preservation of the parks from intrusion and their proper care will be beset with as many difficulties in the future as in the past."[40]

IN JANUARY 1914 Charles Stover returned, unannounced, to the East Side Settlement. He told friends that he'd been touring the nation's municipal park systems, but whatever knowledge he had gleaned went to waste.[41] Stover had surrendered not just his office but his reputation as well, and he was never again an effective advocate.

A few months after Stover's return, the new Fusion administration of Mayor John Purroy Mitchel evicted the Parks Department from the Arsenal and the *Times* demanded that the city raze the building, "which has no historic associations, is not beautiful, and encumbers ground," before anyone could find a new use for it. "The National Academy of Design scheme is not dead, by any means," the paper warned.[42] In fact the academy had had enough. Giving up all hope of a grand new building, it settled rather modestly in a town house on Fifth Avenue at Eighty-ninth Street. Its days of glory were over in any case. The Armory Show of 1913 had sounded the trumpets of the avant-garde, and the National Academy of Design soon degenerated into a sleepy club for elderly conservative artists.

The Arsenal survived, thanks to the fiscal crisis of 1914, but the empty building did indeed attract the notice of "park invaders"—the Museum of Safety tried to move in—and in the 1920s the Parks Department finally slunk back to its old home.

NEW YORK CITY'S parks were neglected through World War I. Many were festooned with signs and barely tended. Union Square had been torn up by subway construction, and a third of it was left as a mud patch for the duration. The lawns of neighborhood parks were turned into liberty gardens, where school-children grew vegetables as part of the war effort. An ugly and far less useful fate threatened Central Park: one Guy Emerson, of the Liberty Loans Campaign, wanted to have schoolchildren dig trenches in the North Meadow; this would help them empathize with the doughboys, Emerson thought, and it would pre-pare them for combat. Horrified by this proposal, Albert Bard asked, "Why not advertise the war by smashing the windows in the City Hall?" Yet the new parks commissioner okayed Emerson's scheme. The civic groups mounted a campaign to head it off in the Board of Estimate, and MAS's Richard Welling went to the *Times* with an idea.

For years Welling and the *Times* had fought to protect the park from projects "in themselves often worthy, oftener grotesque, and frequently purely commercial." Their battles had been waged on a case-by-case basis, with the projects' advocates maintaining that any damage done would be very slight, or insisting that the park was large enough to accommodate just one more "feature." This time Welling talked the *Times* into publishing "a bird's-eye view of Central Park as it would look if all these enterprises had been carried into effect."[43] Actually, there were so many "enterprises" that Vernon Howe Bailey, who produced the drawing, had to leave out a good many. Even so, there was very little park left in his drawing. He showed the speedway, Grant's Tomb, the Cathedral of Saint John the Divine, a stadium, the National Academy of Design, a marionette theater, the Ninety-sixth Street play-ground complex . . . and on and on. The drawing was a useful prop to wave during Board of Estimate hearings, but the final blow to Guy Emerson's hopes came when someone asked him why he'd chosen the newly restored North Meadow. Because of its "rural beauty," he answered, and the audience erupted in raucous laughter.[44]

In itself this battle wasn't terribly important, but Welling and Bailey's aerial view of Central Park would pop up repeatedly in the future. The Municipal Art Society reproduced it in the 1960s, for instance, when it was fighting off the Huntington Hartford Pavilion, a scheme for a café for the park's southeast corner—although by then no one remembered that the drawing had sprung from MAS.[45] And at the time it rang alarm bells in the civic groups. It managed to convey a sense of Central Park's fragility; of how hard it was to maintain the integrity of an artwork made of dirt and trees and shrubs; and of how, over time, even little changes to the park would transform it into something unrecognizable.

After the First World War, MAS realized that the city knew very little about the park's original design; in fact the Parks Department didn't even own a set of plans. In 1912 the landscape architect N. B. Van Ingen looked through the Parks Department archives and came upon the dusty minutes of the old Park Board, which had supervised the design and construction of Central Park. The board was a meddlesome group and chary of funds, and it had forced Vaux and Olmsted to justify each of their countless design decisions in great detail. Buried in the minutes was a weekly account of their work. Van Ingen begged that the papers be collated and indexed to serve as a guide for the park's restoration and maintenance, but predictably, Charles Stover wasn't interested.[46]

Later, however, in 1919, as MAS and the Society of Landscape Architects geared up to press for the park's restoration, they decided to take up Van Ingen's project. Neither the aldermen nor the Russell Sage Foundation would pay for it, so MAS set up a fund-raising committee and asked I. N. Phelps Stokes, the brother of J. G. Phelps Stokes, to join. ("I. N." stood for Isaac Newton, but he never used his full name. It was quite a mouthful, and he found that turn-of-the-century hoteliers looked coldly on men named Isaac, even if "Newton" tagged along.) Phelps Stokes was an architect, a millionaire, a print collector, and a housing activist. At the time he was writing his encyclopedic, six-volume work, *The Iconography of Manhattan Island*, a crucial resource for future preservationists. In the course of his research, he'd found the legendary Greensward drawing—Vaux and Olmsted's first plan for the park. Understanding its value, he rescued it from neglect and saw to its restoration. Now Phelps Stokes turned MAS's publication project in a different direction. He was a friend of Frederick Law Olmsted, Jr., who had landscaped his Greenwich estate, and the Olmsted office, it turned out, had its own archive. It, too, included official papers, but also other writings, among them some fragments of Olmsted's unfinished autobiography.

As a result of this discovery, Van Ingen was dropped from MAS's publication project, and the Olmsted papers were published instead. *Forty Years of Landscape Architecture: Central Park*, edited by Olmsted, Jr., and Theodora Kimball, was finally released in 1928 (and reprinted in 1973). Park preservationists greeted the book as "our bible, our constitution,"[47] and its publication marked the true beginning of the Olmsted cult, in which the man was transformed into an almost mythic figure— while Calvert Vaux, his partner, faded into obscurity.

Long before the "bible" actually made it into print, MAS and the American Society of Landscape Architects had begun a campaign to restore Central Park. They noticed that the police ignored the sort of everyday vandalism and thoughtlessness that could destroy the park, and they suggested that the city create a force of "park keepers." Then there was the question of administration. Parks commissioners changed every few years, often before they'd learned the full complexity of their job. The office of the landscape architect and his power to veto a commissioner's plans had been fatally compromised by Stover's treatment of Parsons and Lay. To remedy this situation, MAS and the Society of Landscape Architects wanted to "take the park system out of municipal politics." They suggested establishing a board of park commissioners modeled on the Art Commission. These commissioners would be chosen in consultation with the art societies and would serve for rotating six-year terms. When Mayor Hylan took the proposal for park keepers "under advisement" without acting on it, and then simply dismissed the notion of an independent park commission, the art societies began lobbying for the necessary change in the city charter.[48]

The park by now was under assault on all fronts, and encroachments soon monopolized MAS's attention. Manhattan's center of gravity had continued to shift northward. Whenever people thought of a new amenity for the East Side, West Side, Harlem, or Midtown, their eyes turned toward this central island of greenery.

In 1919, for example, Julia Rice offered the city a million dollars to build a stadium in Central Park as a memorial to her late husband, Isaac Rice, a life member of MAS whose mansion still stands on the corner of Riverside Drive and Eighty-ninth Street. Mrs. Rice had never had the time to be active in MAS—as president of the Society to Prevent Unnecessary Noise, her hands, or her ears, were already full. Fortunately she was finally persuaded to build her stadium in Pelham Bay Park. It was a monumental structure designed by Herts & Tallant, but the city was careless with its foundations, and it soon began to sink into the swampy soil.[49]

Even though Mrs. Rice's threat had been safely banished to the Bronx, others kept springing up throughout the 1920s to take its place. Mayor Hylan, for instance, wanted to build the Independent subway under the western edge of the park. Putting it there, rather than under Central Park West, would have spared the city any disruption in traffic—not to mention the expense of moving sewers, gas lines, and water mains—but the cost to Central Park would have been enormous. The subway would have flattened the park's topography: hills and valleys would have disappeared; rocky outcrops would have been blasted away; and instead of boulders and cliffs, ventilation grilles and escape hatches would have dotted the landscape. Residents of the Upper West Side threw up their hands in horror; the Parks and Playgrounds Association threatened to sue the city; and MAS announced that it would join the lawsuit. Hylan backed down.

Then the Sixth Avenue Association mobilized. Darkened by an El, that street had long been an ugly duckling, but now a subway was due to replace the El (though years of delay lay in store). The avenue had just been extended to Varick Street, and landowners wanted to give it a northern outlet into the park. Once MAS understood that this wasn't a scheme for a new "commercial thoroughfare," it decided to hold its tongue[50] (although with a little more foresight, it might have seen that the days of pleasure drives were numbered and that "commercial" traffic would soon flood the park). More alarming was Mayor John F. Hylan's plan, unveiled in 1922, for a music and art center.[51] Its centerpiece was to be a new municipal opera house. Dressed in pompous Classical facades by the architect

Arnold Brunner, this enormous scheme was the worst sort of frigid City Beautiful design, very much a forerunner to Lincoln Center. It would have stretched from Fifty-seventh Street to Fifty-ninth and from Sixth Avenue to Seventh, while an elevated plaza would have bridged Central Park South, turning it into a miserable underpass, and extended the axis into Central Park. The proposal for a music and art center would eventually collapse of its own weight, but in 1923 the mayor came up with one last scheme for Central Park: an enormous war memorial.

WAR MEMORIALS had been on MAS's mind since 1918. It knew, as soon as the armistice was signed, that countless monuments would be erected around the country, dozens in the city itself. Every town would want to honor its dead, every neighborhood and every regiment; then there would be a host of private memorials, and somewhere in New York City there would surely be one great monument, a collective symbol of the city's grief. Or would it be a symbol of victory? How should people commemorate a war that was marked by unprecedented slaughter and concluded with a catastrophic peace conference?

MAS had no real answer to this question, save that one should hire an artist. Its booklet on war memorials, designed to warn the public away from the catalogs of metal foundries and stone-carving firms, was distributed around the country. A "stock design," MAS wrote, "is prepared by a draughtsman of a grade no higher than the utmost business economy considers it prudent to risk." Such work was "not worthy of the spirit which made men give their lives to their country" and in time would prove an "ever increasing source of chagrin to the community." But an artist! A Beaux Artist could design anything, from a wayside cross to a carillon tower, from memorial columns to triumphal arches, from stained-glass windows to monumental bridges, art galleries, community centers, auditoriums, even pedestals for captured cannon—"The massive modern howitzer is capable," MAS claimed, "of good use in monumental treatment."[52]

The arts community did enjoy a boom in the monument business, but it was still an open question what sort of war memorial New York City should build. The Municipal Art Society's first idea was for a water gate, an apt choice if the point was to stress America's ties to the Allies (or if one had been dreaming of monumental water gates for the past few years), but not exactly in touch with America's new isolationist mood. There was no public consensus on the issue, only a nagging sense that updating old ideas for monuments was somehow inadequate.

In November 1919 a public meeting was held to discuss the question, and soon MAS was busily conferring with Fiorello La Guardia, president of the Board of Aldermen, and Henry Curran, Manhattan borough president. As City Hall's lone Republicans, however, La Guardia and Curran were politically isolated, and it wasn't very clever of MAS to deal exclusively with two thorns in Tammany's side. Mayor Hylan had formed his own Committee on the War Memorial, but MAS bitterly complained that this body wasn't "representative." Certainly the art societies went unrepresented. The committee did include Paul Bartlett, who'd just stepped down as president of the National Sculpture Society, but he enjoyed a very curious relationship with his own former constituents: he suspected many of them of being "pro-German"—by which he meant any attitude short of a bloodthirsty hatred of the Hun.

Things reached a crisis when the mayor's committee toyed with the idea of simply rebuilding Thomas Hastings's plaster Arch of Victory in stone, and the sculptor Alexander Stirling Calder, whose son would make mobiles, complained that Hastings's design wouldn't do. Calder reminded his colleagues that America had entered the war to make the world safe for democracy. A triumphal arch wouldn't express that idealism; it would merely seem to gloat over a vanquished enemy. When the National Sculpture Society agreed with Calder, the *Herald* ran the headline: "Sculptors Oppose Permanent Arch as 'Rough on Germany.' " The *Herald* was opposed to the League of Nations; it took a paranoid view of Calder's (and President Wilson's) idealism; and it insinuated that the Sculpture Society was treasonous. This smear campaign devastated the National Sculpture Society, and it made life more difficult for the Municipal Art Society as well. For MAS agreed that the Arch of Victory was the wrong monument for World War I, but now it didn't dare say so too explicitly. Instead, MAS suggested an open competition for ideas, accompanied by a referendum of Great War veterans.[53] The competition never came to pass; instead, the mayor's Committee on the War Memorial asked Thomas Hastings to produce a design. MAS feared that he would submit the Arch of Victory again but in 1923 Hastings came up with something much worse: a scheme for a vast Beaux Arts garden in the middle of Central Park.

M A S A N D Thomas Hastings had quarreled long ago over the Manhattan Bridge, and in 1923 they were locked in another heated argument. It centered on Hastings's favorite sculptor and frequent collaborator, Frederick MacMonnies. MacMonnies had begun his career as a protégé of Augustus Saint-Gaudens, who remembered him as "a pale, delicate ... lad sent me by some stonecutter as a studio boy." Mac-Monnies went on to study in Paris and settle in Giverny, and when they met again Saint-Gaudens was startled and a little saddened to find that "the gentle, tender bird I had caressed out of its egg had turned into a proud eagle."[54]

MacMonnies was *very* proud and not much liked by his fellow artists, but in Paris he mastered a dashing, theatrical style of sculpture. His work on the Soldiers' and Sailors' Memorial in Brooklyn's Grand Army Plaza was universally lauded, and in 1893 he startled his colleagues at the Chicago World's Fair with *Columbia Enthroned*, an enormous fountain showing a bare-breasted Columbia on a fantastic barge, like Cleopatra on her way to Tarsus. Father Time steered her ship, the Arts and Sciences worked the oars, Fame blew trumpet blasts from the prow, and sea horses played in the ship's foamy wake. For a time MacMonnies was regarded as the brightest light of his generation, but eventually it became clear that he applied much the same dash to every work, and such Belle Epoque froth dated quickly. His *Nathan Hale* in City Hall Park was generally admired, but his *General Henry Slocum* in Brooklyn annoyed those who knew its subject. It showed Slocum "with his sword pointed to the sky and his mouth opened like the Bull of Bashan's," one man complained, while in truth the general had always been "a gentleman. . . . He never played to the galleries; he never bellowed, never dashed to the front of battle with his sword and his mouth in the air, and he never pointed his sword to the skies."[55]

But this was nothing like the storm that greeted MacMonnies's *Civic Virtue*. It all began with a bequest: a certain Mrs. Angelina Crane left the city $62,000 with which to build a fountain. (She left her daughter just $5.) In 1908 Mayor Mc-Clellan assigned the work to his friend MacMonnies, author of Washington, D.C.'s General McClellan Memorial, and the two picked a site in front of City Hall. After his first sketches were rejected by the Art Commission, MacMonnies recruited Thomas Hastings as his collaborator, and in 1917, nearly ten years after receiving the job, MacMonnies showed their new design to the Art Commission. The scale was colossal, and the Municipal Art Society protested that the fountain would dwarf City Hall itself. Find some other site, MAS suggested, but the Art Commission merely asked Hastings and MacMonnies to shrink their design.[56]

In 1922, when the fountain was finally finished, eyes began to pop and tongues to wag. Hundreds of years before, Michelangelo had startled Florence by giving his *David* not the lithe, princely physique of a Donatello but the hard, muscled body of a street kid. The Florentine working class had recognized David as one of its own, and for once a masterpiece of public art was truly popular. That, it seems, was MacMonnies's ambition—and the measure of his failure. His Civic Virtue was a beefy lad holding a thick, stubby sword. Beneath his feet writhed busty mermaids: the forces of Civic Vice, freshly clobbered. Naturally, people broke into guffaws on seeing the fountain. Some nicknamed it "Big Boy"; others, "Tough Guy." But women, especially, saw a brutal misogyny in it, and having won the vote a few years earlier they were finally in a position to demand action. Prudes complained about Virtue's nudity, and reformers had their own objections; normally happy to wrap themselves in the mantle of civic virtue, they couldn't quite locate their ideal in MacMonnies's cartoonish violence, nor could they identify personally with "Tough Guy." He was too thuggish, too voluptuous, too much a piece of rough trade.

The *Sun* looked at "Tough Guy" and accused Mayor Hylan of an "act of civic indecency." The mayor had known nothing of this fourteen-year-old project until it was ready to be installed in his front yard, and naturally his first thought was to blame the thing on some predecessor. He charged into the Art Commission's office demanding to know "Who ordered that lewd statue, anyway?" None too truthfully, the secretary told him that "Mayor McClellan was *entirely* responsible." Hylan had received his first public office from McClellan, and was too kind to forget it now. "Oh, my God," he murmured, "we must at all costs protect McClellan."[57] So the blame was shifted to the Art Commission—which, after all, had seen and approved MacMonnies's model—and to the artist himself.

The mayor called a special meeting of the Board of Estimate to determine if the Art Commission had "overreached its artful eye."[58] One grateful feminist suggested that a portrait of the mayor himself—clothed, presumably—would make a fine symbol of civic virtue. MacMonnies denied that his work was a slur upon women, but spoke dismissively of the public's "narrow prejudice." The parks commissioner, trying to be helpful, pointed out that mermaids are mythical creatures and not women at all.

In the meantime the Fine Arts Federation rushed to defend the Art Commission, its very own creature. It passed a resolution insisting that MacMonnies's work was indisputably accomplished—in a technical sense—and that the public should take the federation's word for it. It was a haughty statement. The Fine Arts Federation might have pleaded for tolerance; instead it suggested that the public was simply too ignorant to judge an artist's work and should stop being so uppity. This only served to inflame tempers.

MAS was already troubled by the fact that a number of editorials had questioned its silence on the matter, and the Fine Arts Federation's resolution proved to be the last straw. The society's board fired off a letter to the federation ridiculing *Civic Virtue*, questioning the whole notion that the arts community alone could judge public art, and demanding a special meeting of the federation to consider the issue. At least one sculptor resigned from MAS to protest this stance, and Arnold Brunner, president of the Fine Arts Federation, warned that "public discussion of this subject by any society of artists would be most regrettable."[59]

The Municipal Art Society refused to keep quiet, however, and its next bulletin carried an editorial by Mrs. Herbert Keen:

> Artists are not always right nor is the public always wrong. . . . Art Commissions are not infallible. To accept a composition simply because it may be technically excellent is not to exercise that breadth of judgement required for such highly important decisions. . . . There are only two questions to ask. Is Civic Virtue artistically worthy of its supremely important subject and its most conspicuous position? And should any other considerations whatever have been allowed to outweigh these most important aspects of the case? We maintain that every work of art shown in public is a direct appeal to the public judgement and taste, and that the public have a right to express their judgement. In this great city where the quality of civic virtue is the supremely necessary thing in life, it is a deeply regrettable *and hardly endurable thing* that the most important piece of sculpture and the one erected in our most significant public place, should embody what so many people find to be either a ridiculous or a repellent conception of civic duty.

When he read this, Albert Bard erupted in fury. He hadn't been present when MAS first thrashed out its position, but now he demanded that the society reverse its course. No one—not MAS or the Art Commission or the general public itself—had the right to judge the content of a work of art, he argued, and he pointed to the danger in Keen's declaration of the Art Commission's fallibility: here was MAS, that agency's parent and heretofore its constant defender, blithely suggesting that the Art Commission could and should be overruled. If the Art Commission's friends said as much, what would City Hall say? Bard was told he could write an essay for the next bulletin, but that it would be printed as a purely personal statement. He resigned from MAS's board in protest. Within a few years he was drawn back into the society's orbit, however—since he'd never abandoned his work for the City Club, the Fine Arts Federation, and MAS's other allies, he found himself constantly collaborating with the very society he'd just left. But for the next twenty-three years, until Bard rejoined its board, MAS had to do without the constant presence of its most brilliant and impassioned member.[60]

One thing saved *Civic Virtue* from the scrap yard. As the parks commissioner pointed out, New York had accepted Mrs. Crane's bequest and had spent the money on MacMonnies's fee. If *Civic Virtue* were rejected, the city would have to come up with another $62,000 to erect a new fountain. No one was in the mood to pursue this course. Of course, *Civic Virtue* could be moved to a less prominent place, but the problem was finding one. There was some talk of putting it in Foley Square, but that seemed just as conspicuous as the approach to City Hall. As far as MAS was concerned, *Civic Virtue* was now something to lump together with the Tweed Courthouse and the Mullet post office: another eyesore to banish from City Hall Park. Nor did the fountain grow on the Municipal Art Society. In 1928 it convinced the Parks Department that some landscaping might help, but when the city planted ivy and low shrubs, the society protested that it hadn't gone far enough—MAS wanted to hide the fountain in a grove of trees.[61]

In the end, *Civic Virtue* stayed in City Hall Park until 1941, when Parks Commissioner Robert Moses carted it off to a traffic circle in Queens.

THOMAS HASTINGS had once hoped to work with MacMonnies in Central Park. In 1917, when the Catskill Aqueduct Celebration Committee asked Hastings to design a monument celebrating the city's new water system, his mind must have drifted back to Charles Stover's old idea of sunken gardens on the lower reservoir site—or perhaps it was Hastings who had inspired Stover in 1912. At any rate, he drew up plans for a vast T-shaped lagoon surrounded by formal gardens. Sitting in the water was MacMonnies's *Columbia Enthroned*—the sculpture that had adorned the 1893 Chicago fair, now translated from plaster and lath into bronze. At the south end of the lagoon, shallow banked steps would serve as an open-air theater, with a vista of the lagoon and its fountain stretching out behind the stage like a spectacular backdrop.

John Purroy Mitchel's regime was far too stingy to entertain such a scheme, and in any case, the First World War diverted everyone's attention. The war soon claimed Mitchel as one of its victims. When he was voted out of office, he joined the air force as a student pilot. Mitchel's bravado scorned the use of a safety belt, and one day in July 1918, when his plane went into a sudden dive, the former mayor was catapulted from the open cockpit. A foolish death made Mitchel a hero in the eyes of his friends, though not of his enemies, and in 1919 Hastings plucked up his chutzpah and declared that his Central Park lagoon would make a fitting memorial to the man. But Tammany Hall had suffered too greatly at Mitchel's hands to honor him on such a pharaonic scale: a gilded portrait bust would do nicely, the sachems thought, and one was finally erected in 1926, at Fifth Avenue and Ninetieth Street.[62]

Hastings, though, was a persevering sort. He yearned to give New York a great formal garden, and the war memorial seemed to offer him one last chance to unlock the public coffers. In 1923 he redrew his scheme for the lower reservoir, and this time he added playgrounds to the formal gardens and roped off part of the lagoon for use as a public swimming pool. These populist touches were sure to find favor with Mayor Hylan.

Something else had changed since Hastings drew his first plan eight years earlier, however: abused and ridiculed for his *Civic Virtue*, Frederick MacMonnies had sworn he would never again work for the public. Without his old collaborator, Hastings was at a loss to design the war memorial's sculptural climax. He couldn't bear to give up the frolicking sea horses from *Columbia Enthroned*—they would still rise out of the lagoon to spout playful jets of water—but now an open arcade would sit behind them, and in the middle of the arcade, an Arch of Freedom would shelter a sober image of Athena, Greek goddess of wisdom and war.

The sculpture of Athena was an utterly insipid idea, and those sea horses struck a jarring note, but Mayor Hylan wasn't too concerned with iconographic niceties. At least no one could accuse Athena of indecency, wrapped in armor as she was. Better yet, Hastings's swimming pool and playgrounds leavened his Beaux Arts pomp with popular sports.

But while the mayor was enchanted with Hastings's design, the art societies and park advocates were deeply upset. Hastings tried to win them over by saying that he too was philosophically opposed to any encroachment on the park—a difficult statement to believe, or else a very sudden conversion—but that this plan was "the exception." He tried to win the support of the Sculpture Society by dangling the idea of a collaboration in front of them: that screen of arches behind the lagoon, he pointed out, would be a fine opportunity for sculpture. The sculptors held firm, however, in part because their art would play a subordinate role in Hastings's architectural scheme. The Municipal Art Society announced that it too was "unalterably opposed" to Hastings's scheme, and its stance, untainted by professional jealousy, was a little more pure than that of the sculptors.[63] MAS was convinced that two things were terribly wrong with Hastings's plan. First there was the issue of context. MAS had come to accept that Central Park was a work of art, and one was supposed to conserve a work of art, not update it. MAS wanted the reservoir site landscaped in the naturalistic style of Vaux and Olmsted so as to maintain the original sense of a harmony of parts within the park. The second problem was Hastings's evident insincerity. This was the third time that he'd appeared before the public bearing drawings of a lagoon for Central Park. First it was supposed to celebrate a new aqueduct; then to mourn the death of a former mayor; and now, with just a few changes, Hastings tried to pass off his design as a fitting war memorial. Yet nothing about Hastings's lagoon suggested the war. The original design, with *Columbia Enthroned*, might have been the perfect way to celebrate the Spanish-American War: it had the right imperialist overtones, and one could even picture it as a comic allegory of the White Fleet. But the Great War had silenced even Rudyard Kipling; it had left a taste not of conquest or victory but of death, and MAS could find no sense of tragedy in this "fountain with its splashing waters." The design would "speak of the frivolities of life," MAS complained, "not of reverence for the dead."[64]

The Parks and Playgrounds Association organized a special Park Conservation Committee to coordinate the fight against Hastings's war memorial proposal, and MAS appointed Charles Stoughton and Richard Welling as its delegates to that body. Welling proved to be the committee's most valued member and, at one point, gave a brilliant performance before the Board of Estimate.*

In the meantime the Municipal Art Society tried to make the state of the parks into a campaign issue. In October 1925 it demanded that the mayoral candidates commit themselves to removing the El from Bowling Green, restoring the public forum at Union Square, and banning parking in Madison Square. Further, MAS wanted a promise that subways wouldn't intrude on Central Park or Bryant Park, and that Central Park would be restored. Mayor Hylan never bothered to answer MAS, but his opponent, Jimmy Walker, promised the society his full cooperation, and the papers printed the story.

When Jimmy Walker was elected mayor in 1926, the Municipal Art Society felt sure that Central Park was now in good hands. That same year W. B. Roulstone founded the Central Park Association, which was committed to defeating the war memorial project and restoring the park to its original glory. Roulstone commissioned the Olmsted brothers to conduct a survey of the park's needs, and the Olmsteds documented "the cumulative results of many years of parsimonious neglect and abuse." Central Park, they wrote, "is today in more critical and dangerous physical condition than it has ever passed through in the seventy or more years of its existence." They called for restrictions on traffic through the park, the closing of some of its drives, and a million-dollar rehabilitation program, claiming that a quarter of that sum was needed just to replace dead trees. Egged on by the

---

* *The details of Welling's performance are obscure, but the following may give some hint of his character. Welling had served in the navy during the Spanish-American War, and when he realized that America was sure to enter the First World War, he proudly presented himself again to a navy recruiting office. He'd been a wrestler at Harvard, the strongest man in his class, and he was so proud of his body that he had himself photographed in the nude. Yet the navy doctors turned him away: he had a hammer toe, they explained, and the navy couldn't accept such a deformity. Incredulous, Welling demanded to see their regulations, and there indeed it said in black and white that no misshapen toe could disgrace the deck of a navy ship. Welling's legal mind noticed, however, that the regulations didn't say he needed ten toes. Off he went to a surgeon, and off came the toe, but the navy was not amused. Welling filed suit, won his point and, with it, the command of a naval base at Montauk Point—only to find that exercising such undemocratic power made him deeply uncomfortable. Thereafter he governed his base with a policy of "discipline by consent."*

Central Park Association (and MAS, in a supporting role), Walker appropriated the money.[65]

Yet nothing happened. Jimmy Walker had kept Francis D. Gallatin, Hylan's parks commissioner, in power, and as long as he remained in the Arsenal, Hastings's war memorial was still something of a threat. Even more alarming was the growing realization that no one—not MAS, not the newspapers, not even Mayor Walker—knew how Gallatin really meant to spend his million dollars. He promised to produce a plan, but it never materialized.

Walker was beginning to get annoyed when, in 1927, Gallatin tried to remove the newsstands from City Hall Park on the novel grounds that the vendors were derelict in their civic duty: they hadn't been voting. Editors sneered that the parks commissioner should rephrase his complaint: they hadn't been voting *for Tammany*. When Walker realized that Gallatin had a remarkable talent for embarrassing him, the ax fell, and Gallatin was replaced by Walter R. Herrick, a friend of the mayor since they'd served in the state senate together. No one knew it at the time, but Herrick was also one of the mayor's most trusted bagmen.[66]

The Municipal Art Society found it could do business with Herrick. Fortuitously, the society had a new board member: William White Niles. For the past thirty years Niles had devoted himself to Westchester County and his native Bronx.[67] In 1895, as a state legislator, he had introduced the bill creating the New York Zoological Society, and he still served as the zoo's secretary. He was chairman of the Taconic State Parkway Commission, and when he came to MAS he'd just wrapped up his work as chairman of the Bronx River Parkway Commission. After eighteen years, the parkway was finally finished, and Niles—its father, as MAS liked to say—was basking in public accolades. His advice couldn't simply be brushed aside, and since he knew how to be tactful with politicians, he had a good relationship with the new parks commissioner.

One of Herrick's first acts in office was to cancel Hastings's war memorial—in part, no doubt, because it was so closely identified with Hylan—and to promise that the reservoir site would be landscaped naturalistically. Next, Herrick took Niles's advice and put Herman Merkel, the general superintendent of Westchester's park system, in charge of Central Park's rehabilitation. Niles assured MAS that he would keep an eye on his protégé, and Merkel promised the society a thorough restoration. He contemplated a few changes: some new walks where crowds had ground dirt paths into the lawns, some discreet fencing (chains between low iron poles), an underground irrigation system, and a few small playgrounds "in hidden sections." There would be just eight of these, however, and Merkel insisted, to MAS's great satisfaction, that this would have to satisfy the recreation advocates once and for all.[68]

The civic groups and art societies threw themselves behind Merkel's restoration program, and George McAneny, MAS's new president, demanded that Mayor Walker implement it at once. The Board of Estimate appropriated $871,000—Gallatin's $1 million having evaporated—and Merkel went to work.

MAS was happy that he did such a good job of hiding the playgrounds in thickets. People could walk past them and hardly know they were there, and since the playgrounds were near the park's entrances they effectively intercepted noisy children. What MAS didn't understand was that Merkel's shrubbery would present a security problem, especially in the years to come, when the Parks Department had fewer employees and the park acquired a homeless population; Merkel's thickets would soon be uprooted by Robert Moses. Nor did MAS grasp the power of precedent. Merkel had given playgrounds to just eight neighborhoods. Soon others would demand their own. Merkel's "ultimate concession" had in fact represented the opening of a door.[69]

Meanwhile, the lower reservoir site was still a problem. Since the park's defenders didn't trust the city to come up with a design, they resolved to produce one on their own. One of MAS's board members was the landscape architect Arthur Freeman Brinkerhoff. He was best known for designing sumptuous estates on Long Island, but, like I. N. Phelps Stokes and Electus Litchfield, he'd spent the war years working for the U.S. Housing Corporation. Now, as president of the local chapter of the American Society of Landscape Architects, he persuaded MAS to ask the landscape architects to stage a competition for the reservoir site. Brinkerhoff himself developed the winning scheme in consultation with the Parks Department and MAS. His plan replaced the reservoir with a great oval meadow, its outlines softened by clumps of trees. There would be no play areas "except for very young children," and the area would have just one formal element: at the north end of the lawn, a small plaza would rise over the transverse road and look out over the upper reservoir.[70]

The landscape architects unveiled their plan for the "Great Lawn" in March 1930. MAS hailed it as the perfect solution; so did the Park Association, the real estate lobby, the Fifth Avenue Association, and the *Times*. The Regional Plan Association incorporated the scheme into its own master plan for the city. Commissioner Herrick formally adopted the design, and the Art Commission gave its approval. Whenever MAS asked when the city was going to build the scheme, however, it got evasive answers.

Slowly the city began filling the lower reservoir, but soon work stopped altogether. The Depression had halted construction in New York. There were no more excavations going on; no more sources of free dirt.

A shantytown sprang up in the reservoir's bed, the most notorious of all the era's Hoovervilles. Some of the shanties were actually quite solid—one, built of scavenged bricks by unemployed masons, was twenty feet tall. Other homeless people lived like moles in the empty water mains beneath the reservoir. For a time the public was sympathetic to the plight of the Hooverville's residents, but gradually a familiar callousness set in. Fifth Avenue's residents called on the city to evict the homeless. The park advocates and the Municipal Art Society, however, saw a splendid opportunity to put the unemployed to work building the Great Lawn.

But the Arsenal was in turmoil. When Jimmy Walker fell from power he pulled

Walter Herrick down with him—the parks commissioner had been forced to testify at great length about his extracurricular role as the mayor's bagman. John O'Brien, the new mayor, handed control of the Parks Department to John Sheehy, a Tammany district leader with no expertise in the design or care of parks. In fact, Sheehy confessed that he'd never set foot in Central Park before taking up his post.

At last, however, the park became the scene of furious activity. Sheehy borrowed trucks from the Sanitation Department and relief workers from the welfare department, and they began filling in the reservoir. MAS was happy until it found out that Sheehy wasn't building the Great Lawn after all; instead he meant to carpet the site with sporting fields, baseball diamonds, running tracks, and a wading pool.

"This very desirable playground space should be provided elsewhere," Electus Litchfield cried, "and not in Central Park." "We wish to ask Mr. Litchfield," the *Daily News* answered, "where, in God's name, is 'elsewhere' in the borough of Manhattan? There is no 'elsewhere' for Manhattan's young people."[71] The *Daily News* cheered Sheehy on in the name of the "little people," and the neighborhood groups of Yorkville and Harlem vied with one another in lauding his work. But Sheehy had overlooked one detail: he had never submitted his playground scheme to the Art Commission.

The president of the Art Commission was I. N. Phelps Stokes, who had joined MAS's board of directors in 1926. As a director of MAS, Phelps Stokes was committed to the Great Lawn, but his interest in the park went further. His wife's grandmother, Anna Minturn, had launched the original campaign to create Central Park, and Phelps Stokes himself had grown old with the park. When it was new, in the 1870s, it had been his childhood playground—not that Phelps Stokes ever played a vulgar game of baseball. As a teenager, he had come to know Calvert Vaux; the aged architect had taught him how to handle a canoe. In middle age, one of Phelps Stokes's coups as a print collector was to stumble on the original Greensward Plan. Now, in old age, Phelps Stokes looked down on Central Park from his apartment at 953 Fifth Avenue, a building he designed and financed, and he could be found in the park every day, pushing his invalid wife along in a wheelchair.

Phelps Stokes informed Parks Commissioner Sheehy that his ball fields were illegal. Confident that the Art Commission was powerless, Sheehy ignored him, but "Little by little," as Phelps Stokes wrote, "the mayor, Mr. McAneny, Mr. Straus, president of the Park Association, Mr. Ochs, proprietor of the *New York Times*, and many other well-known citizens and organizations have been drawn into the controversy, and the papers, especially the *Times*, have not only exposed the park commissioner's plan, but have upheld the Art Commission in its contention that the proposed development could not legally be started until plans had been submitted to, and approved by, the Art Commission."[72] Finally, a face-saving compromise was reached: Sheehy could keep his playing fields, but only as a temporary solution. (The Art Commission had no jurisdiction over temporary works.) The final plan would be resolved after the upcoming mayoral election.

And so the Great Lawn's fate was to be decided at the polls. The election of

1933 pitted Sheehy's boss, Mayor John O'Brien, against Fiorello La Guardia, Fusion's fiery and populist New Dealer. Since Tammany hadn't risen to the occasion when the Depression struck New York—its work relief programs were generally paltry, mismanaged, and corrupt—Sheehy's ball fields served the hapless O'Brien as a useful symbol of his supposed concern for the average New Yorker. The issue was far more complicated for La Guardia. He had spent years in Congress representing the crowded tenements of East Harlem, a neighborhood starved for recreational facilities, and his well-honed political instincts surely told him that new ball fields would win far more votes than the Great Lawn, but other factors came into play. La Guardia knew that his support within the Fusion Party was thin at best, and that the party leaders had actually offered the nomination to half a dozen other candidates before turning to him in desperation. La Guardia could ill afford to alienate the old reform establishment, and many of Fusion's leaders—men like George McAneny and Nathan Straus, the president of the Park Association—were committed to the Great Lawn. So was Charles Culp Burlingham, the aged president of the New York Bar and one of I. N. Phelps Stokes's closest friends. It was Burlingham who'd finally convinced the bickering Fusion leaders to unite behind La Guardia. So La Guardia made a campaign promise: there would be no "hodgepodge" of ball fields in Central Park.[73] The lower reservoir site would become the Great Lawn after all.

And once he was elected mayor, La Guardia made the fateful decision to install Robert Moses in the Arsenal.

BETWEEN THE WARS

IN 1919 SOLDIERS flooded home from the war, the arms and shipbuilding plants shut down, and the economy was thrown into turmoil. Private builders refused to pay the new, higher, wartime wages, and New Yorkers suffered from both overcrowding and unemployment. It would have been the perfect time for a great campaign of public works, but no plans had been laid. The West Side Improvement project had collapsed in acrimony, and neither the railroad nor the city was eager to revive it. The trains still lumbered down Death Avenue, and "Riverside" Park was still a euphemism. The rail systems of Calvin Tomkins and William Wilgus were still phantoms; the Congestion Committee's hopes for new housing and workplaces in the outer boroughs remained a dream; the Greater City was yet a cipher.

In fact the issue had grown far beyond that of the Greater City. "Region" had become the buzzword of the times, and regional planning meant, in essence, that New Jersey had entered the picture. As much as New York might have liked to ignore its neighbor, the city's lifelines lay in the tangled strands of railroads on the other side of the Hudson. After Calvin Tomkins's fall from power and Mayor Mitchel's trial by fire, politicians were more tempted than ever to evade the railroad issue, but in 1916 the state of New Jersey brought a complaint to the Interstate Commerce Commission. The railroads, it pointed out, charged one rate for all goods delivered to the Port of New York, whether they were bound for the Jersey terminals or required further shipment across the Hudson to New York City itself. In effect, New Jersey was forced to subsidize New York's shipping costs, and it had had enough of such "discrimination." In the name of fairness, it demanded that the ICC force the railroads to use two rates.

In short, New Jersey had declared war, and if the danger wasn't immediately apparent to the city's politicians, it was perfectly clear to the New York Chamber of Commerce. "Splitting the Port," as the *Post* called it, meant that New York's costs would go up and New Jersey's would go down. This would lure ships and factories away from New York and into New Jersey, and it would make Baltimore and Philadelphia, already cheaper ports of call, irresistibly attractive destinations. New York's defense was coordinated by Eugenius Outerbridge, chairman of the city's Chamber of Commerce (and, in 1909, of Fusion's Committee of One Hundred), and Irving Bush, whose vast terminal was threatened with obsolescence. They handed the case to Julius Henry Cohen, making him counsel to both the Chamber of Commerce and the Merchants' Association, and engineering his appointment as New York State's special deputy attorney general.* Cohen convinced the Interstate Commerce Commission that the Port of New York was, in fact, a single economic entity. Where would New Jersey be, he asked, without New York's Erie Canal? Still, Jersey's case had undeniable merit, and it drew attention to the huge costs of lighterage. Even as the ICC found in New York's favor, it strongly advised the two states to work out a joint plan for the port's development.[1]

In 1917 the governors of New York and New Jersey met in the great hall of the Chamber of Commerce and, with Outerbridge, Bush, and Cohen looking on, they pledged to work out such a plan. A bistate commission was formed to study the port, and Cohen, its counsel, was charged with drafting a law that would let the two states cooperate—a tricky problem, both politically and constitutionally. While he studied the issue, America entered the war. A flood of troops, food, and munitions clogged the harbor. The railroad system, strained even in the best of times, collapsed beneath the weight of new traffic, and trains backed up as far as Pittsburgh. Convinced that America would lose the war if the bottleneck wasn't broken, Outerbridge convinced Woodrow Wilson to create the War Board of the Port of New York, a sort of glorified dispatcher with the power to dictate schedules and priorities to the railroad's terminals and shipping lines. Irving Bush became the board's chief executive. Calvin Tomkins took control of New York State's canal system. For once the port worked with some degree of efficiency—as much as one could hope for, given its facilities—and many merchants even hoped this centralized control of shipping would survive the peace.

With the armistice, however, things settled back to their usual simmering chaos. In 1918 Cohen emerged with his draft proposal for the Port of New York Authority, a bistate agency with power over a port district of seventeen counties. This agency would devise a comprehensive plan for the port and would have the power to veto any waterfront construction, public or private, that interfered with the scheme. It would float bonds on self-sustaining projects or, if necessary, borrow on the two states' credit. Mayor John F. Hylan was horrified at such a threat to his own power, but his opposition, Cohen remembered, was "one of our really great aids."[2] If Hylan opposed something, it was a sure sign to the Republican and independent newspapers that the idea must be a good one. Al Smith threw his

---

* Cohen had long been active in the West Side Reform Club, along with Albert Bard and John De Witt Warner; in 1910 he and Louis Brandeis established the garment industry's "Protocol of Peace," which set up an arbitration system for labor-management disputes.

weight behind the scheme, and Belle Moskowitz, the widow of Charles Israels, took the cause directly to the public. Moskowitz had become one of the first public relations counselors—she may have invented the term—and she spearheaded the most elaborate advocacy campaign yet seen. She organized committees of industrialists, handed out prizes to high school essayists, bombarded the media with press releases, and produced one of the first documentary films: *Mr. Potato*, the story of an animated spud from the Jersey meadows. He left the farm "unwrinkled, round, and with bright eyes." It took him three and a half days to journey from the farm to a wholesaler in New York City, and he arrived looking barely edible. Moskowitz arranged to slip *Mr. Potato* into the programs of movie and vaudeville houses. Tens of thousands, if not hundreds of thousands, of New Yorkers saw it and came away convinced.

The Port Authority came into being in 1921, but by then the opposition had succeeded in weakening Cohen's original proposal. The agency had lost its powers to regulate development and to draw on tax revenues. It could still form plans, however, and issue bonds to pay for them, and it still had within its grasp the whole vast port district. And it soon found a partner in the Committee on the Regional Plan.

BACK IN 1901, John De Witt Warner, Calvin Tomkins, and the Lamb brothers had patched together a fragile growth coalition of businessmen and architects. This group had splintered over the competition for funds and the bitter struggle between reform's conservative and progressive wings. Since the Municipal Art Society had abandoned planning, and since the city continued to ignore the issue, a new group was needed to take up the cause. The Committee on the Regional Plan of New York and Its Environs began with Charles Dyer Norton, president of National City Bank. Earlier in life, Norton had been president of the Commercial Club of Chicago, the driving force behind Daniel Burnham and Edward Bennett's famous plan for Chicago. In 1914, Norton, now a New Yorker, joined the Advisory Committee on the City Plan, the group of architects, planners, realtors, and bankers summoned by George McAneny to help thrash out the land-use and height district maps of the 1916 Zoning Resolution. Norton knew full well that the zoning resolution left most of the great questions unanswered. Its crude land-use maps were largely beholden to the status quo. The resolution said nothing of where to build new parks or schools or firehouses. It gave no clue as to how the city could make livable neighborhoods, nor did it deal with the armature of rapid transit lines, freight railroads, and highways. McAneny's work had been aborted by his failure to establish a planning commission and by the hostility of Mayor Hylan. Norton decided that planning advocates should once again draw up their own unofficial master plan for New York. It would be far more detailed and sophisticated than MAS's old efforts, for Norton had two enormous advantages over the early Municipalians. He could call on the services of a whole generation of bright-eyed city planners and experts in municipal statistics, two professions that hadn't existed in 1901, and he had a source of money in the Russell Sage Foundation.

During his lifetime, Russell Sage was the most notorious miser in New York. Even the *Times,* in an otherwise sycophantic article on the charity of millionaires, had to admit that, "In the case of Russell Sage, alms and the man seem widely divergent. . . . But his wife," the paper added, "is diligent in doing good."[3] The crabbed spirit of Sage told in the legendary shabbiness of his house, in the widespread rumor that Mrs. Sage was permitted but two new dresses a year, and in the contempt of countless waiters who'd been insulted by his puny tips. It's tempting to dismiss such stories as urban folklore, but then there's Sage's own voice popping up in the press: he once told the *Times* that granting workers a paid vacation was no better than condoning thievery.

When he died, Sage left his widow $74 million. Far too decent to want such a sum for herself, she created the Russell Sage Foundation, dedicated to improving the living conditions of the masses—while incidentally, perhaps, recouping its namesake's reputation. Its character owed much to Robert W. De Forest, the foundation's first president and the Sage estate's executor. George McClellan, for one, despised De Forest: "He became a sort of first citizen, accepting any appointment he was offered on any committee or board and never pretending to do any work or even attend meetings."[4] There was some truth to the charge. A vice president of MAS for many years, De Forest never attended a single board meeting. On the other hand, the society never complained: MAS benefited from the association far more than De Forest did. For he was indeed a first citizen: chairman of Theodore Roosevelt's Tenement House Commission, first commissioner of the Tenement House Department (thanks to Seth Low), president of the Metropolitan Museum, founder and donor of the museum's American Wing, and a trustee of the Charity Organization Society and half a dozen other philanthropies.

"Charity," however, can mean several different things, and to De Forest it meant a system of relief conducted along "business principles." Since he thought that giving money to the poor would undermine their morals, his "philanthropy" often consisted of granting small loans—loans no commercial bank would contemplate. The same businesslike philosophy was evident in the Sage Foundation's first great work, the construction of Forest Hills Gardens. When the Queensboro Bridge opened in 1909, and the Long Island Railroad tunnel in 1910, much of Queens was suddenly within easy reach of Manhattan. The Sage Foundation bought two hundred acres of land and hired Frederick Law Olmsted, Jr., and Grosvenor Atterbury to design a community of middle-class and wage-earner housing. The public assumed that this meant subsidized housing, but Forest Hills was "neither charitable nor philanthropic," as Atterbury pointed out; instead it was meant as a model for private developers, a demonstration of what good planning and architecture might achieve in free market conditions. In fact the price of the land and the high design standards meant that the houses were far too expensive for wage earners, and Forest Hills became an upper-middle-class enclave. Its looping roads were a compelling indictment of the standard gridiron plan, but it didn't exactly do much for "the masses."

So the Sage Foundation drifted until 1921, when Charles Norton—aided by George McAneny, Alfred White, and Nelson Lewis—convinced it to found, and to fund, the Committee on the Regional Plan of New York and Its Environs. The regional plan would cover more than 5,000 square miles. Long Island, northern New Jersey, Westchester County, and Connecticut fell within its scope. It would cost the Sage Foundation more than $1.3 million, occupy an army of statisticians and economists, draw on the skills of a host of architects (among them, Cass Gilbert, D. Everett Waid, William Delano, Harvey Wiley Corbett, Thomas Hastings, and Electus Litchfield), and fill ten hefty volumes, plus a popular prospectus by the bravely named R. L. Duffus.

The public was stunned by the architects' pretty pictures: the Art Deco fantasies of parkways lined by new skyscrapers, and terraced apartment buildings rising along the waterfronts. Harvey Wiley Corbett and Hugh Ferris contributed their schemes for multilevel streets and arcaded sidewalks. These were drawn from the work of Charles Lamb; Corbett did little more than update the architectural style, while Ferris rendered them dramatically in charcoal. Lamb's influence was evident, too, in a sketch for a new civic center north of City Hall Park. There Francis Swales designed a terraced skyscraper that leaped across the narrow streets on massive arcades.

The heart of the regional plan, however, was an intricate rail network designed by William Wilgus and worked out in concert with the Port Authority. It called for two great rings of train tracks: a belt-line freight system in Manhattan, as Wilgus had proposed in 1908; and an outer belt bypassing Manhattan altogether. The southern arc of this outer belt would pass through Staten Island, Brooklyn, and Queens to Hell Gate, as Calvin Tomkins had proposed, while its northern arm swung past Paterson and Newark to Westchester. Tunnels beneath the harbor and the Hudson would weave the two rings together. Passenger trains would follow the same routes, and highways would run alongside them.

In its broad outlines this rail plan echoed and developed what Calvin Tomkins had sketched fifteen years before. And the Regional Plan Association accepted Tomkins's notion that Manhattan's destiny was to one day free itself from industry: its future was to be a largely white-collar world of business, commerce, culture, and middle-class apartments. The regional plan went far beyond Tomkins, though, in providing a series of ring-shaped rail lines in the outer boroughs; all this was meant to impose a new pattern of development on the city. The subway was a simple radial system, funneling workers to the ever more congested core of Manhattan and simultaneously dooming the outer boroughs to be mere bedroom communities. What the Regional Plan Association proposed was more like a spider net. Concentric belt lines would weave the old spokes together, and it would be possible to go from Brooklyn to Queens, for instance, without journeying to Manhattan first. And where the old spokes met the new rings, land values would concentrate. A series of minor urban nodes would develop as business and commercial centers for the outer boroughs. They would take some of the pressure off Manhattan real estate and provide bulwarks against urban sprawl.

Lewis Mumford wrote that the plan was "conceived first of all in terms which would meet the interests and prejudices of the existing financial rulers: indeed . . . its aim, from the beginning, was as much human welfare and amenity as could be obtained without altering any of the political and business institutions which have made the city precisely what it is." Mumford's verdict has been endlessly repeated, and the regional plan is almost always dismissed as a capitalist tool. Of course it was—not just because it was funded by capitalists but also because it was a plan for a city in a capitalist society. To tamper with that fact would have been foolish; it would have guaranteed that the plan wouldn't work for the city, and, given Benjamin Marsh's experience with the old Congestion Committee, it would have guaranteed that the plan would go nowhere.

The Port Authority sat down with the New Jersey railroads and found that they were no more farsighted than they had been a decade earlier. In the meantime, Gustav Lindenthal was back on the scene, trying to convince the Port Authority that the city needed his railroad bridge instead of tunnels. This idea had haunted Lindenthal for more than three decades, each disappointment serving to inflame his imagination, and in 1920 he'd produced his newest and most mind-boggling design for a bridge. It boasted twelve train tracks and twenty lanes for cars. Each tower was taller than the Woolworth Building, and the anchorage was weighted down with a massive skyscraper half as tall. Lindenthal meant to build this bridge at West Fifty-seventh Street, with a huge ramp slicing through San Juan Hill and flooding Midtown with traffic.

Lindenthal formed a private company to build the bridge, and even obtained a state charter, but sane people simply shook their heads in wonder. That was the reaction of Lindenthal's most brilliant assistant, the Swiss-born engineer Othmar Ammann. He didn't doubt that Lindenthal's bridge would stand up, but the expense was unreasonable, the railroads weren't interested, and the site was disastrous. Also, the War Department added its own, insuperable complaint: that the bridge, if sabotaged or bombed, would trap the fleet in its anchorage opposite Morningside Heights.

Ammann began toying with a more reasonable proposal—a bridge for cars and passenger trains rather than freight, at a more reasonable site, farther north, where the river was narrower, the ground was higher, and the fleet wasn't jeopardized. A bridge at 179th Street would open up a huge new area of suburbs for development and would let traffic between New Jersey, Westchester, and New England bypass much of Manhattan's congestion. In 1923 Al Smith and George Silver, the governors of New York and New Jersey, endorsed Ammann's idea while Belle Moskowitz lobbied for the support of civic groups, including MAS. Two years later the Port Authority agreed to build Ammann's bridge.

The George Washington Bridge was finished in 1931, under budget and eight months ahead of schedule. Such efficiency cast a rosy glow not just on its builders but on the whole notion of entrusting public works to independent public authorities. Franklin Delano Roosevelt would carry the concept with him to Washington a year later, and in 1934 Robert Moses would begin his transformation of the Triborough Bridge Authority into a massive engine for economic development.

Few people noticed, and fewer complained, that the Port Authority had already abandoned its mission to build the freight tunnels and terminals that were so crucial to the city's manufacturing base. It had built an automobile bridge instead, and in the depths of the Depression, that seemed a stupendous achievement—especially if one looked southeast to Randall's Island.

The city had begun building the Triborough crossing in 1925, and after six years of bungling, just one anchorage and a few piers were standing—nothing else. South of the George Washington Bridge lay the West Side's Miller Highway, another monument to ineptitude. That highway had been started in 1928, but the city had run out of money, and in 1931 there were still no access ramps.

AFTER JOHN PURROY MITCHEL fell from power, New York suffered through sixteen years of Tammany rule. First came blustering John Hylan, "the ranting Bozo of Bushwick," as Robert Moses called him.[5] "Tammany has had many things to answer for," wrote the *Herald Tribune* in 1925, "but never have the prosperity and progress of the community received such a serious setback" as Hylan's election. "New subways . . . have been obstructed for no other reason save that Mr. Hylan neither knew how to build them nor was willing to allow anyone else to build them. The Port Authority program, which would have expedited the handling of merchandise and saved the public millions of dollars, was delayed because Mr. Hylan was incapable of understanding it and fearful that if it were worked out by others his own prestige might suffer. For eight years this metropolis, so far as governmental development is concerned, has stood still."[6]

Not entirely still: Hylan spent $198 million on new schools, an investment that was sorely needed after Mitchel's parsimony. Hylan's populism took the form of extravagant gestures—like his promise to build a Music and Art Center on Central Park South and a huge war memorial with swimming pools and playgrounds in the park itself—but he lacked the political skills to turn them into concrete form. He did eventually set in motion construction of the IND subway, and this was a substantial achievement, if a tainted one. Its construction was a shocking boondoggle. Hylan divided the system into short stretches and let separate contracts for each, dispensing patronage far and wide, while his condemnation commissioners handed out ludicrously generous settlements. The subway cost twice what it should have, construction dragged on until 1929, and Hylan burdened his successors with the vexing question of who should operate the new line. He'd floated bonds with the promise that the new subway would be self-sustaining, but he never arranged to let the IND operate in tandem with the privately owned subways. Without such an agreement, it was doomed to run up huge operating deficits.

Yet it wasn't Hylan's incompetence that doomed his career; it was the brutal warfare between his mentor, William Randolph Hearst, and Governor Al Smith. The publisher still hoped to be president. Albany was the essential stepping stone to Washington, and Al Smith stood in his way. In 1919 Hearst unleashed a shameless smear campaign, charging the governor with responsibility for the sale of tainted milk. On her deathbed, Smith's mother was heard murmuring piteously that "my son did not kill those babies," and truly he hadn't. In 1925, when Charles Murphy was dead and Smith had taken up the reins of the Democratic Party, he took his revenge by denying Hylan the nomination for a third term as mayor, and by installing the elegant figure of James J. Walker in his place.[7]

At first Jimmy Walker, the city's one hundredth mayor, was a bit of a mystery to the Municipal Art Society. His father, William Walker, had been a Tammany superintendent of public works until 1907, when the Bureau of Municipal Research exposed a host of irregularities and outright frauds in his department. (Tammany liked to say that William Walker had built the city's first recreation piers, but Fusion heatedly pointed out that the money had been appropriated during the previous administration of Mayor Josiah Strong.) If the elder Walker embodied the old Tammany, his son seemed to be an example of the new, and MAS had reason to hope that he would be a relatively decent mayor. True, he'd started out as a songwriter—author of "Will You Love Me in December As You Do in May?" and "There's Music in the Rustle of a Skirt"—but at least he'd never been an actor.

Charles Murphy had spied the young man's glamour and had seen that he might provide Tammany with a new image. So Walker had ascended through the ranks until, as Speaker of the New York State Senate, he became Al Smith's indispensable ally, pushing piece after piece of the governor's progressive program through the legislature, while young Robert Moses crouched beside Walker's desk telling him what the bills meant. When Walker ran for mayor, then, it was on Smith's record as governor. "Witness laws providing for workers' compensation, widows' pensions, child welfare, shorter hours of work for children in industry," Walker told reporters who asked what he stood for. "I respectfully draw your attention to our stand on woman suffrage, the direct primary, consolidation of our state departments . . . a bond issue of $100 million for the maintenance of that great army of unfortunate wards of the state."[8] He was against Prohibition and spoke out against the Ku Klux Klan, and if that record wasn't enough, there was always Walker himself. He was an exquisite sight: tall and rail-thin, gorgeously attired in suits of his own design (he packed four dozen of them for a European vacation), and blessed with the sharp, chiseled features that looked so apt against an Art Deco background. He was a joy to listen to. Even his enemies admired his charm and his offhand wit—as when he told reporters that he'd appointed John F. Hylan to a sinecure in children's court: "Now the children can be judged by one of their peers."[9] Alas, as Robert Moses pointed out, Walker was "incapable of sustained effort." He was "the product of a crazy age, impish, urbane, polished, sardonic . . . at his best when dependent solely on his wits, when he was unprepared, unrehearsed, and seriousness was purely coincidental."[10]

In later years Walker was remembered for instituting a bread-and-circus regime. He presided over the great age of ticker tape parades. It was only natural that hundreds of thousands of New Yorkers turned out to cheer Charles Lindbergh in 1927, but it was the genius of Grover Whalen, Walker's police chief and chairman of the Mayor's Welcoming Committee, to create artificial festivities. Whalen's "greatest accomplishment," one observer wrote, "was making sure that all motorcades began promptly at twelve noon. While it was not difficult to get New Yorkers to turn out for Byrd, Gertrude Ederle, or Lindbergh, there was understandably less excitement over General Horatio Vasquez of San Domingo, Hassan Tagi Lader of Persia, or George Kojuc, the Ukrainian-American 100-meter backstroke champion. Yet at noon, lower Broadway was always packed with people taking their lunch break. The more obscure the guest, the more he was touched by the warmth of his reception."[11]

Such scenes enjoyed a transient fame in the newsreels, and they were immortalized by the Marx Brothers in *Duck Soup,* but at first there was a more serious side to Walker. He'd learned some things from the New Tammany: that the civic groups, with their access to the editorial columns, were a constituency worth courting; that municipal services could generate good publicity; that party loyalty could be earned as well as bought; and that parks, especially, were a motherhood issue. The tragedy was that his promises were never quite translated into action. In his inaugural address, Walker promised a huge program of parkland acquisition, and the figure of $30 million was bandied about. Some of the parks he mentioned had been a subject of discussion since the 1907 report of the Improvement Commission, and as a start, $4 million was actually appropriated: enough to buy Great Kills and Willow Brook parks on Staten Island, while in Queens the city acquired Highland and Alley Pond parks and enlarged Kissena Park. Staten Island's Wolfe's Pond was mentioned too, but in a few months' time speculators nearly tripled its price, and the city shied away.[12] But nothing was done to landscape these places or to make them more accessible to the general public. Instead the party faithful were allowed to build bungalows and the new parks became, in effect, private resorts for apparatchiks.

In 1926, a few months after taking office, Walker appointed a City Committee on Plan and Survey. Harvey Wiley Corbett, president of the Architectural League, hailed it as "the most significant thing in municipal development that has occurred in the United States."[13] Corbett spoke far too soon. With just a little exaggeration, the group was dubbed the "Committee of 500"—in fact, it had no fewer than 472 members, most of whom "had little previous knowledge of the subjects committed to them," according to Albert Bard, "and . . . even less time or inclination to study them."[14] That might also have described the committee's chairman, Morgan J. O'Brien, a state supreme court judge.

The pressing need, obvious to any serious observer, was for a City Planning

Commission, and most reformers thought this body would have a fairly easy job. As far as the reformers were concerned, the Regional Plan Association had already done the difficult work of drawing up a blueprint of the city's needs, and the City Planning Commission would simply have to implement the plan, ward off any conflicting proposals, and update it as time passed. At the Municipal Art Society, however, some were convinced that the regional plan had never gone far enough in one area: controlling the skyscraper. So while the mayor's Committee of 500 mulled over the Regional Plan Association's plans and drew up recommendations for a City Planning Commission, MAS founded its own Committee on Skyscrapers.

This committee included Richard Welling as chairman, Grosvenor Atterbury, Samuel Ordway, and Charles Stoughton, but it was dominated by Henry Curran, a witty and charming Republican reformer.

Curran's social conscience had been awakened in the 1890s, when he put himself through Yale by working summers for the *Tribune*'s Fresh Air Fund. The search for sob stories confronted Curran with sights few reformers had seen firsthand. Later on, Curran was president of the Board of Aldermen during the Gaynor administration, and he is most often remembered for spearheading an investigation of police corruption, one of the most painful episodes of Gaynor's reign.* He went on to become Manhattan's borough president in 1919, and after a failed mayoral bid in 1921 he was named counsel to the City Club. There he launched a campaign against skyscrapers, revealing himself to be a talented publicist. On December 23, 1926, a slow day for news, he made headlines with a press release announcing that Santa Claus would bypass New York City lest his reindeer choke in the soft coal smoke or collide with a skyscraper. (Curran's childhood had been shattered by his father's early death, and he had something of a Santa Claus fixation. "I can still believe in Santa Claus," he wrote in his memoirs, when he was sixty-four years old, "and I do—ah, yes, I do!"[15]) In his City Club bulletins, Curran aimed straight for the jugular. "Municipal Murder," read one headline; "Latest Casualty List from the Skyscraper–Motor Car Front on the Sidewalks of New York. Killed 54—wounded unknown—this is not a war communiqué of 1918, nor does it refer to American soldiers. . . . It refers to American *children*, who were alive in May and were killed in June . . . [by] the herds of clumped skyscrapers and the packed and pushing motor vehicles that the skyscrapers breed."[16]

Now Curran and Welling steered MAS's skyscraper committee back to Electus Litchfield's old proposal to limit the floor area of buildings rather than their height or shape. It endorsed the floor area ratio, and it wanted a particularly stringent

---

* *The investigation was sparked by the murder of Herman Rosenthal, a gambler and pimp, who was shot down in front of the Hotel Metropole in Times Square. Seven policemen were within a hundred yards of the murder scene, but none intervened; none pursued the assassins; none even bothered to record the license of the getaway car. Curran contended that this lethargy was easily explained: Rosenthal was about to testify that Lieutenant Charles Becker, head of the vice squad, was in fact his business partner. Becker was eventually convicted of the crime and executed in Sing Sing, along with four colorfully named gunmen: Whitey Lewis, Lefty Louie, Dago Frank, and Gyp the Blood.*

Previous page: The Beaux Arts Skyscraper. A detail of Cass Gilbert's Woolworth Building. *This page:* The work of Charles Rollinson Lamb. *Left:* A study of setback skyscrapers, circa 1899. *Below:* Lamb's setback system (on the left) contrasted with Ernest Flagg's city of towers. *Bottom:* Vernon Howe Bailey's 1908 perspective of Lamb's plan for Lower Manhattan. *Right:* Two views of Ernest Flagg's Singer tower.

KING'S DREAM OF NEW YORK

Far left: Charles Lamb's aerial streets popularized in H. M. Petit's drawing, "King's Dream of New York." Left: A 1911 project by E. P. Goodrich, engineer of Manhattan's Department of Public Works, to build Lamb's "Double-Decked Streets for Lower Manhattan." Above: The second Equitable Building (at left) towers over its neighbors.

BULLETIN OF THE

MUNICIPAL ART SOCIETY

NUMBER 23   OF NEW YORK   FEBRUARY, 1923

SCHEME "A"
FOR STANDS UNDER ELEVATED STAIRS

SCHEME "B"
FOR SUBWAY AND ISOLATED STANDS

SUGGESTED DESIGNS FOR NEWSSTANDS SUBMITTED BY THE SOCIETY

Far left: The auditorium of DeWitt Clinton High School, designed by C.B.J. Snyder, with Charles Yardley Turner's murals, The Opening of the Erie Canal. *Left:* Gerald Kaufman's 1921 designs for model newsstands. **Below:** The Chelsea Piers, designed by Warren & Wetmore, blocking West Street's view of the Hudson River.

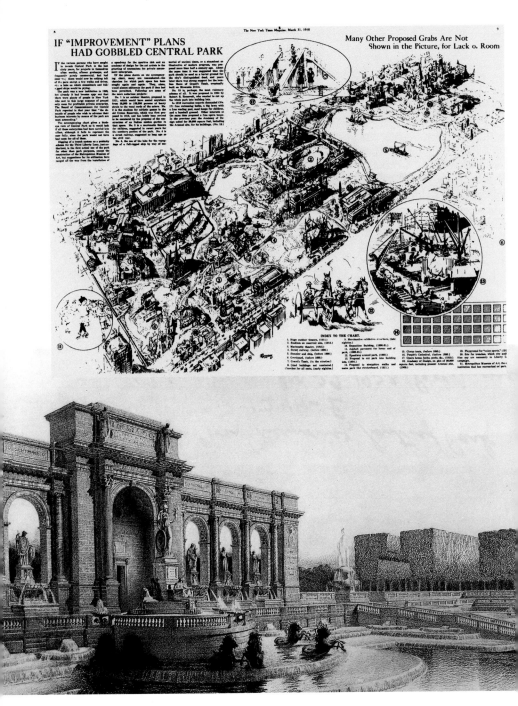

Top: Vernon Howe Bailey's 1918 perspective of "Improvements" proposed for Central Park. Above: Thomas Hastings's 1923 War Memorial project for the lower reservoir site in Central Park. Right: A 1920s view of City Hall Park, with Frederick MacMonnies's Civic Virtue in the foreground, the Brooklyn Bridge Terminal in the middle distance, and McKim, Mead & White's Municipal Building at the rear.

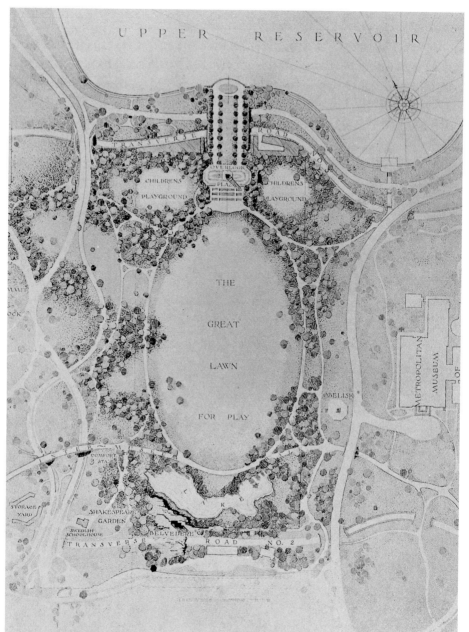

UPPER RESERVOIR

CHILDRENS PLAYGROUND

CHILDRENS PLAYGROUND

OVERLOOK PLAT

THE

GREAT

LAWN

FOR PLAY

OBELISK

METROPOLITAN MUSEUM

STORAGE YARD

COMFORT STA.

SHAKESPEARE GARDEN

SWEDISH SCHOOLHOUSE

BELVEDERE

TRANSVERSE ROAD NO. 2

PLAN FOR DEVELOPMENT OF THE LOWER RESERVOIR SITE

CENTRAL PARK

PRESENTED TO THE COMMISSIONER OF PARKS · BOROUGH OF MANHATTAN
THE NEW YORK CHAPTER · AMERICAN SOCIETY OF LANDSCAPE ARCHITECTS

SCALE OF FEET

MARCH 1ST 1930

Far left: The American Society of Landscape Architects' plan for the Great Lawn on the lower reservoir site in Central Park. *Above:* The same site in 1932, with a Hooverville in the foreground. *Left:* The Balto memorial by Frederick G. R. Roth.

Left: The Regional Plan Association's 1931 scheme for the Chrystie-Forsyth Parkway. **This page:** Two lost landmarks. **Below:** Saint John's Chapel, designed by John McComb, Jr., with Saint John's Park in the foreground. **Right:** Richard Morris Hunt's 660 Fifth Avenue, at left.

Right: The Jefferson Market Courthouse, designed by Frederick Clarke Withers. *Below:* The remains of Colonnade Row, designed by A. J. Davis. *Far right:* Robert Moses's project for the Brooklyn-Battery Bridge, shown in one of Ole Singstad's perspectives. *Below right:* Washington Square North, with its Greek Revival row houses.

Above: *The Seagram Building and its plaza, designed by Ludwig Mies van der Rohe.*
Inset: *Two Fifth Avenue, designed by Emery Roth & Sons, with its low wing in the foreground facing Washington Square.*

formula: an FAR of 6.* Most buildings, then, would be just 60 feet tall, and the rare exceptions—taller buildings with plazas at their feet—would have to go before the Art Commission. "An able body," Curran called the commission, "with proper representation from elements in our city that sponsor something besides trade."[17] The committee's report was mailed off to the mayor, the Board of Estimate, the Committee of Five Hundred, the press, and the whole roster of civic groups. But the report horrified many at MAS. A 60-foot city! The effect on land values and property taxes horrified some, of course, but even an aesthete might question Curran's goals. American architects were just beginning to feel they'd solved the problem of the skyscraper as an architectural form and that, in doing so, they'd finally made a distinctly American contribution to world architecture. The Wool-worth and Metropolitan Life towers had long been world famous for their height, but the former was a magnified Flemish Gothic bell tower; the latter, an overgrown Venetian campanile. Now a new generation of towers hinted at a magnificent advance in style and form. Ralph Walker's Barclay-Vesey Building (1923–1926), Raymond Hood's American Radiator Building (1924), and E. J. Kahn's Two Park Avenue (1926–1929) seemed as American as jazz.

The city was just entering into the great building boom of the late 1920s, and the *Times* captured the manic mood of the day: "The city is in upheaval. . . . In not more than half a dozen years the skyline of Midtown Manhattan . . . has been lifted a hundred feet. American vision, daring, restlessness, engineering skill have all been properly read into this marvelous transformation to Babylon. As for building for eternity, the need does not exist. Thirty years from now they will be tearing up the city once more." And so they would be, and rebuilding it bigger, but not better.

I. N. Phelps Stokes didn't quite share in the *Times*'s euphoria, but he still objected to Curran's report. He feared that, for lack of space, few builders would opt for plazas and that New York would again become a flat-topped city, as dreary as its old brownstone incarnation. He may well have had another objection, since real estate had a place in his investment portfolio.[18] Others feared the report was simply too extreme to have any impact. Samuel Ordway agreed that the city would never adopt anything so radical, but insisted that it was "necessary to aim for the ideal," not just as a matter of principle but because it was MAS's only hope to shift the terms of the debate.[19] The board of directors was torn. Phelps Stokes was named to the Skyscraper Committee, Welling stepped down, and Curran drifted away. The board agreed that MAS should pursue "less radical ideas." In the end the original report was retracted and suppressed, but no new statement of principles was forthcoming.

Lost in the debate was an ominous suggestion. In January 1927 the *Real Estate Record and Guide*, that most sober of magazines, warned that there were already more

* There were other recommendations. MAS wanted most of Manhattan's unrestricted territory reclassified as business or residential districts. A new retail land use would be created, with manufacturing confined to just 5 percent of floor area. Curran also called on the city to revise its subway system. The subways were laid out like radial spokes, with all the lines converging in Manhattan. Curran's model for a subway plan was the spider net, with concentric rings between the spokes.

office buildings in construction than the city needed. The magazine did something almost unimaginable for a real estate trade publication: it called for a construction moratorium "until the space now available or under construction is occupied by permanent tenants." The warning went unheeded. By the time Wall Street crashed in 1929, the amount of office space in New York had risen by 92 percent; another 56 percent was finished after the crash.[20]

"The wonder," Albert Bard wrote, "was not that the committee [of 500's] report should be delayed, but that it ever should have appeared at all." It almost didn't: at one point a good many committee members threatened to "strike" to protest the shoddiness of the whole enterprise. When the report finally did materialize in 1928, "it contained few definite recommendations" and even these were "phrased in broad terms and dealt largely with uncontroversial questions."[21] Other proposals, like the idea to strip the borough presidents of their spending powers, were transparently hopeless. It was a tempting notion, particularly since yet another Queens borough president had just been toppled from power, this time in a sewer scandal, but the borough presidents controlled far more patronage jobs than the mayor did, and this was an arrangement Tammany would never willingly upset.

The one "outstanding conclusion" of the mayor's committee was that New York needed a city planning board. Jimmy Walker told Edward Bassett to write the necessary legislation. Introduced in Albany in 1929, "it did not find favor," as Albert Bard wrote. "It was common knowledge that the proposal was entirely too good and that strong political powers in the city opposed it. Among other obstructions was that of 'borough autonomy.'" It was also common knowledge that Mayor Walker, despite excellent ties to the state legislature, never really pushed the measure. When the Bassett bill died, Walker offered a sop to the civic groups: a Department of City Planning headed by a single commissioner and graced with purely advisory powers. In effect it would simply duplicate the work of the chief engineer to the Board of Estimate. Some civic groups were grateful, seeing it as a step in the right direction; others opposed "a futile gesture . . . designed to give a false impression that something constructive was being done," in Bard's words. Walker went ahead anyway and appointed Major John F. Sullivan, a well-meaning and dedicated engineer, to this commissionership. He was absurdly overworked, however, and he had no staff to speak of and "no guiding principles or plans." In 1932 the Citizens Union issued a paper describing the uselessness of Sullivan's office, and a year later, as the city tottered on the brink of bankruptcy, the department was abolished as an economy measure. "Nobody," Bard wrote, "was sorry to see it go."[22]

Jimmy Walker had no interest in opening up the subject of zoning. The building boom was in full swing, cheered on by the press. Why complain? In truth there were some very good reasons to cheer. The Building Code of 1915 was finally bearing fruit, and the new towers and lofts were far safer than their predecessors. There would be no Triangle fire in the new garment district; no Equitable blaze in the shiny Midtown skyscrapers. The new buildings enjoyed more sun and light, too.

Architects and developers had grown far more subtle; they weren't about to repeat the prewar catastrophe of lower Fifth Avenue, where new office buildings had so suffocated one another that the neighborhood degenerated into a district of unprofitable lofts. The zoning code and the Save New York Campaign had set certain broad land-use rules, of course, but now architects had also learned how to plan and mass buildings so that they would always enjoy enough air, no matter what was built next door.

As one of Jimmy Walker's biographers put it, the zoning code "also gave Tammany politicians, through their influence with the Board of Standards and Appeals, splendid opportunities to increase their net worth by obtaining variances."[23] William E. Walsh, chairman of the board and a dear friend of the mayor, was indicted on bribery and tax evasion charges in June 1930. He was charged with accepting bribes from Bronx builder John "Fishhooks" McCarthy. In return for a series of zoning variances, Walsh took $30,000 plus a $1,500-a-year lease on an apartment worth $4,000 a year. He was never convicted. Meanwhile William F. "Horse Doctor" Doyle, a former veterinarian, had collected $2 million over nine years for representing clients before the Board of Standards and Appeals. Doyle had always insisted on receiving a portion of his fees in cash; he later admitted, in a federal tax case, that he had split those fees with another party whom he refused to name, pleading the Fifth Amendment. Doyle retired to the fashionable beach community of Deal, New Jersey—safe, he hoped, from further subpoenas. Then there was the case of George Olvany, who became the boss of Tammany Hall after Charles Murphy's death in 1924. Olvany was a partner in a law firm, and "Petitioners who retained the firm to request zoning variances were invariably found to be in the right."[24] With such a track record, Olvany's firm earned $5 million in five years, and the evidence of such shady deals is still writ large on New York's skyline. The French Building at 551 Fifth Avenue, for example, is 60,000 square feet bigger than it should have been—thanks to $30,000 in legal fees. Two of Tudor City's buildings grew an extra six floors, and for this developer Fred French had to pay a mere $75,000.

In 1928, with half of Jimmy Walker's first term over, the Citizens Union published an odd evaluation of the mayor. "At times he is tremendously serious," the union wrote, "but too often this seriousness is centered on comparatively trivial items while questions of grave importance are postponed or set aside for a more convenient occasion. . . . His fascinating personal qualities" made his lack of any real achievements "all the more tragic."[25]

Walker's record soon grew worse. As long as Al Smith controlled the state Democratic Party he was able to impose some restraint on Tammany. But in 1928, Smith's career came to grief with his tragic campaign for the presidency. Smith soon found his power crumbling. In Albany, Governor Franklin Roosevelt would build on Smith's legacy while keeping the man himself at arm's length. In New York City, Walker seized the chance to free himself from Smith's shadow. George Olvany, Smith's ally, was forced to retire as Tammany's chief, and Walker installed John

Francis Curry in his place. Olvany himself had been a specialist in patronage and "honest" graft, in which a bribe masqueraded as a legal fee, but Curry was a political Neanderthal. On taking office he announced that "It is fiction, this New Tammany. I will carry out the politics in which I grew up." "The mask is off Tammany," wrote Norman Thomas, who had run for mayor on the Socialist line. "A district leader of the old school sits in the seat of Tweed and Croker. Jimmy Walker is Mayor and Grover Whalen is Police Commissioner. The old gang is on the job. Who cares about . . . the gross waste of an ever-increasing budget?"[26]

Patronage soon began to reach new heights of sleaziness. Bird Coler, who'd been comptroller during the Van Wyck years and now ran the municipal hospitals, admitted he'd never seen anything like it. In the old days, he said, Tammany bosses would call on him with a list of people to hire, but he was always free to veto the incompetents. Now strangers appeared in his office bearing chits from Tammany Hall, and Coler had no say in the matter. Even physicians were not immune from infection: when Dr. Sigismund Goldwater took over the city hospitals in 1934, he discovered that his doctors routinely demanded bribes before agreeing to treat patients.

In the old days, when MAS was almost a branch of the Citizens Union and the Citizens Union was still a political party, the Municipal Art Society used to valiantly battle corruption. But MAS no longer had the stomach for such fights. Its new president was J. Monroe Hewlett, an architect and muralist. He'd served on McAneny's short-lived Advisory Committee on the City Plan, but he'd never been active in MAS, and some members of the board were not happy to have him. In his inaugural speech Hewlett "spoke of his desire that the Society become more active, more vitally interested in things that concern the artistic growth of the city and which will arouse constructive enthusiasm on the part of laymen." It was time to search for "more inspiring activities . . . to interest its membership and the public in informed opinion held by artists and laymen, without itself taking a position in controversial matters." This smacks of constructive engagement, to use an anachronistic phrase, and it was more than the society's secretary, Samuel Ordway, Jr., could bear. Like his father before him, Ordway was a longtime foe of Tammany Hall and, "With apologies for his outspokenness, [he] recorded his dissent, and submitted that 'things which concern the artistic growth of the city and arouse constructive enthusiasm' are nearly always controversial, and as such offer the one opportunity for 'inspiring activity,' which is leadership."[27]

Hewlett's caution prevailed, however. Thus when Charles Stoughton was delegated to study the approaches for the Triborough Bridge, he reported that they were "as good an arrangement as we can probably expect to get." City Hall was such a cesspool that this was technically accurate, but MAS might have said other things. It might, for instance, have drawn the public's attention to an oddity in the bridge's location. The Triborough is really a complex of four bridges linking Manhattan, Queens, and the Bronx, and what's remarkable is that the spans stretching from Queens and Manhattan don't line up with each other: the Manhattan bridge is twenty-five blocks farther north. Most people approach the bridge from the south, and that means they have to drive far out of their way, through congested streets studded with traffic lights, to reach the bridge. This odd location had nothing to do with engineering or soil conditions; rather the site had a long history of ties to Tammany Hall. Sulzer's Riverbank Casino once stood there, and that beer garden was a favorite destination of Tammany's riverboat excursions. Then William Randolph Hearst bought the casino for his Cosmopolitan Film Studios so he could film ponderous costume dramas starring his lover, the charming, stuttering, and hopelessly miscast Marion Davies. When Hearst moved his film studio to Hollywood, Tammany decided to relieve him of an embarrassment of real estate.

By 1929 the corruption of the Board of Standards and Appeals was already well known, at least in architectural and real estate circles, and evidence kept surfacing that Jimmy Walker's new magistrates had paid handsomely for their jobs. Yet the public shrugged off these warning signs and, all unconcerned, reelected Walker. After defeating Fiorello La Guardia by a two-to-one margin, Walker euphorically pronounced the end of New York's reform movement. Never again, he promised, would its citizens have to hear "the timeworn, moth-eaten, imaginary slogan, 'Anti-Tammany.' "[28] It was a moment of hubris, and, predictably enough, Walker's world was about to crumble. In less than a year the appellate division asked Samuel Seabury to probe the magistrates' court.

More admired than liked, Seabury was a distinguished scholar and a retired judge. In his youth he had been a radical—one of Henry George's single taxers—and he brought to his new job a lethal combination of rectitude and frustrated political ambition. His investigations of the magistrates would make him the leading figure in New York's reform camp.

In 1931 the City Affairs Club petitioned Governor Franklin Roosevelt to remove Jimmy Walker from office. It cited fraudulent condemnation awards, the scandal at the Board of Standards and Appeals, corruption in the Docks Department, patronage in the city hospitals, the sale of magistracies, and Walker's own attempts to stifle Seabury's investigation. Roosevelt responded by authorizing a full investigation of every cranny of Walker's regime. Samuel Seabury then demonstrated that Walker himself had taken a million dollars in gifts and bribes or, as the mayor called them, "beneficences." In 1932, Seabury asked Roosevelt to remove Walker from office. Advised by Al Smith that his career was over, Walker resigned and, like so many Tammany officials before him, boarded an ocean liner for Europe.

Walker fled a city that was sinking into political and economic chaos. Charles McKee, president of the Board of Aldermen, stepped in as acting mayor. His hands were clean of scandal, and reformers respected him. In an attempt to put his house in order and reassure the bond markets, McKee appointed George McAneny to the comptroller's office, and reformers were grateful for this as well. But Tammany distrusted McKee's ties to Franklin Delano Roosevelt and to the Bronx Democratic machine; it insisted that a special election was needed to choose Walker's replacement. Fusion had no time to organize behind a viable candidate (Seabury refused the nomination), and though McKee attracted a quarter of a million write-in votes, John P. O'Brien became the new mayor, serving out the last year of Walker's term.

O'Brien had begun his career as George McClellan's private secretary. Later, as corporation counsel, he found a unique way to build himself a political base: he sent out obscenely inflated bills for personal property taxes, and when his terrified victims begged for relief, he kindly granted them "exemptions."[29] O'Brien's cleverness had its limits, however. New York had seen many mayors in its three-hundred-year history, but none with such a talent for inopportune candor or devastating malapropisms. Asked who his police commissioner would be, O'Brien answered truthfully: "I don't know. I haven't got the word yet."[30] Speaking to a Jewish audience, he hailed "the scientist of scientists, Albert Weinstein." He confided to a Hellenic Association that he used to pore over the pages of "that great Greek poet, Horace." And he confessed, before a congregation in Harlem, that "My heart is as black as yours."[31]

This was the man Tammany had chosen to lead the city in its darkest hour. The press was so appalled that it did the cruelest thing possible: it printed O'Brien's statements verbatim. The bond markets were even more unkind. In May 1933 the city nearly defaulted on $100 million in short-term notes. Wall Street had no respect for Keynesian economics, especially in a municipal government, and forced O'Brien to nearly double his interest rates in return for new loans. Five months later the city discovered that it couldn't meet its payroll without more loans. Wall Street demanded new concessions, and now the city was truly governed by its bankers—by the likes of Charles Mitchell of National City Bank, who was convicted of massive tax evasion in 1933; Thomas Lamont of the J. P. Morgan Company, who managed, like the other nineteen partners in that firm, to pay no income tax in 1931 or 1932; and W. W. Aldrich, Chase's new chairman of the board, whose predecessor had borrowed money from Chase in order to sell the bank's stock short.[32] The bankers preached the balanced budget as their solution to the Depression. They praised Herbert Hoover's Reconstruction Finance Corporation—"the millionaires' dole," as La Guardia called it—which loaned money to banks and big businesses, but they frowned on any effort to help the common, unemployed citizen. O'Brien's haplessness gave the bankers the opportunity to rewrite the budget as they saw fit. The salaries of city workers were slashed, construction of public works came to a halt, and even maintenance programs were abandoned.

All this only made the city's pain more keen. When the Depression started, the city had been ill equipped to help its citizens. The charter still said it could give relief to institutions, but not to individuals; unless you were an inmate of the city's farm colony, an orphanage, or an asylum, the city could not help you. In 1931, when the state legislature amended the charter, Jimmy Walker appropriated a mere $2 million for relief, and much of that money was misused. The city hired workers but gave them no equipment, or the wrong equipment—handing out shovels, for example, to dig in land so frozen that only heavy bulldozers could do the job. Naturally the workers burned their shovels to keep from freezing.

Private groups were doing far better: the Emergency Work Bureau, a joint venture of the Association for Improving the Condition of the Poor and the Charity Organization Society, spent more than $8 million putting 37,000 people to work. But soon the unemployed numbered 300,000, and the usual donors were themselves in dire straits. In 1931 there were ninety-five recorded deaths by starvation in New York.[33] By the next spring the charities had exhausted their coffers, and a third of New York's social service institutions had closed their doors.

IN 1933 the Fusion Party drove Tammany from City Hall, and Fiorello La Guardia embarked on his twelve-year reign as mayor of New York. He was an unlikely candidate to head a Fusion ticket, and some of the party's blue-blooded leaders regarded him as "Half Wop, Half American, Half Republican." La Guardia was part Jewish as well, though he rarely mentioned it: he faced enough prejudice as it was. He was born in Greenwich Village to immigrant parents, and after a far-flung childhood went to work as an interpreter at Ellis Island. The year was 1907, immigration was at its peak, and La Guardia would remember that he "suffered a great deal because I could not help these poor people." At night he studied law, and he became a poor man's attorney, representing tenants against landlords, workers against bosses. Fired up by the cause of his union clients, he joined their picket lines and strategy sessions. From activism to politics was a small step, but there was a problem: La Guardia couldn't countenance Tammany's corruption. In an early encounter, he exasperated Jimmy Walker. "What are you in politics for?" Walker demanded. "For love?" And even if La Guardia had somehow quelled his conscience, that Irish machine was still closed to Italians. So La Guardia became a Republican. The affiliation was an absurd misfit, but at first he tried to play the party loyalist, and in 1913 he even refused to join his fellow Republicans in endorsing John Purroy Mitchel, an independent Democrat, for the mayoralty.[34]

Republicans had long played a marginal role in this city's politics, but La Guardia was a master of ethnic politics who could address crowds in German, Italian, or Yiddish, and he was perfectly willing to fight Tammany with its own tactics. When he ran for Congress in 1916, his poll watchers were as burly as the Tiger's, as quick to throw a punch, and just as willing to stuff a ballot box. He won by 357 votes. When he took a turn as president of the Board of Aldermen in 1919, he enchanted reformers by exposing corruption in the County Courthouse contracts (sixty-nine indictments ensued) and scandalized them by brawling with Charles Craig, the Democratic comptroller. La Guardia returned to Congress as a lonesome liberal who denounced his own Republican Party as "the kept woman of big business." It seemed that he would achieve little in Washington, but "The function of a progressive," he told one interviewer, "is to keep on protesting until things get so bad that a reactionary demands reform."[35] His legislative victories came late in his congressional career, when things had gotten bad indeed. In 1932 he led the fight against Herbert Hoover's proposed national sales tax, and he cosponsored the Norris–La Guardia Act, which limited the courts' ability to interfere with strikes.

That same year, in a bitter irony, he was voted out of office in the Democratic landslide.

La Guardia promised that, if elected mayor, he would make New York City "a gigantic laboratory for civic reconstruction." He said he would unify the transit system, clear the slums, build low-cost housing, and put the unemployed to work on building "a great, big beautiful kind New York." La Guardia had been a premature New Dealer, but when he claimed the mayor's office in January 1934, his old agenda had become the nation's policy. A partnership sprang up between Mayor La Guardia and President Franklin D. Roosevelt. Washington offered money to the city in a desperate bid to revive the economy; New York offered concrete plans and programs to put that money to work. The president had embarked on a novel experiment in activist government, and the mayor was desperate to prove the experiment a success. That the mayor happened to be a Republican didn't hurt either. As a result, New York claimed an enormous share of Washington's aid: 17 percent of the public works budget for the entire nation, and a full quarter of its public housing funds.

When La Guardia came to power, the Municipal Art Society had a new president, the architect Electus Litchfield. We first met him in 1907, when Litchfield tried to convince the city that it should limit the volume of buildings by using a floor area ratio. He'd been a member of MAS since 1909, but he'd been active even longer in the City Club (whose clubhouse he designed), and he had close ties to the Fusion Committee, especially to C. C. Burlingham. William Exton, MAS's secretary in the early 1930s, remembered him as "a great and good architect."[36] Harmon Goldstone, a future president of the society, called him "a lovely old gent."[37] I. N. Phelps Stokes counted Litchfield among his few true friends, part of a tiny circle of "fine Christian characters, gentlemen par excellence and scholars—each in his own way—and . . . interested in the deeper things, as well as in the amenities, of life."[38]

Electus Litchfield hailed La Guardia as the first mayor in New York history to display an interest in the fine arts—a distinction already claimed by George McClellan. But La Guardia presented a challenge to the distinguished old gentlemen of MAS. Chasms of social class and ethnicity lay between them, and more. He didn't conform to their model of the "best men"—moneyed, educated gentlemen who saw political office as a public service rather than as a profession. They feared his demagoguery, shuddered at his manners, and winced at the memory of his brawls with the aldermen. The old reformers believed in creating orderly procedures to prevent graft, and La Guardia would find some of these—like the Art Commission's aesthetic review of public works—intolerably annoying.[39]

In the days of Seth Low and George McClellan, the Art Commission had been one of the few weapons available to reformers in their battle against graft. Accountants had since taken over that role, and by the 1920s the Art Commission seemed, quite inadvertently, to play into the hands of Tammany grafters. While the nascent Modernist movement tried to make a new poetry out of functionalism, the conservative Art Commission still upheld the old traditions of municipal art. In 1927, when Borough President Cyrus Miller produced his first design for the West Side Highway, the drawings showed a clumsy, rude structure of steel. The Municipal Art Society begged the Art Commission to "take its time" reviewing the project. The Art Commission rejected the design, and in doing so it gave the city architects, Sloan & Robertson, the opportunity, eagerly seized, to slather the highway ramps in Tammany granite. The revised highway plan was all "very much better than when first submitted," I. N. Phelps Stokes said,[40] but still . . . Two decades earlier, Henry Hornbostel and Gustav Lindenthal had taught New York that steel could be a beautiful and even expressive material. The team of Carrère & Hastings and Leon Morsieff had shown it again at the Manhattan Bridge. But now, it seemed, only a sheath of granite would suffice. The art societies applauded the monumental effect of the stone; the cost-conscious reformers decried its expense; and the avant-garde complained that it was intellectually dishonest.

Modernist voices grew louder in the 1930s. In 1935, Borough President Levy laid plans to encase the East River Drive's steel structure in granite "to give the effect of arched masonry." In its bulletin of November 1935, MAS published an anonymous complaint: "A magnificent opportunity will be lost unless the citizens of the city demand that such projects derive their beauty sincerely as an expression of their function and by utilizing truly logical building materials. What a chance the designers have here to develop a feeling for the sweep of speed and the lithe forms of steel." The society's reply was largely incoherent—"The things which are seen are temporal," it intoned, "while the things which are not seen are eternal"— but eventually it dismissed the comments as "trite" and asked: "We wonder how our correspondent feels about the frank expression of the elevated railways. Certainly the elevated railways on Sixth and Third Avenue are frank expression[s] of structure."[41]

Modernists undermined the Art Commission's moral authority, even among people who didn't actually appreciate the new style, but Mayor La Guardia had a more personal complaint. The president of the Art Commission was Municipalian I. N. Phelps Stokes, and La Guardia despised him at first sight. The mayor was of course very short and portly, and extremely sensitive about it. Phelps Stokes, alas, was very tall and drastically thin, and propped on this scarecrow's body was a bizarrely small head—as a student at St. Paul's he had answered to the name "Chippie," and at Harvard to "Toodles," but Parisians giggled at the mere sight of "*Monsieur tête d'asperge.*"[42] The mayor had always been poor, whereas the commissioner was born rich—though his fortune was melting away, and by the end of the Depression he'd been reduced to dining at Schrafft's and living in a two-room apartment. The mayor was blunt, to say the least; the commissioner was a man of "exaggerated mannerisms." The mayor was the soul of ethnic New York; the commissioner proudly traced his family history back to the Domesday Census. And lastly, the mayor was a populist, and the commissioner privately believed that the nation's only hope was to restrict the franchise to property owners. Thank goodness

La Guardia owned a tiny, heavily mortgaged house in Riverdale, or Phelps Stokes would have denied him the right to vote.

Few mayors ever attended the Art Commission's hearings, but La Guardia made a point of doing so. He began his first meeting with elaborate courtesy, but then, begging leave to address the commissioners, he pulled a note from his pocket and read it aloud: "On my first visit, as mayor, to this office, as I crossed the threshold, I was confronted by an angry group of well-fed cockroaches. Understanding that the City Hall is under the particular care of the Art Commission, I was much surprised to find that conditions had been allowed to reach such a pass."[43]

Phelps Stokes stammered that the Art Commission's role as "custodian" of City Hall meant that it was the building's *curator*, not its *janitor*, but it was no use. He had to appoint one of his commissioners, a venerable gentleman named George Wickersham, to deal with the cockroaches. Each morning Wickersham rushed to City Hall—only to discover that no matter how early he arrived, La Guardia was already there, barking orders at the exterminators and curses at the Art Commission. Wickersham was so unnerved that he resigned, at which point a grim smile was seen to creep across the mayor's face, but La Guardia's terrorism had just begun. In March 1934 he wrote Phelps Stokes: "Frankness requires me to state that I am not at all satisfied with the present Art Commission, or in agreement with its policies. From our conference it seems to me that you gentlemen are living on a memory of the past. I am concerned with the future. The commission, as I have observed it, seems to lack initiative and energy. While impressed with its dignity, I was disappointed in its accomplishments."[44]

La Guardia carried his complaints directly to the press. "During his first year as mayor," Phelps Stokes remembered, "he was critical of the commission's membership . . . its attitude and accomplishments . . . and especially its president." It was a " 'highbrow' or 'top hat' " organization, the mayor charged, unworthy of its power to delay the city's construction crews.[45] Robert Moses, La Guardia's parks commissioner, had taken to submitting designs to Phelps Stokes on the very day that construction began. That way, even if the Art Commission had objections, it was already too late to make changes. At least Moses was still trying to build beautifully, and had a huge team of architects slaving away in the Arsenal.

In contrast, the engineers in La Guardia's Docks Department churned out designs for the new North River piers without any architectural assistance. For some reason the Docks Department was under the impression that the Art Commission had no jurisdiction over "utilitarian" structures. When Phelps Stokes pointed out the department's mistake, the corporation counsel was called in and backed him up. The drawings for the piers were reluctantly submitted and promptly rejected, but the Docks Department went ahead and built them anyway. This was illegal, of course, but Phelps Stokes couldn't very well sue the city. If it had been Mayor Van Wyck, he might have, but La Guardia was a reformer, the greatest New York had ever produced, and he was already talking about the need to write a radically new city charter. If pressed, he would surely seize the opportunity to

abolish the Art Commission. So back at the Municipal Art Society, Electus Litchfield trod very carefully and complained about the piers in a private letter to the
mayor. La Guardia admitted that they were very ugly, and promised to have an
architect "doll up" the next set of docks.[46]

Such was the mayor's opinion of what architects do. "However, his relations with
the Art Commission had already begun to improve," Phelps Stokes wrote in his
memoirs, "and within a year we were staunch friends. I can say with assurance that
the Art Commission has never received from any mayor—not even from Mayor
McClellan—more hearty cooperation and a more sympathetic understanding of its
aims, than from Mayor La Guardia—after the first year of his incumbency."[47]

Phelps Stokes never knew the reason for La Guardia's change of heart. He
thought the mayor had finally realized the value of his work, and those friends who
knew better were too kind to correct him. It was really Phelps Stokes's wife, or,
more precisely, his devotion to her, that saved the Art Commission. He had married
Edith Minturn, the niece of philanthropist Josephine Shaw Lowell and of Robert
Gould Shaw, the Civil War hero. Readers may already be acquainted with her
beauty, as turn-of-the-century artists found in her their ideal of the "new" American
woman. She inspired one of John Singer Sargent's finest portraits, now a gem of the
American Wing of the Metropolitan Museum, in which she looks as young and
radiant and keenly intelligent as a Daisy Miller or an Isabel Archer. (Mr. Phelps
Stokes is also present in the painting, but "purely as an accessory.") Sargent
depicted her in tennis clothes, an informality considered daring and even a little
improper in Phelps Stokes's circle, though luckily not quite as scandalous as *Madame
X*'s drooping shoulder strap. Minturn had already inspired Daniel Chester French:
she was the model for French's *The Republic*, the colossal gilt statue that rose from
the lagoon of the Columbian Exposition in Chicago in 1893. That was more than
forty years in the past, however. In 1935 Edith Phelps Stokes lay abed, left
speechless and paralyzed by strokes. Though doctors had labeled her a "vegetable,"
Phelps Stokes was convinced his wife's mind was intact, even if none of her muscles
answered to it, and he insisted on staying by her side to talk and read aloud to her.
For years this evoked nothing more than the head-shaking pity of his friends; only
later—after this part of our story—was Phelps Stokes confirmed in his belief that
his wife could hear him. One day he surprised his wife with a joke, and she burst
into laughter.

In the meantime Electus Litchfield was trying to convince the mayor that the Art
Commission shouldn't be abolished. He set up a meeting between La Guardia,
himself, the sculptor Attilio Piccirilli, and Charles Culp Burlingham. Piccirilli,
one of the mayor's few true friends, had known La Guardia since his days as a
struggling labor lawyer. Burlingham had coaxed Fusion's leaders into uniting behind
La Guardia, and he was the only person the mayor held in awe (though to Phelps
Stokes, La Guardia's "Mr. Burlingham" was just plain "Charlie"). When the three
made their case for the Art Commission, La Guardia answered by savagely mim-
icking Phelps Stokes until Burlingham broke in. "Fiorello," he said, "did you know

that man's wife has been unable to recognize him, to know him, and he sat by her bedside for four or five years and he has never left her more than two or three hours at a time?"

"That's the way it was with my wife," La Guardia murmured.[48] It was something he almost never discussed, but twenty years before, La Guardia had nursed his child and his first wife as they died of tuberculosis. He'd been shattered by the experience; he's said to have spent the next year in a boozy haze. Burlingham's information was perhaps the one thing that could have touched La Guardia. Ever afterward the mayor was very kind to Phelps Stokes, and the two even grew fond of each other. Phelps Stokes came to call the mayor "Little Flower," and the mayor gently answered with a new nickname, the last in Phelps Stokes's long life: "Old Pomposity."

So the Art Commission was saved from the wrath of La Guardia, but just in time to come under severe attack from other quarters. For the mayor had been perfectly correct when he accused the Art Commission of "living on a memory," and this was particularly sad because the municipal art movement was blossoming as never before.

The Depression had struck the city's artists and architects with special ferocity. By 1934 six out of seven architects were out of work and others were surely underemployed. Private relief programs sprang up during the Hoover years, groups like the Architects' Emergency Committee, which put designers and renderers to work documenting Colonial and Georgian houses. Even Rockefeller Center cleverly publicized its own lavish program of public art as if it were a charitable enterprise.

The government was slow to help the arts community, but in 1932 New York State's Temporary Relief Administration began hiring artists as muralists and teachers. After the Civil Works Administration was created in 1933, MAS persuaded it to hire a team of sculptors to restore the city's vandalized and decrepit monuments. (Later MAS persuaded Robert Moses to put conservators on the Parks Department's regular payroll.) The team was headed by Isidor Konti, Karl Bitter's former assistant, and its first project, recommended by MAS, was the restoration of the *Maine* Memorial in Columbus Circle. Prominent, filthy, mutilated, and covered with graffiti, the *Maine* Memorial was a prime candidate for restoration, but the choice was also part of Litchfield's courtship of La Guardia. The monument's missing limbs had been sculpted by Attilio Piccirilli, the mayor's dear friend. Surveying the repairs with La Guardia at his side, Piccirilli wept with joy.[49]

In 1935, the artist George Biddle, president of the American Society of Mural Painters, convinced his friend President Roosevelt that artists needed their own federal work relief project. Of course the art market had been devastated by the Depression, but there was another point to Biddle's suggestion. Never had a president so needed to build public morale. The nation was facing its gravest crisis since the Civil War; its political and economic systems had never been held in such low repute; and it took no great stretch of the imagination for many to conclude that America was a failed experiment. Artists, however, could paint the glories of American culture, could bring beauty into the daily lives of the public, could hymn the common man and woman. And, being desperate, they would do all this for very little money. Alternatively, if left to starve, artists might lend their eloquence to the radical left.

Biddle had a handy model for his scheme: in the 1920s the Mexican government had hired painters at wage earners' salaries and set them to work painting murals. Aside from the political benefits—murals were an especially important form of propaganda in a nation with such a high illiteracy rate—the Mexican mural movement had resulted in the flowering of a national school of art.*

Roosevelt created the Public Works of Art Program, later known as the Federal Art Program, both of which were divisions of the Works Progress Administration. At its peak, the WPA employed 2,323 New York artists. They were paid a pittance—most received just $23.86 a week—but between 1935 and 1943 two hundred murals appeared in the city's public buildings, and another five hundred in the city's hospitals. MAS played two roles in all this. Its own mural program, abandoned during the First World War, served as an ancestor, an inspiration, and a model for the Federal Art Program. Now, especially at the start, the Municipal Art Society played some role in guiding the federal program by recommending projects to the WPA. Electus Litchfield remembered that the late Guy Lowell had drawn a scheme for painted decoration in the vaulted vestibules of the New York County Courthouse on Foley Square. Like so much else in that sorry building, the murals had been sacrificed to Tammany's "economy" drive. Litchfield tracked down Lowell's drawings and handed them over to the WPA, and they became its first project in New York.[50] Even now, faded as they are, the murals are a welcome relief from the stony architecture of the courthouse.

The WPA later addressed the building's rotunda, with spectacularly vulgar results. Then there was MAS's own abandoned child: the stairwell murals at

---

* *The greatest Mexican muralist, Diego Rivera, was so highly regarded that in 1932 Nelson Rockefeller asked him to paint the lobby of the RCA Building in Rockefeller Center. His assigned theme was "Man at the Crossroads Looking with Uncertainty but with Hope and High Vision to the Choosing of a Course Heading to a New and Better Future." Since Rivera was a Marxist, his intimations of a better future were profoundly upsetting to the Rockefellers. Each new patch of fresco seemed to yield another splash of flagrant red. The last straw came when he slipped in a portrait of Lenin exhorting a group of workers. Rivera was paid off and summarily discharged. As he was escorted from the premises, mounted policemen patrolled the streets to fend off any demonstrators. An account of this development shared the front page of the Times with another headline: "Nazis Pile Books for Bonfire Today." Rivera's dismissal divided the art community. Biddle was one of Rivera's supporters, but the aged Edwin Blashfield endorsed the Rockefellers' actions; the scandal was proof, he said, that people should buy American when it came to art. A few months later the Rockefellers decided not to remove the mural but to pulverize it. To its disgrace, MAS didn't utter a peep of protest. See Irene Herner De Larrea, Gabriel Larrea, and Rafael Angel Herrerias, Diego Rivera's Mural at the Rockefeller Center (Mexico City: Edicupes, 1990).*

Washington Irving High School, which had never been finished. Salvator Lascari now found a place on the WPA payroll and finished the job he'd started two decades before.

As the Federal Art Program matured, it needed—and wanted—less help. Burgoyne Diller, coordinator of the program's New York Mural Division, employed a wide range of artists. MAS complained that the selection was too wide and that Diller had no aesthetic standards. In fact MAS opposed the Coffee Pepper Bills in 1938, which would have made the WPA arts programs permanent. Albert Bard described the bills as "an effort to organize artists in labor groups, affiliating them with labor as labor, not as art, and then give art employment to the greatest possible number—regardless of artistic talent or quality."[51]

It's true that many of the WPA murals were utterly dreadful, but then again, so were many of the art societies' own early efforts. Some of the happiest works of the WPA were the least pretentious. In 1937 Sacha Moldovan painted the auditorium of Brooklyn's P.S. 164 with *Scenes of New York, Old and New.* Moldovan had been a friend of Soutine and had exhibited with Matisse, but his New York scenes are a surprise: the style is American Primitive. In the Children's Ward of Old Gouverneur Hospital, Abram Champanier painted *Alice in Wonderland in New York.* In Champanier's paintings, Wonderland *is* New York, rendered with enormous affection. Some artists, like Frederick Stahr, worked in a modified academic style. Stahr painted *The Evolution of Staten Island from 1620 to 1935,* a set of thirteen murals in the marble corridors of Borough Hall in Saint George. Stahr had first broached the idea in 1903 and been turned away for lack of funds; only now were Carrère & Hastings's intentions finally realized, somewhat updated. The last panel depicts the construction of the Port Authority's Bayonne Bridge, its steel a glowing shade of vermilion.

Many other muralists were drawn to the work of Diego Rivera. Among them was Charles Alston, who painted *Magic* and *Medicine* in the vestibule of Harlem Hospital. This was the first federal commission awarded to an African American, and despite the neighborhood's complexion both the hospital superintendant and the medical board were horrified to learn that Alston meant to celebrate black history. The Artists' Union and the Harlem Artists' Guild had to rally to defend Alston's right to depict the "cultural interest of the people most vitally concerned."

In 1938, James Michael Newell was asked to paint the history of the Bronx in Evander Childs High School on East Gun Hill Road. MAS had once hoped to paint such a mural cycle in Morris High School. Newell, however, had no interest in the sort of quaint colonial scenes MAS always preferred, and he substituted *The Development of Western Civilization* for his assigned theme. At least Newell's history was far more inclusive than the old Beaux Arts conception. His mural culminated in a pair of hands dangling broken chains and framing an open book inscribed with the words of Walt Whitman:

And that where I am or you are this present day
there is the center of all days
all Races
and there is the meaning to us of all that has ever come of races and days
or ever will come.

One will find very little avant-garde art in the WPA murals. The reason for this didn't lie with Diller, a man of broad judgment and catholic taste; it lay instead with I. N. Phelps Stokes and the Art Commission. In his memoirs, Phelps Stokes admitted "abhorring modernistic 'art' in every form," and his colleagues were just as conservative.[52] A very few exceptions slipped through. Ilya Bolotowsky, who'd abandoned figural art after discovering Mondrian and Miró, painted three murals: in the Williamsburg Housing Project, in the Hall of Medical Science at the 1939 World's Fair, and in a lounge in Goldwater Memorial Hospital. The hospital mural, a Suprematist arrangement of floating planes of color, was called *Abstraction*. Bolotowsky stated his intentions in the most modest terms. "A hospital mural," he wrote, "should contain no definite subject matter, but should be generally decorative and soothing in color. Since straight lines are the most restful things to contemplate, this mural is composed of straight lines and geometrical shapes." Phelps Stokes let Bolotowsky's design pass, perhaps because of the painter's therapeutic theory, or perhaps because he mistook the artist's decorative geometry for Art Deco wallpaper.

Ben Shahn, however, was another matter. One of the masterpieces of the federal art program was Shahn's thirteen-panel mural in the Bronx Central Annex of the U.S. Post Office. There, on federal property, he was safe from the Art Commission, but even so, he ran into trouble when he displayed the cartoon for his work. Shahn, too, included a text by Walt Whitman:

Brain of the new world! What a task is thine!
To formulate the Modern out of the peerless grandeur of the Modern
Out of thyself—comprising science to recast Poems, Churches, Art
(Recast—maybe discard them—end them—maybe their work is done, who knows?)
By vision, hand, conception, on the background of the mighty past, the dead,
To learn with absolute faith the mighty living present.

Discard the churches? Sacrilege! So cried Father Ignatius Cox of Fordham University.[53] Shahn's work was suspended for a time while the artist made an eloquent appeal that free speech—vanquished in Germany and Italy, and threatened in the rest of Europe—still be allowed to flourish in America.

Shahn was able to proceed with those murals, but in 1938 Phelps Stokes took pride in rejecting "a series of sordid murals, painted in the crudest and most offensive modernistic style, for the new Riker's Island penitentiary and contrasting the horrors of the old with the scarcely less repulsive new methods of punishment in our prisons."[54] He was referring to Shahn's project to decorate the main hall of the prison, between the cellblock and the chapel. Phelps Stokes insisted that the murals would depress the prisoners. Shahn polled the inmates, and in general they approved of his work, but Phelps Stokes was immovable. The WPA finally handed the commission to a more conservative artist.

Phelps Stokes's treatment of Shahn outraged the arts community—not the fossilized organizations that made up the Fine Arts Federation, but that segment of the art world that was vital and creative. *Art Front* magazine demanded that the federation's grip on the Art Commission be broken; it suggested that the commissioners be democratically elected by all of the city's arts groups. This was an eminently reasonable idea, but by now La Guardia may have discovered some political value in Phelps Stokes's conservatism. Radical young modernists offered La Guardia a far more effective bugaboo than the Art Commission's harmless old fogies. As the years wore on and the mayor's thoughts turned to hopes of higher office in Washington, he took more care to prove that he wasn't a radical. He attacked Communists; he barred Bertrand Russell, whose only crime was that he was irreligious, from teaching philosophy at City College; and now he dismissed the avant-garde's cries of outrage. "Any people," said the mayor in one speech, "that insist on progressive government and maintain conservative art are pretty well balanced."[55] So when a Charter Revision Commission was appointed, Phelps Stokes was allowed to take an active part in its deliberations. He arranged to add a landscape architect to the Art Commission, but otherwise the organization remained untouched. The Fine Arts Federation held on.

DURING LA GUARDIA'S reign, the art societies even managed to tighten their control over municipal architecture. The depredations of Sloan & Robertson—Mayor Walker's favorite municipal architects—had raised an old question: how should the city choose its designers? Back in the 1890s the art societies had assumed that Beaux Arts architects were every bit as virtuous as they were skilled. After all, they were gentlemen, or at least they were moneyed—they had to be to study in Paris for a few years. In its age of innocence, MAS assumed that such fellows wouldn't consort with Tammany, but since then McClellan had co-opted the Beaux Arts style, Beaux Arts gentlemen had proved to be all too human (as when Whitney Warren was found to have embezzled fees from his associates at Grand Central Terminal), and French pedagogy had become the norm in America. Young draftsmen could take night classes at the Society of Beaux Arts Architects or in private ateliers—one of the best was run by MAS's own Harvey Wiley Corbett—or even take correspondence courses. Competence was no longer a class issue, nor did it provide a clue to an architect's political affiliations.

The Civil Service Commission, revitalized by La Guardia after sixteen long years of abuse, had its own answer to the city's architectural dilemma: it wanted to put architects on the city payroll and entrust them with all the city's public improvements. The art societies were horrified. Of course self-interest had its say: architects depended on the occasional public commission to keep their practices alive, especially during the Depression, and didn't want to surrender these jobs to a faceless municipal agency. There were also more noble reasons to question the idea. Art never flowers in a bureaucracy, and it was easy to picture the sort of hidebound, humdrum, hackish work that would emerge from this new class of anonymous civil servants.*

As early as 1902, in the wake of the Horgan & Slattery scandals, Albany had considered creating a "whitelist" of architects qualified and fit to work for the city. Of one hundred names submitted to the mayor—it's unclear by whom—he would pick fifty. The bill raised fears of "a professional 'ring,'" however, and it needlessly eliminated the possibility of open competitions.[56] Rejected in 1902, the idea of a whitelist was revived by Electus Litchfield in 1935. Litchfield went to see La Guardia and convinced the mayor that the best way to choose architects was to let the architectural community do it for him. The American Institute of Architects, the Architectural League, the Municipal Art Society, and a few other groups would set up a jury to weigh the experience, talent, and professional reputation of architects, and then they would narrow the field down to a list of fifty firms eligible for city work.** La Guardia wanted no scandals on his watch, especially with the federal government keeping such close tabs on how its money was spent, and if something did go wrong, this mechanism would provide him with a little cover. So he agreed, putting Litchfield himself in charge of the program,[57] and the whitelist was even written into the new City Charter of 1938.

The problem, of course, was that the architectural community was rife with its own brand of politics. Young architects bitterly protested that they were excluded from the list and that commissions were simply funneled to well-established firms. With no private work to fall back on, the young architects were in a truly desperate plight, and so the whitelist was soon expanded from fifty firms to seventy-five, and eventually to one hundred. This hardly solved the program's other problem, however. That an architect sat on the board of the AIA or the Architectural League was no guarantee of genius, but it did mean that he and his protégés now had an excellent chance of receiving public work contracts. With the best of intentions, Litchfield had simply delivered municipal architecture into the hands of an old boy network.

Of course the Art Commission was still around to uphold standards, and both its power and its endemic conservatism had just been confirmed in the City Charter of 1938. As soon as the Art Commission was safe, however, I. N. Phelps Stokes retired to write his lonesome, mournful memoirs. In retrospect, the Art Commission would miss him. There was a brand of misplaced heroism in Phelps Stokes: he had

---

* C.B.J. Snyder's career with the Board of Education was something of an anomaly, but even his late work is disappointing.
** The mechanism was complicated. The Civil Service Commission prepared a questionnaire for architects. A three-member jury reviewed the responses, the jurors themselves being chosen by a Committee of Eight composed of the presidents of six architectural societies, the Fine Arts Federation, and MAS.

the courage of his convictions, and though he knew painfully well that he was an anachronism, his conscience wouldn't let him compromise. Phelps Stokes's successors on the Art Commission were less sure of themselves. The International Style was becoming the lingua franca of the architectural community, and art commissioners who'd been schooled in the academies knew they would never really understand this language. To distinguish between an economy of means, a poverty of imagination, and simple stinginess was beyond their ken, and their answer was not to try.

After the Second World War the Art Commission would grant pro forma approval to almost any project that passed through its office. By the 1950s the quality of municipal architecture had sunk so low that Hugh Ferris called on the commission to remember that its legal duty was one of aesthetic discrimination, and not mere self-perpetuation. Ferris wasn't attacking the International Style, as some assumed, merely insisting that the public deserved the very best of modern architecture. Ferris's complaints had no effect. By then, MAS had grown distant from its sleepy partners in the Fine Arts Federation, and there was little it could do to bring pressure on the Art Commission.

The full effects of the Art Commission's abdication of responsibility wouldn't be evident for years, but in 1963, just months before his death, Albert Bard endowed a biennial prize for public architecture in New York. The City Club decided to make a big splash of the first awards ceremony. It recruited a distinguished jury and ordered a lavish banquet, but at the last moment the festivities were abruptly canceled. The jury had examined more than two dozen projects built at a total cost of almost $200 million. Eighty percent of those buildings were pure "hack work," one juror said, and the rest amounted to "deadly mediocrity." Not one deserved a prize. "Aided and abetted by municipal bureaucracy," Ada Louise Huxtable wrote in the *Times*, "mediocrity has become a habit."[58]

THE MOST valuable public works of the Depression era were the housing projects. MAS had called on the city to build public housing as early as 1908, but neither the conservative reformers nor the unimaginative machine politicians paid any heed. During World War I the federal government was forced to build housing for workers in the arms and shipbuilding industries, and both I. N. Phelps Stokes and Electus Litchfield took this up as their contribution to the war effort. Litchfield planned Yorkshire Village in Camden, New Jersey, perhaps the best of these instant communities.

Phelps Stokes's involvement in housing went back much further. So far we have seen him as a conservative aesthete who aroused more ridicule and protest than admiration, and later on, we will see him as an early preservationist. Yet Phelps Stokes wished to be remembered as a housing advocate. Religion had called him to public service as a young man. The activist preachers of the 1880s—men like Phillips Brooks and William Rainsford—awakened him to the hellish living conditions of the poor, and their fiery sermons made him want to "jump up and shout

'Hosanna!' and then rush out and do something." And so Phelps Stokes became one of the first Beaux Arts architects to marry his profession to a social conscience. While still a student at Columbia he decided to devote himself to low-cost housing: surely, he thought, one could find ways to build decent but inexpensive housing in a free market. He was encouraged by Seth Low, then president of Columbia, by Robert Fulton Cutting, and by Josephine Shaw Lowell, and in the next few years his research led him down strange paths, some Kafkaesque, and some more suggestive of *Sullivan's Travels*. While a student at the École des Beaux Arts, he dressed as a hobo and slept in a Parisian flophouse, its beds stacked high against the walls like bunks in a slave ship. And one night in New York he appeared, disguised again, at the Charity Organization Society. He'd come too late to chop wood—performing that chore earned one a bed for the night—so he was shown to the refectory and slept on a table between two drifters. Their last jobs had been walking the line out west, and they asked if Phelps Stokes had ever worked for a railroad. "Yes," he answered—truthfully, for at the time he was the president of the Nevada Central Railroad Company.[59]

Phelps Stokes ended up building new headquarters for the Charity Organization Society, and in 1901 he designed the Tuskegee Model Tenements—in its day, philanthropy's lone attempt to house the city's African-Americans. Phelps Stokes was also one of two architects who served on the state's Tenement House Commission, and in that capacity he drafted some of the crucial technical paragraphs in the New Tenement Law of 1901. After that, confident that no one could build "really bad" housing in the future, he decided to give up the field.*

In the meantime other architects were learning how to improve on the New Law tenement model. Building simply and on a large scale in Jackson Heights, architects like Andrew J. Thomas managed to provide "at least the illusion, if not the reality, of the house in a garden." So did Clarence Stein and Henry Wright, who designed the City Housing Corporation's Sunnyside project in Queens.

Nevertheless, by the mid 1920s the housing situation in New York was, in some ways, worse than it had ever been. The model tenement movement never seemed able to produce housing rent for less than eight dollars a month per room, when seven dollars would have been a much more useful target. Even at eight dollars, the lucky tenants, carefully screened and policed by the building managers, were hardly the most desperate of New Yorkers. And private builders without the capital to build on a large scale were rarely able to achieve such economies.

Much new housing had been built in the outer boroughs, however; some of it fine, some dreary, and most of it far too expensive for the poor. By the mid 1920s

---

* Until the First World War he had a fairly conventional practice with John Mead Howells; their masterpiece was Saint Paul's Chapel at Columbia University, a gift of the Phelps Stokes family. They won second prize in a lot of competitions, a much more cherished distinction than it sounds, for it was a commonplace in Beaux Arts circles that first prize went to the safe, competent scheme, but the second prize was awarded to the bold and the brilliant. Phelps Stokes was especially proud of his entry in the Municipal Building competition. It was a Gothic skyscraper, and Phelps Stokes pointed out its influence on Cass Gilbert's Woolworth Building and, even more convincingly, on Harvey Wiley Corbett's Bush Terminal Tower.

the middle-class market was actually saturated, and by 1927 there were 83,000 vacant apartments in New York. But for the poor, things had gotten worse: more people lived in Old Law tenements in 1925 than in 1909.

In 1926 August Heckscher, a German immigrant grown rich in real estate, joined Mayor Jimmy Walker's Committee of Five Hundred. Heckscher's mission was to study the city's housing problem, and he pithily summed it up as "a disgrace to the city and the nation." Heckscher, whose philanthropy is remembered in Central Park's Heckscher Playground and Long Island's Heckscher State Park, called on the city to spend half a billion dollars over five years to build new housing in the slums. Half the money could be raised by public-spirited citizens—or so Heckscher thought. Astors, Vanderbilts, and Rockefellers had indeed funneled money into the model tenement movement, but they'd never contemplated anything like this scale of investment. (Besides, they weren't Democrats, and only a fool would have trusted Tammany with money.) Jimmy Walker didn't come up with his share, either, but the city did promise to press ahead with a single demonstration project, and a site beckoned.

Through the early years of the century the city had ignored the Municipal Art Society's demands for new avenues to funnel traffic to the Manhattan Bridge, but in 1928 it finally widened Chrystie and Forsyth streets, and in 1929 it used the power of excess condemnation to clear away the buildings between the two streets. Now the city owned a plot of land seven blocks long and 125 feet wide. The Regional Plan Association had its own ideas for the site: one of its most seductive drawings pictured a sunken parkway between the two streets, while the neighboring tenements gave way to glistening Art Deco skyscrapers, complete with beacons flashing from their roofs. This was an alarming image, too, since it imagined the Lower East Side as a gentrified paradise. Mayor Walker ignored the RPA and decided to build housing instead of a highway. It was a great opportunity, and Walker might have gone down in history as the man who built the first public housing project in America. He boasted of the project before a spade had been turned, and in 1929 it was Heckscher who led the movement to "draft" the supposedly reluctant mayor for a second term of office. He deserved reelection, Heckscher said, because of all the "magnificent improvements under way and in contemplation."

"Who can say no?" Walker replied.[60]

Yet Chrystie-Forsyth was an opportunity squandered. The condemnation commissioners began handing out suspiciously lavish sums to the landowners—and this brings us to the subject of Joseph Force Crater, whose fate was one of the great unsolved mysteries of the day. An attorney, Crater was appointed to administer the bankrupt Libby Hotel, which stood on the Chrystie-Forsyth site. It was appraised at $1,200,000, but in June 1929 Crater arranged for its sale to the American Bond and Mortgage Company for a mere $75,000. Two months later the city bought the same building for the amazing sum of $2,850,000. Early the next year Crater was appointed to the State Supreme Court, reportedly kicking back a year's salary in return for the honor. He shouldn't have bothered, since his tenure didn't last so long. One night in 1930 Crater dined with friends, stepped into a cab, waved good-bye, and vanished. He left a note for his wife that the American Bond and Mortgage Company owed him "a very large sum." She was unable to collect it, and Crater was never found. In all, the city spent more than $16 million acquiring the Chrystie-Forsyth site.

A second problem arose when Tammany announced that Sloan & Robertson had won the competition to design the Chrystie-Forsyth project. The architectural firm of Sloan & Robertson had by now become the Horgan & Slattery of Jimmy Walker's reign, but with a difference: at least Sloan and Robertson were fairly talented designers. Their most famous work is the French Building on Fifth Avenue, the livid Babylonian headquarters of Fred French's real estate empire.[61] Early in their career, Sloan & Robertson bid on a number of city projects. At first the partners couldn't understand why they never received any work, but their luck changed when they began making campaign contributions to Tammany Hall. Soon they were donating $10,000 a year to the Democratic machine, but in return they received a flood of lucrative commissions, like the Women's House of Detention at Jefferson Market and the Hospital for Chronic Diseases on Welfare Island. Nor was Tammany's tribute much of a burden, since the architects boldly charged their campaign contributions to the city as reimbursable expenses. Their logic was indisputable, and their profits were outrageous. In one case an investigator discovered that Sloan & Robertson had charged $90,000 in fees for some work on Riker's Island, when the construction itself should have cost no more than $22,000.[62]

Even if they'd approached the Chrystie-Forsyth project with the best of intentions—and there's no evidence they did—Sloan & Robertson had no experience in the housing field and no knowledge of those little tricks of design and construction that could keep the price of apartments down to a reasonable level. Their scheme would have rented at $10.75 a room per month—far beyond the means of neighborhood residents. (A. J. Thomas's competition entry came in at $8.31 per room—still too high, but presumably the best that could be done, given the absurd land costs.) Ironically, such high rents would have fit right into the Regional Plan Association's agenda, but Litchfield, Phelps Stokes, and MAS protested. It was a crime, Phelps Stokes thought, to tear up a neighborhood for the sake of progress and then deny the benefits to the original residents. The point, he insisted, was not to drive people away but to improve their lives. That principle was to be tragically ignored in the city's later urban renewal programs, but for the moment economy, if not decency, carried the day. As the Depression deepened Heckscher's housing scheme collapsed. The Chrystie-Forsyth site remained a vacant wasteland until 1934, when Robert Moses turned it into the hapless Sara Delano Roosevelt Park, named for F.D.R.'s mother—and Eleanor Roosevelt's nemesis.

After this false start, public housing had to wait until 1934, when the state passed the Municipal Housing Authority Act. It let cities set up their own housing authorities to build low-cost apartments using municipal bonds or federal money from the Public Works Administration. The New York City Housing Authority was created the same year, and in 1934 Frederick Ackerman, its technical director, drew up a program for Williamsburg Houses. Sixteen blocks of tenements would give way to four "superblocks" with housing, parks, a school, and a community center. Ackerman arranged a competition with a twofold purpose: to find a design for the site, and to assemble his own whitelist of architects eligible to work for the Housing Authority. He assembled a distinguished jury dominated by the Swiss-born Modernist William Lescaze to judge the entries. Of almost three hundred entrants, twenty-two were declared eligible to work for the Housing Authority. One was MAS's Electus Litchfield, whose scheme was organized on a monumental Beaux Arts axis. He did not, however, supply the aesthetic revolution Lescaze desired; nor did any of the other finalists. So "extraordinary influence" was brought to bear, in the words of historian Richard Plunz. "The stakes were high in the struggle for jobs and for design ideology alike," and the jury decided not to hire any of the finalists, but to seize the commission itself.[63] Lescaze dominated the design process as he had the jury. He carpeted the site with twenty-four low buildings, each shaped in plan like a bumpy, off-kilter H, and the whole complex was turned fifteen degrees on its site, making a sawtooth pattern on the neighboring streets. The rationale for this was "scientific": it improved the apartments' orientation to the sun, Lescaze said. But his courtyards also trapped the bitter winter winds and blocked the cooling summer breezes. The plan was neither "inviting nor informal," Talbot Hamlin wrote; instead of streets and grassy courtyards, there was only amorphous space.

Williamsburg set a pattern in motion. The old architects were shoved aside and, with them, the rich legacy of 1920s housing experiments and of traditional urbanism. As the housing program matured, it was given to ever more reductive schemes of brick barracks standing in a sea of greenery. Low density and open space were the order of the day. The street, traditionally the living room and plaza of working-class communities, was largely banished. Superblocks would supposedly eliminate "wasteful" asphalt and "dangerous" traffic, but in fact the greenery would prove to be far more perilous. Where streets were perceived as public places, policed by their own residents and shopkeepers, the new "parkland" was perceived as a no-man's-land. The sense of communal space was fractured.

It didn't have to be so. There were obvious alternatives. One was rehabilitation, and Electus Litchfield tried valiantly to interest the city in this course. He acted after Langdon Post, the housing commissioner, inadvertently plunged the city into a new housing crisis in 1937. There were still tens of thousands of horrific Old Law and even pre-law tenements in the city, and Post issued new orders to force landlords to bring them up to date. He didn't demand anything luxurious: just one toilet in each apartment and fire-retardant walls around the stairwells. (The Old Law tenements were supposed to have stairs made of fire-retardant materials, but Tammany's Building Department had often ruled that hard pine qualified.) The landlords' response was predictable. Some evicted their tenants, remodeled their buildings, and then let them at much higher rents. Others simply shuttered their tenements. Post was widely criticized for not having foreseen what would happen, and La Guardia soon forced him from office. But as far as Litchfield was concerned, the problem with Post was that his reforms didn't go far enough.

Litchfield pointed out that the old buildings were so deep, and their rear yards so shallow, that sun and air could never penetrate the apartments within. He wanted the city to condemn a swath of land through the interior of each Old Law tenement block, making sixty- or eighty-foot-wide courtyards open to the avenues at either end. In effect, the old backyards would be enlarged, combined, and turned into public parks and playgrounds. "Backyards," Litchfield insisted, were relics of the "horse and buggy age," when they'd served as convenient places to install latrines. "The time has come to plan for blocks and not simply for individual lots or houses. Let us strike at the darkness and congestion which produce the slums. Let us 'Let in the light.' "[64]

The *Times* and the *Herald* publicized Litchfield's scheme, and the Brooklyn Slum Committee called on the Board of Aldermen to put it into effect. But two years earlier, in 1935, the city had tried its hand at rehabilitation with the First Houses project. The site, at Avenue A and East Third Street, was just half a block wide, so the city tore down every third tenement rather than enlarging the rear yards. Since the old buildings relied on their party walls for support, this introduced structural complications, and the city ended up virtually rebuilding what was left. And since the motivation behind the project was work relief, not housing per se, unskilled laborers were used. Their inefficiency helped make the project very expensive, and the effect was to leave the city very cool toward rehabilitation.

Phelps Stokes had a different solution: to build at much higher densities. He complained that the Housing Authority, "like so many other groups of amateur 'reformers,' has many Utopian and impracticable ideas."[65] The Housing Authority insisted that 250 people per acre was the highest density acceptable in its projects. Such a low limit meant that it couldn't operate in what Phelps Stokes called "the real slums on the Lower East Side," since the rent roll wouldn't pay off the land costs without a huge subsidy. But subsidies weren't available, Phelps Stokes didn't want them in any case, and he didn't think they were necessary. If one built eight- to ten-story elevator buildings, he pointed out, one could house 675 people per acre and charge them seven dollars per room.

Phelps Stokes produced detailed drawings and cost estimates of his scheme. His buildings hugged the street lines and had internal courtyards; they looked much like some of the larger 1920s middle-class housing developments—like the London Terrace apartment complex, for instance, which fills the block between Ninth and Tenth avenues, Twenty-third and Twenty-fourth streets. That may have been one reason why his ideas found no favor with the Housing Authority. That agency was committed to wide open spaces, and it was mesmerized by the work of the European Modernists, but it was also very careful not to arouse the taxpayers' antagonism. It didn't yet dare to give the poor a luxurious status symbol like elevators, and it saw a certain political wisdom in building housing that looked like barracks for the indigent.

THE HOUSING AUTHORITY was soon laying plans for the reconstruction of vast areas of the East Side waterfront and of scattered sites in Harlem and the outer boroughs, but at first it had no master plan, and once again the civic groups called on City Hall to establish a planning commission.

In the meantime, MAS and its allies were growing alarmed by a vast concentration of power in the hands of Robert Moses, who was now both the parks commissioner and the chairman of the Triborough Bridge Authority. When the civic groups complained about Moses's projects they were often greeted with silence, contempt, or ad hominem attacks. At best Moses might release a little information that was carefully colored, impossible to confirm, and designed to prove that there were no viable alternatives to his own original scheme. Furthermore, the civic organizations were given little advance knowledge of his plans, and without a master plan for the city, they found it hard to judge the impact of Moses's highways, or even to set priorities. In the meantime the mayor and the Board of Estimate were so concerned with putting the unemployed to work that they could barely pause to weigh the planning issues of the day. If Moses found the money to build a project—almost any project—La Guardia had little choice but to grant his approval.

The mayor, however, had taken office in 1934 with a promise to rewrite the city charter. After myriad revisions, the charter had grown into a vast document of 1,700 sections and 400,000 words. Few people ever read the full text, but those who did discovered that their industry had unexpected rewards. The tired scholar might stumble on a hoary old statute that barred sheep and goats from boardinghouses. Another, written in the dim days of New York's early history, governed a fine point of etiquette: anyone abandoning a dead horse in a dark street was asked to leave a lamp on the carcass.

The new charter took effect in 1938. It gave the Board of Estimate new powers; the boroughs lost some of their autonomy; and the sixty-five aldermen gave way to a twenty-nine-member City Council. The council was elected on a complicated system of proportional representation—instead of organizing elections by district, parties ran a slate of candidates for each borough—and this was, in La Guardia's words, "the greatest progressive step for labor and minority groups of all types that has ever been offered to the citizens of New York."[66]

As far as the Municipal Art Society was concerned, the great feature of the new charter was that it finally established a City Planning Commission—MAS's goal since the 1890s. The new commission had eight members; they were appointed on a rotating schedule for six-year terms (so no one mayor could stack it with his cronies); and they were given the job of producing a master plan for Greater New York. Its first chairman was Adolph Berle, one of La Guardia's most trusted advisers, but Berle soon moved on to Washington to become the assistant secretary of state. His successor was Rexford Tugwell, a brilliant New Dealer and an eloquent advocate for planning.

MAS and its allies greeted Tugwell with a long list of demands. They wanted the master plan to foster coherent neighborhoods—arrondissements, as Stanley Isaacs called them—each with its own full menu of public amenities within easy reach. They noted that the old Zoning Code of 1916 represented an "absurd exaggeration" of the city's needs: there was room within the setback zoning envelopes to build homes for 77 million residents, which was roughly the population of the nation east of the Mississippi; and factories or offices for 340 million workers, more people than lived in the entire hemisphere. MAS called for a radical downzoning of the city: Ralph Walker, who advised La Guardia on how to set up the planning commission, suggested that the city plan for a population of twelve million. "The area now zoned for residence," he told the American Institute of Architects, could house that many people "in buildings of about three stories . . . with half of the land left for gardens and open spaces. A business population natural to a community of its size could be housed properly on about ten percent of the area now zoned for business."[67]

Tugwell started work on his master plan, and over the course of a year and a half he drew up detailed land-use maps to refine and correct the crude diagrams in the 1916 Zoning Resolution. He failed to reach out, however, to his natural allies. Until MAS and the civic groups raised their voices in complaint, the City Planning Commission didn't even publish its agendas in advance, and so no one knew what issues Tugwell had slated for discussion.[68] Electus Litchfield found that Tugwell's interim land-use reports were absolutely unintelligible: they weren't even illustrated with maps. At the same time rumors of new height and density controls alarmed the real estate community, and Robert Moses came to see the planning commission as a threat to his independence. Moses denounced Tugwell as "a planning red" and the master plan as a socialist assault on American liberties. Tugwell soon found that he'd lost the mayor's support. There was an element of personal jealousy in this estrangement—delegating power to commissioners didn't come easily to La Guardia—but it also testified to the raw power Moses had been able to accumulate. The mayor's relationship with Moses was also tortured, but at least it was productive, and since Moses had the money to put people to work *and* the power to withhold that money from the city, La Guardia couldn't afford to upset him.

The planning commission soon discovered that it was expected to rubber-stamp Moses's projects, and in 1941 Tugwell gave up hope and took a post with the federal government. Moses himself was appointed to the City Planning Commission that same year, and this meant that he could propose and dispose of his own projects. MAS bitterly protested Moses's appointment as a violation of the spirit of the city charter, but to no avail. One year later, in 1942, the city announced that it was abandoning all work on the master plan, and the power to shape the city was left in the hands of one imperious man: Robert Moses.

ROBERT MOSES

IN JANUARY 1934, when Robert Moses joined the La Guardia administration, he seemed to be the very flower of New York's reform movement. His mother had been the driving force behind Madison House, one of the great settlement houses. He had studied at Yale, Oxford, Columbia, and the Training School of the Bureau of Municipal Research. His dissertation, on the British Civil Service, had concluded that an aristocratic class of well-bred public-spirited Ivy League men should rule America—a notion dearly held by many members of the Municipal Art Society.

Moses's career began in 1914, when he joined the Bureau of Municipal Research. The bureau had been responsible for Fusion's victory in 1910, and the sweetest part of that success was the election of George McAneny, one of the bureau's founders, as Manhattan borough president. When Moses joined the bureau, Mayor John Purroy Mitchel had just asked it to revamp the entire municipal bureaucracy. Moses was assigned to work with Henry Moskowitz on the Civil Service Commission, and, cheered on by Samuel Ordway, MAS's counsel and the spokesman for the Civil Service Reform Association, he produced the most elaborate system of employee classification and ratings yet devised. Almost a parody, it so outraged city workers that Mayor Mitchel never dared to implement it.

Moses himself grew disenchanted with the bureau. He desperately wanted it to take a stand on the great issues of city planning and public works, and the debate over the West Side Improvement fired his imagination as a new accounting technique never could. After work he would often take a cab uptown and roam across Riverside Park, and one Sunday in the summer of 1914 he stood on a ferry with a friend, Frances Perkins, the future secretary of labor, and pointed to the West Side's muddy shore and clattering trains. "Isn't this a temptation to you?" he asked. "Couldn't this waterfront be the most beautiful thing in the world?"[1]

It would be a long time before Moses had the chance to act on his dream of being a master builder. With Tammany's triumph in 1917, the Bureau of Municipal Research was again barred from the corridors of power, but Moses was rescued from unemployment by Belle Moskowitz. She'd been close to Al Smith since the Triangle fire of 1911, and they cemented their relationship when Smith ran for governor in 1918. Women had just won the vote in state elections, and Moskowitz became Smith's liaison to the women's civic groups and then a member of his kitchen cabinet. In 1919 Moskowitz made Moses secretary of the State Reconstruction Commission, which would become the cornerstone of Smith's career. It designed a new blueprint for the state government, streamlining the bureaucracy down from nearly two hundred separate agencies to a mere sixteen, and vesting executive power in the governor rather than the legislature. Good government groups had long dreamed of such constitutional reform, but it was Moskowitz who sold the idea to Tammany as a cold political calculation: the scheme would attract independents, she pointed out, and drive a wedge through the Republican Party. It was Moskowitz, too, who explained to Moses just what powers and perks the legislature could afford to surrender and which it would have to retain. She gave him his first education in power politics.[2]

It took years to get this program approved, years Moses spent in Albany as one of Smith's most trusted and loved lieutenants—and in building his own relationship with the state legislature. In 1923, while vacationing on Long Island, Moses discovered a new passion: he became entranced with the wilderness of dunes, inlets, and meadows, all within thirty miles or so of Manhattan. He organized the State Council of Parks, became its chairman, and persuaded Governor Smith to agree to a $15 million bond issue for new parks. Moses envisioned a great state park on Fire Island and another chain of parks on the North Shore, and to make them all accessible to the public he laid out Long Island's Southern State and Northern State parkways.

MAS could claim a very faint measure of credit for Moses's achievements on Fire Island. It couldn't help but notice that his roads were inspired by the Bronx River Parkway, William White Niles's pride and joy, and that Moses had even recruited Niles's landscape architect, Gilmore Clarke. If MAS had had a longer memory, it might have reminded the public that Moses's plan had other ancestors as well. Fire Island State Park first appeared as the result of a medical emergency. Cholera broke out aboard a German ship in 1892, and the state bought a Fire Island hotel and 200 acres of land for use as a quarantine area for the passengers. Once the danger of contagion had passed, the hotel was abandoned and the land was declared a park, but it was "an isolated, swampy sandbar, accessible only by small boats and infrequent ferries, inhabited by fishermen and loners, surf casters and assorted oddballs."[3] Such a park seemed a useless luxury, and in 1907 the state was about to sell it until Calvin Tomkins went to Albany. Yes, he admitted, Fire Island was deserted, and it lay far beyond the traffic arteries of New York City. But that would change, Tomkins predicted, and Fire Island would be needed as a metropolitan park. Many laughed, but in 1908 the sale was canceled.[4]

Three years later Charles Lamb first suggested a way to link the barrier islands to the metropolis. In 1911 Lamb formed an alliance with the Reverend Dr. Newell Dwight Hillis, pastor of the Plymouth Church (now the Plymouth Church of the Pilgrims) on Orange Street in Brooklyn Heights. It was a pulpit with a celebrated tradition of activism, the place where Henry Ward Beecher had preached for forty years and where he once staged the mock auction of a slave "dressed in virginal white" to purchase her freedom.[5] Hillis's activism took a rather different form. "Brooklyn Beautiful" was the text for his sermons and lectures, and his campaign played to the frustrations of developers and landowners who'd spent years speculating in the borough's empty or underdeveloped land, only to watch in dismay as "the transit situation [was] throttled by some mysterious power." Someday, Hillis prophesied, Brooklyn would receive the refugees from Manhattan's doomed residential districts, the borough would become the new center of New York's urban culture, and Long Island would find its destiny as the chic resort of transatlantic travel. "Long Island, I maintain to be the porch of the entire United States," he told the Nineteenth Ward Improvement Association. "Manhattan Island eventually will only be the doorknob leading into Long Island, the beautiful."[6]

The Brooklyn Beautiful campaign was meant to hasten that day. Alfred Steers, the borough president, set up a citizens' committee to help Hillis "stir up sentiment," and Daniel Burnham, coordinator of the Chicago fair and author of many City Beautiful plans, was brought in to make suggestions. Burnham didn't stay long; the plan he left behind was a mere sketch; and it fell to Charles Lamb and Nelson P. Lewis, the chief engineer of the Board of Estimate, to supplement his ideas. They drew schemes for bridge terminal plazas, for boulevards converging on a new business center at the Flatbush Avenue station of the Long Island Railroad, and for a Shore Drive. In Columbia Heights, this would take the form of an esplanade elevated over Furman Street and graced with a ribbon of parks carved out of the backyards of houses on Columbia Street (officially these yards sat on city land, but they'd been fenced off by homeowners). Beyond Brooklyn Heights the drive would return to earth; then it would stretch from Coney Island down the central spine of Long Island's barrier islands all the way to Montauk.[7]

One cannot prove that Moses ever saw Lamb's sketches, but his basic concept of a great ocean drive stretching the length of Long Island became Moses's goal. He was never able to see the whole scheme through to fruition, but he achieved enough to amaze his contemporaries. Moses patched together his state park system from an odd variety of sources. Some of it was condemned land; some was wrested from local villages in a bruising fight; some already belonged to New York City's water department; and one parcel was a sandbar that had washed up around a coast guard station. To get this last bit, Moses had to convince Herbert Hoover, then the secretary of commerce, that the federal government could afford to give up its windfall. Hoover's secretary was Harold Phelps Stokes, Moses's Yale classmate, a sometime Municipalian, and the brother of I. N. Phelps Stokes. As Moses put it, "personal friendship, not super duper planning," won the day.[8]

The Long Island parks and parkways opened in 1929, in the last, heady summer before the stock market crashed. Three hundred thousand New Yorkers made their way to Jones Beach that first year, and such numbers put the city's own haphazard planning schemes to shame. (New York had purchased Jacob Riis Park seventeen years earlier, for instance, yet there was still no easy route to the Rockaways.)

Moses's success on Long Island taught New York's politicians that parks were a true motherhood issue (Roosevelt, who inherited the parks program from Smith, would later carry the lesson to the White House), and in 1933 the parks nearly catapulted Moses into the mayor's office. Only Samuel Seabury stood in his way. In Seabury's unforgiving eye, Moses was Al Smith's creature, and Smith was guilty of two sins: his very virtues provided a fig leaf for Tammany's endemic corruption; and his election as governor and his nomination for the presidency effectively shut Seabury himself out of both those offices. When the Fusion Committee tried to nominate Moses for the mayoralty, Seabury threatened to split the party into two warring factions. A "harmony committee," chaired by Charles Culp Burlingham, finally picked La Guardia as a last resort, and La Guardia, eager to heal the wounds in the Fusion coalition, offered Moses the Arsenal.

Moses set conditions for taking the Parks Department job, explaining that he wanted "unified power over all the city parks and, even then, only as part of the unified control of the whole metropolitan system of parks and parkway development."[9] This meant that he wanted to be the city's sole parks commissioner; that he intended to stay on as head of the State Council of Parks and the Long Island State Parks Commission; and that he wanted control of two public authorities: the languishing Triborough Bridge Authority and a new entity that would build the Marine Parkway Bridge to the Rockaways. With all that power, he could forge the city and state parks into a single "metropolitan" system. La Guardia agreed, and Moses himself wrote the bill reorganizing the city's Parks Department. Now there would be just one parks commissioner instead of four, and he would have virtually untrammeled control over his domain. He could, at will, raze any building in the parks. No landscape architect could veto his decisions, and no one—not even the mayor—could interfere with his administrative decisions.

This was an enormous amount of power for a political appointee—especially, it seemed to MAS, if his appointment wasn't going to be vetted by the art and park societies. The Parks Committee of the City Club opposed the bill; MAS didn't, but only because of the unique situation. Moses himself was the "ideal" choice for parks commissioner, as Electus Litchfield said in a letter to the mayor; and then there was the atmosphere of the times: the sense that an overwhelming crisis justified desperate measures. Two years before, President Roosevelt had been given unprecedented powers to deal with the national emergency; now MAS was willing to let Moses assume an even more dictatorial sway over the parks. The society knew he'd put the unemployed to work and rescue the parks from years of Tammany neglect, and those were both urgent matters. And there was one last factor: no one expected Moses's tenure to last. Moses himself told MAS that "possibly, after two years," it could have its wish for an independent parks council, and Litchfield believed him.[10]

The Parks Department seemed too narrow a field of endeavor to satisfy Moses for long. It was no secret that he was politically ambitious, and he was so universally admired that he could surely claim the governorship if he wished. Or so it seemed. When Moses did run for governor in the fall of 1934, he was so haughty, so contemptuous of the public, and so vicious toward his opponent that he seemed to lose support every time he spoke. The man was clearly unelectable, and he would end up holding the reins of the Parks Department for more than a quarter century. This didn't mean, however, that his career had come to a standstill. Rather, he found a unique route to power, adding one agency after another to his résumé until he held twelve city and state jobs at once. Nothing in the city charter or the state constitution had foreshadowed this possibility. Moses now ruled a government within the government—a private empire.

The full danger wasn't clear in 1934, though, and MAS's qualms were centered on the fear that some *future* parks commissioner might abuse his power. Municipalians trusted Moses, even worshiped him, and in the mid 1930s any other attitude would have seemed churlish. Suddenly thousands of CWA and WPA workers were pruning, planting, and building, and parks that had languished through the Walker years were now the scene of frantic activity. Bryant Park was rebuilt, not exactly as MAS had hoped—it had warned that there were too few entrances in the design— but much as Carrère & Hastings had wanted. In the Bronx, at Orchard Beach, there was no old design to serve as a crutch for Moses's inspiration: there he came up with the idea of linking Rodman Neck, Twin Islands, and Hunters Island to create a huge new bathing facility on Long Island Sound. The Prospect Park and Central Park zoos were rebuilt to the witty design of Aymar Embury. In every park in the city, every building was repaired, stripped of graffiti, and repainted. The work lasted all through the bitter cold winter of 1934, with three shifts working around the clock, and in the spring of 1935 the Great Lawn in Central Park was finally finished, almost exactly as MAS and the Society of Landscape Architects had proposed.

There were a few murmurs at the Municipal Art Society. Merkel's eight playgrounds in Central Park—"the ultimate concession" to recreation advocates—had now become nineteen, but MAS was too happy with its Great Lawn to raise the issue publicly. It was especially delighted that, in deference to La Guardia's campaign promise, Moses had barred all active recreation from the Great Lawn. Little did MAS know that in the 1950s Moses would carpet the lawn with dusty ball fields.

Just one thing was truly troubling: Moses had torn down Central Park's Casino. Calvert Vaux had designed the building as a Ladies' Refreshment Salon, but in 1929 Joseph Urban, designer of the *Ziegfeld Follies*, had transformed the interior into a chic Art Deco nightclub. A steep cover charge was imposed, bootleg liquor flowed copiously, and the Casino became the stuff of New York folklore. The concession was held by Sidney Solomon, a man with unsavory friends; the financier was allegedly Arnold Rothstein, the gangster who had fixed the World Series of 1919 and who served as Tammany's liaison to the underworld;* and the driving force behind the project was Mayor Walker himself. "The Casino will be our place," Walker told his mistress, and Solomon provided the couple with their own lavish private suite upstairs.[11]

La Guardia tried to turn the Casino into a campaign issue in 1929, but at the time his tales of dirty money, private rooms, and a secret stairway were dismissed as the paranoid rantings of a demagogue. People were sadly wiser in the 1930s, though, when Moses canceled the lease and demolished the building. There was no place in the park, he said, for an elitist and corrupt establishment, nor would he tolerate this "encroachment" on the park's greenery. The City Club and the Citizens Union were distressed, however. They were glad to see the lease canceled, but far from being an encroachment, the Casino was part of the park's original design. They wondered, too, why it was necessary to tear down a remarkably beautiful building that belonged, after all, to the public, not to the crooked restaurateur. The Park Association added its own complaint when Moses announced that he would build a playground on the site—the first playground in the park's interior.

In private, Moses's aides explained that the Casino had to disappear as a matter of private revenge rather than public policy: the commissioner wanted to punish Jimmy Walker for betraying Al Smith. "God, he wanted to get Walker!" one source told Robert Caro. Moses's motive seems to have been an open secret at the time, but none of the civic groups or art societies wanted to embarrass their hero by referring to it publicly. Nor did they feel that they could support Sidney Solomon—tainted as he was—in a lawsuit aimed at saving the Casino. Granting an injunction against Moses, State Supreme Court Justice John F. Carew wrote that "The commissioner has no more power to destroy the Casino than he has to destroy the obelisk, to fill in the reservoir or the lake, to tear down City Hall, the Arsenal [or] the many historic buildings, monuments, structures, statues in the many other parks of the city, the treasured relics of generations here. He is only to hold office for a brief term. He is the passing creature of a day. He will, in time, and that not long, be superseded. He may not 'waste' the heritage of New York. In the meantime . . . he must restrain his extravagant, excessive energy and zeal or he must be restrained."[12]

Technically, however, City Hall doesn't sit in City Hall Park, so that landmark at least was forever safe from Moses's whims. And for all of Judge Carew's eloquence, he was wrong about those other monuments as well. The appellate court soon wrote, in a remarkable decision, that Moses's powers were far too broad and ought to be reined in by the legislature, but for now the law was explicit: Moses had the power, if not the moral right, to tear down the Casino.

✳   ✳   ✳

* When Rothstein was murdered in 1929, the police were careful not to search his apartment until all his files had been spirited away by unknown parties—one of the many scandals of Jimmy Walker's reign. Rothstein lives on as "The Boss" in Damon Runyon's short stories, and Jimmy Walker's love affair with Betty Compton—with the Casino as a backdrop and the homeless lurking in the bushes—inspired Al Jolson's musical Hallelujah! I'm a Bum!

COMMAND OF the Arsenal was an important post, but the core of Moses's empire was the Triborough Bridge Authority. As promised, La Guardia named Moses to its board in 1934, and the other commissioners were soon forced out for squandering public money. Moses fired the original engineers and brought in Othmar Ammann and Aymar Embury to redesign the bridges. He canceled all the contracts for Tammany granite, and with the savings, plus an infusion of federal relief money, he set about expanding an already immense project. Besides building four bridges, he enlarged Randall's Island, built a sports complex there, and erected the huge Downing Stadium. He accomplished all this in just two years.

The Triborough complex opened in 1936, and by then the civic groups had helped Moses survive one of the great crises of his career: FDR's attempt to wreak a petty revenge. The two men had despised each other since the 1920s, when Roosevelt sat on the Taconic Parkway Commission with MAS's William White Niles. Roosevelt saw how Moses sapped that agency of funds in order to build his own pet projects. Moses, in turn, hated Roosevelt for consigning Al Smith to political exile, held him in contempt for his physical disability, speculated on his virility, and delighted in saying unprintable things about Eleanor Roosevelt. Once Moses's popularity had taken a beating in the gubernatorial race, the president saw a chance to strike back. In December 1934 the Interior Department issued a new rule, Executive Order 129, which stipulated that the Public Works Administration would no longer give money to any public authority "created for a specific project wholly within the confines of a municipality" if any of its directors also held public office "under said municipality."[13] In the whole country this applied to just two people, both New Yorkers: Langdon Post, who doubled as tenement commissioner and head of the Housing Authority; and Moses, who ran Triborough and the Parks Department. When Washington informed La Guardia it would make an exception for Post, there could be no doubt of Roosevelt's true target.

Desperate to keep federal money rolling into New York, La Guardia was willing to go along with this. When Moses stubbornly refused to resign from Triborough's board, the mayor worked out a compromise with Roosevelt, promising not to reappoint Moses when his term expired in 1935. But Moses leaked the story to the press, and the response was one of universal outrage. Moses was clearly doing a brilliant job; he was dedicated, energetic, and apparently incorruptible. Indeed he was that rarest of creatures: a visionary who could translate his plans into reality. To punish such a man due to a private grudge was a misuse of power, as C. C. Burlingham said, worthy of George III. One hundred and forty-seven civic and business groups, including the Municipal Art Society, joined together to pass a resolution: better to turn down Washington's money, they told La Guardia, than submit to tyranny.

With his own constituency up in arms and his enemies on the lookout for signs of a dictatorship, Roosevelt was forced to retreat: Executive Order 129, he announced, wouldn't be applied retroactively. The civic groups were as delighted as Moses himself, and thought they'd cemented a public-private partnership.* And in Flushing Meadow, there was visible proof of the collaboration between Moses and the civic groups. There a wasteland was being turned into a world's fairgrounds and, everyone hoped, into the most splendid of parks.

THE NEW YORK World's Fair of 1939 was the idea of Joseph Shadgren, an immigrant from Luxembourg, "a man of modest means, a civil engineer without excessive forcefulness of personality and without wide acquaintanceship among the great or even the near great."[14] In 1934, while reviewing his daughter's grade school lessons, Shadgren realized that the 150th anniversary of George Washington's inauguration was fast approaching. With all the ardent patriotism of a new citizen, he decided that New York should celebrate the occasion with a world's fair. The exposition became his one-man crusade, but Shadgren was dismissed as an eccentric until 1935, when someone suggested he seek out George McAneny, now president of both the Title Guaranty and Trust Company and the Regional Plan Association.

McAneny cared about history, but he also saw that a fair meant construction jobs and tourist dollars. McAneny convinced the city's business leaders that a world's fair was precisely what New York needed, and he convinced Robert Moses that it would be the perfect opportunity to transform Flushing Meadow into a park. That area of Queens was deceptively named; it was a meadow "where ashes grow like wheat," as F. Scott Fitzgerald wrote.[15] Cinders blanketed the earth, the thirty years' harvest of Brooklyn's incinerators. The city had already agreed in principle to reconstruct the meadow, but the task was so herculean that nothing had been accomplished. "I told Mr. McAneny," Moses wrote later, "that I would stop at nothing to help him . . . if the fair were actually to be in Flushing Meadow, and if from the beginning the project was planned so as to insure a great park in the geographical and population center of the City."[16] And it was Moses who then sold the idea to La Guardia. Flushing Meadow was in the geographical heart of the city, he pointed out, and it was far larger than Central Park. Moses's planners pictured a marina, an arboretum, two man-made lakes, bridle paths, and an "active recreation" center with athletic fields, swimming and wading pools, a model yacht basin, and an outdoor amphitheater.

---

* MAS wanted to celebrate by giving Moses an award, but Moses was apparently determined to prove that he hadn't needed any help, and he became elusive. Other groups were facing the same problem; finally fifteen of them rented the Rainbow Room for a joint ceremony. Aside from MAS, they were the City Club, the Park Association, the Regional Plan Association, the Architectural League, the Art Commission Associates (composed of retired members), the Central Park West Association, the Columbus Avenue Association, the National Academy of Design, the National Sculpture Society, the American Institute of Architects, the American Society of Landscape Architects, the New York Society of Architects, the Outdoor Cleanliness Association, and the Fine Arts Federation. Moses promised to attend, but when the date came around, he was having a spat with La Guardia, and since the mayor was going to give a speech, Moses decided not to show up. (MAS Minutes, May 22, 1935.)

Meredith Michael Hare, MAS's secretary, arranged a dinner at the New York Civic Club for "progressives in the arts."* Among the speakers were Harvey Wiley Corbett, the industrial designers Gilbert Rhode and Walter Dorwin Teague, and the planner Henry Wright, but their ambitions were summed up by the critic Lewis Mumford. "The story we have to tell," Mumford announced, "is the story of this planned environment, this planned industry, this planned civilization. If we can inject that . . . as a basic notion of the fair, if we can point it toward the future, toward something that is progressing and growing in every department of life and throughout civilization . . . we may lay the foundation for a pattern of life which would have an enormous impact in times to come."[17] That night Hare founded the Fair of the Future Committee, an ad hoc group, to develop the theme.

This committee came up with two ideas. In the past, world's fairs had resembled enormous trade shows where manufacturers could learn about the latest products and the newest technologies, but the world was a smaller place now, and Hare realized that this should be the first "consumers' fair." Instead of talking to one another, manufacturers would demonstrate how their products could improve people's lives. And this would be tied into the fair's overarching theme, "Building the World of Tomorrow."

The Program Committee kept the "progressives" happy, and to satisfy the art societies, there was a Board of Design to oversee the work of individual architects. Aside from Teague, the board members were predictably conservative, and their influence told in the tepid classicism of the fair's official buildings. The most talented designers of the day had to use all their tact and diplomacy to sidestep the art societies' deadening influence. Harmon Goldstone, a future president of MAS, was then a young draftsman in the office of Wallace K. Harrison, architect of the Theme Pavilion. Harrison yearned to build an "emotional symbol" for the fair, Goldstone remembers, but the Board of Design handed him "a very conventional program," the sort that demanded "columns, and steps, and lions." "The first thing we did was throw out the program," Goldstone says; the next thing was to set up so many meetings with the individual board members that "they got the feeling they were participating" in the design.[18] In the end, there were no lions in the Theme Pavilion; there weren't even any steps. Harrison produced the celebrated Trylon and Perisphere—a pinnacle and a sphere. The entrance was the world's largest escalator; the exit was an immense spiraling ramp.

Inside the Perisphere was a space twice as large as Radio City Music Hall, and there, as if through a hole in the clouds, crowds looked down from balconies on Henry Dreyfuss's vision of the World of Tomorrow, a huge model of Democracity. Home to 1.5 million, powered by hydroelectric dams, Democracity was a cluster of separate communities. Centerton was the business and cultural district, with a single

---

* In many discussions of the world's fair, Hare is mistakenly identified as the secretary of the Municipal Art League, which was founded at La Guardia's request to encourage the performing arts; its most visible monuments are the School for the Performing Arts and City Center.

skyscraper at its heart. Scattered through a greenbelt were Pleasantvilles, bedroom communities for the middle class, and Millvilles, designed for industry and workers' housing. Highways linked these satellite towns. But this vision of the future was rather alarming. Democracity's careful separation of land uses, a product of the Garden City movement, meant that its residents would always be commuters driving from one segregated zone to another. While visionaries like Charles Lamb, and the Regional Plan Association after him, had always worried about how to improve the existing city, Democracity was a new city on an imaginary site. It suggested that New York's problems were so intractable that there were only two possible solutions: demolish the city, or escape it.

Both alternatives would be pursued after the Second World War when the city's old neighborhoods were earmarked for destruction—or for "urban renewal," in the euphemism of the 1950s—and when the middle class was encouraged to settle in new suburbs. These suburbs wouldn't be the tightly planned greenbelted communities suggested in Democracity, but sprawling speculator-built suburbs. They would be created not by city planners but by highway engineers. And it was a sadly prophetic fact that the 1939 fair's most popular exhibit was not Democracity or the earnest art exhibits, but General Motors' Futurama.

Futurama called on all the talents of Norman Bel Geddes, the celebrated scenic and industrial designer. At this exhibit people boarded a moving platform and were treated to an imaginary plane ride over the continent as it might appear in 1960. This was a future where cars were shaped like teardrops and ran on liquid oxygen and where atomic power was being used "cautiously." It was a future crisscrossed with highways that cantilevered off the sheer faces of mountains and leaped over rivers on streamlined bridges; a future where cities had been rebuilt from scratch around highway interchanges. As Walter Lippmann wrote, "General Motors had spent a small fortune to convince the American public that if it wishes to enjoy the full benefits of private enterprise in motor manufacturing, it will have to rebuild its cities and its highways by public enterprise."[19]

WHEN THE New York World's Fair opened in 1939, highways could still seem glorious and romantic, and Robert Moses had just built a parkway as lyrical as anything in Bel Geddes's Futurama: the Henry Hudson Parkway had opened in the fall of 1937, and Riverside Park finally stretched over the railroad tracks and into the river. Almost four decades had passed since MAS first embraced Milton See's scheme for an Italian garden at the Hudson's edge; a quarter of a century had gone by since Charles Stover started work on the seawall; and it had been two decades since John Purroy Mitchel produced his ill-fated West Side Improvement project.

Moses has often been blamed for building the Henry Hudson Parkway at the water's edge, and so depriving the public of its chance to actually get to the water. Yet in that instance there was no ideal solution—either the road would take the waterfront or it would split the park in two—and Moses had a history of expert advice to back him up. In 1932 an official board of advisers that included Herman

Merkel, a great favorite of MAS, had recommended the waterfront route for the road. By then another controversy had already arisen around Inwood Hill and the city's plans for the Henry Hudson Bridge.

In 1901 bridge designer Alfred P. Roller proposed that a bridge carry Riverside Drive over Spuyten Duyvil Creek. The bridge would serve as a memorial to Henry Hudson and, he hoped, be ready for the Hudson-Fulton Celebration of 1909, when New York meant to honor its two great navigators. Roller planned to build great stone bastions rising out of the water to buttress a 500-foot steel arch. Atop the abutments rose twin copies of the Dewey Arch. When MAS exhibited the project in 1904, it was described as "a dignified affair of stone arches and handsome super-structure." But the *Times* reported that "the Roman triumphal arch, besides its general triteness and banality in connection with a twentieth century piece of engineering, had nothing at all to do either with the specific achievement it was meant to commemorate or with the romantic and picturesque character of the gorge it was to mark."[20]

Nothing happened until 1906. With the Hudson-Fulton fete approaching, Man-hattan Borough President Ahearn was pushing to extend Riverside Drive north from 135th Street to Lafayette Boulevard, and the bridge project was revived. Roller and the architects Walker and Morris presented a new design for an 800-foot arch of steel. The riverbanks themselves would serve as abutments, which meant that the entire width of the Harlem Ship Canal would be available for navigation and there was no need for piles of Classical architecture rising above the roadbed.

The Board of Aldermen set aside a million dollars to start work on the bridge, but the Municipal Art Society was unhappy with the bald, utilitarian design. Had the bridge been but a bridge it might have passed muster, but it was still supposed to do double duty as a memorial, and that seemed to require more majesty. The Art Commission agreed and rejected the design. "What we want," one member told the *Times*, "is a bridge that is imposing and magnificent and worthy of the city. We do not want a bridge built after any such plans as those now before us. Such a bridge would not be imposing enough. It is not monumental and magnificent. In fact, it is generally inartistic."[21] The Art Commission even specified exactly what it wanted: a stone arch. An 800-foot arch of stone was an impossibility, however, and this left just two options: a stone veneer over a steel framework, which outraged all those, including the editors of the *Times*, who'd come to regard steel structures as both beautiful and honest; or an arch of reinforced concrete, which demanded enormous foundations and was probably beyond the capabilities of the fledgling concrete industry. Either would be far more expensive than Roller's design, and it seemed impossible to redesign the bridge and still finish it in time for the Hudson-Fulton Celebration. The city's editors were up in arms, and it was a lucky stroke for the Art Commission that a taxpayers' suit forced Ahearn to suspend work on the Riverside Drive extension.

By the time Ahearn fell from power only one thing had been accomplished: William Muschenheim—who had paid for MAS's Times Square electroliers—organized a public subscription to build a memorial column on the Spuyten Duyvil bank. There was never quite enough money to add the finishing touch, however, and the crowning statue of Hudson was still missing.

By the early 1930s doubts had arisen about the bridge, and especially about running a road through Inwood Hill. When Henry Hudson sailed up the North River, MAS noted, he saw "as beautiful a land as the foot of man can tread on," and something of that still existed on Inwood Hill. Here one could still find "virgin forest, steep wooded hillsides, silicate and granite, glacial potholes—through gnarled trees the immemorial river, and distant towers; here is every characteristic of wild country—on Manhattan Island. Many a New Yorker, taken there blindfolded, would imagine himself hundreds of miles away." In the early 1900s this had seemed expendable, but after three decades of apartment building in upper Manhattan, Inwood Hill was the last bit of true nature left on the island. Inwood Hill had also become a park (through gift and condemnation) and the sacred principle of preserving parkland forced MAS to reconsider the issue of the highway and its bridge. "Must citizens go afield," MAS asked, "to the Palisade Park, to Indian Point, or to Bear Mountain to come into close contact with 'tor and tree'? What would be the verdict fifty years from now?"[22]

Inwood Hill became the "center of a controversy of long standing, and of acrimony unusual in such matters." It was a matter of particular concern to MAS, since "Across the Harlem converge the magnificent parkway systems leading to New York, creations in part of the genius of William W. Niles, one of our Directors." Niles proposed his own alternative plan for Inwood Hill. He would separate the north- and south-bound traffic and divert them around the hill. Clinging to the hill's "nether slopes," the drives would leave much of the forest intact. Two roads would certainly have been dramatic, but very expensive. By 1931 the civic groups had come to prefer a single road skirting the eastern edges of Fort Tryon Park and Inwood Hill Park. Anything else, they agreed, would be an "indefensible park invasion."[23]

Robert Moses plotted just such an invasion, however. He shifted the route back to the ridge of Inwood Hill and aimed his high bridge straight at Muschenheim's lonesome column. The civic groups were tempted to defer to his judgment until two young architects, William Exton and Robert Weinberg, launched a crusade. Both were active in the Citizens Union, the City Club, and the Parks Association; Weinberg worked for the Parks Department, though he'd become disenchanted with the Arsenal's increasingly thoughtless designs, and Exton was MAS's secretary and the youngest member of its board. Weinberg was especially worried about Riverdale and Spuyten Duyvil, then still a village within the city. At the very least, he thought, some planning controls ought to be imposed so that these neighborhoods wouldn't be ruined by promiscuous development. But even this modest and sensible proposal ran counter to Moses's agenda: he was trying to minimize local opposition by keeping the exact route secret for as long as possible, and the last thing he wanted was to open up the question of the highway's impact on Spuyten Duyvil. Exton's first concern was Inwood Hill, his favorite retreat from a life hectic with civic work and a great many love affairs. Exton began cajoling people to visit Inwood Hill and see it for themselves. He showed them the stillness and beauty of the forest, and from the hilltop he pointed out the better route at the park's edge. Not just trees were at stake, he pointed out; across the Harlem River, the alternate route would run through mud flats and a shantytown, sparing Spuyten Duyvil. Comptroller McGoldrick was immediately convinced, but the board of the Municipal Art Society took a little longer. "Old Electus Litchfield ... said what a beautiful view there was from the road," Exton remembered. "I said that *from* the road there is a beautiful view, but *to* the road there is a lousy view. And I still remember some of the old-time architects and Beaux Arts boys who were on the board saying, 'Hear, hear!' "[24]

MAS voted to support Exton in defense of Inwood Hill, and it joined the Citizens Union, the Parks Committee of the City Club, and the Regional Plan Association in demanding a thorough examination of Moses's plans. Moses answered with a smear campaign against Exton and Weinberg. They were pushing for the new route, Moses charged, because it would enhance the value of land Weinberg owned in Spuyten Duyvil. "It was a lie, a goddamned lie," Exton told Robert Caro years later. Weinberg *had* inherited a little land in Spuyten Duyvil, but it was near Moses's route, not the alternate; if anything, Weinberg had been acting contrary to his own financial interest. The City Club investigated and exonerated the two men, but doubt remained in the public mind, and poor Exton felt tarnished for the rest of his life.[25]

Exton and his colleagues didn't understand that Moses *couldn't* explain the real reasons behind his plan. His great talent was in finding ways to finance things. He had mastered the art of lulling the city and state into appropriating funds for a project by concealing its ultimate cost. One year he would ask for money to build a park; the next, for money to build access roads, without which the park was useless. What politician could refuse? For the Henry Hudson Parkway, Moses managed to tap twenty-two different sources of city, state, and federal money. His six-lane highway would run through Inwood and Van Cortlandt parks so Moses could classify these stretches as park access roads eligible for federal funds. If the issue were examined closely, the CWA and WPA might well withdraw their support. Also, Moses didn't want to say that Wall Street was responsible for the high bridge. The bridge was going to be financed by a bond issue backed up by toll revenues, but the bankers had doubts about its profitability. They pointed out that there was already a bridge on Broadway, near Exton's route, and it was free. That bridge was a notorious bottleneck, but the bankers were nonetheless convinced that a toll bridge would never make money unless it were built farther away—and that meant in Inwood Hill Park. Of course, if Moses had been willing to wait a year or two, until the city had the money to build the bridge itself, Inwood Hill could still have been saved, but patience was never one of Moses's virtues.

✳   ✳   ✳

IN THE MID 1930s a new cast of characters appeared at MAS: the architects Harvey Wiley Corbett, Ralph Walker, and Ely Jacques Kahn. The three were masters of the Art Deco style. Corbett had become famous in the early 1920s for his celebrated zoning studies, rendered by Hugh Ferris. His best-known building is the Master apartment house on 103rd Street and Riverside Drive, built for the strange and somewhat sinister theosophist Nicholas Roerich. Kahn's oeuvre was concentrated in the garment district. Walker designed the epoch-making Barclay-Vesey Building—the first New York skyscraper to break with historicism—and the sublimely beautiful headquarters of the Irving Trust Company at One Wall Street. All three of these architects had ignored the Municipal Art Society during the 1920s, but although they'd been too busy for civic work in the boom years, they now had a great deal of time on their hands. Kahn, in fact, was spending his lunch hours, not with clients, but telling anecdotes of the architectural scene to his receptionist, a young writer named Ayn Rand, who used them as background material for her delirious novel, *The Fountainhead.*

Kahn's ascendancy at MAS was a bit ironic. In his memoirs he remembered returning to New York from a triumphant career as a student at the École des Beaux Arts only to find that none of the city's prestigious firms would hire him. He'd imagined for himself a typical career: do well at the école, apprentice at a prestigious firm, and then build country houses and libraries and museums. But a Jew couldn't get a job at firms run by "the scions of well known families," and Kahn had to make a career for himself designing speculative lofts for Jewish developers—the sort of work that, until the 1920s, never got published in the architectural journals.[26] Kahn became famous by accident, as it were: the business culture of the boom years and the fad for Art Deco rescued him from a profitable obscurity. Yet there remains a haunting bitterness in Kahn's memoirs, and one hopes he took particular pleasure in becoming president of MAS, for it was largely composed of the very sort of blue bloods who had wounded him so deeply.

Schooled in the ways of real estate developers, MAS's new directors were a much cannier crew than the gentle old men who had run the society in the 1920s, yet they were still at a loss when faced with a mind as cunning and a power as far-flung as that of Robert Moses. "No law, no regulation, no budget stops Robert Moses in his appointed task," La Guardia once crowed.[27] The statement was too literally true, but what the mayor didn't admit was that Moses himself was largely free to decide just what constituted his "task." In the mid 1930s, when the state revised the charter of the Triborough Authority, some apparently innocuous amendments actually granted the authority astonishing new powers. The Triborough Authority had been created to build the bridge complex; it was supposed to collect tolls until it paid off its bonds, and then go out of business. Yet the new charter let Triborough issue new bonds whenever it chose and collect tolls for as long as it wished; it granted the authority the power to build virtually any sort of "facilities for the public" (parks, highways, housing, etc.); and it said that these new powers would be "part of the contract with the holders of the bonds." Laws can be repealed, and charters can be amended or revoked, but contracts can be broken only with the consent of both parties: now the Triborough Authority could be restrained only if the bondholders and the authority itself gave their assent.[28]

So long as bankers were willing to buy its bonds, Moses could capitalize the Triborough Authority's revenues and spend the money much as he pleased, for while the city had to approve each of his projects, no power on earth could force Moses to spend money on a project he didn't like. Time and again the city was faced with a terrible dilemma: build what Moses wanted, how he wanted it, and when he wanted it, or watch him snatch the money away—and not just the money but also the jobs it would create, the contracts and fees, the tax revenues, and the opportunity for politicians to claim credit for a new public work.

As a result, MAS was in an odd position. Much of its old program was carried into effect during the Depression. There were new parks and highways, playgrounds and swimming pools and the city's first housing developments for the poor, and yet none of these new realities quite fulfilled the old dreams. The new housing typically displaced more people than it resettled. The apartments themselves may have been better than quarters in the old tenements, but the buildings impoverished the public realm. As for all the new greenery, it was clear to MAS that the budget of Moses's Parks Department contained a fatal flaw: there was money to buy and to build parks but not to maintain them. Acres and acres of land had been added to the Arsenal's preserves, but there was no new army of workers to tend them, and the effect soon told on the parks themselves. The new parks were landscaped for low maintenance, and the old were altered to achieve the same grim efficiency. Pads of concrete appeared beneath Central Park's benches, where grass had grown until now. An arm of the lake was amputated. The cave was sealed off with concrete blocks. Elsewhere, sheer neglect took its toll. The Loch was left to choke in debris until the bubbling stream turned into a muddy trickle; the Cascade ran dry. Quantity was winning out over quality, political effect over good governance.[29]

Then there were the highways, and here the real point seemed to escape MAS. Moses was carrying out a plan of arterial highways much like the old Regional Plan Association schemes, but the RPA had always meant to build rail systems at the same time. Most people would travel by train, MAS assumed; cars were the luxurious option. But now only highways were built, partly because of the temper of the times. Detroit's massive advertising campaigns had identified cars with modernity, had even succeeded in making them emblems of status: owning a car was enough to establish someone as a member of the middle class. There was another reason not to build train tracks, and that was the railway companies themselves. They'd thwarted the Port Authority through the 1920s, and by the 1930s every bureaucrat and planner knew that highways were easier to build than railroads: one didn't have to negotiate with private operators.

The very nature of New York's roads was changing before MAS's very eyes. Roads were no longer pleasure drives where people drove slowly for recreation, to appreciate the view, and discursively, with stops. Instead, they were highways in the modern sense: great asphalt arteries for express traffic, carrying the full burden of the city's commuters and a growing amount of its truck traffic. Landscaped as they were, they were purely functional elements of the city plan. A certain confusion still reigned, however. The new highways retained certain vestiges of the old conception of drives and parkways. They were laid out as if to link the various parks in one metropolitan system, and often they sliced through the parks themselves. By 1938 MAS was beginning to realize that something was going wrong.

The turning point was Moses's announcement that the Bronx River Parkway would be rebuilt, just thirteen years after its completion. William White Niles had died in 1935, and Moses, having ignored Niles's advice while he was alive, unveiled a flagstaff dedicated to his memory in 1938. He even delivered a nice little eulogy.[30] Yet already, as Albert Bard wrote, "A sinister report is heard that this roadway, which now follows the turnings of the river and the contours of the singularly beautiful valley, will have to be straightened and widened, its bridges scrapped—in short, made into a speedway to carry the volume of traffic coming upon it. The same engineering may be invoked to 'improve' the Bronx River, which now meanders with gentle flow beside the drive, so that its waters also may get faster to the Sound."[31] As Moses prepared to put this plan into effect in 1940, Charles Stoughton urged MAS to try to stop him. Stoughton lived in the Bronx and had been a friend of Niles, and he knew from experience that it was already possible to drive at forty miles an hour for nearly the entire length of the parkway. E. J. Kahn wrote of MAS's position: "World renowned for its beauty," the Bronx River Parkway "should be retained as a work of art." This time the answer came not from Moses himself but from Gilmore Clarke, Niles's erstwhile landscape architect. The Bronx River Parkway was Clarke's own masterpiece, but he'd since been absorbed into Moses's machine, where duplicity was apparently a matter of course. The contemplated changes in the parkway, Clarke wrote, "are more in the nature of restoration than destruction."[32]

Reading this, Kahn thought MAS must have misunderstood what was going on—an understandable mistake, since the full plans had never been released to the public. But when A. F. Brinkerhoff took charge of a special committee to study the issue, he found a situation even more drastic than Stoughton and Bard had imagined. In fact, little would be left of Niles's work when Moses was finished, and that little would be a mere service road sitting next to a new highway. The ribbon of park that graced the old road would be reduced to tatters, and Moses was claiming additional land from the Bronx Zoo and the Botanical Garden in order to extend the route farther south. The plan was a disaster, Brinkerhoff thought, and yet he had to advise MAS to drop its protest. Nothing could be accomplished, he said. Contracts had already been let, and Moses had carefully crafted a situation in which he was virtually exempt from public review.[33]

In 1938 the Fine Arts Federation printed a white paper on the city's public works policy, and MAS thanked the author, Albert Bard, for capturing its views so well. It was the first time the art societies had dared to question the principles behind Moses's work. "The use of the parks for the new roads built for modern traffic presents an unexpected problem," Bard wrote. The scale of the new highways was shocking, especially the area devoted to interchanges with their ramps, clover-leafs, and bridges. Few people anticipated how small would be "the scraps of grassland left when the roads have taken what they want," Bard went on:

> For the most part what remains of the ostensible park has become simply the embellishment of the drives and this the motorist accepts with composure as he is only concerned with racing through them where no traffic lights interfere. The surrounding country being gone, why linger to see the road? This is equally true of small areas such as the islands that would have been parks—now lying under the extension of the Triborough and New Haven Railroad bridges—a good part of whose remaining grass plots are rendered sunless under the shade of the overhead structures. Our pleasure at the acquisition of so many new parks is somewhat cooled in finding that many are but stepping stones for high-ways and bridges which spoil the view and monopolize the spaces that would have been the plantation. The park and bridge are mutually antagonistic. . . . [Ward's Island and Randall's Island] were very precious spots. . . . No one would think of that aspect now; when they are already almost obliterated . . . by the march-past over them of the New Haven Railroad and the Triborough bridges and a proposed footbridge . . . by a stadium on Randall's and a sewage disposal plant on Ward's Island, leaving but thirty-seven acres for park on the south-eastern corner of the latter.

Bard complained that "The city cannot keep off its own grass." Indeed it couldn't keep off its own streets: Moses was laying plans for new elevated highways. The irony was that the city was now spending tens of millions to free its avenues of elevated train tracks. Said Bard,

> Removed, they leave the avenues, made usable and pleasant, open to the upper light and air. Let us enjoy this unexpected opportunity of looking upward while we may. For we are now called upon to replace the railroads by elevated highways for motor traffic over the avenues, of which the first, four and one-half miles long, already built at a cost of about $3,550,000 a mile, is the West Side Express Highway. . . . These elevated roadways will obstruct the light even more than the present open elevated railroad structures, for their roadbeds, being solid, will let no light through. It would be better for the lighting of the streets to retain the present lighter framework of the railroads in place and endure their noise and ugliness in order to keep these darker covers out.[34]

By 1938 the city had made enormous progress on its system of waterfront ring roads. Moses had finished the Henry Hudson Parkway; the Miller Highway was finally in operation; Stanley Isaacs was building the East River Drive; and Moses was ready to proceed with the Belt Parkway. In 1936 La Guardia had created a Tunnel Authority to build the Queens-Midtown and Brooklyn-Battery crossings. But the latter would be useless without a connection to the Belt Parkway, and despite Washington's largesse, La Guardia was short $50 million. Only Moses, with his Triborough revenues, could provide such a sum. He set his own price for cooperating: he wanted control of all the river crossings, whether tunnels or bridges. La Guardia agreed. But others began to question the city's priorities. The Belt Parkway and its link to the Battery tunnel was a huge project—so big, Comptroller McGoldrick warned, that if the city proceeded it would exhaust its entire capital budget for the next two years: "Not a single new school, not a single new hospital, not a new police station or firehouse, not even a health station would be provided," McGoldrick pointed out. "These are essentials, and in my considered judgment, we cannot embark upon new ideas until we meet these basic needs."[35] McGoldrick, Stanley Isaacs, and Newbold Morris thought the Belt Parkway could wait. Between them, the comptroller, the borough president, and the president of the Board of Aldermen had enough votes on the Board of Estimate to block the project, but La Guardia informed them that if they didn't yield he would break with the Fusion Party. McGoldrick and his allies backed down. There would indeed be no new clinics for two years—and by then there would be new highways to build.

Electus Litchfield had asked his colleagues at MAS to support McGoldrick, but after some hemming and hawing the board decided to side with Moses, at least tacitly.[36] The Municipal Art Society didn't know yet that a change was brewing in the plans for the Brooklyn-Battery crossing. Moses had a deeply romantic side; its outlet was a fascination with suspension bridges and a corresponding horror of tunnels. As far as Moses was concerned, a tunnel was but a nasty hole in the ground: claustrophobic, tiled like a bathroom, and foul with exhaust fumes. The suspension bridge was a different matter: a blend of art and science as finely calibrated as a Gothic cathedral. To drive through a tunnel from the Battery to Brooklyn would mean a few minutes of tedium. But to drive across a bridge, to soar above the upper harbor and look down at New York as if it were a child's toy—now *that* would be exhilarating.

In January 1939, Moses announced that the Brooklyn-Battery crossing would be a bridge designed by Othmar Ammann and Aymar Embury. Planners were puzzled by this announcement. A bridge would be a bit cheaper to build than a tunnel, but more expensive to maintain. Theoretically the bridge could carry more traffic, but it would be subject to the weather. Then, the planners realized, one had to consider the bridge's effect on lower Manhattan. Its vast approach ramp—eight lanes wide and as much as a hundred feet tall—would start at Rector Street; then, passing south, it would darken thousands of windows and deafen countless tenants with the rumble of traffic. The city would have to reassess all the buildings nearby, and this introduced another hidden cost to the bridge: according to one estimate, New York would lose $29 million in real estate taxes over the next ten years—and that figure was calculated in the depths of the real estate depression, when assessments were miserably low. (They didn't begin to recover until 1941.) Then another issue had to be considered: Battery Park had only recently been liberated from the elevated tracks that used to snake their way to Whitehall Street, and now Moses meant to build an infinitely more massive ramp in the park itself, plus an anchorage of solid concrete some ten stories tall—an odd thing for a parks commissioner to propose.

Finally there were issues harder to quantify, but no less powerful. The tip of Manhattan was a paradoxical place. On the one hand it was steeped in history: there was Bowling Green, for instance, the oldest public park in the city, where the gilt statue of George III had briefly reigned; there, in Battery Park, was Castle Clinton, the scene of innumerable public festivals; and beyond the castle lay the harbor with its vista of sea and sky and commerce. Visitors could stand on the seawall and find that the noise of the city was muffled by splashing waves, the cries of seagulls, and the sonorous rumble of foghorns. Behind them stood the skyscrapers, proudest symbol of man's mastery, but before them reigned the elements in all their majesty.

From the harbor, the impression was very different. The skyline of lower Manhattan, as seen from the upper bay, was the great iconic image of the city. Mention London and people pictured the tower of Big Ben or the dome of Saint Paul's; speak of Paris and they would imagine the Eiffel Tower. A reference to New York conjured up the prow of Manhattan, with its beetling skyscrapers rearing up from the flood. Countless tourists rode the Staten Island Ferry just to catch a glimpse of that view; countless writers hymned the sight. To Eric Mendelsohn, the German Expressionist, it seemed "the joy-cry of Wealth and Power, the victory cry over old Europe and the whole world."[37] For others, it seemed proof of one of the great skyscraper myths. "They did not grow thus to astound foreigners or to overawe immigrants," wrote Paul Morand, the French writer, of the Battery's towers. "They have climbed these heights because the last fragment of a rock which was running short had perforce to be utilized: they have risen naturally, as the level of a stream rises when it is cramped within enclosing banks. . . . All the crazy lust for growth which sprawls towns flatly over the Western plains and makes that infinite pullulation of their viviparous suburbs, here finds expression in a vertical drive. From these great folios New York derives her grandeur, her strength, her aspect of tomorrow. Roofless, crowned with terraces, they seem to be awaiting the rigid balloons, the helicopters, the winged men of the future."[38]

Now Robert Moses meant to put a bridge in the foreground of this picture, in effect writing his name in gigantic letters across the skyline. But would it be an artist's signature, or a vandal's? When a public work is pending, a handsome artist's rendering is usually released to titillate the voters, and renderers are paid handsome sums to make even the most banal project look glamorous. But Moses published just two small and terribly dry drawings of the bridge: a plan and an elevation, neither of them rendered, and neither very informative. In the plan, the bridge amounted to just a few delicately drawn lines on a map. In the elevation, the context was conspicuously absent. Such reticence convinced William Exton that Moses was hiding something. He suggested to Ole Singstad, the engineer who had designed the Battery tunnel, that he take Moses's drawings and draw perspectives of the bridge. Singstad took up the idea "with alacrity," as Exton told MAS's board, and produced two sets of views—one from the harbor, as if you were standing on the Staten Island Ferry; the other a set of worm's-eye views from the lawn of Battery Park.[39]

Singstad's drawings were devastating. From the park the prospect back toward Manhattan was now a view of the underside of a massive overpass. From the harbor it looked as if the fabled skyscrapers were corralled behind a colossal fence. Moses insisted the drawings were "completely phony," and his biographer, Robert Caro, offers that there was "something funny" about the perspectives, but if so, Moses's staff could never pin it down, and when Aymar Embury was interrogated by his colleagues at the Architectural League, they wrung from him a reluctant confession that the drawings were "approximately accurate."[40]

One civic group after another objected to Moses's scheme, and their protests were coordinated by the Central Committee of Organizations Opposing the Battery Toll Bridge. Its chairman, Albert Bard, dispatched speakers to every civic group and art society he could find, and he sent C. C. Burlingham, now eighty-one years old, to speak to the mayor. La Guardia agreed to stall for time, and he promised Burlingham that if the city could find another source of money—one not controlled by Moses—he would build the tunnel instead. At that time, Albany was considering two bills: one authorizing the Triborough Authority to build the Battery bridge; another canceling the Tunnel Authority's permission to build a tunnel. La Guardia announced that, while he backed the first bill, he would take no position on the second. But Moses, on vacation in Florida, telegraphed an ultimatum: if La Guardia didn't commit himself to the bridge Moses would drop the entire project. The mayor backed down.

The reformers still trusted in the City Planning Commission, however, and Bard marshaled his troops. The civic groups begged for an impartial study of the alternatives: either Singstad's tunnel or a Regional Plan Association scheme to slap a toll on the Brooklyn Bridge and rebuild its decks so they could carry more cars, making a new crossing unnecessary. But the City Planning Commission, under pressure from Moses and the mayor, took a narrow view of its duties. Neither a tunnel nor a rehabilitation scheme was formally on its docket, said the planning commission; it could consider the merits of the bridge but not of any imaginary alternatives. The City Planning Commission then voted to approve the bridge, and so did the Art Commission—with Phelps Stokes retired, its days of courage, sometimes misplaced, were largely over.

These were hard blows. "The planning and art commissions have been faithless servants," C. C. Burlingham mourned in the *Herald Tribune*. "What justification can there be for men whom we have trusted to preserve the beauty of New York . . . to destroy or risk the destruction of any feature of beauty?"[41]

There was just one hurdle left in the city's approval process: the City Council still had to pass a home rule message informing Albany that it approved of those two bills in the state legislature. The day before the City Council hearing, the Fine Arts Federation warned that the bridge would "disfigure perhaps the most thrillingly beautiful and world-renowned feature of this great city." Moses, when asked for a comment, said, "The same old tripe."[42]

Manhattan Borough President Stanley Isaacs took charge of presenting the opposition's case. Isaacs was already in political trouble, having made the political mistake of hiring for his staff a brilliant young man, Simon Gerson, who happened to be a member of the Communist Party. Isaacs hoped that Gerson's radicalism would "leaven" his own conservative instincts, but the Hearst papers didn't see the point of such a dialogue, and they were baying for the borough president's blood. Nevertheless, at the City Council hearing, Isaacs put his troubles aside for the moment and calmly called one witness after another to poke holes in Moses's argument. A long line of planners, engineers, accountants, and assessors pointed out that Moses had overstated the tunnel's cost and understated the cost of a bridge; that his budget simply left out one $11 million item—the elevated link to the West Side Highway—and that he'd ignored the bridge's impact on property taxes. In the end, Isaacs called on George McAneny to testify. He was seventy years old and looked even older—Joseph McGoldrick remembered him as "old and wrinkled and very shrunken." McAneny spoke not just as president of the Regional Plan Association but as one of the great figures in the battle to make New York a more livable place and a more just place—as someone who had been a young crusader for the civil service, once Moses's cause; who had helped pull Tammany from its throne in 1910; who had shepherded the zoning code and the Dual Contracts into being. He reminded the City Council that money wasn't the only issue. "What all this would do to the values of real estate," said McAneny, "some of it the most valuable in the world, I leave to others. But that the city would permit its famous Battery to be dealt with in such a fashion seems to me an incredible thing. I am in fact of the opinion that if the plans under discussion are seriously pressed, there will be an uprising of public opinion the like of which has not been known since, forty years ago, some well intentioned gentlemen in office proposed that the City Hall be torn down to make way for something more modern in the skyscraping line."[43]

Surely, McAneny concluded, there were enough questions about the bridge for the city to conduct an impartial study of the alternatives. At the very least, Moses should provide a breakdown of his budget estimates. All he was asking for, McAneny said, was a little time, a little information, a chance for reason to prevail.

Moses didn't appeal to reason when he testified, however. Instead he flaunted his power, and he repeated his discredited cost estimates. He claimed the Regional Plan Association had opposed him fifteen years before over the creation of Jones Beach—which was not true. He threw in the comment that civil service was "a racket," and he accused Stanley Isaacs of being a Communist. Appalled, the reformers booed and hissed, but Moses went on, unashamed. Referring to the RPA plan, he insisted that

"No man in his right mind" would put a toll on the Brooklyn Bridge. McAneny didn't have to worry about such political realities, he said. "He's not going to run for public office again." Then he turned to look at McAneny, who was sitting in the audience. "He's an extinct volcano," Moses said. "He's an exhumed mummy." There were no hisses this time; just stunned silence. And finally Moses presented the City Council with an ultimatum. "This is a showdown project," he warned. "Either you want it or you don't want it. And either you want it now or you don't get it at all."[44]

Years later Joseph McGoldrick told Robert Caro that, yes, he'd been afraid of Robert Moses. "I was there that day, you know, sitting in the audience, when he said that to George McAneny.... And when Moses called him an 'exhumed mummy,' I saw the expression on his face. I saw it, you know. So I was afraid of him."[45]

The home rule message passed, the legislature hurriedly approved the bills, the governor signed them, and the battle seemed lost. The War Department still had to certify that the bridge wasn't a hazard to navigation, but this seemed a mere formality. Since the Brooklyn Navy Yard was upstream, Moses had already investigated the point. His bridge easily cleared both river channels, and the air force told him not to worry about air raids: a bomb would have to sever one of the cables to block the river, and the odds of that happening in the days before smart bombs were 1 in 100,000. Besides, there were already two suspension bridges between the harbor and the navy yard.

But if Moses could misuse his power, the reformers could retaliate in kind. C. C. Burlingham, asked if there was any hope left, thought for a moment before breaking into a smile. "Call Eleanor," he advised. On April 5, 1939, Mrs. Roosevelt's newspaper column, "My Day," wandered off the subject of the president's grandchildren.

> I have a plea from a man who is deeply interested in Manhattan Island, particularly in the beauty of the approach from the ocean at Battery Park. He tells me that a New York official, who is without doubt always efficient, is proposing a bridge ... over Battery Park. This, he says, will mean a screen of elevated roadways, pillars, etc., at that particular point. I haven't a question that this will be done in the name of progress, and something undoubtedly needs to be done. But isn't there room for some consideration of the preservation of the few beautiful spots that still remain to us on an overcrowded island?[46]

There were other pleas from New York. Burlingham—"At the risk of being called an extinct firecracker," he said—kept the debate going in the letters column of the *Herald Tribune.* He demanded that Moses release a detailed budget for the bridge, and he followed up with another letter, this one written "in graveyard confidence" and addressed to the president:

Dear Franklin:

Now please *stop* and read my letter to the *Herald Tribune*. . . . Nobody fit to have an opinion wants the Battery Bridge except Bob Moses.

. . . The War Department can stop it . . . *verb. suf. sap.*, especially when the sapient being is a lover of New York, as well as President of the United States and Commander in Chief of the Army.[47]

A word to the wise is sufficient, and FDR quietly passed that word to Harry Woodring, his secretary of war.

All summer long Moses muttered darkly that Washington's red tape was holding up his bridge, but this delay was calculated to give the impression that the army engineers were carefully studying an issue that had, in fact, already been decided. In July 1939 Woodring finally announced that the Brooklyn-Battery Bridge would be a hazard to navigation. Luckily, he added, there were alternatives.[48]

Moses spluttered and raged, but he was trapped. There was no evidence to tie FDR to the War Department's decision. The civic groups had whipped up public opinion to rescue Moses from Executive Order 129, but now they all lined up against him; not one pointed out the patent absurdity of the War Department's stance. And the mayor refused to fight Washington. "We must go on to the next thing," he told Moses.[49]

THE NEXT skirmish erupted over Washington Square. For Municipalians, Washington Square represented the heart of genteel old New York. Its southern boundary, where Stanford White's Judson Memorial Church was crowded by loft buildings and apartments, was already ruined, but the Greek Revival row houses to the north still spoke of another age. For Robert Moses, however, Washington Square represented a traffic problem. It marked the south end of Fifth Avenue, and except for buses, all traffic was routed to the narrow streets ringing the park. As a result, most drivers preferred other routes south. But if Fifth Avenue continued through the park, Moses figured, the cars could be funneled onto West Broadway, and Manhattan would have a major new traffic artery at a tiny cost. Of course the park, sliced in two, would be ruined; the quiet neighborhood would be flooded with through traffic, and developers would soon pounce on Washington Square. This little band of asphalt could spell the doom of much of Greenwich Village. Since the new connecting road would lie within a park, Moses insisted that its construction was an administrative matter for the Parks Department alone to decide. The Washington Square Association endorsed Moses's scheme, but Stanley Isaacs rallied the civic groups, including MAS, to stop the project.

Borough President Isaacs won this battle, but his willingness to fight Moses came at a terrible cost to his career. When the "Gerson affair" first broke in the newspapers, La Guardia (who had approved the appointment) told Isaacs that "This won't last. They'll find another victim, and Gerson will be forgotten."[50] Moses, however, was determined to remind the papers. Whenever he spoke of Isaacs, the words "Gerson" and "Communist" were sure to follow. "The claque complaining about Robert Moses is headed by Stanley Isaacs, who ... gave employment to Simon Gerson, who was a Communist"—so read a Parks Department press release in 1956, two decades after the storm first broke.[51] Isaacs's home was picketed; he was denounced in churches, and the American Legion suggested that patriotic "shock troops" should storm his office. La Guardia, terrified of being tainted himself and of losing the Catholic vote, forced Isaacs off the Fusion ticket. The smear campaign, revived periodically, kept Isaacs from ever climbing higher than a seat on the City Council.[52]

IN 1940 the Belt Parkway was finished, and at the opening ceremonies Mayor La Guardia announced that the Reconstruction Finance Commission would lend New York City the money to build the Battery tunnel. Everyone cheered, except Robert Moses.

Not long afterward, Moses announced that he was going to tear down the Aquarium in Battery Park. It was a curious building with a long and checkered history. It had started life as Fort Clinton, and was finished just in time for the War of 1812; as a result, New York was spared a second occupation. Fort Clinton stood in the harbor, a little round island of sandstone linked to the Battery by a wooden causeway and drawbridge. When peace came, the fort became a breezy public promenade and a water gate for distinguished visitors: Lafayette was welcomed there, deliriously, on his return to America. In 1824 the first in a series of dance and concert halls was built within the old walls. The name Fort Clinton gave way to Castle Clinton. Barnum reigned at the Castle, and Jenny Lind sang there. By the 1860s the island had been engulfed in landfill as Battery Park was enlarged. Castle Clinton became an immigrant station, and after Ellis Island opened in 1896, the Zoological Society installed the Aquarium. A flimsy tin-roofed structure rising out of Castle Clinton's massive walls, the Aquarium was no architectural gem, but it was immensely popular. Two and a half million people visited it every year, and this constant stream of sight-seers brought a pleasant bustle to Battery Park. Mothers brought their children throughout the day; adults came at lunchtime, on weekends, or after work. Many couples went to the Aquarium on dates: admission was free, and it was dark enough inside for couples to kiss but public enough to reassure everyone concerned that necking wouldn't blossom into sex.[53]

Now Moses announced that the building had to come down: its roof was leaky and its ventilation poor, he said, and construction of the Battery tunnel would undermine its foundations. He claimed that the building was already settling and pointed out that the Aquarium's floor was a bit below ground level. Once again, Moses's explanation made no sense. Ole Singstad, the tunnel's engineer, pointed out that the tunnel came nowhere near the Aquarium, that the fortress walls rested solidly on bedrock, and that the Aquarium hadn't settled into the ground—rather, the landfill had partly buried the building. Castle Clinton had been built to withstand bombardment by heavy cannons, and Singstad gave his guarantee that it would surely survive the tunnel excavation. As for the roof and the ventilation system, those could be fixed for far less than the $2 million Moses planned to spend on a new aquarium.

The Municipal Art Society lodged a protest with the Board of Estimate:

> We have no suggestion to make as to the disposition of the fish nor any criticism of the loyal and extremely capable work that Mr. Moses has done and is doing. There is a question, however, in the minds of many citizens as to the advisability of the removal of one of the few historic relics in the City.
>
> It appears that from an engineering angle the old fort does not interfere with the new tunnel or its approaches. . . .
>
> Whatever its final use, it does not seem necessary to destroy the building, in spite of recent action of the city authorities. The Society registers its protests, not only for its members, but for many citizens outside of New York City who have expressed their regret at the destruction of the old fort.[54]

William Exton described this protest as "a namby-pamby, weak-kneed, sniveling, futile, ineffective specimen of 'appeasement.' "[55] It was time, Exton thought, for MAS to face some unpleasant truths about Moses: he was the enemy of good planning, he was a tyrant, and he was tearing down the beloved old Aquarium to revenge himself on those who had blocked the Brooklyn-Battery Bridge. MAS already knew that Moses was egotistical and ruthless; still, Exton's friends had trouble believing that Moses was revenging himself on the poor Aquarium. It seemed too petty, too mean to be believable. But it soon became clear that there was no other possible explanation.

In September Moses told the Board of Estimate that he was closing the Aquarium on October 1. It was an administrative decision, he said, which he alone had the right to make. He asked that the Aquarium's budget be transferred to the Bronx Zoo so some of the fish could be stored there. Moreover, he announced that Battery Park would be closed to the public as a safety measure during the tunnel's construction. Closing the entire park was apparently his way of forcing the Board of Estimate's hand: if no one could visit Battery Park, there'd be no reason to keep the fish there. The board agreed, but the civic groups pointed out that the city had a contract with the New York Zoological Society and that only the Board of Estimate—not a parks commissioner, no matter how high-handed—had the right to terminate it. Albert Bard obtained a show cause order requiring the city to explain why "the members of the Board of Estimate should not exercise the discretion invested in them by law."[56] This maneuver worked, but only briefly: in October the board bowed to Moses, canceled the contract, and authorized the Aquarium's demolition. Even La Guardia, who was fond of the old Aquarium, voted for demolition. Apparently he'd decided that he needed Moses's help in his reelection campaign.

The fish tanks were emptied, but the outbreak of World War II interfered with

Moses's plan. Heavy equipment was suddenly such a precious commodity that it was hard to find someone willing to undertake the heroic task of demolishing the fort's eight-foot-thick walls—the very walls that Moses claimed were dangerously fragile. In 1942 a demolition crew settled for pulling down the Aquarium's roof, interior walls, and fish tanks. The debris was heaped up around the fort, and the park was fenced off, but the court battle still raged. George McAneny and his allies sought to stop any further demolition on the grounds that Moses had won the Board of Estimate's consent through "false and fraudulent representation."* They fought their way up to the court of appeals, losing each time, but by 1943, when the last decision was handed down, the war effort was in such high gear that Moses had to postpone his revenge.

The war offered Moses other opportunities, however. In 1942 he was named to head the city's industrial scrap metal drive, and he seized the opportunity to lay claim to the Battery tunnel's cast iron lining. Actually, the metal was useless for the war effort—the army needed steel, not cast iron—but Moses succeeded in suspending construction and thus throwing the Tunnel Authority's finances into some doubt. Then he launched a quiet smear campaign against Ole Singstad, the tunnel's engineer, questioning his skills, which were impeccable, and digging up some suspicious old real estate maneuvers by Singstad's brother-in-law, even though an investigation had already exonerated Singstad. And finally Moses kept insisting that the Tunnel Authority would never be financially viable. There was only one solution, he said: let the Triborough Authority build the tunnel. In 1945 La Guardia agreed to this proposal, and Robert Moses gobbled up his rivals.

Here was a new source of revenue for Moses's coffers—for in fact the Brooklyn-Battery Tunnel would later prove very profitable—and an opportunity to punish Ole Singstad. Moses built Singstad's tunnel, but credited the design to his own engineers. And though Singstad's services were in great demand around the world, Moses saw to it that he never built another public work in the state of New York.

Peace revived the controversy about Castle Clinton. Many who'd once wanted to save the Aquarium were less sure about trying to restore the fort to its original appearance. After all, whatever charm it once had was lost when its little island was engulfed in landfill. After some debate, MAS resolved to continue its support of McAneny, and for the next eight years, whenever it seemed useful, MAS restated its position. The Park Association took a different tack, however. Its independence was fatally compromised by the fact that Moses sat on its board of directors and by the fact that its president, Iphigene Sulzberger of the *Times* dynasty, was one of the few

---

* McAneny had already played a key role in saving superb landmarks in New York and Philadelphia. More than any other single figure, he had been responsible for persuading the federal government to save Federal Hall on Wall Street. That splendid Greek Revival temple, once the Custom House, stood on the site where George Washington was inaugurated as the first president. It was going to be sold as surplus federal property until McAneny, the Scenic and Historic Preservation Society, MAS, and other groups intervened. In 1938 the Philadelphia Custom House—another Greek Revival masterpiece—was also threatened. McAneny stepped in as president of the Carl Schurz Memorial Foundation, and the government agreed to make it a memorial to McAneny's mentor.

people whom Moses bothered to court instead of bully. The Park Association had remained neutral during the earlier Aquarium debate, but now it backed the scheme to raze the fort with all its might. So whenever McAneny told the tale of Castle Clinton frightening away the British Fleet, the Parks Association sneered that the English had really feared navigating the lower bay. Whenever McAneny spoke of Barnum and Jenny Lind and Lafayette, the Park Association replied that they would never recognize the site now. And whenever McAneny remembered the fort's days as an immigrant station, "the Plymouth Rock" of countless Americans, the Parks Association answered that Castle Clinton had been "a disgrace to the nation and the city," a place where "new arrivals received the most scandalous treatment."[57]

McAneny, however, was a great debater. One of his opponents quoted Tennyson to justify the fort's demise: "The old order changeth, yielding place to new." McAneny promptly answered with Scripture: "Remove not the ancient landmark which thy fathers have set."[58] In an effort to cut off the debate, Moses now announced that almost nothing was left of Castle Clinton—just two walls, teetering on the verge of collapse. So much time had passed since the Aquarium's demise that most people accepted this without question, but McAneny convinced Walter Binger, La Guardia's public works commissioner, that he should go look for himself. Binger climbed the heap of rubble and saw that the fort was still intact. He went back a second time with C. C. Burlingham, who was finally disillusioned with Moses, and McAneny brought their report to Harold Phelps Stokes, who was now working for the *Herald Tribune*. The paper hired a plane to fly over the Battery, and the next day its front page carried an aerial photo showing the old fort safe and sound behind a ring of rubble. Though caught in a bald-faced lie, Moses refused to either apologize or surrender. One Friday afternoon he persuaded the Board of Estimate to authorize demolition again. Robert Dowling of the City Trust Company (he was also a lay member of the Art Commission) put up money for another suit; Paul Windels warned the lawyer not to wait till Monday, but to "bring this to court in half an hour."[59] He did, yet by the time the injunction was served, the great wood and iron doors of the fort had already been burned.

Moses's eagerness to destroy the old fort was due to the fact that McAneny had been busy. The fight against the Brooklyn-Battery Bridge had taught him that no power in New York City was sufficient to stop Moses, so McAneny abandoned the notion of home rule—normally a sacred principle to the reform movement—and turned again to Washington. Privately, Harold Ickes, Roosevelt's secretary of the interior, promised that the National Park Service would take over the fort as a national historic monument, but that the transfer of jurisdiction would be time-consuming. The city and state would have to transfer the fort to the federal government, and then Congress would have to come up with an appropriation. For four years McAneny led troops of aged reformers and preservationists down to Washington and up to Albany, trying to convince legislators that Castle Clinton was indeed historic, and for those four years he fought a rear-guard action in New York City to stave off Moses's wrecking crew.

With his sheer eloquence, McAneny extracted Mayor William O'Dwyer's promise to save Castle Clinton, but O'Dwyer always wanted to be liked and was famous for sending away every petitioner with a smile. Soon he broke his word, and in 1947 he asked the Board of Estimate to authorize demolition. He was stopped by action in an unexpected quarter: the attic of City Hall, where the Art Commission had its office. The Art Commission at last found the courage to remind the mayor that Castle Clinton was "a work of art" or "monument" within the definition of the city charter—any public building was—and thus couldn't be "altered" without the Art Commission's written consent. Surely the fort's demolition was an alteration of the first order, and the Art Commission would have to vote on the matter.

Never before had the Art Commission claimed jurisdiction over demolitions—it had not spoken out, for instance, when the Central Park Casino was destroyed—and though this was a novel legal argument, it seemed so obviously right that Albert Bard couldn't resist tweaking the mayor. Of course the Art Commission had to vote, he wrote in letters to the papers, and "as an ex officio member . . . Mayor O'Dwyer should know this." From Washington, the Interior Department lodged its own protest. It had been drawing plans for the fort's restoration, and now it promised publicly to provide "all the funds required to restore the ancient structure as a Castle Clinton National Monument" as soon as the local authorities agreed to transfer ownership.[60] Embarrassed, O'Dwyer reversed course and asked the Board of Estimate to cancel the demolition. The state senate voted to transfer the fort to the federal government, but Moses succeeded in bottling up the bill in the assembly's Rules Committee, and the measure failed.

At that point the preservationists nearly gave up. The city authorized another assault on the fort in 1948, and this time only a "miracle of maneuvers" could save it. Since the demolition plan still hadn't been submitted to the Art Commission, McAneny greeted the bulldozers with yet another lawsuit, this one grandly filed in the name of Alexander Hamilton, the great-great-grandson of the statesman and the treasurer of the American Scenic and Historic Preservation Society. An injunction was granted, and the judge went beyond the legal issue at hand to offer his own opinion on the proper fate of Castle Clinton. "Upon all the circumstances," he wrote, "I am satisfied that it is a monument of significant and architectural value. . . . I think there is still room for values which, while they may fail to impress in a material sense, nevertheless make for a fuller national community life. A people indifferent to the landmarks and monuments of its past will not long retain its capacity to achieve an honored future."[61]

The appellate division wasn't convinced, however. Apparently its judges had never seen the Parthenon or the Roman Forum, for in 1949 they ruled that Castle Clinton was a "ruin," and that a ruin couldn't be a "monument." Only if Castle Clinton were restored to pristine condition would it qualify, but that would cost money, the court pointed out, and the Art Commission had no power to compel the Board of Estimate to make an appropriation.[62]

Hamilton's petition was denied, but in 1950 the Brooklyn-Battery Tunnel finally opened, and the walls of Castle Clinton had stubbornly refused to fall down. That same year Congress at last passed a bill ordering the Interior Department to take possession of Castle Clinton and providing money for its restoration. President Truman had promised McAneny that he would sign the bill, but at the last moment he called Mayor O'Dwyer and offered to veto it. O'Dwyer happened to be quarreling with Moses at the moment, and perhaps remembering his own broken promises to McAneny, he told Truman to sign the bill. The interior secretary described the deliverance of the fort as "a victory of wide importance and interest in the cause of historical preservation. After years of struggle and debate in New York City, in the courts, in the state legislature, and in Congress, the saving of Castle Clinton evidences a new and deeper recognition of the need of preserving the diminishing landmarks of our history as an essential part of our national heritage."[63]

It was a bittersweet victory, however, for Castle Clinton makes a rather depressing monument, one that people rarely visit twice. There isn't much to look at; it's far too clean and neat to make a convincing fortress; and it's too thoroughly reconstructed to seem genuinely antique. To truly restore the fort would have meant carving away at Battery Park so the tides could once again splash against Castle Clinton's ramparts. It would have been better, of course, if Moses had left the Aquarium alone. As it happened, the new aquarium at Coney Island cost $10 million to build, not the $2 million Moses had promised. Admission is charged to recoup the cost, but nothing can be done about the fact that Coney Island is far away and hard to reach.

VENERABLE TRADITIONS: THE EARLY DAYS OF THE PRESERVATION MOVEMENT

AMERICA'S PRESERVATION MOVEMENT began in 1850 when the state of New York bought the Hasbrouck House in Newburgh and turned it into a museum. In this modest structure Washington had disbanded his victorious army and handed over the reigns of power to Congress.

For the next century the preservation movement remained a sort of patriotic cult. In the North it worshiped the Founding Fathers; in the South it kept alive the myth of a chivalrous culture destroyed in the Civil War. Fueled by bitterness, loss, and poverty, this southern cult was by far the more vital, and it had taken such a hold that by the early years of this century southerners were startled to see how carelessly New York treated its past.[1]

Because of the diligence of southern historians, the landscape of Virginia was haunted by the memories of settlers and landed gentry, of revolutionaries and presidents, of battles and statesmen. But New York's best-known historian was Washington Irving, a satirist, and by nineteenth-century standards, the city's past was barely worth recording. It had seen few battles, produced no great Founding Father. Its commercial life hardly counted in the heroic, romantic, or moralistic modes of nineteenth-century authors. In 1903, Senator Chauncey Depew went so far as to describe the Morris-Jumel Mansion, Fraunces Tavern, and Saint Paul's Chapel as the city's "only" historic monuments.[2] Washington had used the Morris-Jumel home as his headquarters, had said farewell to his officers in Fraunces Tavern, and had worshiped at Saint Paul's on the day of his inauguration. Such scenes were indeed the stuff of dramatic tableaux or, later, of heart-stirring moments in MGM biopics. They'd have made fine subjects for the Municipal Art Society's public school murals. Humbler histories were still ignored.

New York saw its first great preservation battle in 1893, when the city tried to tear down City Hall to make room for a new municipal building. City Hall, as we have seen, only narrowly escaped, and two years later New York acquired its first organized preservation lobby, the American Scenic and Historic Preservation Society. It was founded by Andrew Haswell Green; its first, honorary president was J. P. Morgan; and for many years its secretary was Edward Hagaman Hall, the husband of Irene Hall, MAS's resident green thumb. Hall worked out of a tiny office on Nassau Street whose walls were hung with "dusty relics of the past—pictures of primitive mansions, facsimiles of historic parchments, national emblems, faded and tattered, aboriginal weapons, grinning skulls centuries old."[3]

In one sense the Preservation Society's program was very broad—it mixed conservation, archaeology, and historic preservation—but in another, very narrow. It was trying to preserve for future generations some sense of America as it was when the colonists and Founding Fathers still walked the earth. It fought to make public parks of those rare remnants of the revolutionary past: the Billopp House in Staten Island, Fraunces Tavern, the Morris-Jumel Mansion, Hamilton Grange, Castle Garden, Inwood Hill's virgin forest and Indian remains, the ruins of Fort Washington, and the old Hall of Records in City Hall Park.

The Preservation Society was one of MAS's allies and a regular partner in its coalitions; its membership was drawn from the same small circle of civic-minded reformers and artists—people like Charles Lamb, Robert De Forest, and George McAneny. There was a different emphasis at each group, however. The Preservation Society cared more about history and patriotism; MAS cared more about architecture and the cityscape. In 1902 the two groups actually went to battle against each other. MAS's civic center scheme—the gargantuan Post-Lindenthal-Hornbostel project—involved clearing City Hall Park of all buildings save City Hall. The Preservation Society objected, pleading for the preservation of the old Hall of Records.[4] It wasn't pretty, but it was sacred. Preservationists dubbed it the Martyrs' Prison in honor of the Revolutionaries who died there during the British occupation.* The Municipal Art Society was unmoved though, because the building was "an ugly and flimsy sham," as the *Times* put it, and because it stood in the way of MAS's dream of a splendid Beaux Arts civic center worthy of one of the great cities of the world.[5]

Yet at the same time MAS was involved in its own odd preservation project, one that received no help from the Historic Preservation Society. The Colonnade Hotel was slated for destruction, a casualty of speculation in the wake of subway construction. The hotel occupied about half of Lafayette Street's celebrated Colonnade Row, designed by A. J. Davis in 1831, a set of nine private houses linked by a superb Corinthian colonnade. In Davis's design the streetscape was more important than the individual house, and that was something close to MAS's heart. The society couldn't save the hotel, but Calvin Tomkins tried to raise enough money to at least buy the columns. He hoped to reerect them in Bryant Park, screening the

---

* Honoring victims of the British occupation was much in the air. There was an old monument to the "martyrs" in Trinity churchyard—a Gothic catafalque built in 1856—but since then Andersonville had made more vivid the miserable fate of prisoners of war. A campaign was already under way to build the Prison Ship Martyrs' Monument in Fort Greene Park, which McKim, Mead & White completed in 1908. Many of those working to save the old Hall of Records, like Mrs. Schuyler Van Rensselaer and Edward Hall, were MAS members.

hideous, noisy iron cage of the Sixth Avenue elevated line. The *Times*, however, was brutal in its opposition to the idea: "Let the dead past bury its dead."[6]

That attitude was widely shared in those days, yet at the same time Seth Low was implementing the city's first preservation program. He never admitted to having a preservation policy, but he tried to use the city's small parks program to save old landmarks. In 1903 the American Scenic and Historic Preservation Society begged him to purchase the Morris-Jumel Mansion and its grounds before the subway arrived in the neighborhood. That house posed a little dilemma for the city's reformers, though. It was built in 1765 by Roger Morris, a colleague of Washington in the Indian Wars, and Washington used it as his headquarters after the Battle of Long Island in 1776. All that was well and good, and so was the fact that Washington had once courted the future Mrs. Morris. The problem, as the *Times* put it in 1903, was that for generations the home had been "absurdly miscalled the 'Jumel Mansion,' " a name by which it was "much belittled." The paper's quarrel was not with Stephen Jumel—the wealthy merchant who remodeled the house in 1811, transforming it from a Colonial mansion to a very elegant Federal-style villa—but with his widow, née Betsy Brown. She'd started life as a poor seamstress. Her beauty, charms, and intelligence had provided her with a path to wealth of which the *Times* disapproved: she had been Jumel's mistress for a decade before becoming his wife. Furthermore, her second husband was Aaron Burr. Worse yet, she had glittered in Parisian society, and, though there's no corroborating evidence, she had boasted of an affair with Napoleon. This was not the sort of history that Seth Low, the *Times*, and the city's patriotic societies wished to remember. Their solution was simple, if not very elegant: the city bought Madame Jumel's house but effaced her memory. For years the place was known as the Morris Mansion, and the grounds are still called Roger Morris Park—though Morris's ghost might not recognize its home.[7]

While the history of the Morris-Jumel Mansion was being sanitized, preservationists were trying to rescue and prettify another landmark. Since Washington's farewell in 1783, Fraunces Tavern had been burned, rebuilt, extended, and converted into a tenement. It was so "alienated and 'soiled,' " as Montgomery Schuyler put it, that one could only guess at its original form, but authenticity was hardly the preservationists' goal. The American Scenic and Historic Preservation Society wanted the city to buy the entire block bounded by Coenties Slip and Broad, Pearl, and Water streets. The tavern would be "restored," and the rest of the block would be cleared of buildings and turned into a park. At first glance this park seems a peculiar and extravagant idea: the reconstructed tavern would have emerged looking like a grand manor house sitting in a garden. On the other hand, this greenery would have let preservationists tap into the $1 million a year small parks program. The adjoining businesses supported the plan. Comptroller Edward Grout was sympathetic but worried about the debt limit. The result was a tie vote on the Board of Estimate, and the measure failed. All was not lost, however: Grout promised to change his vote once the city's finances improved, and he suggested the preservationists try again next year. They did, but fruitlessly, and when Fusion was voted out of office the outlook for preservation grew very dim.[8]

Tammany could be just as sentimental as the reformers, but its familial ties were more likely to be with the Old World than the New. New York's Dutch or British history had little appeal, and even the American Revolution had less political value than the ongoing struggles that filled New York with political and economic refugees.* In such a climate Fraunces Tavern seemed doomed until Charles Lamb appealed to the Sons of the Revolution. Lamb himself was a member—General Frederick Stymetz was an ancestor and his brother's namesake—and in 1904 he persuaded his confreres to buy the tavern.[9] (They couldn't afford to purchase the rest of the block.) The architect William Mersereau restored the tavern. His work was, necessarily, rather imaginative. In 1907 the building was opened as a museum, and that same year the Daughters of the American Revolution opened a museum in the Morris-Jumel house.

In 1908 the Board of Estimate rejected a very modest preservation scheme. It would have cost a pittance to buy Poe Cottage—the rude farmhouse in the Bronx where Edgar Allan Poe wrote "The Bells," cared for his dying wife, and lived "in direst want"—and move it a few blocks to a safe location in Poe Park. The idea was broached by Edward Hagaman Hall, who promised that the American Scenic and Historic Preservation Society would install "rare daguerrotypes and other relics" so visitors would have "something more to see than the bare walls and roof which sheltered this man who lacked wanted bread but not an immortal name."[10] The city turned Hall away.

Private money was required to spark the restoration of City Hall, too. Fire had swept through the building in 1858, destroying its cupola and ruining much of the interior. The reconstruction wasn't very sensitive to Mangin and McComb's delicate, French-inflected Federal architecture. The rebuilt cupola was botched, for instance, when someone decided to include a clock in the design. In 1908 the city announced that it was going to redecorate the Governor's Room—really a suite of three reception rooms just above City Hall's front door. The *Times* demanded that the project receive "the close attention of the Art Commission, with the assistance of the Municipal Art Society. . . . If Aldermanic taste prevails, or Tammany architects are called in, we shall have a gorgeous and bizarre room in the old hall, instead of the buff walls and horsehair furniture of Architect McComb's era."[11] As if in answer, Mrs. Russell Sage stepped in with an offer to pay for a true restoration of the room, and she brought in her own architect, Grosvenor Atterbury. Some of Mangin's original drawings turned up at the New-York Historical Society; the McComb family unlocked its archive; and Atterbury filled in missing details as best he could by consulting McComb's own dog-eared annotated copy of Sir William

---

* *The reformers had trouble enough trying to stop people from renaming the city streets and thus effacing a little bit of New York's already tenuous memory. They managed to ward off attempts to rename the Bowery, so redolent of Peter Stuyvesant, but the new Kenmare Street, an extension of Delancey, grated on their nerves: its name commemorated Big Tim Sullivan's Irish birthplace.*

Chambers's *Treatise on the Decorative Part of Civil Architecture*, published in 1791. When the Governor's Room was finished, an MAS *Bulletin* records, "it was realized how beautiful the building must have been when first erected."[12]

A year later George McAneny, the new borough president, turned his eyes to the old Council Chamber. The noble domed hall had long ago been cut up into offices. McAneny tore them out and the architect William A. Boring restored the chamber as a committee room for the Board of Estimate. Tammany's return to power meant the end of city funds for restoring the building, but in 1918 Mrs. Sage and Atterbury returned to the scene and rebuilt the cupola. Atterbury went back to Mangin's original drawings and found a much more sensitive way to include a clock.

It may have been his work on City Hall that converted George McAneny into a preservationist. Then again, a number of his friends and allies at MAS and the City Club were active in the American Scenic and Historic Preservation Society. McAneny eventually became that group's president. As borough president he'd already begun putting its program into effect. He rescued Poe Cottage in 1913, and he began buying up Inwood Park, with its ancient forest and Indian remains. (When he commissioned a plan for the area from Arnold Brunner and Frederick Law Olmsted, Jr., they perversely recommended crowning Inwood Hill with monumental Beaux Arts buildings.) McAneny also played a role in the heroic struggle to save Saint John's Chapel, the city's most beautiful church.

SAINT JOHN'S Chapel was the masterpiece of John McComb, Jr., one of the designers of City Hall. It was built by Trinity parish in 1803, and it looked out over a four-acre park known as Hudson Square or Saint John's Park, which was bounded by Varick, Beach, Hudson, and Laight streets. All this land belonged to Trinity, part of the square mile or so of property that Queen Anne had granted the parish in 1705. For a time, Hudson Square was the jewel of Trinity's possessions. Fenced with iron and lined by brick row houses, with the great Georgian spire and portico of Saint John's commanding its axis, it looked like a genteel quarter of London. By the 1860s the area was no longer fashionable, however, and Trinity sold the park to Cornelius Vanderbilt in 1867. There he built the ghastly Hudson River Railroad Freight Depot, southern terminus of the Death Avenue line; it plunged the neighborhood deeper into a spiral of decline, and by 1895 the state of Trinity's tenements had become a full-fledged scandal—to think that all the High Church pomp of Trinity's services rested on a slumlord's fortune! Dr. Morgan Dix, the rector, defended the church by arguing that the death and illness rates in its tenements were no higher than those in other crowded quarters. Of course the death rate in an *average* tenement was appalling, but this did not trouble Dr. Dix, and the tenement reform movement took its inspiration from other pastors.

When the *Times* launched an investigation in 1908, it found that Trinity had made no improvements; instead, it had tried to conceal its ownership by listing lots in the names of lessors. By then the area was a mix of factories, stores, warehouses, and "old dwellings transformed into tenements, gorged with life. . . . To squalor are added dark halls and stairways, windowless interior bedrooms, sinks in back yards, and more dwellings in rear courts approached through narrow passages." Most of the residents of the area were native-born descendants of Irish and German families that had arrived two or three generations before, and had stayed in the neighborhood "because 'they have always lived there.' "[13] But alas, they were not Episcopalians, and it seems that no one explored the possibility of saving the church by transferring it to another denomination, even though there was no other church for a considerable distance—apparently Trinity didn't rent to the competition.

Saint John's Chapel looked much like Saint Paul's Chapel, which still survives on lower Broadway, but it was a finer building: its tower was taller and more elegantly proportioned, and its portico was far more suavely handled. Saint Paul's, however, had been built a little earlier—early enough for George Washington to have visited—and thus it belonged to the sacred past of the Founding Fathers. For this reason Trinity would never have torn down Saint Paul's, but in 1908 it announced that services would cease at Saint John's.

A campaign to save the chapel was launched by I. N. Phelps Stokes, who presented a petition "To the Rector, Church Wardens, and Vestrymen of Trinity Church":

> Gentlemen:
>
> The recent announcement of the Vestry that on February first next the work of Saint John's Chapel, Varick Street, will be abandoned, and the natural inference which follows, that the church building will be demolished, comes as a surprise and shock to the community, saddening the hearts of those who reverence the ancient monuments of our city, and believe in the uplifting power of venerable traditions and accumulated effort, and the refining and ennobling influence of dignified and beautiful architecture.
>
> Since the action was taken, many questions have been publicly raised as to the adequacy of the reasons for a step of such grave importance, affecting, more deeply perhaps than had been realized, the feelings of the community, and the civic pride in a building which, by common consent, ranks second only to Saint Paul's Chapel, among the very few remaining monuments of our past. These questions will, we doubt not, receive your further thoughtful consideration.
>
> In our country there exists no public tribunal charged with the care of our national monuments, and upon you, therefore, as sole trustee, devolves, in this case, a double responsibility, a responsibility which we believe you fully appreciate and will wisely discharge.[14]

The first signature on the petition was that of President Theodore Roosevelt; the second was Mayor McClellan's; and dangling below were the names of Seth Low, Robert Fulton Cutting, Elihu Root, Robert W. De Forest, John Bigelow, Joseph Choate, J. P. Morgan, William Dean Howells, Charles Follen McKim, George Post, Thomas Hastings, and many others. It was an impressive roster of first citizens, old family names, great fortunes, and the very pillars of Episcopalian culture in New York. Quite a number of signers were Municipalians. Phelps Stokes, it seems, was determined to bring his biggest guns to bear on the parish, but in doing so made a tactical mistake: the *Times* calculated that if these gentlemen felt so strongly about Saint John's, they could well afford to purchase it themselves. The clergy wasn't quite so blunt, but the rector of Grace Church did suggest that these were "the very men, by nature of their prominence," to lead a subscription drive to buy the chapel. Something similar had happened in Boston, he pointed out, when Old South Church was purchased, "after much tribulation, by the united efforts of all Boston." South Church was now a monument, museum, and lecture hall, and that might have been the happy fate of Saint John's as well, but the *Times* didn't exactly assist in forging a united effort. "Any expression of public sentiment against the removal of stately or comely landmarks with historical allusions is wholesome," wrote the editors, but the sentiment behind this particular campaign seemed "elusive." "It is *just* a century old," they wrote of Saint John's, and though a structure of "some" distinction, "it stands in an unlovely neighborhood where it is no longer needed."[15]

Phelps Stokes's petition seemed to bear fruit, however. Trinity agreed to continue services for the moment and the parish promised that it had no immediate plans to destroy the chapel. Trinity wasn't acting out of a sense of altruism; rather, the parish realized that the chapel's fate was tied to the subway. Building the Dual System subway forced the city to extend Seventh Avenue southward from Eleventh Street to Carmine Street and to widen Varick Street, just as MAS had long demanded. The neighborhood's pre-law tenements would come tumbling down, Varick Street would become a major thoroughfare—a perfect location for big new lofts—and if Trinity were patient, it would be able to sell off its embarrassing little slum at a hefty profit. There was another, political advantage in waiting: the chapel's portico stood in the bulldozers' path, and Trinity was perfectly happy to let the city take the blame for destroying Saint John's.[16]

In 1913, when people realized what was afoot, there was a great uproar. Phelps Stokes protested, and the Municipal Art Society organized a committee, chaired by architect Harry Alan Jacobs, to back him up. Even Nelson Lewis, chief engineer to the Board of Estimate and no sentimentalist, was shocked by the parish's failure to make "some effort" to preserve "one of the most artistic buildings in the city." A Trinity spokesman was forced to admit "the rare beauty of the building," but "Who will see it?" he asked. "The crowds who fill the downtown streets," Annie Gould answered in a letter to the *Times*—and all the families who filled Trinity's tenements, she might have added. The chapel's neighbors "have eyes and brains," Gould wrote, "and an object of beauty does make an impression and help develop some genius, besides giving wholesome pleasure to the less gifted. The acoustics of Saint John's are very good. It would make a capital People's Forum and social center. Our democracy needs such civic temples scattered throughout the town, emphasizing the dignity and worth of good citizenship. Lectures, music, voting, social reunions, free speech allowed—would not this justify the city in buying the Chapel?"[17]

A La Guardia might have taken up Annie Gould's challenge, but twenty years and a political revolution would have to pass before the city started thinking along such lines. Phelps Stokes spoke of raising money to buy the chapel from Trinity, but as a first step he had to rescue it from the city's wrecking crew. He drew a plan showing that it was still possible to save the chapel. There would be a bulge in Varick Street's new curb line, but no great harm would be done if the parking lane disappeared here and if the new sidewalk passed through the chapel's portico. He brought his plan to George McAneny, now the borough president and the man responsible for widening Varick Street. McAneny had already disfigured many a landmark with his street widenings (at least *today* we consider them landmarks), but he agreed to let Saint John's remain where it stood, the building line be damned. The Municipal Art Society breathed a sigh of relief, but a new problem arose when engineers warned that the chapel's foundations would give way as the subway was excavated. Trinity wouldn't spend a dime to shore them up, nor would the contractor, so McAneny agreed that the city would put up the money.[18]

That should have been enough to secure the future of Saint John's—except that Trinity was determined to do away with the building. In 1916, McAneny left politics, and two years later Tammany returned to City Hall. The Great War was on, and the defenders of Saint John's Chapel were distracted or far away: McAneny was in the army, and Phelps Stokes was working for the Housing Department of the U.S. Shipping Board—so feverishly that he collapsed of exhaustion. It was then, in 1918, that Saint John's met its fate. Four years earlier, McAneny had promised that the city wouldn't demolish the chapel, but now, as the last step in Varick Street's reconstruction, Tammany did just that. In effect, the city agreed to take the fall for Trinity. Why it did so remains a mystery.

WHILE BATTLING to save Saint John's, I. N. Phelps Stokes did succeed in rescuing two other landmarks—indeed the expense involved may have hampered his efforts to buy the chapel. One was actually British: High-Low House, a half-timbered Tudor mansion near Ipswich, England. Phelps Stokes was already building himself a house—he owned 175 acres in Greenwich, Connecticut, landscaped by Frederick Law Olmsted, Jr.—but, in 1910, after reading that High-Low House was going to be torn down, he decided to roll up his plans, buy the old house, and ship it across the Atlantic. Another emergency beckoned in 1916: the old Assay Office on Wall Street, built in 1823 by Martin Thompson as a branch of the ill-fated Bank of the United States, was about to disappear.[19] It had a very beautiful facade, which Phelps Stokes bought from the Treasury Department, meaning to rebuild it as part of the Grolier Club's new home, but that project fell through. "With the connivance" of Robert De Forest, president of the Metropolitan Museum, Phelps Stokes stored the dismantled stones on a vacant lot belonging to the museum.[20] The Assay Office was finally reerected as the south facade of De Forest's American Wing in 1923. Today it stands in an unworthy glass-roofed courtyard.

Phelps Stokes's greatest contribution to the preservation movement was, however, a literary effort. In 1908, when the doomed campaign to save Saint John's Chapel had just begun, the city was already gearing up for the next year's Hudson-Fulton celebration. The festival's organizers, many of them Municipalians, prayed that it would awaken New York's interest in its own history, and they seem to have succeeded beyond their wildest dreams: the Metropolitan Museum mounted its first exhibit of early American painting and decorative art, an event that drew throngs of visitors and inspired Robert De Forest to found the museum's American Wing; shops and department stores took Old New York as their marketing theme, and it seemed that every shop window was full of old prints of New York, stripped from dusty parlor walls or salvaged from attics. Phelps Stokes already had a "desultory" interest in such local artifacts, but faced with this sudden embarrassment of riches he "rushed from dealer to dealer, and spent every spare moment delving through portfolios and drawers of old stock." Inspired by what he found, he decided to write "a book on the history of New York prints."

It was called *The Iconography of Manhattan Island*, but it is an injustice to describe this work as a "history of prints." Prints served as his window on the physical history of New York. His images captured a moment in time, but his erudite notes traced the history of the particular site before and after that moment. His research carried him all the way back to the earliest newspapers published in New York in the 1700s, and the book grew larger and larger as Phelps Stokes's passion for his subject took hold. In 1915 one volume was ready, and he planned to finish in three more. In the end he filled six hefty volumes, the last not issued until 1928. Only a few hundred copies were printed, and they were treasured by libraries and museums; some years ago a reprint was issued, but again in such limited quantities that it qualifies as a rarity in its own right.[21]

By the time Phelps Stokes finished *The Iconography* the past had engulfed his interior life. He dreamed, by day and night, only of old New York. "I usually start from some point in the modern city," he wrote, "and on my way—perhaps to keep an appointment at some other well-known point—I am tempted to try a short-cut." Invariably it led him into the past.

I wander over the hills and valleys, and often through virgin forests, and sometimes come out on the shore of the Hudson or the East River where I recognize the topography from the old maps, and take great pleasure in searching for landmarks which I know exist—or at least existed at the time pictured in my dream. Sometimes I find them, and am thrilled by the discovery, but curiously they are almost never inhabited. Although the streets are sometimes populated, I generally pass unnoticed—apparently unseen!

My last dream . . . occurred only a few nights ago. I went to see Jack Morgan at our old house on Madison Avenue and Thirty-seventh Street. He received me in the scarlet uniform of a general of Revolutionary times. We went together to my old rooms in the rear of the house on the third floor, and from the windows looked over the wooded parklands to Kipp's Bay, where a number of British warships lay at anchor in the sun.[22]

There was a note of sadness in all this. At the end of his life Phelps Stokes concluded that *The Iconography* "interfered, more than a little, with my professional career, as well as making sad inroads upon my 'fortune.' ... I now realize that it involved an expenditure of time, energy, and money, which was probably out of proportion to the results achieved, and consumed many hours which should have been devoted, not only to my office, but to my family, and to social amenities, so that, on the whole, I suspect that it has proved a rather selfish, perhaps even a narrowing, influence on my life."[23] Later preservationists would disagree.

AFTER 1910 the *Times* began reporting the steady disappearance of old land-marks as the business district crept northward. In 1911, for instance, it described the loss of the Lenox house on Fifth Avenue and Twelfth Street, the Schermerhorn mansion on Twenty-third Street, the Cyrus Field house on Gramercy Park, and the Van Buren house on Fourteenth Street.[24] Its tone was typically one of bittersweet nostalgia, as if to say that these losses were as sad, but every bit as inevitable, as the onset of old age.

At the Municipal Art Society these casualties were still barely noticed. The artists of the American Renaissance honored the fine Classical traditions of Colonial and Federal buildings. Indeed they pored over their details, and as the Beaux Arts Baroque came to seem vulgar or dated, more and more architects specialized in these styles. They became true connoisseurs, searching out old buildings, measuring them, and publishing detailed drawings as models for designers. The Greek Revival was much less popular—the Beaux Arts architects favored Latin precedents. American architecture since the 1850s was simply dismissed as an artistic wasteland. The eclecticism of post–Civil War architecture—the crude Italianate, the brittle Gothic, the gloomy Romanesque, and the turbid brownstone—seemed provincial and barely literate. Few Beaux Artists complained when the eclectic landmarks of Midtown or lower Manhattan disappeared, but even above Fifty-ninth Street, Fifth Avenue was being transformed, and here a newer strata of Beaux Arts monuments was endangered. Though no one tried to save the old Lenox house in 1911, that year saw the doomed attempt to save Richard Morris Hunt's Lenox Library, not because it was historic (it was only thirty years old), but because it was beautiful. And when 1911 brought news that McKim, Mead & White were designing an apartment building at 998 Fifth Avenue, on the corner of Eighty-first Street, the *Times* erupted in outrage. This skyscraper, however handsome, was "another instance of the persistent defiance of all plan and purpose in building up Manhattan ... an act of deliberate incivicism, and as such honestly to be condemned. Without confessing to any worship of wealth," the *Times* maintained that Fifth Avenue, "one of our treasured sights ... might well be preserved for one distinctive purpose."[25]

Nothing could be done for Fifth Avenue while the city still lacked even a zoning code, but one of the ironies of the 1916 Zoning Resolution was that it actually *encouraged* the demolition of Fifth Avenue's mansions. It was framed as an effort to ensure that people had light and air in their private quarters, and since there was plenty of light and air in the parks, the zoning code let people build especially tall buildings overlooking them. By the end of World War I, MAS and the Fifth Avenue Association realized that a building boom was in store for Fifth Avenue. They joined together to demand a new zoning district on Central Park's eastern edge, with a strict, seventy-five-foot height limit. MAS said it was trying to protect the park rather than Fifth Avenue—to save the "umbrageous" skyline that Olmsted intended—and that was an honorable goal, but scarcely a credible explanation of the Municipal Art Society's motives. For the measure would have affected only Fifth Avenue—not Central Park West, North, or South. It was really meant to preserve the Fifth Avenue mansions by making the construction of apartment buildings less profitable. Given the astronomical cost of land on Fifth Avenue, the seventy-five-foot height limit might, in fact, have succeeded in banning them.

The Board of Estimate refused to act on this measure, however, and through the 1920s Municipalians watched with horror as the great monuments of their past came tumbling down. In their youth, when the Lambs, Blashfield, Cox, and the younger Hunts had set out to make an American Renaissance, they fully expected it to last as long as its Italian namesake. But by the end of their lives they were confronted by an uncomfortable fact: the rest of the world regarded their work as just another fashion whose time had passed. Charles Lamb had been in his early thirties when the original Waldorf-Astoria was built, and at that time, the hotel had seemed a triumph of all that was new and beautiful and hopeful in American life: a miracle of technology, social organization, and art. Its architect was Henry Hardenbergh, one of MAS's founders; its murals by Edwin Blashfield and Kenyon Cox represented the idealistic collaboration of artists that had led them to found the Municipal Art Society in the first place. Lamb was nearly seventy when the hotel was torn down, and aside from his own sad letter to the newspapers, its passing was hardly mourned.[26] Its turrets and domes struck a younger generation as fussy and gloomy; its ballrooms and corridors spoke of ladies in bustles, not of flappers; its allegorical murals provoked giggles.

Farther up Fifth Avenue, mansions gave way to apartment buildings as MAS watched helpless. One couldn't prevent the rich from moving to apartments, from fleeing to Greenwich, from dissipating their fortunes, or from selling off their fabled châteaux. In 1925 Richard Howland Hunt, MAS's president, begged the city to preserve his father's finest house, built for William K. Vanderbilt at 660 Fifth Avenue, as a museum.[27] No one listened. The younger Hunt was hampered, no doubt, by the fact that the Vanderbilts were still around, still immensely rich, and still deeply and deservedly unpopular. They didn't offer to give the house to the city, and it's hard to imagine an elected official paying millions for a permanent shrine to the authors of Death Avenue—not in 1925, when the trains were still claiming victims. All MAS could do was fall back on nostalgia. When the Cornelius

Vanderbilt II house on the Plaza was demolished, Charles Lamb wrote to the papers once again.[28] When the house was finished, he remembered, Vanderbilt had invited the city's artists to come see how well their peers—Post, Hunt, La Farge, Saint-Gaudens, and Bitter—had done at conceiving a house as a work of art. Now, alas, the same house was treated as a curiosity, or as so much junk. It was thrown open one last time as a benefit for the Charity Organization Society, and tens of thousands of New Yorkers wandered through it, agape at the sheer excess of it all. Before the demolition crew arrived, the Metropolitan Museum laid claim to a Saint-Gaudens fireplace and a La Farge lunette, and the iron gates eventually found their way to the Conservatory Gardens in Central Park. But taste had followed the trickle-down theory, and the more exotic elements of the Vanderbilt houses now appealed, not to museum curators, but to the movie mogul Marcus Loew. The immense "Moorish" chandelier from One West Fifty-seventh Street found a home in the Loew's State Theater in Syracuse; a Moorish room was shipped from 660 Fifth Avenue to the Midland Theater in Kansas City; and the Vanderbilts' furniture was scattered across the country to the farthest reaches of Marcus Loew's empire.[29]

THROUGH ALL these years New York's landmarks had been the victims of progress, an enemy as implacable as it was abstract. Fighting it was like setting oneself against a law of nature or, worse yet, like questioning the American dream. One can't overthrow the laws of nature, only suspend them here and there. One can put an endangered animal in a zoo and transform it from a wild animal into a pampered specimen, and similarly one could save a few old buildings. The city or private groups could turn them into museums, install furniture, set up wax figures in period dress, and dress docents in old costumes. By the 1910s, when the Americanization movement was in full flood, New Yorkers had gotten rather good at this, as patriotic societies and wealthy old families devoted themselves to rescuing the past. They themselves took on the expense and later transferred their work to the city. In 1915, for example, the Dyckman House on Upper Broadway, the last Dutch farmhouse left in Manhattan, was saved by members of the Dyckman family. They restored it, furnished it, and gave it to the city. In 1919 the American Scenic and Historic Preservation Society bought the site of Fort Washington—MAS helped it raise the money—and Jane Taylor restored the Abigail Adams Smith House on East Sixty-first Street, which the Colonial Dames opened to the public in 1924. That same year George Baker, Sr., and J. P. Morgan, Jr., bought the Grange, Alexander Hamilton's villa on Convent Avenue, for the American Scenic and Historic Preservation Society. Staten Island's Billopp House, where Benjamin Franklin and John Adams tried to negotiate peace with Lord Howe, was finally restored in 1926 by the Conference House Association, and Staten Island was soon the scene of the most ambitious preservation program in the city. The Richmond-town Restoration began in 1933, when the Staten Island Historical Society restored the old county courthouse; over the years more and more of the village's buildings were restored, and others were trucked in from other sites.

Up through the 1930s, preservation meant condemning historic buildings to the eerie half-life of a house museum. There was never money for more than a few such establishments, nor was there much demand for them. And there was no hint of another strategy for saving landmarks, no suggestion that the city interfere with property rights to save historic buildings. But the rampages of Robert Moses set people thinking about the city's history and the beauty of its old neighborhoods.

THE LANDMARKS LAW

WHILE MCANENY BATTLED Moses to save the ruins of Castle Clinton, MAS realized that there must be a way to stop such situations from occurring again. In 1941 Ely Jacques Kahn formed a committee to work for the preservation of "New York's remaining historic buildings, as well as areas" still graced by the "architectural charm of the past."[1] Kahn worked with two Columbia professors, Carl Feiss and Talbot Hamlin, and with Gardner Osborn, curator of the Federal Museum in the Subtreasury Building and secretary of the group fighting Moses's Battery bridge. Feiss soon left New York, and Hamlin pleaded that he was too ill to join MAS's board, though he agreed to help "unofficially." Two things came of this committee. The Battery tunnel approach obliterated the Syrian Quarter, a cluster of old houses between State and Washington streets. Many dated back to 1800–1830 when the neighborhood was a fashionable residential quarter. They were fine Federal-style buildings, and Gardner Osborn arranged to have them documented before they disappeared. Photographs were taken of the houses, and researchers compiled family histories of their occupants up to the year 1830. No one asked the Syrians for their tales.[2] Osborn's research was donated to the Library of Congress.

Hamlin's contribution was to draw up a list of New York buildings worth saving. The most recent buildings dated from 1860. Maybe he meant to ensure that the buildings were indisputably historic, but more likely this was a reflection of Hamlin's own aesthetic and social biases. For him the Greek Revival was "the last moral American style," destroyed, like the Jeffersonian culture it represented, by the industrialization of America that followed on the heels of the Civil War.[3] Hamlin's selection crystallized a philosophy of preservation that ruled MAS's thought for the next three decades. It marked the birth of the "masterpiece theory," in which the finest works of each age and style—"a few gems," as one Municipalian later put it—would be saved for posterity. *Just* the gems, though: the notion of preserving entire neighborhoods, so central to the preservation movement's eventual success, wasn't yet part of MAS's program.

The masterpiece theory was seemingly made for connoisseurs, and it was in developing such a class of specialists that Hamlin made his great contribution to the preservation movement, for he transformed the study of American architecture into a discipline that was both respectable and interesting. Historians had long dismissed American architecture as the crude parroting of European styles. Seen in that light, the field wasn't a very rewarding one: a historian would spend his life enumerating the "mistakes" of rude craftsmen. Hamlin set out a far more seductive thesis: that in America, the old styles were often stamped with a creativity and a naive genius missing in hidebound Europe. This theme was sounded most vividly in Hamlin's *Greek Revival Architecture in America*, the first masterpiece of American architectural history, and also in his biography of Benjamin Henry Latrobe, which won a Pulitzer Prize.[4] Moreover, Hamlin became a mentor for a generation of young historians—people like Wayne Andrews, W. Knight Sturges, and Alan Burnham. One result of this newfound interest in American architecture was the founding of the Society of Architectural Historians in 1946, a group that soon joined MAS in the battle for a preservation law.

WHEN THE Second World War ended, New York was the "town of all towns," Jan Morris writes in *Manhattan '45*, "the supreme and symbolical American city. All the signs were that it would be the supreme city of the Western world, or even the world as a whole. . . . Everywhere, emblazoned across the city by its unrivaled advertising industry, were the signs of boom times coming." That year, the Gallup Poll reported that 90 percent of New Yorkers considered themselves "happy."[5] But if the population was cheery, the city itself didn't look it. Little had been built since 1930. There was hardly a building in the city that wasn't at least fifteen years out of fashion. Few had been well maintained; fewer still had been cleaned.

The old reform movement was looking shabby as well. La Guardia left office in 1946, an exhausted man soon to die of cancer. The Fusion movement produced no worthy successor. La Guardia had never minded railing against enemies, but he'd been far too domineering to tolerate partners or rivals in the Fusion movement. On the loftiest of grounds he'd withheld patronage from the Fusion Party, blighting that shaky organization before it had a chance to grow corrupt, and he'd sabotaged his allies either by lending them no support in their races for higher office or by damning them with faint praise. Tammany Hall had suffered too. Starved of patronage by both La Guardia and Roosevelt, Manhattan's Democrats couldn't even keep up with the mortgage payments on their Union Square clubhouse, and they lost the building in 1945. Other machines were waiting in the wings, however. Roosevelt had funneled Washington's largesse through the Bronx and Brooklyn, and even without his help, the fortunes of outer-borough clubhouses were on the rise as the population shifted away from Manhattan.

The Democrats produced Mayor William O'Dwyer in 1946. Born in Ireland and graced with a brogue, O'Dwyer had been a cop, a judge, and the Brooklyn district attorney. He was famous for his investigation of Murder, Inc., and for the present that served to cloak his own ties to the underworld. During the campaign, O'Dwyer took pains to assure the public that electing a Democrat didn't mean reopening the floodgates of corruption, and since no public servant had a higher reputation for honesty than Robert Moses—and he was, as one discriminating politico told Robert Caro, "*money* honest"[6]—O'Dwyer promised to keep Moses in office. In return, Moses endorsed O'Dwyer. He saw in O'Dwyer's victory the opportunity to vastly increase his own powers. Already in control of the Parks Department and the Triborough Authority, and still a member of the City Planning Commission, Moses persuaded O'Dwyer to appoint him to the Housing Authority, to name him chairman of the Mayor's Slum Clearance Committee, and to make him nothing less than the city's "construction coordinator."

Moses had now succeeded in concentrating a vast amount of discretionary power in his own hands—more, perhaps, than any Tammany ringleader had ever enjoyed. He had control of Triborough's coffers, and thus of a far larger construction budget than the mayor himself. He had a planning staff far, far larger than that of the City Planning Commission, and he could set it to work on any project he wished. He had behind him a coalition of bankers, insurers, and labor unions whose income depended on a steady flow of massive construction projects. All of this meant that Moses, not the mayor, shaped the city after the war, and that Moses's agenda prevailed. Highways were built; schools weren't. The subways were milked for money. It cost the city about six cents per passenger to run the subways in those days. Moses persuaded O'Dwyer to raise the fare from a nickel to a dime. This made them "self-sustaining," so the city could float bonds on subway fares. Calvin Tomkins had wanted to capitalize subway revenues in 1909—with a crucial difference: Tomkins meant to use the money to build more subways, but now the funds were siphoned away. The fare was raised, as Stanley Isaacs wrote, "so the city can borrow more money, which will be invested in highways, parkways, etc., . . . for which the motorist will not be asked to contribute a nickel. Why the motorist should be given a free ride and the straphanger asked to pay the full capital cost of the subway investment certainly cannot be explained decently."[7] Despite the fact that the city now made a profit on every token, by 1956 it was cutting back on routine maintenance. The subways had begun a twenty-year period of decline, and if the new highways gave the middle class the means to escape the city, the steady deterioration of the subways gave them a reason.

The fact that Moses held so many jobs subverted the whole system of checks and balances that reformers had built into New York's government over the years. Nor did he just control the city's construction programs. As head of the Slum Clearance Committee, Moses was in charge of implementing the federal government's urban renewal program, known as Title I. Title I was the sort of ingenious scheme that would have made Charles Lamb or Calvin Tomkins envious. The idea was to build new housing in the crowded inner-city slums where it was most needed. The stumbling block to construction of this sort had always been the high cost of land. Under Title I, however, the federal government paid two-thirds of the city's condemnation costs, and then the city turned the land over, at its discounted price, to private developers for reconstruction.

In effect, Title I put the city's awesome power of condemnation at the service of private interests, the projects' "sponsors." Of course there were federal controls on the budgets involved, on the standard of living accommodations, and so forth, but many of the normal local controls didn't apply. There were also questions of social justice, architectural quality, and planning. Private landlords, unlike the Housing Authority, were still free to discriminate on the basis of race, and the Title I program spurred Stanley Isaacs's heroic campaign to ban racial discrimination, first in subsidized housing and then in all housing. MAS mailed off a resolution in support of Isaacs's campaign, but, as always, the society concentrated on the physical issues. Seeing these dreary brick barracks rise across the city, Albert Bard tried to have the Art Commission's jurisdiction extended to include "private properties of public or quasi-public nature." If the city subsidized a project, used eminent domain to claim the land, granted it a tax exemption or a zoning variance, then, Bard argued, "the city becomes in a sense a partner in the project and may properly have some control of the exterior design in which the public has an interest."[8]

Bard's colleagues no longer placed much hope in the Art Commission, however; they were more worried about the City Planning Commission. But it was Moses's Slum Clearance Committee, not the CPC, that decided where to put renewal projects; lacking a master plan of its own, the planning commission merely rubber-stamped what was set before it. Even before Title I went into effect it was clear that the CPC had neither the staff nor the independence to do its job. MAS came back to life in 1946, resurrected by the architect Charles A. Platt (no relation to Charles C. Platt, the noted country house architect, or to his descendants Geoffrey and Charles Platt, who figure later in MAS's history). Platt decided that the solution was to create an official Advisory Commission for the City Planning Commission. Of course it wouldn't just advise; it would also provide the CPC with its own organized constituency, ready to fight for the commission's prerogatives. In 1946 Edwin Salmon, the CPC's chairman, welcomed the idea, and Manhattan Borough President Rogers went so far as to accept MAS's slate of candidates. But Salmon was one of Moses's cronies and, despite his pleasantries, saw to it that nothing happened. Platt realized that MAS needed to shift its tactics: reform would have to spring from the grass roots rather than from the head of the planning commission. He noted "the ever increasing tendency displayed by civic groups, notably the Citizens Union . . . to divide the city up into small sections in an endeavor to get citizen interest in community planning."[9] Realizing that its only hope was to bring political pressure to bear, the Citizens Union, the Regional Plan Association, and MAS's Civic Design Committee called a meeting of twenty-five civic and neighborhood groups in late 1946. The meeting was "stimulated by the Municipal Art Society but not sponsored by it," according to MAS's records, and it led to the birth of the Citizens' Conference on City Planning. McKim Norton took charge of this group and found some money to finance it.

In the meantime, Albert Bard was working with the Citizens Union on two ideas for charter revision. The first would have required the borough presidents to set up community planning councils so that neighborhood residents could advise the City Planning Commission on matters affecting them. The second required the planning commission to "prepare plans for the harmonious and integrated development of a community or neighborhood; and providing wherever possible for the preservation of historic and aesthetic features of the neighborhood."[10] This last idea was still a hopeless cause—there was no constitutional foundation for the CPC to take aesthetics into account—but the civic groups did make some headway in giving a voice to the communities. When Robert Wagner, Jr., became chairman of the planning commission in 1948 he was enthusiastic about MAS's efforts on behalf of community planning,[11] and that same year there was a "Better Communities for New York City" conference, an all-day affair at the Roosevelt Hotel, at which Henry Bruere (then head of the Bowery Savings Bank) gave advice on how to deal with the CPC and Stanley Isaacs spoke on "How Can We Fit the Big City to the Citizen?"[12]

All this talk and agitation seemed futile until 1950, when two things happened. First, Robert F. Wagner became Manhattan's borough president, and he set up his own unofficial community boards. Cynics suggested that they were just a way for Wagner to broaden his political base, and there was a good deal of truth in that, but an important precedent had been set.

Also in 1950, and over Moses's objections, Mayor O'Dwyer installed his campaign manager, Jerry Finkelstein, as chairman of the City Planning Commission. Finkelstein was an ambitious young man. On the advice of the Citizens Union, he set about reviving the long-dormant project to draw a master plan for the city. He didn't have much trouble building a case for the idea. He could point to the school system—to the overcrowded classrooms in new neighborhoods, packed tight with kids because no one had planned for a shifting population—and to the utter confusion reigning in the city's bureaucracy. He identified a site where one city agency was planning to build a sewage treatment plant, a second was planning a library, and a third was designing a school.[13] Finkelstein asked the Board of Estimate to more than triple his budget, and the old reformers gathered together to back up his request: C. C. Burlingham, Nathan Straus, Stanley Isaacs, Henry Bruère, and George McAneny formed the Committee for an Adequate City Plan. The *Times* joined in: "The noble purpose set forth in the Charter of 1938 . . . has never been realized," the paper wrote. "We support without reservation the principle involved."[14] Finkelstein got his appropriation. Zoning was thrown open to discussion—as it should have been in 1917—and the City Planning Commission began work on Stanley Isaacs's old scheme to divide the city into "arrondissements," giving each neighborhood a voice on local improvements. It seemed that reason might finally prevail.

The Municipal Art Society was in favor of all this, but there was already such a broad consensus on this agenda that the society felt free to concentrate on another issue: it wanted the City Planning Commission to downzone the streets around

New York's parks. It wanted to protect the parks' scale and their sunlight, but mixed up in this there was also a preservation issue: MAS wanted to discourage builders from setting their eyes on Washington Square North and its handsome Greek Revival row houses, artifacts of the old New York glorified by Henry James.[15] Some were owned by Sailors' Snug Harbor, and in 1939 MAS had persuaded the harbor not to demolish them. The architect Harvey Wiley Corbett, an MAS board member, converted the houses into apartments; tragically, most of the interiors were lost in the process, but at least the facades, the scale, and the rhythm of the street were left untouched. Washington Square was still in danger, though: Moses still dreamed of a traffic artery through the park, and he was scheming with New York University to "renew" the blocks south of the square; but what worried MAS most was Washington Square North.

While MAS was talking to the City Planning Commission, the news broke that a towering apartment house would replace the old Rhinelander houses at the west corner of Fifth Avenue and Washington Square North. This was exactly what MAS had feared. Samuel Rudin was the developer, and his architect was Richard Roth, the untalented son of the great Emory Roth, designer of the twin-towered San Remo and El Dorado apartment buildings on Central Park West. Shaped by the 1916 Zoning Code, the new building at 2 Fifth Avenue would be a massive setback structure of gray brick. Horrified Villagers formed the Committee to Save the Rhinelander Houses and called on the city to buy and preserve the old houses. Albert Bard wanted MAS to tap into this outrage. Here at last, he thought, was the opportunity to launch a popular crusade for preservation.

MAS would have been delighted to see Bard and this committee succeed, but that possibility seemed so unlikely that the society pressed a very different course. Rudin's building was perfectly legal, but the City Planning Commission was appalled by its scale and, as Harvey Wiley Corbett put it, "Of its own volition, without fanfare or publicity, arranged for a meeting of a few men representing both sides to sit down and talk the matter over." Corbett was one of them. He helped work out a compromise in which the building's bulk was redistributed. Now a low wing on the south would hew to the cornice line of Washington Square, while the mass of the building was concentrated in a tower behind it, away from the park. At this point the planning commission, having stretched its zoning powers as far as they could go, gave its blessing to the scheme. Corbett, however, tried to go further. While helping Roth rework his apartment plans, he kept pressing for a solution that would be sympathetic not just to the scale of Washington Square but to its architectural character as well. He came away from one meeting with high praise for Roth: "No architect could make a more serious and conscientious effort to preserve the north side of the Square," he told his colleagues at the Municipal Art Society. "The cornice line and other details, including small entrances of Colonial design, conform to the existing building." Roth's intentions were better than his client's, however, and the Committee to Save the Rhinelander Houses soon told MAS that the design had been changed. The new building's cornice no longer quite aligned with those of its neighbors, the small entrances were gone, and balconies had appeared. When MAS learned this, it suddenly reversed course and called on the city to purchase the Rhinelander houses. Use them for some public purpose, MAS said, or transfer them to the National Trust for Historic Preservation.[16] That didn't happen.

Two Fifth Avenue might easily have been a better building, but even in its compromised form it remained a kind of triumph for the Municipal Art Society, for Finkelstein, for the planning commission, and even for Sam Rudin, who was spared the odium of having *utterly* ruined Washington Square. MAS waited expectantly for the planning commission to apply this lesson to the new zoning code, but that was not to be. While Corbett was meeting with Roth, and while Finkelstein's planners were drafting their new code, teams of investigators were probing Mayor O'Dwyer. There were hints of payoffs by the Firemen's Association, of cash contributions from bookmakers, of bribery in the top ranks of the police department, and of ties to the gangster Frank Costello. O'Dwyer began looking for ways to escape the spotlight, and in August 1950, just eight months into his second term, he accepted an appointment as ambassador to Mexico. It seemed a strange career move at the time; not until 1951, when O'Dwyer nervously testified before the Kefauver Commission, did the public understand his reasons.

When a mayor retires, he is succeeded by the City Council president until a special election can be arranged. In 1950 the council president was an especially obscure figure. Five years before, when the Democratic leaders had decided to nominate an Irish mayor from Brooklyn and a Jewish comptroller from the Bronx, they realized the ideal City Council president would be an Italian from Manhattan. They couldn't think of a sufficiently trustworthy specimen, however, until someone pointed out that the legal secretaries of state supreme court judges were very well paid, and that such jobs were handed out only to the safest sort of clubhouse crony. Pulling out a city directory, they came upon the name of Vincent R. Impellitteri, secretary to a certain Judge Schmuck. Assured by his district leader that Impellitteri was a loyal fellow, the Democrats conferred on him the second most powerful elected office in the city.[17]

As City Council president, Impellitteri had faithfully executed O'Dwyer's orders, but now, unfortunately, he was mayor: a sweet, kindly, dim-witted fellow with almost no knowledge of how to govern a city. His position was precarious. A windfall had descended on him, but in three months' time there would be a special election, and Impellitteri was barely known to the public. He had to develop a track record of instant achievements, but he had no time to do anything, only to take credit for projects long in the making and now coming to fruition. His political survival depended entirely, in other words, on Robert Moses. And Moses took up Impellitteri's cause, providing the acting mayor with all the photo opportunities and ribbon cuttings he needed, praising his hard work and "courage," and offering his hearty endorsement. Of course Moses would exact a price for his support, and when Impellitteri was elected mayor in November 1950, Robert Moses became, in effect, his grand vizier.

Part of Moses's bargain with Impellitteri was that Finkelstein would have to go. Moses had been enraged when Finkelstein's planning commission started showing signs of independence, and his anger had reached a peak early in 1950, when the Triborough Authority unveiled plans for a Mid-Manhattan Elevated Expressway. The scheme was an urbanist's nightmare. A 160-foot-wide highway over Thirtieth Street, it would have been a wall of overpasses, access ramps, noise, and shadow slicing Manhattan in two. Local businesses and Borough President Robert Wagner begged the city to build a tunnel instead of an El, and they insisted that the planning commission examine this option before acting on Moses's plans. Finkelstein agreed with them. Mayor O'Dwyer had temporized: with one hand, he gave Finkelstein permission to launch a study of the tunnel; with the other, he vetoed the essential appropriation. This mere breath of opposition so piqued Moses that he canceled the expressway project just three weeks after it was first announced.

The cancellation exposed Mayor O'Dwyer's impotence, annoyed the construction unions, and convinced some newspapers that the City Planning Commission stood in the way of progress. O'Dwyer was reportedly furious with Finkelstein, but let him keep his job. Impellitteri fired him as soon as he took office. Over the strenuous objections of MAS and the other civic groups, Finkelstein was replaced by Colonel John Bennett, a former state attorney general who, thanks to Moses, soon became the sponsor of a lucrative Title I urban renewal project. The master plan and zoning studies were shelved again; the public hearings were canceled; the planning staff was dispersed. The window of opportunity was shut tight.

WITH THE City Planning Commission back in the clutches of Robert Moses, MAS turned its full attention to preservation. Unable to shape the new city in any positive way, the members decided that they might at least save the best bits of the old. The loss of the Rhinelander houses had piqued their interest again, and they were shocked when Warren & Wetmore's Ritz-Carlton Hotel was torn down in 1950. In 1951, Edward Steese revived MAS's Committee on Historic Architecture. An architect and "a fiery, touchy character," Steese dusted off Talbot Hamlin's ten-year-old list of aesthetic structures.[18] MAS and the Society of Architectural Historians formed an alliance to update and extend this list from Hamlin's cutoff date of 1860 to 1918, and later to 1930. Municipalians were sent out to "inspect, photograph, and so far as possible to supply accurate documentation on each of these structures." A book was planned, and MAS meant to place a medallion on each of its honored structures. The society went about its work at a sleepy pace, only to be rudely awakened in 1955, when William Zeckendorf unveiled plans to replace Grand Central Terminal with an eighty-story skyscraper. The architectural community erupted in outrage, but when Zeckendorf's project proved to be a phantom, the architects retired once again into their usual silence. MAS, however, seized the moment to go public with its preservation program, and on November 24, 1955, the *Times* kindly printed a long boxed letter to the editor that appealed for money and for new members willing to work for historic preservation. MAS also experimented with corporate memberships. Board member Walter Mack approached his colleagues at the Stock Exchange, for instance, and Whitney North Seymour, Sr., the society's president, sent out a letter to lawyers and judges. Many responded to his call. Seymour was a pillar of the legal community and was expected to sit on the U.S. Supreme Court someday, although he was never, in fact, appointed. He was "very grand," Brendan Gill remembers—"He loved his cutaway and striped trousers"—and as a lawyer, "he was accustomed to the posture of defense," precisely what the preservation movement needed.[19]

"Only a handful, a tiny handful of people" were interested in the history of New York, Harmon Goldstone once said, and the prevailing image of preservationists was of "ladies with floppy hats and tennis shoes, joined by a few crackpots."[20] Such people, along with others, found a home at MAS. One was Nathalie Dana, who actually did have an extraordinary hat collection.* Although she left a rather faint impression on the official records of the Municipal Art Society, Dana hovered over MAS for years like a guardian angel, shaping its board if not its policy. When she felt MAS was languishing, she brought in new blood; when she felt it was losing its focus, she coolly dispatched the regime in power and brought in still fresher faces. She was "*formidable* in figure *and* manner," said Goldstone, with a "brusque, iron-mask front" that masked a deep shyness. She'd grown up in a different age. Dana had been born in 1878, in the "brown decades"; been raised in a Queen Anne house that McKim, Mead & White decorated long before they discovered the Renaissance; and been educated at Brearley when its long white spartan hallways seemed modernistic, and when that school itself was an avant-garde institution. As a distant relation of the Hunts and as a young friend of the Blashfields, the Bitters, the Coxes, and Mowbray, she'd seen the American Renaissance come and go. She even remembered that her grandmother's shoes were made to order by Mr. Saint-Gaudens, the sculptor's father. But if Nathalie Dana appreciated the past, she had little nostalgia for it, and certainly no desire to return to it. "I knew I was unfeminine," she wrote of her youth, "and therefore a problem," and while an I. N. Phelps Stokes might mourn the passing of the nineteenth century, Dana, nine years younger, greeted it as a personal liberation.[21] It gave her the freedom to pursue a life of the mind, and though she wasn't quite talented enough to be a concert pianist, she became an amateur chamber musician of the first order. She was active in the Mannes School and in the Dessoff Choir, which was pioneering the early music repertory. She grew up to the strains of von Suppé; she grew old to the sound of Schoenberg.

---

* Her late husband, Richard Henry Dana, was an architect who specialized in the Colonial Revival. (He was named for his paternal grandfather, the novelist; his mother was the daughter of Henry Wadsworth Longfellow.) Dana was one of the guiding forces of Great Georgian Houses of America, a two-volume work published in 1933 and 1937. Financed by subscribers as a benefit for the Architects' Emergency Committee, the project was designed to put architectural draftsmen to work "and in so doing improve their morale, giving them training in an exact and serious technique and rendering financial aid." An example of the private efforts to fund work relief that had sprung up during Hoover's administration, it was a model for the great WPA programs that followed. Its focus was on documenting the past rather than preservation per se. William Lawrence Bottomley, Preface, Great Georgian Houses, vol. 2 (1937; reprint, New York: Dover, 1970), 8.

"This Society needs young people, active people," Nathalie Dana told Harmon Goldstone.[22] Many of those new members turned out to be second-generation Municipalians, and in the next decade half-familiar names like Ruth McAneny Loud, Bancel La Farge, and Allyn Cox would dot the membership rolls, while two generations of the Sulzberger family, which published the *Times*, made their appearance. Other members had a more distant connection to MAS's history. Harmon Goldstone, for instance, was the son of Lafayette Goldstone, a prolific designer of apartment buildings, a close friend of Electus Litchfield, and, during World War I, Litchfield's colleague at the U.S. Shipping Board. The younger Goldstone remembers growing up in a circle of public housing advocates; they expected architects to have a civic conscience, and it wasn't hard for Nathalie Dana to recruit him.[23] Dana also drew on her contacts with the summer arts colony of Cornish, New Hampshire. The most important of these was the architect Geoffrey Platt. He shared a firm with his brother, William; their father was Charles A. Platt, who was celebrated at the turn of the century for his garden and country house designs. While Goldstone happily identified with the Modernist movement and spent much of his career in the office of Wallace K. Harrison, Geoffrey Platt had been schooled in the traditional styles and was never entirely comfortable working in the International Style. Platt's masterpiece was the Art Deco Steuben Glass Building on Fifth Avenue, a very chic design of streamlined forms and glass blocks. "It would have been preserved now," remembers Charles Platt, William's son, but in the 1960s it was destroyed by Harry Winston, "who got a prize for improving Fifth Avenue."[24]

Part of the Municipal Art Society's task was to erect a scholarly foundation for the preservation movement. Among the society's chief assets was the architect Alan Burnham. Like the Lamb brothers long before him, Burnham specialized in ecclesiastical work, perhaps because the traditional styles had never entirely disappeared from that field. His career never flourished, however. He was "the most invisible person imaginable," says Goldstone, "a scholar at heart. He retreated from public view." Burnham's most congenial commission was at Biltmore, the enormous château that Richard Morris Hunt built for another Municipalian, George W. Vanderbilt, in Asheville, North Carolina. When Hunt died and Vanderbilt's finances turned sour, Biltmore's music room was left unfinished until Burnham designed it in 1976. It's a tribute to his skill and modesty that one would never know that the room didn't come from Hunt's own atelier.[25]

Despite all its efforts to find new members, MAS remained a tiny organization of roughly five hundred people. "It was as if we were taking names off tombstones in Staten Island," says Brendan Gill, who joined MAS in the mid 1950s. "Yet the politicians never challenged us. No one did, not even reporters." MAS was "such a funny, stuffy old organization," Goldstone remembers. When he took office he explained that "before we lay out a program for the year, I'd like to know how much money we have." Whereupon Irene Walsh, MAS's secretary and sole employee, produced a battered little cardboard box of petty cash. "That was our working capital," Goldstone says. But if MAS had no money, it did have other assets. "That generation," Harmon Goldstone remembers, "had a kind of idealism and a sense of social responsibility that I think has largely gone out of the world."[26]

Mrs. Dana produced a new board member, William Jayme, who'd led a tree planting campaign in the Carnegie Hill district. Jayme worked for CBS, and he arranged for MAS to go on the radio with Russell Lynes, author of *The Tastemakers*, and the historian Agnes Gilchrist. Lynes was the moderator; a new guest was invited each week, and each fifteen-minute program was devoted to a building MAS wanted to preserve for posterity.[27] In 1955, they went on the air on WQXR, the radio station of the *Times*, with a fifteen-minute talk on the houses of Washington Square.

In 1957, the New York Community Trust took up MAS's idea of putting bronze plaques on historic buildings, and the unveiling ceremonies provoked a steady trickle of items in the newspapers. That same year, MAS published its list of historic buildings. A little mimeographed booklet called *New York Landmarks*, it was mailed out to MAS members and to libraries. MAS's counsel was so nervous about the booklet that he insisted on adding a disclaimer in which the Municipal Art Society absolved itself of responsibility for any fluctuations in property values as a result of its work. (He assumed that the mere suggestion that a building be preserved would drive its price down.) Introducing the list, Edward Steese noted that many buildings once included on the list had already been demolished:

> Missing . . . are such structures as the Produce Exchange Building, the United States Trust Company and others destroyed in the march of progress. Among such, as an area now destroyed, might well be Park Avenue below Fifty-ninth Street, which in its heyday had a distinction different from, but equal to, that of Gramercy Park or Washington Square, opulent in design and scale, and the first planned boulevard in the city. That once residential district (which most of us have seen grow up and die) is now replaced by office structures built in recent years. Similarly, the great houses on Upper Fifth Avenue have been replaced by new apartments—with low ceilings—as a result of changed economic conditions.[28]

Edward Steese persuaded the University Club to mount a small exhibit of New York landmarks in 1953, and the response was so enthusiastic that the club offered MAS a thousand dollars to mount a larger show. Eldridge Snyder, chairman of the University Club's Art Committee, recommended that his friend Henry Hope Reed assemble the next exhibit. The pity was that the University Club isn't open to the public; only the club's members saw this remarkable exhibit of precious original drawings. Many of them wouldn't have survived much longer if Reed hadn't come along. Richard Morris Hunt's drawings had found a safe refuge with the American Institute of Architects in Washington, but Reed was the first person who ever asked to see them. He found other drawings in the cluttered attics and garages of their creators' children or grandchildren, and persuaded the owners to donate their archives to the New-York Historical Society or the Smithsonian. Reed also found

Whitney Warren's first sketch for the facade of Grand Central Terminal, Hunt's sketches for the Statue of Liberty's pedestal, and Charles McKim's studies for the University Club. Reed displayed his drawings in four groups: buildings of national importance were shown in frames draped in red, white, and blue; those of local importance in the city's blue and orange; those that had been demolished in black; and those that were threatened in an alarming shade of red.[29]

Reed was drawn into the Municipal Art Society's Historic Structures Committee, but he soon grew tired of its meetings and of talking about what ought to be saved while those same buildings were tumbling down in the streets. He wanted to take the society's case directly to the public, to share MAS's knowledge and love for the city with a wider audience. Russell Lynes's radio program certainly helped, but the best way to open people's eyes to a building's beauty is to stand them in front of it, so in 1956 Reed pioneered the walking tour. Since then, a walking tour industry has sprung up in New York, and on any given weekend the papers list half a dozen or so tours sponsored by MAS, by museums, or by neighborhood groups. At first Reed hoped to get people into buildings that were normally closed to the public—the clubhouses, for instance—but when none would cooperate, Reed took to the streets.

When Municipalians speak of Henry Hope Reed they use words like "a fanatic," "a tiger," or "a crazy," but they almost always speak of him with affection. Reed is a truly remarkable person. His aesthetic sensibility might have belonged to a typical Municipalian circa 1900. His life is ruled by the belief that the rise of Modernism marked the onset of another Dark Age, and that our only hope is to recover the legacy of Classical architecture. His favorite insult is to call someone "a hopeless modernist," a phrase that may have begun life as a pun, but crops up so frequently in Reed's conversation—to describe almost everyone he's ever known—that it seems more like a tic.

So long as Reed focused on preservation, MAS welcomed him as its most passionate and eloquent spokesman, but Reed went much further. He didn't simply want to save old buildings while contemporary architecture went to hell; he wanted to create a second American Renaissance just like the first. Nor could he bear to see landmarks mistreated and abused, and his passionate indignation spilled out on his walking tours. Goldstone began demanding that Reed hand in scripts of his tours so he could edit anything "libelous." "He made my life hell," Reed says, and in any case Reed didn't always stick to his scripts; he'd get carried away as he spoke. As he guided tours through Central Park, for instance, he couldn't help pointing out how Vaux and Olmsted's design had been manhandled. The sight of fresh asphalt or chain link or some chunky new recreation building would launch him into a slashing attack on the last forty years of philistine parks commissioners, including the Arsenal's present administration. Goldstone took to shadowing him, standing in the back of the tour group and glaring whenever he suspected that Reed was about to say something indiscreet.[30]

Reed's attacks on modern architecture eventually grew worrisome for the Municipal Art Society. Some feared that the public would regard MAS as an anti-quarian society, unqualified to comment on present-day developments; others were committed Modernists themselves and regarded Reed as some hoary mastodon come back to life. In search of balance, Harmon Goldstone decided that MAS should conduct tours of the city's Modernist architecture. To guide these tours the Museum of Modern Art recommended Ada Louise Huxtable, then a little-known member of its staff, and Goldstone found some grant money to pay her. (Her tours were later published as a book.) The decision to hire Huxtable still irks Henry Hope Reed, both because Huxtable was paid while he wasn't, and because he'd inadvertently boosted the career of yet another "hopeless modernist."[31]

Huxtable soon began writing articles about architecture for the *Times*. By the early 1960s she was penning occasional unsigned editorials for the paper, and in 1963 she became its first full-time architecture critic—the first on any American news-paper. The *Times* "never wanted serious criticism," says Brendan Gill, but Huxtable was "very strong, the exact opposite of what they expected when she showed up in her little lace knits."[32] "She created the post," Goldstone remembers, "and gave architectural journalism a tremendous boost in prestige in the newspaper world," especially when she won the first Pulitzer Prize for criticism.[33] Soon after that she joined the board of MAS.

All this attention didn't do much to save landmarks from demolition or alter-ation, however. Often it just made their loss seem all the more painful. Still, MAS went on struggling to save buildings where it could—whenever moral suasion, the society's only weapon, might work. And in 1955, MAS did manage to save the rooftop sculptures of the Appellate Courthouse. They were the pride of MAS's first generation—of Bitter, Ruckstuhl, French, and their contemporaries—but the city wanted to remove them rather than maintain the building properly. MAS and the judges demanded their restoration; the result was a refurbishment of the entire building. Henry Hope Reed gave tours of the building and produced a little pamphlet on its precious store of sculpture and murals. When the restoration was finished in 1957, the judges celebrated by throwing an open house.[34]

Downtown, though, more sculpture was in danger. In 1957, Meyer Berger of the *Times* reported that Western Electric was going to tear down the Saint Paul Building on lower Broadway. This was an early skyscraper by George Post, and a very ugly one, but it boasted four heroic atlantes by Karl Bitter: hunched, muscular nudes straining to support a balcony over the entrance. Berger wondered if they might be rescued, and Whitney North Seymour took this as a cue. At his request, Western Electric agreed to remove the figures intact if MAS could find a new home for them. The sculptor Paul Manship took up this task and saw Bitter's work off to India-napolis, where the figures now grace a fountain in a public park. (Manship went on to found an independent organization, the Committee to Preserve American Art.[35])

In the meantime, MAS had turned its attention to the Old Merchant's House, an astonishing time capsule at 29 East Fourth Street. The old merchant was Seabury Treadwell, who moved into the house in the early 1830s and whose daughter remained there till her death in 1933. She left behind a Greek Revival row house complete with its original decor and furniture, and George Chapman, a banker and lawyer, bought the house and kept it intact. With his death, however, the house was left without a protector. In 1957 the Historic Landmark Society was created to buy the house and all its furniture. Its finances were terribly rickety, though, and MAS continued its appeal for help.[36]

THERE WAS little else that MAS could do without a landmarks law. Other cities had already moved to protect their historic neighborhoods. The first was Charleston, which had been protecting its historic center since 1931.* In 1937 New Orleans had transformed the Vieux Carré into a historic district, and Boston eventually followed suit with Beacon Hill. Each of these cities created a special zoning district with a commission, either elected or appointed, that could veto any exterior alterations. The courts upheld these historic districts, not because they preserved the beauty and historic character of neighborhoods, but for the sake of more concrete and mercenary benefits: in return for surrendering a certain amount of freedom, owners enjoyed increased property values, tourism flourished, and both the benefits and burdens fell on every property owner within the district.

MAS's problem was that it wasn't really thinking about historic districts. It did speak of protecting Washington Square, but it's not at all clear that it meant to include Greenwich Village in the same package. MAS focused on saving individual masterpieces of architecture, and at the time no zoning code could accomplish that. As far as the courts were concerned, the city had no business looking for masterpieces or historic structures unless it meant to buy them. The courts were also very stern on the subject of "spot zoning": cities could invent special rules for whole neighborhoods, but they couldn't arbitrarily single out particular buildings or lots for special treatment. That would be unfair, the courts said, and it would open up an enormous amount of room for abuse by crooked politicians and builders. So it seemed that MAS had no legal recourse.

Albert Bard had been pondering such legal issues for decades. By the mid 1950s he was "a very frail little man," Harmon Goldstone remembers. "A breath of wind would have blown him away." Cataracts had left Bard nearly blind, and he was very deaf. He would come to MAS board meetings, lay his bulky hearing aid on the table, and say, to no one in particular, "Let me know when there's something worth hearing and I'll turn it on." But he was still "a fighting cocker," says Goldstone.

The modern skyscraper city so disgusted Bard that he had moved to Hoboken, but as he walked from the PATH tubes to his office he still waged a daily war on the world of advertising, stripping the lampposts of fliers as he passed. He hadn't come to terms with the International Style, either. "His tastes were formed before I was born,"[37] Goldstone says, and this was literally true: Bard had first joined MAS's board

---

* This was well known to Municipalians: I. N. Phelps Stokes had family in Charleston, and his former partner, William Dean Howells, the novelist's son, had bought and carefully restored one of that city's finest mansions, the Colonel John Stuart House.

in 1911, the year of Goldstone's birth, and at age ninety he still yearned for the Beaux Arts and the City Beautiful. If he'd had the power, he would have gladly passed a law requiring the construction of none but Beaux Arts buildings.

One of the things that frustrated him was the courts' refusal to admit that the state had *any* legitimate interest in the appearance of things. It's true that when the courts upheld zoning laws they sometimes mentioned in passing that zoning produced handsomer cities, but legally, beauty was still irrelevant—a pleasant side effect, but nothing more. Justice really has to be blind, said the courts, and the city could exercise its "police power" only for the sake of public health and safety.

Bard had been trying to change this for much of his life. Back in 1913, in the thick of MAS's campaign against billboards, Bard first proposed an "aesthetic amendment" to the state constitution, a simple affair that would have given cities the right to restrict development for the sake of beauty, just as they could act in the interests of fire safety or hygiene. MAS and Mayor Gaynor's Billboard Commission endorsed that proposal, and George McAneny's Fifth Avenue Commission yearned for such an amendment. Yet no one expected Bard to succeed in Albany, and even if he had, they knew the U.S. Supreme Court would surely object.

Bard waited a quarter of a century before reviving the idea of an aesthetic amendment. In 1938, New York finally had a planning commission, the city was gearing up to produce the first official master plan since 1907, and there was much talk of revising the zoning code. So Bard dusted off his proposed amendment and announced that it was time to extend zoning "into the aesthetic field. The present laws condition the use and restrain the abuse of private property," he wrote, and they enhance property values by making it "safe to buy." Yet there remained "neglected principles of beauty as important as those of use. . . . Design has been heretofore, and still is, an almost unknown factor in planning."[38] This was answered with the usual mumblings about the U.S. Constitution, however, so in 1939 Bard tried a new tack. At the time, Robert Moses was waging his first assault on Washington Square, and MAS and the American Institute of Architects were both wondering what to do with the miserable fiasco that was Foley Square. The civic groups were afraid that the streets around the two squares would soon be rebuilt, and they realized that the zoning code wasn't stringent enough to protect the scale and character of these public spaces. Now Bard lobbied for the "aesthetic zoning of private property where it abuts" a public improvement, whether a park or a public building.[39] His theory was that, since public improvements enhanced the value of neighboring lots, the city had a legitimate interest in how that land was exploited, if only to protect its own investment. Again Bard's friends nodded their heads in sympathy, privately concluding that his ideas were so much pie in the sky. And so they were until 1954.

The Great Depression had brought about a revolution in constitutional law. The Supreme Court had set out to undo the New Deal in 1935, and had changed its mind after the Democratic landslide one year later. Where the rights of employers and property owners had once reigned supreme, they would now be balanced against the rights of labor and a broader sense of the public interest. It took years for the Court to work out the full implications of this shift, but in 1954 the justices finally took up an issue close to Albert Bard's heart: the extent of the state's "police power." The case of *Berman v. Parker* involved a slum clearance project in Washington, D.C. A local businessman decided to fight the condemnation of his property. The project had been authorized to eradicate "urban blight," he noted, and that term might well have described his neighbors' property. But *his* business was thriving, his building was sound, and in taking it away, the government was motivated by an aesthetic impulse not recognized in the law. As Justice William O. Douglas summarized Berman's case, "To take [property] for the purpose of ridding the area of slums is one thing; it is quite another, the argument goes, to take a man's property merely to develop a better balanced, more attractive community." The lower courts had agreed with Berman and ruled that the police power could be invoked only to remove conditions "injurious to the public health, safety, morals and welfare." The Supreme Court found that "These are some of the more conspicuous examples of the traditional applications of the police power to municipal affairs. Yet they merely illustrate the scope of the power and do not delimit it. It is well within the power of the legislature to determine that the community should be beautiful as well as healthy, spacious as well as clean, well-balanced as well as carefully patrolled."[40]

"*The community should be beautiful*": that was an epoch-making phrase. It meant two things to Albert Bard: first, that the city could legislate beauty—could, for instance, order the Art Commission to review the design of each and every structure, public or private, built in New York. This was "an ambitious idea," he admitted, "but one that ought to come [to pass] in New York if the citizens have any respect for the city." Second, he saw the possibility of a landmarks law, for if the city could *make* beauty, surely it could also *protect* beauty where it already existed.

Bard was so excited that he wanted the city to start exercising its new preservation powers at once. His colleagues at the Municipal Art Society suggested that he'd better draft an amendment to the General City Law. Bard did so, and his amendment was introduced in 1955 by State Senator MacNeil Mitchell. It allowed municipalities to enact "special regulations" for the "protection, enhancement, perpetuation or use [of] places, buildings, structures, works of art and all other objects having a special historical or aesthetic interest or value." Bard explained the constitutional issues in *The American City* magazine, which carried his article "Esthetics and the Police Power," and MAS mailed reprints to its members, begging them to write Albany and demand passage of the bill. "Its implications are far reaching and a new milestone in a direction in which we are all most concerned," MAS explained. "It will give power to the legislature to take special action under special circumstances and would give the City power to make exceptional provisions in areas involving preservation of historic structures."[41]

"Special action under special circumstances" was a marvelous legal formula: it sounded so innocuous that the bill sailed through the legislature. But it was vetoed by Governor Averell Harriman. He said it was "vague." That, Bard shot back, was precisely the point.[42] It was only enabling legislation, after all, designed to let municipalities shape their own preservation policies. When the bill passed again in 1956, Harriman signed it. The passage of this bill was a momentous event, but Harmon Goldstone remembers that it was "little noticed at the time."[43] Even at MAS the law's implications were still barely appreciated. Its passage went unmentioned at the next annual meeting until, late in the ceremony, Bard himself strode to the microphone. He didn't mention his own role in shaping the law, but he was horrified that no one had remembered to thank Senator Mitchell.[44]

The Bard Law, as it came to be known, secured the immortality of at least one Municipalian. It became the essential foundation for every preservation law in New York State, and it served as an example and inspiration for communities around the country. Almost a decade would slip by before Bard's work bore fruit in New York City, however, and Bard, who died in 1963 at the venerable age of ninety-six, never saw his day of triumph.

"AN EDUCATED public and enabling legislation were not enough," Harmon Goldstone has written. "The political pressure of an aroused public was needed. By 1958, ten percent of the buildings on the Municipal Art Society's highly selective list had already been torn down."[45] A year later it had become clear that the public was rousing itself. Brooklyn Heights emerged with the first grassroots campaign to put the Bard Law to work, and Greenwich Village mobilized to save the Jefferson Market Courthouse. The mood was changing. In 1959 the great Title I scandals broke open—after many years of probes and jabs in the Post, at last the story exploded. It had several components. One was sheer corruption—the revelation of financial ties between Title I projects' sponsors, politicians, and Moses's aides. The most dramatic scandal was also the most petty: the revelation that Manhattan Borough President Hulan Jack, the first African American to achieve that position and a vigorous supporter of the Riverside-Amsterdam urban renewal project, had let the sponsor of that project, a notorious slumlord named Samuel Ungar, remodel his apartment for free. Perhaps the most poignant element in Jack's downfall was Ungar's initial defense: he claimed to have done the work as a friend, and to have concealed his generosity with phony receipts to protect Jack, since no one would believe in a friendship across racial boundaries.

Such a clear-cut impropriety led to closer examination of other Title I sponsors, some of whom had used the program to buy tenements at a discount and milk them for revenue—without ever lifting a finger to rebuild the sites. It was clear that Title I had often been perverted. Sponsors were chosen *before* a particular plan was decided upon, and urban renewal had become, in effect, a mechanism for enriching a new generation of slumlords rather than improving slum areas. The displacement of a vast segment of New York's population had in fact been creating new slums, so that urban renewal had become a kind of low-intensity war against the poor: uproot them, disperse them, and repeat the procedure wherever they regroup. So tainted had the program become that at last—after years of futile protests from displaced tenants, after years of complaints and doubts—cracks began to appear in the armor of urban renewal.

One finds, interspersed with reports in the *Times* of the scandal, a number of articles on rehabilitation as opposed to renewal. James Felt, the new city planning commissioner, began to experiment with more modestly conceived projects, and there were significant signs of grassroots support for rehabilitation. In the Village, landlords were issuing wholesale eviction notices and tenants were taking to the streets with picket signs, demanding that the city downzone the neighborhood to preserve both its character and its social fabric.

A love of one's neighborhood—of its architectural character, its texture, and its social fabric—was hardly a new development in the life of New York, nor was the will to fight for it, as Charles Lamb learned when the Lower East Side stymied his schemes for broad new avenues in lower Manhattan. This fighting spirit was especially strong in Greenwich Village. Margot Gayle, a Municipalian and Villager, insists this was mere luck: articulate, caring people just happened to live in the Village. Jane Jacobs, the great urbanist and activist, would argue that the neighborhood's spirit was the product of the Village itself—that the scale of the streets and the vibrant mixture of uses created a strong public life. As far back as 1916, when plans were announced for a fourteen-story loft on Washington Square South, the *Times* had carried a letter of protest from one Solomon Toledano. He apologized for the fact that he was not a landowner; perhaps, Toledano wrote, a bohemian had no right to complain that "the tumbledown picturesqueness of Washington Square South is to be 'improved' . . . by the erection of fourteen-story buildings. I am only one of those who have made Greenwich Village and the Washington Square District what it is—who are Greenwich Village—and of those who by their vision of beauty have created America's first home for iridescent souls, first real art center, first 'republic in the air,' as one of our number has termed it. An atmosphere such as exists nowhere else in America, which it has taken many years to build, can be destroyed very quickly. Is it only commercial values that are worth saving, only real estate that is to be protected? Will none raise a hand to save from profaning modernization the temple of the soul?"[46]

Toledano would find an answer to his prayers more than half a century later in the writings and activism of Jane Jacobs, and in the works of Margot Gayle, who raised her hand to save the Jefferson Market Courthouse.

THE JEFFERSON Market Courthouse was designed in 1875 by Frederick Clarke Withers and Calvert Vaux. It was originally part of a true little civic center comprising a courthouse, a jail, and a public market; its tall belfry, adorned with a magnificent clock, served as a fire warning tower. An 1885 poll of American architects singled out this complex as one of the finest buildings in the country, but the popularity of Victorian Gothic withered in a very few years. The market and jail were torn down in the 1920s, replaced by Sloan & Robertson's Women's

House of Detention. (Their Art Deco design was nice in itself, but not a very good neighbor for a Gothic Revival courthouse, and in fact MAS had asked the Art Commission to insist on something more sympathetic.) In 1945 the courts moved out, and a long series of transient tenants passed through the building. The Police Academy used it for a time—for riot training, it was whispered—but by 1958 the building was empty. Routine maintenance came to a halt. The clock stopped. The city offered the building to its agencies, but none wanted it. A local bank set its eyes on the site and made plans to put up an apartment building. A little before Christmas 1959, a model of the scheme appeared in the bank's front window, and a few nights later, Margot Gayle arrived at a Christmas cocktail party to find the room full of Villagers "clucking their tongues and saying, 'Isn't it a pity?' "[47]

Gayle lived on West Ninth Street, just around the corner from Jefferson Market. She was active in the Democratic reform movement and had run for City Council in "a hopeless campaign" against Stanley Isaacs—"Mr. Republican, a wonderful person," Gayle says. For a time she was the district leader for Gramercy Park, and in the fifties she worked for Mayor Wagner's Department of Commerce and Public Events. It was the age of decolonization, when one new nation after another entered the United Nations, and protocol demanded that Gayle arrange a ticker tape parade for the head of each new and obscure state. This was ideal training for an early preservationist: she had to learn how to conquer the public's monumental indifference and ignorance.

Gayle had joined the Municipal Art Society in 1957 at a time when MAS wasn't used to women activists. In such a milieu Gayle rarely dared tell men what they ought to do; instead, she would *ask*, as a personal favor, and depend on their notions of chivalry. And MAS presented her with other problems as well. "When I joined, I especially wanted to be involved with the Historic Buildings Committee. I was told, 'Well, you certainly belong on that committee, Margot, but I don't think that you can attend because all our meetings are at lunchtime at the Century Club.' " Gayle swallowed her pride. She peppered the committee with suggestions, and they were discussed, without her, in the exclusively male precincts of the Century. She helped Alan Burnham work on *New York Landmarks*, she lent the society her considerable talent for public relations, and she worried about Jefferson Market. "It bothered me very much," she says, "to see that building unused." In 1958 she persuaded Brendan Gill to write about the building in *The New Yorker*, and Alan Burnham took him on a tour. "I remember climbing the tower," says Gill, "through what must have been a foot of bird shit . . . this slippery guano."[48]

At that Christmas party in 1959, Gayle realized that stronger measures were required. "It set me thinking," she says. "What can we do about it? Why don't we organize? Why don't we form a committee?" She knew that saving the courthouse would be a major enterprise, but a more manageable project suggested itself, one that would let the city know that Villagers valued this quirky, disheveled structure. Gayle suggested that people focus on the courthouse clock. Towering over the corner of Sixth Avenue and Tenth Street, the clock hovered above a subway stop, a PATH station, and a school yard, and it was visible for blocks up and down Sixth Avenue, but it had been stuck for years at twenty minutes after three. "Everyone looked up at that gloomy clock," and every glance was answered with a visible symbol of neglect. This was Gayle's hook. The Village Neighborhood Committee for the Clock on the Jefferson Market Courthouse was born, with Harold Birns as chairman and Gayle as vice chairman. Jane Jacobs was a member, as were Philip Weinberg, Whitney North Seymour, e. e. cummings, and Marianne Moore. The group's name didn't even suggest an acronym—"We didn't think like that yet," says Gayle—but its very clumsiness caught the eye of *Times* columnist Meyer Berger, who hailed the longest committee name yet spawned by Greenwich Village.[49]

Gayle started her campaign by firing off a telegram to Mayor Wagner. "What we want for Christmas," she told him, is a working clock. "Some people in city government approved of our goal," she says, and let the committee lease the tower for a dollar a month. To raise money, the committee sold Jefferson Market Christmas cards and postcards—the artists and printers donated their work. Seven hundred dollars in repairs set the clock in motion again, but despite the best efforts of George Spinnig, an expert in antique clocks who volunteered his services, the old hand-wound works kept terrible time. It cost $4,300 to have the timepiece electrified, but finally, in September 1961, the clock was illuminated and the courthouse bell, the second largest in the city, rang in celebration for the first time since Dewey's victory at Manila.

The clock was but "the thin edge of the wedge." The committee's ultimate goal was to save the building itself, and this was far more controversial. In those days there was "no community planning board of any consequence," Gayle remembers, "no infrastructure of groups: no local historical society, no Landmarks Commission, no conservancies, no historic district councils." There was just the Municipal Art Society, and Gayle appealed for its support. MAS was "very, very helpful in holding our hands as a local group down there," she remembers, both in dealing with myriad government agencies and in making the case that the courthouse was an important building. Brendan Gill remembers "the incredulity on the part of the public that this hideous building was being put up for preservation. People truly didn't have an eye, a feeling, for Victorian architecture." Ada Louise Huxtable remarked that "If you can save *that*, you can save anything." A *Herald Tribune* editorial labeled the building "a monstrosity." "Today, it's fashionable to call it a monstrosity," Alan Burnham admitted, "but it's functionally beautiful and very picturesque." In *The New Yorker*, Gill went much further in singing the building's praises. He called it an "invincibly romantic confection."[50]

"Opinions differ radically as to whether it is architecturally handsome or architecturally ugly," Jane Jacobs wrote of Jefferson Market. "However, there is a remarkable degree of unanimity, *even among those who do not like the building as a building,* that it must be retained and used for something."[51] Villagers cherished the building as a landmark in the most literal sense of the word. The extension of Sixth Avenue in the 1920s had been a slash-and-burn affair, and when the El came down in the

1930s, the city didn't bother to build malls in the middle of the thoroughfare. Sixth Avenue was no boulevard, like upper Broadway, but a highway. And after all these years it remained, as *Progressive Architecture* wrote, "an intrusion into the Village, broad and noisy and without any particular character, on which people loiter rather than live; and the presence of this handsome piece of architectural fantasy, obviously old and particularly gratuitous, was recognized as a saving grace."[52]

Stanley Tankel of the Regional Plan Association came up with the idea of getting the New York Public Library interested in Jefferson Market. The library wanted a big new branch in the Village, but when it was first shown the courthouse "it okayed the site but wanted to demolish the building," Margot Gayle remembers. The Pratt Institute agreed to do a feasibility study for adapting the courthouse, and Harmon Goldstone led the city's commissioner of real estate through the building to convince him that it could, without too much trouble, be brought up to the modern fire code. Ada Louise Huxtable suggested the perfect architect to do the job: Giorgio Cavaglieri. She knew he loved the building, and he'd just designed two branch libraries. Cavaglieri told the library that renovating the courthouse would cost twice as much as a standard-issue branch but that it would be a larger and infinitely more distinguished facility. The library quailed at the extra cost, and pressure was required. So 10,000 people and 500 businesses signed a Save the Courthouse petition; and 62 organizations backed the effort, including local civic groups, the community boards, the Citizens Union, the Village newspapers, B'nai B'rith, the local schools and PTAs, the American Legion, the NAACP, the local political clubs, and even the Gotham Kennel Club. Mayor Wagner finally agreed to present the library with an ultimatum: it could have money for a new branch only if it saved the courthouse. "This is a neighborhood created and sustained by the people themselves," Wagner said, "and the remodeling of the courthouse into a library is New York's contribution to the preservation of its essential values."[53]

The Public Library was forced to cooperate, and Cavaglieri went to work. He could never understand the American mania for tearing buildings down; he liked to point out that he was born in Venice in a fourteenth-century house with eighteenth-century additions. His father had been the general manager of the Assicurazione Generale, Italy's largest insurance company, which had a clear architectural policy: whenever possible its branch offices were located in a distinguished old palazzo in the very heart of the city's *centro storico*. To Cavaglieri it seemed only natural to remodel a fine old building. Jefferson Market made him the most famous preservation architect of the 1960s—a bit of typecasting he found a little bittersweet[54]—and his celebrity resulted in his becoming MAS's president. His transformation of Jefferson Market wasn't finished until 1967, well after the landmarks law was in place, but the fight to save the courthouse served as a backdrop to the ongoing landmarks debate. It was the perfect illustration of MAS's goals: a distinguished old building, a masterpiece of its sort, saved because the community had come to realize that it enriched the cityscape. Moreover, when Cavaglieri was finished, the library stood as an indictment of the modern library branches. They offered banal functionalism while Jefferson Market was graced by a generosity of scale and a richness of craft and detail that New Yorkers never expected to see duplicated in their lifetimes.

IN THE fall of 1956 a young lawyer named Otis Pratt Pearsall moved into a basement apartment in Brooklyn Heights. It was "a fortuitous movement," he remembers. The Heights had been shabby for years, and many of its row houses had been converted into rooming houses, but young professionals began to appear there in the early 1950s, lured by the low rents and the easy commute to lower Manhattan. "We didn't know we were yuppies then," Pearsall remembers, and "gentrification" was still an uncoined word.

The preservation movement started shortly after that, in 1958, when it became clear that the renaissance of Brooklyn Heights was fraught with danger. As people moved in, Pearsall realized, property values would rise and developers would pounce. "They would want, not the old neighborhood, but big buildings taking advantage of that view." In fact, the process was already beginning: a developer had torn down five houses in 1953; the Watchtower Society was ready to demolish more; and Robert Moses was planning to seize the neighborhood's northeast corner for the Cadman Plaza Housing Project. The Brooklyn Heights Association didn't quite see the threat—"They were well intentioned, but set in their ways," Pearsall says—and so thirty or forty people, mostly newcomers to the Heights, organized the Community Improvement and Conservation Council—or CICC, pronounced "kick"— and arranged a public meeting just before Christmas 1958. CICC wanted many things. It wanted better services, and it wanted tree planting—Irene Hall's trees had long since disappeared. It wanted to change the program of Cadman Plaza from efficiency apartments to larger units, which were in short supply in the neighborhood. And finally, it wanted to make Brooklyn Heights a historic district. "Our houses," wrote the *Brooklyn Heights Press*, "and the architectural character of the Heights must be rigidly preserved, and safeguards must be developed to this end."[55]

Pearsall wanted to create a special Historic District Commission to govern development in Brooklyn Heights. By now there were about fifty historic districts "scattered around the country. The statutes were all simple, short things which gave control of exterior features within the district to a commission whose members were either appointed or elected." Gladys James—heir to the Underwood Typewriter fortune, the grand old lady of Brooklyn Heights, and an MAS board member— introduced Goldstone to Pearsall, "the Young Turk." Goldstone put him in touch with Albert Bard, Henry Hope Reed, and Alan Burnham, "who gave us moral support. Bard's presence was what he really contributed to it. The thing that was important was that the Bard Law was named after him, and he was enthusiastic about what we were doing. Here was a man in his mid-nineties by then, and he was like a boy. Eventually everyone, even the real estate people, was universally in favor of a Heights [historic] district. In the beginning, though, we needed this boost— Burnham, Reed, Bard. They didn't do anything physical to assist, but we didn't need that, we had all this energy." They did at least one thing, though: they explained to Pearsall that he needed a good architectural historian to build the case for a historic district, and they were able to recommend the perfect person: Clay Lancaster, who lived in Brooklyn Heights. "We ferreted out Lancaster," Pearsall remembers, and recruited him to the cause; his research was eventually published as a book, *Old Brooklyn Heights*.

The Heights Association was "gung-ho, ready to go. We were really the only grassroots preservation organization in the city"—not like Greenwich Village, Pearsall says, where "some individuals" were active but weren't "organized or influential." MAS still approached preservation from an "intellectual, elitist perspective" that focused on individual landmarks and not on historic districts. Pearsall pursued his own course in defense of the Heights. He began with James Felt, the new planning commissioner. "We beat up on Felt, talked to him, had panel discussions on the radio, and eventually got him to take a public position on behalf of the Heights and landmarks. In 1962 we drafted and proposed our own legislation. Eventually it became clear that Platt and Goldstone had a broader agenda: a citywide preservation statute. MAS came to fear we would threaten this agenda."

Goldstone didn't want the city to end up with several historic districts, each governed by its own law, its own standards, and its own set of commissioners. He may also have feared what would happen if Brooklyn Heights, home of the best-organized and most vocal preservationists in the city, made a separate peace with the city. As Pearsall says, there was "a crucial synergy between the Heights and MAS in getting this thing off the ground. [The Municipalians] had no political base, but they knew some people. [MAS was] a simple civic organization with a truly elitist perspective and no grassroots support, and then, out of the blue, we came along and gave the politicians courage. They saw [that preservation] was popular," and enough votes were at stake to provide "a political counterforce to the developers." But if Brooklyn Heights won its own district, the neighborhood might be satisfied. The residents would still support a citywide landmarks law, but not with all of their passion and energy, and support for preservation would not serve as their litmus test for politicians. "I begged Pearsall to wait for a law," Goldstone says, promising in return that Brooklyn Heights would be the first historic district designated. "I don't think he was very happy about it."

Indeed he wasn't. "We were interested in the entire city," Pearsall says, but "we didn't understand why there was a conflict. Goldstone was able to hold us off because we were politically naive. Later, when we had much closer relations to elected officials, it wouldn't have worked." For the moment, however, it was Goldstone who had James Felt's ear and through him "a much deeper reach into the city government than we did."

Pearsall bowed to the pressure. "There was a particularly painful period of three or four years. We didn't just sit sullen, we worked for a citywide law." But in those years, "We lost two houses on Orange Street . . . a humongous apartment building went up," and there were many "little erosions" all over the Heights. Stoops disappeared, cornices were shorn from facades, and here and there buildings grew extra floors. "It was a hard time for us."[56]

WHILE PEARSALL was organizing Brooklyn Heights, MAS had been busy trying to shape the new zoning code. The Zoning Code of 1916 had gradually acquired a terrible reputation. It had shaped a city that was too dense, with streets too much like canyons, and a cityscape lacking in the grace notes of parks and trees and plazas. All of that might have been addressed by reforming the code, but other factors demanded a more revolutionary approach. America had imported the International Style just as avidly as it had taken to the Beaux Arts sixty years before. But the new style was a poor match for setback zoning. Modernism was supposed to be rational, pure, efficient, and hygienic. Setbacks weren't pure or efficient or even terribly rational. They complicated a building's steel structure, they made complex forms, and the cornice lines were set far too high to produce sunny streets. The Art Deco architects had delighted in turning setbacks into massive sculpture, but the Modernists yearned to build crisp, pure volumes floating in space. The new curtain walls of glass and steel looked terrible on setbacks.

In 1955 the planners Harrison, Ballard & Allen drafted a new zoning code based on the floor area ratio principle, which encouraged the construction of pristine towers on very low bases. MAS backed the plan because it allowed "the lowering of the cornice line," as Harvey Wiley Corbett put it.[57] But the draft also tried to encourage more community participation in the planning process, and this was enough to damn it in the eyes of Robert Moses. The City Planning Commission rejected the proposed code, and Moses devoted himself to seeing that Ballard didn't receive any more work from the city. The planner did, however, find a haven of sorts at the Municipal Art Society, and he helped shape its policy on planning and zoning issues.

A year later the Seagram Building was designed by Ludwig Mies van der Rohe and Philip Johnson. Like the first Equitable Building it was a fabulously expensive stunt, but this time the client built less than usual, not more. Mies took the 25 percent tower allowance and left out all the setback masses that usually sat beneath it. He was left with a pristine form commanding an open plaza. The beauty of its proportions and materials—the building is clad in bronze—made up for any paucity of detail, and the old buildings that lined three sides of the plaza, especially McKim, Mead & White's Racquet and Tennis Club across Park Avenue, ensured that the plaza was a perfectly defined outdoor room, rich in detail.

Of course the Seagram Building was unique. Money was no object, and the owners were actually penalized by a city tax on the use of luxury materials, like bronze, in construction. They were penalized again, year in and year out, by the city's assessors, who taxed the building as if it filled its zoning envelope. For years MAS fought this as a senseless impediment to public-spirited architecture, but the courts ruled that Seagram had shown bad business sense and must pay the price. Despite all this, the Seagram tower was a seductive image of Modernism. People ignored the fact that it was successful precisely because it played off the fabric of the dense old stone city. The Seagram Building, which could never be duplicated, became the prototype for the Zoning Code of 1961. This code was supposed to free architects from the tight, "unimaginative" constraints of the old rules. It took years for the city to learn that few architects, and very few developers, deserve so much freedom.

MAS was fully behind the idea of "plaza zoning," but at the preliminary hearings in 1959, and again at the public hearing in 1960, Geoffrey Platt kept demanding something more complex—"some kind of aesthetic zoning" that would let the city protect "historic or architecturally significant neighborhoods and buildings." MAS's ideas on how to achieve this were still very vague, however: Platt merely pointed out that enabling legislation already existed in the form of the Bard Law and that the city could take advantage of "the good offices of the Art Commission." James Felt, the city planning commissioner, warned Platt that opening up the subject would "scuttle the whole thing." Felt asked MAS to support the new zoning code as it stood, and promised in return to take up the subject of preservation at a later date.[58] Platt agreed, though he probably didn't put too much weight on Felt's promise. The new code took effect a year later, and on May 8, 1961, MAS presented Felt with its highest honor, the President's Medal, for having created "the framework on which a finer city of the future will take form."[59] That, at least, was the confident assertion inscribed on his medal. Felt's acceptance speech surprised the members. Instead of dwelling on the zoning code, he spoke of the need to do "something" about historic preservation. "New Yorkers are becoming aware of their roots and are proud of them," he said. "We owe it to ourselves and to posterity to capture whenever possible those true symbols of the city's past and present which have important cultural, aesthetic, and historic values, and preserve them in a meaningful way."[60] The next day, Felt lunched with Platt and Goldstone at the Century Club, and they talked about writing a landmarks law.

James Felt has a very mixed reputation today. He and his family were in the real estate business; he was a governor of the Real Estate Board and had assembled the land for Peter Cooper Village and the Riverton housing project. He was active in Jewish philanthropies, and he'd long demanded that the City Planning Commission be better funded so it could finally do its job.[61] Felt's appointment was Mayor Wagner's response to the growing torrent of criticism of Moses's tyranny, and it came after consultation with the Citizens Housing and Planning Council, of which MAS was a member. Implicit in Felt's appointment was the idea that the setback zoning code would finally be changed, that urban renewal would be handled more sensitively, and that the city would explore rehabilitation programs. Jane Jacobs, however, found that Felt's urban renewal policies amounted to more of the same. The idea of mixing commercial and residential uses in a single street still seemed dangerous, dirty, and perverse to Felt's generation, and for years the planning commission thwarted Jacobs's scheme for rehabilitating the West Village. Felt's 1961 zoning code is now seen as a disaster—"a destructive document," as MAS's

Philip Howard calls it.[62] Yet without Felt there would have been no landmarks law in 1965.

Harmon Goldstone found in Felt "a warmth and a wisdom" unusual in city government. "To our surprise, he was sympathetic to our objective, and more important, had the knowledge, which none of us amateurs did, of how to achieve it," Goldstone wrote. "He had been working in the back of his mind, anxious for a way to save landmarks and historic districts." It was as if "we were looking for one another." With a candor born of sympathy for the cause, Felt told Platt and Goldstone that "If you're willing to give the mayor credit for this activity, we can do something." They promised that Wagner would get "all the credit he wants," and Felt suggested the first step: Goldstone was to write the mayor and ask that he appoint a committee to examine the preservation issue. "I will see that he gets the letter," Felt promised, "and I will see that he does something about it."[63]

Wagner loved appointing such committees. In 1961 two hundred mayoral committees were studying various issues. "Some never met," by one account. "Most had no effect at all, except to invent the illusion of action."[64] But Felt was serious; he was convinced that a landmarks law would be Wagner's crowning achievement—"the thing he'll be remembered for"—and he walked Goldstone's letter through City Hall.[65] Within a month Wagner had appointed the Mayor's Committee for the Preservation of Structures of Historic and Aesthetic Importance. "In a city being rebuilt as rapidly as New York," Wagner said, "there is a constant danger that structures of historic interest or high aesthetic value may be overwhelmed by the rebuilding rush. We cannot and should not ignore the past history of our city, nor permit its beauty to vanish if they [sic] can be preserved."[66]

Geoffrey Platt was the committee's chairman and Goldstone its secretary, and they were joined by Arthur Holden, Whitney North Seymour, Sr., McKim Norton, Robert S. Curtiss, Robert W. Dowling, Luther Gulick, Stanley Lowell, Clarence Michaels, Bethuel Webster, Morgan Dix Wheelock, and Frederick Woodbridge. In November the committee called on the mayor to create an Advisory Landmarks Preservation Commission to conduct a survey of buildings worth saving and to draft legislation to protect them. Wagner agreed.

The advisory commission was given three years to complete its work. Platt asked for $35,000 in funding, and was astonished to receive $50,000 instead. He needed an architectural historian to "run this thing," and when he asked James Grote Van Derpool for recommendations he was astonished again: Van Derpool, one of Columbia University's great architectural historians, offered to take the job himself, though it meant giving up his academic career, his tenure, and the chance to become dean of his school. Of course Van Derpool's reputation brought enormous prestige to the advisory commission.

And so the advisory commission set to work, and the prospects for a preservation law seemed fairly rosy. Felt gave Platt some advice: "Make yourself known. Don't surprise anyone." And he added a kindly warning: "You're going to lose some buildings during this period," he said, "and don't let it bother you. . . . You're going to lose them."[67] Felt is dead now, and no one can say if he had a particular building in mind, but fate had a cruel trick in store for New York's preservationists: the city was about to lose Pennsylvania Station, its greatest work of public architecture, and the prime mover behind this vandalism was James Felt's brother Irving, president of Madison Square Garden.

Pennsylvania Station had long been in danger. It was no secret the railroad held the building, and its own customers, in utter contempt: the evidence was written in filth and grime, in a jumble of billboards and an amazingly hideous new ticket counter. The *Times* first reported that the station was threatened in 1955, when the peculiar partnership of Billy Rose* and William Zeckendorf—a Broadway vulgarian and a "visionary" developer—wanted to put up a two-story merchandise mart. They called it "The Palace of Progress"—no doubt that was Rose's idea—and their architect was I. M. Pei.[68] That project came to naught, but in 1962 Irving Felt conceived a more plausible and massive scheme called Penn Plaza. The abbreviation was all too telling. The project featured a massive, glassy office building and a new sports arena, while the railroad station itself—the gateway to the city—was tucked miserably underground.

The threat to Pennsylvania Station finally shook the architectural community awake. In 1955 the architects had protested when Grand Central Terminal was in danger, but since then they'd been largely silent on the subject of preservation. Now, thanks to two young architects named Norval White and Elliot Willensky, the Action Group for Better Architecture in New York (AGBANY) sprang up to save the station. Its most prominent member was Philip Johnson (Mies van der Rohe's disciple and a pillar of American Modernism), but it also included Paul Rudolph (chairman of Yale's Architecture School and the most brilliant figure in the younger generation) and I. M. Pei, who'd apparently come to regret his own involvement in the Palace of Progress scheme just seven years earlier. AGBANY organized petitions: Charles Platt (Geoffrey's nephew) remembers pounding the hallways of the old Architects' Building to collect signatures, and he still wonders at the fact that the young architects were all eager to sign, whereas "the old fogies"—trained decades earlier in the Beaux Arts system and now glumly aping the International Style—threw him out of their offices.[69] There were even protests, and New York had never seen demonstrators quite like these: young intellectuals in thin ties and dark-rimmed glasses carrying neatly lettered placards demanding "Action, Not Apathy."

AGBANY had only a slim chance of saving Pennsylvania Station. Since Madison Square Garden would seat more than 2,500 people, the normal occupancy limit for an arena, the project needed a zoning variance. AGBANY begged the City Planning Commission to withhold the variance: consider what will be lost, the architects pleaded. MAS and AGBANY met with the mayor's office and the Advisory Land-

---

* Rose achieved a certain notoriety when he suggested turning Central Park into an amusement park. That, he said, would drive away the "rapists and perverts." Even Robert Moses was appalled by this proposal. More quietly, Rose later engineered the destruction of Joseph Urban's Ziegfeld Theater.

marks Preservation Commission to see if the city couldn't at least delay the project until studies were made.[70] Geoffrey Platt's appearance surprised many people in city government: this was not the sort of thing an advisory landmarks commission was supposed to be doing. In future, Platt would be much more discreet. The deputy mayor insisted that "financial considerations" made it unwise to delay the project, while the planning commission explained that its civic conscience was touched but that its powers were limited by law: it could weigh the *proposed* use of land, but not its current use. "Even if the Parthenon itself stood on the chosen site," Huxtable wrote, the planning commission would be powerless to save it.[71] In January 1963 the CPC voted unanimously to grant the variance. Even Harmon Goldstone, who'd joined the planning commission a year earlier, felt he had no choice but to cast his vote in favor of Madison Square Garden.

The demolition of Penn Station began in August 1963 and dragged on until 1965. "Until the first blow fell," wrote the *Times*, "no one was convinced that Penn Station really would be demolished or that New York would permit this monumental act of vandalism. Any city will get what it admires, will pay for, and ultimately deserves. Even when we had Penn Station, we couldn't afford to keep it clean. We want and deserve tin-can architecture in a tin-pot culture. And we will probably be judged not by the monuments we build but by those we have destroyed."

WHILE PENNSYLVANIA Station was being reduced to rubble, the Advisory Landmarks Preservation Commission built the case for a preservation law. It began by documenting the extent of the destruction. "A 1941 survey across the United States had listed some 6,400 structures as worth saving," Goldstone wrote, but "by 1963, 2,560, or forty percent of them, were gone." It noted that many other cities had already taken action: "In 1945, only two of our cities had any sort of legal protection for landmarks; twenty years later, there were sixty-four."[72] And it conducted its survey of New York City in search of buildings worthy of preservation.* This was the easy part. It was far harder to actually frame the legislation. Those sixty-odd cities with preservation policies had created historic districts in their zoning codes, and MAS was thinking in terms of an amendment to the zoning law that would designate individual landmarks as well as entire neighborhoods. But the corporation counsel insisted that preservation must be kept quite separate from zoning. Goldstone was stunned by this at first; it took him a while to see that preservation and zoning were two separate issues and that the City Planning Commission and preservationists would inevitably have conflicting agendas.

The bill was rewritten to create a separate, independent Landmarks Preservation

---

* Van Derpool's survey, of course, was based on MAS's list of historic and aesthetic structures, and in 1963 this was finally published in book form as New York Landmarks. Goldstone had "shamed" Burnham into finishing it. Tired of reporting "progress" on the book every year, Goldstone finally announced at one annual meeting that, "Based on the percentage completed as of this morning, it will be ready for the printers in 175 years." MAS subsidized the book's publication (and won an award for "inventive publishing") in order to keep its cover price low.

Commission. It would have eleven members, including at least three architects, one landscape architect or city planner, an architectural historian, and someone from real estate. The commission would single out buildings that "represent or reflect elements of the city's cultural, social, economic, political and architectural history," and also districts that "have a special character or special historic or aesthetic interest or value." The commission would have to hold a public hearing before designating a building, so that owners had a chance to voice their opinions. Once designated, a landmark couldn't be demolished, nor could its exterior be altered, unless the commission granted the owner a "certificate of appropriateness." There were two major checks on the commission's power. First, the Board of Estimate had to ratify each designation; second, there was an escape clause. In hardship cases, when an owner couldn't obtain a 6 percent return on his property, the Landmarks Commission had eleven months in which to find a buyer willing to preserve the structure. (At first, the 6 percent return applied even to nonprofit institutions.) If no buyer materialized, the landmark designation was rescinded and the building was left to its fate.

While the legislation was being thrashed out at the advisory commission, Platt and Goldstone continued meeting with James Felt. He arranged for Goldstone to join the City Planning Commission, and in the meantime Felt was working on his friends at the Real Estate Board. At first, there was "intense, behind the scenes real estate opposition,"[73] but this was muted by a new provision in the bill, the so-called moratorium clause. Builders had complained that the Landmarks Commission would surprise them, halting projects with sudden last-minute designations. So the commission's power was drastically curtailed. It would hold public hearings for the first eighteen months of its existence, but then a new schedule would take effect: six months of hearings would alternate with three years of silence. During those long hibernations no new designations could be considered: it was open season for historic buildings. The moratorium ensured that the landmarks law would be "a paper tiger," as Brendan Gill says. It limited how much and how quickly the commission could designate, and ensured that the commission couldn't step in in emergencies.

In May 1964 Platt delivered a draft of the bill, "which was about three inches thick," to Mayor Wagner. All through that summer it sat on the mayor's desk—"just inertia," Platt said later.[74] "Wagner was always asleep at the switch," growls Brendan Gill.[75] While the mayor still slept, the *Times* announced that the Brokaw mansion at 1 East Seventy-ninth Street was slated for demolition. Designed by Rose & Stone in 1887, the house was one of the last great Fifth Avenue mansions and the cornerstone of a superb blockfront.[76] An especially awful apartment building was due to replace it. Wagner took no notice for the moment and a few days later he blithely issued a proclamation: September 28 to October 4 would be Preservation Week in New York City. The irony, or hypocrisy, was inescapable: while the Brokaw mansion was in danger, and while Wagner celebrated preservation, he was still sitting on the landmarks law. "It was pointed out forcibly to the mayor that he had a draft of the legislation on his desk," Platt remembered, and on October 6 the mayor finally presented the bill to the City Council.

The bill was sponsored by Councilman Seymour Boyers of Queens—ironically, a borough that has often shown little sympathy for preservation. The City Council tinkered with it in two ways: it insisted that each borough contribute at least one landmarks commissioner, and it threw away one clause. Platt and Goldstone had expected the City Council to find some problem with the bill, and they had provided a sacrificial lamb: originally the Landmarks Commission was supposed to review all construction within four hundred feet of a landmark. The City Council deleted that clause.* When the council members asked just how extensive the city's preservation program would be, James Van Derpool sought to put them at ease. His survey had identified some 750 individual landmarks, he testified, though more would undoubtedly come to light in the future. (Actually, the survey already listed 1,200 structures.[77]) As for historic districts, well . . . there was Greenwich Village, Brooklyn Heights, and "perhaps" a cast iron district in SoHo. Just those three.

There was very little opposition to the bill. Thanks to the moratorium clause, the Real Estate Board sent just one minor official to testify against it. He made a "pro forma speech," which Goldstone had "already heard about seventy-five times." Clearly the board's heart wasn't in the fight, but it just "wouldn't have been natural" if it hadn't complained. There were more objections from the other end of the spectrum. Councilman Paul O'Dwyer, brother of the former mayor, argued eloquently that the Landmarks Commission should have jurisdiction over the city's historic parks. The West Side Democratic Club wanted to give Landmarks the power to protect interiors. MAS grumbled that the landmarks law's best friends might prove to be its worst enemies. Afraid of awakening Robert Moses, the Municipal Art Society shied away from O'Dwyer. (Moses had resigned from his city posts to lead the 1964 World's Fair Corporation, but he still ruled the Arsenal through his successor, Newbold Morris.) As for interiors, "We all said, that's going to be hopelessly difficult," Goldstone remembers. "That's going to be an invasion of privacy. We'd better stay away from that hornet's nest." Some Municipalians also thought that interior designations were "unwarranted." Giorgio Cavaglieri, for one, insisted that "buildings must be kept alive with present day uses," and that "a landmark was not 'something under a glass bowl.' "[78]

While the City Council deliberated, scaffolding went up around the Pyne-Davidson Row on Park Avenue between Sixty-eighth and Sixty-ninth streets. This was actually a set of four Georgian mansions, two designed by McKim, Mead & White, the others by Delano & Aldrich and Walker & Gillette. No two were exactly alike, but they formed a glorious ensemble and were prime candidates for land-marking. The city was still powerless to act, but James Van Derpool moved in wealthy circles and "made a phone call."[79] "Suddenly it was announced that an anonymous patron, described as a 'person of immense goodwill,' had bought the

---

* This wasn't a frivolous provision. Insensitive neighbors can make any landmark look like a lost little toy.

houses from Sigmund Sommer, who was razing them to make way for a 31-story apartment house." The *Times* discovered that the patron was the Marquesa de Cuevas, granddaughter of John D. Rockefeller, Sr. Her good deed cost two million dollars, but as the *AIA Journal* tartly wrote, "If the City Council would pass the Landmarks Preservation Bill, which it has been contemplating for over two months, the city could act in the interest of its citizens, instead of the reverse, as is presently the case."[80] In the meantime the fate of the Brokaw mansion hung in the balance. There were rallies outside the empty building, and then, one weekend in February, the demolition crew arrived: "A dandy way," wrote Huxtable, "to do enough damage at a time when no normal channels are functioning."[81] Geoffrey Platt got a desperate call from the mayor's office offering to stop the demolition work for the weekend if he could think of some way to save the house.[82] This time, however, no marquesa was available.

BY A UNANIMOUS vote, the landmarks bill passed in April 1965, two months too late for the Brokaw House. MAS gave awards to Councilman Boyers and Mayor Wagner, feting them in the Seventh Regiment Armory, in the fabled Tiffany rooms that would one day be the subject of another prolonged preservation fight; James Felt went unrewarded at this celebration, while the politicians collected their tribute. Soon Wagner had the honor of appointing the first Landmarks Commission, which was well stocked with Municipalians.* Geoffrey Platt was its chairman, a post Harmon Goldstone took over in 1966 when John Lindsay became mayor. Van Derpool took charge of the staff and was a skillful, charming administrator, and he brought in Alan Burnham as his assistant.[83] Burnham gave up his architectural practice, "though it was never much of one," as Goldstone says; the pity is that in the press of work Burnham never found the time to finish his monumental study of the life and work of Richard Morris Hunt. When Van Derpool retired, Burnham became head of the historic research department. Frank Gilbert, a lawyer and the grandson of Chief Justice Brandeis, joined the staff to ensure that the commission always acted with due process. He was also a voice of caution, doing his best to steer the commission clear of lawsuits, and this aspect of his job would soon become controversial. Below that level, however, "The city was so penny-pinching there was no one to help," Goldstone remembers. "I had the worst civil service hacks." Preservation, after all, was still a new discipline.**

The Landmarks Commission held its first public hearing in September 1965, but that sensational event was barely reported at the time—the newspapers were on strike. Nevertheless, the Board of Estimate chamber was overflowing when the

---

* *The first commission also included J. Woodbridge, Juliet Bartlett, Russell Lynes, Loring McMillen, Stanley Tankel, William R. Fisher, Helen Swenson, J. Clarence Davies, Jr., L. Bancel LaFarge, and Samuel J. Lefrak.*
** *He remembers how grateful he was when a friend, Martha Dalrymple, came on board as a volunteer spokesperson. She'd learned her craft working for Nelson Rockefeller. "It was like a Baroque painting: the skies opening." In 1974 they coauthored the first book-length guide to the city's landmarks: Harmon H. Goldstone and Martha Dalrymple,* History Preserved: A Guide to New York City Landmarks and Historical Districts *(New York: Schocken Books, 1976).*

hearing began at ten in the morning, and it took eleven hours to hear that day's testimony. What's striking about the Landmarks Commission's first hearings is that so many of the buildings on its calendar were about to be torn down. The trustees of Sailors' Snug Harbor in Staten Island meant to do away with their complex of Greek Revival temples. The Quakers had already signed a contract to sell the Friends Meeting House on Gramercy Park to a developer; so had the Hebrew Immigrant Aid Society, owners of the Astor Library. The Lutheran church was about to demolish the Morgan mansion at Madison Avenue and Thirty-seventh Street; and the Manhattan Club was negotiating the sale of its home, the former Jerome mansion on Madison Square.

None of these buildings would have survived without the landmarks law. One didn't survive with it. The Manhattan Club was able to prove hardship, and when the Landmarks Commission couldn't find a buyer for the Jerome mansion—the price was just $750,000—the stately Second Empire mansion came tumbling down. This was a bitter blow, but in hindsight it seems to have served as a very useful symbol. Later court decisions would take note of the Jerome mansion's fate, and as Harmon Goldstone wrote, "the hardship clause, originally mistaken for a weakness in the law, has proven to be a hidden strength. It has demonstrated that the preservation law is reasonable and fair." The residents of Gramercy Park and Murray Hill were fighting proposals to rezone their neighborhoods at far higher densities; they showed up in great numbers to save the Morgan mansion and the old Friends Meeting House, and this helped give the commission the courage to go ahead and designate.[84] The Morgan mansion, where I. N. Phelps Stokes grew up—it was built by his grandfather—survived through sheer good luck, however. The Lutheran church was also able to prove hardship, but by the time the court case was resolved in 1974, the economy had turned sour, redevelopment was postponed, and eventually the Morgan Library purchased the mansion, thus securing its future. The Friends Meeting House was saved in a different fashion. The Quakers opposed designation on the loftiest of grounds: "Tangible things are not important in themselves, but as means to ends," a representative told the Landmarks Commission.[85] But tangible things mattered so much to the building's neighbors that a group called the Friends of Gramercy Park sprang up. Its guiding spirit and principal funder was Benjamin Sonnenberg, the legendary pioneer of public relations and an MAS board member. He lived in enormous splendor at 19 Irving Place, a forty-room mansion filled with precious things. (Brendan Gill once tried to talk him into bequeathing the house to the Municipal Art Society.) Sonnenberg and his neighbors bought the Friends Meeting House. Sensitively restored by another Municipalian, architect James Polshek, it's now a synagogue.

A last-minute rescue of the Astor Library was an even happier story. The Hebrew Immigrant Aid Society had bought that building in the 1920s for use as a processing center for immigrants. By 1965 the demographics of immigration had changed, however, and the aid society was ready to sell out to a developer who had ideas about a new apartment house. The contract had already been signed when the Landmarks Preservation Commission designated the building. The developer slipped out of his contract, but this was merely a reprieve for the building. Unless the Landmarks Commission could find a new buyer within a year, the designation would have to be rescinded. At the last moment, Joseph Papp appeared on the scene. Papp had made his name with free Shakespeare productions, and he'd become the darling of New York's liberals in 1958, when Moses's Parks Department suddenly tried to bar his temporary stage from Central Park. The department's objection? That years earlier Papp had refused to name names before the House Un-American Activities Committee. MAS was just one of countless civic groups that rallied behind Papp, and for once the Arsenal backed down. Moses himself arranged for the construction of the Delacorte Theater, the gift of philanthropist George Delacorte.* The administration of Mayor John V. Lindsay was even friendlier to the Shakespeare Festival (its easy mix of culture and populism was the sort of thing Lindsay aspired to, but rarely achieved), so much so that Papp was ready to take a great leap forward and provide his actors with an indoor home. He was looking for a landmark, and the Landmarks Commission had a problem on its hands in the old Astor Library. At first Papp was skeptical, but it was suggested that, if he wanted the city's help, he'd best help the city first. Papp bought the building in the "belief, amply supported by Mayor Lindsay's actions, that the city would buy the Public Theater and lease it back to Papp at a nominal sum."[86] *Architectural Forum* wrote that "The eleventh hour rescue marks the first successful attempt by the Landmarks Preservation Commission to use the city's new law, and marks the continuing attempt to do the impossible by Joseph Papp."[87]

Sailors' Snug Harbor, on Staten Island, was "one of my favorite buildings," Goldstone says; it seems that the Harbor's unity and austerity appealed even to Modernists. The Harbor was entrusted to a board of trustees composed entirely of ex officio positions—the head of the chamber of commerce, the mayor, the Episcopal bishop, and so forth. Normally the mayor resigned at once; the remaining board members naturally wanted to perform their pro forma duties with as little fuss as possible, and so the Harbor was really run by its executive director, an "old curmudgeon of the worst kind" who regarded the buildings as a maintenance problem and nothing more. He took Goldstone through the site one day to show him all the rot; in the meantime a buyer was waiting in the wings ready to carve the place up for housing.[88]

When Goldstone designated the buildings, the trustees of Sailors' Snug Harbor went to court, arguing that the landmarks law was unconstitutional. The lower court agreed with them, finding that the burden of designation outweighed any

---

* Designed by MAS's own Giorgio Cavaglieri, the Delacorte Theater enjoys a beautiful view of Belvedere Castle. Then again, it spoils the view from the castle. Cavaglieri himself was disappointed with the theater. Its light stanchions were supposed to be retractable, disappearing into low concrete pylons when not in use, but in order to avoid complaints about encroachments in the park, the city insisted on maintaining the fiction that the Delacorte is a "temporary" structure (in fact the Shakespeare Festival has a ninety-nine-year lease), and concrete sounded permanent. Now the tall, ungainly light towers stick out like sore thumbs night and day, season after season. (Giorgio Cavaglieri, interview by author.)

public benefit. For the appeal, MAS put together a pro bono legal team to write an amicus brief. Its head was Terence Benbow, a Wall Street lawyer and Staten Islander; he worked with Ralph Menapace, MAS's brilliant counsel, and a young volunteer named Paul Byard (another family friend of Nathalie Dana). Byard haggled over the language with Menapace. Should they say that the lower court decision would "gut," "eviscerate," or "disembowel" the law? Byard insisted on "eviscerate," and he was delighted when the appellate court not only upheld the landmarks law but quoted his words in its decision. "It was very unusual," Byard says, and he adds, "the appellate division and the court of appeals were always very good courts."[89]

Sailors' Snug Harbor was still in grave danger, however. While the appellate court upheld the landmarks law—"certain of the basic questions," it wrote, "are no longer arguable"—it ordered a new round of discovery to determine whether this particular designation inflicted undue hardship on the owner. The guaranteed 6 percent return needn't apply to a charity, the court ruled, but the question remained whether maintaining Sailors' Snug Harbor "either physically or financially prevents or seriously interferes with carrying out [its] charitable purpose."[90] After decades of neglect, maintenance was indeed a problem at the Harbor. The trustees, still determined to sell, scheduled a vote to authorize the next round of legal action, but as they gathered on Wall Street, Harmon Goldstone paid a desperate visit to the mayor. Lindsay had once told him that if "a *real* problem came up" he should "just yell for help." Goldstone told him, "I'm yelling right now." Lindsay had resigned from the Harbor's board, but the two of them set out for Wall Street, Lindsay striding down Broadway while Goldstone ran along beside him to fill him in on the details. The mayor burst into the meeting. He was resuming his seat on the board, he announced. As an ex officio member, he pointed out, he had every right to do so, and he was going to vote against the sale. The very idea was "disgraceful," he said. "What studies have been made?" he demanded to know. Lindsay then announced that the city would "buy the buildings rather than see them disturbed."

The executive director was "open-mouthed," Goldstone remembers, but the trustees were "swept off their feet." With Lindsay's backing, the city then took the land. The trustees had a site in mind in South Carolina, next to a veterans' hospital, and the city's purchase helped make the move possible.[91]

Saving Sailors' Snug Harbor and the Astor Library were only the most dramatic triumphs of the early days of the Landmarks Commission. But if Goldstone and his colleagues felt a certain euphoria, it was mingled with a good deal of fear. They'd embarked on an experiment in constitutional law, and it seemed wise to delay their day of judgment for as long as possible. So the Landmarks Commission stood by as the Singer Tower, Ernest Flagg's masterpiece, was torn down to make way for the headquarters of the U.S. Steel Corporation, an awful hymn to the brute strength of steel beams. The commission also looked away as Joseph Urban's fabled Ziegfeld Theater gave way to another glass box. And by a six-to-five vote, the Landmarks Commission declared that the Metropolitan Opera House was *not* a landmark.

This last decision was perhaps the most painful moment in the early history of the Landmarks Commission. The battle pitted a citizens' group, Save the Met, against the Metropolitan Opera Company, which was playing with a stacked deck. It had to sell the old opera house to pay for its new home in Lincoln Center, and it feared that if the old auditorium survived, some new impresario might challenge the Met's monopoly on grand opera (as Oscar Hammerstein once had, to the great benefit of opera, if not of the Met). So when the Met contracted to sell its home to developer Irwin Chanin, it inserted a clause requiring him to demolish the building. Failure to do so would void the sale, and that would mean bankruptcy for the Met. In essence, the Met threatened to commit suicide unless it had its way. The Landmarks Commission was swayed by this curious form of blackmail, and so, regrettably, was the Municipal Art Society. It kept ignoring Save the Met's agonized pleas for support—even after the AIA came up with a scheme to preserve the auditorium in a new tower. Some board members were disgusted by MAS's timidity, and at the last minute the society finally endorsed Save the Met's goals, but this was too little too late to be of any use.

The destruction of the opera house also testified to one of the gravest flaws in the landmarks law. The building's exterior was famously ugly, and some commissioners let their aesthetic standards take precedence over any consideration of the building's historic and cultural significance, and voted against designation. The pity, of course, was that the Met's architectural glory was its auditorium, decorated in 1903 by Carrère & Hastings, and *that* the commission couldn't protect.

THE SENSIBLE
LANDMARKS LAW

THE MUNICIPAL ART SOCIETY had spent a quarter century working for a landmarks law, and when it was finally passed in 1965 the society wondered what to do next. There was a period of "backing and filling and being very unsure," Margot Gayle remembers. A certain amount of passion was gone, and Harmon Goldstone, Geoffrey Platt, and Alan Burnham had left MAS to join the city government. Having a landmarks law changed the tenor of the preservation movement. As Goldstone says, "We were looking for a way to create a dispassionate, orderly procedure in the statute. The process plods along without any whoop-de-do. We took all the fun out of it." A different sort of advocacy was now required. MAS had to recruit people to testify at hearings, propose new landmarks and historic districts, and help the city fight off any legal challenges. It had to keep an eye on the day-to-day activities of the Landmarks Preservation Commission, offering praise and criticism, prodding it along. It had to coax the Board of Estimate to ratify the commission's designations and to grant it a decent budget. And it had to pay political tribute to City Hall, since the best way to interest a mayor in preservation is to make sure it generates good publicity.[1]

In the mid 1960s, however, MAS was still "sort of a social organization," a member recalls. "You were invited to join, and there was a sort of a social aura to it." Otis Pratt Pearsall, who joined the board at this time, remembers it as "a sort of Victorian remnant, a nice board, but not a powerful board." Nathalie Dana grew unhappy. She knew the "gentleman-amateur" approach would no longer work and that MAS wasn't capitalizing on its success. The landmarks law had created a huge reservoir of goodwill toward MAS. Now was the time to expand the society and broaden its scope, but the opportunity was slipping away. Dana decided that the root of the problem was MAS's president, Ruth McAneny Loud.[2]

Loud was the first woman to head the Municipal Art Society, and it was typical of the group's stodginess that this breakthrough came about by accident. She slipped into the role when Whitney North Seymour, Jr., was elected to the state senate and gave up his post as MAS's president. Loud, then vice president, stepped into his place and was later elected to two more terms in her own right. She was the daughter of George McAneny and the guardian of his memory. Perhaps she played this role too enthusiastically; she idolized her father and worried that a biographer would be more critical than she, and so kept too tight a rein on his papers. The result is that there is no biography of McAneny, and he is almost forgotten. (She thought Robert Caro's tone in *The Power Broker* was exactly right, but since she couldn't bear to read about Moses—"that bastard"— she just looked up her father's name in the index.) Aside from telling tales of her father, Loud's great joy was to throw parties. "It's what I do best," she said, and her parties were splendid affairs. Feminism horrified Loud, but she used MAS's annual meetings to get women into places ordinarily denied them—like the Century and the Players clubs—and she took an impish delight in dancing in such sacred quarters.[3]

Perhaps this impishness grated on Nathalie Dana. Dana was brusque and serious while Loud had a childlike enthusiasm for life and a bubbling sense of humor—she once opened a home furnishings shop with Karl Bitter's widow because, she said, she couldn't resist naming it "Bitter and Loud." Dana decided to recruit yet another old friend, the lawyer David Prager, to bring some professionalism to MAS. She talked the society's treasurer into resigning and then proposed that Prager take his place (administering an annual budget of "something like $10,000").

Prager set two conditions for joining the board: MAS had to hire an executive director and set up an executive committee. Loud agreed, but she picked the director herself and presented him to the board as "a sort of fait accompli." His name was Fred Williams; he was a friend of Loud's, the director of "some amateur theater enterprise in which she was involved." Williams found MAS an office at 41 East Sixty-fifth Street, in the American Federation of the Arts Building. It was a tiny space, but the building was full of arts groups—the old Society of Mural Painters, the Architectural League, and others—and there was a pleasantly clubby bar. The executive committee met in Prager's law office, and the board assembled for lunch at the Overseas Press Club, in the Wilkie Building on Fortieth Street. "One couldn't always hear through the din of lunch plates," Prager remembers, and "staff members . . . sometimes voted, and no one really noticed."[4]

Such a casual approach irritated Dana and Prager, and then there was the question of Fred Williams. By all accounts he was a troubled man, and he was proving to be "totally ineffectual."[5]

In 1968 Nathalie Dana learned that Loud wanted another two years in office, that she'd picked a nominating committee, and that this committee had already voted to reelect her.* It was an excellent committee—it was chaired by Brendan

---

* MAS had an arcane method of selecting officers. The current president drew up a list of names for a nominating committee, the board (always) voted its approval, the committee nominated one person for each vacancy, the board approved (almost always), the nominees were presented to the members at the next annual meeting, and finally the secretary stood up and single-handedly voted them all into office "on behalf of" the membership.

Gill, and Ada Louise Huxtable was a member—but there was a tradition at MAS that presidents served for four years at most. Loud had already served five. And technically the board of directors, not the president, was supposed to appoint the nominating committee—but an election had already occurred. At the next meeting, Loud asked the board to confirm her candidates for the nominating committee. She mentioned nothing about an election having already taken place. David Prager summoned up all his courage—"I'm diffident by nature," he says—and gently suggested that the procedure seemed "undemocratic." Since Loud was a candidate for office, shouldn't she recuse herself? Loud was furious, Brendan Gill felt his good faith had been questioned, and the meeting broke up in acrimony. Scathing correspondence was passed around, and finally Bronson Binger, Nathalie Dana, Harmon Goldstone, and Whitney North Seymour, Sr., asked Loud to withdraw her candidacy. She had no choice but to agree, and Charles Evans Hughes III succeeded her.

Prager refers to these events as the "palace revolution." "It cleared the air for a new procedure," he says, "and brought MAS into the twentieth century." At least it cleared the way for a new executive director. Fred Williams had grown even "more peculiar," as one source puts it. A search committee was formed to look for a replacement, and Joan Davidson, a new board member, produced a young man named Kent Barwick. "I didn't invent him," Davidson says, but she did "discover him." Davidson was the daughter of J. M. Kaplan, "a crusty old philanthropist" who'd made his fortune with the Welch Grape Juice Company; she became the head of the J. M. Kaplan Fund—the angel of virtually every preservation group in the city. Barwick, her discovery, was a tall young man raised on Long Island and in Cooperstown. He'd drifted into copywriting and, "as is only possible in advertising . . . was an immediate success."[6] By the time he was twenty-eight he had a wife and two kids, he was the creative director of an ad agency, and he was miserable—"dying to get into the nonprofit field." He joined the Friends of South Street Seaport, a band of volunteers who created a maritime museum on South Street, and he helped arrange an exhibition on the Port of New York. It was hands-on work; Joan Davidson, another Friend of the Seaport, met Barwick when she walked into the museum's bathroom and found him painting the floor. A few months later she suggested he "leave the greasy world of business" and come work for MAS. He couldn't afford to at first, but some money was raised, largely from J. M. Kaplan. It was enough to offer Barwick "an excellent opportunity" and a tiny salary.[7]

Barwick took the job because he was flattered that such a distinguished group of people had asked him aboard. Only later, looking through MAS's records, did he discover that his rivals for the post fell into two camps: those who weren't alcoholics were standing on their last legs. It was a strange little group Barwick had joined. Charles Evans Hughes III, MAS's president at the time, was an architect with Skidmore, Owings & Merrill. His masterpiece was the Manufacturers Hanover Trust Company Building at the corner of Fifth Avenue and Forty-third Street, one of New York's great Modernist landmarks. Hughes was a "wonderful man" but a "bumbling presenter," Barwick remembers. "A pacifist, not a firebrand," says Brendan Gill. Barwick had a part-time secretary and the volunteer help of Ronald Friedlander, whose father designed the Bronx County Courthouse and the Museum of the City of New York. Friedlander had spent most of his life in nonprofit work; now retired and in his seventies, he produced a program called *The Livable City* on WNYC. Pat Jones, a writer for Mobil Oil and producer for PBS, helped out as a consultant. As for the society itself, it was still suffering from a "hangover," Barwick says. It was "the vestige of a club. It was very Waspy when I joined." One might add that Barwick himself is very Waspy, and this surely recommended him to the board.[8]

In 1968 a *Times* editorial heralded the news that MAS was "turning to the total urban environment."[9] Now the Municipal Art Society had room to look at other issues again. It began to make its voice heard on zoning and planning issues, subjects it had long neglected, but its attention was drawn back again and again to the inadequacies of the landmarks law. Platt, Goldstone, and Felt had managed to forge a consensus behind the preservation law in 1965, but only at the cost of sundry compromises, and the most ironic of these had to do with the city's historic parks.

M A S   H A D   talked about preserving Central Park as far back as the 1920s, long before it dreamed of a landmarks law, and it was the bad taste of Robert Moses and his untrammeled power as parks commissioner that sparked the modern preservation movement in 1941. Yet the Landmarks Law of 1965 made no mention of parks. The power to designate scenic landmarks "hadn't been forgotten" when the law was written, Goldstone says. It had been "left out . . . because we thought it was going to be so difficult to get it through."[10]

In the 1950s, when the landmarks law was just a gleam in the eyes of a few Municipalians, they didn't dare mention scenic landmarks. To do so would have invited the parks commissioner's wrath, and MAS knew how easily Moses could quash its movement. When Moses stepped down from his city posts in 1960 it looked as if MAS had more room to maneuver, but in fact little had changed at the Arsenal. Moses had picked his own successor: Newbold Morris, an old pillar of the Fusion movement who still stood out in the political landscape, according to the *Times*, as a "reformer and an idealist." Even his friends admitted, however, that Morris had a strong streak of naïveté—his enemies called him a Boy Scout—and somehow Moses tapped into both that idealism and that innocence. Morris idolized Moses—some said to the point of self-abasement—and proudly described himself as the master builder's "disciple."[11] And so the new parks commissioner kept Moses's staff intact and even referred all major decisions to his predecessor. It was as if Moses had never given up his post; even in 1965 he would have seen the designation of scenic landmarks as a threat to his power, and that would have been fatal to the landmarks law.

Moses left the Parks Department with an ambiguous legacy: hundreds of acres of new greenery, but most of it of a very low aesthetic quality. He'd once been a brilliant designer, as Jones Beach and the early parkways still attest, but the parks had long since fallen into the hands of a giant bureaucracy that valued engineering more than aesthetics and efficiency more than charm. The Arsenal churned out parks in ever more standardized designs, each with its own allotment of recreational facilities, whether needed or not; its little brick rest rooms, which were never maintained; and its concrete park benches laid out by the linear foot. There was always too much asphalt and too little shrubbery, and a late Moses park was a dreary thing: an open, windswept landscape meant to deny hiding places to muggers, it also denied people any sense of shelter.

These attitudes had spilled over into the city's historic parks. There was no Samuel Parsons to fight tooth and nail for the parks' integrity; Moses's landscape architects were cogs in an assembly line, and their power to veto the commissioner's schemes had been stripped away in 1934. Over a thirty-year period Central Park was remade in "the worst taste of suburbia," as Lewis Mumford wrote in *The New Yorker*; the idyllic landscape was littered with "firm, man-made boundaries—iron fences, concrete curbs," and "dull buildings and prisonlike enclosures."[12] And after the Second World War, Moses ushered in Central Park's age of "aggressive philanthropy," as Henry Hope Reed called it, throwing the grounds open to foundations and to philanthropists who yearned for immortality.[13] The Wollman Skating Rink was built in 1950, for example, and the Hans Christian Andersen statute was installed in 1956. The Alice in Wonderland group—"beloved by children, if not by art critics," as one Municipalian noted—appeared in 1959, and the Delacorte Theater in 1963.

MAS kept quiet about these projects, in part because the civic groups had few tools with which to block them, and Moses simply snarled at critics. The Art Commission, which could have intervened, had degenerated into a secretive, timid body, too terrified to exercise its veto.[14] The City Planning Commission played a purely advisory role in shaping the Parks Department budget, and since many encroachments were gifts to the city, they never even appeared in the budget. The civic groups' only hope, therefore, was to influence donors, and this strategy worked once, in 1955, in the protest against the Lasker Senior Citizen Center. The Lasker plan called for fourteen acres of the Ramble to be fenced off to create a reservation for the elderly—and to keep out muggers, the Parks Department said. If any aged visitors actually managed to climb the Ramble's steep slopes, they would have found a sprawling suburban ranch house designed by Moore & Hutchens, where they were expected to amuse themselves with horseshoes, shuffleboard, croquet, and a television room. The Lasker Foundation was eventually persuaded to withdraw its grant—not so much by MAS's complaints as by the desperate protests of the Linnean Society, a dedicated group of bird-watchers.[15]

Donors wouldn't always listen, however. In 1960, when Harmon Goldstone was still an officer of the Municipal Art Society, he inaugurated the fight to stop another encroachment, the Huntington Hartford Pavilion. If ever a man was the victim of inherited wealth, it was surely Hartford, heir to the $100 million A&P supermarket fortune. A biography, aptly titled *Squandered Fortune*, garishly describes his slide into a spectacularly sordid existence.[16] When MAS confronted him, however, Hartford was still a respectable figure, though he was engaged in an eccentric campaign to make his mark in cultural philanthropy. In the 1950s he built the Huntington Hartford Museum of Representative Art, that odd little white marble building on the southern edge of Columbus Circle (the art inside was even odder), now occupied by the city's Cultural Affairs Department. In 1960 Hartford decided to build inside the park itself: a 1,000-seat café, designed by Edward Durell Stone, overlooking the pond at Fifty-ninth Street and the Plaza. The pond itself was to be jazzed up with fountains, and Stone wanted to train multicolored floodlights on the jets of water. Moses loved the idea, which meant that Newbold Morris loved it too, and the Art Commission gave its seal of approval to the design—but only, one member admitted, after it decided "to judge the ... café in terms of its design, and not to weigh its appropriateness to a Central Park location."[17]

The Hartford Pavilion was "an emotional issue" for Harmon Goldstone; Central Park had been his childhood backyard. "I *worked* on that one. I made a sidewalk survey, a block-by-block count of restaurants and their cuisines and their costs" to prove that people in the park weren't exactly the famished, thirsty hordes pictured by the café's advocates. Goldstone republished Richard Welling's old drawing of proposed improvements to the park, and he tried to discuss the issue with Hartford, but the man "had an awful lot of money and a lot of power and a lot of ego. It was always impossible to meet or talk with him on the phone. I don't think we ever met."[18]

MAS pointed out that Olmsted and Vaux had placed a restaurant beneath the terrace of Bethesda Fountain. That café had been shuttered for decades, and Bethesda's arcade had seemed dark and ominous ever since. Why not revive it? MAS asked, but Hartford, Moses, and Morris brushed that suggestion aside. Then, in 1963, Walter Hoving, president of Tiffany's and éminence grise of the Fifth Avenue Association, filed a lawsuit charging that the city had no right to use parkland for a café "which would not serve even one incidental park purpose."[19] MAS contributed money and expert witnesses to the suit, but the legal argument rested on the fact that the proposed café's main entrance would be on Fifty-ninth Street rather than inside the park. The café, lawyers argued, wasn't meant for people using the park; it would really belong, in some sense, to the streets of the Upper East Side. This was a shaky foundation for a lawsuit, and it failed to convince the courts. Outside the courtroom, Hoving warned that the café might bring an undesirable crowd to Fifth Avenue and so lower property values—an argument that made MAS squirm.[20]

While the suit wound its way through the court system, the National Park Service declared Central Park a national historic landmark (a toothless honor) and mayoral candidate John Lindsay issued a white paper on the parks. This was written by Thomas Hoving, Walter's son, and naturally, it called on the city to abandon

Hartford's café project. Young Hoving also made two other recommendations that cheered MAS: he urged that Central Park be named a scenic landmark, which would mean amending the landmarks law, and he said the city should appoint a "curator" to supervise "exact reconstructions" of the original Olmsted and Vaux design. "Lindsay was the darling of the Municipal Art Society," Kent Barwick remembers; Whitney North Seymour, Jr., prominent in both MAS and the Parks Council, was "a Lindsay person"; and Hoving's white paper delighted Municipalians.[21] Yet when Lindsay won the election and Thomas Hoving became his parks commissioner, Central Park became a battlefield all over again. Construction of Hartford's café was indeed canceled, and Henry Hope Reed was named Central Park's first (unpaid) curator, but neither Lindsay nor Hoving nor Goldstone moved to create the new category of scenic landmarks.

Hoving had his good points. In 1966 he joined with MAS and a coalition of environmental groups in a campaign to reroute the planned Richmond Parkway. The original plan called for the route to plow through Staten Island's most beautiful and environmentally sensitive wilderness areas, land through which Frederick Law Olmsted used to hike. In 1967 Hoving, Lindsay, and the city planning commissioner, Donald Elliott, led a crowd of six hundred hikers along the parkway's path. The state finally compromised on a less destructive plan; the city showed a newfound sensitivity to New York's remaining wilderness; and the parkway battle eventually led to the establishment of Staten Island's Greenbelt and the Gateway National Park.

As Central Park's curator, Henry Hope Reed found himself in the position Samuel Parsons had occupied half a century before: he was charged with preserving and restoring the park, while Hoving was a populist in the tradition of Charles Stover. Hoving staged concerts and "happenings" that brought tens of thousands to the park and that left Reed worrying about the lawns and wondering how people could contemplate the subtleties of the landscape amid the din. Both Hoving and Reed lamented the miserable quality of Moses's encroachments, but whereas Reed wanted to rip out Moses's harsh and dreary playgrounds, Hoving's solution was to redesign them as "adventure parks" for youngsters. MAS and the Parks Council applauded Hoving's innovations, to Reed's dismay. Reed, however, was the president of the Friends of Central Park, a dedicated band of preservationist "park radicals." Since this was a single-issue group, the Friends of Central Park were far freer than MAS to engage in no-holds-barred fights with the city, and their spokesman, Robert Makla, could be both eloquent and savage.*

It was Reed who briefed MAS on Thomas Hoving's project for the Central Park Stables, a scheme that started out as an answer to a little problem and then mushroomed until it threatened acres of parkland. The only stable left in Man-

---

* Both Hoving and his successor, August Heckscher, complained bitterly about the Friends of Central Park, and they reproached Reed for presiding over this noisy band of critics while working for the Arsenal. Where did his loyalties lie? Had he never heard of a conflict of interest? Reed claimed that his position with the Friends was purely honorary, and he added that there could be no meaningful conflict of interest when neither the Friends nor the city paid him a cent.

hattan, the Claremont on West Eighty-ninth Street, sat on a block that was slated for urban renewal. Without a stable, Central Park's bridle paths would have been abandoned, so Hoving decided to build a new facility in the park. Then stables for the police department's mounted squad were added to the project, plus new headquarters for the Twenty-second Precinct, and finally an enormous exercise ring. Hoving persuaded Stephen Currier, the owner of *Architectural Forum* magazine, to pay for an architectural competition. The winner was Norval White, coauthor of the *AIA Guide to New York City*, cofounder of AGBANY, and one of MAS's directors. White did his best to minimize the project's impact on the park. His scheme was described as an "underground" structure, but more precisely, it was to have steep banks of earth piled around its walls and, as August Heckscher put it, "a sort of meadow on the top." Almost at once Hoving found himself in political trouble. It started with that exercise field: "The idea got around, given credibility by a notation on the original architectural drawings, that this field was to be used for polo." The Lindsay administration was already having trouble with its elitist image—aside from Hoving's Tiffany connection and Lindsay's own silk stocking background, the city's new transportation commissioner was a Russian prince—and now Lindsay's critics trumpeted the news that the city was about to build a polo field. "Hoving tried to redeem the situation by insisting it was really intended for tiddlywinks," but voters resent flippancy in public servants, so Hoving solemnly promised there'd be no polo and insisted that polo had never entered his mind.[22]

MAS didn't particularly care what games were played on the field; the plan still threatened to set a series of horrifying precedents. It would have been the park's first indoor sports facility, the first intrusion of unrelated city services, and the first underground structure in any established park. This last point was especially dangerous, MAS thought, since it was also battling an attempt to build a garage beneath Madison Square. Kent Barwick was new to MAS when the board of directors ordered him to launch a campaign against the stables, and what astonished him was that Norval White was in the room at the time. White had watched friends and colleagues reject all his arguments, but "he didn't whine or scream or walk out of the room," Barwick remembers. He took the blow with grace, and that civility left a deep impression on Barwick.

A new twist was introduced in 1967 when Thomas Hoving resigned as parks commissioner to head the Metropolitan Museum of Art, and August Heckscher, MAS's vice president, became the new parks commissioner. Heckscher staged the first "wed-in" in the city parks—"For nine couples," sneered the *Times*, "all was free, loud and televised."[23] He horrified Henry Hope Reed by making Doris Freedman, a great patron of modern art, his cultural affairs commissioner; and he let men take off their shirts for the first time in the parks' history. One of Heckscher's first acts in office was to suggest a closer collaboration between MAS and the Parks Department, and in some areas this was fruitful: it was during his regime that the Parks Department took title to two Staten Island landmarks, Sailor's Snug Harbor and the Alice Austen House. But Heckscher had also inherited the Central Park Stables project from his predecessor, and he fought hard for it.

It was a "quasi-political" battle, Barwick remembers, and the forerunner of many to come. MAS was "not the sole force, but it fell to us to organize. We organized a coalition, we had a slogan."[24] The society's new newsletter presented both sides of the debate fairly, with David Todd writing in support of the stable. The idea was to keep separate the society's two different roles: MAS would be an advocate, but it would also report the issues more dependably, and in more depth, than the daily papers. The civic groups succeeded in politicizing the battle. One faction of the City Council favored the new police quarters but nothing else; another supported just the recreational facilities; and a third agreed with MAS that none of these things belonged in Central Park. As a result, the Central Park Stables were voted down in the City Council.

At the Metropolitan Museum, however, philanthropy was getting aggressive again. In 1876 the state of New York reserved a large section of Central Park for the museum: it could build anywhere between Eightieth and Eighty-fifth streets, Fifth Avenue and the Park Drive. Frederick Law Olmsted later regretted that he'd gone along with this, but the law remained on the books. Thomas Hoving, the museum's new director, had great plans for the Met; he was determined to transform it into a vast encyclopedia of art. So in 1967, when Egypt offered to give the Temple of Dendur to an American museum, Hoving was eager to get his hands on it. Since this was a gift to the American people, in recognition of assistance in saving Abu Simbel and other monuments from the floodwaters of the Aswan Dam, the Smithsonian thought it should have the temple, but Hoving won the prize by promising to build a separate wing for it. He had other additions in mind, too. Nelson Rockefeller had given money for a wing of primitive art, a memorial to his son Michael, who'd reportedly been killed by cannibals in New Guinea. Also, the American Wing had outgrown its quarters, and in 1969, after years of delicate negotiations, Robert Lehman had left his art collection to the museum with two provisos: that it be displayed in its own wing and, ridiculously, within reconstructed rooms from Lehman's town house. (Alas, the financier had tacky taste in decor.)

Hoving's plans for expanding the Met raised a host of issues for the Municipal Art Society. Any new wings would cover up the old Victorian facades by Vaux & Mould and Theodore Weston (built before Richard Morris Hunt arrived on the scene). These facades were landmarked; the city wasn't bound to listen to the Landmarks Commission's complaints, but it would set a very poor example if it flouted the spirit of the preservation law. And then there was Central Park. The state land grant might have seemed sensible back in 1876 when the park was still fringed with farms. Nearly a century had passed, however, and the farms had given way to high-rises. Greenery was an infinitely more precious commodity now, and sacrificing part of Central Park for new buildings, no matter how distinguished their contents, no longer seemed to be in the public interest. Finally MAS and its allies took up Mayor Lindsay's cry for decentralization and wondered why it shouldn't apply to the Met. Lindsay was committed to decentralizing the school system, expanding the power of the community boards, and setting up "little city halls." When news first broke of Hoving's plans for the Temple of Dendur, Robert Makla insisted that "Cultural decentralization is the only worthy policy. Entire communities are still untouched by the cultural explosion which has enriched central Manhattan."[25] The Metropolitan already had one branch facility, the Cloisters, so why not another for the Temple of Dendur? The city could use the temple, the *Times* added, "as a city planning tool, a cultural focus and point of beauty for any one of the many parts of New York that need it far more than Fifth Avenue and Central Park."[26] At the time the city was also wondering what to do with Roosevelt Island, and in 1968 the landscape architects Zion & Breen suggested that the tip of that island would make a better home for the temple. It would draw visitors to the new park there, and the temple itself would confront, if not the Nile, at least a river. Ada Louise Huxtable pushed this scheme in the *Times*, and the City Planning Commission asked the Met to consider other sites, but the Met rejected them all.

When the museum announced in 1969 that it was going to build the Lehman Pavilion as well, Parks Commissioner Heckscher wanted to know just how far Hoving meant to go. He insisted that the museum produce a master plan, and Hoving unveiled this in 1970, the Met's centennial year. The work of Kevin Roche and John Dinkeloo, designers of the Ford Foundation headquarters on East Forty-second Street, the master plan increased the museum's bulk by a third. (It's almost touching to read the architects' original description of their design: the steel and glass curtain walls were an homage to Victorian architecture, they said, and they would be so light and transparent that the museum would seem to dissolve into the landscape.) The city accepted the plan with the proviso that the museum agree never to expand farther into the park, but the Municipal Art Society was horrified. Hoving started work by cutting down the trees in front of the Met, claiming they were "diseased." That was "the wrong lie," Barwick says: the logs were left lying on Fifth Avenue and it was a simple matter for MAS to have them examined. Healthy trees were sacrificed for a banal new plaza. Meanwhile MAS still hoped the Landmarks Commission would put a wrench in the Lehman wing project. The museum was, after all, a landmark, and the law called for the commission to deliver a nonbinding advisory opinion on any changes to a city-owned landmark. Harmon Goldstone had in fact already issued a negative recommendation, but no one knew it, because the city never published it.

The Friends of Central Park resorted to picketing the Met's centennial celebrations. The Parks Council and the Municipal Art Society "adopted a more effective and costly strategy," Heckscher remembers: they went to court. Their lawyer was Leonard Sand, who went on to become the judge in the Yonkers housing case, and the dispute bore the "Pickwickian name" of *Tuck and Gill v. Heckscher.*[27] "Gill" was Brendan Gill, who remembers that for the sake of publicity, "It had to be personal:

'Brendan Gill is suing Augie Heckscher.' It was a terrible thing. We were classmates at Yale."[28] The legal battlefield was an arcane clause in the city charter which said that the Board of Estimate had to approve any public improvements paid for with private funds. The corporation counsel insisted this clause didn't apply to philanthropic gifts, that it was only meant to stop developers from installing substandard sewer lines. Of course MAS had no guarantee that the Board of Estimate would actually vote against the Lehman wing, but at least there'd be a public debate, and the city would be more thoughtful about accepting future gift horses. The case went to three courts, and the city finally prevailed with the argument that the mayor did have sole power to accept gifts to the city. The Lehman Pavilion was a gift that Lindsay was happy to accept.

"Nothing positive came of the lawsuit except public alarm," Barwick says. In his notoriously unreliable memoirs, Hoving gloated that MAS merely succeeded in delaying the project until the recession forced building costs down. The Landmarks Commission did manage to shame the museum into leaving the Met's old Victorian facades exposed within the new building, and when the Lehman Pavilion finally opened in 1975, critics agreed that the handsomest thing about its architecture was the one wall designed by Calvert Vaux and Jacob Wrey Mould.[29] Something more did come of the lawsuit, however. It focused MAS's attention on the need for two revisions to the landmarks law: first, the society was determined to establish the new category of scenic landmarks; second, it meant to force the city to publish the Landmarks Commission's advisory opinions.

In 1971, in the middle of MAS's quarrel with the Metropolitan Museum, Harmon Goldstone visited Kent Barwick and asked for the society's help in amending the landmarks law.[30] The Penn Central railroad was about to file suit challenging the law's constitutionality. So far Goldstone had managed to stop the railroad from building a tower above Grand Central Terminal, but Penn Central was still completely free to do whatever it wished inside that building. Goldstone wanted a new category of interior landmarks to save the city's great public rooms: spaces like Grand Central's concourse and the floor of the Stock Exchange. MAS pressed him to go further: the society wanted scenic landmarks, too; it wanted to repeal the moratorium clause; and it thought the city should publish the Landmarks Commission's advisory reports. Goldstone explained "his difficulties." His budget was tiny, and his lower-level staff had no training in preservation, architectural history, or even architecture. This wasn't the time to take on too many new tasks, Goldstone said.[31] Barwick, however, was convinced that Goldstone was really afraid of pushing City Hall too far. He feared that the Lindsay administration wasn't in the mood for a new fight with developers and that it wouldn't countenance scenic landmarks if that meant handing a new weapon to critics of the Metropolitan Museum.

IN FACT Goldstone and his colleagues at the Landmarks Commission were exceptionally busy. The preservation movement was becoming far more popular than Goldstone had ever expected. Back in 1965 he'd known that Van Derpool's survey of potential landmarks was incomplete; new gems would turn up as people learned more about the city and its architectural history. What surprised Goldstone was that people kept coming to the Landmarks Commission with ideas for new historic districts.

Goldstone had promised that Brooklyn Heights would become the city's first historic district, and he kept his word in November 1965. "In no time at all," Pearsall remembers, "we discovered the compromises in the landmarks law. Light, bulk, and use were still ruled by the zoning laws. It was difficult for us. The Watchtower was planning a building, and we realized it was hard to block under the landmarks law. We felt we wouldn't be able to use the landmarks law to block a high building if they got to use the hardship clause to tear down the old houses there. The 6 percent return applied at that time to nonprofit organizations, too. We went to the planning commission for a limited-height district, an amendment to the citywide zoning law, and we won in a close Board of Estimate hearing. The Watchtower caught up with us at the last minute. We worked out a compromise— the Watchtower project was exempted, in a sense. They got their approval, and *then* the new limits took effect; in the meantime we negotiated a much lower solution for their building." The community provided the Watchtower Society with a list of distinguished modern architects, and the Watchtower chose Ulrich Franzen. His building turned out to be "very elegant," says Pearsall, and "not intrusive at all."[32] By today's standards, though, it seems a very halfhearted attempt at contextualism.

Brooklyn Heights was easy. There was enormous community support for designation, Clay Lancaster's research was impeccable, and the neighborhood was a sterling candidate for protection: it had long been a fairly homogeneous neighborhood of high architectural quality, and all those years of shabby gentility meant that it had suffered relatively few inroads. When the Landmarks Commission turned to Greenwich Village, however, the ground suddenly seemed less steady.

In 1965 the Landmarks Commission held hearings on a sixty-five-block historic district for Greenwich Village. Lawsuits were threatened by a group touting itself as the Committee for Responsible Landmarks Preservation, and Goldstone still remembers one long conversation with a man who swore he'd go to court to recover his property rights. When all other arguments failed, Goldstone invoked the favorite bugaboo of 1960s city planners: "We're protecting you from having a glue factory next door," he said. The fellow wasn't convinced; maybe he'd read Jane Jacobs's book, in which she pointed out that there *was* a glue factory on her block and that it was perfectly odorless.[33]

Alarmed by the opposition, the Landmarks Commission decided that if it singled out just the best pockets of the Village it would have a stronger footing in court. Many "dogs," as Goldstone put it, were scattered through the neighborhood. There were taxpayers, old row houses long since mutilated, and modern apartment buildings with white glazed-brick facades. Goldstone worried that these buildings might vitiate the idea that the neighborhood was a single coherent unit. How much diversity could the Landmarks Commission tolerate in a historic district? Goldstone began whittling away at his map of the Village, and in 1966 he unveiled a scheme to break up the neighborhood into eighteen tiny separate historic districts. Together they would cover just two-thirds of the district proposed the year before. The new map looked like a jigsaw puzzle with a third of its pieces missing; it showed a neighborhood riddled with unprotected lots. "Dismay was mingled with surprise" in the Village, and the Greenwich Village Historic District Council announced that it would fight for the whole sixty-five blocks.* The Villagers didn't dispute that many buildings in the neighborhood were unworthy of protection, but Goldstone's compromise seemed to miss the point of the historic districts clause: that there was a public interest in ensuring that future development respected the scale and character of the genuinely historic fabric. The corporation counsel agreed: historic districts were easier to defend in court when, as in a zoning district, neighbors shared the burdens and benefits alike. He advised Geoffrey Platt that the Landmarks Commission should designate the whole area, but he recommended that it prepare "the most detailed report on the whole district that you can possibly imagine. You've got to overwhelm them with detail."[34] It took Alan Burnham two years to finish the report.

The charms of Greenwich Village were evident to everyone, but SoHo appealed only to those whose taste ran more toward the avant-garde. In 1947 the Washington Square Association had commissioned a planning study from Arthur Holden, who worked long and hard for a preservation law at MAS, and his recommendations were typical of the blind spot that still afflicted even relatively enlightened circles. Holden called for preserving the low-scale residential character in Greenwich Village by downzoning the area, but the whole neighborhood south of Washington Square was slated for demolition. The park itself would have been extended southward as a mall, so that New York University would have an identifiable campus. SoHo's lofts, dismissed as obsolete, were slated for urban renewal, and Broome Street was to be the site of a crosstown expressway.

This proposed Lower Manhattan Expressway, an elevated six-lane highway, was first drawn by Robert Moses in 1940. It was meant to link Long Island and New Jersey, and its octopus arms would stretch out to the Manhattan and Williamsburg bridges, the West Side Highway, and the Holland Tunnel. Sixteen years later the expressway qualified for federal funding, and in 1960 it was officially entered on the city map, but when the Board of Estimate was asked to condemn land along the expressway route, the neighborhood rose up. At least 2,000 families faced the loss of their homes, and 10,000 jobs would disappear. Such devastation was nothing new in the Bronx and still went unnoticed in the press, but this was Manhattan. Eleanor Roosevelt, Lewis Mumford, and Congressman John Lindsay denounced the scheme. The Board of Estimate decided not to act at that time, but in 1964 the

---

* The council started out as an alliance of the Association of Village Home Owners, the local planning board, the West Village Committee, the Greenwich Village Association, and the Village Independent Democrats.

construction unions threw their weight behind the project. With the world's fair just finished, the building industry was sluggish, and the unions were perfectly willing to trade 2,000 temporary construction jobs for those 10,000 permanent positions.

Again the Board of Estimate shied away from authorizing condemnations, however, and in 1966 the neighborhood was momentarily cheered by John Lindsay's election because, as a congressman, he'd opposed the expressway. Now, as mayor, he revamped the proposal, and in 1967 he unveiled a new plan in which most of the road lay underground in tunnels and open cuts. Though Lindsay's scheme would have left fewer visible scars on lower Manhattan, it involved just as much devastation and job loss. "We're not fools," said Jane Jacobs. "We know it's a version of the old Moses scheme."[35]

The fight continued. In a celebrated incident Jacobs appeared at a public hearing and unwound the stenographer's tape: without a record of the proceedings, the city was forced to schedule another hearing. (When Jacobs was arrested, Margot Gayle raised money for her defense, but years later MAS refused to give Jacobs an award for her life's work. Some board members simply couldn't countenance her civil disobedience.) Jacobs's act was prompted by desperation: she had concluded that since the city had no intention of actually listening to the opposition, guerrilla tactics were fully justified. But in 1969, John Lindsay lost the Republican primary and was forced to run for a second term on the Liberal Party line. His opponents were John Marchi, a conservative Republican from Staten Island, and Mario Procaccino, an even more conservative Democrat. If coaxed to abandon Procaccino, liberal Democrats could provide the swing vote in such an election. "The overlap between liberal Democrats and expressway opponents was too large to ignore," writes historian Rebecca Read Shannor, and Lindsay suddenly announced that the highway was "dead for all time."[36]

Politics, not reason, had saved SoHo from the expressway, and MAS hadn't played a terrifically enlightened part in the campaign. For a long time its protests were limited to the complaint that the Haughwout Building, at Broadway and Broome Street, stood in the expressway's path. That building was featured in Alan Burnham's *New York Landmarks* as the masterpiece of cast iron architecture, and it was worth fighting for, but much more was at stake.

For decades, SoHo had lived under the threat of demolition. Real estate had been frozen. Marginal businesses struggled on. Those that could afford to move did so, and they were replaced by artists. The old studio neighborhoods on Fifty-seventh Street and in the West Sixties had long since become too expensive for artists, but the empty lofts of SoHo made perfect studios, and may artists found it highly convenient to live cheek by jowl with industrial supply stores. Living in these commercial lofts was illegal back then, but the artists had no place else to go, the landlords had no alternative tenants, and the city chose to look the other way. It seemed to be a temporary situation: the artists' rent payments ensured that SoHo generated some tax revenue, and the artists' illegal status meant that they would be all the easier to evict once construction started on the highway.[37]

In 1969, after Lindsay canceled the expressway, MAS demanded that the city propose a historic preservation program for the area. The city legalized the artists' lofts a year later, and art galleries, boutiques, and restaurants began to open in the neighborhood. Prices were rising, and when the Board of Standards and Appeals approved a twenty-one-story sports center on West Broadway, it began to look as if SoHo had been spared the highway only to fall victim to a real estate boom.

Burnham was one of the first New Yorkers to show much interest in cast iron architecture; he was joined by William Knight-Sturges, Henry Hope Reed, and James Marston Fitch. Their scholarship was complemented by Margot Gayle's activism. A loyal Democrat, Gayle had lost her post as a spokesperson for the City Planning Commission when Lindsay was elected. "The upshot was that I became a full-time preservationist. It's still politics," she says. "Why not?" By then her interest in the Jefferson Market Courthouse had blossomed into a more general fascination with Victorian architecture. The period was still unloved except by the art directors of horror movies; the Victorian age seemed "as exotic and unfathomable to most Americans," Huxtable wrote, "as the puberty rites of far off tribes."[38]

In the early years of the Landmarks Commission, MAS had to work especially hard to win designations for Victorian buildings. There were bitter arguments, for example, over the James H. McCreery store at 801–807 Broadway and over three grand buildings on Lafayette Street: the Puck and DeVinne Press buildings and the loft building at No. 376. Gayle has a certain fascination for underdogs, and in 1966 she was one of the founders of the Victorian Society, an organization that grew indirectly out of MAS. (Brendan Gill and Charles Evans Hughes III were also founding members.) Shortly afterward Gayle met Nicholas Pevsner, the great German-born architectural historian, and the encounter transformed Gayle's hobby into a crusade. Pevsner was a Modernist who, anxious to discredit the Beaux Arts, turned to the study of Victorian architecture. He made heroes of the Victorian engineers who first explored the possibilities of iron and glass, and he presented the stylistic foibles of Victorian architects as a heroic search for individualistic expression. Pevsner warned Gayle that "If you Americans don't save your nineteenth-century buildings, you don't have much more to save." He insisted that "we had a responsibility to do something," Gayle remembers. She was still pondering Pevsner's advice when James Marston Fitch addressed the Victorian Society on cast iron buildings, and then Gayle went along on Henry Hope Reed's first walking tour of SoHo.[39]

All this led Gayle to found the Friends of Cast Iron Architecture. Pevsner and the American historian Henry Russell Hitchcock agreed to be its honorary chairmen. Michael Brooks, an NYU professor, led walking tours through the district, and Gayle passed out little magnets so people could test for themselves whether a building was iron or stone. MAS helped arrange a grant from the National Science Foundation to hire a team of researchers from Pennsylvania State University. They were led by Winston Weisman, an architectural historian who'd done pioneering work on cast iron buildings. MAS sponsored lectures by Weisman and Fitch at the Film Makers' Cinematheque on Wooster Street.[40] The Municipal Art Society offered "a safe haven," Gayle says: "facilities, a space for lectures, moral support, advice. They'd issue a press release." The society's involvement brought a local battle to the attention of the entire city and offered a statement that the neighborhood's case wasn't a purely parochial concern.

There was never much doubt that the Landmarks Commission would save some of the Cast Iron District, but as with Greenwich Village, Goldstone's instinct was to save the best parts of SoHo, and the community was determined to save it all. So the first stage of the campaign focused on getting the full twenty-six blocks scheduled for a public hearing. The Landmarks Commission bowed to the argument that it could still pick and choose what to designate. Once that was achieved, preservationists were free to make their case that the whole neighborhood should be a single historic district. Every Sunday during this period the Friends of Cast Iron Architecture and the SoHo Artists Association set up bridge tables on the street to hand out buttons and collect signatures for a petition to Mayor Lindsay. Gayle knew that mayors were deluged with petitions, so to give hers some bulk she had each person sign a separate card, and then she packaged them in exquisite boxes handcrafted by a local artist. One day she carted the boxes down to City Hall and asked the policemen on duty if she could leave these "gifts" for Mayor Lindsay. The officers knew Gayle and let her pile the boxes on Lindsay's desk. The idea was that when he arrived "he'd rush to see what lovely presents someone had given him"—and find the petition calling on him to save SoHo. At least he would notice it. "That was the scenario," Gayle says. "I don't know if it worked or not."[41]

IN GREENWICH VILLAGE and in SoHo, preservationists and community activists pushed the Landmarks Commission further than it was inclined to go. There was a slight element of charade in this—it's not as if Harmon Goldstone was *unhappy* when these districts turned out larger than he had proposed. The activists' pressure tactics were in fact useful to the Landmarks Commission; they counterbalanced developers' complaints, and they convinced the mayor that preservation was politically wise. Yet Goldstone's hesitations and doubts about these larger districts were genuine. At heart he still believed in the masterpiece theory of preservation. This was "an intellectual bias characteristic of that generation," says Charles Platt, and it was a bias Goldstone shared with his fellow commissioner, Geoffrey Platt (Charles's uncle). They were connoisseurs, ready to protect the very finest buildings of the past, but indifferent to the rest. The landmarks law did not demand that a building be a masterpiece, only that it be "characteristic" of a bygone age, but Goldstone and Platt had seen that kind of language as a way to avoid legal challenges. They didn't want the courts weighing the fine points of architectural history, with expert witnesses for either side debating, say, whether a particular building was one of the *best* examples of the Greek Revival row house.

By 1973 Brooklyn Heights, Greenwich Village, and SoHo had become historic districts. Back in the 1960s before the landmarks law took effect, these were the only neighborhoods that MAS thought of protecting. Since that time, however, preservationists had grown much more ambitious. The concept of historic districts wasn't novel anymore; it had proved itself. Many observers found coherent, preserved neighborhoods a more attractive idea than lone masterpieces scattered to and fro. The public's notion of what's historic and what's beautiful began to expand. At first the most obvious candidates for designation were the upper-class residential neighborhoods, but with time and with education, people began to see the beauty of more modest buildings as well. Brownstones, once thought to epitomize the gloomy bad taste of bourgeois Victorians, came to be regarded as a precious stratum of New York's legacy. People learned, too, that there was a type of beauty—and a record of a more inclusive, democratic history—in the city's gritty old commercial buildings.

MAS's own eyes opened wider with time. Back in 1957 one John E. Nicholson showed the society's board of directors photographs of the area near Peck and Coenties slips and suggested that the Municipal Art Society try to save one entire block. The board sent him away. "As the structures were built as warehouses," MAS felt, "and . . . are slated for demolition in the slum clearance project, the society should not attempt to preserve any of the blocks as mentioned. If further research indicates one building of historic or architectural importance, however, the society should consider what it might do to help. Mention was made of the desirability of preserving the quality of an area, but that effort should not be wasted on outworn structures per se."[42]

Eight years later, in 1965, Whitney North Seymour, Jr., presented MAS with the idea of saving Schermerhorn Row, between Fulton, Front, and South streets, the "one remaining block in this area that is still a legitimate landmark." MAS obtained a grant from the New York State Council on the Arts for a feasibility study to convert the buildings. Another group was working toward the same end, however, and with far more zeal.

The Friends of South Street Seaport, a private nonprofit group, was founded in 1967 by Peter Stanford to create a maritime museum. In 1968 MAS, the Friends of South Street, and the State Council on the Arts cosponsored an exhibit on "The Destruction of Lower Manhattan." That same year, the Landmarks Commission saved Schermerhorn Row from demolition. The city took over the property (and sold off its air rights) as the home of the seaport's maritime museum. Soon it no longer seemed right to save just Schermerhorn Row. The streets and slips to the north were still steeped in nautical history: there was a whole neighborhood of Greek Revival shipping offices and decrepit, ancient taverns. Melville's New York was still largely intact in this place, and when one stood in Peck Slip and looked at the Brooklyn Bridge soaring above that tumbledown, earth-hugging cityscape, one could practically see the modern age dawning. None of this was "beautiful" in the conventional sense, and no earth-shattering events had occurred in South Street's warehouses, but the landmarks law didn't set such high standards: it merely asked that a neighborhood be "characteristic" of a vanished age. By 1970, preservationists were calling for the creation of a South Street Seaport Historic District stretching from Schermerhorn Row north to the Brooklyn Bridge. Ada Louise Huxtable wrote some of her most eloquent columns on South Street. It took a long time to build a consensus behind the South Street Seaport Historic District; it wasn't designated until 1977, after Goldstone retired and two decades after Nicholson first broached the subject.

Goldstone did, however, act on many other neighborhoods. There was Cobble Hill, "really an expansion of Brooklyn Heights," as Goldstone wrote, "both geographically and in time sequence"; the Charlton-King-Vandam District, where a cluster of Federal-style houses had miraculously survived; Chelsea, where rows of Greek Revival houses confronted the Gothic campus of the General Theological Seminary; and Park Slope, with 1,900 houses. Two historic districts—Stuyvesant Heights and Saint Nicholas—were middle-class black enclaves, and it seemed a tribute to the power of great architecture that those two neighborhoods had been so carefully tended while their surroundings fell into decay. (The Saint Nicholas District, with its row houses by McKim, Mead & White and James Brown Lord, is better known as Strivers' Row.) Other districts were already governed by restrictive covenants. Turtle Bay Gardens, once a humdrum block of brownstones, was remodeled in 1919 by Mrs. Walter Martin. She created a beautiful common garden out of the rear yards and imposed a careful system of design controls. In such a case, landmarks designation was hardly more restrictive than what the owners already faced. Turtle Bay was another example of rehabilitation long before that word came into use. So was the Macdougal-Sullivan Gardens Historic District, where William Sloane Coffin created another joint garden in 1920, and Sniffen Court, a blind alley off Thirty-sixth Street, where carriage houses were converted into artists' studios in the 1920s.

The new historic districts were "certainly not foreseen," Goldstone wrote. "People gradually came to realize that a neighborhood in which there is strict control over architectural appropriateness tends to stabilize in other ways. Historic district designation was ... soon welcomed by city planners as one of the most effective techniques available for urban stabilization." Yet as far as Goldstone was concerned, this raised a troubling issue: he worried about misusing historic districts as a city planning tool. This was one of the most frequent complaints lodged against the Landmarks Commission. Whenever a new district was proposed, real estate interests argued that the neighborhood wasn't, in truth, architecturally distinguished or historically interesting, and that the residents were just using the landmarks process to ward off big buildings. This analysis amounted to a terrible indictment of the City Planning Commission—it meant that body was doing such a poor job of shaping a livable city that people were forced to seek relief in other quarters—but the developers never suggested amending the zoning code. Their argument was blind to another fact as well: people saw their neighborhoods in terms fat subtler than those of the zoning code. They wanted to save the architectural riches that a mere zoning amendment would ignore: the cornices and doorways, the stoops and bay windows, the patina of weathered stone and old brick, the play of light and shade, and the sense that a neighborhood had evolved over time.

Back in 1965 the fledgling Landmarks Commission thought it was going to create just three historic districts in the entire city. In the next eight years it designated twenty-four of them. Goldstone felt generous, but the Municipal Art Society was absorbed in new plans. Some districts, like Carnegie Hill, were far smaller than MAS wanted. Seven more were awaiting action by the Landmarks Commission, and Goldstone didn't seem enthusiastic. When asked to designate the Beaux Arts row houses of West 105th Street, he was dismissive. As far as he was concerned, the houses were typical work of his father's generation, not exemplars. It was "a nice part of the city, but we were looking for *distinction.*" Moreover the landmarks law seemed like "a very delicate vessel," and the elder Platt spoke privately of his fear of "wrecking the law on some rock that would do it away forever." Goldstone was no less "terrified that if he misstepped, the whole thing would come crumbling down." Charles Platt remembers his uncle Geoffrey promising that "someday" commercial buildings, "like the Empire State Building," might be designated.[43] A younger generation was convinced that that day had already dawned.

Goldstone would never quite come to terms with this new, broader concept of preservation. He still holds to the masterpiece theory, and the newfound popularity of historic designation puzzles him. In retrospect, says Goldstone, "I can't say I regret it. In general, it's been a very healthful development—it infused culture and history into city planning. I'm always for cultural continuity. I never expected it to come out this way." Yet he still speaks ambiguously: the "perversion" of the law's "pure intent," he says, "is very good."[44]

THE ANSONIA HOTEL became a symbol of the Landmarks Commission's timidity. Like the Jefferson Market Courthouse, this building was a landmark in the most literal sense, for its silhouette served to orient pedestrians far up and down Broadway. It looked like a Parisian building that had grown to skyscraper proportions, and surely that mixture of cultural insecurity and technical prowess was characteristic of an epoch in American history. Then there was the Ansonia's role in New York's musical life. Its soundproof walls had attracted musicians and impresarios—like Caruso, Gatti-Casazza, and Ziegfeld—since the day it opened. Lincoln Center's construction revived the Ansonia's musical tradition, but it also put the building in grave danger.

As the Upper West Side began its renaissance in the early 1970s, the Ansonia's owner, Jacob Starr, was tempted to demolish the hotel; he could have built a forty-story tower on the lot. Starr's lawyers dismissed the building's aesthetic merits as "a question of taste and . . . a matter of debate" and they denied that it possessed "any particular historic significance." Lawyers always say such things, of course, but

Starr's attorneys also insisted that the building realized little or no profit. "The only sound solution," they concluded, "is the demolition of the hotel and the replacement by a structure in keeping with the needs of the neighborhood."

The Landmarks Commission never questioned these financial statements; instead, Goldstone challenged the *community* to demonstrate the building's "viability." The community was more than willing to do so. West Siders first amassed evidence that the Ansonia was profitable, leading Starr to drop his claims of hardship; then they lined up foundation support and offered to buy the building. Starr refused to sell, but the Landmarks Commission still refused to act. Finally a group of activists, led by Rita Aid of the local community board, went to see Goldstone. They threatened to go to the Board of Estimate and testify that the Landmarks Commission was so irresponsible that it didn't deserve full funding. They also said they'd file suit to force the commission to live up to its "responsibility to designate." A few weeks later, by unanimous vote, the Ansonia became a landmark.[45]

Winning a designation for the Ansonia had taken, Roberta Gratz wrote, "seven years, two commission hearings, more than 25,000 petition signatures, a foundation-financed publicity effort, support from Senators Javits and Buckley, John D. Rockefeller III and other luminaries, and—most crucially—a threatened community lawsuit."[46] Her account of this battle formed the centerpiece of a series of articles on landmarks in the *New York Post.* Together they constituted a damning indictment of the Landmarks Commission's timidity. Gratz described "an extreme reluctance on the part of the commission to designate in the face of even mild opposition, a reluctance to designate properties that might stand in the way of anticipated real estate development and a reluctance to designate sites where property owners simply threaten a lawsuit. . . . Some critics have gone so far as to say that [the Landmarks Commission] is the worst enemy of the work it professes to do."[47] Gratz summarized her case:

> Item: For seven years the city has had a landmarks preservation law and a Landmarks Preservation Commission.
> Contradiction: The law which created the commission effectively prevents it from fulfilling its purpose.
> Irony: Considerable evidence exists that the commission likes it that way.

It was a magnificent series, and it gave an immense boost to MAS's campaign for a new, more powerful landmarks law, but Gratz also presented the society with an awkward problem. Most of her sources had insisted on anonymity—some were current or former landmarks commissioners—and Kent Barwick was the most talkative exception. The frequency with which his name popped up made the articles seem like his personal attack on Harmon Goldstone. Barwick's "behavior shocked a lot of people," Charles Platt remembers, and at least one commissioner was "apoplectic" at the thought of "this young guy . . . vilifying Harmon Goldstone." Goldstone himself took Barwick's remarks personally. "He's a brilliant political engineer with an absolute horror of the press," says Barwick. "Harmon deserves sainthood instead of grief, but it was inevitable that the subject would be politicized." Yet the fact that all this criticism came from MAS, or seemed to, was especially painful to Goldstone.[48]

Mayor Lindsay's response to the *Post* series was to tell Goldstone to work out a new law with the private groups. Goldstone did so, but his draft had no provision for scenic landmarks or for repealing the moratorium clause. He sent a rather oily letter to Brendan Gill, thanking MAS for its "interest" in the landmarks law, but adding that this was not the time to push matters too far.[49] The result, as Bronson Binger noted, "was a deep loss of confidence in Mr. Goldstone."[50] Councilman Carter Burden introduced a draft of MAS's own legislation, and Barbara Lee Diamondstein, a landmarks commissioner, went to Dick Aurelio, Lindsay's deputy mayor, and convinced him that the mayor should appoint a new commission to study the competing amendments. The commission was chaired by Whitney North Seymour of the Municipal Art Society. Seymour guided the new commission toward MAS's goals, not Goldstone's. Its draft of the new law eliminated the three-year moratorium, ordered the city to publish the Landmarks Commission's advisory opinions,* and allowed for scenic and interior landmark designations. The draft wasn't quite MAS's ideal: only "publicly accessible" interiors, as defined in the Civil Rights Act, were eligible; the interiors of banks, restaurants, theaters, museums, and even the lobbies of office buildings could be designated, but never the inside of a house or a private club. The battle to save the interiors of the Villard houses, as we'll see, would be waged more in the court of public opinion than in a court of law. But still, this was a triumph.

THIS ''SENSIBLE'' landmarks law passed late in 1973. Within a few months, Central Park became the city's first scenic landmark (for which MAS credited Whitney North Seymour), and the New York Public Library, the finest Beaux Arts building in New York, was named the first interior landmark. The library designation eventually inspired that building's spectacular restoration, and that, in turn, led to the renaissance of Bryant Park. In the spring of 1974 the Municipal Art Society celebrated by giving Roberta Gratz an award recognizing her role in changing the law. And that same evening MAS presented Harmon Goldstone with its highest honor, the President's Medal. This was a poignant attempt to patch up a badly bruised relationship and put a painful quarrel in perspective, but it didn't entirely succeed. Goldstone wouldn't speak to Kent Barwick for years and refuses to speak *of* him even now. If pressed, he'll refer vaguely to "activists." "I'm sure I was reviled as too expedient," he offers. "They still hate me."[51]

By the time MAS honored him, Goldstone had stepped down from office. Abraham Beame was elected mayor in November 1973, and Goldstone, eager to

---

* *The law doesn't force the city to comply with the Landmarks Commission's advisory opinions, but the mere threat of bad publicity for the city is usually effective.*

return to the relatively quiet life of a practicing architect, offered to resign whenever the mayor-elect wished. Months later he read in the papers that he'd been replaced by Beverly Moss Spatt. Neither MAS nor Goldstone had been consulted; this was a patronage appointment—Spatt's father, Brooklyn's surrogate judge, had brought Beame along in the clubhouse—and yet Spatt was well qualified for the job. She was a planner and had been a dissident member of the City Planning Commission. She was "vexatious to work with," Brendan Gill remembers—"brilliant" and "difficult," Barwick offers—and she "viewed the Municipal Art Society as socially objectionable." But she launched the first of a series of campaigns to streamline the commission's procedures and tried valiantly "to bring the Landmarks Commission into the twentieth century."[52]

Spatt's boss was another matter, however. Abe Beame was "a boor of the first order," says Harmon Goldstone.[53] In 1954, when Beame was the city's budget director, the Soldiers' and Sailors' Monument was threatening to collapse unless major repairs were undertaken. Beame suggested spending the money on a "more utilitarian structure."[54] He turned a deaf ear on the Municipal Art Society's complaints, and only the grousing of veterans, more numerous and politically powerful than MAS, convinced him that a restoration was in order.

As mayor, Beame's most notable contribution to the preservation movement was to save the Tweed Courthouse, but even then his motives were unsettling. In its old Beaux Arts days, MAS wanted the building destroyed, and even in the 1960s it supported a dreadful civic center project, which would have bulldozed the courthouse and much else besides. But Henry Hope Reed had already begun to feature the building on his walking tours, and eventually preservationists noticed that this maligned and scandal-tainted structure was a rather handsome "Palladian country house."[55] So in 1974, when the *Post* reported that Beame was going to replace the courthouse with a "new, more economical annex" to City Hall, MAS, the Victorian Society, the AIA, and the Fine Arts Federation begged him to reconsider.[56] Beame insisted the building was an eyesore and, though his enemies suspected that he was merely calling the kettle black, labeled it a symbol of corruption. All the more reason to save it, the preservationists replied: New Yorkers needed to remember that the price of good government is undying vigilance. This argument marked a certain maturity in the preservation movement, a recognition that history didn't have to be edifying to be relevant, but Beame wasn't convinced: he still preferred the improbable role of an honest man horrified by a relic of clubhouse politics.

The mayor's stance posed a delicate problem for the Landmarks Commission. It could designate the courthouse and issue an advisory opinion against demolition, but to do so would anger Beame without guaranteeing the building's survival. Beverly Moss Spatt went behind the mayor's back to ask MAS for more help—send letters, she begged, with copies to the mayor—and a Save the Tweed Committee was organized by Paul O'Dwyer and Brendan Gill.

Finally the mayor did cancel the demolition, and Margot Gayle still regrets that Beame—"such a modest man"—has won very few plaudits for this change of heart.[57] MAS, however, was in no mood to lavish praise on City Hall. It noted Beame's true reason for sparing the Tweed: the city had entered its epic fiscal crisis and couldn't spare half a million dollars to tear the building down.[58] It was the only good thing to come of New York's bankruptcy.

Such a victory could hardly disguise the fact that the number of new landmark designations plummeted during Beame's reign.[59] (Indeed the Tweed Courthouse wasn't actually designated until 1984.) The mayor was unsupportive, Spatt was preoccupied with her efforts to rework the commission's internal procedures, and the fiscal crisis brought devastating budget cuts that crippled the staff. There was just one saving grace to the situation: the terrible recession gripping New York had stilled wrecking balls around the city. But one frightening specter still hovered over the city's landmarks, for just when the landmarks law became an effective instrument, the preservation movement was confronted with the most serious threat in its history: the court battle over Grand Central Terminal.

IT WAS the peculiar fate of the New York Central railroad that, in the end, its real estate proved far more valuable than its train tracks. Through the first third of the century the region's railroads squandered every opportunity to reorganize or consolidate their operations, and though World War II brought an ephemeral prosperity, afterward the railways began to slide into bankruptcy. Many customers disappeared as factories moved on to the Sunbelt, land of cheap wages and resources. Truckers, glorying in cheap gas and in the subsidized highway system so kindly provided by Washington, took the rest of the customers away. In 1962 the Port Authority took over the insolvent Hudson and Manhattan railroad, renaming it the PATH system. Six years later, when the MTA was organized, it took over the Long Island Railroad commuter trains. When the surviving railroads did at last reorganize, it was a case of bankrupt companies merging only to drown in their pooled liabilities. In 1968 the New York Central and Pennsylvania railroads joined hands to become the Penn Central Railroad Company, and a year later the bankrupt New Haven line was absorbed, but this conglomerate was, in the words of railroad historian Carl Condit, a "mutilated dinosaur" crippled by decades of "gross managerial errors," crumbling facilities, and "concentrated railroad pathology."[60] So desperate was the situation that Congress intervened. Amtrak was organized in 1971 to operate the nation's passenger system, and in 1976 ConRail took title to freight operations. Penn Central survived, however: a sort of corporate phantom, its facilities leased to various arms of the government and its trains operated by Washington. But it still owned New York City real estate. On the West Side lay the Penn Yards, and soon young Donald Trump, fresh from Queens, was stumbling over the rusty train tracks and wondering what he could build there. And in Midtown, on some of the most valuable land in the world, sat Grand Central Terminal.

In the 1860s the state had ordered the New York Central to keep its trains north of Forty-second Street, which was then far from the densely settled part of the island. The first Grand Central Terminal was built soon afterward, and its train tracks stretched north to Fifty-sixth Street. Within a generation, however, the city had caught up with the terminal. The train yards, blanketing Park Avenue and more than a dozen cross streets, became a fantastic impediment to traffic and a prime example of urban blight. The Park Avenue Association—founded by Everett Wheeler, Nathalie Dana's uncle—waged a long campaign to force the railroad to electrify its tracks and move them underground; this bore fruit in 1902, after an accident in a steam-filled tunnel killed seventeen people. The result was a new terminal, with sumptuous facades and decor by Warren & Wetmore, and this jewel of public architecture was given an appropriate setting in the form of "Terminal City," the enormous real estate development built above the train yards. Albert Bard, who hated all skyscrapers, fumed in 1929 when the railroad built the New York Central Building—now the gilded Helmsley Building—which straddles Park Avenue. Since it stood above a public street, Bard said, the Art Commission ought to be able to stop it. Obviously the commission didn't intervene, and it's just as well, for the Central Building proved to be an exemplary skyscraper. Park Avenue was cleverly threaded through its base, the building's low wings tied it to the long line of offices and apartments marching up Park Avenue, and the tower marked the avenue's axis without entirely blocking it.

After the Second World War, as the railroad business declined, the New York Central looked for new sources of revenue. During the war patriotic billboards had infiltrated most public spaces in the city, and what Washington had requisitioned, Madison Avenue soon rented. The east wall of Grand Central's concourse was seized by the war bond campaign and then turned over to the custody of Kodak. Billboards sprang up weedily all over the terminal. In the meantime, tenants stripped the old shopfronts. The roof leaked. The building's skylights, painted black during the war, stayed that way even after the skies were safe again. Grime took its toll. Whitney Warren's color palette, once shockingly pretty, turned dull and filthy with the years: butter yellow stonework darkened to ochre; creamy plaster curdled to a wan tan; and the gilt and aqua sky of the concourse ceiling came to look as turbid as New York's polluted rivers.

Neglect saved pennies in the short term; the real money lay in Terminal City's real estate. In the 1950s, "The Central hired a real estate butcher to cut up its magnificent Grand Central City like a carcass," wrote critic Douglas Haskell. "Piece by piece, individual lots were sold for individual office buildings, mostly cheap ones." The first was the Union Carbide Building, rising fifty-three stories tall between Forty-seventh and Forty-eighth streets. By 1979 fifteen buildings had been demolished and Park Avenue's coherence as a great urban street was irrevocably tarnished.

The choicest piece of real estate remained the terminal block itself. In 1954 William Zeckendorf proposed an eighty-story office tower over the baggage-handling area. I. M. Pei, his architect, came up with a circular plan and a novel structural solution: the building would have looked like the cooling tower of a nuclear reactor. Nothing came of this grim monument, but the project should have served as a warning to the city. Certainly the citizens' groups understood the danger. In 1955 Giorgio Cavaglieri pleaded with the City Planning Commission to down-zone the Grand Central neighborhood, already the most congested in the city. If necessary, said Cavaglieri, the city should simply purchase the terminal's air rights.[61] The planning commission ignored him, and the railroad, delighted with this neg-ligence, began exploring its options more seriously. In 1960 the railroad came up with its most comical and bizarre scheme: it wanted to install three new floors of bowling alleys in the lofty waiting room. MAS helped kill this project with the only appropriate weapon—sheer ridicule—but could only watch helplessly as the Pan Am Building rose behind the terminal in 1962. It was designed by Walter Gropius and Pietro Belluschi, both celebrated modern architects, but for all their vaunted talent they succeeded in ruining the grandest vista in New York.

With Pan Am in place, there was just one major parcel left for Penn Central to develop, and that was the site of the terminal itself. The landmarks law had passed by the time the railroad was ready to proceed. The railroad asked Goldstone not to designate the terminal, assuring him that "nothing would happen."[62] This was scarcely credible, however, and Grand Central became a landmark in 1967. None too soon! That very same year the railroad came back to the Landmarks Commis-sion, this time bearing plans for a $100 million, fifty-five-story tower rising above the terminal. Morris Saady, a British developer, had hired the architect Marcel Breuer. Breuer brought to the project a reputation as one of the pioneers of the International Style—a reputation worn a little thin by the 1960s, but still consid-erable. Breuer was convinced that preserving Grand Central was a meaningless and sentimental gesture, but given the politics of the situation he made some effort to be respectful. His design left the terminal's facade alone—but a concrete skyscraper would hover just above the old copper roof. Much of the terminal's interior would be destroyed as well, but in 1967 the Landmarks Commission still had no authority over interiors. The railroad claimed this tower would have "no exterior effect" on the terminal. There was some trepidation at Landmarks, and Goldstone remembers one of his "key people" saying, " 'We can never stand up to this power; we're going to have to knuckle under on this one,' . . . But when it came to Grand Central, I said, we may well be torpedoed, but let's go down with all flags flying."[63] In 1968 the Landmarks Commission rejected the scheme, describing it as "nothing more than an aesthetic joke. . . . The tower would overwhelm the terminal by its sheer mass . . . and would reduce the landmark itself to the status of a curiosity."[64]

Rebuffed once, Saady and Penn Central came back in 1969 with a second scheme. By now they'd realized that Breuer's first project would have been hugely expensive: it was a delicate task to thread the pillars and elevators of a huge office building through the terminal. The second scheme threw caution to the winds, and now Breuer proposed demolishing the terminal's south facade. In its place the tower, now fifty-nine stories tall, would rise on slender pilotis. Penn Central asked the Landmarks Commission for a certificate of appropriateness. As the *Times* dryly observed, "The owners implied that they were actually improving the site." The railroad's lawyers summoned up all their professional chutzpah and insisted that the terminal was virtually invisible. "The aesthetic quality of the south facade is obscured by its engulfment among narrow streets and high-rise buildings," they wrote. "It is hardly seen at all except for a short distance to the south on Park Avenue, and even there the view of the facade is intersected by the encircling roadway and by the tall buildings that line Park Avenue."[65] Once again the landmarks commissioners unanimously rejected Breuer's design, and this time Saady and Penn Central went to court, charging that the city had "taken" property without just compensation.

So the Landmarks Commission was confronted with its most ferocious challenger to date. MAS entered the case as a friend of the court, and its brief bore the names of some of the city's most influential legal and political minds: Whitney North Seymour, Jr., then the U.S. attorney for the Southern District of New York; Robert Wagner, the former mayor, still a power in the Democratic Party and a fixture in the permanent government; plus a former presiding justice of the appellate division; a former president of the New York Bar; and a former counsel to presidents Roosevelt and Truman.[66] The trial was held in 1972. Months passed, then years, and still no decision was handed down. "Judge Saypol . . . wished he'd never got mixed up in it," Geoffrey Platt remembered. "He sat on the case . . . and I think he wished it would go away."[67] In the fall of 1974 rumors began to fly that a decision was imminent, and Kent Barwick asked to see the City Planning Commission's file on the case, just in case something terrible was in the offing. On top of the bulging file sat the newest entry, a confidential memo from Corporation Counsel Burke to Mayor Beame. It reported that Judge Irving H. Saypol had decided against the city and that the railroad's lawyers were offering a deal: if the city didn't appeal, Penn Central wouldn't sue for damages. If it did appeal, the railroad would demand $60 million. Burke advised Beame to drop the case.[68]

At MAS the mood was very grim. If Saypol's ruling stood, the historic districts might still survive, but the whole category of individual landmarks—MAS's single greatest contribution to the preservation movement—would be obliterated. The situation was critical; it called for the city to launch the most vigorous appeal, but the society had little confidence that this would happen. Burke privately believed that the landmarks law was unconstitutional, and so did the chief of his appeals division. Mayor Beame, no friend to historic preservation, had the soul of an accountant. For $500,000 he had canceled his cherished plan to tear down the Tweed Courthouse; for $60 million he just might gut the whole landmarks law.

MAS's first task was to put so much pressure on the city that it wouldn't dare drop the case. The society quietly warned City Hall that it regarded the Grand Central case as a life-or-death issue. Stanley Friedman, the deputy major (and later a figure of scandal), promised to consult MAS before reaching a decision, and the Municipal Art Society began marshaling its forces. It roped together a gilt-edged Citizens Committee to Save Grand Central, and it reconvened its lawyers' committee to plot the legal strategy for an appeal.

McKim, Mead & White's
Pennsylvania Station. **Previous
page:** A view of the waiting room.
Above: An overall view. **Right:**
AGBANY protesting the station's
demolition in 1962.

Left: The demolition in progress.
Below: The station's rubble, discarded in the Hackensack Meadows.

Below: The Brokaw Mansion, designed by Rose & Stone, at Fifth Avenue and Seventy-ninth Street. Right: The Public Theater installed in the old Astor Library. Far right: The Public Theater's Newman Auditorium, designed by Giorgio Cavaglieri.

Above: Kent Barwick addressing a landmarks rally. Right: Mayor Robert F. Wagner signing the Landmarks Law of 1965 as Harmon Goldstone (left) and Geoffrey Platt look on. Far right: A detail of the Haughwout Building, the masterpiece of SoHo's cast iron historic district.

Grand Central Terminal.
Above and right: *Two views
of Warren & Wetmore's facade,
with Walter Gropius and Pietro
Belluschi's Pan Am (now
MetLife) Building looming in
the background.* **Facing page:**
*Marcel Breuer's second scheme
for a tower over the terminal,
and,* **inset**, *a view of the terminal's concourse.*

This page: McKim, Mead & White's Villard Houses. *Above:* A view of the courtyard, with Saint Patrick's Cathedral across Madison Avenue. *Right:* The entrance to the Urban Center. *Facing page:* Saint Bartholomew's Church. *Top:* Two pages from Tim Prentice's St. Bart's Scrapbook. *Below:* MAS's candlelight vigil protesting plans for a skyscraper on site.

Times Square. **Far right**: The Times Tower before Cyrus Eidlitz's facade was stripped in 1966. **Top**: Times Square in the 1940s. **Above**: A New Year's celebration. **Left**: Times Square in the 1980s, in the throes of reconstruction.

*Top: Three stages of the Coliseum Center design. **Left to right**: Moshe Safdie's original project; David Childs's first effort; and Childs's final design, which settled the lawsuit. **Above**: A photomontage showing the shadow Safdie's design would have cast on Central Park.*

Above: *The Upper West Side, in a view north from Broadway and Seventieth Street.* **Left:** *Roz Chast's cartoon, "Introducing the Midstreet," donated to MAS's City for Sale auction.*

Above: A model of Television City, Donald Trump's first scheme for the Penn Yards site. *Inset:* Paul Willen's original proposal for Riverside South. *Right:* A model of the final project.

Judge Saypol finally handed down his decision in February 1975. "I'll never forget the day as long as I live," says Laurie Beckelman, who had joined MAS's staff two years earlier. The *Times* carried a front-page article. It quoted Barwick, and he and Beckelman spent the day "sitting in this tiny office answering a phone that never seemed to stop ringing. A woman called and asked to speak to Kent Barwick. She claimed to be Jackie Onassis." Beckelman was sure it was a crank, but Barwick took the call. It *was* Mrs. Onassis, who wanted to know how she could help. Barwick asked her to join the citizens committee. She did so, and within a year she had a seat on MAS's board of directors. As Beckelman puts it, it was "the coming-out, in a way, of Jackie Onassis in New York. Because of *her*, people popularized preservation. Every magazine in America and Europe knew about Jackie and Grand Central." This had its dangers—some used Mrs. Onassis's involvement to paint preservation as the hobby of people who never rode the subways—but these were far outweighed by the advantages. Jacqueline Onassis brought to MAS a visceral belief in preservation, but more important, she attracted news cameras as a flame draws moths. People hesitated to rebuff her. They took her phone calls. Even Abe Beame was susceptible, and in the end, according to Beckelman, "A nicely placed phone call from Jackie Onassis may have been what finally convinced the mayor" to file the appeal.[69]

Behind the scenes, MAS was pulling every string it could think of. It sent an emissary to A. M. Rosenthal to ask for more complete coverage in the *Times.* It contacted the House Appropriations Committee, which was framing the emergency bailout bill for the railroad, and the committee's report included a statement—not a binding one, but surely influential—that the railroad shouldn't touch the terminal until the courts had their final say. MAS contacted Edward Koch, still a congressman then, who expressed his concern to the secretary of transportation. The society reached out to the MTA, which leased Grand Central Terminal, and which now became MAS's "underground ally." And when a new, more sympathetic corporation counsel came on board in 1975, MAS persuaded him to assign his very best lawyers to the case.

No one knew how the courts would decide the case. The landmarks law had survived all legal challenges to date. The Manhattan Club had launched the first challenge to the law's constitutionality, but the state supreme court (the lowest in New York's judicial system) upheld the law in 1966, and the club didn't appeal. As we've seen, the clubhouse was later demolished under the hardship clause, but that loss seemed to prove that the landmarks law did in fact respect the rights of property owners. When the trustees of Sailors' Snug Harbor sued, they triumphed in the lower court, only to see that ruling reversed by the appellate division in 1968. The city's purchase of the Harbor prevented the case from going back to trial. But in 1973 this record of success took an alarming turn. In *Lutheran Church in America v. City of New York*, the court of appeals ruled that the Morgan house had been unjustly "taken" from the church. That decision was narrowly focused on the Morgan house, but the court used very harsh language to describe the burden of landmarks designation on property owners. Preservationists worried that the court might seize the next opportunity to overturn the law itself.

Theoretically the courts shut their eyes to public protests and solemnly weigh cases against the abstract principles of law. Had the Municipal Art Society believed this, it could have rested content with its amicus briefs. But the society was sure that justices are alive to the political ramifications of their decisions, and a challenge to the landmarks law seemed to demand a vigorous display of public indignation. The law rested on the notion that a preservation program was such a boon to the public that it justified placing modest burdens on private property owners. But how could MAS demonstrate that public interest? It was far easier to measure the benefits of historic districts than of individual landmarks. But if the threat to Grand Central were answered with a great chorus of public indignation, if the terminal's fate became the talk of the town and the nation, then that in itself would serve as evidence of the public interest. It wasn't, admittedly, the sort of evidence the city's lawyers could introduce in court, but it would serve as a context of public opinion within which the judges would act.

In essence, MAS transformed itself into a public relations firm, its insensible clients being the terminal itself and, by extension, all other landmarks. It was only natural that in choosing a new president during this period, MAS settled on a brilliant figure in the advertising world. Frederic Papert was a partner in one of the first ad agencies to go public, and for a time he was the darling of Wall Street. In the early 1970s he initiated the campaign to create a Carnegie Hill Historic District, and that battle had drawn him into MAS's orbit. Something else recommended Papert as well. He'd been active in Robert Kennedy's political campaigns and remained close to the Kennedy family. Mrs. Onassis was now the star of MAS's press conferences, and the society's dependence on her posed a delicate problem. Cursed with celebrity, she was correspondingly wary, and after settling in New York she had fallen back on a fairly closed circle of old friends and trusted advisers. Papert was one of this set; since he was the only Municipalian she trusted implicitly, he became the society's "operative contact" with its star attraction.

Papert proved himself, in the words of one admiring preservationist, "one of the best street fighters in New York," and "one of the great hustlers of all time. He hustled *great* things for preservation." There was a newfound energy at MAS as the society sought to keep Grand Central in the public eye. Laurie Beckelman found Barry Lewis, a fellow from Kew Gardens with a thick New York accent, to conduct tours of Grand Central. They were such a success that weekly tours of the terminal continue to this day, and they're still led by volunteers. Papert got the city's permission to close the Grand Central viaduct for a concert, and he opened a bookstore on the ground floor of the Biltmore Hotel. It sold books on New York and its architecture. Ivan Chermayeff designed a logo and stenciled it on the window. Laurie Beckelman recruited her younger brother, who was just out of college, to run the shop. "Very well known people were coming to this seedy bookstore," she remembers; later it moved to the terminal's basement, near the shuttle trains. J. Walter Thompson, the ad agency, signed on early pro bono—"They were in the Graybar Building [adjacent to the terminal] and really cared." They came up with a slogan: "No More Bites Out of the Big Apple." Volunteers sold buttons and Grand Central T-shirts at the terminal every morning as the commuters arrived, and they passed out free apples on the street. "Come to the rally," they chanted. "No more bites!" To rub the message in, J. Walter Thompson found ties decorated with little apples, each with a bite missing, and this mildly flirtatious neckwear suddenly acquired a very different meaning. "In a way it was very patriotic," says Beckelman, "motherhood and apple pie." For someone like Beckelman, who'd been active in the antiwar movement, the campaign was an exhilarating experience, and for once the heady feeling of being active in a great public cause was hardly marred by contention.

Obviously the railroad and Saady had their own point of view, and Ada Louise Huxtable reported that the real estate community had concocted its own strange domino theory to predict what would happen if the landmarks law were upheld. Preservationists would lose all restraint, the builders warned, and designate buildings and districts right and left until developers, barred from the city center, were forced to take their expertise to the suburbs. Jobs, investment, and the whole white middle-class tax base would follow; behind its stately, landmarked facades, the city center would decay into a vast ghetto.

There was a certain cleverness in the way this theory tapped into racist nightmares, but by the mid 1970s the general public was already convinced that preservation promoted stability; developers had already lost the battle for public opinion. Save for the railroad and a few rabid members of the real estate community, no one wanted to see Grand Central torn down. There was so little controversy that when Lord & Taylor threw a benefit for MAS, it felt comfortable using the event to introduce a new perfume. The cause was so popular that a con artist set up his own "Save Grand Central" table on the sidewalk. MAS set the police on him, only to see him reappear a few months later collecting money to "Save the Whales."[70]

In December 1975 the appellate division concluded that "The need to preserve structures worthy of landmark status is beyond dispute," and overturned Saypol's decision. Ralph Menapace was happy to see that MAS's amicus brief was "cited extensively in the decision," but he worried about the court of appeals and warned MAS that there was only a fifty-fifty chance that the landmarks law would survive.[71]

At this point, MAS stepped up its public relations campaign. It held a press conference in the Oyster Bar at which Hugh Hardy presented a slide show on the station's history. Beckelman made sure the press got to interview everyone they wanted: Brendan Gill, Philip Johnson, Jackie Onassis . . . Philip Morris gave $5,000 to light the terminal's facade at night, and Albert Sanders gave $1,000 to pay for the electricity.

In 1977 the court of appeals upheld the law unanimously. There was no need for the city to pay "just compensation" to the railroad, the court found, because the landmarks law didn't confiscate property. True, the railroad had been denied the opportunity to build a skyscraper, but it could still use the terminal. It was even guaranteed a 6 percent return. Nor was the law discriminatory, the court found: "Discriminatory zoning is condemned because there is no acceptable reason for singling out one particular parcel for different and less favorable treatment. When landmark regulation is involved, there is such a reason: the cultural, architectural, historical or social significance attached to the affected parcel."[72]

Penn Central decided to pursue its suit all the way to the U.S. Supreme Court. In questions of state law, the Supreme Court usually defers to the state's highest court, especially when there has been a unanimous decision. A shiver went through the preservation movement when the Supreme Court agreed to hear the railroad's case. Suddenly Grand Central's fate was truly a national issue, for every preservation law in the country was at risk. The Sierra Club, the National Trust for Historic Preservation, the states of New York and California, and the City Bar Association joined in the amicus brief. Ed Koch, the new mayor, promised that his administration wouldn't drop the ball, and in early 1978 he made Kent Barwick chairman of the Landmarks Preservation Commission. Meanwhile, Hugh Hardy laid plans for a major exhibit on the terminal at the New-York Historical Society, and Mrs. Avery Brooke contributed the seed money to publish a handsome book.

For a finale, J. Walter Thompson suggested an old-fashioned whistle-stop railway tour from New York to Washington on a special Landmark Express train. The plans had just been finalized when Whitney North Seymour, Sr., who'd organized MAS's team of lawyers, begged the society to cancel the tour. "Whitney was just astounding," Beckelman remembers. "He used to lunch with the justices, socially—he wasn't lobbying. I remember when he quietly told us the issue would go to the Supreme Court before it had been announced." Now he told MAS *when* the Supreme Court would hear arguments in the case; by a bizarre coincidence, it happened to be the day after the Landmarks Express tour. Suddenly the trip looked like a very crude attempt to pressure the justices. Seymour "was absolutely mortified," and Harmon Goldstone is still indignant: "I know you have to take care of your constituency," he says, but "It was an idiotic thing to do." When Seymour couldn't persuade MAS to cancel the railway tour, he pleaded with Kent Barwick to stay home—after all, he pointed out, as the city's landmarks commissioner, Barwick was a party to the case.[73]

MAS and Barwick plunged ahead with plans for the tour, however. "There were these wonderful train enthusiasts who got involved," Beckelman remembers, "among them Rogers Whitaker, who wrote for *The New Yorker*," and so the Landmark Express provided an odd spectacle: chugging along behind the standard-issue Amtrak train was a motley collection of antique railroad cars. Ticketron sold tickets; Mobil Oil donated a free ad on the Op-Ed page of the *Times*, and small ads were placed by J. Walter Thompson. Mimes, musicians, and jugglers were recruited to entertain the passengers. "We learned the night before that tickets were sold out," says Beckelman, "and this was a minor crisis: people expected to join the train at its way stops. We called Robert Wagner to get him to call Ed Koch to call the MTA to add more cars." There was a symbolic send-off from Grand Central—the train actually left from Penn Station—and Mayor Koch was there. The Landmark Express stopped along the way picking up people, and as Hugh Hardy remembers, "The pols came out at every stop" to meet Mrs. Onassis. Senator Moynihan and Joan Mondale, the vice president's wife, met the train in Washington, and there was a big rally. "The press was international," says Beckelman. "It was *covered*."

The next day was the Supreme Court hearing, and many Municipalians decided to stay in Washington and attend. Paul Byard had himself admitted to the Supreme Court Bar just so he could be there. His wife had a school friend named Powell; Justice Lewis F. Powell, Jr., got a phone call explaining that the courtroom was going to be packed: could some friends sit in his private box? Powell was surprised; he hadn't realized "anyone was interested" in the Grand Central case. Oral arguments before the Supreme Court are "wonderful . . . so compressed," Kent Barwick remembers. It seemed as if just a few minutes passed before the hearing was over, a new case was called, and everyone got up to leave. The justices were startled. "You could see them look up," Barwick says, and the next case was heard in a nearly empty courtroom.

The Supreme Court upheld the landmarks law, and MAS celebrated by making a movie about Grand Central Terminal and its own role in saving the building. It aired on PBS and featured James Earl Jones, narrating in his most majestic voice; Jacqueline Onassis, lending a touch of glamour; Kent Barwick, looking sheepish and earnest; Robert Wagner, droning on as only a politician of the old school could; Brendan Gill, seemingly crazed with indignation at the thought that the terminal might be destroyed; and, in its most bizarre episode, Philip Johnson making a valiant effort to enact the building's spatial drama with his own body. The film made cunning use of Hollywood film clips to make the case that Grand Central was deeply rooted in the nation's cultural memory, and it also cheated shamelessly: much of that footage was actually set in Pennsylvania Station, and the film's climax was James Earl Jones reading Thomas Wolfe's meditation on the train station and eternity from *You Can't Go Home Again*. That, too, was an homage to McKim, Mead & White's lost masterpiece.

The landmarks law had survived its great challenge. One after another, the courts noted that the law had proved to be a great benefit to the public: neighborhoods had stabilized and regenerated, blight and decay had been averted, property values had risen, tourism had flourished. They spoke of the "burgeoning awareness that our heritage and culture are treasured national assets," and such comments raised some interesting questions: If the landmarks law had reached the Supreme Court earlier—before it had a chance to prove itself, before that still burgeoning interest had taken hold in the public—would it still have been upheld? Did the Court's decision mean that Goldstone's agonized caution had been unnecessary, or did it constitute his vindication? Goldstone himself refuses to hazard a guess, but even as he waves the question away, his eyes shine and a contented smile spreads across his face.

BACK AT the Municipal Art Society, Kent Barwick had been replaced by Margot Wellington. One board member remembers her arrival as "a breath of fresh air . . . Dazzling . . . I've never forgotten." Wellington was raised in California, the daughter of transplanted New Yorkers, and some of their nostalgia for the city had rubbed off on her. She had a degree in anthropology, she'd worked in an architect's office, and she wanted to be a city planner. She arrived in New York during John Lindsay's first campaign for mayor, lived in the Village, and reveled in "the atmosphere of the sixties" when the mood was "Can do!" and the city was filled with "great hope." She found a job as vice president of the Downtown Brooklyn Association, a group founded in 1968 to lure office development back to the borough. Brooklyn "had lost its ball team, its department stores, its cachet, even its newspaper," she says, "and you don't exist anymore in New York without a newspaper. There was a population shift out to Staten Island and Long Island. We had to win over the neighborhood, developers, and politicians." She knew it would take years. Wellington had nothing but the support of local businessmen and some money, but she "invented or reinvented" the classic techniques of 1960s revitalization programs. She inaugurated an ambitious public art program, which brought her into Doris Freedman's circle; she fought the Linear City project and, as a Villager, the Lower Manhattan Expressway. MAS thought Wellington's activism would be useful, and since she'd dealt with "every group there was in Brooklyn" the society hoped she could build bridges between MAS and the outer boroughs—or "*other* boroughs," as Wellington prefers to call them.[74]

When she joined the Municipal Art Society, the group had "two publics," Wellington remembers: "most of the world, which had never heard of it, and a tiny public in Manhattan that thought it was powerful, or at least prestigious." The society had a tiny office at Rockefeller Center, and a staff of four, one of whom ran the Grand Central storefront. The board of directors was made up of architects, activists, socialites, and historians. "Most weren't real donors, except in extremis, but they had access," and a few—Whitney North Seymour, Brendan Gill, Doris Freedman, and William Bernbach—had "exceptional access. There was one degree of separation instead of six. What was extraordinary was the volunteer aspect. People were donating their time," often very valuable time, but there was "an artistic style of management. I spent a year trying to find out what my job was." Wellington invented a more formal management structure, though she "knew nothing about it," and a more systematic approach to fund-raising.

Wellington presided over the Municipal Art Society through most of the Grand Central battle, which was a watershed in the group's history. When that was all over, J. Walter Thompson arranged a meeting for MAS's directors and papered a whole conference room with news clippings on the Grand Central case. There was a message in all this: for the first time in its history, MAS had moved out of the back room and emerged as a quasi-political force. Could it sustain that position? MAS's only daily contact with the general public was through the tiny bookstore in Grand Central Terminal.

Even before the Supreme Court handed down its decision, MAS had realized that the store was draining its coffers and would have to close. But Fred Papert understood that the bookstore had given MAS "a public face" for the first time in its life, and he didn't want to see the society retire again into quiet obscurity. He came up with the idea of an urban issues center: MAS would find a nice landmarked town house and put in a bookstore, offices, meeting rooms, and maybe a bar. Margot Wellington wrote up Papert's idea. She pictured the center as an "open, accessible place for all sorts of interactions: some educative, some confrontational, some attempts at mediation." MAS thought a town house would cost about $60,000—money the society didn't have—but one day David Prager got a call from a friend, Arthur Tourtellot, president of the CBS Foundation and William Paley's "intellectual conscience," as Brendan Gill puts it. Tourtellot had money to dispose of and was looking for "a big philanthropic idea." Papert wanted to ask for $40,000, but in the end, CBS provided $200,000 in seed money. "It made everything else possible," Wellington remembers. In the meantime, someone gave the office a Sol Steinberg poster—his famous New Yorker cover showing a Manhattanite's mental map of the world—and since Papert's skills as an adman hadn't abandoned him, he called on the magazine's business department. The New Yorker agreed to run a free ad: join MAS and get a free Steinberg poster. "It was one of those horrible summers when we barely paid the staff," Wellington says, but ten days after the ad ran, a sack of mail arrived at her door, and in short order the campaign raised $140,000. "It helped the whole thing take off," Wellington says. "It gave us a lot of energy," and it brought in a lot of new members, too, though many never renewed—they just wanted the poster.[75]

Wellington began shopping for an East Side town house, but Bill Shopsin, an architect who was active in MAS, came up to someone at the annual meeting and said, "Talk to Helmsley. He doesn't know what to do with the north wing of the Villard house." The Villard houses—there were six of them, grouped around a common courtyard on Madison Avenue between Fiftieth and Fifty-first streets—were among the supreme masterpieces of McKim, Mead & White. The facades, designed by the brilliant, short-lived Joseph Wells, marked the firm's turn toward Italian Renaissance sources, but the true glory of the complex was its courtyard. Its wings seemed to embrace Saint Patrick's Cathedral, which stands across the street.

It seemed faintly miraculous that the houses had survived so long. They were built at the command of Henry Villard, a railroad tycoon who soon suffered financial reverses, and within a generation "fashionable" New York had relocated far uptown. "We looked at the old lease," Wellington remembers, "a restrictive covenant of 1919, which was signed by all the owners, both wife and husband. It was to last twenty-five years, and it said the houses couldn't be altered outside." Nor could they be converted into flats, a museum, or a hotel.[76] The complex sat half empty through the 1930s and 1940s. In 1935, when La Guardia first broached the idea of a municipal art center, Electus Litchfield suggested he buy the Villard houses. Otherwise, Litchfield warned, "there will be a temptation to demolish these buildings some day."[77] The covenant forbade such a conversion, but then again it kept the houses from being replaced with a taxpayer. When the covenant expired, in 1944, Joseph Kennedy helped the Roman Catholic archdiocese buy the houses. Offices were installed, and the north wing was leased to Bennett Cerf, the celebrated publisher, for twenty-five years.

In 1968, the first rumors that the Villard houses were in danger prompted MAS to send emissaries to the archdiocese, and Giorgio Cavaglieri even contacted the Vatican. Remember, MAS said, an air-rights sale might be arranged. MAS extracted a promise that the houses were safe for the foreseeable future, but a few years later Cerf's company, Random House, was gobbled up by RCA and decamped for new quarters. And when Cardinal Spellman died, a spokesman for Terence Cardinal Cooke announced that "with all our schools and responsibilities, at some point we would have to wonder whether we are justified in keeping property as valuable as this." Soon the developer Harry Helmsley arrived with plans for a hotel.[78]

So began a long, tortuous series of negotiations between preservationists, the archdiocese, the Landmarks Commission, and Harry Helmsley. "The landmarks law couldn't help the Villard houses because they weren't economically viable," Wellington remembers, and the lawyers for the archdiocese kept reminding MAS of the Lutheran church case. There was "an odd twist," though: it was clear that Helmsley didn't bear the Villard houses any ill will; he only wanted to tear them down so he could use the area for a plaza and win his 20 percent zoning bonus. "The idea was to give him the bonus if he agreed *not* to tear them down." The city agreed to this swap. The Landmarks Commission forced Helmsley to set the new tower far back on the site so it wouldn't overwhelm the courtyard, and it insisted on a neutral, dark facade so the hotel would seem like a backdrop to the landmark houses. But one troublesome problem persisted: Helmsley still meant to gut the interiors. The south wing, once the Whitelaw Reid house, included some of the finest rooms Stanford White had ever designed. Its jewels were the library and a ballroom, the famous Gold Room, named for the dull glow of gold leaf that adorned its walls, and graced with precious carvings and with murals by John La Farge. Preservationists insisted that these rooms would make extraordinary additions to any hotel. The Landmarks Conservancy suggested that the Gold Room would make an incomparable bar, but Helmsley rejected that idea on the theory that you can walk down into a bar, but not up going out of it. Since these interiors had never been accessible to the public, the Landmarks Commission was powerless to protect them, but private groups were much freer: they could make such a ruckus that the whole city would regard both Helmsley and the archdiocese as cads if they destroyed them.

Helmsley finally bowed to the pressure. He ran into Brendan Gill at a benefit and challenged the preservationists to come up with a plan. If they could show him how to incorporate the Gold Room into a bustling hotel, he said, he would be willing to save it. The Architectural League took up the gauntlet and prepared a plan. Helmsley was won over, and the great rooms were saved. "The whole episode was thrilling to me," says Gill, "because it was the first time that everyone got together and compromised and bettered from it." When the hotel was finished, Gill was pleasantly surprised that the tower "didn't seem to be toppling over into the courtyard," as he'd feared. Even Helmsley was happy, boasting that after all the controversy, the end result was "the perfect hotel."[79]

That still left the north wing of the Villard complex, for which Helmsley had no use. Its interiors were designed by Charles Platt, Geoffrey Platt's father, and they were far more modest than anything in the Reid house: no gilt, no mosaics, no bas-reliefs, just the comparatively quiet elegance of Louis XVI. Margot Wellington went to look at them. By that time, the house had been unoccupied for years. There was no heat, and long strips of paint hung from the ceilings or crunched underfoot. The great rooms had been divided into cubicles, and ceilings had been dropped, but the old ornament behind was still intact. "I really felt very strongly about this building," Wellington remembers, but it had three weaknesses: there was no streetfront store for MAS, the building was much bigger than a town house, and it wasn't for sale. "It seemed silly, out of the question, too big to handle," Wellington says, but "my greatest asset was total ignorance, and stubbornness."[80]

Helmsley offered to give MAS the building rent-free for two years. MAS still wouldn't be able to amortize its renovation costs, but the offer got the board members interested, and Fred Papert kept pressing them to take a great leap of faith. The negotiations continued. Helmsley agreed to lease the house to MAS for a long period; the rent would start at less than four dollars a square foot, and escalate over time. That left the question of what to do with the space, since MAS could use just three of the six floors. Wellington recruited other not-for-profit groups. "We discovered you had to have exhibits all the time to make an exhibit space work," she says, and the tenants were chosen with the idea that they were likely to contribute exhibits to the galleries. Wellington recruited the AIA, the Parks Council ("Freedman was very active in it"), and the Architectural League ("which wasn't as quiet then"). It was Papert who thought of putting commercial tenants as well as art groups in a not-for-profit building. They would help pay the rent, particularly over time. "So we undertook it, which was genuinely heroic."

Wellington compares the Urban Center to the Museum of Modern Art: there was interest in modern art long before the museum opened its doors, but MoMA became "a center for its experience, its social life, its business." MoMA had it comparatively easy, though: it had the support of the Rockefellers. The Urban Center had no single angel, but as Wellington says, "A really strong idea is the best thing you can have when you are fund-raising." Mobil Oil gave the center a grant—its public relations officer, Herb Schmertz, sat on MAS's board. Philip

Morris agreed to finance the first season of exhibits. The National Endowment for the Arts gave a challenge grant. The Ford Foundation paid for a direct mail campaign. Brendan Gill escorted Brooke Astor through the filthy, cobwebby, ice-cold building. It was "macabre," he remembers. "You expected Vincent Price to appear at every landing." After their tour they crossed the courtyard to the White-law Reid wing, where Helmsley's workers were busy restoring the Gold Room. "She remembered going to a ball in that house," Wellington says, "a party in the 1920s, when she was very young. She walked as if still young. Brendan sang 'Danny Boy' to her. I think that's why she gave a grant." Gill says it was to silence him.[81]

As for the bookstore, "we always wanted it," Wellington says, "but feared we couldn't do it at the first push." In those days there were very few architectural bookstores, and Joan Davidson saw the need for one that offered a complete stock, from coffee table books to foreign magazines and technical manuals. So the Kaplan Fund gave MAS the money to go ahead, and it has continued to support Urban Center Books. John Frazier ran the bookstore for years. "It gives people a reason to go there anytime," Wellington says of the bookstore—assuming they know it's there. Thanks to Leona Helmsley, however, many people don't.

The Helmsleys' marriage was a subject of debate among Municipalians. Fred Papert, on the one hand, belonged to the camp that admired Harry Helmsley and blamed Leona for his downfall. "He was a man of honor," Papert says. "He was so pleased when he ended up with the perfect hotel that he offered us the north wing almost for free, I think as a sort of thank-you." Margot Wellington, on the other hand, always suspected that "Harry has a great technique: dirty deeds are done by henchmen so he can seem to be a nice old man." Tim Prentice tells the story of his first real meeting with the couple, when he was MAS's president. At that time, the hotel was still in construction, and the Municipal Art Society thought it would be a wonderful coup if it could hold its next annual meeting in the newly restored Gold Room. But how to make the scheme attractive to the Helmsleys? "A seduction" was arranged. Benjamin Sonnenberg invited Prentice, Gill, and the Helmsleys to have a glass of sherry at 19 Irving Place. Few turned down Sonnenberg's invitations, but the Helmsleys were unusually avid guests: they arrived with *two* lawyers. As soon as his guests were assembled, Sonnenberg decided to retire, leaving Gill to turn his charm on Harry and Leona. He explained that MAS wanted to meet in the Gold Room, and he dangled a lure before their eyes: Mrs. Helmsley, he said, could co-chair the evening with Mrs. Onassis. The lawyers broke in. No, they said, it was impossible: insurance difficulties. After a few minutes of awkward small talk, the Helmsleys offered Gill and Prentice a lift uptown in their limousine. As soon as the car doors were closed, Leona turned to Gill. She was furious at the suggestion that she should share the spotlight with Jackie Onassis: "That bitch! That climber!"[82]

Now Leona had become the Municipal Art Society's landlord, and it was a strained relationship. As east Midtown began to boom in the 1980s and Madison Avenue became more posh, she seemed to regret that the society had ever been invited to take over such a prominent corner. It didn't help that MAS had rented space to Celine. "It was the only first class tenant in the area," Papert remembers, "and it was ours." Leona had another complaint, as well. She once planted daffodils around the edge of the courtyard, a bit of landscaping kitsch that seemed out of place in the urbane architecture of McKim, Mead & White, and the landmarks commission made her pull them up. "It was an asshole thing to do," Papert maintains.[83] She took her revenge on preservationists by forbidding MAS's bookstore to hang a sign on the building or even to place one in a window. A sign, she said, would get her in trouble with the Landmarks Commission. Desperate to let people know that the bookstore existed, the society equipped a mime with a sandwich board and had him walk up and down Madison Avenue, but mimes expect a salary, and the experiment was discontinued.

The Urban Center opened its doors in 1980 with an exhibition on the Villard houses. A fine monograph by Bill Shopsin and Mosette Glaser Broderick served as a catalog.[84] "There was a sense of family in creating this from nothing," Tony Wood remembers of the Urban Center's early days, "a small town feeling that doesn't exist at MAS anymore." Wood, who was a new member of MAS's staff, adds that so much energy had gone into creating the Urban Center that the society "lost its advocacy push at first." It took some time to learn how to use the Urban Center. Margot Wellington had inherited a mission of "basic public education" in the city's architecture and history. "The genius of MAS is to romanticize New York," she says, "and to counter the usual syndrome of romanticizing some other place." MAS still offered weekly tours of Grand Central, however—they started as part of the "war strategy" and have continued ever since—and on Sundays there were walking and bus tours under the aegis "Discover New York." By the mid 1980s there were new exhibits on current issues every month or six weeks; there was "a more focused approach" toward using exhibits as advocacy tools.

Kent Barwick had left MAS during the Grand Central battle. When Joan Davidson, his mentor, became head of the New York State Council on the Arts, she took Barwick along as her executive director. Davidson didn't last long in Albany, though—"she's not diplomatic," one observer says—and Barwick was left without a job. He went to Harvard as a Loeb fellow and then returned to New York at "a very bad time." Doris Freedman, MAS's president, came to his rescue in 1978. Freedman had raised money for Ed Koch since his days as a liberal congressman, and she supported him again in the mayoral campaign of 1977. Koch was "beholden [to Freedman] and knew it," one Municipalian says. She wanted to head the Cultural Council, a prestigious dollar-a-year position, but Edward Villela got the job instead. Since Koch didn't know Villela, much less owe him a political debt, at least one observer concluded that some strange character flaw had led him to betray Freedman. "She must have found some way to get her hands around Koch's neck," one source speculates, because he tried to make amends. He asked if some other favor would suffice. She told him to make Kent Barwick chairman of the Landmarks Commission.

During Barwick's reign as chairman, an ideological shift occurred in the Landmarks Commission. In the 1960s Giorgio Cavaglieri was MAS's model of a good preservation architect. He approached his job like an art conservator: he preserved but never restored. If Cavaglieri had to alter an old building or add to it, the new work was carried out in the International Style—"the architectural expression of our times," Cavaglieri insists. "I'm still an idealist," he adds.[85] Cavaglieri's approach to preservation is a principled one, and he sticks to it even though it horrifies a younger generation of preservationists. The shift away from Cavaglieri's approach was "partly due to Fitch," Charles Platt says, "though he wouldn't like it."

James Marston Fitch, a member of MAS's board in the late 1960s, began teaching preservation courses at Columbia University in the late 1950s. His classes evolved into Columbia's School of Historic Preservation. Over twenty years, Fitch produced "a whole group of students educated and equipped to deal with [preservation] issues as professionals, albeit at first very callow individuals." When Platt joined the Landmarks Commission in 1979, "it amazed me how much people knew. My generation didn't [study] the history of architecture." In these younger students, familiarity with old architecture bred acceptance, not contempt, and soon the Landmarks Commission began insisting on a higher quality of design. It encouraged restoration of missing elements of facades, and when a building's appearance was poorly documented, it was grateful to architects who designed in the style of the original.

In 1982 the Landmarks Commission designated Lever House, New York's first great Modernist building. But Barwick "ran into a buzzsaw," Tony Wood remembers. The building was owned by the Fisher brothers, a family of developers who were not shy about exerting political pressure. They sought to head off the designation at the Board of Estimate. MAS held a rally at Lever House, and, with the Landmarks Conservancy, sponsored a press conference and ran an ad in the *Times*. Margot Wellington noted that Andrew Stein, the Manhattan borough president, seemed remarkably "unimpressed" by Lever House, and this was alarming, because if Stein voted against the designation, the other borough presidents would probably defer to him. MAS realized it would lose Lever House unless it could win over Jay Golden, the city comptroller, and so Mrs. Onassis went down to the Board of Estimate and visited him. "There weren't supposed to be any photographers present," Tony Wood says, "but somehow there were," and the next day the papers carried a photo of Mrs. Onassis bestowing a kiss on Golden's cheek. The designation passed on Golden's two votes; that photograph was celebrated in preservation circles as "the Kiss That Saved Lever House."[86]

Margot Wellington was exhausted by the time the Urban Center opened its doors. She thought of resigning. Her husband dissuaded her, but two of her protectors on the board of directors, Doris and Alan Freedman, had died. On the one hand their death left a leadership vacuum on the board; on the other, Wellington's style grated on David Prager, Tim Prentice, and Fred Papert, three former presidents of MAS. (Wellington describes her relationship with Papert as "seven and a half years of conflict.") In 1983 they forced Wellington out of office (she became a board member) and asked Kent Barwick to come back to MAS. They offered him a far higher salary than he (or Wellington) had earned in the past, but Barwick wasn't interested in being an executive director again. He was running a city agency; he didn't want to go back to serving "at the pleasure" of a board of directors, as their servant rather than their equal. To lure Barwick back, MAS revised its way of doing business. Barwick became its first paid president, "a first among equals" on the board of directors.

Barwick once described himself as a "creature of MAS," a staff member recalls. "He was nurtured by it, shaped by it," but his return was "a major sea change," a public statement that MAS was taking itself more seriously: "He was the preeminent figure in Landmarks in New York." And one board member says, "He knew everyone in the city government." After Barwick's return, there was a sudden escalation in MAS's influence, but there was also a downside. At first Barwick couldn't testify at the Landmarks Commission. "He was effectively silenced," says Tony Wood, and this at a time when things were changing for the worse at the Landmarks Commission.[87] Barwick says that City Hall never interfered when he presided over the Landmarks Commission. In those days, for example, the Koch administration was hell-bent on demolishing the Helen Hayes theater. Nevertheless, Barwick signed the forms identifying it for listing on the National Register of Historic Places—fearing that his career in government would come to an abrupt end. But not a word of complaint came from City Hall. Barwick, however, had the luxury of heading the Landmarks Commission during a real estate depression when few people were building. Once the building boom of the 1980s began, preservation became a far more contentious issue, and Gene Norman, Barwick's successor as landmarks chairman, clearly enjoyed far less freedom.

To the annoyance of many activists, Barwick refused to criticize Gene Norman, despite the fact that the number of landmarks designations per year suddenly sank to its lowest level ever. In a three-year period Barwick had designated almost 3,000 landmarks; in the next three years, Norman designated only 317.[88] At the same time construction was booming, and so many worthy buildings were threatened that preservationists simply couldn't keep up. Buildings began slipping through the cracks. The most embarrassing case was that of the Wilkie Building on Fortieth Street, overlooking Bryant Park. It had started life as the New York Club, and Henry Hardenbergh had given the building a wonderfully strange facade with a Baroque loggia and Flemish stepped gable.[89] MAS knew the building well: in the 1960s it had held its board meetings there, in the Overseas Press Club. The Landmarks Commission knew the building, too, and identified it as a prime candidate for preservation. But no one noticed when the owners of the Wilkie Building obtained a permit to alter its facade. They set jackhammers to work, mutilating the building's columns and arches and balconies. By the time the dust had settled, there was nothing left worth preserving. The only thing preservationists could do was to arrange for a new layer of record-keeping: in the future the Buildings Department would have to warn the Landmarks Commission if anyone wanted to alter or demolish one of its candidates for preservation.

The most bitter dispute centered on the Rizzoli and Coty buildings, two shops located on Fifth Avenue between Fifty-fifth and Fifty-sixth streets. "It was a great campaign," Tony Wood remembers, "but the end result wasn't." Despite the best efforts of the Fifth Avenue Association, that street had been getting tawdry since the 1970s. Fast-food chains made their appearance below Central Park, and more and more shops seemed to be tourist traps with "Sale: Going Out of Business" signs permanently affixed in the windows. Fifth Avenue's stature as a "high end" shopping street was slipping, and a new threat appeared: skyscrapers. The Olympic Tower rose next to Saint Patrick's Cathedral at Fifty-first Street. A hulking monolith of black glass, it was an alien intrusion in a cityscape of pearly marble, granite, and limestone.

Donald Trump picked up this somber theme in the 1980s when he tore down the Art Deco Bonwit Teller store on Fifty-sixth Street and put up Trump Tower. Bonwit Teller was another building that should have been a landmark but wasn't, and Trump, adding insult to injury, reneged on his promise to save the store's bas-reliefs for the Metropolitan Museum. Extricating the great stone slabs proved too expensive, he explained, after they'd been shattered.* Trump Tower was a fifty-five-story essay in mirrored black glass with shopping in its base and apartments above. The shops were in an atrium, a strategy MAS disliked, fearing that it drained the surrounding streets of vitality. And MAS heartily disapproved of the scale of Trump Tower: it brought to mind Charles Lamb's old warnings that the skyscraper would kill Fifth Avenue.

MAS formed a Committee for the Future of Fifth Avenue. There wasn't much it could do about the tone of Fifth Avenue's tourist shops. (But when Scribner's abandoned its bookstore at 597 Fifth Avenue, a landmark designed by Ernest Flagg in 1913, MAS launched a campaign to find another bookseller to take the space. Brentano's eventually moved in.) Nor did the society succeed in persuading the Landmarks Commission to create a Fifth Avenue Historic District. The neighborhood certainly merited designation—after all, the Fifth Avenue Association had spent decades encouraging fine architecture on the street—but the Landmarks Commission shied away from the issue.

In the midst of all this a pair of developers, David Solomon and G. Ware Travelstead, decided to build a tower at 712 Fifth Avenue between Fifty-fifth and Fifty-sixth streets, demolishing the Rizzoli and Coty buildings. The Rizzoli Building had started out as a rather frothy Beaux Arts town house. It had a very pleasant facade, but not a great one. The Coty Building looked far less inter-

---

* Many thought Trump had already practiced enough economy: the demolition crew of Polish émigrés slept in the store as they ripped it down; a lawsuit, still in progress, charges that they were exposed to asbestos in the process and that their Social Security taxes were never paid.

esting; it had been built as a shop, with a simple grid of frosted-glass windows lighting three floors of lofts above. When MAS heard about this new tower it reiterated its pleas for a Fifth Avenue Historic District, to no avail. It asked the Landmarks Commission to at least designate this one blockfront, including the Harry Winston store and the church, but that request, too, was rejected. It didn't look as if the commission would designate just the two buildings, either—certainly the Coty Building didn't seem to merit the august status of an individual landmark. But MAS had hired Andrew Dolkart, the architectural historian, to look into the building's history, and Dolkart discovered that its windows were the work of René Lalique, the celebrated French artisan. They were so filthy that no one had noticed anything remarkable about the frosted glass, but they were actually an enormous bas-relief of sculpted glass. Dolkart's discovery convinced the Landmarks Commission to schedule a public hearing to consider if the Rizzoli and Coty buildings should become individual landmarks. The Municipal Art Society mounted an exhibit on the buildings, and on Lalique, at the Steuben Glass showroom, and the society's lawyers prepared injunctions to ward off any late-night demolition. "There was a certain level of sophistication" in MAS's campaign to save these shops, Wood remembers.

The summit of this sophistication was MAS's alliance with Donald Trump, who suddenly joined the Committee for the Future of Fifth Avenue and swore to help protect the Rizzoli and Coty buildings. MAS, which hadn't forgotten the sad story of the Bonwit Teller bas-reliefs, bore its new ally no love, and the society assumed that Trump's newfound interest in preservation was purely selfish. The proposed tower, after all, would sit cattycorner to Trump Tower, and MAS believed that Trump wanted to save his building's view. This, it turned out, was a correct assumption, but MAS didn't realize just *how* selfish his motives were. Trump had actually met with Travelstead a few months earlier. According to Wayne Barrett, his biographer, he told Travelstead, "I can't imagine a tower going up on that site that would block the view of the people who bought apartments from me—unless, of course, my name were on the project." In other words, Trump wanted a stake in 712 Fifth Avenue. How large, he never said, nor did he mention paying for it, but he did point out that he had "the political clout to tie you up forever." Travelstead didn't want such a presumptuous partner and rejected the idea. "I hope you don't have any problem," Trump said, "with the Municipal Art Society."

Trump provided MAS with his own lawyer, Allan Schwartz, and with $50,000 for Schwartz's fee. A former corporation counsel, Schwartz was close to Ed Koch, whom he still represented in private matters. He was a "player," someone that City Hall would listen to, and he was aggressive, hinting darkly of some irregularity in Travelstead's permits. The Landmarks Commission voted to designate the Rizzoli and Coty buildings as individual landmarks. The *Times,* which didn't think that either building was distinguished, and which objected to the last-minute designation, replied with a cretinous editorial that accused the Landmarks Commission of standing in the way of "useful development." (The Landmarks Commission might have spared itself this assault had it done the right thing and included the two buildings in a larger historic district.)

MAS girded itself for a fight at the Board of Estimate, which could deny the designations. Volunteers were posted outside the Rizzoli Building; they passed out postcards calling on the board to save the buildings. The developers, at this point, unveiled a new scheme for the site. (There were rumors all along, denied by the developers, that this second scheme already existed.) It preserved the two facades, with a new tower set back behind them. If there was to be a tower, MAS thought it should be much smaller and set much farther back from Fifth Avenue. The Landmarks Commission was eager for a compromise and gave its approval to the second scheme.* "I don't think Kent ever thought the Landmarks Commission would certify the tower as appropriate," Tony Wood says. "He expected a battle at the Board of Estimate. He was screwed."[90]

The fight concerning 712 Fifth Avenue resulted in a very mixed victory for MAS. By the time the tower actually opened, the cast of developers had changed; the tower, planned as a hotel, had become an office building; and the building's base, conceived as a shopping mall, had turned into a department store—a new home for Henri Bendel. The new tower was unfortunate, but there were things to admire: the Coty Building had been gutted to form a soaring atrium for Bendel's, and one wall of this great room was truly splendid, for here were Lalique's windows, cleaned, restored, backlit, and glowing in the night.

IT'S SAID that Paul Byard's father was the first person to suggest that landmarking a church might infringe on the free practice of religion. The elder Byard, also a lawyer, was representing Trinity Parish in 1965, and his suggestion so alarmed Frank Gilbert, the Landmarks Commission's counsel, that he held up the designation of Trinity Church for a year.[91] The issue seemed to evaporate, however. Churches, synagogues, temples, and mosques all had to comply with the zoning, fire, and building codes; landmarking was just one more regulation.

Even in its most timid days, the Landmarks Commission was especially fond of designating churches. This was only natural, for until very recent years, sacred buildings called forth the best architectural efforts of each generation. Moreover, churches seemed to be relatively safe choices. After all, they weren't in the real estate business.

Or were they? Ecclesiastics, like other property owners, were tempted to skimp on repairs—to remove an old cornice, say, instead of repairing it, or to replace a leaky tile roof with one made of asphalt. Nor were churches immune to the pressures of the real estate market. Congregations moved or died away; churches

---

* At this time, Mayor Koch was considering Giorgio Cavaglieri for a post on the Landmarks Commission. Koch asked Cavaglieri how he would vote: would he let the tower rise over the Rizzoli and Coty buildings? One must decide if the buildings are really worthy of being landmarked, Cavaglieri said. If so, then no tower was acceptable; if not, tear them down and build the tower. Cavaglieri knew as he spoke that he was casting his commissionership away. The first solution would have outraged developers, the other would have enraged the preservation community, and Koch was looking for a compromise.

were left empty, and suddenly the land on which they stood seemed more valuable than the buildings themselves. After World War I, New York had seen a fad for "skyscraper churches." Old congregations cut deals with developers, tore down their roomy sanctuaries, and put up an apartment or office building with a church auditorium tucked into its base.[92] This fad ended with the crash of 1929, only to be revived in the 1970s by Saint Peter's Church on Lexington Avenue, which found a new home huddled at the base of the Citicorp tower. Saint Peter's used this real estate deal to fund its celebrated jazz concerts; in the 1980s, other parishes looked for ways to fund sorely needed social programs, and the idea of cashing in on the real estate market seemed irresistible.

By the time Kent Barwick took office, churches had become a problem for the Landmarks Commission, and Barwick thought it would be a good idea if one of his commissioners happened to be a vestryman. Of course Barwick wanted someone he could count on, so Whitney North Seymour arranged for the writer Joseph Mitchell to join the vestry of Grace Church, although the ecclesiastical authorities might have thought him an odd choice. Mitchell came from a "divided family"—with a Baptist father and a Presbyterian mother—and was best known for hanging around a different category of landmark. His most celebrated book was *McSorley's Wonderful Saloon,* and MAS first recruited Mitchell when that celebrated bar was threatened with demolition. Seymour worked his magic, however: Mitchell joined both the vestry and the Landmarks Commission, and Barwick looked forward to the day when he could display the commission's new sensitivity to churches. The first case to come up was a project to build a bridge over Church Street, linking Trinity Church with the parish office building. The architect's first design was blatantly inappropriate. Barwick watched as each commissioner criticized the design, and as Trinity's representatives sank into an ever more visible fury. At last it was Mitchell's turn to comment. "It's just like Trinity," he snarled. "They always were arrogant." And off he went on a tale of Trinity's iniquities.

Trinity got to build its bridge—with a new design that gently alluded to Victorian architecture—but the city's churches grew every more vocal about the burdens of historic preservation. The Church of Saint Paul and Saint Andrew, one of the ornaments of West End Avenue, insisted that caring for a landmark building created an unbearable financial hardship. The parish had actually rejected all offers of assistance, and it was unable to prove its point. The longest, bitterest case was that of Saint Bartholomew's Church on Park Avenue. The church was designed by Bertram Grosvenor Goodhue and finished, after his death, by his successor firm, Mayers, Murray & Philip. The complex combined a garden, a community house, and the church itself in one extraordinary composition that climaxed in the church's polychromed dome. So compelling was the architects' achievement that it set a standard for the rest of the block. In 1929, when Cross & Cross designed the General Electric Building behind the church, they were careful to match Saint Bart's salmon brick and to take Goodhue's Byzantine exoticism one step further into the weird forms of German expressionism. In the 1960s, when a new office building was built next to the GE Tower, similar care was taken. The same brick was used, and the building was kept low so as not to overwhelm the church. Now, however, the church was threatened by its own rector. Reverend Thomas Bowers was an activist minister who had expanded the parish's social programs. To pay for them, he'd come to an arrangement with developer Howard Ronson. They planned to put up an office building on the site of Saint Bart's community house. Its base would contain expanded facilities for the parish, and the offices above would subsidize its good work to the tune of $9.5 million a year.

When MAS first heard of the scheme it sent a delegation to Bowers. Mrs. Onassis and Brendan Gill suggested that there was another option: if the church left its building alone, they pledged to lead a major fund-raising drive to support the outreach programs. Brooke Astor, one of the city's great philanthropists, was willing to help, and the church was surrounded by vastly wealthy corporations whose largesse had never been tapped—companies with a stake in the neighborhood's quality of life. The meeting seemed to go well. "They thought afterward that they'd made some headway," Wellington remembers. But Bowers's answer came a little later when, standing in his pulpit, he denounced Onassis and Gill as "architectural idolators." The battle was on.

MAS was shocked by Bowers's behavior. As Margot Wellington remembers, "To divide the flock, and then go beyond that and divide the city, and attack people who came to you as emissaries"—it seemed so "extreme." MAS replied with an exhibit of scathing cartoons by Tim Prentice in which he mockingly explored "sensitive" ways to turn the church into a skyscraper. The *real* project, designed by Peter Capone of the firm Edward Durrell Stone, Architect, seemed satirical in its own right. Apparently inspired by the Citicorp tower, which is poised atop massive legs, Capone's scheme for Saint Bartholomew's exhibited a similar structural bravado. The project was awful: a faceted, fifty-nine-story glass tower partly cantilevered over the church. Philip Johnson justly said that it would be better to tear Saint Bart's down. The Landmarks Commission scheduled a hearing for January 31, 1984, and that morning's papers carried photos of a candlelight vigil held in front of Saint Bart's the night before. As the commissioners and witnesses arrived, they were greeted by the spectacle of an MAS press conference on the steps of City Hall—it was a "soup-to-nuts" campaign, says Tony Wood. Landmarks rejected Capone's scheme.

A year later the church came back with a new design, which it trumpeted as a more sensitive solution. True, the cantilevers were gone and the materials were more sympathetic, but all in all the scheme was only a little better than the first. The parish knew full well that the Landmarks Commission would never certify it as appropriate, and its lawyers had already laid plans for hardship proceedings to overturn the designation. They presented a pathetic picture of the parish's finances and of the costs of maintaining a landmark church, but MAS contacted Touche-Ross, the accounting firm, which conducted its own pro bono review of the parish's financial statements and found that they overstated the parish's plight. Moreover, the church was still rebuffing the preservationists' offer to raise funds for the parish—conditional on there being no new tower. The Landmarks Commission rejected the hardship application. Blocked on one front, Saint Bart's pursued other tactics.

Meanwhile, churches across the state insisted that landmarks designation was an unbearable burden, even an impediment to worship, and the Interfaith Coalition Against the Landmarking of Religious Properties took their complaint to Albany. The churches realized if they could amend the state law that enabled cities to adopt their own preservation laws, they could change every preservation law in the state in one fatal stroke. "It was a very smart strategic move," says Tony Wood, the MAS staff person in charge of the issue, and Albany was "very ripe territory for the church to play its political game."[93] The churches' instrument was the Flynn-Walsh Bill, named for its sponsors, which quite simply exempted religious properties from preservation laws. Public hearings were held around the state. The first, in Ithaca, went very well for MAS: one churchman arrived to testify in support of the bill, and twenty preservationists showed up to oppose it.[94] Wood flew around the state to help rally local preservationists. The climax was a big public hearing in Albany in February 1984, and MAS decided it was time to resort to "our own historic tradition." The Grand Central Landmark Express had been "one of the great advocacy moments," Wood says, so a new whistle-stop tour set out for Albany. This event wouldn't have been complete or newsworthy without Jacqueline Onassis. She called Wood late one night, agreeing to go, but mentioned in passing that she didn't plan to actually testify. "Of course!" said Wood, "but inside, I just screamed—we'd been planning on it." When they arrived at the state capitol, however, the corridors and balconies were packed with people straining for a glimpse of Mrs. Onassis, and when she walked through the crowd it was "kind of like the Red Sea parting. She was so moved by all the people that she agreed to testify." Hundreds of people testified, Wood remembers, "but Jackie caught their imagination." Afterward Mrs. Onassis visited the governor and the speaker and made the rounds of legislators' offices. "She didn't have to put up with this shit," says Wood. "All the politicians were there with their wives, dogs, and secretaries. It was remarkable that so many offices suddenly sported pictures of JFK, dug out of storage."[95]

That second Landmark Express train was "a unifying experience for a lot of preservation people in the state," Wood remembers, and the Flynn-Walsh bill went down in flames. The churches didn't give up, however. Unable to prove economic hardship to the Landmarks Commission, but still unwilling to compromise, Saint Bartholomew's decided to press the First Amendment argument that landmark designation infringed on the free practice of religion. The lower courts rejected the church's arguments, however, and agreed with MAS that any hardship was partly fictional and partly self-inflicted. The Supreme Court refused to hear them.

When the court battle was over, MAS made contact again with Thomas Bowers, the rector of Saint Bart's. Kent Barwick is fond of gestures of reconciliation, and the parish was now in need of a new direction. So MAS's annual meeting of 1990 was held in Saint Bartholomew's, and the result was one of the more awkward gatherings in the society's history. There were rumors beforehand that Bowers might say something nasty. Some vestrymen reassured MAS that Bowers would merely welcome the society and that friendlier parties would take charge from there, but in the end Bowers did speak at length, and gracelessly. MAS had won its court case, he said, and now it was the society's duty to face the consequences. He laid the parish's financial difficulties at MAS's door: clear up the mess you've made. His remarks went unchallenged until much later in the evening, when Brendan Gill found himself standing in the very pulpit from which Bowers had denounced him as an "architectural idolator." That had been Gill's thanks for offering to do then what Bowers demanded that he do now: to raise money for the church's repair and the parish's social work.

SMALL URBAN PLACES

THERE'S A BITTERSWEET irony to the preservation movement. The land-marks law was founded on the notion that great architecture and urban design contributed to the public well-being. The Landmarks Commission singled out neighborhoods for their human scale, their individual character, their wealth of architectural detail, and the eloquence with which they spoke of New York's history. It said that these were precious qualities that made life in New York a richer and more humane experience. Politicians admitted as much when they passed the landmarks law, and they upheld the notion every time the Board of Estimate or the City Council ratified a landmarks designation. The courts had been convinced that great architecture and urbanism merited protection. Even the Internal Revenue Service agreed. Yet the virtues of old landmarks and historic districts were nowhere to be found in new construction. It was as if, in protecting the past, the city had given up all hope for shaping a better future.

Part of the problem lay in the Zoning Code of 1961. At the time, it seemed to be supremely well intentioned, and the civic groups were convinced, as Giorgio Cavaglieri put it, that the new code would "inevitably" result in "imaginative solutions" and "a handsome New York."[1] But there was a basic conflict in the new zoning. The City Planning Commission had recognized that New York was over-building and that its streets were barren, inhospitable places for the public. It tried to answer the first problem by modestly reducing the city's density: it set an FAR of 15 for commercial districts. That was the median bulk of post–World War II office buildings. But it also encouraged a richer elaboration of public space. Since Charles Stover took charge of the small parks movement at the turn of the century, New York had spent untold millions to create public spaces in the heart of the city, yet the outlay had never been proportionate to the need. Now the city decided to shift this task to the private sector with a system of incentives. The 1961 Zoning Code traded higher densities for public amenities, especially plazas, and there were two ways for a developer to earn a bonus. The builder could negotiate with the city, applying for a special permit and submitting to a long public review process now known as ULURP, the Uniform Land Use Review Process. Most builders took the second, simpler course: by following a set of guidelines, they could build "as of right," with no public review required. The guidelines established a simple equation: for each square foot of plaza, a developer won ten square feet of extra floor. The bonus amounted to an extra 20 percent of buildable space, and the real FAR was no longer 15, but 18.

This was the same method of zoning that Electus Litchfield had first proposed back in 1907. At the time Litchfield had won the support of the Congestion Committee, but the architectural community understood that the FAR granted builders far too much liberty. The Beaux Arts architects knew that a plaza, if carefully conceived in relation to its surroundings, could immeasurably enrich the cityscape; the Villard houses and Rockefeller Center are triumphant examples. But if all builders were encouraged to create open space, and if the size and shape of each plaza was determined by the square footage of individual lots rather than by some larger vision of urban planning, then the result would be sheer chaos. In 1961 such fears were brushed aside, however, and MAS blindly trusted that architects would behave responsibly. It didn't realize that the system of zoning bonuses meant that architects were effectively trapped.

Had the plaza been an option, with no financial rewards attached, architects might have been able to consider whether it was a good idea for a particular site. Developers, too, could have weighed their own attitudes toward the general public; instead of building open spaces that were actively hostile to passersby, they might have just scrapped the whole idea. But the bonus precluded any such considerations. It cost almost nothing to build plazas, but in return, developers won the right to build extra floors that would generate revenue, foot by foot, year after year. This was an irresistible bargain, and by 1973 New York had acquired 1.1 million square feet of new open space. But what sounded like a great boon was often, as Ada Louise Huxtable wrote, "an environmental tragedy."[2]

IT TOOK time for New York to face up to the myriad problems of plaza zoning. The 1960s and early 1970s were an era of rich experiment in urban design, and New York's civic groups and art societies were preoccupied with the notion of humanizing the city with great new outdoor spaces. Americans flocked to the piazzas of Rome and the cafés of Paris, they pointed out, while a harsher urbanism still prevailed at home. In the early 1960s the civic groups united in a campaign to create "oases in the asphalt desert," as MAS's former president, Ely Jacques Kahn, put it. "New Yorkers dwell . . . in a rectilinear world of glass and geometry, amid hard surfaces, crowded streets and sooty air," Kahn wrote in the *Times*. "New York needs dozens of small parks—parks close to home, where the young can play and their elders relax—parks close to work, where a moment in the sun can brighten a day: parks to please the eye, parks to rest the feet, parks to fill the lungs."[3]

The idea of parks in business districts was new to New York, and the notion ran up against an obstacle in the City Planning Commission. The planning establishment insisted that three acres was the minimum size for a useful park, and this maxim established a fabulous price tag for Midtown parks, ensuring that the most congested parts of the city went without relief. Then the landscape architects Robert Zion and Harold Breen pointed out that Midtown was sprinkled with parking lots, most measuring about 40 by 100 feet, and they suggested a new notion of "the Midtown parklet" as a "small outdoor room, human in scale, with walls, floors and a ceiling."[4] Their prototype design was an exercise in studied simplicity. Its floor was paved, its "roof" was the leafy canopy of a grove of trees, and its furniture was a set of movable chairs. At the back was a "waterwall"—a cascade running the full width of the park. The glint of sunlight on water would lure pedestrians into the park, while the sound of falling water would muffle the traffic noise. The Architectural League and the Park Association exhibited Zion's Midtown parklet scheme in the 1960s, and Ely Jacques Kahn published it in 1963 in the Sunday *Times* magazine. Nothing happened, however, until MAS revived the project in 1971, featuring it in an exhibit called "Streets for People" at Union Square. William Paley, the founder of CBS, decided to build the project, and Paley Park, on Fifty-third Street, became the most elegant and popular of New York's urban oases.

There were also more ambitious schemes to green Midtown. In 1961 the AIA began talking about pedestrian malls, and this evolved into a project sponsored by MAS and a coalition of civic groups, and designed by Simon Breines, called Five and One Half Way. This plan solved the old problem of the daunting length of the Midtown blocks. Charles Lamb had proposed zigzagging malls early in the century; Mayor Gaynor had dreamed of a new Midtown avenue in 1910; the Rockefellers had made a start with their private street at Rockefeller Center; and Jane Jacobs had written of Midtown's withered street life in *The Death and Life of Great American Cities*. Breines called for a pedestrian walkway running from Bryant Park to Central Park and tracing "a sinuous course" along the "most feasible path"—sometimes cutting through parking lots and service alleys, other times threading through parcels soon to be developed. There would be as little condemnation as possible. But the City Planning Commission took a more modest course, involving no condemnation at all, when it set guidelines for a network of passages threaded through Midtown blocks. These could be parklets or covered arcades; whenever possible they were supposed to align with one another, but they never did function as a continuous mall: pedestrians didn't dare brave the traffic that separates one passage from another.

The most attractive experiment of the era, and the most heartrending for the Municipal Art Society, was the ill-fated Madison Avenue Mall. It began with the first celebration of Earth Day in 1971. While MAS celebrated the event with the Streets for People exhibit, Mayor Lindsay marked the occasion by announcing that midday traffic would be barred for a week from Madison Avenue between Forty-second and Fifty-seventh streets. Pedestrians flooded the avenue, basking in the April sunshine. Instead of traffic, there were Frisbees; instead of blaring horns, there were picnics. The city decided to bar traffic for a second week, and so was born the notion of a Madison Avenue Mall. William Whyte, an urban critic active in MAS, set up time-lapse cameras to monitor the experiment. "The number of people on the street more than doubled," he reported, "going from nine thousand to nineteen thousand. And this was not at the expense of activity on neighboring streets. The flows there were about as high as they usually were."[5] As Whyte told the *Times*, the experiment "lasted only two paltry weeks, was restricted to 12–2 P.M., had a smattering of old benches for street furniture, and the second week it rained. But on the whole it was a whale of a success." Lindsay ordered the Office of Midtown Planning and Development to draw up plans for a permanent mall. Madison Avenue would be shut to all but crosstown traffic, buses, and emergency vehicles, and the city would widen the sidewalks, plant trees, encourage cafés, and even sprinkle the street with public art. All this would restore a sense of balance between pedestrians and autos, said the city; it would bring greenery into the heart of Midtown Manhattan at little cost, and make New York a more livable and humane city.

MAS staked its hopes on the Madison Avenue Mall, but a powerful coalition was rising up to fight the project. The avenue's merchants cried out that the "quiet and dignity" of their neighborhood would give way to a "carnival and street fair" atmosphere; they spoke of "undesirables" and wondered how their customers would arrive if not by car—a curious delusion, since no one drives to Madison Avenue to shop. Nightmares of a lowered "tone" in Midtown drew the Fifth Avenue Association into the fray; the Automobile Club issued dire forecasts of traffic bottlenecks; and finally the Independent Taxi Owners Council rose up in arms. This last group, five thousand strong, regarded traffic flow as the prime directive in urban design, and it was already disgusted with Lindsay for banning cars from Central Park on weekdays. In the face of all this opposition, Lindsay struggled to forge a compromise. He suggested a three-month trial run for the mall in the hope that merchants would discover new customers walking through their doors. This proposal, however, was greeted with a lawsuit. Nineteen plaintiffs—among them, Brooks Brothers and the Fifth Avenue Association—went to court, and in 1973 they obtained a ruling that even a temporary mall must have the Board of Estimate's approval. This spelled the project's doom. (Ironically, putting an issue before the board was the same strategy MAS had tried, unsuccessfully, in its battle with the Metropolitan Museum over its expansion into Central Park.) The mayor tried to mollify the taxi industry, promising a crackdown on gypsy cabs and even offering to lift the restrictions on cars in Central Park, but by the time the issue reached the Board of Estimate, Lindsay was a lame duck mayor, elections were approaching, and serious debate gave way to political calculation. The taxi owners had a friend in Comptroller Abe Beame—they had supported him in the bruising mayoral primary—and the presidents of the outer boroughs knew they had little to gain by satisfying Manhattan's hunger for greenery and much to lose by angering cabbies who lived in their own bailiwicks.[6]

The Madison Avenue Mall did set a precedent, however. Brooklyn's Fulton Street was later converted into a mall, and this rejuvenated a neighborhood that had seemed doomed to decay. Another mall appeared in the financial district: Nassau Street was too narrow, twisting, and congested with pedestrians to be of any use to the taxi industry, and it was transformed into a pedestrian mall in 1977, almost seven decades after Charles Rollinson Lamb first proposed such a thing.

WHILE THE civic groups sketched their oases and malls, the 1961 Zoning Code was riddling the city with new plazas, and the experiment was proving disastrous. On Sixth Avenue one could see the new zoning code shaping block after block of the city. Beginning in 1961 and continuing for a decade, a wave of new construction swept up Sixth Avenue from Forty-seventh to Fifty-fourth Street. The buildings were brute slabs rising forty or fifty stories with nary a setback. The open spaces huddled at the towers' feet amounted, as the critic (and Municipalian) Peter Blake wrote in 1965, to "a chaotic conglomeration of piazzas, piazzettas, piazzetines, arcades, and courts."[7] The new Sixth Avenue offered the first warning that the new zoning code was ruinous when applied wholesale to an entire neighborhood, but worse still was the effect of lone buildings rising in established neighborhoods. The notion of the street as an outdoor room was sacrificed as plazas turned the street wall into a jagged line; the ugly, scarred party walls of old buildings were exposed to view; and the new towers, with all their volume concentrated in a single mono-lithic slab, dwarfed their neighbors. Ada Louise Huxtable pointed to Fifth Avenue and Seventy-ninth Street, site of the late, lamented Brokaw mansion, where devel-oper Anthony Campagna built a bulky new apartment tower with a "wraparound corner plaza." Here, she pointed out, one could see "the destructive force of the new zoning when it is applied literally and without adjustment to specific urban con-ditions. Open plazas opposite the open space of Central Park are an absurdity. But the awkward, meaningless windswept setback from the street gives the builder a bonus of extra rentable floors in a taller tower. Builders, notoriously, are not urbanists. This trend can destroy the little that New York has of genuine urban elegance or greatness, its few handsome avenues and sophisticated plazas."[8]

Just as inept was the new General Motors Building, which rose on the full block between Fifth and Madison avenues, Fifty-eighth and Fifty-ninth streets. It took the place of McKim, Mead & White's Sherry Netherland Hotel, a beautiful homage to Henry Hardenbergh's Plaza Hotel. Together with Bergdorf Goodman, the two hotels had formed the walls of New York's best outdoor room: Grand Army Plaza, better known as "the Plaza," so handsomely designed by Karl Bitter and Thomas Hastings. When General Motors announced that it would build on this crucial site, MAS, the AIA, and the Fifth Avenue Association had set up a committee of architects to consult with Edward Durell Stone, GM's designer. Stone rushed ahead, however, and the *Times* leaked his design before the architects could even set up a meeting.[9] GM simply told MAS not to worry, that its plaza would be "the brightest" and "most expensive" in the city.[10] Perhaps it was all that, but in its merry vulgarity General Motors completely missed two rather important points, and its plaza was a disaster: depressingly sunk a floor below street level, it never attracted visitors, not even after the owners went to the desperate extreme of installing AstroTurf; and worse, it ruined Grand Army Plaza, just as any room would be ruined if someone tore out a wall and left a gaping hole in its place.

Harmon Goldstone, who joined the City Planning Commission in 1962, remembers that he and his colleagues were horrified by what was happening, especially since GM was on Fifth Avenue. He likens it to seeing someone's teeth kicked in. The planning commission realized early on that the plaza "had been a trap, and the destruction of the street was very disturbing. What seemed like this dream . . . didn't work out." Yet the commission was reluctant to admit its mistake, much less rectify it. "It's hard for the city to admit it's wrong," Goldstone says. "You need an excuse to make a change." It found one excuse in the construction of Lincoln Center, where a Special Zoning District was created in 1967. Buildings on Broadway were required to have six-story bases "built out" to the street line, and developers received bonuses for building ground-level arcades. "We were trying to recapture the street wall" and the human scale of traditional streets "while keeping the wider sidewalk," says Goldstone.[11]

Despite Goldstone's best efforts, Lincoln Center was soon surrounded by hideous and overbearing apartment buildings, in part because, to MAS's fury, the Board of Standards and Appeals began handing out zoning variances. The arcades quickly proved to be a disappointment. They had a long family tree—its roots stretched back to Charles Lamb at the turn of the century and to Harvey Wiley Corbett in the 1920s—but those two visionaries meant to build arcades *over* the sidewalks; here, arcades sat *next to* the sidewalks. Pedestrians shunned them except in heavy rain, and they found their best use as open-air cafés during the summer months.

For the moment, the Lincoln Center guidelines marked the limit of the planning commission's appetite for reform. MAS spent the late 1960s criticizing builders for putting plazas on Broadway and Park Avenue (both wide boulevards whose chief virtue, up to now, had been their regularity) or facing the city's parks. A plaza next to a park was at best redundant; at worst, as at the General Motors Building, it ruined the park's spatial definition. By 1972 MAS realized that mere criticism was futile, and that the builders themselves weren't really to blame. The city encouraged these plazas, and the zoning bonus was now so routine that its value was reflected in the price of land. MAS began meeting with Raquel Ramati, a young architect on the staff of the planning commission, and the society agreed that "Builders should be encouraged to make architecturally sound decisions and not simply attacked as the enemy."[12] Ramati's solution was to ban plazas from Broadway and from Park and Fifth avenues. "The builder will be required to build to the lot line," Mary Perot Nichols wrote in the *Village Voice*, "returning to the straight building line of an earlier and more elegant age."[13] A zoning bonus would still be available, but now developers would earn it by donating money to a Parks Improvement Trust Fund.

This fund was administered by a mixed group of city officials, community board members, and representatives of civic groups; its mission was to supplement the Parks Department's official budget.

WHILE NEW YORK grew more particular about where plazas should be built, it was also learning how to shape the zoning code to foster a vibrant street life. Street life had two great champions in these years. The first was Jane Jacobs; the second was William Hollingsford Whyte, universally known as Holly. "No profession can be said to contain him," writes Brendan Gill, who ranks Whyte with such great "learned amateurs" as Jacobs, Lewis Mumford, and Frederick Law Olmsted. An editor at *Fortune* for many years, Whyte became famous for his book *The Organization Man*, a pioneering study of America's executive class and its suburban lifestyle. In 1959 he began working in open-space conservation, but soon he turned to the urban environment, "subjecting the city to a scrutiny as close as that to which Thoreau . . . subjected Walden Pond and its environs."[14]

In 1969 Donald Elliott, the city planning commissioner, invited Whyte to work on New York's master plan. Whyte was tempted, since Elliott promised to address one of New York's great problems: the fact that communities had so little voice in the planning process. (Elliott went on to set up the system of community boards in 1971.) But Whyte had a different idea: he wanted to conduct a study of the city's plazas. Developers' fondness for plazas "should have been seen as an alert," he realized. "When a building rents out very quickly, real estate people figure they might have set the rents too low. The planning commission might well have concluded that it had underpriced the bonus. It certainly seemed clear that the benefits for builders were great. Some suspected they might be scandalously so."[15] When Whyte wondered how much the public benefited from these plazas, it turned out that no one knew. The planning commission had never tried to evaluate the program.

Whyte set up the Street Life Project in 1969 and, working with students from Hunter College, trained time-lapse cameras on plazas. He learned that some of the spaces worked; some didn't. People were obviously drawn to the Seagram building, and "At lunchtime on a good day," Whyte reported, "there would be 150 people sitting, sunbathing, picnicking, and schmoozing. People also flocked in great numbers to the open space at 77 Water Street, known as swingers' plaza, because of the raffish young crowd it attracted." At any given moment of a balmy lunch hour, Whyte could count 160 people using 77 Water Street. Yet other places, equally sunny, were deserted. On average, just 17 people braved the plaza at 280 Park Avenue, for example. "If places such as Seagram and 77 Water Street could work so well," Whyte asked, "why not others?" Size, he discovered, didn't correlate with popularity; sunlight seemed to matter in the spring and fall, when temperatures were chilly, but not in summer; it was the design of the plazas that made the difference.[16]

Whyte talked Donald Elliott into watching his films, and he suggested to the planning commissioner that "the city was being had. For the millions of dollars of extra floor space it was handing out to developers, it had every right to demand much better space in return."[17] Whyte offered to conduct a more thorough study and to quantify what made successful plazas attractive to the public. Then the city could draw up design guidelines for plazas, and at last the public investment in new open space, paid for with precious sun and sky, might bring a decent return. With Elliott's blessing, Whyte took to the streets again. He set up cameras on sidewalks, perched them on rooftop aeries, and dangled them from window ledges. This time his lenses were trained on sixteen plazas and three small parks. He talked to doormen, security guards, and shop owners, and he spent countless hours simply watching what people did—where they walked, sat, ate, and talked; where they stopped and where they hurried on. Whyte's time-lapse cameras made patterns of all this movement, and the picture they presented was startlingly at odds with the tenets of modern urban planning.

Whyte demonstrated that people are far more social animals than planners had realized. Architects still spoke sneeringly of congestion and crowded sidewalks, yet Whyte could show that, in the real world, people were instinctively drawn to crowds. Unconsciously, they gravitated to the more congested sidewalks. They held the most intimate conversations while standing astride the very center of crossing paths of circulation. In other words, people attracted people. Yet Whyte found that a contrary suspicion of crowds was also at work, and while the architectural elite yearned for a European street life, old prejudices still reigned in the popular imagination. Shopkeepers and building managers muttered about "undesirables," and when asked for specifics, they pointed out hippies and blacks, drug dealers and youths in general, and even Whyte's own student volunteers. Whyte had isolated the real reason why so many plazas lay empty: it was fear—and it was hideously counterproductive. In the name of warding off undesirables, builders had devised all sorts of strategies to keep people away from their plazas: seats were banished; ledges and planters were edged with spikes; plazas were raised above the sidewalks or sunk below the street; security guards were ordered to keep people moving; stores were displaced in favor of banks or monumentally empty lobbies; and when all else failed, fences were erected. The product of builders' suspicion had a certain poetic justice: the general public was driven away, leaving just the criminals to brave the empty concrete wastes. Drug dealers *liked* the most inhospitable parklets since their customers could easily find them, and their view of advancing policemen was unobstructed by crowds.

Whyte handed the City Planning Commission a long list of proposed design guidelines. Buildings would have to devote half their ground-floor frontage to shops. Plazas would need one linear foot of seating for every thirty square feet of open space. Whyte set standards for the height and depth of benches, just to make sure they would be really useful, and he banned the spikes and railings that made so many ledges useless for sitting. Noticing that movable chairs make for the best seating of all, since people can group them as they want or pull aside a single chair for privacy, he put a premium on them. Food kiosks were no longer classified as obstructions, but rather encouraged. He required trees—one for each twenty-five feet of sidewalk and six for each five hundred square feet of plaza—and they had to be planted in the ground, not in planters, so they would grow tall enough to actually produce shade.

The civic groups rallied around Whyte's proposals. Ironically, it was the community boards that objected: they feared that Whyte was imposing a straitjacket on architects. The AIA put them at ease, however, by explaining that architects would be grateful for the guidelines. Without them, developers would make all the decisions. Whyte's reforms were adopted in 1975. Since then they've set a standard for designers around the country. Whyte summed up his life's work in a book, *City*, published in 1988, but he's best known to the general public through a film, *The Social Life of Small Urban Places*, which first aired on PBS's *Nova* in 1980. As the film's distributor, "MAS got some credit," Laurie Beckelman says, "but Holly did all the work."[18] Many of Sixth Avenue's dismal plazas were redesigned as Whyte suggested. On the other hand, some developers hewed to their old-fashioned ways, and MAS helped organize local "plaza patrols" to ensure that builders lived up to their legal obligations.[19]

The finest demonstration of Whyte's techniques, however, was the rejuvenation not of a plaza but of a public park. Bryant Park had been a troubled place for much of its history, a focus for the local drug trade and an eyesore to its neighbors. It was rescued by the Bryant Park Restoration Corporation, a privately funded group organized by local businesses. The entrances were made more inviting, food kiosks were installed, public rest rooms were added (by the J. M. Kaplan Fund), and new herbaceous borders were planted. But the most brilliant and successful touch was the simplest: the park's Great Lawn, once a vast, dull expanse of grass, was provided with lawn chairs. In the summer of 1993, when the park reopened, the lawn was revealed as one of the great urban parks, and MAS chose the site, and the occasion, to give Whyte a medal for his lifetime achievement.

THE GLOBAL CITY

HOLLY WHYTE'S WORK in the early 1970s offered New York's civic groups a new sense of optimism about their ability to shape a more livable city, but their hopes were soon dashed. His guidelines were adopted in 1975 at the very moment when New York lost control of its destiny. The occasion was the collapse of the Urban Development Corporation, a public authority created in 1968 by Governor Nelson Rockefeller. The UDC was his answer to Richard Nixon, who had slashed the public housing budget, but two things distinguished the new authority from earlier public housing ventures: most of the apartments it built were for the middle class rather than the poor; and the state declared that it had a moral obligation, rather than a legal one, to back up the authority's bonds. This was a shrewd way of ensuring that the UDC's debt didn't appear on the state's own books. Inflation turned the UDC's ledgers into a sea of red ink, but the public authority kept building, and the banks kept buying its bonds in the expectation that Rockefeller would enforce the state's moral obligation. When the governor resigned in 1973, however, the banks grew worried; they panicked when his designated successor, Malcolm Wilson, lost the election; and they began bailing out in 1974. One year later, the Urban Development Corporation defaulted on a hundred million dollars in notes.

This was the biggest default of a government agency since the Great Depression, and bankers recognized that if reality could catch up with the UDC, then New York City's bonds weren't safe, either. The city had amassed a vast amount of debt since 1965, when Robert Wagner drew up the last budget of his twelve years in office and couldn't make it balance. Rather than ruin his exit with budget cuts or tax increases, Wagner worked out a deal with Rockefeller. The governor won Democratic support for a state sales tax; the mayor got a small increase in the city sales tax and, fatally, the right to borrow against future *estimated* revenue. "A good loan is better than a bad tax," the mayor explained. At the time, John Lindsay and Abraham Beame were vying to succeed Wagner, and both denounced the new policy as a Pandora's box. Yet these same two men later found it terribly convenient to take a rosy view of the future when estimating revenue. Optimism might have been justified in the 1960s, when the city's economy was still booming, but by 1969 the city had begun losing jobs to the Sunbelt and tax revenues to the segregated suburbs. The city, convinced that the downturn was temporary, continued to borrow. By the mid 1970s, even routine operating expenses were funded from the capital budget.

In the year following the UDC's collapse, the big banks sold more than $2 billion in New York securities, transferring their risk to the innocent small investor. When the market became saturated, the banks complained of a "panic" and demanded that Mayor Beame bail them out. Beame had been elected on the premise that, having long been the city's comptroller, he "knew where the money was," but in fact he'd been so expert at hiding the city's budgetary problems that the full scope of New York's deficit escaped him. Given the mayor's incompetence, the reins of government were effectively seized by an ad hoc coalition composed of the governor, Wall Street bankers, and union chiefs. A state agency was created to oversee the city's budget. The unions risked their pension funds to make loans to the city. Some 65,000 municipal jobs were eliminated, wages were frozen, the subway fare was hiked, welfare grants were slashed, and tuition was imposed at City College. Despite all this, federal loan guarantees were needed to stave off bankruptcy. The Republican administration in Washington chose to use New York's difficulties as an indictment of liberal government, and in 1975 President Gerald Ford promised to veto any bailout. The *Daily News* replied with a celebrated headline: "Ford to City: Drop Dead." Wall Street gave its answer the same day as stocks plummeted, the price of gold soared, and the value of the dollar declined. Wall Street had understood the problem better than Washington: New York's debt was held by hundreds of banks, insurance companies, annuity funds, and retirees. Default would send seismic waves through the nation's economy. So a loan package was very grudgingly approved—at a percentage point above the prevailing Treasury rate.[1]

Despite this last-minute rescue, New York's future hadn't seemed so bleak since 1934. The budget cuts affected every segment of society—except, perhaps, the banks—and years of austerity lay ahead. The city was in the midst of a recession that would ultimately cost it more than half a million jobs. Not a single new office building opened its doors in 1976. Through the mid 1970s, the newspapers carried grim reports of a corporate exodus as one company after another shut its New York headquarters and moved to the suburbs—searching, they said, for better transportation, lower taxes, and a decent quality of life.* After decades of "deferred maintenance," the subway system finally reached a point of crisis, and a token bought admission to a Kafkaesque dream world: passengers could only guess if a given train would ever reach its destination or if its doors would actually open on command.

---

* In 1976, Holly Whyte found that these companies usually had a still more pressing motive to move. He studied thirty-eight corporations that left New York; in thirty-one cases the new headquarters was "a place close to the top man's home. Average distance: about eight miles by road." William H. Whyte, City: Rediscovering the Center (New York: Anchor Books, 1988), 288.

In the *Times*, Roger Starr preached the odious gospel of "planned shrinkage," arguing that the city should foster "internal resettlement." Rebuild the city center at higher densities, he said, and withdraw services from troubled neighborhoods until the land lay fallow.

In 1977, after the crest of the fiscal crisis, Edward I. Koch was elected mayor. "After eight years of charisma and four years of the clubhouse," his ads had asked, "why not try competence?" The Municipal Art Society liked Koch at the time. Margot Gayle had known him since the 1960s when they were both up-and-coming figures in the reform camp of the Democratic Party. Doris Freedman had been raising money for Koch since 1968, when Greenwich Village sent him off to Congress to mount a valiant struggle against the Vietnam War. (Koch's opponent in that election was MAS's own Whitney North Seymour, Jr., whose politics were lamentably conservative.) Koch had always been friendly to the preservation movement, as one would expect of a Villager. As a congressman, and then as a new mayor, he threw his weight behind MAS's campaign to save Grand Central Terminal, and we've already seen that he named Kent Barwick chairman of the Landmarks Preservation Commission. When Koch took office he spoke kindly of the community boards as a necessary counterforce to developers. He was even persuaded to revive the long moribund Art Commission. Yet even in the first months of the Koch administration there were troubling signals that something was amiss in City Hall. As a candidate, Koch had promised to purge the city government of clubhouse politics. MAS knew where he could start: through the Beame years, the society had bitterly complained about the Board of Standards and Appeals. MAS noted the lucrative zoning variances handed out so regularly to the politically well connected, the ease with which insiders were able to prove economic hardship, and the tendency of the board to set its own zoning policies in utter disregard of the planning commission. The board operated "in a closed circle of intimacy with its plaintiffs, almost as if it were a private rather than a public body," MAS noted, and it waited expectantly for the new mayor to clean house, but then it watched in horror as Abe Beame's appointees managed to keep their jobs.

Koch's first years in office were a grim period, but austerity budgets were better than imminent bankruptcy. The mayor was widely seen as a responsible man doing well in bad circumstances, and his colorful speaking style made him a national celebrity. If some heard faint echoes of Jimmy Walker in the mayor's pithy sound bites, they still prompted memories of Walker's wit, not his ethics. The dilemma facing Koch was how to revive the local economy when industry was fleeing and Washington was steadily pulling out of the public housing business. The Koch administration pictured New York as a global city, a center of high finance and white-collar services, and the city coddled these industries while it left others to their own devices. Rather than shore up the city's shrinking manufacturing base—by building, for instance, a rail link and new freight terminals in the Bronx—City Hall declared that New York was a "post-industrial" city. Factories and small businesses were left to flounder while large corporations were granted tax abatements to expand or update their facilities. The real estate industry was assigned the task of building the new global city of high-rise offices and luxury apartments, and whenever possible the city would leverage its limited resources to catalyze private investment.

The outlines of this policy became clear early in Koch's first term, when the mayor reversed a long-held position and threw his weight behind Westway, a project celebrated as, inch per inch, the world's most expensive highway design to date. The Westway proposal dated back to the Lindsay administration, and the intentions behind the scheme were admirable: to reclaim the West Side waterfront from the abandoned piers and the rusting Miller Highway and to bring the public in contact with the water by submerging the highway below grade. Westway would stretch from the Battery to Forty-second Street—a six-lane road, 4.2 miles long, buried beneath 181 acres of landfill in the Hudson. State parks would sit on the water's edge; inland, there would be new real estate. The price tag came to $4 billion, 90 percent of it paid by Washington, the remainder by the state, but critics of the proposal expected it to cost far more.

West Siders worried, however, that the project would funnel new traffic into their neighborhoods and that the new real estate would spark a dramatic surge in development nearby. Others suggested that the money would be better spent on the deteriorating mass transit system, and they begged the city to "trade in" the money for the subway. Environmentalists, in turn, discerned that the landfill would destroy the breeding area for striped bass. And it was this environmental detail, the city's cover-up of the facts, and the intervention of New Jersey's congressional delegation that finally killed the project in 1982.

The Municipal Art Society did a poor job of listening to the complaints about Westway. When Fred Papert became the society's president in 1976 he told the members that MAS had to be "the spokesman for a citywide point of view in matters of land-use planning, particularly when many of the newly empowered community boards were using their powers parochially, when developers were scarce, and when the city administration was preoccupied with high finance. We are trusted and respected by all three . . . and therefore have a special responsibility—a special opportunity, really—to save New York." A few months later, MAS endorsed Westway. One hundred fifty members resigned in disgust.[2]

It was a "bloody confrontation," Margot Wellington says. "There's no such thing as an activist who hasn't made a great mistake. I didn't do the right thing either. I thought [Westway] was a good thing for the Village, particularly in the beginning, when I knew some of the planners and I knew they really did intend to build a new city." Before joining MAS, Wellington had fought the Linear City Project in Brooklyn and the Lower Manhattan Expressway. Both would have devastated vast areas of decent occupied buildings. By comparison, Westway seemed a blessing. Since it was in the river, there wouldn't be any demolition. The waterfront would be within reach for the first time in memory. The planners spoke of matching the scale of the existing neighborhoods. The director of the project presented it to MAS's board, and "it seemed a model." Ada Louise Huxtable admired the scheme and urged John Oakes, her colleague at the *Times*, to support it. But, as Tim Prentice later complained, MAS had never heard both sides of the debate; it had never invited Westway's critics to present their case.

It's also clear that the Municipal Art Society took its position far too early. When Ada Louise Huxtable wrote about Westway in 1977, she praised the concept but also pointed out what remained to be done: the city needed to design a park worthy of Olmsted; to zone the newly created land to respect the character and scale of the Village, TriBeCa, and Chelsea; and to protect those old neighborhoods from the impact of new construction to the west. "Westway must not be just a real estate gimmick for developable land," Huxtable wrote. "It must be planned, designed, and controlled in the interest of a better city, not of a better tax base. . . . Someone will have to set standards. And those standards will have to be translated into superior and binding legal and architectural solutions."[3] Those standards never were set, however. The parks were placed in the deserving hands of architect Robert Venturi, but the planning controls and architectural guidelines never materialized.

"We didn't *campaign* for Westway," Wellington points out, speaking of MAS. "Every word of testimony was fought over," especially by Fred Papert and David Prager, who supported the project, and Doris Freedman, who was "very upset and angry over the society's position and tried to reverse it. . . . If she'd lived longer," says Wellington, "I think she would have." Wellington believes that Westway was "probably right overall," but it was "bad for MAS to endorse it. You need someone to take a *pure* position," to stand up as the voice of "a pure conscience," and then "maybe you can help shape a compromise. If you start out as the voice of 'citizen reason,' where will the compromise come from? MAS has to go too far. I never considered it bad when someone said our position was too extreme. It changes the place a discussion starts from."[4]

In the 1980s there were new tax exemptions and loans for business, new efforts to raise venture capital, and new abatements for developers. And with Ronald Reagan's election, Koch himself moved further and further to the right. Koch won the plaudits of developers, investment bankers, corporations, and the rising class of yuppies—the very groups that benefited from his policies. Between 1982 and 1985, sixty office buildings went up. The Jacob K. Javits Convention Center—first planned in the Lindsay years—was finally built, and half a dozen hotels opened. A wave of co-op conversions swept the city. Subsidized by the J-51 program's tax abatements, they testified to a promising development: urban life was becoming fashionable again for the middle class, in large part because of the preservation movement. But all this new prosperity was thinly based. Small businesses foundered, driven under by chain stores and rising rents. The city's stock of SRO hotels was savaged by new construction and co-op conversions, and the disappearance of these single-room-occupancy buildings had a devastating effect. They had provided shelter for the working poor, for the elderly, for those on public assistance, and for patients brusquely discharged from the state's mental institutions. Homelessness flourished when the SROs disappeared; New York was becoming a Dickensian city.

The city's finances, to be sure, were still straitened, and even the economy's revival after 1979 couldn't make up for the fell effects of Washington's "disinvestment" in the cities. The shortfall in revenues was answered—sporadically—by a new vigor in the private sphere. One could see it in the soup kitchens and shelters operating out of church basements, founded because congregations couldn't bear to watch idly as the city let people shiver and starve in the streets. And new business districts sprouted up across the city as local businesses petitioned the city to assess special taxes on their neighborhoods. They used the money for private security guards, trash collectors, new sidewalks—whatever seemed necessary to stave off a sense of urban decay. New philanthropies were organized to fill the vacuum in government funds. Alan Freedman, Doris Freedman's husband and MAS's president from 1982 until his death in 1983, set up the WNYC Foundation in 1978 to rescue the municipal radio and television stations from oblivion. The Central Park Conservancy was founded in 1980 to rescue the park from chronic, and worsening, neglect. (That organization now raises half the park's budget.) And the Municipal Art Society pioneered new ways to salvage the city's crumbling legacy of parks, monuments, and public spaces.

In 1977 MAS invented the Adopt-a-Station program for the city's subway system. At the time the MTA was consumed with the onerous task of rebuilding an ancient infrastructure, and the stations themselves were of necessity neglected. MAS started out by hiring artists to redesign four "culture stations": they worked with minimal budgets, and some of the supergraphic designs look dated today, but at the time few New Yorkers expected that the 1980s would bring a revival of craft and historicist design.[5] The most charming project was for the West Eighty-first Street station on the IND line: paintings of dinosaurs filled the station's advertising space and hinted at the relics upstairs, in the Museum of Natural History. At first, MAS found that the MTA saw "a problem for every solution," but the Transit Authority gradually came to see that spiffy new stations had a direct appeal to the public.

MAS embarked on the Adopt-a-Station program in the hope that "money would pour into the project," as Laurie Beckelman remembers.[6] Surely, MAS thought, the city's great corporations would want to invest in New York's most heavily trafficked public places. But that was an almost sterile hope. MAS was able to supervise the redesign of the Clark Street station in Brooklyn, and Chase Manhattan Bank subscribed to the renovation of the IRT's Wall Street stop, but other donors shied away. Instead, the program prompted the city to invent a new category of zoning bonus, and the city's sunlight was soon being sacrificed, at bargain prices, for improvements to the subway stations.

Similar programs sprang from MAS through the 1980s. In 1987 MAS, the Parks Department, and the Art Commission launched the Adopt-a-Monument program, which found private donors to restore the city's aging and vandalized works of public art. MAS painted a depressing picture of the state of the city's monuments with its exhibit "Monumental Woes." The project led to the restoration of the Minerva clock in Herald Square, the Columbus Memorial in Columbus

Circle, and, its most ambitious feat, the Plaza at Fifth Avenue and Fifty-ninth Street.* The Adopt-a-Mural program was launched four years later, and Edward Simmons's murals in the Criminal Courts Building—MAS's first gift to the city—were restored to their original glory in 1993, the society's centennial year.

Privatization left its mark on the New York skyline as well. The building boom of the 1980s marked the mad apogee of incentive zoning. Two trains of thought were at work. On the one hand, the City Planning Commission kept expanding the menu of public spaces that qualified for a zoning bonus. A builder could win extra bulk in return for providing a plaza, an arcade, a through-block passage, or an atrium—and yet another bonus for putting shops in the atrium. On the other hand, the city seized on the opportunity to transfer items from its own capital budget to the private sector. The era of building great new public works had ended when Ronald Reagan abandoned the nation's cities to their own devices, and New York was struggling just to maintain its aging infrastructure.

Meanwhile the MTA had its own problems. It was spending vast sums on the most basic subway improvements, like new switches and switching equipment, and had no money to spruce up decrepit stations. So the city was eager to dispense a new sort of zoning bonus—so eager that it sold the sky for fire sale prices. When Harry Macklowe built River Terrace, for instance, he spent $1.7 million to repair the East River Esplanade, and received a bonus worth $13 million. William Zeckendorf, who built the Copley apartments on West Sixty-eighth Street, made half a million dollars in repairs to the Sixty-sixth Street subway station; his bonus was worth $8 million. All these bonuses made the zoning code itself something of a fiction. Each new tower, each package of bonuses, was negotiated, first by the City Planning Commission and then, if the developer wasn't satisfied, by the Board of Standards and Appeals.

The Koch administration's "only piece of constructive zoning," says Margot Wellington, was the crackdown on sliver towers. In the early 1980s slender towers began sprouting from the twenty-foot-wide lots of East Side side streets. Most people assumed that they were the product of the skyrocketing cost of land—that lots were now so dear that only towers could turn a profit. But in fact a seemingly innocent change in the zoning code had sparked the fad. In the name of the Clean Air Act, the Environmental Protection Agency had pressured New York to do *something* about its air pollution problem. Environmentalists wanted the city to discourage traffic by putting tolls on the East River bridges or by banning cars from parts of lower Manhattan. Either course would have been politically costly, however, and the planning commission settled on an apparently painless gesture: it eliminated parking requirements for apartment buildings. Garages, however, had long served as a crucial check on developers. Architects had never been able to fit parking spaces into a twenty-foot-wide apartment building. Now they didn't need to, and sliver towers made their appearance. They provoked such widespread

---

* A guidebook was also published: Margot Gayle and Michele Cohen's The Art Commission and the Municipal Art Society Guide to Manhattan's Outdoor Sculpture (*New York: Prentice-Hall Press, 1988*).

disgust, especially on the politically powerful Upper East Side, that the city agreed something must be done, and MAS was instrumental in getting the subject on the planning commission's agenda.[7] The planning commission was ready to set a minimum forty-foot width for towers, but the civic groups pointed out that it's fairly easy to buy two adjacent brownstone lots. They insisted on a forty-five-foot minimum. Developers would then have to buy three lots, and that was a much more difficult proposition. The civic groups won their point and, as Wellington says, "the whole thing stopped."

The Koch administration showed its character more clearly, however, with the Midtown Zoning Resolution of 1982. Its origins dated back to 1978 and to a new organization of civic groups. In 1978, when MAS was looking for tenants for the Urban Center, it organized a group of like-minded organizations—"Not the Real Estate Board," as Wellington says, "but groups sensitive to the issues we were interested in: the Landmarks Conservancy, the Regional Plan Association, the AIA, and others. We realized we didn't know a lot about these groups, so we set up an informal breakfast club composed of the presidents and the executive directors of various groups. It was called the Presidents' Council, and like the Fine Arts Federation at the turn of the century it gave the advocacy groups a chance to coordinate policy." The subject of East Midtown soon came up. A crisis was in the making in that area: the city was letting too many buildings stretch the already generous zoning code. So far only a few buildings were in construction, "but people had seen plans," Wellington remembers, and the members of the Presidents' Council agreed to take a common step to relieve some of the pressure on the East Side.[8]

In 1979 the Presidents' Council sent a delegation to the planning commission and asked it to approve a study of Midtown zoning. It was supposed to be finished by April 1980, since speed was essential if the city was to head off the East Side mega-projects already in the works. The Kaplan Fund and the Rockefeller Brothers Funds would provide the money; the staff would be drawn from experts chosen by both the civic groups and the City Planning Commission. Robert Wagner, Jr., chairman of the planning commission, was open to the idea. Holly Whyte, Abraham Barkham (a realtor from James Felt & Co.), and the architectural firm of Davis, Brody & Associates were named to conduct the study. Wagner soon left the planning commission to become a deputy mayor, and his replacement was Herbert Sturz, from the Ford Foundation's Vera Institute of Justice. "What Sturz ... had in the way of planning background has never been clear," one critic writes,[9] and Margot Wellington and Fred Papert, so often at odds on planning issues, would soon share a deep dislike for the man. Sturz was an ardent devotee of the notion that the real estate industry offered the key to New York's prosperity, and he was convinced that the planning commission's function was to catalyze construction. The study was delayed, and what finally emerged from all the hearings and negotiations was the infamous Midtown Zoning Resolution of 1982. "We got it on the agenda," Wellington says of the Midtown Zoning Resolution, "and then it got out of our hands. The CPC co-opted the study and twisted it around."[10]

There were some good points embedded in the Midtown Zoning Study, most of them due to Holly Whyte. His job was to evaluate the public benefits of zoning bonuses. He pointed out that it was absurd to hand out bonuses for through-block passages: if a builder's site faced two streets, he'd be a fool not to connect them. Arcades had never worked out, Whyte noted, and atriums and galleries drained so much commercial activity from the streets that they shouldn't be encouraged. All these bonuses were eliminated outright (developers were simply required to build through-block passages) and the bonus for plazas was reduced by two-thirds. All new buildings would also have to have shops on the street (with transparent glass windows) in order to preserve "retail continuity."[11]

One might applaud the elimination of these bonuses, except for the twisting-around that Margot Wellington mentioned. The original point of the zoning study was to save East Midtown from overdevelopment, and the planning commission did cut density in a zone stretching from Third to Sixth avenues between Thirty-ninth and Fifty-ninth streets. At the same time, however, it decided to boost density between Sixth and Eighth avenues. The West Side's standard FAR climbed from 15 to 18, and the planning commission added a generous program of tax abatements for new West Side buildings started before May 1988.[12] There was an obvious fallacy in all this: if overdevelopment was bad for the East Side, it could hardly be good for the West Side. The City Planning Commission insisted, however, that extra bulk and tax incentives were needed to conquer developers' historic prejudice against building on the West Side, and so the mayor sent Herb Sturz to pressure MAS to approve the proposed changes. Wellington remembers Sturz's negotiating tactic: "No changes! It's gotta go through. We've gone too far now. It's better than nothing."[13] MAS caved in and endorsed the new Midtown Zoning Resolution.

Supposedly the Municipal Art Society was exchanging a reduction of density on the East Side for more density on the West Side. In fact, "everyone on the East Side got a chance to grandfather their plans," Wellington remembers. Three years had passed since MAS and its allies first pleaded for a Midtown zoning study. It was an emergency, they said then: act now or a wave of new construction will swamp the East Side. Three years, of course, was time enough for most developers to get their projects in the ground. Twelve new office buildings opened in 1981 and 1982; others were still rising into the sky, and when they were finished it was hard to find a good place to build on the East Side: the neighborhood was already saturated.[14]

The new zoning and tax incentives would lead to a massive wave of development on the West Side as well, and horrible situations were in the making. The Clinton area, with all its low-cost housing and its sizable elderly population, was suddenly placed in peril. Maps of the new Midtown Zoning District showed a little finger stretching north to Columbus Circle and roping in the Coliseum, the city's old and obsolete convention center. That site was so large and was now so liberally zoned that, as one city official crowed, it could support a 130-story tower. And in the heart of the Midtown zone sat Times Square.

TIMES SQUARE

BY THE 1980s Times Square had come to mean two very different things. Tourists thought of the Broadway theater, glitzy musicals, and nights on the town. New Yorkers and the patrons of the Port Authority Bus Terminal thought of Forty-second Street as a world of peep shows, prostitutes, drugs, and muggers.

When Times Square was in its heyday, before the Depression, MAS had never appreciated the place; it raised the hackles of people like Albert Bard. Times Square stood for popular culture, bright lights, billboards, and the messy vitality of commercial culture—for everything the Beaux Arts aesthetes deplored.[1] At the turn of the century, when the Municipal Art Society started campaigning against outdoor ads, it pictured Times Square as the deepest circle of billboard hell. The society published photos of local buildings that were entirely blanketed in signs; even their windows were not spared. With the help of Jacob Cantor, such extremes were soon outlawed, but Times Square's great glory was its kaleidoscope of electric signs, especially the flashing, "moving" sky signs, and these flourished despite the best efforts of the Municipal Art Society. MAS tried to ban all sky signs in 1902, and it succeeded, for a while, in limiting their size. It wasn't until the courts overturned that regulation in 1909 that Times Square truly blossomed. That same year, Heatherbloom Petticoats ("Silk's Only Rival") built a fifty-foot electric sign showing "a girl caught in a storm, with her skirts fluttering back and forth at the mercy of swirly rain and gusts of wind."[2] Those were the days when leering young men gathered at the base of the Flatiron Building hoping that an updraft would lift a woman's skirt and give them a glimpse of petticoat or leg; since the Heatherbloom Girl performed even when real skirts were becalmed, she caused something of a sensation. The lesson wasn't lost on advertisers: the Heatherbloom Girl sparked a boom in moving signs, and by 1912 Times Square had exploded in lights. One sign depicted a bareback rider; another, a chariot race. A winking girl sold chewing gum, a fountain spewed sparkling water, a thirty-foot kitten toyed with a spool of thread, and a pair of boxers sported "summer underwear."

Yet the seeds of Times Square's decay were already present. It wasn't just the movies and television that did in Broadway; Lee Simonson, the celebrated scenic designer who was active in MAS in the 1930s, placed the blame squarely on the theater owners. By his account, Times Square's decline was a function of steel and marketing. When MAS was founded, New York's theaters were much like the old Baroque auditoriums of Europe, with tier upon tier of shallow balconies ringing the auditorium. They had terrible sightlines, but the upper balconies were full of very cheap seats—cheap enough for the working class, for families with children, and for students. Those seats developed the theater's future audiences. In an odd way these auditoriums were more democratic than the Broadway theaters of today. Their tiers separated the audience into different classes, but on the other hand rich and poor still took their entertainment together, in the same room, if not on the same floor level. That was, in fact, part of the theater's attraction: the poor went to a play to ogle the rich, and the rich went to strut.

When steel came into use, the balconies didn't have to cling so close to the walls. Times Square's first theaters, built around 1900, had just two big balconies: the audience had better sightlines, but the cheapest seats were gone forever. By the 1920s theater owners had decided to concentrate on the high end of the market, and in Times Square's second generation of theaters there was just one enormous balcony. Now every seat was fairly expensive, and the Children of Paradise were driven away. One had to be prosperous to go to the theater regularly; and those who went occasionally, as to an event, demanded to see nothing but hits. When the Depression struck in 1929 there were already more theaters than hit plays to fill them, and Hollywood struck in that moment of weakness. What hurt wasn't just the popularity of the new talking movies but also the fact that the Hollywood studios bought up legitimate theaters around the country so they could monopolize film distribution: by shutting theaters in faraway places, they crippled Broadway's road shows, and producers were no longer able to recoup their investment by taking a show on tour.

Forty-second Street began its downward slide during the Depression as the street's theaters succumbed to burlesque. "Not for Your Aunt from Dubuque," boasted Minsky's ads; not for New Yorkers either, said La Guardia, who outlawed burlesque in 1940. "Without this cause célèbre," Morton Minsky insisted, "he would not have been reelected."[3] Thirteen theaters were padlocked, and "the culture of Forty-second Street," Brooks Atkinson wrote, "collapsed rapidly." Grind houses moved in, showing movies around the clock, and the street's "ranking cultural institution" was now Hubert's Museum, popularly known as the Flea Circus.[4] Times Square itself struggled on. Many of its theaters were dark, but "the theater" was still healthy—Broadway was still creative, and its musicals were still genuinely popular. Given the narrow audience of the Broadway theater, however, this couldn't last. Musicals became more and more the province of tourists and a rather small cult of admirers. The spoken theater moved Off Broadway and even Off-Off Broadway. In 1966, a new genre of theater arrived to fill the vacuum on Forty-second Street:

peep shows made their debut. The Supreme Court loosened the obscenity laws a year later, and the peep shows flourished.

The year 1966 also saw the mutilation of Times Square's great symbol: the very building that had given the square its name. The Times Tower was always an odd building, and compared to the Flatiron Building it was terribly clumsy, but its architect, Cyrus Eidlitz, had given it pleasant Italian Gothic facades, and the very awkwardness of the building's silhouette made it memorable. Since 1905, when election results were first beamed from the tower's roof, the building had been the backdrop of so many great crowd scenes that it was ingrained in the public's imagination as a key image of New York. But in 1965 the Allied Chemical Company bought the Times Tower, and a year later it stripped off the old facade and sheathed Eidlitz's steel skeleton in a stark new skin of white marble. The Landmarks Commission could have stopped this, but in those days the masterpiece theory of preservation still ruled, and the commission still shied away from designating commercial buildings.

By 1967 the Lindsay administration had finally recognized that Times Square was in trouble, and it invented a Special Theater District "to preserve, protect and promote the character" of the neighborhood. The intention was admirable, but the effect was perverse. Now a developer could win a zoning bonus by building two new theaters: one commercial and the other not-for-profit. The new bonus spawned the Minskoff and Uris theaters, both cavernous auditoriums cursed with terrible acoustics. (Their nonprofit siblings, the Circle in the Square and American Place theaters, were much more successful.) The Uris (now the Gershwin) was housed in an egregious black glass tower on an especially inhospitable plaza—although it's better now, having recently been renovated in accord with Holly Whyte's guidelines—while the Minskoff rose on the site of the splendid old Astor Hotel, whose ballrooms, bars, and restaurants were probably more important to the culture of Time Square than any single theater.

One obvious flaw in Lindsay's incentive program was pointed out in 1976 by the city planner Kenneth Halpern. "There are still no provisions . . . to save existing theaters, many of which are fine old buildings," he wrote in *Urban Design* magazine. "These theaters are an integral part of New York's cultural life and certainly an effort should be made to preserve them." Halpern's "extremely simple" solution was to give the same zoning bonus to developers who preserved and renovated old theaters.[5]

Halpern's recommendation was ignored; developers were more interested in another line of thought. As part of its 1969 master plan, the Regional Plan Association came up with a ludicrous, fantastic scheme for a Modernist city stretching from end to end of Forty-second Street.[6] None of it saw the light of day, but the scheme had an insidious effect. The RPA pictured Times Square as an underdeveloped and undervalued area; it argued that the city should think of the neighborhood as an extension of the Midtown business district—as Lebensraum for the white-collar world. Developers thought this a charming notion and began assembling parcels of Times Square real estate. They had no stake in the entertainment industry, and since their long-range goal was to redevelop the entire area, they didn't bother to maintain their recently acquired buildings in the short term.

Nor did they much care about the character of their tenants. In 1972, when Gail Sheehy rummaged through the city's real estate records, she found that the owners of pornographic theaters and hourly rate hotels included members of the Association for a Better New York, some Park Avenue banks, and even members of the mayor's Times Square Development Council. Edward R. Finch II rented quarters to some of the worst porn-stores in Times Square. Finch was the son of an appellate court judge, a well-known lawyer in his own right, and the uncle of President Nixon's son-in-law. From the late 1950s until 1966 he had served as counsel to the Municipal Art Society. Sol Goldman of Goldman-DiLorenzo, one of the largest property owners—and tax delinquents—in the city, rented space to more than a dozen peep shows, massage parlors, and houses of ill repute. Ian Woodman, a builder of "high social polish," owned the Raymona Hotel on Eighth Avenue where, by one account, "a thousand tricks a day were turned."[7]

"Our brightest memory was looking like a bomb," Fred Papert says of Times Square.[8] His response was to found the Forty-second Street Redevelopment Corporation. The city's response was the Marriott Marquis Hotel, the so-called Portman Hotel.

''THE PORTMAN HOTEL,'' says Margot Wellington, "is a very uncomfortable subject" for the Municipal Art Society.[9] The project dated back to the Lindsay years, and it was Lindsay's campaign manager, the developer and hotelier Peter Sharp, who first assembled the site on the west side of Broadway between Forty-fifth and Forty-sixth streets. In 1973 the mayor held a press conference to unveil plans for the "Times Square Hotel."[10] It was unusual for a privately financed scheme to receive such a spotlight, but the mayor explained that the hotel would serve the city's new convention center and spark a revitalization of Times Square. The design was by John Portman, an Atlanta-based architect and developer rolled into one. Portman was the apostle of the atrium: each of his projects boasted a soaring, yawning void lined by balconies and wanly animated by glass elevators. At the time, Portman's work was widely praised, and projects like the Peachtree Center in Atlanta and the Renaissance Center in Detroit were touted as tools to revitalize decaying cities. The City Planning Commission approved the hotel in less than a month—astonishing speed—but the economy was grim, construction of the convention center was delayed, and late in 1974 Portman pulled out of the project.

"I knew," says Wellington, "when Portman left, blustering that he'd be back, that it was important to him to crack the New York market." For the Koch administration, it was equally important to clean up Times Square. Aside from the commuters and tourists who passed through the area, aside from the jobs and tax dollars that would flow from new construction, the area had become a national embarrassment: a favorite scene for exposés on the prostitution racket. Something had to be done, and in 1978 New York decided to lure John Portman back to town. The city's barker was Kenneth Halpern, now director of the Office of Midtown Planning, and a great admirer of Portman's work. (Portman later hired him.) But the developer was playing hard to get. The economy was still sour, the site of the convention center had been shifted farther south, and since Portman had let his options on the land lapse, regaining control of the site would be expensive, perhaps impossible. To win him over, the city and state put together a package of incentives. They waived the sales tax on construction materials, arranged for the federal government to kick in a grant worth $21.5 million, and agreed that the Urban Development Corporation would use its power of condemnation to take the site. The hotel wouldn't have to pay rent to the UDC for seven years; afterward, it would pay rent out of its profits, if there were any. In all, taxpayers would end up subsidizing the hotel to the tune of $100 million. Portman could hardly refuse such an offer. He pulled the old blueprints out of his files, and since Halpern had seen another opportunity, he reworked them. The city's Urban Design Group had long wanted to "rationalize" Broadway's traffic by creating a pedestrian mall in Times Square, so Portman was offered one last bonus: a little bit of Broadway. The hotel would include a low wing sitting on the new mall itself, interrupting the longest continuous street in the country. "He offered *city* land to the hotel," Wellington says of Halpern, her voice still quavering with rage after all these years, "offered to close the street, and if it was a mistake there was no way to undo it."[11]

Things had changed since Portman's first appearance in New York, however. People had begun to look more closely at his hotels. Once praised for revitalizing cities, they'd come to seem more like alien colonies. Since everything was oriented inward toward the atrium, rather than outward toward the streets, Portman's projects actually drained the life out of their neighborhoods. For another thing, the preservation movement had sunk deeper roots into this city since 1973. "People are still hung up on the goddamn corny image of what's there in Times Square," Portman once complained. "There's not one great thing about it."[12] But preservationists pointed out that two great theaters, the Helen Hayes and the Morosco, stood on Portman's site. The first was designed by Herts & Tallant, the leading theater architects of belle epoque New York, authors of the Brooklyn Academy of Music, the gorgeous Lyceum on Forty-fifth Street, the New Amsterdam on Forty-second, and the Booth and Shubert theaters on Shubert Alley. The Helen Hayes, with its splendid terra-cotta facade, was one of their most spectacular designs. The Morosco was designed by Herbert J. Krapp, an architect of much more modest talents, but actors and directors insisted that this theater was the true treasure. With its intimate scale and perfect acoustics, the Morosco was an ideal setting for spoken drama, and it had seen the premieres of seventeen Pulitzer Prize–winning plays.[13]

The Landmarks Commission knew that the Helen Hayes was worthy of protection—an internal document called it "one of the finest theaters" in New York—but it refused to hold a public hearing on the issue or even to evaluate the Morosco. The city promised that, in recompense for the two theaters' destruction, it would renovate nine small theaters on Forty-second Street. The arrangements were very vague, however, and the scheme seemed pointless when the city could simply move the site of the Portman Hotel; now that the Urban Development Corporation was involved, it could condemn another site as easily as this one. Activists suggested that Portman build a few blocks to the north, on Broadway between Forty-eighth and Forty-ninth streets, but he refused. Nor would he consider the slightly smaller site of the Bond Building, on the opposite side of Times Square. The city could have easily pressured Portman to reconsider, but Mayor Koch was determined to push the hotel through. "He was never approachable with the idea that . . . you could reshape a project," Wellington complains. "There was never any pursuit of a compromise. [Projects] were always pushed through as formulated by a developer with one motive: profit."[14]

In desperation, activists tried to work out one more compromise with Portman. For the sake of his zoning bonus, Portman was planning to build a new theater into the base of his hotel, and massive trusses, spanning 120 feet, would support the tower above. The architect Lee Harris Pomeroy suggested that Portman build over the old theaters instead. MAS had learned all about transfer trusses two years before, when Rockefeller Center threatened to build an office building on the site of Radio City Music Hall. Municipalian Lewis Davis had sketched an alternative: a tower perched on four massive legs that straddled the auditorium, leaving that great interior landmark intact.* Pomeroy was proposing a similar solution for the Helen Hayes and Morosco theaters. The scheme was feasible, Portman admitted, but he insisted that redesigning the hotel would take eighteen months and that his financing would crumble in the face of such a delay.

Joan Davidson saw the Portman Hotel as a threat to more than just two theaters: she understood that it was meant to spark a massive reconstruction of Times Square. Wellington arranged for her to meet Richard Kahan of the UDC, and Davidson pleaded with him to "rethink the whole thing." Kahan would go on to shape the master plan for Battery Park City, to join MAS's board of directors and to lead its negotiations over Riverside South, but back then he was "young and cocky and arrogant and powerful"—and he was "furious" at her suggestion, Wellington remembers. "I *like* Richard, but this was not one of his best moments."[15]

Davidson kept trying. She didn't sit on MAS's board at the time, but she came to a meeting and pleaded with the society to take a stand. She and Wellington pinned their hopes on Brendan Gill, "a real friend of many art forms," as Wellington says, but he disappointed them both. "If he had taken on the leadership, joined with Joe Papp, the society would have really moved. Papert, however, was calling the shots." Papert's was a simple argument: "If the city can't keep its word,

---

* "For some reason," says Margot Wellington, her nose wrinkling with distaste, MAS's campaign to save the Music Hall "concentrated on the Rockettes." Actually, the dancers' peril provided the story with enough bathos and glitz to make the eleven o'clock news. As MAS investigated the project it realized that Rockefeller Center's internal accounting methods exaggerated the cost of running the Music Hall. Moreover the staff kept booking terrible films. Rockefeller Center changed its policy, brought in new management, and restored the Music Hall. It's been a success ever since.

how can you do business?"[16] The mere utterance of that line is almost always conclusive evidence that something truly terrible is in the offing. It worked its fell magic on MAS, however, and at Papert's "insistence," the society refused to help. "Joan Davidson was devastated," Carole Rifkind remembers. Ralph Menapace, then president of the board, was "deeply upset," and he went on to testify personally on behalf of the theaters. Tim Prentice was "ashamed" of MAS, and Margot Wellington wept.[17]

Joan Davidson describes the Portman Hotel as the Municipal Art Society's "one major lapse. There was a moment when, had all the major forces joined, I think then we could have forestalled everything that has come in [the hotel's] wake. Nobody got the point except a few theater people." Actors Equity and Joe Papp understood the threat perfectly, she says. Tim Prentice was "definitely on the barricades," and the Kaplan Fund, which Davidson heads, "gave a lot of money." But the *Times* didn't help; Ada Louise Huxtable was "late," and MAS was concerned "not to unduly antagonize the big players. We felt terribly abandoned."[18]

FRED PAPERT had his reasons for not wanting to annoy the city or the Urban Development Corporation. In 1976, he recruited Lewis Davis, Donald Elliott, and "other Lindsay holdovers," as Kent Barwick puts it, and founded the Forty-second Street Redevelopment Corporation. Its mission was "to rescue West Forty-second Street from four decades of misuse and neglect . . . to reverse Forty-second Street's fall from grace . . . creating in time a river-to-river grand boulevard that would become a magnet for private investment, visitors, jobs and tax revenues, and have a major impact on the economy of New York City and the tristate region."[19] Papert describes MAS as "the parent of this organization," though this particular child was largely raised by other hands, and Papert's initial money came from the Ford Foundation. He started out with $150,000 and a board of directors that included Father Rappleyea, the pastor of Holy Cross Church, from which Father Duffy once battled the gangs of Hell's Kitchen; Gerald Schoenfeld, the chairman of the Shubert Organization; and Jacqueline Kennedy Onassis.

Papert started by taking over the Crossroads Building at Broadway and Forty-second Street. In the words of journalist Josh Alan Friedman, "A sawdust peep scumatorium, where kiddie porn had been available, was evicted and replaced by a police substation." Papert hired Richard Haas to paint a mural atop the building, and Haas responded by re-creating, in trompe l'oeil, the old Italian Gothic facade of the Times Tower. Papert and his allies ran the building at a great loss, but "the cops and the painting, both temporary, were 'symbolic,' they said, of things to come."[20]

Papert's new job provided him with an interesting education not just in the complexities of real estate but in human nature as well. He was soon warning his friend Brendan Gill never to trust developers because "They're all pirates and savages."[21] Papert's conversation on this subject can turn into a litany of betrayals. "We had an option to buy a parking lot for a million dollars," but it slipped out of his hands, the Milsteins bought it for $5 million, and Papert watched it climb in value. "It's now worth thirty," he said in 1992. Then there was the case of Harry Macklowe. When Doris Freedman was MAS's president, she thought the society should have a developer on its board, and she recruited Macklowe. ("Macklowe was family to Doris," one Municipalian remembers; he had a collection of "important" modern paintings.) Papert says he seemed like an "enlightened, civilized fellow," and he was the "best board member you can imagine." He played a crucial role in creating the Urban Center, since no one else at MAS knew how to negotiate leases with Harry Helmsley or with the society's commercial tenants, and in 1980 he tried his best to convince the real estate community to support the designation of the Upper East Side Historic District. (He failed in that task as developers had their hearts set on rebuilding Madison Avenue.[22]) Only when Macklowe left MAS's board did Papert learn that "Real property brings out the worst in everyone." The Forty-second Street Redevelopment Corporation was interested in an empty lot on Eleventh Avenue. "We had an option about to expire," and an arrangement with a developer who was going to build apartments on the corner, bringing a permanent, twenty-four-hour-a-day population to the neighborhood. At the same time Philip Morris was going to build a theater next door, a Hugh Hardy design based on an unbuilt project by Joseph Urban. The theater's air rights would be sold to the apartment project, and the Forty-second Street Redevelopment Corporation would end up with a 25 percent interest in the tower. But at the last moment the developer backed away from the project. Macklowe offered to pick up the pieces of the deal, "but he wanted the twenty-five percent equity interest back, and immediately began to screw us."* There was a lawsuit, which Papert won, "but by then our financing had disappeared."[23]

Despite all this, Papert made enormous progress. Apartments were built on that Eleventh Avenue corner—though not by Papert, and without a theater. By 1978, Papert had transformed the seedy buildings that lay between Ninth and Dyer avenues. The block was home to the French Palace, the Mermaid Bar, the Studio $10 ("Complete Satisfaction Featuring the Most Beautiful Conversationalists"), plus one anachronistic institution: Playwrights Horizon. The theater group had lost its old quarters in 1974 and had settled among the peep shows in sheer desperation.[24] Papert took its presence as a cue, and turned the peep shows and massage parlors into Theater Row, a collection of not-for-profit theaters and restaurants. (Across the street sits Manhattan Plaza, public housing for the arts community.) Dyer Avenue, the approach to the Lincoln Tunnel, became a great outdoor canvas for the muralist Richard Haas. The avenue had been brutally sliced through the blocks, leaving blank, scarred walls on either side, but Haas gave them some trompe l'oeil pomp, painting stone walls and Art Deco pylons—municipal art in two dimensions. Farther west, the McGraw-Hill Building, Raymond Hood's blue-green

---

* Macklowe would soon become notorious for his involvement in the illegal demolition of a pair of single room occupancy hotels on West Forty-fifth Street.

Art Deco tower, had been empty for years. Papert's group restored it—without, alas, the original gold and green window shades, an integral part of Hood's color scheme.

After his success with Theater Row, Papert turned his eye toward the most critical block in the area, the stretch of Forty-second Street between Seventh and Eighth avenues. At one end lay Times Square; at the other, the Port Authority Bus Terminal. Thousands walked that block every working day, pushing past drug dealers, porn theaters, peep shows, and sex-toy shops. Most commuters were too stunned by the onslaught to notice that the street was also peppered with first-run movie theaters. That one block of Forty-second Street shaped an image of the entire city as an ugly, dangerous, and sleazy place.

In 1978 Papert produced a plan to revitalize the block. It meant taking over the seedy buildings, throwing out the porn shops, and bringing in new tenants— restaurants, movie theaters, shops, perhaps an Imax screen—that would keep the street lively twenty-four hours a day. The old buildings would be spruced up. Some facades would be restored, and others would be turned into giant billboards. The idea was to improve the neighborhood incrementally, and Papert was determined to start with the block's cornerstone, the New Amsterdam Theater. The Ford Foundation offered to lease the theater for five years as a home for modern drama companies, but the owner wouldn't lease the building. He was willing to sell it, but the price was a problem: the city said $1 million was fair, but the owner wanted $8 million.[25]

This stumbling block changed Papert's thinking. To justify a higher level of city investment, he came up with a plan to revamp the whole block in one stroke. The idea of incremental improvements gave way to "The City at Forty-second Street," a scheme for an urban theme park that Papert now describes, a little wryly, as "high-class Disney." It would feature a museum, a fashion center, a hotel, and an amusement ride that "simulated movement through layers of New York, from the subway to the tip of a skyscraper."[26] When Ed Koch saw the model at the Ford Foundation he was rightly horrified. "New York isn't orange juice," he insisted. "It's seltzer." (*Seltzer?*) Papert was struggling with another problem as well: no one would lend money to the project on the basis of prospective ticket sales—at least not enough to finance the debt for renovating the theaters and the subway station. So Papert shifted tactics again. Now the idea was to move the block's development rights to the corners, where developers would build new offices and a merchandise market, and these would pay to fix up the theaters.

Koch approved of this scheme in principle, but he decided that the city should have more direct control over the project. In 1980 the mayor and Governor Cuomo agreed that the planning commission and the Urban Development Corporation would take over the project, develop a new program, and recruit developers.[27] Once it was placed in the UDC's hands, the project ballooned. Now four office towers were planned for the southern end of Times Square. A hotel would sit on the northeast corner of Forty-second Street and Eighth Avenue. A vast two-block-long merchandise mart would tower over Eighth Avenue and bridge Forty-first Street. The Times Square subway station would be rebuilt, and nine theaters would be restored on Forty-second Street.

This scheme had its virtues. Richard Kahan, who was still the head of the UDC, brought in the planning firm of Cooper-Ekstut to prepare a set of design guidelines. This was the same cast of characters that had been responsible for the superb master plan of Battery Park City, and as Kent Barwick understood it, the guidelines were meant as "mitigation for the loss of the Helen Hayes and the Morosco," and for the brutal scale of the Portman Hotel.[28] The new buildings were to be carefully sculpted with setbacks to give them a human scale and, at the same time, a dramatic profile; they would have glass street walls and neon signs in deference to the neighborhood's character. The guidelines were "not discretionary," according to the UDC.[29]

The state, however, chose George Klein of Park Tower Realty to be the principal developer. Klein had a reputation for putting up good buildings by distinguished architects; unfortunately, as Halina Rosenthal once complained, he likes to build them in the wrong places.[30] His scheme for a mid block tower on East Sixty-second Street helped spur preservationists to create the Upper East Side Historic District,[31] and a later project for a condominium tower atop the Metropolitan Club came to grief before the Landmarks Commission. Klein's marketing strategy was to lure large law firms to Times Square, and his research told him that such tenants liked big, open floors. Setbacks interfered with big floors, and the Cooper-Ekstut guidelines called for many setbacks. Klein's solution was to ignore the guidelines and to provide himself with a fig leaf by recruiting the architect Philip Johnson.

Johnson has had a long, distinguished, and controversial career. He's "the prince of foxes," Brendan Gill once said, "always ahead of the pack."[32] At the time, Johnson had recently reinvented himself as a Post-Modernist, and his design for the AT&T headquarters had landed him on the cover of *Time* magazine. MAS had just organized a retrospective of Johnson's work—the leftover photographs still decorate its offices—and it had just thrown him a party for its annual benefit, a $1,000-a-plate dinner at the Four Seasons.[33] (Johnson was honored not just for his buildings, but also for his interest in preservation: for picketing the demolition of Pennsylvania Station, and for speaking out for Grand Central Terminal and Saint Bartholomew's Church.[34]) That benefit had been splattered all over the society pages thanks, in part, to the fact that Mrs. Onassis arrived on Johnson's arm. Aside from his fame, Johnson brought two other valuable credentials to Klein's project. More candid than most architects, he has famously described himself as a "whore," and he was apparently perfectly willing to do Klein's bidding and discard the Cooper-Ekstut guidelines. He's also, as Margot Wellington marvels, "so good at convincing people." (It's clear she means "manipulating" them.) "He's charming at it and he doesn't get you nearly as angry at him as you'd think."[35]

Yet no amount of "convincing" could obscure the fact that Johnson's design was appalling, or that very little "design" was actually involved. His towers were bulky boxes in a tinselly gift wrap of stone and reflective glass. Aside from their mansard roofs, the towers seemed to have been shaped purely by Klein's desire for big floors. Not one was handsome in and of itself, and having four of them, each a different size, certainly didn't help. To make matters worse, Johnson and Klein soon decided that the old Times Tower should be demolished. They wanted to replace it with a plaza or a monument, something to lend their cluster of towers a focus, and they spoke dreamily of their project as another Rockefeller Center.

In the *Times*, Paul Goldberger gingerly admitted that Johnson's towers had been greeted with "a mixed response," but in fact it was hard to find anyone who actually admired them.[36] Their defenders spoke in terms of the project's dubious economic benefits and of the need to do something to clean up Forty-second Street. The *Times* hauled out its biggest editorial guns: "Get Out of the Way of Times Square," one editorial thundered. "Born Again or Porn Again" was the headline on another. Johnson, as always, proved deft at deflecting criticism. "Joan Davidson tried to take him on," one Municipalian remembers. She complained that his facades were sterile, that there was too little going on at street level, that they were out of place in the dynamic, vulgar, populist ethos of Times Square. "He twisted what she said and offered her a clock," Wellington says, "which isn't what she'd asked for at all."[37] The City Planning Commission elicited just a few trivial concessions: the towers were pushed back five feet and their bases became faintly livelier. But the buildings remained deadly dull, and in a way Johnson had inadvertently performed a public service. The miserable quality of his design awakened people to the project's deeper flaw: New York City was about to sacrifice its precious entertainment district and replace it with a dreary new world of office buildings.

BY 1984 it was clear to MAS that 1978's decent, modest project to reinvigorate Forty-second Street had turned into a scheme to rebuild Times Square. "Rehabilitation" had turned into "urban renewal of the worst sort."[38] Yet at MAS, Kent Barwick recalls, "The stage was not set for adversarial relations." Barwick had just returned to MAS from the Landmarks Commission, having left the Koch administration "in good order, with a big party at Gracie Mansion." For a brief time he was serving as both landmarks commissioner and president of the Municipal Art Society, and it was even suggested that there was no inherent conflict.

There was much angry talk at MAS about Klein's decision to scrap the Cooper-Ekstut guidelines. Theoretically, Klein's proposal should have been ruled *hors concours* by the UDC, yet both the city and the state had happily accepted the plan. Some members of MAS's board thought there were grounds for a fight in this, but Barwick is "very astute politically," says Papert. "He has a good sense of what will or won't wash." Barwick didn't want to wage a battle over the aesthetics of setbacks. "It wasn't a broad public issue that we could get people excited about," he says, especially "in the unusual situation we found ourselves in." The *Times*, the mayor, and the governor—"the Holy Trinity"—were all committed to the plan, and it was "clear we weren't going to carry the Board of Estimate."[39]

"No one wanted to oppose Fred Papert and their good friend Philip Johnson," says Wellington. "We're wimps," Carole Rifkind would later complain. (Rifkind, a preservationist, sat on MAS's board in 1984.) "It was never something that was thrashed out. Our Forty-second Street policy was formed in 1977 or 1978, and it's never since made it back to our attention. At one meeting, Richard Kahan suggested we sue the hell out of them, but it was finessed. There was no vote taken, and the board didn't have the depth of knowledge to understand how the project has departed from its original intentions." Other board members are far harsher. Tim Prentice insists that the board understood the issues full well, and he bitterly regrets the fact that Papert, his close friend, talked him out of insisting that MAS take a stand. For there was a point when it seemed that a consensus had been reached and that MAS would launch a campaign against the project. That moment passed. Papert, says Wellington, "is a genius at doing something I've tried to learn: making a meeting come out the way you want it. He can reopen a subject and so phrase the issue that people end up retracting their own statements." Privately Papert would speak bitterly of the UDC project—what started out as "blight removal" had become "urban development"; what had once been welcomed was now "perceived" to be "a puffy real estate deal." But at that board meeting, Papert insisted that the project had ultimately sprung from the Municipal Art Society and that if MAS moved against the scheme its word would be worthless. His colleagues backed down. "Kent kept them in line," says Papert, while Barwick explains that Papert "kept reminding us this was our project."[40]

There was one more factor in MAS's timidity. Answering the storm of criticism that greeted the UDC's scheme, Herb Sturz, the planning commissioner, had promised to reopen the issue of planning in Times Square as a whole. In November 1984 he set up the Times Square Advisory Committee, better known as the Bow-Tie Committee, in reference to the square's actual shape. Fred Papert, Kent Barwick, and Paul Byard were members, but it got off to "a very slow start, and not an auspicious one." There was talk of condemning the Times Tower and reconstructing it "in some form," but the larger issue of Times Square's zoning was ignored. Barwick complained of "a three-card monte atmosphere—the spirit of our agreement was not met. We relied on Sturz's assurances that there would be some amelioration," he remembers. "We accepted that something would be done. I had no reason to distrust the administration I had just left." But gradually he decided that Sturz had "no intent to deliver at all." "A moving target is the most difficult to deal with," Papert says, adding that Sturz "sets up all these committees and it's only months later that you find out what he's doing."[41]

MAS decided to prepare its own zoning scheme and to "become an aggressive proponent of a master plan for Times Square."[42] If it couldn't stop the towers on Forty-second Street, it could at least make sure that they didn't become a model for the entire district's reconstruction. This was "very difficult," Wellington says, "because MAS had supported the Midtown Zoning Resolution. The problem was in part our own doing." Back in 1982 MAS hadn't realized that the resolution's

West Side zoning incentives would lead to the wholesale reconstruction of Times Square, or that blockbusters would become the standard. By the mid 1980s the measure's full effects were too obvious to ignore. As Paul Goldberger wrote, "The fallacy was in [the city's] belief that any such incentive was needed at all. Had the city merely reduced zoning on the East Side . . . development would have moved westward anyway. To have added this huge incentive seems, in retrospect, to have simply been a gift. Because it is now possible to build unusually high skyscrapers in the Times Square area, land values have gotten even bigger than they might otherwise have been and a . . . cycle of speculation has been set up—making the construction of more and bigger towers seem almost inevitable."[43] The results were already evident on West Fifty-second Street, which had been transformed by skyscrapers from Fifth to Seventh avenues. "Once," wrote Maureen Dowd, the street was "wild and low, a night street with a row of Victorian brownstones that, two steps down, offered jazz and comedy and strip joints. It was called 'swing street' and 'the street that never sleeps.' "[44] Now the nightclubs were gone, and names like Leon & Eddie's had given way to others like Equitable and E. F. Hutton. It was a cityscape that "real estate developers celebrate," Goldberger wrote, "a part of town with nothing but skyscrapers . . . set cheek by jowl from one block to the next," and into this canyon "the sun seldom penetrates."[45] Now developers were ready to push development just a little farther west, into the very heart of the theater district.

Architect Hugh Hardy had joined the Municipal Art Society during the Grand Central battle and found he liked the organization: "It gets reinvented all the time by different people," he says. Now it was Hardy's turn to reinvent the society: "I'm the one who promoted the idea that you couldn't *have* New York without Times Square." Hardy and the landscape architect Nicholas Quennell became cochairmen of a new Entertainment District Committee at MAS. As the committee pored over Times Square's real estate records it discovered some twenty-five "soft sites"—large parcels of land that were clearly awaiting redevelopment. Their development would permanently alter the scale of the district, and since the zoning code permitted office buildings on all these sites, even the use of Times Square was in danger. As Philip Howard put it, "The future may be preserved theaters with nothing around them to support them in a cultural sense, and our theater district could become a kind of Houston."[46]

As MAS took a closer look, it discovered that Times Square was a far more complex and vital neighborhood than Municipalians—or the city—had ever realized. The Landmarks Commission was taking halting steps toward designating some of the old Broadway theaters, but the theaters themselves were only the most visible facet of the entertainment industry. As Margot Wellington put it, "All the little specialized businesses that make up this vast machine, the people who supply amplifiers, gels, props, sets, costumes, lights, the places where someone can get a fitting—that's what the real industry is." Those businesses were crowded into the shabby, low-rent offices of Times Square. Few could afford the high rents of new buildings, nor could they survive if forced to relocate far from the theater district.

For that matter, MAS realized that there was more to Times Square than just the Broadway theater industry. Kent Barwick remembers touring the bars of Eighth Avenue. They were thriving places full of middle-class black patrons. Barwick had never known that this scene existed. Had the crowd been white, he realized, he would have heard about it—if not from friends, then from the media.[47] So MAS looked further. It found that "many of Times Square's businesses are family-owned and have been around almost as long as the theaters," as Tony Hiss wrote in *The New Yorker*. "Most still cater to a middle-class and family crowd, and an increasing number of these middle-class customers are black families, Hispanic families, and Asian families." MAS cast an eye on the neighborhood's first-run movie theaters and found that they sold more tickets than all the movie theaters in the rest of the city combined. And they played an important role in New York: the movie chains had long since pulled out of the city's poor neighborhoods, and Times Square had become a regional entertainment district, drawing audiences from all the boroughs. Times Square was on its way, wrote Hiss, "to becoming the first fully integrated American entertainment center."[48]

All of this was in danger now, but the city was barely aware of what it was about to destroy. MAS began asking if the city's plans weren't "inadvertently racist."[49] It was as if City Hall and the media—and, up to now, MAS—shared a crude vision of Times Square in which the place was home to just two industries, Broadway and sleaze, and two audiences. One audience was conspicuous enough: the white middle-class crowd pouring out of the Winter Garden at 10:30 P.M. But the people of color who lined up to see Steven Spielberg movies were left out of the city's equation. They were assumed to belong to that other, illicit Times Square.

MAS began pointing out that Times Square wasn't as terrible a place as New Yorkers assumed. "It wasn't a one-dimensional issue," says Barwick. Tourists understood the point: MAS discovered that when Europeans were asked where they'd like to stay in New York, they answered "Times Square" more often than any other choice. They were looking for a splash of neon, a little chaos, a bit of tawdriness—all the things they associated with America. But New Yorkers were astonished when MAS said there were good things about the place. "People wondered what we were doing," Barwick says. " 'The buildings are junk,' they'd say. 'Do you want to preserve pornography? White slavery?' " "It was a shocking idea to people," Philip Howard remembers. "Until we took up the cudgel, the idea that Times Square's lights, glitter, and tawdriness needed to be preserved was simply not the public attitude. A variety of public relation things, stunts organized by MAS, changed public consciousness."[50]

Electric signs were something the public could immediately understand. "Lights are superficial," Barwick admits, "and we've been criticized for troubling over details, but we found a way of shorthanding the issue." In November 1984 MAS and eleven other civic groups organized a half-hour blackout of Times Square's electric signs, a chilling preview of what awaited the square if the city didn't reform its zoning code. Only one sign stayed lit—the "Spectacolor" on the Times Tower flashed a message to Ed Koch: "Hey, Mr. Mayor! It's dark out here. Help keep the bright lights in Times Square."[51]

MAS decided to sponsor a competition for the Times Tower site in cooperation with the National Endowment for the Arts to focus attention on "the future of this volatile project." Contestants were free to choose whether the Philip Johnson project would ever be built. Entries poured in from around the country, and Hugh Hardy rejoiced in the evidence that Times Square was "*not* a universal symbol of crime and destitution. It's about all the wonderful motherhood issues of enjoying yourself." The jury was "very distinguished," Barwick remembers, but "hopelessly divided. Committed Modernists couldn't countenance a historic preservation solution." At least one board member objected to the whole idea of the competition: "It blew my mind. How could we take a neutral position—a blind taste test?" But Barwick doesn't regret the exercise. "It worked because it was a prolonged public relations device. It got people talking and asking questions."[52]

MAS eventually developed a two-pronged approach to Times Square. First it wanted the old theaters landmarked—less for aesthetic reasons than for their cultural significance. Designating the interiors was very controversial, however. Broadway musicals compensated for their insipid music with lavish spectacle, and this tendency reached an extreme with the fad for "environmental" stage sets that wrapped around an audience. It was an old technique, first seen in New York in 1924 when Norman Bel Geddes and Max Reinhardt transformed the stage and auditorium of the now vanished Century Theater into a Gothic cathedral. Bel Geddes restored the theater afterward, but Broadway's theater owners wanted to save that expense. Preservationists didn't see why irreplaceable architecture should be sacrificed so casually; they didn't think it wise to ruin a theater forever for a show like *Starlight Express.* They pointed to the auditorium of the ANTA Theater, once the charming home of the Theater Guild, whose stucco walls and beamed ceiling had all been stripped away; that house was now as dreary as a high school gymnasium. Without the protection of a landmark designation, every Times Square theater might eventually succumb to the same fate.

Landmarking the theaters would, however, have a perverse side effect. Their air rights could be transferred to neighboring sites, and all this extra volume would be piled atop the already huge zoning envelopes. So the new landmarks made it even more difficult for MAS to achieve its goal: to preserve the neighborhood's character from the impending development.

"There is a movement afoot to readdress zoning in New York," says Hugh Hardy. "The values of the 1916 Zoning Code have reemerged." Modern zoning was all about the square footage of buildings, but by now Hardy and others had realized the virtues of the old approach. The early setback legislation let the city control the shape and scale of towers. As far as Hardy was concerned, the issue wasn't Times Square's "bowl of sunlight," as Tony Hiss described it. Instead Hardy was simply trying to ensure that the inevitable office towers didn't overwhelm the billboards and electronic signs. He wanted mid-rise buildings of fifteen or twenty stories on Broadway and Seventh Avenue. The FAR would be six or seven, and the buildings would have a distinctive massing: a four- or five-story base with signs atop a broad setback, and then towers on top.[53]

To dramatize his case, Hardy called on San Francisco's Environmental Simulation Laboratory—Sim Lab, for short. This lab had been set up with a grant from the National Science Foundation to answer an age-old problem of city planners: they relied on models, but models are always disarming. People like miniatures and are easily seduced by a model maker's craftsmanship. Then, too late, they're often horrified by the built project. Even architects are often deceived by models—but of course, they often use them to manipulate clients and planners. Architects tend to build rather abstract models, with the existing neighborhood depicted as a collection of stark cardboard boxes with no detail, while their own building appears in full flower, as if singled out in glowing spotlights. Sim Lab went two steps further in realism. First, it laminated all those cardboard neighbors with color photos of the actual buildings. Then it mounted a movie camera, fitted with a periscope, on a little computer-driven crane. The camera could glide through the model and record its experience from any viewpoint or speed, whether that of a pedestrian strolling along the sidewalk or of a motorist bowling down the street. These movies gave a wonderfully accurate impression of what a project would really look like—before it was built.

For the Times Square Project, Sim Lab built an elaborate model of the neighborhood some fifteen feet long. All the buildings could be removed, new designs could be slipped into place, and the model could assume three different permutations. The first showed Times Square as it was in 1985, in all its messiness. The second depicted what would happen if the neighborhood were fully redeveloped under the existing zoning code: huge towers rose straight up from the sidewalks; billboards and lights gave way to the sterile curtain walls of a corporate cityscape. The third stage was Hugh Hardy's "ideal world" of setback towers and flashing neon signs. Sim Lab also made a twelve-minute movie, narrated by Jason Robards, that captured each version of Times Square from a pedestrian's viewpoint. Hardy's vision of the square allowed for substantial growth, as the city demanded, but it also preserved the human scale of the neighborhood and its character as the city's glittering nightspot. Even MAS's board of directors was surprised by the film. Elliot Willensky, whose office enjoyed a panoramic view of Times Square, commented that it was "tempting to say it is too late to save the district, but the film demonstrates how much can still be saved."[54]

MAS hauled Sim Lab's model down to City Hall for one of the City Planning Commission's hearings, and Barwick persuaded the cast of the musical *Big River* to make an appearance: their job was to rearrange the model from its "present" to its "possible" and its "ideal" permutations. Barwick forgot to warn Herb Sturz that he'd planned such an entertainment, however, and "when Sturz arrived, he was *furious.* The nerve of us to set this up in his hearing room!"[55] Yet the planning commission was clearly fascinated. The model and film created a far more vivid impression of the neighborhood and its possible fates than any dry assortment of zoning diagrams. The commissioners began referring to Times Square as an "entertainment district," and that in itself was a modest triumph: they were finally acknowledging that the neighborhood played a unique role in New York.[56]

To keep Times Square in the news, MAS organized an inauguration for the new Canon sign, and shortly afterward, MAS won the support of Community Board Five, which voted to support downzoning.

In January 1986 the planning commission proposed a set of policy changes for Times Square, and MAS noted that "Much of their language and many of their proposals are identical or similar to the goals of our own committee." The new guidelines would require setbacks and electric signs, as MAS had proposed. (For maximum visibility, MAS wanted the signs set at an angle to the street line, but the planning commission wouldn't countenance anything so messy.) And MAS was cheered when, shortly afterward, the Board of Estimate approved the landmark designations of the Broadway theaters, including their auditoriums. These interior designations were "precedent setting," a "major victory for preservationists."* But in the spring of 1986, while the City Planning Commission was still mulling over the zoning guidelines, Barwick announced that "our worst fears have been realized": the most sensitive sites in Times Square had been sold and were soon to be developed. Six projects, MAS learned, were in the final stages of planning, and some demolition had already begun. At least one developer meant to pacify MAS by hanging signs on his new facades, but the Bow-Tie Committee warned that "the overall bulk and configuration of his building will be a disaster for Times Square, the beginning of the Sixth Avenue Canyon we all fear." "The situation is drastic," Philip Howard declared. "The developers are forging ahead and unless pressure is brought to bear immediately, all will be lost."[57]

MAS demanded that the planning commission impose a moratorium on construction in Times Square until it formally adopted the new zoning guidelines. The threat of a moratorium was enough to convince some developers that they had better redesign their projects. In the meantime the planning commission began its public hearings, and Paul Byard noted that MAS's cause was helped by the "righteousness" of the opposition. Morgan Stanley was threatening to leave New York if it had to put signs on its tower. Developers decried the vulgarity of neon and billboards and insisted that the answer was "tasteful building lighting" instead of commercial signage.[58]

On January 22, 1987, the Board of Estimate met to vote on the Times Square guidelines. MAS held a press conference in the rotunda of City Hall beforehand, and that stately chamber echoed with the sound of a tinkling piano as celebrities

---

* The theaters' owners challenged the designations in court, arguing that the theater industry as a whole had, in effect, been singled out for an unprecedented degree of burdensome regulation. The designations were upheld in 1992, however.

sang of the delights of Broadway. There was excellent coverage, not only in the *Times* but in *The New Yorker*'s "Talk of the Town." Two weeks later, the Board of Estimate gave its approval to the guidelines.[59]

So what did MAS achieve? In the next two or three years the guidelines certainly produced some strange buildings. One of the first was the clumsily named Holiday Inn Crowne Plaza Manhattan Hotel, designed by Alan Lapidus (son of Morris, the architect of Miami's Fountainbleau Hotel). It was a jukebox of pink brick and purple glass, and its base was decorated with a flashy, pulsing grid of twinkling light bulbs. Lapidus's design would have been more at home in Las Vegas or Atlantic City, but it's "much better than it would be without the light bulbs," Hardy offers. At 1585 Broadway, architect Charles Gwathmey went to the other extreme: his tower was "shockingly pristine," Carole Rifkind says.[60] The developer seemed embarrassed by Times Square, and his brochure advertised a "local ambience" set by a wide range of attractions: "from the Whitney Museum and Museum of Modern Art to Carnegie Hall and Radio City Music Hall"—all of which were rather distant from 1585 Broadway.[61] The builder's fastidiousness was evident in Gwathmey's design as well: he arranged to put the required signage behind glass, making it invisible during the white-collar working hours. The handsomest of the new towers was Fox & Fowle's Embassy Suites Hotel, a thirty-eight-story building cantilevered over the landmark Palace Theater. The building was marred by one peculiar feature, however: its lobby had no windows. Apparently the architects never realized that they could work them into the signage. "No doubt," says Hardy, "they'll blame it all on MAS."[62]

Ada Louise Huxtable wrote a measured appraisal of Times Square's new zoning:

> In fairness, one must say that this is an unusually skilled and thoughtful set of urban design rules. More creative, groundbreaking guidelines through innovative zoning have yet to be devised. Never was a barn more splendidly locked after the horse was out. Ironically, this is important legislation because it is on the leading edge of the art of place-making through visual and physical means. New York, as usual, has delivered something special. And it has demonstrated, once again, its absolute mastery of Catch-22: The zoning defines the characteristics of the area brilliantly and supplies the criteria meant to protect and preserve those characteristics; but because they are being destroyed by the new construction, and because the new construction is also destroying the place that supplied the characteristics, recreating them is an exercise in artifice and futility. They become a kind of splendid wallpaper, or light show for a performance that isn't there.[63]

"There ought to be more than aesthetic legislation," Hugh Hardy admits. "The real problem is that Times Square has lost its energy." If the place were still a focus of popular culture, as it was in the 1920s, "there'd be no problem." As it is, the narrowness of the theater audience is "a very deep problem, and just fiddling around with light bulbs isn't the solution. There's a question of how far aesthetics can go. Land use is the larger planning issue, and no city agency will deal with this." Carole Rifkind is more positive. Considering what would have happened to Times Square without MAS's intervention, she describes the campaign as "probably one of our finest hours in terms of explaining urbanism to a large number of people. We *do* live in a democratic city, despite the politics. Public servants are not deaf, and a certain education takes place too." Rifkind sees the Times Square guidelines as an important precedent: the notion that the zoning code can be rewritten to capture or enhance the character of particular neighborhoods is something "that will come to the fore in the future."[64]

"There are mixed signals still in Times Square," Barwick said in 1993. "Maybe it still has a life."[65]

CITY FOR SALE

In 1985, while the Municipal Art Society was still mired in its battle to save Times Square, the city unveiled plans for a ghastly leviathan on the site of the Coliseum at Columbus Circle. Municipalians had been worrying about Columbus Circle since the turn of the century, and the society's early history was dotted with schemes to improve one of the few great public places in an otherwise dreary street grid. There was William Laurel Harris's project in 1898, and Charles Lamb's in 1901; and in 1959 Henry Hope Reed trumpeted a Baroque design by his friend and colleague, John Barrington Bayley. One of the founders of Classical America, Bayley wanted to ring Columbus Circle with a "colossal portico with enclosed galleries."[1] Bayley's scheme was meant as a critique of Robert Moses's Coliseum. In the early 1950s Moses had offered the site to the Metropolitan Opera Company, but Washington told him he couldn't build an opera house as part of a federally financed housing scheme. Moses was forced to shuffle his deck of cards. It took him another decade to build the opera house—half a mile north, at Lincoln Center—and in the meantime he'd come up with another plan for Columbus Circle: a convention center with a housing project behind it. MAS was unhappy to hear that the convention center would block Fifty-ninth Street. It was already difficult to navigate around Central Park, and this was about the last place in New York where a superblock was needed. On the other hand, the use of Fifty-ninth Street gave Albert Bard some hope: since the street was city land, at least the Art Commission would have jurisdiction over the new building. So Bard thought, and so the law seemed to say, but Moses brushed this suggestion aside, and the Art Commission itself shrank away from any confrontation. MAS begged Moses to at least hold a competition among the city's finest architects, but Moses shrugged off that idea, too. Competitions, he said, arouse "bad feelings." No, MAS replied, it was the practice of handing out such plum jobs to an in-house design team that created resentment.[2]

When the *Times* published a perspective of Moses's Coliseum, MAS was appalled: what a banal building for such a prominent site! Only its name hinted at grandeur: the convention facilities would be housed in a windowless box of beige brick, while the office building next door suggested the lowest level of speculative building. The building wouldn't even answer the curve of the site: Columbus "Circle" might still exist on a street map and in the arc of the sidewalk, but the building itself defined an amorphous, shapeless place.

Having failed to sway Moses, MAS sought out Aymar Embury, one of the numerous figures listed as having had a hand in the design. Embury had started out as a draftsman in Electus Litchfield's office; he'd gone on to be a fine country house architect and had done some lovely work for Moses in the 1930s—the grace notes in the Central Park Zoo, for instance, are largely his achievement. By the 1950s, however, he was a dissipirited cog in the Moses machine. Behind Moses's back, Embury showed MAS his first sketches for the Coliseum. The surviving descriptions are very vague, but MAS liked the design: it was recognizably a *public* building, it had some sense of occasion, and it even called for monumental sculpture. All these virtues had apparently fallen victim to a meager budget, however. It's not clear why Embury cooperated with MAS—whether he hoped to reopen the issue or just clear his own name.[3] In any case, MAS redoubled its criticisms of the Coliseum's design, and Moses's reply came in a letter to the *Herald Tribune.* He ridiculed these "premature, captious criticisms and disputes about matters of taste." The Coliseum was "not a museum of abstract art or an open prize competition for a civic monument to civic virtue," Moses wrote. It was "a business enterprise."[4]

Thirty years later the city still thought of this site as just a business venture. The MTA had inherited the building in 1968, when Nelson Rockefeller tricked Moses into surrendering the Triborough Authority's independence. Once the Jacob K. Javits Convention Center opened, the Coliseum wasn't needed anymore. The city had prepared for this moment in 1982, when it gerrymandered the Midtown Zoning Resolution to include the Coliseum site. Three years later, the MTA issued a request for proposals (or RFP), asking developers to submit bids and designs. The document required retail space on Columbus Circle and said that the new building should "relate" to the Hartford Museum, but it was mute on all other issues of urban design. There were, however, two crucial clauses in the RFP. One baldly announced that "the amount of the purchase price offered . . . will be the primary consideration" in selecting a developer. The other clause required developers to apply for the full 20 percent zoning bonus in exchange for renovating the Columbus Circle subway station. The point, clearly, was to make the building—and thus the purchase price—as large as possible.

In answer to the request for proposals, developers paired off with architects. Some of the designers were quite distinguished, but as the RFP made plain, the city wasn't interested in architectural talent, just money, and all the entries tried to fill every square inch of a hideously inflated zoning envelope. The winning team consisted of developer Mortimer Zuckerman, of Boston Properties, and architect Moshe Safdie. Zuckerman was best known in New York as the publisher of *The Atlantic.* (Later on, he would buy the *Daily News.*) He bid a staggering $455 million for the site, and his scheme was backed up by a commitment from Salomon Brothers to rent space in the project. Safdie had achieved fame in 1967 when he designed Habitat, a prefabricated housing project built for Montreal's world's fair. Canada still considered Safdie an interesting architect, and Zuckerman was a Canadian. For the Coliseum, Safdie designed two towers—68 and 58 stories tall—containing offices, apartments, movie theaters, and a shopping mall; in all it amounted to 2.7 million square feet of space. With sloping roofs and diagonal wind bracing, Safdie tried to evoke a crystalline geometry. The end result, said one MAS board member, would have looked at home at Cape Canaveral.[5]

MAS and the Upper West Side were both horrified by the project and tried to head it off at the Board of Estimate. The neighborhood could picture all too vividly what would happen at every rush hour as crowds poured out of Safdie's towers and tried to board the overburdened IRT. It knew, too, that traffic generated by the scheme would compound Broadway's air pollution problem. And as planners scanned the drawings more carefully they realized that Safdie's towers would blanket acres of Central Park in shade. The shadow studies were alarming: in March, when the sun was low in the sky, the shadow would stretch the width of the park and even touch Fifth Avenue. The Board of Estimate brushed the neighborhood's complaints aside, and when MAS sent a board member, Philip Howard, to testify that the project was unconscionably large, he was "beaten up" by city officials. They reminded him brusquely that MAS had endorsed the Midtown Zoning Resolution of 1982, the fatal document that produced Zuckerman's zoning envelope. How, they asked, could MAS be so inconsistent?[6]

The Board of Estimate approved the Coliseum Center, and Philip Howard spent his vacation glumly rereading press clippings on the project. He treasured Salomon's threat to leave the city if the building was reduced "by one square foot." It was "a classic case of developer hubris," says Howard, but it struck him that something was deeply amiss. "The community had done a fantastic job exploring the problems of this project. Seeing them slapped down was galling. Usually developers propose, everyone complains, and there's a compromise: the end result [is] only two-thirds as bad as the original." But this time there'd been no compromise; the city had approved the original project in all its "unalloyed evil," and Howard wondered "why the process, as imperfect as it is," hadn't worked. For the moment, Howard didn't have an answer. He was convinced that MAS should fight the project. ("Howard likes to sue," one colleague observes. "He's very aggressive.") But by Howard's own admission, his first "impassioned pleas" to the board were "so obviously emotional" that no one wanted him to talk about the Coliseum.[7]

"The board was very hemmy and hawy at first," Joan Davidson remembers. It knew the project was dreadful, but it didn't know if MAS should take a leading role in the fight. Davidson and Paul Byard agreed that MAS had to do so. Byard was no stranger to big projects himself: he'd worked at the Urban Development Corporation for years. "I like making new things," he says, and "fighting the Coliseum was a hated task. Davidson was crucial: if she thought [a campaign] was important she would pay for it. She was at the other end of the table, and she winked, and so I went ahead." Davidson dropped a very broad hint that the Kaplan Fund would provide money, and the board agreed to investigate a suit. "Without the lesson of Times Square, we never would have sued," Kent Barwick says. "Having been burned and lied to, it very much affected our attitude to the Coliseum project. We were prepared to be feistier ... when we saw that same cast operating even more arrogantly at the Coliseum. We decided that it had to be stopped."[8]

But on what grounds? Byard was interested in the Coliseum because it presented the "generic issues" of overbuilding. "The real issue was the zoning code," Byard realized, and at least one board member saw MAS's work on Times Square and the Coliseum site as the first blows in a larger campaign to downzone the city. "But that was not the issue people really wanted to address," Byard says.[9] In part this was due to MAS's original support of the Midtown Zoning Resolution, a decision it had bitterly come to regret. But the society also knew that a broad attack on the zoning code would lead to a battle with the entire real estate community, a fight MAS didn't think it could win, and it knew that the best hope to stop the Coliseum Center was to find an issue it could bring to court.

John Low-Beer, MAS's Menapace Fellow,* began to research the issue, and there seemed to be valid, substantial claims against the project's environmental impact statement. The new towers, the statement claimed, would have no substantial effect on air quality, but it assumed that cars would flow through Columbus Circle at a steady, constant rate of twenty-five miles per hour. This was absurd: "The circle's traffic does nothing but start and stop," as Howard says. The air quality might be "twice as bad" if the towers were built, and the impact would spread north to Lincoln Center, which was already one of the worst air quality "hot spots" in Manhattan.

MAS hired Peter Paden, a well-known environmental lawyer, to look into a suit. As Paden looked at MAS's legal options, the discussion turned to how MAS could force the city and Zuckerman to build a smaller building. Zuckerman had offered so much money to buy the site that he couldn't afford to just lop off some floors. Paden mentioned in passing that the purchase price would be reduced if the city gave Zuckerman a smaller zoning bonus. "Can they do that?" Howard asked. Paden said, "It's done all the time," though in this instance, the city had actually instructed developers to apply for the full bonus. And then it dawned on Howard why the normal review process had been such an abject failure this time: the city wasn't granting a zoning bonus; it was selling it to the highest bidder.

It struck Howard that this must be unlawful. "I just *knew* it was wrong; it was really just *obvious*," he says. The whole point of zoning was that the light and air and sky belong to the public, and that there's an upper limit to what a developer could rightfully take away. The City Planning Commission could grant a bonus in return for some other public benefit, but it was supposed to weigh whether these amenities were

---

* *The Menapace Fellowship, named in honor of MAS's late president, lawyer Ralph Menapace, provides a two-year internship in urban land use law.*

worth the sacrifice. This balancing act was purely theoretical, of course. In practice, bonuses were granted almost automatically, and amenities that cost a pittance yielded a windfall in extra space. But at the Coliseum the situation was different. The city had created an impossible conflict of interest for its own planning commission; it was "prejudicing the outcome of a purportedly democratic decision-making process."

Before going to court, MAS met with both Zuckerman and Salomon Brothers. Their attitude, Howard says, was that "You're a nice young man, but we have the opinions of five of the best law firms in New York." The condescension in their voices only whetted Howard's appetite for litigation. To prevail over those law firms would be "satisfying in and of itself," but on the other hand, Howard didn't want to actually face them in court. "There was a question of who to sue," he remembers. "I didn't want to sue Boston Properties; they had all those high-priced lawyers. I wanted to sue as few people as possible, and preferably those with limited resources. I wanted to sue the city."

MAS filed its lawsuit in June 1987. The *Times* reported the news on its front page. The article noted that MAS was hardly a radical or litigious organization; it even said that this was the first time in its ninety-odd years that MAS had gone to court. That wasn't true, but it *was* helpful: it made the Coliseum project sound like an unparalleled outrage. The tone of the coverage, Howard says, showed how useful it was "to have a conservative board" of civic leaders willing to sue when "unconscionable" acts are about to be committed. "There's power in conservatism, and it's a legitimate power. The Municipal Art Society should not often sue—only when we're right, not only morally, but right on the law. And so far we've held to that." There's a broader point here, Howard says. "In New York there is no power anyplace. Power is what you make of it. It's a perception of public will, an intangible thing manipulated by the media. By being articulate, by being conservative, we're able to influence things."[10]

The battle, of course, was also waged in the court of public opinion. The city meant to use half of Zuckerman's $455 million to balance its budget and half for improvements to the subway system, but it often tried to leave the impression that all the money would go to mass transit, and it accused MAS of putting aesthetics before the welfare of New York's straphangers. Considering that the Koch administration had bitterly fought trading in Westway funds for mass transit, MAS thought that this outrage rang a little hollow. City Hall also insisted that MAS was exploiting a technicality: the city granted zoning bonuses all the time, it pointed out. Why couldn't it sell one?

Aside from upholding a legal principle, MAS had to demonstrate the project's impact on the city at large. It planned two public relations extravaganzas to get its message across to the general public. One was the "City for Sale" auction, which highlighted the fact that the city was behaving like the most rapacious real estate developer. Thirty architects and artists ranging from Roz Chast to Keith Haring responded to a mock request for proposals for city-owned land, and their work was auctioned at Christie's to help pay MAS's legal bills. In October 1987 the society staged a more populist event, the "Stand against the Shadow" rally in Central Park.

Thousands of New Yorkers arrived at Columbus Circle with black umbrellas in hand, and then they traced the shadow's path clear across Central Park.

On December 6, 1987, Judge Lehner ruled against the city, finding that it had no right to sell a zoning bonus. The city, of course, filed an appeal. Zuckerman, for his part, decided to find another architect. Until now, he'd defended Safdie's design as if it were an avant-garde breakthrough. When he realized that almost everyone else thought the building was horrifically ugly, and when he also realized that this contributed to his opponents' passion, he dropped Moshe Safdie and turned to David Childs. A partner in the vast firm of Skidmore, Owings & Merrill, Childs was one of the original competitors for the Coliseum commission, and his scheme was widely thought to be "one of the better entries" in that miserable lot.[11] He was also a member of MAS's board of directors, and one of the few who'd argued against filing the lawsuit. Once he was hired by Zuckerman, Childs naturally announced his resignation from MAS, but he was convinced to stay with the proviso that he excuse himself whenever the Coliseum project was discussed.[12]

In June 1988, Zuckerman unveiled Childs's new design for the Coliseum Center. This time, to satisfy the court, there was no zoning bonus. Childs had reduced the building's height from 925 to 850 feet. He'd shifted the towers on the site so that most of the shadow was concealed within the shadow of the Gulf and Western Building. The new design was also more attractive than the first: it echoed the Art Deco towers of the Century apartment building on Central Park West. Without the issue of the zoning bonus and without the shadow, MAS realized that it would be harder to drum up wide support for another fight. And as the city struggled with a budget deficit, the Board of Estimate was growing ever more anxious to lay its hands on Zuckerman's millions. Nevertheless, the project was still grotesquely large, and the environmental issues were still unresolved. MAS felt it couldn't accept Childs's project. It would have to resume the legal battle.

For once the *New York Post* and the *Amsterdam News,* newspapers that rarely see eye to eye, found some common ground.* "The nay-sayers never give up," complained the *Post,* and it went on to accuse MAS of exploiting "a procedural technique" to block "any development at all. . . . Sweating straphangers are, to be sure, of little interest to the elite Art Society crowd. They tend to travel around town—when in town—in considerably more comfortable conveyances. . . . The members of this outfit are knee-jerk nay-sayers. They *say* they favor responsible, measured development. But they've never met a development proposal they liked."[13]

The *Amsterdam News* accused MAS of a "vicious assault" on Boston Properties,

an essentially innocent and honest outfit from Canada that did not know of the shark and barracuda infested municipal waters here in New York City.

---

* *The* Post *was then owned by developer Peter Kalikow, and MAS was battling his plan to tear down much of the York Avenue Estate, a full block of model tenements dating from the early 1900s. In the midst of an endless crisis of homelessness, the model tenement movement seemed to be one chapter of New York's history that was worth remembering.*

Should the Municipal Art Society cost the development team more money, a suit against them [MAS] should be considered, for they have been too long arbiters of what should happen, mostly in midtown Manhattan, and have virtually ignored the outer boroughs, except for an odd landmark designation.

Powerful white civic groups often backed by the *Times* have run rough-shod over honest developers and powerless citizens as well. With the kind of power . . . the [members of the] Municipal Art Society seem to have, would it not seem appropriate and practical for them to turn their attention and considerable talent to housing the homeless, providing resources for the rebuilding of the Harlems of this city, and ridding New York of the narcotics disaster even in their own back yards?[14]

Those accusations—that MAS is a predominantly white organization, that it focuses on Manhattan below Ninety-sixth Street, and that it had done nothing for the homeless—were all true. It was odd, however, to hear MAS described as an "arbiter" and to read that it was "often backed by the *Times*." That hadn't been true since the *Times* stopped printing Ada Louise Huxtable's editorials, and at the time of the Coliseum conflict the paper's land-use policy was shaped by Roger Starr, with whom MAS never agreed.

As the battle heated up again, the city offered to work out a settlement with MAS. Another 100 feet was knocked off the towers' height. (The project was now 700,000 square feet smaller than the Safdie scheme.) The city also agreed to create 120 subsidized apartments in the neighborhood and to provide community space in the new building. Finally the mayor promised, at MAS's insistence, that in future the city would "give full recognition to the planning and design concerns which should govern the development of major sites." The apartments and community space were mere tokens, MAS thought, and it didn't place much faith in the mayor's promise to do better next time. ("It's just a piece of paper," Paul Byard said.) The project was still far bigger than MAS wanted, and the whole process disgusted the society: the city had whittled the project down to a point where it was no longer illegal, but it had never once tried to determine how the site could be developed in the public interest. Still, MAS agreed to settle.

Paul Goldberger wrote in the *Times* that the Municipal Art Society had become "the conscience that we once expected our planners and city officials to be." The *New York Observer* wrote that every time Zuckerman's architects went back to the drafting board, the building got smaller, prettier, and better—and that it was worth sending them back a few more times to see what happened. Many activists felt that MAS had settled "short of the line," Tony Wood remembers. "Many are West Siders without a citywide perspective, but it has given some activists the idea that MAS may be a good partner, but it has to be watched." And Howard explained, "There was a problem in that the site was zoned for more density than was eventually agreed on. After we won [the first round] they took away the bonus. We would have had to fight on these 'gray areas' of environmental law. . . . They would simply have done a new environmental impact statement and 'fixed' it." Howard thought it was "quite an effective settlement. There are always people who want to see the building not built, but unfortunately the zoning was in place."[15]

The Coliseum towers will never be built, however. The stock market crash of October 1987 convinced Salomon Brothers to withdraw from the project, and as the city's economy spiraled downward it grew ever more unlikely that Zuckerman could find tenants for the building. In retrospect, Zuckerman might well be grateful to MAS for delaying construction, and to State Senator Manfred Ohrenstein and the Coalition for a Livable West Side. *They* filed a second lawsuit against the project in 1990, waging their battle on the very environmental issues that made Philip Howard so uncomfortable. The coalition triumphed in the lower court but lost on appeal. By then a vast amount of New York's office space sat empty. Theoretically, Zuckerman was obliged to either proceed with construction or surrender $30 million to the MTA. The city was reluctant to press either point—Zuckerman had since purchased the *Daily News*—and in 1994 the project was finally canceled.

THE COLISEUM project represented just one of the dangers facing the Upper West Side in the 1980s. There was a flurry of proposals to build atop Central Park West's landmarks: James Polshek designed a tower for the site of the Second Church of Christ Scientist; Hugh Hardy designed an apartment building to sit atop the New-York Historical Society; and a third tower was proposed for Shearith Israel. MAS successfully opposed all these schemes—even though Hardy was a board member at the time and Polshek used to be one. The Landmarks Commission estimated that more than half of the Upper West Side's 2,400 buildings might be worthy of protection, but by 1983 just 26 individual landmarks had been designated, while three small historic districts included another 125 structures.

MAS lent its expertise, its exhibition halls, and its publicity machine to Landmark West, a preservation group founded by West Side activist Arlene Simon. It also joined with Columbia University and Planning Board Seven to develop a new zoning strategy for the neighborhood. "The idea," says Barwick, "was based on the liberal belief, the 1960s belief that I hold dearly, that if you give people the ideas, the technical help, etc., they're perfectly capable of designing the future of their own neighborhoods and they'll behave responsibly." The neighborhood was very attractive physically, with two great parks, but its diversity was threatened by new development, and the task was to find a level of sustainable growth, growth that would "build in" housing for blacks, Hispanics, and the poor. On a formal level, the study sought to sustain the character of the streets and avenues, and particularly to protect the low scale of Columbus Avenue. The side streets and Columbus Avenue would be downzoned to protect their low scale. Broadway and Central Park West would actually be upzoned so that new buildings would match the context of pre–World War I and 1920s apartment buildings. At the same time, mandatory inclusionary housing would ensure a varied population. The idea was to make the West Side "more of what it was."[16]

The planning study led MAS to focus on one of the sorry legacies of urban renewal: the West Side's pollution problem. Robert Moses's superblocks in the West Sixties and Nineties disrupted vehicular traffic and funneled cars onto Broadway, which had a terrible air-quality problem. And as MAS looked for ways to ease the neighborhood's traffic, it turned its attention to the Penn Yards site.

Penn Yards had once been the bustling freight yard of the New York Central railroad. When the city built the Miller Highway in 1928 it had to lift the road high above a morass of train tracks. The elevated highway was still there in the 1980s, but the trains had vanished when the railroad went bankrupt, and the site was left a weedy garbage dump. Its potential was enormous, however. Seventy-six acres of Hudson River waterfront could become a splendid new neighborhood, a boon to the entire city. Or it could become yet another urban disaster.

The Penn Yards site was now in the hands of Donald Trump, the heir to an outer borough real estate empire. The elder Trump, who was periodically accused of misusing federal subsidies to amass his fortune and of ruining Coney Island with his grim housing projects, had close ties to the Queens Democratic machine. These ties served young Donald well in his Manhattan debut, the "renovation" of the Commodore Hotel on East Forty-second Street. A grand old building, the Commodore was stripped and gutted and finally resurfaced in a mélange of reflective glass, polished marble, shiny brass, and mirror. It emerged in 1978 as the Grand Hyatt Hotel. The approvals for that project, including a forty-two-year $160 million tax abatement, were pushed through in the last days of the Beame administration by Deputy Mayor Stanley Friedman. It was the largest tax write-off up to that time. Lest it seem too partial to Trump, the city announced that the new Hyatt was just the first project of a new "Business Incentive Program." On Beame's last day in office, Friedman added a final sweetener: a special permit to let Trump extend the hotel's restaurant over the Forty-second Street sidewalk. At the time, such generosity was explained away by the desperate need to set New York's economy on its feet again, but in fact, when Friedman pulled his strings for Trump, he'd already arranged to become a partner in the firm of Trump's lawyer, the notorious Roy Cohn.[17]

Trump was hailed as a hero at the time. Construction was at a standstill in New York, and in those days of fiscal crisis, politicians and the press alike trumpeted any signs of a resurgent economy. Governor Hugh Carey turned Trump's ribbon-cutting ceremony into a campaign appearance.

After the Hyatt, Donald Trump went on to build Trump Plaza and Trump Tower; to gut, mutilate, and then gild the lovely old Barbizon Plaza on Central Park South; and to buy, for an absurd sum, the storied Plaza Hotel. He made his wife, Ivana, a present of Mar-a-Lago, the inanely vulgar Palm Beach house of Marjorie Merriweather Post, and he bought himself the world's largest yacht, once the plaything of Adnan Kashoggi. Fatally, perhaps, he extended his reach to Atlantic City, pouring millions of dollars into the construction of the troubled Taj Mahal casino. All this activity, and each new acquisition, was duly celebrated by a well-oiled public relations operation. By the mid 1980s Trump had achieved a celebrity unmatched by any other developer, and he was even mentioned in some circles as a possible presidential candidate.

Trump had first cast his eyes on the Penn Yards in 1976.[18] With the railroad bankrupt and the city mired in a depression, the land was available for a song. Trump's first impulse was to move the Miller Highway. With the trains gone, there was no reason for an elevated highway to stand like a giant fence between the city and its precious waterfront. Tampering with the highway would have introduced all sorts of complications, however, so Trump abandoned the idea, and after three years of fruitless negotiations he let his option to buy the train yards lapse. A year later, in 1980, the city brushed aside a report recommending that it buy the yards and build new freight facilities on the site. And soon, a new set of developers came along: Francisco Macri, an Argentinean banker; and Abraham Hirschfield, who'd made a fortune building ghastly garages but was better known for his quixotic pursuit of political office. (In 1993 his brief and stormy reign as the *New York Post*'s publisher would lead to a staff revolt.) In 1982 Macri and Hirschfield wrested city approval for a 7-million-square-foot project named Lincoln West and, in return, agreed to undertake a package of public improvements worth $100 million. When Macri's financing evaporated, Trump reappeared on the scene, and in 1985 he paid $115 million for the Penn Yards. Six years earlier, he could have had the land for just $28 million, but in the gold rush days of the 1980s few people questioned Trump's financial acumen.

Yet there was every reason to question Trump's skills as an urban planner. He was planning to build 15 million square feet on the site—more than twice the density of Macri's Lincoln West proposal. Trump's project called for a phalanx of seventy-story towers and a 130-story skyscraper—the tallest building on earth—and all this would rise from an immense, monolithic podium raised as high as the Miller Highway. Within the podium, Trump planned an enormous "regional" shopping mall, vast garages, and a million square feet of television studios. A park would sit atop this platform, but given its height above ground and the difficulty of access from the streets, this patch of greenery looked suspiciously like a private preserve for Trump's tenants rather than a truly public amenity.

Trump dubbed the project Television City, and he staked his hopes on NBC. The network's studios were antiquated, and despite a long lease at Rockefeller Center, NBC was making overtures to New Jersey. Threatening to move across the Hudson had become a standard ploy for big corporations, and it always seemed to shake loose a bounty of tax abatements from City Hall, but NBC's threat was especially worrisome. Losing the network would be a tremendous embarrassment, on a par with losing the Brooklyn Dodgers. Columnists and political rivals would trumpet the news that Ed Koch's New York was no longer a cultural capital. Losing NBC was politically unacceptable to the mayor, and Trump was playing on that fear.

The scale of Television City was necessary, Trump insisted, to subsidize NBC's rent. And to assure the skittish network that the project would proceed, the Urban Development Corporation would have to get involved: Trump wanted to transfer the land to the UDC and thus sidestep the normal public review process. And finally, Trump said, he would need tax abatements to proceed. When the city added up everything the developer wanted, it discovered that Trump was asking for a billion dollars in tax breaks. This was outrageous, even by Koch's standards, but with NBC at stake, City Hall was soon abuzz with negotiations. Koch's deputies presented the mayor with a more modest incentive package: $700 million in up-front tax breaks, which Trump would pay back over time. Koch rejected the deal.

This may have been an act of good governance on Koch's part, or of political calculation, given the West Side's hostility toward the scheme, but the mayor's harshest critics insisted that his veto was simply spiteful. It's true that Koch had come to loathe Trump. In 1980 the city had begun a reconstruction of Central Park's Wollman Skating Rink. Everything went wrong, the new cooling pipes were riddled with leaks, and after six years of cost overruns the city produced, not ice, but slush. Trump offered to manage, pro bono, the rink's second reconstruction, and he finished the job in six months. The ribbon-cutting ceremonies in November 1986 marked the crest of Trump's public reputation, and a turning point in his relations with the mayor. Trump crowed about his success, and every boast he uttered underlined the fact that the city had originally bungled the job. Publicly, Koch couldn't afford to seem churlish; privately, he was said to be furious. In any case, Koch set out to disarm Trump by undoing the link between Television City and NBC, and in 1987 he came to an agreement with the network. NBC would renovate its Rockefeller Center studios in return for an immense package of tax abatements and exemptions. The pact set yet another record for corporate tax breaks, and it marked the first time the city had paid a company to stay put, but at least it didn't add any new skyscrapers to the skyline. Once NBC had been satisfied, the mayor announced that he would oppose any Penn Yards development that was "substantially" larger than the Lincoln West scheme. Trump called Koch a moron. "Piggy, piggy, piggy," replied the mayor.

When NBC slipped through his fingers, Trump renamed his Penn Yards project—Television City gave way to Trump City—but physically the scheme was little changed. The Municipal Art Society was glad that, after two years of silence on the subject, Mayor Koch had finally admitted that Trump's proposal was much too big, but it seemed to MAS that "piggy, piggy, piggy" hardly constituted a planning strategy. Developing Penn Yards could have a terrible impact on a neighborhood already burdened with too much traffic pollution and too little public transportation. On the other hand, the site presented a unique chance to bring the public in touch with the waterfront. Despite the dangers and the opportunities latent in Penn Yards, the city had never assessed what ought to be built there; it had never drawn a plan of its own or even considered trying to formulate the public interest in the site. In the meantime the city was about to rebuild the Miller

Highway, and that meant that the elevated road would probably blight the waterfront for another fifty or sixty years.

In 1989 MAS decided that it was "time to meet a gap in government awareness," as Philip Howard phrased it, and in the city's "willingness to act."[19] That fall, MAS, the Parks Council, and the Regional Plan Association unveiled their own idea for the Penn Yards. The scheme sprang from the architect Paul Willen: it was called Riverside South; and the name aptly summarized Willen's strategy. He suggested extending Riverside Park to Sixty-first Street, echoing the park's famous curving cliff of apartment buildings. While he was at it, Willen realized that this was an opportunity to correct the problem with Riverside Park: the fact that a highway at the water's edge prevented people from getting close to the river. Willen's solution was to sink the highway below grade and let it curve inland. "The simplicity of the idea carried it," Barwick says. "People could comprehend it immediately. The *Times* even wrote an editorial in our favor—a rare occurrence."[20]

In the meantime, Koch's reign was drawing to a close. "Corruption is like a great aquifer beneath the city," says Brendan Gill. When Koch first assumed office, he had "no particularly evil intent, but he's a slob, and the aquifer took him over."[21] In January 1986, Donald Mannes, the borough president of Queens and a close ally of the mayor, had been found in his car, dazed and bleeding from knife wounds. He told a bizarre tale of kidnapping and assault, but the police concluded that Mannes had attempted suicide. Mannes, it turned out, had been running a bribery ring out of the Parking Violations Bureau, and he'd just learned that the FBI was on his trail. He succeeded in a second attempt at suicide two months later. By then the "aquifer" was fairly oozing out of the ground, and over the next three years one corruption probe spilled over into another. Officials of the Transportation Department, the city's leasing office, the Board of Standards and Appeals, the Marine and Aviation Department, and the Health and Hospitals Corporation left office in disgrace or in handcuffs. The most prominent victim was Stanley Friedman, the Bronx County leader who'd once been so useful to Donald Trump. The oddest was Bess Myerson, the cultural affairs commissioner who'd played the role of Koch's "partner" in the 1977 election campaign. She was charged with trying to influence the judge presiding over her lover's divorce trial—the lover being a crooked sewer contractor with ties to the mob. After each new indictment or resignation the mayor expressed his horror and astonishment, and the columnist Murray Kempton finally suggested that New York adopt as its civic motto "whatever the Latin is for 'I am shocked.' "[22] There was never a hint that Koch himself was corrupt, but as reporters reconstructed the history of his regime it became clear that the scandals' roots dated back to 1978 when Koch, freshly elected as a reformer, made peace with the clubhouses by granting them control of entire agencies.

Corruption wasn't the only issue in the mayoral primary of 1989. MAS, of course, blamed Koch for the horrors of the building boom. A much wider segment of the population blamed him for exacerbating racial tensions, especially between blacks and Jews, and held him responsible for the proliferation of homelessness in

New York. MAS placed its hopes for change on David Dinkins, the borough president of Manhattan. Critics dismissed him as a clubhouse hack; MAS praised him as a "healer." He'd supported MAS on planning issues, and in 1989 he railed against Koch's attitude toward Penn Yards. "It is incomprehensible," Dinkins said in a campaign speech, "that the city did not propose a plan for a site with the size and impact of the West Side rail yards. . . . Reacting to a developer's plans in this way is an abdication of responsibility."[23] When Dinkins became mayor, "we seemed to have a very warm relationship with the administration," Barwick remembers. "We shouldn't have taken this personally. The administration listened to us, but did nothing."[24]

David Dinkins had arrived in City Hall just as the recession struck New York in full force. The financial services and real estate industries, the twin cornerstones of Ed Koch's "global city," had both collapsed. Tax revenues plummeted, the budget deficit soared, and the city's credit rating tottered. The mayor struggled to maintain control over New York's finances, and his first budget appalled many of his closest supporters; it opted for across-the-board cuts with scant consideration of the human costs involved. Dinkins was in no mood to listen when MAS and its allies suggested that the city consider buying Penn Yards. Calling the site "an extraordinary opportunity," Borough President Ruth Messinger, State Senator Franz Leichter, Assemblymen Jerrold Nadler and Richard Gottfried, and City Council members Ronnie Eldridge and Carolyn Maloney called on the city to condemn the land and plan it properly. Riverside South, they pointed out, already offered "one vision" of what might be built there. Paul Goldberger wrote about the idea in the *Times*, and there was a period of "intensive letter-writing" to Dinkins, but the mayor resisted the idea of massive city investment.

In September 1990, MAS met with Barbara Fife, the deputy mayor for planning and development; Richard Schaeffer, the planning commissioner; and Lucius Riccio of the Transportation Department. "We asked for a six-month delay to study moving the highway," Barwick says. "It turned into a city idea for a three-month study, with no study of public ownership." MAS agreed and thought it had a deal, but around Thanksgiving, the city suddenly backed out. MAS could interpret this in only one way: as a sign that the city was preparing to embrace Trump's plan. Of course the planning commission would scale down the project and exact other concessions as well. But the Trump plan was so fundamentally flawed that no amount of tinkering would suffice. Their negotiations in ruins, MAS, the Parks Council, and Westpride (a coalition of neighborhood groups) went to court to stop the Miller Highway's reconstruction on the grounds that the city and state had never done an environmental analysis of alternative highway designs. As David Dunlap wrote in the *Times*, the suit worked "a rupture in relations" between Dinkins and "the civic leaders who had earlier cheered his pronouncements on city planning and community involvement in land-use issues. 'The honeymoon is over,' said Kent L. Barwick. . . . 'The great disappointment is to find ourselves in court so soon after the nuptials.' "[25]

"There was hostility between us and the city at that time," Barwick remembers, and since City Hall wouldn't talk to MAS, a new idea emerged: "Why not talk to the owner?" Stephen Swid, the chairman of MAS's board, knew Trump socially and called him up. Then Swid, Barwick, Philip Howard, Bruce Simon, and Richard Kahan met with Trump. The Municipalians suggested that Trump abandon his plan and adopt theirs instead. They would fight Trump City tooth and nail, they explained; Trump might win in the end, but at best, there'd be years of lawsuits ahead. On the other hand, if Trump decided to build Riverside South, the civic groups would fight *for* him.

"The idea of having us as supporters, not litigants, interested Trump," Barwick says. "He was attracted from the very beginning by the public relations aspect of it. He was intrigued enough to agree to a few more meetings." So a consortium of six civic groups—MAS, the Regional Plan Association, the Parks Council, the Natural Resources Defense Council, the Riverside Park Fund, and Westpride—met with Trump at the law offices of Cravath, Swaine & Moore. Action in another quarter had just given the civic groups a boost. The Coalition for a Livable West Side, which had never accepted MAS's decision to settle the Coliseum lawsuit, had just gone to court to challenge Mortimer Zuckerman's environmental impact statement. Many of the coalition's members lived in Lincoln Towers, the housing project next door to the Penn Yards. Their lawsuit offered a hint of the kind of guerrilla warfare Trump himself could expect to face, and it made the six civic groups sitting in Cravath's office seem comparatively reasonable: Trump could either deal with them, or find himself picked apart by the radicals.

Richard Kahan took part in the negotiations as a volunteer, but he became indispensable to the civic groups because "he knew development," as Barwick says. "He called on his former associates from Battery Park City and the UDC so we could understand the economics. He had the confidence of the civic groups, he could be tough with Trump, and he could tell us when we were wrong. It was the most informed discussion I ever saw." In the meantime MAS and the Natural Resources Defense Council were also meeting with Vincent Tese of the Urban Development Corporation. The Defense Council presented the Penn Yards project as an important environmental issue, and the group represented an important constituency for Governor Mario Cuomo. Tese saw advantages in a sunken highway and promised that if the civic groups could "deliver" the community and Trump, "he'd deliver the state."

Back at Cravath, Swaine & Moore, a compromise was slowly taking shape. Trump's original plan called for 15 million square feet of space. Clearly that was a bargaining position, and he fully expected the city to whittle it down. "I don't know what Trump [really] hoped for," Barwick says. "Maybe eleven million square feet." The civic groups wanted 7.2 million. The two sides met at 8.2.[26]

Trump held a press conference to announce that he'd adopted the civic groups' plan. MAS was euphoric. "It's like a miracle, a huge success," Philip Howard said at the time. It illustrates the "power of putting pen to paper ... the power of the plan."[27]

But so far, Riverside South was just a rough outline. Months of planning lay ahead until it became a concrete proposal. There was a highway to design, a park, and sixteen apartment complexes. The civic groups wanted to build on Kahan's work at Battery Park City, where design guidelines governed everything from building materials to window types and air-conditioner grilles. All these details assumed new importance once the civic groups realized that Trump himself would probably never be able to build the project alone. By any reasonable definition of the term, Trump seemed to be bankrupt. His casinos were losing money; the Plaza Hotel couldn't generate enough revenue to fund its debt; and in the sinking real estate market, many of Trump's properties were now worth less than the mortgages they carried. If he kept his head above water it was only because his creditors didn't want to seize overvalued property in the middle of a recession. Trump had managed to renegotiate much of his debt, but he might well need to sell most—maybe all—of Penn Yards. If he could win the city's approval of a plan, that would boost the prices he could command. The new master plan made his plight easier in another way as well. With their massive podiums, both Trump City and Television City had been monolithic projects, difficult to break down into pieces for individual developers. The new Riverside South, with its traditional city blocks, could easily be sold one piece at a time.

A set of detailed ironclad design guidelines would control the project no matter who actually built it, but there was another worrisome factor to deal with. Theoretically, any number of civic groups could have formed their own coalition and gone to Trump with a similar deal—satisfy us and we'll help you—and they might have placed very different demands on the developer. Instead of a park, they could have demanded low-income housing or transit improvements or funds for the rail link so desperately needed by New York's industry. MAS knew that as the project moved forward, Trump would be barraged by civic and community groups with new demands. "It would be hard to control Trump," Barwick realized. He might well agree to new amenities, like subway renovations, and then insist on more bulk to pay for them.

MAS and its allies realized that their work with Trump wasn't finished yet. They wanted to be intimately involved in the design's development. Finding a mechanism for this was difficult. Richard Kahan was uneasy about continuing with the project. He didn't want to be pictured as Trump's tool, and he certainly didn't want to work for Trump. The only solution, it seemed, was to create a new entity to plan and design Riverside South. To that end, the Riverside South Planning Corporation was formed as a not-for-profit group with seven partners—the civic groups plus Donald Trump. "It's perilous," Barwick admitted shortly afterward. "The developer has more cards, in that he owns the property, but both sides feel we need one another." Trump would pay all the bills for the planning group, but he had to put the money in escrow to insulate the civic groups from undue pressure. "All the parties have the opportunity to walk away without any obligation."

News of the Riverside South Planning Corporation created a sudden shift in public attitudes, however. New Yorkers were used to a state of open warfare between communities and developers; when this partnership was announced, many concluded that the civic groups had sold out to Trump. WNYC's radio talk shows buzzed with angry talk of betrayal; civic groups that had once said kind things about Riverside South were now scathingly critical. MAS was caught unawares by this shift in tone; Kent Barwick had never looked more miserable, or more angry. "He sold out to *us*," he insisted, speaking of Trump. "He endorsed *our* plan." But Trump had become New York's most visible symbol of greed and hyperbole. He seemed to epitomize the callous 1980s, and his new financial and romantic difficulties inspired sheer glee in many quarters. Now that Trump was on the edge of ruin, Brendan Gill couldn't understand why MAS would "pull one of the costliest of his many misadventures back from the brink of total failure. . . . Let Trump sell the property to the city at a low price," Gill wrote, "or give it to the city, and gain fame by being among the most generous of our benefactors."[28] Wayne Barrett, Trump's biographer, was convinced that Trump was merely using a group of naive do-gooders to stave off foreclosure; others insisted that the community could have killed Trump City and then forced the city to come up with its own plan.

The Riverside South Planning Corporation unveiled its final project early in 1992, and over the next seven months it held more than six hundred meetings with city officials, advocates, and neighborhood groups. The drawings and an elaborate model showed a broad, concave arc of buildings facing the new waterfront park. The buildings had grown taller since Willen first imagined the scheme. At either end they climbed as high as forty and forty-nine stories, but they were lower in the middle of the bow to let the morning sun into the widest stretch of the park. A series of small parks dotted the complex's inner edge, engaging the existing neighborhood. The riverfront park sought to capture the mixture of naturalistic planting and recreation that made Riverside Park so successful, but its waterfront was designed as a "soft" edge: it would seem less like a seawall than a natural shoreline.

There were, however, some serious issues raised by the project. There was that extra million square feet of space above and beyond what the city had approved for Lincoln West. Trump, having paid too much for the site, needed the extra space to make a profit, and MAS believed that the new park was worth the extra density. There was also the question of transportation. At least ten thousand new residents of Riverside South would rely on the IRT station on West Seventy-second Street, already a perilously overcrowded place. MAS could hardly deny that the subway station needed to be rebuilt, but it took the position that the MTA shouldn't rely on developers to perform one of its own basic functions.

In the meantime the state had gone ahead with the $85 million reconstruction of the Miller Highway, a monumental waste of federal money. The civic groups insisted that the highway could be rebuilt again, in its proper place, in ten years' time. Surely, they said, the state's congressional delegation could make this come to pass. Others weren't sure. "Do *you* think anyone will knock it down in ten years?" asked Brendan Gill.

The project's environmental impact was a source of growing concern. At first, planners assumed that the new North River Sewage Treatment Plant would handle the project's waste, but that assumption proved extremely optimistic. In truth, the sewage plant was a monument to West Side politics. When first proposed in the 1960s, it was meant to sit in the river at West Sixty-third Street. (Harmon Goldstone sat on the planning commission when the project was approved. "Son," he told a young friend, "in two years you'll be able to swim in the Hudson."[29]) But the Upper West Side succeeded in moving the project to Hamilton Heights. As a concession to that community, and in recompense for the fact that the desperately overcrowded neighborhood had no Riverside Park of its own, the state agreed to build a park on the plant's roof. The city promised that the facility would be odorless, but in 1987, when the plant finally went into operation, noxious fumes wafted across the neighborhood. Furthermore, the sewage plant was soon running at full capacity, meaning it couldn't accommodate the flushing toilets of 5,700 new luxury apartments. The plant was "continuously polluting the air over hundreds of acres of West Harlem," wrote Brendan Gill. "How on earth can it be expected to accept as much as a teacup more of our sewage and wastewater?"[30]

The community board voted to oppose the project. Ruth Messinger, the Manhattan borough president, announced that she couldn't support it without certain concessions: there could be no net increase in sewage to the North River plant; there had to be a specific promise of low-cost apartments; she demanded a guarantee that the park would be built as the buildings went up rather than years later; and she wanted the builders' obligations to construct the park and follow the guidelines made absolutely clear.

The last two requests were comparatively easy to fulfill despite Trump's resistance—and, it was said, that of his banks. The park design and guidelines were written into the city's permit and the deed for the site. The low-cost units, however, remained a much more tentative proposition, since they depended on the availability of subsidies. Sewage also presented a dilemma, and Trump agreed to contribute to a new fund to help retrofit plumbing fixtures across Manhattan.

Riverside South was at last approved by the city. No one seemed to be in a hurry to begin construction in the middle of a depressed market, and moving the Miller Highway remains a long-term goal—or so it seems in an impatient, forgetful age. When professors teach the urban history of Rome or Paris, ten, twenty, even fifty years slip by in the blink of an eye as one slide gives way to the next. Abram Hewitt, the visionary nineteenth-century mayor, once said that "Everything takes ten years," and if anything, that seems too little.

ON OCTOBER 29, 1993, the Municipal Art Society celebrated its centennial at Grand Central Terminal. The building and the society had become linked in the public mind, and the one thing most people knew about MAS was that it had once saved the terminal. Grand Central was still in the early stages of a glorious restoration. Municipalians danced that night in the waiting room amid pastel yellow walls and newly gilded chandeliers, and they applauded as a freshly cleaned patch of the concourse ceiling was unveiled: a brilliant rectangle of aqua dotted with gold stars.

A few blocks to the west, Times Square was aglow with neon. The new hotels were flourishing, and MAS's billboards and moving signs almost managed to conceal the fact that the new office towers sat empty and bankrupt. The building boom had gone bust: all the tax incentives of the 1980s had built, not prosperity, but useless space. The towers' dark windows announced that Forty-second Street itself was lined with shuttered stores. The state had just announced that its redevelopment project would be postponed till after the turn of the century, and MAS had emerged as a forceful voice on the issue: *Cancel* the office buildings, it said. It pointed to the state's interim project as the ideal solution: new shops, restaurants, theaters, and hotel rooms were in the works. Billboards, bright lights, and a vibrant street life were the keynotes of the scheme. In the meantime, there were other signs of new life for the neighborhood. Attracted by the new billboards and bargain prices, the music industry was moving to Times Square, and the Disney Corporation was thinking of restoring the New Amsterdam Theater. It seemed that Forty-second Street might find its way again.

To the northwest, Riverside South was quiet, but Donald Trump was soon leading Philip Johnson on tours of the site: they were exploring, they said, a scheme for subsidized housing, and Trump was scouring the globe for new financial partners. In the Bronx, the Municipal Art Society had been asked to design a new master plan for the troubled Hunts Point district, and the society was proud to think that it had shed its elitist image and that it might find a broader public in the future.

And all across the city there were landmarks and historic districts, parks, plazas, monuments, and skyscrapers that had been touched by the Municipal Art Society.

NOTES

CHAPTER I

1. Chauncey Depew, address at the opening of the New York State Pavilion, reprinted in *Report of the Board of General Managers of the Exhibition of the State of New York at the World's Columbian Exposition, Transmitted to the Legislature April 18, 1894.*

2. Paul Bourget, "A Farewell to the White City," *Cosmopolitan*, December 1893, p. 186; Mariana Griswold Van Rensselaer, "The Artistic Triumph of the Fair Builders," *Forum*, December 1892, p. 539; and Henry Adams, *The Education of Henry Adams: An Autobiography* (Houghton Mifflin: Boston, 1918), 340, 343.

3. Edwin Howland Blashfield, "Biographical Sketch of Evangeline Wilbour Blashfield," unpublished manuscript in the New-York Historical Society, 7.

4. Edwin Blashfield, "A Plea for Municipal Art," paper read at the first meeting of the Municipal Art Society, March 22, 1893, reprinted in Barr Ferree, ed., *Yearbook of the Art Societies of New York: 1898–1899* (New York: Leonard Scott, 1899), 94–98.

5. Daniel H. Burnham, "White City and Capital City," *Century*, February 1902, p. 619; and Will H. Low, *A Painter's Progress* (New York: Garland, 1910), 251.

6. Rodman Gilder, *The Battery* (Boston: Houghton Mifflin, 1936), 74–75, 85–86.

7. Quoted in Francis R. Kowsky, "The Central Park Gateways: Harbingers of French Urbanism Confront the American Landscape Tradition," in Susan R. Stein, ed., *The Architecture of Richard Morris Hunt* (Chicago: University of Chicago Press, 1986), 79–89.

8. Frederick E. Church, Calvert Vaux, and Henry G. Stebbins, "Report of the Committee on Statues in the Park," April 25, 1873, reprinted in Frederick Law Olmsted, Jr., and Theodora Kimball, eds., *Frederick Law Olmsted, Landscape Architect, 1822–1903* (New York: Benjamin Blom, 1970), 488–93.

9. Blashfield, "Biographical Sketch," 7½.

10. Ibid., 2.

11. Evangeline Blashfield, address to the Nineteenth Century Club, March 12, 1895, reprinted in *How to Make New York a Beautiful City* (New York: Nineteenth Century Club, 1895).

12. Blashfield, "Biographical Sketch," 7.

13. Edwin Blashfield, "A Plea for Municipal Art," reprinted in Barr Ferree, ed., *Yearbook of the Art Societies of New York: 1898–1899* (New York: Leonard Scott, 1899), 94–98.

14. "A Lively First Annual," *New York Times*, April 25, 1893, p. 2.

15. "To Make the City Beautiful," *Times*, April 20, 1893, p. 6.

16. "A Move to Beautify New York," *Times*, January 3, 1894, p. 4.

17. Ibid.

18. Arnold W. Brunner, speaking in Boston in 1915, quoted by J. Horace McFarland, "The City Planner," in Robert I. Aitken et al., *Arnold W. Brunner and His Work* (New York: AIA, 1926), 29.

19. The presidency was offered to Augustus Saint-Gaudens, but he declined because he was "frightened to death" of making speeches: "I should demoralize everything within sight and hearing." Augustus Saint-Gaudens, letter to Hamilton Bell, reprinted in Homer St. Gaudens, ed., *The Reminiscences of Augustus St. Gaudens*, vol. 2 (New York: Century, 1913), 115.

20. Morrison H. Heckscher, "Hunt and the Metropolitan Museum of Art," in Susan R. Stein, ed., *The Architecture of Richard Morris Hunt* (Chicago: University of Chicago Press, 1986), 172–87.

21. Michele H. Bogart, *Public Sculpture and the Civic Ideal in New York City, 1890–1930* (Chicago: University of Chicago Press, 1989), 158–65.

22. "Art Notes," *Times*, March 25, 1901, p. 8.

23. Calvin Tomkins, *Merchants and Masterpieces*, rev. ed. (New York: Henry Holt, 1989), 91.

24. Bogart, *Public Sculpture*, 163–64.

25. Tomkins, *Merchants and Masterpieces*, 80.

26. MAS Minutes, November 24, 1958. Joseph Howland Hunt was president from 1916 to 1917 and again from 1919 to 1923; his first term was shortened by illness. Richard Howland Hunt served from 1926 to 1927.

27. Concerning Tammany's confusion of artist and artisan, see H. A. Caparn, Letter to the Editor, "The Artist and the Artisan," *Times*, February 2, 1902, p. 14.

28. "To Promote a Neglected Art," *Times*, May 29, 1893, p. 4.

29. "The Question of a Site," *Times*, March 29, 1895. Clipping in the Seeley-Lamb Collection.

30. Quoted in Bogart, *Public Sculpture*, 64.

31. "The Question of a Site," *Times*, March 29, 1895. Clipping in the Seeley-Lamb Collection.

32. Samuel Parsons, Jr., Letter to the Editor, "Save Mount Tom," *Times*, February 21, 1899, p. 6.

33. "New Site for a Monument," *Times*, November 1, 1899, p. 14.

34. "Riverside Park Monument," *Times*, October 6, 1899, p. 6.

35. "The Question of a Site," *Times*, March 29, 1895. Clipping in the Seeley-Lamb Collection.

CHAPTER 2

1. Candace Wheeler, speech to the Nineteenth Century Club, March 12, 1895, reprinted in *How to Make New York a Beautiful City* (New York: Nineteenth Century Club, 1895), 28.

2. Doreen Bolger Burke et al., *In Pursuit of Beauty: Americans and the Aesthetic Movement* (New York: Rizzoli, 1987), 481–82.

3. Richard Guy Wilson, Diane H. Pilgrim, and Richard N. Murray, *The American Renaissance: 1876–1917* (New York: Brooklyn Museum, 1979), 19, 230.

4. "Architectural Aberrations No. 10: The New Criminal Court Building, New York," *Architectural Record* 3 (April–June 1894): 429–32.

5. "The Building Department," *New York Times*, November 13, 1901, p. 8.

6. "All Ordered Out of Criminal Courts," *Times*, November 4, 1909, p. 1. Also see "Criminal Courts Now Safe," *Times*, March 22, 1912, p. 18.

7. "Embellishing the City," *Times*, August 10, 1899, p. 6.

8. Ibid.

9. John G. Agar, quoted in "Says the Mayor Is Arrogant," *Times*, March 19, 1899, p. 3.

10. "Embellishing the City," *Times*, August 10, 1899, p. 6.

11. "Horgan and Slattery," *Times*, March 4, 1902, p. 8.

12. For samples of Horgan & Slattery's work, see "Fire Engine House No. 22, East Twelfth Street, New York, N.Y.," *American Architect and Building News* 64 (November 2, 1901): plate; "Water-Tower No. 3, and Hook and Ladder House No. 24, New York, N.Y.," *American Architect and Building News* 75 (February 8, 1902): plate; and Robert A. M. Stern, Gregory Gilmartin, and John Montague Massengale, *New York 1900* (New York: Rizzoli, 1983), pp. 72–73.

13. John De Witt Warner, "Bridges and Art," address delivered before the National Sculpture Society, December 19, 1899, reprinted in *Public Improvements* 2 (January 1, 1900): 97.

14. "Meeting of Architects," *Times*, January 4, 1899, p. 7.

15. George B. McClellan, Jr., *The Gentleman and the Tiger: The Autobiography of George B. McClellan, Jr.*, ed. Harold C. Syrett (Philadelphia: Lippincott, 1956), 52.

16. MAS Minutes, April 30, 1906.

17. *Times*: "Panels for City Hall," August 5, 1903, p. 14; "Art Commission Meets," August 12, 1903, p. 9; "Art Notes," October 25, 1903, p. 8.

18. "City Hall Art Censured," *Times*, December 1, 1903, p. 16.

19. "Powers of the Art Commission," *Times*, December 3, 1903, p. 8.

20. Margot Gayle and Michele Cohen, *The Art Commission and the Municipal Art Society Guide to Manhattan's Outdoor Sculpture* (New York: Prentice-Hall, 1988), 283–86.

21. Ruth McAneny Loud, interview by author.

22. The fullest account of the Plaza is provided by Michele H. Bogart, *Public Sculpture and the Civic Ideal in New York City, 1890–1930* (Chicago: University of Chicago Press, 1989), 205–17. For Bitter's career, see Ferdinand Schevill, *Karl Bitter: A Biography* (Chicago: University of Chicago Press, 1917); and James M. Dennis, *Karl Bitter: Architectural Sculptor, 1867–1915* (Madison: University of Wisconsin Press, 1967).

23. Ruth McAneny Loud, interview by author.

24. Schevill, *Karl Bitter: A Biography*, 24.

25. Karl Bitter, "From Battery to Harlem," *Municipal Affairs* 3 (December 1899): 635.

26. Letter, Karl Bitter to Herbert Adams, quoted in Dennis, *Karl Bitter: Architectural Sculptor*, 233.

CHAPTER 3

1. MAS Minutes, April 29, 1901.

2. "Municipal Art Society," *New York Times*, April 30, 1901, p. 9.

3. Charles de Kay, "Civic Art in New York," *Times*, August 11, 1901, p. 12.

4. Ibid.

5. MAS Minutes, June 25, 1902; and Calvin Tomkins, "Review of the Work of the Municipal Art Society by the President," *MAS Bulletin* no. 24½ (1905).

6. MAS Minutes, April 27, 1907.

7. "Public Improvements Planned and in Progress in the City of Greater New York," *Times*, August 11, 1901, sec. 4, p. 15.

8. David C. Hammack, *Power and Society: Greater New York at the Turn of the Century* (New York: Russell Sage Foundation, 1982), 193.

9. John De Witt Warner, "Matters That Suggest Themselves," *Municipal Affairs* 2 (March 1898): 123–32.

10. Hammack, *Power and Society*, 226.

11. "To Improve New York," *Times*, April 20, 1902, p. 6.

12. George B. McClellan, Jr., *The Gentleman and the Tiger: The Autobiography of George B. McClellan, Jr.*, ed. Harold C. Syrett (Philadelphia: Lippincott, 1956), 166.

13. M. R. Werner, *Tammany Hall* (Garden City, N.Y.: Doubleday, Doran, 1928), 424–26.

14. "To Improve New York," *Times*, April 20, 1902, p. 6.

15. "Municipal Art Societies," *Times*, June 2, 1901, p. 6.

16. "Municipal Embellishment," *Times*, January 1, 1902, p. 6.

17. "A New Municipal Building," *Times*, September 28, 1902, p. 6.

18. Lawrence Veiller, Reminiscences. Oral History Collection, Columbia University.

19. Richard Skolnik, "Civic Group Progressivism in New York City," *New York History* 51 (1970): 41–59.

20. MAS Minutes, June 25, 1902.

21. Quoted in Skolnik, "Civic Group Progressivism," 44.

22. James K. Kettlewell, *Saratoga Springs: An Architectural History* (Saratoga Springs: Lyrical Ballad Book Store, 1991), 88–90.

23. *Who's Who in New York City and State* (New York: Hamersley, 1904), 615.

24. B. F. Cresson, "Calvin Tomkins, Affiliate," *American Society of Civil Engineers: Memoirs of Deceased Members*. Collection of the New-York Historical Society.

25. Ibid., 2.

26. The major source of information on the Lambs is the Seeley-Lamb Collection, which includes Charles and Ella Condie Lamb's correspondence and scrapbooks (they used a clipping service). I am grateful to Charles Lamb's granddaughter, Mrs. Barea Lamb Seeley of Tenafly, New Jersey, for access to the collection. Mrs. Seeley is preparing a biography of the painter Ella Condie Lamb, Charles Lamb's wife, who worked in the J. & R. Lamb Studios. For Charles Lamb, see George R. Collins and Carol Willis, *Visionary Drawings of Architecture and Planning* (Cambridge: MIT Press, 1979). For Frederick Lamb, I have also relied on an unpublished manuscript by David Adams, "Frederick S. Lamb's Opalescent Vision of 'A Broader Art': The Reunion of Art and Craft in Public Murals."

27. Lamb, "The Beautifying of Our Cities," 172, 175, 185, 188; and Adams, "Lamb's Opalescent Vision," 26.

28. Frederick S. Lamb, "Lessons from the Expositions," *Craftsman* 3 (October 1902): 49–58; Adams, "Lamb's Opalescent Vision," 6.

29. Clippings in the Seeley-Lamb Collection.

30. Douglas Gilbert, "Lamb, the Builder, Envisions a City of Towers," *New York Telegram*. Clipping in the Seeley-Lamb Collection.

31. Ibid.

32. Ibid.

33. "The President Arraigned," *Times*, July 5, 1899, p. 1.

34. "Sculptors to the Front," *Times*, July 30, 1899, p. 14.

35. "The Dewey Arch," *Times*, September 27, 1899, p. 6.

36. "The Dewey Arch," *Times*, September 3, 1899, p. 16.

37. "A Permanent Dewey Arch," *Times*, October 3, 1899, p. 3.

38. "Preserve the Arch!" *Times*, October 12, 1899, p. 6.

39. "Would Beautify the City," *Times*, December 20, 1899, p. 9.

40. "To Build No Naval Arch," *Times*, December 17, 1901, p. 3. So powerful was the memory of the Dewey Arch, and of that rare union of art and public euphoria, that the idea kept returning to haunt New York. As soon as Nicoll's committee abandoned the idea, it was taken up by the Naval Academy Alumni Association, who hired Ernest Flagg, designer of the Naval Academy in Annapolis, to produce his own design. In 1905 the idea of the arch was revived, this time for the Hudson-Fulton celebration. Yet another arch was proposed for the Battery in 1919, and that same year Thomas Hastings designed a triumphal arch on Madison Square, just where Dewey's had been, to welcome the troops home from World War I.

41. "To Embellish the City," *Times*, December 24, 1899, p. 22.

. Charles Rollinson Lamb, *The Possibilities of the Esthetic Development of Our City* (New York: unicipal Engineers of the City of New York, 1908), 189. Seeley-Lamb Collection.

. "Meeting of Architects," *Times*, January 4, 1899, p. 7.

. "Water Front Discussed," *Times*, February 23, 1899, p. 8.

. "Sculptors and Painters Dine," *Times*, May 6, 1899, p. 7.

. Julius F. Harder, "The City's Plan," *Municipal Affairs* 2 (March 1898): 24–45. Also see bert A. M. Stern, Gregory Gilmartin, and John Montague Massengale, *New York 1900* (New rk: Rizzoli, 1983), 28–29.

. Barr Ferree, "In Streets and Papers," *Architects' and Builders' Magazine*. Clipping in the eley-Lamb Collection.

. "Architectural League's Regular Ticket Wins," *Times*, May 3, 1905, p. 18.

. Charles Follen McKim, quoted in William H. Wilson, *The City Beautiful Movement* (Baltimore: hns Hopkins University Press, 1989), 293.

. Russell Sturgis to Charles Rollinson Lamb, December 20, 1901, and Lamb to Sturgis, ecember 28, 1901. Letters in the Seeley-Lamb Collection.

. "Manhattan's Quiet Eddy in Gramercy Park," *Times*, September 24, 1905, sec. 3, p. 7.

. For Lamb's feminism and his role in the National Arts Club, interview with Barea Lamb eley.

HAPTER **4**

. "Art Notes," *New York Times*, March 25, 1901, p. 8.

2. "Municipal Art Society," *Times*, March 17, 1903, p. 2.

3. "Municipal Art Society," *Times*, June 21, 1901, p. 6.

4. M. R. Werner, *Tammany Hall* (New York: Doubleday, Doran, 1928), 166–67.

5. A.D.F. Hamlin, "Report of Committee on Decoration of Public Buildings of the MAS," *AS Bulletin* no. 7 (March 1904): 7.

6. "Report of the Model City Committee," MAS Minutes, April 29, 1902. Also see William Crandall, "The Model City: A Suggestion for the St. Louis Exposition," *Municipal Affairs* 5 Fall 1901): 670–74.

7. William H. Wilson, *The City Beautiful Movement* (Baltimore: Johns Hopkins University Press, 989), 45. Also see Mel Scott, *American City Planning Since 1890* (Los Angeles: University of alifornia Press, 1969), 69–71.

8. Charles de Kay, "Civic Art in New York," *Times Magazine*, August 11, 1901, p. 12.

9. "Growth of the Block Beautiful," *Times*, January 25, 1903, p. 28.

0. Irene Hall, "Report of Committee on Flowers, Vines, and Area Planting," *MAS Bulletin* o. 12 (April 25, 1904).

. Letter to the Editor, "Not a Friend to Tree Planting," *Times*, April 28, 1901, p. 21.

2. "Shade Trees in Cities," *Times*, August 7, 1903, p. 6.

3. Irene Hall, "Report of Committee."

4. MAS Minutes, November 11, 1907.

5. "Street Signs," *Times*, March 3, 1902, p. 8.

6. Letter to the Editor, "Names on Street Lamps," *Times*, July 24, 1899, p. 6.

7. "To Change Street Lamp Signs," *Times*, July 14, 1899, p. 12.

8. Letter, "Names on Street Lamps."

9. Letter to the Editor, "Street Sign Discussion," *Times*, May 17, 1901, p. 8.

20. Charles de Kay, "Civic Art in New York," *Times*, August 11, 1901, sec. 5, p. 12.

21. "Improved Street Signs," *Times*, May 22, 1901, p. 6.

22. "Topics of the Times," *Times*, May 23, 1901, p. 8.

23. "Signs on Street Corners," *Times*, July 11, 1901, p. 6.

24. "For More Street Signs," *Times*, January 6, 1906, p. 5.

25. George B. McClellan, Jr., *The Gentleman and the Tiger: The Autobiography of George B. McClellan, Jr* ed. Harold C. Syrett (Philadelphia: Lippincott, 1956), 201.

26. "Improving Columbus Circle," *Times*, January 5, 1902, p. 6. Also see "Municipal Embellishment," *Times*, January 8, 1902, p. 6.

27. "The Eighth Avenue Circle," *Times*, September 21, 1902, p. 6. Also see "Eighth Avenue Circle," *Times*, April 16, 1903, p. 8.

28. "Improving Columbus Circle," *Times*, January 5, 1902, p. 6.

29. "Municipal Art Society Prizes," *Times*, June 28, 1902, p. 8.

30. MAS Minutes, June 30, 1902.

31. "Times Square Sees Electroliers Unveiled," *Times*, March 17, 1905, p. 6.

32. "Regulating Traffic in Times Square," *Times*, May 14, 1905, p. 14.

33. In 1913 Borough President George McAneny, a longtime Municipalian, tried to replace th electrolier, but the city had sold its remains for scrap metal, and the Mott Iron Works had lost the molds from which it was cast. "Report of Fixtures Committee," MAS Minutes, October 21 and November 24, 1913.

CHAPTER 5

1. John De Witt Warner, "Municipal Betterment in the New York City Elections," *Municipal Affairs* 5 (1901): 625–27.

2. "Unlovely New York," *New York Times*, February 11, 1903, p. 2.

3. " 'Imagination' vs. Honesty," *Times*, February 13, 1903, p. 8.

4. Charles Rollinson Lamb, *The Possibilities of the Esthetic Development of Our City* (New York: Municipal Engineers of the City of New York, 1908), 113–14. Seeley-Lamb Collection.

5. Photographs and clippings in the Seeley-Lamb Collection.

6. Thomas Collier Platt, *The Autobiography of Thomas Collier Platt*, ed. Louis J. Lang (New York: Dodge, 1910), 40.

7. Joshua Henry Cohen, *They Builded Better Than They Knew* (New York: Julian Messner, 1946), 43–44.

8. Lincoln Steffens, "New York: Good Government in Danger," *McClure's*, November 1903, pp. 84–92.

9. Quoted in "The City Beautiful," *Times*, March 15, 1903, p. 6.

10. Henry Curran, *Pillar to Post* (New York: Scribner's, 1941), 55.

11. Steffens, "New York," 86.

12. George B. McClellan, Jr., *The Gentleman and the Tiger: The Autobiography of George B. McClellan, Jr.*, ed. Harold C. Syrett (Philadelphia: Lippincott, 1956), 171.

13. Steffens, "New York," 87.

14. MAS Minutes, April 27, 1903.

15. Tom Buckley, "A Reporter at Large: The Eighth Bridge," *New Yorker*, January 14, 1991, pp. 37–59.

16. "More Justices Must Sit in Packed Court House," *Times*, May 27, 1906, p. 6.

17. "Horgan and Slattery," *Times*, March 5, 1902, p. 8.

18. "To Embellish the City," *Times*, February 1, 1902, p. 8.

19. "The Need of Public Baths," *Times*, March 18, 1902, p. 8.

20. Jacob Riis, *The Battle with the Slum* (New York: Macmillan, 1902), 282.

21. "Roger Morris Park," *Times*, December 30, 1903, p. 6.

22. "Coney Needs Cleansing," *New York Tribune*, July 15, 1901, quoted in Kathy Peiss, *Cheap Amusements: Working Women and Leisure in Turn-of-the-Century New York* (Philadelphia: Temple University Press, 1986), 133.

3. *Times,* July 14, 1899, p. 6.

4. "Mr. Coler's Coney Island Project," *Times,* June 13, 1899, p. 6.

5. "Would Save Lung Block," *Times,* November 14, 1903, p. 16.

6. Riis, *The Battle with the Slum,* 67.

7. One other visitor to the graveyard was a pious young man named William Seabury, who was appalled by the disinterment of his ancestors' remains. This was only his first taste of Tammany's power: Seabury lived to lead the investigation that destroyed Jimmy Walker's career. Gene Fowler, *Beau James: The Life and Times of Jimmy Walker* (New York: Viking, 1949), 5–26, 29–30; George Walsh, *Gentleman Jimmy Walker: Mayor of the Jazz Age* (New York: Praeger, 1974), 221–22; Robert Stern, Gregory Gilmartin, and John Montague Massengale, *New York 1900* (New York: Rizzoli, 1983), 136–37.

8. Riis, *The Battle with the Slum,* 309.

9. David Dunlap, *On Broadway: A Journey Uptown over Time* (New York: Rizzoli, 1990), 13–22.

0. Lamb, *The Possibilities of the Esthetic Development,* 9.

1. Curran, *Pillar to Post,* 114–15.

2. Homer St. Gaudens, ed., *The Reminiscences of Augustus St. Gaudens,* vol. 2 (New York: Century, 1913), 296.

3. Lamb, *The Possibilities of the Esthetic Development,* 89.

4. "Where Shall the Building Be?" *Times,* May 10, 1894, p. 4.

5. Matthew P. Breen, *Thirty Years of New York Politics Up-to-Date* (New York: Breen, 1899), 70.

6. "New Municipal Building," *Times,* March 6, 1903, p. 2.

7. Ibid. Also see *Times:* "The New Hall of Records," May 26, 1899, p. 3; and "Decoration of Public Buildings," May 27, 1899, p. 6.

8. "The Hall of Records," *Times,* March 13, 1901, p. 6.

9. "Plaster for Marble in Hall of Records," *Times,* December 16, 1906, p. 13.

0. Breen, *Thirty Years,* 766–69.

1. Quoted in Michele Bogart, *Public Sculpture and the Civic Ideal in New York City: 1890–1930* (Chicago: University of Chicago Press, 1989), 141.

2. Quoted in Bogart, *Public Sculpture,* 142.

3. Quoted in Bogart, *Public Sculpture,* 144.

4. "Horgan and Slattery Chuckle with Glee," *Times,* March 8, 1903, p. 12.

5. McClellan, *The Gentleman and the Tiger,* 172.

6. *Times:* "No Hall of Records for a Year More," May 31, 1905, p. 16. Also see "Hall of Record Bids," June 24, 1905, p. 4.

7. A.D.F. Hamlin, "Report of Committee on Decoration of Public Buildings of the MAS," *MAS Bulletin* no. 7 (March 1904): 6–7.

8. "Plaster for Marble in Hall of Records," *Times,* December 16, 1906, p. 13.

9. Hamlin, "Report of Committee," 6–7.

0. "City Hall Park," *Times,* July 19, 1902, p. 8.

1. Calvin Tomkins, Charles C. Haight, and Charles R. Lamb, "Memorial of the Municipal Art Society Relative to Proposed Changes in and About City Hall Square in New York City," *MAS Bulletin* (September 1, 1902).

2. *Times:* "New Bridge Department Architect," June 28, 1902, p. 16; and "For an Artistic Bridge," December 20, 1902, p. 10.

3. "The Architectural Embellishment of the New Williamsburg Bridge," *House and Garden,* March 1903, pp. 141–45.

4. Montgomery Schuyler, "Our Four Big Bridges," *Architectural Record* 25 (March 1909): 49–60.

55. Calvin Tomkins, "Manhattan Bridge Connections, Report of the Committee on City Plan," *MAS Bulletin* no. 6 (March 11, 1904).

56. "City Hall Terminal and Offices Planned," *Times*, March 28, 1903, p. 16.

57. H. G. Wells, *The Future in America* (1906; reprint, New York: St. Martin's Press, 1987), 29–30.

58. "Grand Jury Makes a Bridge Presentment," *Times*, May 3, 1901, p. 6.

59. *Times:* "Experts for Bridge Plans," September 12, 1902, p. 16; and "Plan for Bridge Relief," September 30, 1902, p. 16.

60. "Tammany Brigandage," *Times*, February 25, 1892, p. 4.

61. Buckley, "A Reporter at Large," p. 56.

62. *Times:* "Plan City Buildings at Cost of $50,000,000," July 2, 1903, p. 2; "Commissioner Lindenthal's Plan," July 3, 1903, p. 8.

63. *Real Estate Record and Guide* 72 (July 4, 1903): 1; and (July 11, 1903): 45.

64. Calvin Tomkins, "Memorial from the MAS to the Board of Estimate," April 27, 1903. MAS Archives.

65. "Report of City Plan Committee of the Municipal Art Society on City Hall Square and Brooklyn Bridge Terminals," *MAS Bulletin* no. 2 (October 5, 1903).

66. Tomkins, "Memorial from the MAS."

67. McClellan, *The Gentleman and the Tiger*, 170.

68. "Grout," *Times*, October 2, 1903, p. 6.

69. McClellan, *The Gentleman and the Tiger*, 170.

70. "Low Administration's Legacy to McClellan," *Times*, November 10, 1903, p. 1.

71. *Times:* "Mr. Low's Legacy," November 11, 1903, p. 8; "Defers Big Improvements," December 2, 1903, p. 9.

72. The new borough president of Manhattan, John F. Ahearn, endorsed the civic center even before assuming office. See "City Hall Park," *Times*, December 30, 1903, p. 6.

CHAPTER 6

1. "The Expansion of New York," *New York Times*, March 29, 1903, p. 6.

2. "Aldermen in Plea for Board's Life," *Times*, March 28, 1915, sec. 3, p. 4; and Henry H. Curran, *Pillar to Post* (New York: Scribner's, 1941), 127–43.

3. "To Improve New York," *Times*, April 20, 1902, p. 6.

4. *Who's Who in New York City and State* (New York: Hamersley, 1904), 107–08.

5. "To Embellish the City," *Times*, February 1, 1902, p. 8.

6. Quoted in Harvey Kantor, *Modern Urban Planning in New York City: Origins and Evolution, 1890–1933* (Ph.D. diss., New York University, 1971), 73–74.

7. "To Lower Forty-second Street," *Times*, July 24, 1903, p. 6.

8. "Money for New Bridges," *Times*, July 26, 1902, p. 2.

9. Charles Rollinson Lamb, *The Possibilities of the Esthetic Development of Our City* (New York: Municipal Engineers of the City of New York, 1908), 95, 97. Seeley-Lamb Collection.

10. "Central Park and Blackwell's Island Bridge," *Times*, April 26, 1903, p. 6.

11. "The City's New Bridges," *Times*, May 31, 1903, p. 29.

12. "Blocks Street Widening," *Times*, July 23, 1903, p. 14.

13. "New Bridge Approaches," *Times*, November 20, 1902, p. 6.

14. MAS Minutes, November 12, 1902.

15. "To Improve the City," *Times*, December 2, 1902, p. 8.

16. "Plan to Beautify New York," *Times*, November 30, 1902, p. 16.

17. Frederick Stymetz Lamb, "New York City of the Future," *House and Garden*, June 1903, p. 299.

18. Quoted in MAS Minutes, December 20, 1902.

19. "Municipal Art," *Times*, April 17, 1904. Clipping in the Seeley-Lamb Collection.

20. Frederick Stymetz Lamb, "City of the Future," 300.

21. "To Replan the City," *Times*, April 24, 1903, p. 8.

22. "To Make the City Beautiful," *Times*, April 29, 1903, p. 9.

23. "To Replan the City," *Times*, April 28, 1903, p. 8.

24. "Changes in the City Map," *Times*, May 2, 1903, p. 3.

25. Benjamin R. C. Low, *Seth Low* (New York: Putnam, 1925), 70–71.

26. "To Improve the City," *Times*, December 2, 1902, p. 8.

27. MAS Minutes, December 16, 1903.

28. Ibid., January 20, 1904.

29. George B. McClellan, Jr., *The Gentleman and the Tiger: The Autobiography of George B. McClellan, Jr.*, ed. Harold C. Syrett (Philadelphia: Lippincott, 1956), 180.

30. *New York Evening Telegram*, May 27, 1900, quoted in McClellan, *The Gentleman and the Tiger*, 11–12.

31. Letter, F. D. Millet to McClellan, March 2, 1908, quoted in McClellan, *The Gentleman and the Tiger*, 32.

32. "Mayor Gets Gold Medal from Architects," *Times*, January 29, 1908, p. 3.

33. Ibid. Also see "No City Architect Needed," *Times*, January 31, 1909, p. 10.

34. McClellan, *The Gentleman and the Tiger*, 95.

35. Ibid., 181.

36. Ibid., 173.

37. Ibid., 181.

38. "Mayor Names Men to Make City Beautiful," *Times*, March 13, 1904, p. 12.

39. McClellan, *The Gentleman and the Tiger*, 241.

40. "Municipal Art," *Times*, April 17, 1904. Clipping in the Seeley-Lamb Collection.

41. *Report of the New York City Improvement Commission*, 1904.

42. C. R. Lamb, *The Possibilities of the Esthetic Development*, 99–100.

43. Photograph in the Seeley-Lamb Collection.

44. "Subway a Year Old: What It Has Done," *Times*, October 27, 1905, p. 9, col. 3.

45. MAS Minutes, April 25, 1905.

46. Ibid., November 11, 1907.

47. See Montgomery Schuyler, *Sticks and Stones* (New York: Boni & Liveright, 1924), 18.

48. *Times*: "Don't Like the Park Wall," April 16, 1905, p. 14. Also see "Would Raze Park Wall," May 2, 1905, p. 12.

49. "Keep the Park Intact," *Times*, May 25, 1905, p. 6.

50. "A Bad Feature," *Times*, January 8, 1905, p. 8.

51. Frederick Stymetz Lamb, "New York City Improvement Report," *Charities* 19 (1908): 1536; quoted in Mel Scott, *American City Planning Since 1890* (Berkeley: University of California Press, 1969), 82.

52. "Costly City Beautiful," *Times*, November 11, 1907, p. 3.

53. "Ninety-eight Million Dollars for Improvements," *Times*, November 10, 1907, sec. 5, p. 6.

54. "Suggests Vast Scheme for Greatest City," *Times*, January 3, 1905, p. 6.

55. John De Witt Warner, et al., "Report of the Committee on Charter Revision," reprinted in *MAS Bulletin* no. 40 (November 30, 1908).

56. "Liberal Plan for the Terminal of the New Bridge," *New York World*, October 15, 1906, clipping in the Seeley-Lamb Collection; and Lamb, *The Possibilities of the Esthetic Development*, 96.

57. Lamb, *The Possibilities of the Esthetic Development*," 104.

58. "Says Chelsea Park Is Costing City Dear," *Times*, September 10, 1906, p. 2.

59. "Liberal Plan for the Terminal."

60. MAS Minutes, January 9, 1906.

61. MAS Minutes, April 30, 1906.

CHAPTER 7

1. New York spent $45 million more in 1909 than in 1904, and its borrowing capacity was growing by $40 million a year. "Mayor's Message Reviews His Work," *New York Times*, January 5, 1909, p. 4.

2. MAS Minutes, April 30, 1906.

3. *Times:* "Jefferson Park Opens with a Field Day," October 8, 1905, p. 6. Also see "A New $3,000,000 City Playground," October 15, 1905, sec. 1, p. 8.

4. "Jefferson Park Opens."

5. C. R. Lamb, *The Possibilities of the Esthetic Development of Our City* (New York: Municipal Engineers of the City of New York, 1908), 88. Seeley-Lamb Collection.

6. "Tell How to Make the City Beautiful," *Times*, October 21, 1908, p. 4.

7. "The Palisades Park Project," *Times*, April 1, 1901, p. 8.

8. Henry H. Klein, *My Last Fifty Years: An Autobiographical History of "Inside" New York* (New York: Klein, 1935), 54–56; George Walsh, *Gentleman Jimmy Walker: Mayor of the Jazz Age* (New York: Prager, 1974), 51.

9. Letter, Charles Stover to M. H. Morgan, filed with MAS Minutes, April 18, 1907. Also see "Urge Quick Action on Ocean Park Site," *Times*, November 29, 1909, p. 5.

10. Kathy Peiss, *Cheap Amusements: Working Women and Leisure in Turn-of-the-Century New York* (Philadelphia: Temple University Press, 1986), 122.

11. *Times:* "Divergent Views of Seaside Park," December 3, 1909, p. 7. Also see "The Rockaway Park," December 3, 1909, p. 10; "Objection to Seaside Park," December 5, 1909, p. 2; "Defends Seaside Park," December 9, 1909, p. 4; "Rockaway Park Purchase Laid Over," December 18, 1909, p. 9.

12. Klein, *My Last Fifty Years*, 49, 138–41.

13. Excursion boats did arrive. Kathy Peiss, *Cheap Amusements*, 122, 140.

14. Charles de Kay, "Manhattan Beautiful," *Times*, April 1, 1905, sec. 4, p. 8.

15. Submission form for the Slocum Memorial Fountain. Files of the Art Commission of the City of New York.

16. Margot Gayle and Michele Cohen, *The Art Commission and the Municipal Art Society Guide to Manhattan's Outdoor Sculpture* (New York: Prentice-Hall Press, 1988), 87.

17. "Metz Heckled at City Plan Meeting," *Times*, May 6, 1909, p. 2.

18. Walter Cook, "Report of a Committee of the Art Commission," February 6, 1906. Files of the Art Commission of the City of New York.

19. "Low Administration's Legacy to McClellan," *Times*, November 10, 1903, p. 1; Harvey Kantor, *Modern Urban Planning in New York City: Origins and Evolution, 1890–1933* (Ph.D. diss., New York University, 1971), 46.

20. *Times:* "Rushing Work on New Court House for Queens," April 11, 1909, p. 13; "Dead Man Carried on Queens Pay Roll," November 2, 1910, p. 8; "Queens Building Inquiry," November 3, 1910, p. 5; Christopher Gray, "Beneath the Grime, Corruption," December 15, 1991, sec. 10, p. 5.

21. "City Architects," *Times*, July 2, 1905, p. 6.

22. "A New Public Bath," *Real Estate Record and Guide* 84 (July 3, 1909): 9–10.

23. Henry Rutgers Marshall, address to the Nineteenth Century Club, March 12, 1895, reprinted in *How to Make New York a Beautiful City* (New York: Nineteenth Century Club, 1895), 7.

24. "Wood Pavements Downtown," *Times*, June 20, 1905, p. 8.

. Charles Rollinson Lamb, "Report of Thoroughfares Committee," MAS Minutes, April 30, 06.

. Quoted in M. R. Werner, Tammany Hall (New York: Doubleday, Doran, 1928), 515–16.

. Henry Bruère, quoted in "Novel Bureau That Will Make an Organized Hunt for Municipal rafters,'" Times, April 8, 1906, sec. 3, p. 6. Also see Robert Caro, The Power Broker: Robert Moses 1 the Fall of New York (New York: Vintage, 1975), 60–63.

. John De Witt Warner, "Civic Centers," Municipal Affairs 6 (March 1902): 23.

. "Architects Appeal for Municipal Art," Times, November 9, 1905, p. 18.

. "Civic Centers," Times, March 16, 1905, p. 8.

. MAS Minutes, December 18, 1906.

. Mardges Bacon, Ernest Flagg: Beaux-Arts Architect and Urban Reformer (New York: Architectural istory Foundation, 1986), 6–16, 72.

. Ernest Flagg, "Report of the Staten Island Committee," MAS Bulletin no. 25 (September 19,)05).

. Matthew P. Breen, Thirty Years of New York Politics Up-to-Date (New York: Breen, 1899), 722.

. Ibid.

. Ibid., 723–27. Also see Evelyn Gonzalez, "From Suburb to City: The Development of e Bronx, 1890–1940," in Timothy Rub, Richard Plunz, and Evelyn Gonzalez, Building a rough: Architecture and Planning in the Bronx, 1890–1940 (New York: Bronx Museum of the Arts,)86), 8–28.

7. Quoted in Gonzalez, "From Suburb to City," 10.

8. Breen, Thirty Years, 747–48.

9. "Bronx's Grand Boulevard," Times, October 29, 1899, p. 15.

). Times: "President Haffen's Fight for Big Bronx Concourse," April 6, 1902, p. 3; "Bronx oncourse Act Signed," July 22, 1902, p. 14.

1. "New York's Great New Driveway," Times, August 17, 1902, p. 24.

2. "Bronx Building," Times, August 28, 1921, quoted in Richard Plunz, "Reading Bronx Iousing, 1890–1940," in Rub, Plunz, and Gonzalez, Building a Borough, 38.

3. Albert E. Davis, "Report of the Bronx Committee," MAS Minutes, January 9, 1906.

4. Ibid.

5. Edward Hagaman Hall, Letter to the Editor, "Rodman Drake Park," Times, March 29, 909, p. 12.

6. MAS Minutes, November 7, 1907.

7. Montgomery Schuyler, "Along the Harlem River Branch," Architectural Record 24 (December 908): 417–29; Robert A. M. Stern, Gregory Gilmartin, and John Montague Massengale, New ork 1900 (New York: Rizzoli, 1983), 44–45.

8. MAS objected in principle to the fact that it was a state commission, which seemed to iolate the principle of home rule, but given the fact that the parkway extended well into Vestchester County it was silly to demand city control of the project.

9. "Claims the Laurels for Courthouse Plans," Times, March 17, 1905.

0. Louis L. Haffen, "Bronx Only Beginning Its Era of Prosperity and Development," Times, ebruary 25, 1906, sec. 5, p. 7.

1. J. G. Phelps Stokes, "Report of Civic Center Committee of MAS," February 8, 1904; eprinted in MAS Bulletin no. 4 (1904). MAS Archives. Also see MAS Minutes, October 28, 903; November 25, 1903; and August 9, 1904.

52. Henry Rutgers Marshall, Loyall Farragut, and William J. Coombs, "Report of a Committee of the Art Commission," June 3, 1903. Files of the Art Commission of the City of New York.

53. Times: "Claims the Laurels." Also see "Architect Wins Suit," June 9, 1909, p. 5.

54. Edwin R. Lewinson, John Purroy Mitchel: The Boy Mayor of New York (New York: Astra Books, 1965), 43–44.

55. "The Parks for Public Use," *Times*, June 4, 1908, p. 2.

56. "Park Privileges," *Times*, June 7, 1908, sec. 2, p. 8.

57. *Times:* "Gov. Hughes Ousts President Haffen," August 30, 1909, p. I. Also see "City Paid $252,118 for a $4,300 Marsh," March 24, 1908, p. 14.

58. Lewinson, *John Purroy Mitchel*, 44.

59. Timothy Rub, "The Institutional Presence in the Bronx," in Rub, Plunz, and Gonzalez, *Building a Borough*, 84, 87, 90.

CHAPTER 8

1. Edward Cohen and Othmar Ammann, quoted in Tom Buckley, "A Reporter at Large: the Eighth Bridge," *New Yorker*, January 14, 1991, p. 51.

2. "To Relieve the Bridge Congestion," *New York Times*, April 23, 1902, p. 8.

3. "Manhattan Bridge," *Times*, January 11, 1906, p. 8.

4. "Bridge Engineer Resigns," *Times*, April 13, 1902, p. 4.

5. "Manhattan Bridge."

6. "More Justices Must Sit in Packed Court House," *Times*, May 27, 1906, p. 6.

7. "Civic Center," *Times*, March 16, 1905, p. 8.

8. "Score Hurt in Bridge Crush," *Times*, June 24, 1905, p. I.

9. "New Terminal to Solve Brooklyn Bridge Congestion," *Times*, August 6, 1911, sec. 5, p. 3.

10. Ibid.

11. Letter, Gustav Lindenthal to the Art Commission, July 12, 1904, reprinted in "Discussions of Manhattan Bridge Plans," *MAS Bulletin* no. 13 (1904): 15.

12. Letter, Lindenthal to Art Commission, 13–16.

13. Buckley, "Reporter at Large," 56.

14. MAS Minutes, April 19, 1904.

15. Letters of William H. Baur and J. Burkitt Webb to Calvin Tomkins, July 9 and 11, 1904, reprinted in "Discussion of Manhattan Bridge Plans," *MAS Bulletin* no. 13 (1904): 9–13.

16. Letter, Lindenthal to the Art Commission, 13–16.

17. Calvin Tomkins, record of testimony before the Art Commission, Municipal Art Society File, Archives of the Art Commission of the City of New York.

18. "Resolutions of the Municipal Art Society Regarding the Bridge Design," Municipal Art Society File, Archives of the Art Commission of the City of New York.

19. "Lamb Scores Audience," *Times*, January 20, 1905, p. 16.

20. Arnold Brunner, Letter to the Editor, "Mr. Lamb and the Architectural League," *Times*, January 21, 1905, p. 8.

21. Charles M. Shean, Letter to the Editor, "Justice to Mr. Lamb," *Times*, January 22, 1905, p. 8.

22. *Times:* "Manhattan Bridge," December 9, 1905, p. 6. Also see "Manhattan Bridge," January 11, 1906, p. 8.

23. M. R. Werner, *Tammany Hall* (New York: Doubleday, Doran, 1928), 346.

24. "Manhattan Bridge," *Times*, March 15, 1906, p. 8, and March 31, 1906, p. 8.

25. "Manhattan Bridge," *Times*, April 5, 1906, p. 8.

26. McClellan's account of the controversy in his memoirs is so wildly inaccurate that it cannot be the result of a fading memory: it is a pack of lies. George B. McClellan, Jr., *The Gentleman and the Tiger: The Autobiography of George B. McClellan, Jr.*, ed. Harold C. Syrett (Philadelphia: Lippincott, 1956), 246.

27. Montgomery Schuyler, "Our Four Big Bridges," *Architectural Record* 25 (March 1909): 149–60.

28. "Wanted—A Plan," *Times*, March 29, 1908, sec. 2, p. 8.

9. "Repeating Old Errors," *Times*, December 16, 1905, p. 10.

10. "The Manhattan Bridge Terminals," *Times*, December 20, 1905, p. 10.

11. "Interborough Transit," *Times*, August 17, 1908, p. 6.

12. Calvin Tomkins, "Shall Brooklyn Be Held Back for New Jersey?" *MAS Bulletin* no. 27 (1906).

13. Letter, Calvin Tomkins, chair of the Committee on City Plan, to the Honorable Public Service Commission for the First District, City of New York, July 23, 1907; reprinted in *MAS Bulletin* no. 32 (1907).

14. "Millions Wasted, but No Money for Subways." Clipping in the Seeley-Lamb Collection.

15. "Why the East Side Rejoices—A Lesson," *Times*, May 12, 1908, p. 6.

16. "A Memorial Tower, the East Side's Gift," *Times*, May 17, 1908, sec. 4, p. 8.

17. Ibid.

18. Frank Bailey, "Transit Improvements to Benefit Brooklyn," *Times*, January 5, 1908, sec. 2, p. 14.

19. "Wanted—A Plan."

20. "McAneny Approves Tunnel for BRT," *Times*, December 24, 1913, p. 14.

21. "No Money for Subways."

22. "A Speculation for the City," *Times*, May 8, 1908, p. 6.

23. "New Yorkers Are on the Move," *Times*, April 3, 1908, p. 8.

24. "No Money for Subways."

25. Jenna Weissman Joselit, "The Landlord as Czar," in Ronald Lawson, ed., *The Tenant Movement in New York City 1904–1984* (New Brunswick, N.J.: Rutgers University Press, 1986), 39–44.

26. W. H. Chesebrough, "Influence Affecting Business of New York," *Times*, January 5, 1908, sec. 2, p. 14.

27. Bailey, "Transit Improvements."

28. Joselit, "Landlord," 44.

CHAPTER 9

1. Evangeline Blashfield, address, March 12, 1895; reprinted in *How to Make New York a Beautiful City* (New York: Nineteenth Century Club, 1895), 35.

2. H. G. Wells, *The Future in America* (1906; reprint, New York: St. Martin's Press, 1987), 114.

3. The saloon law was revised in 1905 to exclude hotel bars. "The Church and the Hotel," *New York Times*, May 27, 1905, p. 8.

4. "To Embellish the City," *Times*, December 24, 1899, p. 22.

5. "Street Signs," *Times*, April 15, 1902, p. 8.

6. John Martin, "Report of the Committee on Advertising Signs," *MAS Bulletin* no. 23 (April 1905), 6.

7. "Street Signs."

8. *Times*: "Mr. Rives on 'Sky Signs,'" April 24, 1902, p. 16. Also see "The Sky Signs," April 25, 1903, p. 8.

9. Barr Ferree, "In Streets and Papers," *Architects' and Builders' Magazine.* Undated clipping in the Seeley-Lamb Collection.

10. George B. McClellan, Jr., *The Gentleman and the Tiger: The Autobiography of George B. McClellan, Jr.,* ed. Harold C. Syrett (Philadelphia: Lippincott, 1956), 187, 189.

11. Ibid., 209.

12. Ibid., 209–10.

13. John Martin, "Report of the Committee on Advertising Signs," *MAS Bulletin* no. 23 (April 1905), 1, 3.

14. Quoted in Brian J. Cudaby, *Under the Sidewalks of New York*, rev. ed. (New York: Stephen Greene Press, 1989), 32.

15. Martin, "Committee on Advertising Signs," 9.

16. "A Way Out," *Times*, January 20, 1905, p. 8.

17. Calvin Tomkins, "Memorial from the Municipal Art Society to the Rapid Transit Commission," *MAS Bulletin* no. 16 (November 9, 1904), 1–3.

18. "Company Has 48 Hours to Move Subway Signs," *Times*, February 4, 1905, p. 16.

19. *Times*: "Court Halts City in Subway Sign War," February 8, 1905, p. 8. Also see "The Subway Advertising," February 8, 1905, p. 8.

20. MAS Minutes, April 25, 1905.

21. Letter to the Editor, "A Brief for Subway Signs," *Times*, February 13, 1905, p. 6.

22. Quoted in Cudaby, *Under the Sidewalks*, 32.

23. "Subway Advertising Upheld," *Times*, December 11, 1906, p. 7.

24. *Times*: "Forbids Auto Coach 'Ads,'" January 6, 1909, p. 1; "Can't Advertise on Buses," Ma 30, 1911, p. 1.

25. *Times*: "Good Advice from the Mayor," April 21, 1910, p. 10. Also see "Not So Sure Tha They Pay," June 14, 1910, p. 6.

26. "No 'Ads' On Streetcars," *Times*, November 17, 1911, p. 9.

27. Cudaby, *Under the Sidewalks*, 32, 187.

28. Quoted in "Favor Signs in Subways," *Times*, April 26, 1905, p. 2.

29. Martin, "Report of the Committee," 1, 3.

30. MAS Minutes, May 14, 1907.

31. "Municipal Art Society," *Times*, April 1, 1905, p. 11.

32. Martin, "Report of the Committee," 5, 6.

33. "Advertising Art Shown," *Times*, January 10, 1909, p. 12.

34. "War on Advertising Signs," *Times*, May 28, 1907, p. 14.

35. MAS Minutes, April 9 and May 14, 1907.

36. MAS Minutes, December 27, 1909.

37. *Times*: "Autoists Begin War on Highway Signs," August 31, 1911, p. 5. Also see "Autoists Plan Raid on Highway Signs," July 23, 1911, p. 5.

38. "Sign Smashers Out on an Auto Truck," *Times*, September 2, 1911, p. 3.

39. MAS Minutes, October 21, 1913.

40. "All Now in Accord on Billboard Rules," *Times*, May 11, 1914, p. 7.

41. See Everett P. Wheeler, Letter to the Editor, "Encroachments on Streets," *Times*, May 21, 1906, p. 8.

42. *Times*: "Klaw and Erlanger's Ruse," March 13, 1903, p. 2; and "That New Theater Front," March 14, 1903, p. 7.

43. Benedetto Gravagnuolo, *Adolf Loos* (New York: Rizzoli, 1982), 125–33.

44. "The New Fifth Avenue," *Times*, June 27, 1909, sec. 5, p. 1.

45. Ibid.

46. "London and Paris Beaten for Traffic," *Times*, February 2, 1916, p. 9.

47. McClellan, *The Gentleman and the Tiger*, 261.

48. "Like Fifth Avenue Congestion," *Times*, January 16, 1909, p. 10.

49. "Organize to Fight Fifth Ave. Bridge," *Times*, December 2, 1908, p. 2.

50. "Business Men Protest," *Times*, January 26, 1909, p. 18.

51. "Fifth Ave. Bridge Enjoined," *Times*, January 30, 1909, p. 4.

52. "Trial Demanded for Wider 42nd Street," *Times*, December 6, 1908, sec. 2, p. 14.

53. Benjamin Blom, *New York: Photographs, 1850–1950* (New York: Dutton, 1982), 322–23. William Ordway Partridge's Tilden Memorial finally found a home in 1926 at Riverside Drive and 112th Street. As far as I know, no statue of Cleveland was erected.

4. "New Building Rule Hits Whole City," *Times*, May 12, 1909, p. 5.

5. "Eliminating Encroachments beyond the Building Line," *Times*, April 28, 1912, sec. 8, p. 11.

6. *Times:* "Building Projections," June 11, 1916, p. 7. Also see "Building Projections," June 3, 1916, sec. 3, p. 4.

7. "Changes in Lafayette Street," *Times*, June 15, 1912, sec. 8, p. 1.

8. "Thousands of Feet Restored to the Public by the City on Forty-two Thoroughfares," *Times*, November 13, 1912, sec. 8, p. 2.

CHAPTER 10

1. Robert A. M. Stern, Gregory Gilmartin, and John Montague Massengale, *New York 1900* (New York: Rizzoli, 1983), 145.

2. Montgomery Schuyler, "The 'Skyscraper' Up to Date," *Architectural Review* 8 (January–March 1899): 231–37.

3. Harvey Wiley Corbett, "New Stones for Old: Part 2," *Saturday Evening Post*, May 8, 1926, p. 27. Corbett took part in an MAS exhibit as early as 1904, but didn't become active in the Municipal Art Society until the early 1930s.

4. "Discussing the Height of Buildings," *New York Tribune*, April 5, 1894; and "Limits for High Buildings," *New York Times*, April 5, 1894. Clippings in the Seeley-Lamb Collection.

5. Charles Rollinson Lamb, "Civic Architecture from Its Constructive Side," *Municipal Affairs* 2 (March 1898): 46–72.

6. Photographs and clippings in the Seeley-Lamb Collection and in the Charles Rollinson Lamb Collection, Drawings Collection, Avery Library, Columbia University. Also see George R. Collins and Carol Willis, *Visionary Drawings of Architecture and Planning* (Cambridge: MIT Press, 1979).

7. Louis H. Sullivan, "The High Building Question," *Graphic* 5 (December 19, 1891): 405; reprinted in Donald Hoffman, "The Setback Skyscraper City of 1891, an Unknown Essay of Louis H. Sullivan," *Journal of the Society of Architectural Historians* 29 (1970): 181–87.

8. Charles Lamb, *The Possibilities of the Esthetic Development of Our City* (New York: Municipal Engineers of the City of New York, 1908), 101. Seeley-Lamb Collection.

9. "Place Height Limit on New Buildings," *Times*, January 14, 1912, sec. 9, p. 1.

10. "Unlovely New York," *Times*, February 11, 1903, p. 2.

11. Ray Stannard Baker, "The Trust's New Tool: the Labor Boss," *McClure's*, November 1903, pp. 30–43.

12. Paul Starrett, *Changing the Skyline: An Autobiography* (New York: Whittlesey House, 1938), 118.

13. "Reform in Civic Art," *Times*, May 9, 1906, p. 18. Emphasis added.

14. Lincoln Steffens, "New York: Good Government in Danger," *McClure's*, November 1903, p. 84.

15. "The Building Department," *Times*, November 13, 1901, p. 8.

16. "Attack Code Revisers," *Times*, January 29, 1907, p. 4.

17. For an account of Israels's career, see Elizabeth Israels Perry, *Belle Moskowitz: Feminine Politics and the Exercise of Power in the Age of Alfred E. Smith* (New York: Oxford University Press, 1987), 23–26.

18. MAS Minutes, February 12, 1907.

19. "Influence Affecting Business of New Year," *Times*, January 5, 1908, sec. 2, p. 14.

20. MAS Minutes, November 11, 1907.

21. "To Kill New Building Code," *Times*, December 11, 1907, p. 6.

22. "The New Building Code," *Times*, December 17, 1907, p. 10.

23. "To Kill New Building Code."

24. Benjamin Marsh, "City Planning in Justice to the Working Population," *Charities* 19 (February 1, 1908): 1514–18.

25. One of Folks's triumphs was to separate the city's Department of Charities and Correction into two separate agencies, one of them dispensing relief, the other punishment.

26. "Lamb Scores Audience," *Times*, January 20, 1905, p. 16.

27. "Baths before Books Is Maxwell's Maxim," *Times*, September 12, 1908, p. 6.

28. Unidentified clipping in the Seeley-Lamb Collection.

29. MAS Minutes, March 10, 1908.

30. "Puts Tenements before Civic Art," *New York Herald*, 1910. Clipping in the Seeley-Lamb Collection.

31. "There Is Money in Beauty." Unidentified clipping in the Seeley-Lamb Collection.

32. "The Congestion Exhibits," *Times*, March 29, 1908, sec. 2, p. 8.

33. "The Tuberculosis Prizes," *Times*, March 16, 1908, p. 6.

34. "City's Congestion Shown in Models," *Times*, March 14, 1908, p. 3.

35. Ibid.

36. "The Congestion Exhibits."

37. "Would Send Poor to the Suburbs," *Times*, March 12, 1908, p. 2.

38. "City's Congestion Shown in Models."

39. "New York Laid Out All Wrong, He Says," *Times*, March 15, 1908, p. 5.

40. "A Round City," *Times*, March 22, 1908, sec. 2, p. 8.

41. *Times*: "City Planning Exhibit," May 2, 1909, sec. 2, p. 4; and "The City Beautiful on View Tonight," May 3, 1909, p. 5.

42. Clippings in the Seeley-Lamb Collection.

43. "Planning Great Boulevards for New York City," *Times*, August 9, 1908, sec. 5, p. 1.

44. Alan Benson, "The New Ideal in the Building of Cities," *Times*, February 21, 1909, sec. 5, p. 5.

45. "6,000,000 More Here in 1930," *Times*, March 27, 1909, p. 3.

46. "Plan New Exhibit on City Congestion," *Times*, February 7, 1909, p. 5.

47. "Plan Cities Better Abroad," *Times*, May 14, 1909, p. 7.

48. "Forethought in Building a City," *Times*, May 2, 1909, sec. 2, p. 10.

49. Benson, "The New Ideal."

50. "For a City Plan Commission," *Times*, April 11, 1909, sec. 2, p. 4.

51. Marsh, "City Planning," 1515.

52. MAS Minutes, January 15, 1907.

53. Marsh, "City Planning," 1515.

54. Marsh also demanded that elevator capacity be fixed by formula rather than according to the whim of the builder, and that rush-hour traffic be banned on some streets in the business district in order to accommodate the flood of pedestrians. "Would Colonize the Skyscrapers," *Times*, August 7, 1908, p. 5.

55. "City Club Talk on the City's Future," *Times*, January 6, 1909, p. 8.

56. "Morgenthau Fights Evils of Congestion," *Times*, May 4, 1909, p. 18.

57. "Metz Heckled at City Plan Meeting," *Times*, May 6, 1909, p. 2.

58. Unidentified clipping in the Seeley-Lamb Collection.

59. Montgomery Schuyler, "To Curb the Skyscrapers," *Architectural Record* 24 (October 1908): 301.

60. *Times*: "Mr. Flagg's Building Ideal," March 11, 1908, p. 6; "To Limit Skyscrapers," March 7, 1908, p. 3; "Would Limit High Buildings," May 6, 1908, p. 9; "Skyscrapers and the Skyline of the Future," May 10, 1908, sec. 5, p. 1. Also Mardges Bacon, *Ernest Flagg: Beaux-Arts Architect and Urban Reformer* (New York: Architectural History Foundation, 1986), 209–33.

This alarmist argument became a common one. See, for instance, George Ford's remarks in
ls Skyscrapers Poor Investments," *Times*, August 6, 1915, sec. 2, p. 11.
"New York's Growth Will Soon Require a 'Fourth Dimension,' " *Times*, December 23,
5, sec. 3, p. 3.
Lamb, *The Possibilities of the Esthetic Development*, 97–98.
"Double-Decked Streets for Lower New York," *Times*, August 6, 1911, sec. 5, p. 5.
M. H. Morgan, Letter to the Editor, *Real Estate Record and Guide*, November 9, 1909.
ping in the Seeley-Lamb Collection.
Count Henry de la Vaulx, "What You May See before You Die," *New York American*,
ust 12, 1908, reprinted in *The Power of the Press*, 1908. Pamphlet in the Seeley-Lamb
ection.
Morgan, Letter to the Editor.
de la Vaulx, "What You May See."
"Ritz Hotel Plans Filed," *Times*, July 11, 1908, p. 14.
"Building Plans for Equitable Block Will Be Watched with Keen Interest," *Times*, January
1912, sec. 9, p. I.
"The Tall Buildings," *Times*, August 7, 1908, sec. 2, p. 8. Also see *Times*: "909 Foot
scraper to Tower above All," June 30, 1908, p. I; "Plumbing for Sixty-two Stories," July 4,
8, p. 2; and "Equitable May Build Soon," December 4, 1908, p. I.
"New City Building Contract Held Up," *Times*, December 21, 1909, p. 8.
George B. McClellan, Jr., *The Gentleman and the Tiger: The Autobiography of George B. McClellan, Jr.*,
Harold C. Syrett (Philadelphia: Lippincott, 1956), 215–16.
"Aldermen's Records under Searchlight," *Times*, September 20, 1909, p. 18.
Henry H. Curran, *Pillar to Post* (New York: Scribner's, 1941), 145.
"The Building Code," *Times*, May 23, 1912, p. 12.
Quoted in Perry, *Belle Moskowitz*, 82. The death toll rose later to 147.
The cause attracted the wives of other Municipalians as well, like Mrs. George McAneny.
group's motives went beyond puritanism. It hoped to save young women from falling into
hands of prostitution rings. Mayor Gaynor, convinced that typical dance halls hosted
gies," briefly threw himself into the campaign. Kathy Peiss, *Cheap Amusements: Working Women*
Leisure in Turn-of-the-Century New York (Philadelphia: Temple University Press, 1986),
–84; and Perry, *Belle Moskowitz*, 41–57.
Times: Beat Building Code Only after Riot," December 30, 1911, p. I. Also see "The
ding Code's Defeat," December 31, 1911, sec. 2, p. 10.
Lately Thomas, *The Mayor Who Mastered New York* (New York: Morrow, 1969).
Ibid., 56–77.
Clippings in the Seeley-Lamb Collection.

APTER 11

The Memorial Meeting in Honor of George McAneny, pamphlet in the collection of Ruth Loud.
"New York, the Dream City," *New York Times*, March 29, 1910, p. 10.
"New Commission to Develop a City," *Times*, December 20, 1910, p. 22.
Benjamin Marsh, Letter to the Editor, "Marsh on Congestion," *Times*, August 12, 1910,
5.
Ibid.
Harvey Kantor, *Modern Urban Planning in New York City: Origins and Evolution, 1890–1933*
.D. diss., New York University, 1971), 128.
Ibid.; and MAS Minutes, December 18, 1911.

8. MAS Minutes, February 26, September 28, and October 18, 1912; and "Power Over Skyscrapers," *Times*, February 8, 1912, p. 12.

9. John De Witt Warner was horrified that the Municipal Planning Commission Bill would have allowed cities to pay their commissioners. He warned that these jobs would simply beco sinecures, but Bard persuaded MAS to endorse the bill nonetheless. MAS Minutes, April 28, 1913.

10. "Interboro Bids for Subways," *Times*, February 29, 1912, p. 1.

11. Lewis Mumford, *The Culture of Cities* (New York: Harcourt Brace, 1938), 238.

12. "Bridge or a Tunnel Is Richmond's Need," *Times*, December 30, 1915, p. 8.

13. "Marsh Is Expelled from the City Club," *Times*, March 4, 1913, p. 9.

14. "The Building Zone Ordinances," *Times*, June 2, 1916, p. 10.

15. "City Beauty Board Urged by McAneny," *Times*, January 27, 1912, p. 5.

16. This idea was first broached to MAS by Samuel Rea, vice president of the Pennsylvania Railroad. The railroad offered to build the first block of the new thoroughfare, from Thirty-fourth Street to Thirty-fifth, at its own expense. See MAS Minutes, December 12, 191 "New Avenue to Times Square," *Times*, December 14, 1910, p. 1; and "A New Street to Reli Broadway's Congestion," *Times*, January 8, 1911, sec. 5, p. 1. Also note McKim, Mead & White's 1910 presentation drawing in Richard Guy Wilson, Diane H. Pilgrim, and Richard Murray, *The American Renaissance: 1876–1917* (New York: Brooklyn Museum, 1979), 107. For an earlier project, see "C. R. Lamb Suggests Traffic Changes," *Times*, December 5, 1909, sec. p. 4.

17. "Double-Decked Streets for Lower New York," *Times*, August 6, 1911, sec. 5, p. 5.

18. George McAneny, letter to Robert Fulton Cutting, January 21, 1912, quoted in Kantor, *Modern Urban Planning*, 151.

19. MAS Minutes, September 25, 1911.

20. "McAneny Speaks for City Planning Board," *Times*, May 8, 1912, p. 11.

21. Sally A. Kitt Chappell, "A Reconsideration of the Equitable Building in New York," *Jour of the Society of Architectural Historians* 99 (March 1990): 90–95.

22. "Building Plans for Equitable Block Will Be Watched with Keen Interest," *Times*, January 14, 1912, sec. 9, p. 1.

23. *Times*: "Finds Much Wrong in Building Code," June 30, 1912, p. 9; "Reforms Are Need to Prevent Disastrous Fires," January 14, 1912, sec. 5, p. 1.

24. "Chief of Big Skyscrapers Would Curb Heights," *Times*, February 13, 1916, sec. 5, p. 18.

25. "Place Height Limit on New Buildings," *Times*, January 14, 1912, sec. 9, p. 1.

26. Kate Simon, *Fifth Avenue: A Very Social History* (New York: Harcourt Brace Jovanovich, 1978), 116–18.

27. "Equitable to Sell Its Present Site," *Times*, February 16, 1912, p. 18.

28. "Building Plans for Equitable Block."

29. He was one of the investors in the Empire State Building, and in 1919 he built the Capi Theater on Broadway and Fifty-first Street, the biggest and most elegant movie palace of its d Robert A. M. Stern, Gregory Gilmartin, and Thomas Mellins, *New York 1930* (New York: Rizzoli, 1987), 247, 254–56.

30. *Times*: "Wants Equitable Site for Broadway Park," November 28, 1912, p. 1; and "The Equitable Park Plan," November 29, 1912, p. 14.

31. "Plan to Divide Equitable Block with a Thirty-Foot Street to Relieve Congestion," *Times*, December 22, 1912, sec. 8, p. 1.

32. Chappell, "A Reconsideration," 91–92.

33. "Place Height Limits on New Buildings," *Times*, January 14, 1916, sec. 9, p. 1.

34. John Foreman and Robbe Pierce Stimson, *The Vanderbilts and the Gilded Age: Architectural Aspirations, 1879–1901* (New York: St. Martin's Press, 1991), 41–43.

5. "The New Fifth Avenue," *Architectural Record* 22 (July 1907): 1. Also see "Fifth
venue—From Forty-second to Sixtieth Street," *Times*, September 13, 1908, sec. 5, p. 1.
6. "The New Fifth Avenue," *Real Estate Record and Guide* 74 (December 17, 1904): 1346.
7. "Want Fifth Avenue Beautiful," *Times*, March 31, 1908, p. 2.
8. "Fifth Avenue Improvement," *Times*, January 13, 1909, p. 5.
9. "Fifth Avenue Exhibit Planned," *Times*, October 2, 1912, p. 10.
0. Clipping in the Seeley-Lamb Collection.
1. MAS Minutes, October 21, 1913.
2. "Fighting to Beautify Fifth Avenue with Trees," *Times*, April 30, 1911, sec. 5, p. 3.
3. Alan L. Benson, "The New Idea in the Building of Cities," *Times*, February 21, 1909, sec. 5,
. 5.
4. By 1915 real estate taxes were so high that the Allied Real Estate Interests demanded a
ate income tax in order to relieve the pressure. "State Income Tax Is Strongly Urged," *Times*,
)ctober 7, 1915, p. 5.
5. "Shall Fifth Avenue Be a Skyscraper Canyon?" *Times*, November 24, 1912, sec. 5, p. 9.
6. Edwin R. Lewinson, *John Purroy Mitchel: The Boy Mayor of New York* (New York: Astra Books,
965), 121.
7. "The 'Zoning' of the City," *Times*, March 12, 1916, p. 18.
8. "Home Dwellers Have Almost Deserted Fifth Avenue's Busy Retail Center," *Times*, January
1, 1912, sec. 7, p. 1.
9. "Far Famed Fifth Avenue in Peril from Sweatshops," *Times*, December 31, 1911, sec. 5, p. 7.
0. *Times:* "A New Avenue Proposed by Mayor Gaynor," May 29, 1910, sec. 5, p. 1; "Mayor's
lea for New Thoroughfare Revives Seventh Avenue Extension Plan," May 29, 1910, sec. 6, p.
; and "Mayor for the New Avenue," June 15, 1910, p. 3. Also see two Letters to the Editor:
lermann De Selding, "The New Avenue," June 9, 1910; and Real New Yorker, "What's
100,000,000?" June 11, 1910.
1. "The Mayor Chills Fifth Avenue Feast," *Times*, November 21, 1912, p. 10.
2. "Fifth Avenue Only a Dignified Street," *Times*, March 24, 1912, sec. 2, p. 9.
3. *Times:* "Fifth Avenue's Welfare," November 23, 1911, p. 16. Also see "Citizens to Advise
ifth Avenue Changes," November 10, 1911, p. 11; "To Increase Beauty of Fifth Avenue,"
lovember 22, 1911, p. 22.
4. "Fifth Avenue Only a Dignified Street."
5. "Shall Fifth Avenue Be a Skyscraper Canyon?"
6. "Far Famed Fifth Avenue in Peril from Sweatshops."
7. "Building Limit on Fifth Avenue," *Times*, May 25, 1912, sec. 8, p. 1.
8. "Fifth Avenue Report Taken Up," *Times*, May 10, 1912, p. 9.
9. "Skyscrapers and the Skyline of the Future," *Times*, May 10, 1908, sec. 5, p. 1.
0. Charles R. Lamb, Letter to the Editor, "Skyscrapers in Block Center," *New York Herald
ribune*, 1931. Clipping in the Seeley-Lamb Collection.
1. "Business Notes," June 18, 1912. Clipping in the Seeley-Lamb Collection; and "City
lanning Lectures," *Times*, October 13, 1912, sec. 8, p. 1.
2. MAS Minutes, March 2, 1914.
3. Report of the Commission on Building Districts and Restrictions, quoted in " 'A City of
lomes' Aim of Zoning Plan," *Times*, March 12, 1916, p. 13.
4. Ibid.
5. "City Building Zones Divide Realty Men," *Times*, March 28, 1916, p. 22.
6. "Get Many Requests to Restrict Areas," *Times*, March 29, 1916, p. 14.
7. "Urges Parks' Protection," *Times*, March 6, 1916, p. 20.
8. "Plans Park for North End of Manhattan Island," *Times*, March 24, 1912, sec. 6, p. 7.
9. "Zoning Commission Hears Park Plans," *Times*, March 30, 1916, p. 9.

70. "Heart of the City Saved from the Factory Blight," *Times*, October 22, 1916, sec. 5, p. 1

71. "Out of Town Firms Aid City 'Zone' Idea," *Times*, March 9, 1916, p. 21.

72. "To Quit Forbidden Zone," *Times*, March 7, 1916, p. 16.

73. "To Save Fifth Avenue," *Times*, April 3, 1916, p. 15.

74. "Big Employers Act 'To Save New York,' " *Times*, April 2, 1916, sec. 9, p. 1.

75. "Fifth Ave. Deadline Set for Factories," *Times*, March 5, 1916, p. 15.

76. *Times:* "Increasing Demand for Homes in Washington Square Section," March 12, 1916, sec. 3, p. 8. Also see "Washington Mews to Become a Latin Quarter," December 19, 1915, s 4, p. 8; and "Made Over Houses Now Show Profit," December 5, 1915, sec. 7, p. 1.

77. *Times:* "The Zone and Use Regulations," November 22, 1916. Also see "Homecoming Season in Murray Hill—Interesting Changes in Old Center," October 22, 1916, p. 4.

78. "Transforming the Old Shopping District," *Times*, August 13, 1916, p. 2.

79. *Times:* "Combine to Protect Retail Shopping Zone," October 13, 1916, sec. 3, p. 4. Also see "To Send Factories South of 22nd Street," April 21, 1916, p. 7.

80. "Six Lofts in 'Penn' Zone Designed for Millinery Trade," *Times*, September 10, 1916, sec 3, p. 2.

81. "Skyscrapers and the Skyline of the Future," *Times*, May 10, 1908, sec. 5, p. 1.

82. *Times:* Editorial reprinted in "McAneny's Work," October 21, 1915, p. 10. Also see "McAneny to Resign to Join the *Times*," October 20, 1915, p. 1.

83. Gay Talese, *The Kingdom and the Power* (New York: World, 1969), 174. McAneny would later work for Robert Goelet's Ritz-Carlton Corporation and for the Title Guarantee and Trust Company (whose board included a number of wealthy Municipalians, like Robert W. De Forest). He also served as a paid lobbyist for the Pennsylvania Railroad.

CHAPTER 12

1. Herman Melville, *Moby-Dick* (1851; reprint, New York: Oxford University Press, 1988), 1–2.

2. For a history of the waterfront, see Ann L. Buttenwieser, *Manhattan Water-Bound: Planning a Developing Manhattan's Waterfront from the Seventeenth Century to the Present* (New York: New York University Press, 1987).

3. "A Death a Day in the Streets of Crowded Manhattan," *New York Times*, November 1, 1908, sec. 5, p. 1.

4. "Eleventh Avenue Settlement," *Times*, January 16, 1916, sec. 2, p. 3.

5. Ibid.

6. *Times:* "The Central's Plan Will Aid Factories," January 23, 1916, p. 11; and "New Track to Cut Slow Freight Costs," January 25, 1916, p. 11.

7. "Is New York to Lose Commercial Supremacy?" *Times*, December 8, 1907, sec. 5, p. 1.

8. *Times:* "Elevated Water Front Line," February 4, 1908, p. 2; and "Fight Elevated Line on Eleventh Avenue," February 11, 1908, p. 5.

9. Clipping in the Seeley-Lamb Collection.

10. Buttenwieser, *Manhattan Water-Bound*, 95–100.

11. "Big Steamship Lines Want Chelsea Piers," *Times*, December 22, 1903, p. 11.

12. George B. McClellan, Jr., *The Gentleman and the Tiger: The Autobiography of George B. McClellan, J* ed. Harold C. Syrett (Philadelphia: Lippincott, 1956), 248.

13. Charles R. Lamb, "Report of Thoroughfares Committee of Municipal Art Society," *MAS Bulletin* no. 5 (1904).

14. *The Report to the Honorable George B. McClellan, Mayor of the City of New York, and to the Honorable Board of Aldermen of the City of New York . . .*, December 14, 1904, 7–8, plates.

15. MAS Minutes, November 11, 1907.

6. "A New and Great Work for New York City," *Times*, December 27, 1908, sec. 5, p. 3.

7. Clipping in the Seeley-Lamb Collection.

8. Tom Buckley, "A Reporter at Large: The Eighth Bridge," *New Yorker*, January 14, 1991, 37.

9. "Gigantic Plan to Relieve Street Congestion," *Times*, October 4, 1908, sec. 5, p. 10.

10. Lately Thomas, *The Mayor Who Mastered New York* (New York: Morrow, 1969), 290–91, 410, 494. Also see *Times:* "Tomkins Lets Out 61 Men," March 10, 1910, p. 7; and "$300,000 Saved to the City," April 24, 1910, p. 10.

11. Calvin Tomkins, "Terminal Needs of New York City," *Times*, April 23, 1911, sec. 8, p. 9.

12. "Planning to Make New York a Beautiful City," *Times*, April 16, 1911, sec. 5, p. 6.

13. "Tomkins Urges His Plan," *Times*, December 12, 1911, p. 11.

14. Tomkins, "Terminal Needs."

15. "For a City Beautiful," *Times*, December 19, 1906, p. 2.

16. Advertisement for Bush Terminal, *Times*, March 14, 1911, p. 6.

17. *Times:* "Tomkins Now Plans to Buy Bush Stores," February 15, 1911, p. 6. Also see "City Plans to Buy Brooklyn Bay Front," March 27, 1911, p. 16.

18. "Planning . . . a Beautiful City."

19. "$73,000,000 Plan to Improve Harbor," *Times*, July 23, 1911, sec. 2, p. 7.

20. "Legislation for Terminals," *Times*, March 23, 1911, p. 7.

21. "New York and New Jersey," *Times*, June 1, 1916, p. 10.

22. "How North River Piers Will Look with New Giant Piers," *Times*, February 9, 1913, sec. , p. 1.

23. "McAneny and Tomkins Clash," *Times*, May 10, 1912, p. 3.

24. "Tomkins Explains Why He Was Ousted," *Times*, April 4, 1913, p. 6.

25. "West Side Terminal Receives a Setback," *Times*, March 31, 1911, p. 8.

26. "Hits Tomkins Death Avenue Bill," *Times*, April 20, 1911, p. 3.

27. "Attacks Tomkins' Plan," *Times*, April 23, 1911, sec. 2, p. 14.

28. "Tomkins Wants to Be Heard," *Times*, October 2, 1911, p. 15.

29. "Mitchel Tilts at Tomkins for Delay," *Times*, December 13, 1912, p. 11.

30. "New York's Waterfront," *Times*, April 4, 1913, p. 8.

31. "Tomkins Explains." Also see "Tomkins Put Out, Smith in His Place," *Times*, April 3, 1913, p. 1.

32. "Money Ready for Stadium," *Times*, March 6, 1906, p. 7. Also see "A $1,000,000 Stadium for Columbia Athletes," *Times*, March 5, 1906, p. 1; and Robert A. M. Stern, Gregory Gilmartin, and John Montague Massengale, *New York 1900* (New York: Rizzoli, 1983), 414–15.

33. "Columbia's Stadium Held up by State Law," *Times*, March 21, 1906, p. 10.

34. "Plan a Great Riverside," *Times*, January 9, 1911, p. 12.

35. "Agree on $10,000,000 Riverside Pantheon," *Times*, December 3, 1912, p. 12.

36. "Stadium and Pantheon," *Times*, December 14, 1912, p. 14.

37. "Stover Would Turn Speedway over to Automobiles," *Times*, August 27, 1911, sec. 5, p. 3.

38. "City's Progress in Art," *New York Evening Post*, April 6, 1911. Clipping in the Seeley-Lamb Collection.

49. "Stover Insists He's a Good Park Head," *Times*, October 6, 1911, p. 16.

50. MAS Minutes, April 28, 1913, and April 27, 1914.

51. "West Side Track Plan Is Agreed On," *Times*, January 16, 1916, sec. 2, p. 1.

52. *Times:* "Attack Central Franchise," June 12, 1916, p. 6; "Sees a Monopoly in New York Central's Plan," January 31, 1916, p. 17; and "The West Side 'Monopoly,' " February 2, 1916, p. 10.

53. "Central Plan Finds Merchants Alert," *Times*, January 29, 1916, p. 16.

54. "Central's Bargain May Change Parks," *Times*, January 22, 1916, p. 12.

55. *Times:* "Riverside Improvement," February 6, 1916, sec. I, p. 6. Also see "Tracks Plan Ma‹ without Park Map," February I, 1916, p. 22.

56. "Exodus Threatened on Riverside Drive," *Times*, June 21, 1916, p. 9.

57. "Women Will Fight West Side Plans," *Times*, June 14, 1916, p. 13.

58. MAS Minutes, May 22, 1916.

59. "Woman's Wit Turns on Alderman Quinn," *Times*, July 12, 1916, p. 4.

60. "Attacks Central's West Side Titles," *Times*, July 22, 1916, p. 11.

61. "Woman's Wit." Also see *Times:* "Exhibit a Model of New Riverside," July 14, 1916, p. 3‹ and "The Riverside Park Model," July 15, 1916, p. 8.

62. "Thompson Attacks West Side Plans," *Times*, July I, 1916, p. 11.

63. *Times:* "Public Bodies Act on West Side Plan," June 26, 1916, p. 13; "Reports in Favor of West Side Plan," June 30, 1916, p. 17; "Endorses West Side Plan," July I, 1916, p. 15.

64. "Objectors Assail West Side Report," *Times*, May 16, 1916, p. 7.

65. For the 1917 election, see Edwin R. Lewinson, *John Purroy Mitchel: The Boy Mayor of New Yor‹* (New York: Astra Books, 1965), 206–47.

66. Quoted in Lewinson, *Mitchel*, 237–38.

CHAPTER 13

I. *New York Times:* "East Side Parents Storm the Schools," June 28, 1906, p. 4; and "Throat-Cutting Rumours Revive School Rioting," June 29, 1906, p. 9.

2. Charles M. Shean, "Mural Painting from the American Point of View," *The Craftsman* 7 (October 1904): 21. Also see David Adams, "Frederick S. Lamb's Opalescent Vision of 'A Broader Art': The Reunion of Art and Craft in Public Murals," unpublished manuscript.

3. Quoted in Adams, "Lamb's Opalescent Vision," 12.

4. George B. McClellan, Jr., *The Gentleman and the Tiger: The Autobiography of George B. McClellan, Jr.,* ed. Harold C. Syrett (Philadelphia: Lippincott, 1956), 270.

5. A.D.F. Hamlin, "Report of Committee on Decoration of Public Buildings of MAS," *MAS Bulletin* no. 7 (March 1904): 23.

6. David C. Hammack, *Power and Society: Greater New York at the Turn of the Century* (New York: Russell Sage Foundation, 1982), 259–99.

7. Daniel Coit Gilman, quoted in Hammack, 295–96.

8. Diane Ravitch, *The Great School Wars, New York City, 1805–1973: A History of the Public Schools as Battlefield of Social Change* (New York: Basic Books, 1974), 161–94.

9. George E. Bissell, "Report of the Committee on Decoration of Public Schools," *MAS Bulleti‹* no. 8 (1904).

10. Ibid.

11. "Public School Decoration," *Times*, January 23, 1904, p. 16.

12. Mariana Griswold Van Rensselaer, *Henry Hobson Richardson and His Works* (1888; reprint, New York: Dover, 1969). Also see Cynthia Doering Kinnard, *The Life and Works of Mariana Griswold Van Rensselaer, American Art Critic* (Ph.D. diss., Johns Hopkins University, 1977); and Richard N. Murray, "Painting and Sculpture," in Richard Guy Wilson, Dianne H. Pilgrim and Richard H. Murray, *The American Renaissance: 1876–1917* (New York: Brooklyn Museum 1979), 167.

13. Jacob Riis, *The Battle with the Slum* (New York: Macmillan, 1902), 353.

14. MAS Minutes, April 25, 1904.

15. Quoted in Harmon Goldstone and Martha Dalrymple, *History Preserved: A Guide to New York City Landmarks and Historic Districts* (New York: Schocken Books, 1976), 356.

6. Kenyon Cox, *The Classic Point of View* (1911; reprint, New York: Norton, 1980), 70. Also
se "Historical Painting," *Times*, July 16, 1911, sec. 2, p. 8.

7. "Educators Dedicate Clinton High School," *Times*, December 19, 1906, p. 11.

8. "For a City Beautiful," *Times*, December 19, 1906, p. 2.

9. Margot Gayle and Michele Cohen, *The Art Commission and the Municipal Art Society Guide to
Manhattan's Outdoor Sculpture* (New York: Prentice-Hall Press, 1988), 285.

0. Julius Henry Cohen, *They Builded Better Than They Knew* (New York: Julian Messner,
946), 42.

1. MAS Minutes, April 25, 1934.

2. MAS Minutes, October 9, 1911.

3. "Mrs. Mitchel Raises Flag," *Times*, June 13, 1914, p. 10.

4. "Miss Wilson Backs Labor Forum Stand," *Times*, March 25, 1916, p. 20.

5. "Art for Public Schools," *Times*, March 11, 1908, p. 6.

6. David Adams, "Frederick S. Lamb's Opalescent Vision of 'A Broader Art': The Reunion of
Art and Craft in Public Murals," 25, 37, 74. Unpublished manuscript.

7. MAS Minutes, April 27, 1908, and April 26, 1915.

8. Edwin Blashfield, "Biographical Sketch of Evangeline Wilbour Blashfield," unpublished
typescript in the Blashfield papers, New-York Historical Society, 10.

9. *MAS Bulletin* no. 19 (third and fourth quarter, 1919). MAS Archives.

0. "Municipal Art Society Prize," *MAS Bulletin* no. 2 (April 1915). MAS Archives.

1. MAS Minutes, May 27, 1930, and January 20, 1931.

32. *Times*: "Municipal Art Society Members Exhibit Their Work," April 23, 1916, p. 18. Also
ee "Municipal Art Society," March 22, 1911, p. 12.

33. MAS Minutes, May 28, 1917.

34. Ibid., January 26 and February 25, 1918.

35. Ibid., October 28, 1918.

36. *MAS Bulletin* no. 18 (second quarter, 1919).

37. MAS Minutes, September 30, 1918.

38. Interview with Barea Lamb Seeley, Lamb's granddaughter, based on family correspondence
in her possession.

39. Leo Stein, "The Arch in New York City," *New Republic*, January 11, 1919, p. 304.

40. Phillip P. Fehl, "Propaganda and the Integrity of Art: Notes on an Exhibition of War
Posters, 1914–18," in *The World War One Propaganda Poster: A Selection from the Bowman Grory
Collection* (Chapel Hill: Auckland Art Center, University of North Carolina, 1969), n.p., quoted
in Leonard N. Amico, *The Mural Decorations of Edwin Howland Blashfield, 1848–1936*
(Williamstown, Mass.: Sterling and Francine Clark Art Institute, 1978).

41. MAS Minutes, November 25, 1918.

42. Albert Bard, "Editorial Note," *MAS Bulletin* no. 18 (second quarter, 1919).

43. MAS Minutes, March 15 and April 19, 1920.

44. Ibid., March 14, 1924.

45. "No Billboards in Zone Districts," *MAS Bulletin* no. 16 (fourth quarter, 1918).

46. I. N. Phelps Stokes, *Random Recollections of a Happy Life*, rev. ed. (New York: I. N. Phelps
Stokes, 1941), 83.

47. Joseph A. Spencer, "New York City Tenant Organizations and the Post-World War I
Housing Crisis," in Ronald Lawson, ed., *The Tenant Movement in New York City, 1904–1984* (New
Brunswick, N.J.: Rutgers University Press, 1986), 51–93.

48. The phrase is Brendan Gill's, from an interview.

49. MAS Minutes, November 13, 1921, September 18, 1923, December 21, 1932, and
February 16, 1933.

50. Ibid., December 19, 1934; and Gayle and Cohen, *Guide to Manhattan's Outdoor Sculpture*, 202.

Chapter 14

1. Frederick Law Olmsted, quoted in "The Man Who Lived in the Octagonal Cupola," *Village Views* 4 (Spring 1987): 7.
2. "The Constant Fight to Save Central Park," *New York Times*, April 11, 1909, sec. 5, p. 1.
3. "Tearing Up the Park," *Times*, January 5, 1911, p. 12.
4. "Stover Would Turn Speedway Over to Automobile," *Times*, August 27, 1911, sec. 5, p. 3.
5. Letter to the Editor, "Mr. Stover's Candidacy," *Times*, October 13, 1907, p. 8.
6. McClellan did put him on a committee to study whether underutilized parcels of city-owned land could be transformed into playgrounds. "City Playgrounds Inquiry," *Times*, April 29, 1909, p. 18.
7. Lately Thomas, *The Mayor Who Mastered New York: The Life and Opinions of William J. Gaynor* (New York: Morrow, 1969), 204, 207.
8. *Times*: "Recreation for All Planned by Stover," February 15, 1910, p. 4. Also see "Recreation Official Wanted," April 10, 1910, p. 12; and "To Supervise Playgrounds," April 15, 1910, p. 6.
9. *Times*: "Stover Park Head; Lederle Is Placed," January 10, 1910, p. 1. Also see "$150,000 for New City Park," February 3, 1910, p. 1.
10. Lincoln Steffens, *The Autobiography of Lincoln Steffens* (New York: Literary Guild, 1931), 636–40.
11. Roy Rosenzweig and Elizabeth Blackmar, *The Park and the People: A History of Central Park* (Ithaca, N.Y.: Cornell University Press, 1992), 412.
12. "San Juan Hill Gets a Fine Playground," *Times*, September 10, 1911, p. 5.
13. Harmon Goldstone and Martha Dalrymple, *History Preserved: A Guide to New York City Landmarks and Historic Districts* (New York: Schocken Books, 1976), 461–62; and Tony Hiss, *The Experience of Place* (New York: Knopf, 1990), 108.
14. Frederick Law Olmsted, Jr., and Theodora Kimball, eds., *Forty Years of Landscape Architecture: Central Park* (1928; reprint, Cambridge, Mass.: 1973), 157.
15. Goldstone and Dalrymple, *History Preserved*, 405–8; Robert A. M. Stern, Gregory Gilmartin, and John Montague Massengale, *New York 1900* (New York: Rizzoli, 1985), 132–34.
16. "Plan for New Park Entrance Revives Old Controversy," *Times*, January 26, 1913, sec. 5, p. 7.
17. "*Maine* Monument Site," *Times*, March 18, 1911, p. 22.
18. "*Maine* Shaft to Rise in Columbus Circle," *Times*, August 6, 1911, p. 5.
19. Ibid.
20. "Urge City against Popularizing Parks," *Times*, March 28, 1911, p. 6.
21. Harold A. Caparn, Letter to the Editor, "The Parks in Spring," *Times*, March 14, 1911, p. 10.
22. *Times*: "The Manhattan Parks," January 3, 1903, p. 8. Also see "To Improve Central Park," January 3, 1903, p. 16.
23. "The 'Subordinate Disposition,'" *Times*, May 13, 1911, p. 12.
24. "Fosdick Advises Parsons's Dismissal," *Times*, May 11, 1911, p. 3.
25. "Finds Against Parsons," *Times*, June 6, 1911, p. 2.
26. "Mr. Parsons and the Parks," *Times*, April 7, 1911, p. 12.
27. "The 'Subordinate Disposition.'"
28. "*Maine* Shaft to Rise in Columbus Circle."
29. *Times*: "Stover Insists He's a Good Park Head," October 5, 1911, p. 16; "C. D. Lay Named Park Architect," August 11, 1911, p. 6; and "Mayor Reinstates Man Stover Put Out," August 18, 1911, p. 6.

Times: "No Park Invasion," January 4, 1911, p. 8; "The Academy of Design," February 10, 10, p. 6; "Rescue the Old Arsenal," May 25, 1914, p. 10.

Times: "$2,400,000 from Frick to Go for Library Books," December 17, 1906, p. 2; and all Out to Oust Park Department," June 21, 1912, p. 24.

Times: "Call Out to Oust Park Department": "Park Must Be Saved, Says Designer's Son," ie 24, 1912, p. 7; and editorial note, June 12, 1912, p. 12.

"Stover Advocates Park Link between Big Museums," *Times,* March 10, 1912, sec. 5, p. 3.

Times: "Park Must Be Saved, Says Designer's Son," June 24, 1912, p. 7; "The City's Parks :ing a Crisis," June 23, 1912, p. 12; and "Noted Men to Lead Park Defense Fight," June 25, 12, p. 22.

Times: "The Busy Park Destroyers," April 2, 1913, p. 10; "Stover Again Loses His Park chitect," May 2, 1913, p. 1; and "The New Landscape Architect," June 14, 1913, p. 10. Also "A Landscape Architect for the Parks," May 10, 1913, p. 10; and "Pilat Park Architect," ie 13, 1913, p. 13.

Times: "May Ask for Police Search for Stover," November 23, 1913, sec. 3, p. 1; "Think over Safe and Deep in Books," November 19, 1913, p. 1.

Times: "Hear Stover Is Married," November 4, 1913, p. 18; "Coroner Says Body Looks like over," November 11, 1913, p. 1; "Find Drowned Man Is Unlike Stover," November 16, 13, p. 11.

Times: "Moving Pictures to Find Stover," November 25, 1913, p. 1; "Stover Resignation ceived by Kline," November 29, 1913, p. 1.

"Goodbye to Mr. Stover," *Times,* November 30, 1913, sec. 3, p. 6.

"Stover Has Come Back," *Times,* January 29, 1914, p. 1.

"Remove the Old Arsenal," *Times,* May 25, 1914.

"If 'Improvement' Plans Had Gobbled Central Park," *Times,* March 31, 1918, sec. 5, p. 8. so see Albert Fein, ed., *Landscape into Cityscape* (New York: Van Nostrand Reinhold, 1967), –18.

. Albert Bard, Editorial Notes, *MAS Bulletin* no. 14 (Second Quarter, 1918).

. Harmon Goldstone, interview by author.

. MAS Minutes, November 17 and December 15, 1919; "Park Plans Discovered," *Times,* .arch 20, 1912, p. 5.

. Quoted in Rosenzweig and Blackmar, *The Park and the People,* 433.

. MAS Minutes, October 18, 1920.

. MAS Minutes, November 15, 1933.

. MAS Minutes, January 15, 1924.

. B. M. Steigman, "Precursor to Lincoln Center," *American Quarterly* 13 (Fall 1961): 376–86; ictoria Newhouse, *Wallace K. Harrison, Architect* (New York: Rizzoli, 1989), 199.

. "War Memorials," *MAS Bulletin* no. 17 (first quarter, 1919). MAS Archives.

. MAS Minutes, December 15, 1919; and Michele H. Bogart, *Public Sculpture and the Civic Ideal New York City: 1890–1930* (Chicago: University of Chicago Press, 1989), 276–82.

. Homer St. Gaudens, ed., *The Reminiscences of Augustus St. Gaudens,* vol. 2 (New York: Century, 913), 6, 10.

. Hugh Hastings, Letter to the Editor, "Slocum Statue Criticized," *Times,* February 2, 1902, 14.

. George B. McClellan, Jr., *The Gentleman and the Tiger: The Autobiography of George B. McClellan, Jr.,* . Harold C. Syrett (Philadelphia: Lippincott, 1956), 266; and MAS Minutes, November 26 nd December 17, 1917.

. McClellan, *The Gentleman and the Tiger,* 266. Emphasis added.

. Bogart, *Public Sculpture,* 268.

. MAS Minutes, September 19, October 17 and 28, and December 19, 1922.

59. Ibid., January 16 and February 20, 1923.

60. Ibid., April 17, 1928, and February 19, 1929.

61. Margot Gayle and Michele Cohen, *The Art Commission and the Municipal Art Society Guide to Manhattan's Outdoor Sculpture* (New York: Prentice-Hall Press, 1988), 229.

62. MAS Minutes, February 14 and March 14, 1924.

63. Ibid., February 10, 1926.

64. *Times*: "Puts Central Park Needs at $1,000,000," July 20, 1926, p. 5; "Central Park Crisis Acute," July 25, 1926, sec. 2, p. 1; "A Million Dollar Prescription," July 22, 1926, p. 18; "T Report on the Park," July 27, 1926, p. 16; "A Million Dollars for the Park," December 4, 1926, p. 16; and "Ask $1,000,000 Fund for Central Park," December 3, 1926, p. 1.

65. George Walsh, *Gentleman Jimmy Walker: Mayor of the Jazz Age* (New York: Prager, 1974), 11.

66. MAS Minutes, October 19, 1938.

67. MAS Minutes, September 20, October 18, and December 20, 1927.

68. *Times*: "Architect Envisions Finer Central Park," October 4, 1927, p. 31; "Details Remodeling for Central Park," December 20, 1927, p. 22; "The Central Park Program," December 21, 1927, p. 24; "Park Defenders Hail Merkel Data," December 21, 1927, p. 11; and "Sees Central Park Unrivaled in Land," December 29, 1927, p. 8.

69. "Art Society Endorses Central Park Plan," *Times*, December 23, 1927, p. 10; "Central Park Wins," *Times*, January 28, 1928, p. 14; and Henry Hope Reed and Sophia Duckworth, *Central Park: A History and a Guide* (New York: Clarkson N. Potter, 1967), 47–49.

70. MAS Minutes, March 19 and May 27, 1930.

71. Quoted in Rosenzweig and Blackmar, *The Park and the People*, 446.

72. Isaac Newton Phelps Stokes, *Random Recollections of a Happy Life*, rev. ed. (New York: I. N. Phelps Stokes, 1941), 259.

73. Rosenzweig and Blackmar, *The Park and the People*, 447.

CHAPTER 15

1. Julius Henry Cohen, *They Builded Better Than They Knew* (New York: Julian Messner, 1946), 247–88.

2. Ibid., 293.

3. "How Our Men of Wealth Give Away Millions," *New York Times*, October 15, 1905, sec. p. 4.

4. The dispute went back to 1904. In his memoirs, McClellan claims he offered to let De Forest stay on as tenement house commissioner and that De Forest, anxious to score a political point for Fusion, went ahead and announced he'd been discharged. George B. McClellan, *The Gentleman and the Tiger: The Autobiography of George B. McClellan, Jr.*, ed. Harold C. Syrett (Philadelphia: Lippincott, 1956), 239.

5. Robert A. Caro, *The Power Broker: Robert Moses and the Fall of New York* (New York: Vintage, 1975), 357.

6. George Walsh, *Gentleman Jimmy Walker: Mayor of the Jazz Age* (New York: Prager, 1974), 58.

7. For Mayor Walker's career, see Gene Fowler, *Beau James: The Life and Times of Jimmy Walker* (New York: Viking Press, 1949); and Walsh, *Gentleman Jimmy Walker*.

8. Quoted in Walsh, *Gentleman Jimmy Walker*, 58.

9. Fowler, *Beau James*, 198.

10. Walsh, *Gentleman Jimmy Walker*, 40.

11. Ibid., 114.

12. "Richmond Park Site Frowned on by City," *Times*, November 12, 1926, p. 41.

13. "Business Men Laud Civic Survey Plan," *Times*, June 16, 1926, p. 26.

. Albert Bard et al., *Review of City Development, New York City, 1935–38* (New York: Fine Arts deration, 1938), 4.

. Henry Curran, *Pillar to Post* (New York: Scribner's, 1941), 6–7.

. Henry Curran, quoted in Rebecca Read Shanor, *The City That Never Was* (New York: king, 1988), 16.

. "The Skyscraper: Babel or Boon?" *Times*, December 5, 1926, sec. 4, p. I.

. Before the First World War, for instance, Phelps Stokes had formed a partnership with ouglas Elliman and the Phelps Stokes estate and had speculated heavily in Park Avenue corner ts. He was waiting for Grand Central's reconstruction to spark a boom, but the estate decided pull out of the market before that moment arrived. Through the 1920s, Phelps Stokes and liman watched others reap the fruits of their investment scheme, and glumly toted up the llions they might have made. I. N. Phelps Stokes, *Random Recollections of a Happy Life*, rev. ed. Jew York: Phelps Stokes, 1941).

). MAS Minutes, May 17, 1927.

). "As to Overbuilding in Manhattan," *Real Estate Record and Guide* 119 (January 29, 1927): 5.

. Bard et al., *Review of City Development*: 4. Also see *Times*: "Endorses Reforms in Estimate ard," December 27, 1927, p. 9; "A Useful Report," December 27, 1927, p. 18; "City rough Rule Barred in New Plan," December 28, 1927, p. 25; and "Borough Government," ecember 30, 1927, p. 18.

2. Bard et al., *Review of City Development*, 5.

3. Walsh, *Gentleman Jimmy Walker*, 51.

4. Ibid., 216–17.

5. "Walker's Record Held Disappointing," *Times*, January 16, 1928, p. 23.

6. Walsh, *Gentleman Jimmy Walker*, 185.

7. MAS Minutes, January 22, 1930.

8. Quoted in Walsh, *Gentleman Jimmy Walker*, 204.

9. Walsh, *Gentleman Jimmy Walker*, 333.

0. Caro, *Power Broker*, 325.

I. Thomas Kessner, *Fiorello H. La Guardia and the Making of Modern New York* (New York: McGraw-Hill, 1989), 246.

2. John Kenneth Galbraith, *The Great Crash: 1929* (Boston: Houghton Mifflin, 1972), 148–72.

3. Kessner, *Fiorello H. La Guardia and the Making of Modern New York*, 170.

4. Ibid., 24, 36–37, 239.

5. Ibid., 124, 192.

6. Quoted in Caro, *Power Broker*, 547.

7. Harmon Goldstone, interview by author.

8. Phelps Stokes, *Random Recollections*, 213.

9. Electus Litchfield, "Address of the President of the Society at the Meeting of the Board of Directors," September 28, 1932. Pamphlet in MAS Archives.

0. MAS Minutes, September 18, 1928.

I. "The New East River Drive," *MAS Bulletin* (November 1935): 2.

2. Phelps Stokes, *Random Recollections*, 34, 56, 112.

3. Ibid., 205.

4. Ibid., 262.

5. Ibid., 202.

6. MAS Minutes, November 20, 1935.

7. Phelps Stokes, *Random Recollections*, 205.

8. Charles Culp Burlingham, Oral History, Columbia University.

9. Kessner, *La Guardia*, 308.

0. MAS Minutes, December 20, 1933, and February 28, 1934.

51. *MAS Bulletin* (May 1938).

52. Phelps Stokes, *Random Recollections*, 104; Phyllis Samitz Cohen, *Adopt-A-Mural* (New York: Municipal Art Society and Art Commission of the City of New York, 1991).

53. "Whitman Censored," *Art Digest*, January 1, 1938, p. 14; and Robert A. M. Stern, Gregor Gilmartin, and Thomas Mellins, *New York 1930* (New York: Rizzoli, 1987), 107.

54. Phelps Stokes, *Random Recollections*, 268.

55. Quoted in Kessner, *La Guardia*, 440.

56. "Horgan & Slattery," *Times*, March 4, 1902, p. 8.

57. MAS Minutes, March 20, 1935. Also see "Mayor La Guardia's Service for Better Architecture," *MAS Bulletin* (November 1935).

58. *Times:* "City Held Failure in Architecture," May 14, 1963, p. 28; Ada Louise Huxtable, "Architectural Dynamite," May 14, 1963, p. 28.

59. Phelps Stokes, *Random Recollections*, 85.

60. Kessner, *La Guardia*, 159.

61. Stern, Gilmartin, and Mellins, *New York 1930*, 594, 597.

62. Kessner, *La Guardia*, 209–10.

63. Richard Plunz, *A History of Housing in New York City: Dwelling Type and Social Change in the American Metropolis* (New York: Columbia University Press, 1990), 220.

64. MAS Press Release, filed with MAS Minutes, March 1, 1937.

65. Phelps Stokes, *Random Recollections*, 264–65.

66. Kessner, *La Guardia*, 405.

67. Bard et al., *Review of City Development*, 8.

68. MAS Minutes, September 21 and October 19, 1938.

CHAPTER 16

1. This chapter relies heavily on Robert A. Caro, *The Power Broker: Robert Moses and the Fall of New York* (New York: Vintage Books, 1975). Quotation appears on p. 67.

2. Elizabeth Israels Perry, *Belle Moskowitz: Feminine Politics and the Exercise of Power in the Age of Alfr E. Smith* (New York: Oxford University Press, 1987), 115–39.

3. Robert Moses, "The Building of Jones Beach," in Joann P. Krieg, ed., *Robert Moses: Single Minded Genius* (Interlaken, N.Y.: Heart of the Lakes Publishing, 1989), 135–40.

4. MAS Minutes, November 11, 1907, and November 25, 1908.

5. Harmon Goldstone and Martha Dalrymple, *History Preserved: A Guide to New York City Landmarks and Historic Districts* (New York: Schocken Books, 1976), 426–27.

6. "Brooklyn Has Many Plans for the Approaching Year," *New York Herald*, December 31, 1911; and "Hillis Sees Vast Population Here," *Brooklyn Standard-Union*, December 20, 1911. Als see "Brooklyn Beautiful Next," *New York Times*, December 22, 1911. Clippings in the Seeley-Lamb Collection.

7. "Brooklyn Has Many Plans for the Approaching Year," *Herald*, December 31, 1911; and "Now on Brooklyn Heights May Arise a Worthy Rival of Riverside Drive," *Tribune*, December 24, 1911. Clippings in the Seeley-Lamb Collection. Also see drawings in the Charles Rollinson Lamb Collection in the Archives of Avery Library, Columbia University.

8. Moses, "Jones Beach," 138. For Moses's master plan, see John A. Black, "Robert Moses: Long Island's First Environmentalist," in Krieg, ed., *Robert Moses*, 141–50.

9. Caro, *Power Broker*, 360.

10. MAS Minutes, January 17, 1934.

11. Robert A. M. Stern, Gregory Gilmartin, and Thomas Mellins, *New York 1930* (New York: Rizzoli, 1987), 270, 280–81, 288; and Gene Fowler, *Beau James: The Life and Times of Jimmy Walker* (New York: Viking Press, 1949), 246–50.

2. Quoted in Caro, *Power Broker*, 398, 400.

3. Ibid., 430.

4. "Report of the Committee on Theme of the Fair to the Board of Design," July 16, 1936, quoted in Alice G. Marquis, *Hopes and Ashes: The Birth of Modern Times, 1929–1939* (New York: Free Press, 1986), 187–88.

5. F. Scott Fitzgerald, *The Great Gatsby* (New York: Scribner's, 1925), 27.

6. Quoted in Helen A. Harrison, "From Dump to Glory: Robert Moses and the Flushing Meadow Improvement," in Krieg, ed., *Robert Moses*, 91–100.

7. Quoted in Joseph P. Cusker, "The World of Tomorrow: Science, Culture, and Community the New York World's Fair," in Helen A. Harrison, ed., *Dawn of a New Day: The New York World's Fair, 1939–40* (New York: New York University Press, 1980), 4.

8. Harmon Goldstone, interview with author.

9. Walter Lippmann, "Today and Tomorrow," *Current History* 50 (July 1939): 51.

10. *Times:* "Art Notes of Interest," September 24, 1905, sec. 3, p. 7; "Proposed Henry Hudson Memorial Bridge," February 25, 1906, sec. 3, p. 2; "The Hendrick Hudson Memorial," February 16, 1906, p. 8.

11. "Art Board Rejects Memorial Bridge Plans," *Times*, September 20, 1906, p. 7. Also see *Times:* "$1,000,000 to Start Hendrick Hudson Bridge," December 9, 1905, p. 15; Edward P. North, Letter to the Editor, "Hudson Memorial Bridge," September 22, 1906, p. 6; and "The Hudson Memorial Bridge," September 23, 1906, p. 8.

12. "Inwood Hill: An Approach to the City?" *Toward a City of Beauty* (New York: Municipal Art Society, January 1932).

13. Ibid.

14. Quoted in Caro, *Power Broker*, 547.

15. Ibid..

16. Ely Jacques Kahn, unpublished autobiographical manuscript in the Prints and Drawings Collections, at Avery Library, Columbia University. Also see Stern, Gilmartin, and Mellins, *New York 1930*, 551–58.

17. Quoted in August Heckscher, *When La Guardia Was Mayor: New York's Legendary Years* (New York: Norton, 1978), 55.

18. Caro, *Power Broker*, 625–31.

19. Henry Hope Reed and Sophia Duckworth, *Central Park: A History and a Guide* (New York: Clarkson N. Potter, 1967), 50–53.

20. MAS Minutes, October 19, 1938; "A Memorial to William White Niles," *MAS Bulletin* (December 1938): 4.

21. Albert Bard et al., *Review of City Development, New York City, 1935–38* (New York: Fine Arts Federation, 1938), 13.

22. MAS Minutes, April 21 and April 23, 1941.

23. MAS Minutes, December 17, 1941.

24. Bard et al., *Review*, 10, 11.

25. Quoted in Caro, *Power Broker*, 643.

26. MAS Minutes, October 19, 1938.

27. Eric Mendelsohn, quoted in Herman G. Scheffauer, "The Skyscraper Has Found No Favor in European Cities," *Times*, August 27, 1926, sec. 6, p. 11.

28. Paul Morand, *New York* (New York: Book League of America, 1930), 29, 39.

29. MAS Minutes, March 15 and April 19, 1939.

30. Caro, *Power Broker*, 676.

31. Quoted in ibid., 672.

32. Quoted in Thomas Kessner, *Fiorello H. La Guardia and the Making of Modern New York* (New York: McGraw-Hill, 1989), 456.

43. Quoted in Caro, *Power Broker*, 666.

44. Quoted in ibid., 666–68.

45. Ibid., 668.

46. Ibid., 671.

47. Quoted in Kessner, *La Guardia*, 457.

48. Caro, *Power Broker*, 673–74.

49. Kessner, *La Guardia*, 458.

50. Edith S. Isaacs, *Love Affair with a City: The Story of Stanley M. Isaacs* (New York: Random House, 1967), 48.

51. Caro, *Power Broker*, 993.

52. Isaacs, *Love Affair*, 46–53.

53. Rodman Gilder, *The Battery* (Boston: Houghton Mifflin, 1936).

54. Typescript in MAS Archives.

55. Letter, William Exton to the board of directors of MAS (September 30, 1941). MAS Archives.

56. "Aquarium Safe until October 30," *New York Sun*, October 21, 1941. Clipping in the MAS Archives. Bard's client was Pierce Trowbridge Wetter, treasurer of the Greenwich Village Historical Society.

57. "Statement of Park Association's Opposition to Castle Clinton National Monument"; and letter, John Gilland Brunini to A. Carl Stelling, September 25, 1946. MAS Archives.

58. Quoted in Ronald F. Lee, "Unfailing Counselor," in "The Memorial Meeting in Honor of George McAneny, Held in the Federal Hall Memorial," December 10, 1953. Pamphlet in the collection of Ruth McAneny Loud.

59. Caro, *Power Broker*, 685.

60. "New Reprieve Due for the Aquarium," *Herald Tribune*; and Albert S. Bard, letter to the editor, "Removal of Fort Clinton," *Times*, August 7, 1947. Clippings in MAS Archives.

61. Quoted in the draft of a letter to the editor of the *Herald Tribune*, December 17, 1948. MAS Archives.

62. "Appellate Division, First Department: Municipal Corporations—'Monument.'. . ." *New York Law Journal* 121 (May 11, 1949): 1.

63. Oscar L. Chapman, quoted in Caro, *Power Broker*, 686.

CHAPTER 17

1. Gaston Lichtenstein, letter to the editor, "Staten Island's Relics," *New York Times*, August 8, 1911, p. 8.

2. "Roger Morris Park," *Times*, December 30, 1903, p. 6.

3. "New York's Historic Landmarks," *Times*, January 28, 1905, sec. 3, p. 1.

4. *Times*: letter to the editor, "Plea for the Old Hall of Records," May 4, 1902, p. 5. Also see "Alderman Bridges a New Lion of Society," May 3, 1902, p. 8.

5. "Two Unwise Propositions."

6. *Times*: "Two Unwise Propositions"; "Roger Morris Park." Also see "Colonnade Hotel Sold," January 26, 1902, p. 1.

7. *Times*: "The Jumel Mansion," January 8, 1903, p. 8; and "Roger Morris Park." Also see Harmon Goldstone and Martha Dalrymple, *History Preserved: A Guide to New York City Landmarks and Historic Districts* (New York: Schocken Books, 1976), 296–97.

8. Montgomery Schuyler, "The Reconstruction of Fraunces Tavern, "*Architectural Record*: 24; *Times*: "To Save Fraunces Tavern," December 5, 1901, p. 14; "To Save Fraunces Tavern," July 11, 1901, p. 6.

9. Interview with Barea Lamb Seeley, Lamb's granddaughter, based on correspondence in the Seeley-Lamb Collection.

0. "To Move Poe's Cottage," *Times*, January 12, 1908, sec. 2, p. 6; Goldstone and Dalrymple, *History Preserved*, 347–48.

1. *Times*: "The Governor's Room," January 5, 1908, sec. 2, p. 10; "New Governor's Room Open," May 28, 1909, p. 5.

2. "The Restored City Hall," *MAS Bulletin* no. 5 (First Quarter, 1916). MAS Archives.

3. "Trinity Parish, Its Millions and Its Tenements," *Times*, July 19, 1908, sec. 5, p. 3.

4. I. N. Phelps Stokes, *Random Recollections of a Happy Life*, rev. ed. (New York: I. N. Phelps Stokes, 1941), 53.

5. *Times*: "Sentiment and Utility," December 18, 1908, p. 8; emphasis added. Also see "Dr. Huntington on Saving St. John's," December 19, 1908, p. 5; and "St. John's Not Historic," December 24, 1908, p. 3.

6. "Great Destruction in Old Greenwich," *Times*, November 23, 1913, sec. 9, p. 1.

7. *Times*: "To Save St. John's Chapel," December 21, 1913, sec. 4, p. 4; letter to the editor, "Save St. John's Chapel," December 31, 1913, p. 8.

8. "To Save St. John's Chapel," *Times*, December 21, 1913, sec. 4, p. 4; MAS Minutes, April 7, 1914.

9. *Times*: "Old Landmark to Go," January 7, 1908, p. 6; "Wants New Assay Office," April 5, 1916, p. 6.

0. Phelps Stokes, *Random Recollections*, 43–45.

1. Ibid., 140; "Valuable Iconography of Old Time New York," *Times*, December 19, 1915, sec. 4, p. 8.

2. Phelps Stokes, *Random Recollections*, 136.

3. Ibid., 143.

4. "Trade Pulling Down Famous Landmarks," *Times*, October 16, 1911, p. 20.

5. "Fifth Avenue Flats," *Times*, March 31, 1911, p. 10.

6. Clipping in the Seeley-Lamb Collection.

7. MAS Minutes, May 16, 1925.

8. Clipping in the Seeley-Lamb Collection.

9. John Foreman and Robbe Pierce Stimson, *The Vanderbilts and the Gilded Age: Architectural Aspirations, 1879–1901* (New York: St. Martin's Press, 1991), 67.

CHAPTER 18

1. MAS Minutes, October 22, 1941.

2. Ibid., May 26, 1942.

3. Talbot Hamlin, *Greek Revival Architecture in America* (1944; reprint, New York: Dover, 1964), 335. Also see Kenneth Frampton, "Slouching toward Modernity," in Richard Oliver, ed., *The Making of an Architect* (New York: Rizzoli, 1983), 151.

4. Talbot Hamlin, *Benjamin Henry Latrobe* (New York: Oxford University Press, 1955).

5. Jan Morris, *Manhattan '45* (New York: Oxford University Press, 1987), 6–8, 11.

6. Robert A. Caro, *The Power Broker: Robert Moses and the Fall of New York* (New York: Vintage, 1975), 403. Emphasis added.

7. Quoted in Edith S. Isaacs, *Love Affair with a City: The Story of Stanley M. Isaacs* (New York: Random House, 1967), 92–93.

8. MAS Minutes, September 24, 1951.

9. MAS Minutes, November 24, 1947.

10. MAS Minutes, October 23, 1947.

11. MAS Minutes, February 19, 1948.

12. MAS Minutes, April 22, 1948.

13. Caro, *Power Broker*, 780.

14. Ibid., 782–83.

15. Charles Lockwood, *Bricks and Brownstones: The New York Row House, 1783–1929* (New York: Abbeville Press, 1972), 82–86.

16. MAS Minutes, May 15, 1950, and March 19, 1951.

17. Caro, *Power Broker*, 787–88.

18. Anthony Wood, "Taking the Long View: An Interview with Harmon Goldstone," *Village Views* 4 (Summer 1987): 17–42.

19. William N. Jayme, letter to the editor, "To Save City Landmarks," *New York Times*, November 24, 1955, p. 28; and Brendan Gill, interview by author.

20. Harmon Goldstone, "The Future of the Past," address presented to the graduating class of the Restore program, 1978, reprinted in *Village Views* 4 (Summer 1987): 10–16.

21. Nathalie Dana, *Young in New York: A Memoir of a Victorian Girlhood* (Garden City, N.Y.: Doubleday, 1963), 157. Also Brendan Gill and Harmon Goldstone, interviews by author.

22. Wood, "Taking the Long View," 17.

23. Harmon Goldstone, interview by author; and "Landmarks Guardian: Harmon Hendricks Goldstone," *Times*, August 27, 1969. Clipping in MAS Archives.

24. Robert A. M. Stern, Gregory Gilmartin, and Thomas Mellins, *New York 1930* (New York: Rizzoli, 1987), 306; and Charles Platt, interview by author.

25. Harmon Goldstone, interview by author; and John Foreman and Robbe Pierce Stimson, *The Vanderbilts and the Gilded Age: Architectural Aspirations, 1879–1901* (New York: St. Martin's Press, 1991), 303.

26. Brendan Gill and Harmon Goldstone, interviews by author.

27. MAS Minutes, October 26, 1954.

28. Edward Steese, *New York Landmarks* (New York: Municipal Art Society, 1957). Pamphlet in MAS Archives.

29. Letter, Henry Hope Reed to author, August 20, 1990; "Monuments of Manhattan: An Exhibition of Great Buildings in New York City, 1800–1918," catalog in Henry Hope Reed's collection; also H. H. Reed, interview by author.

30. Harmon Goldstone and Henry Hope Reed, interviews by author.

31. Henry Hope Reed interview.

32. Brendan Gill interview.

33. Harmon Goldstone interview.

34. MAS Minutes, September 23 and December 16, 1957.

35. MAS Minutes, December 16, 1957; January 27, 1958; May 26, 1958.

36. MAS Minutes, September 22, 1958.

37. Harmon Goldstone, interview by author.

38. Albert S. Bard et al., *Review of City Development, New York City, 1935–38* (New York: Fine Arts Federation, 1938), 14–15.

39. MAS Minutes, December 13, 1939.

40. Quoted in Geoffrey Brown, "Preservation, Private Property and the Law," *Village Views* 4 (Spring 1987): 25.

41. MAS Minutes, October 26, 1954, and March 1955.

42. MAS Minutes, 1955.

43. Goldstone, "Future of the Past," 12.

44. MAS Minutes, May 15, 1956.

45. Goldstone, "Future of the Past," 12.

46. Solomon Toledano, letter to the editor, "Washington Square Changes," *Times*, April 5, 1916, p. 12.

47. Margot Gayle, interview by author.

48. MAS Minutes, April 29, 1957; Margot Gayle and Brendan Gill, interviews by author.

49. Letter, Margot Gayle to Harmon Goldstone, March 28, 1961, and Margot Gayle, interview by author.

50. "The Return of Old Jeff," *Progressive Architecture* (October 1967): 175–78; Brendan Gill and Harmon Goldstone, interviews by author; MAS Minutes, March 23, 1959; and clippings in MAS Archives.

51. Jane Jacobs, *The Death and Life of Great American Cities* (New York: Random House, 1961), 387. Emphasis in original.

52. "The Return of Old Jeff," 175.

53. Margot Gayle, interview by author; "Village Opens Fight for 'Old Jeff,'" *Herald Tribune*, June 11, 1961, clipping in the MAS Archives; Giorgio Cavaglieri, "Address on December 13, 1968, at the Jefferson Market Branch Library, N.Y.C.," typescript in Mr. Cavaglieri's files; and press release from the office of the mayor, August 23, 1961, in the MAS Archives.

54. Giorgio Cavaglieri, interview by author.

55. Otis Pratt Pearsall, interview by author; and Clay Lancaster, *Old Brooklyn Heights: New York's First Suburb*, rev. ed. (New York: Dover, 1979), x.

56. The material in this section is based on the author's interviews with Otis Pratt Pearsall and Harmon Goldstone.

57. MAS Minutes, April 20, 1955.

58. Anthony Wood, "An Interview with the late Geoffrey Platt, the first Chairman of the Landmarks Commission," *Village Views* 4 (Winter 1987): 7–38.

59. MAS press release, May 9, 1961, MAS Archives.

60. Obituary, James Felt, *MAS Newsletter* (Spring 1971).

61. *Times*: "Three New Appointees All Born in City," December 13, 1955, p. 28; and J. Clarence Davies, Jr., letter to the editor, "Felt Appointment Praised," December 24, 1955, p. 12.

62. Philip Howard, interview by author.

63. Goldstone, "Future of the Past," 13.

64. Jack Newfield and Paul Du Brul, *The Abuse of Power: The Permanent Government and the Fall of New York* (New York: Viking Press, 1977), 142.

65. Harmon Goldstone, interview by author.

66. "Mayor Appoints 13 to Help Preserve Historic Buildings," *Times*, July 12, 1961. Clipping in MAS Archives.

67. Wood, "Geoffrey Platt," 10.

68. Ibid., 10, 24.

69. Charles Platt, interview by author.

70. MAS Minutes, December 17, 1962.

71. Ada Louise Huxtable, *Goodbye History, Hello Hamburger: An Anthology of Architectural Delights and Disasters* (Washington, D.C.: Preservation Press, 1986), 47–49.

72. Goldstone, "Future of the Past," 11.

73. Evelyn Hayes, quoted in Roberta B. Gratz, "Landmarks: A Rating after Ten Years," *New York Post*, January 12, 1973. Clipping in MAS Archives.

74. Wood, "Geoffrey Platt," 14.

75. Brendan Gill, interview by author.

76. Nathan Silver, *Lost New York* (New York: Weathervane Books, 1967), 127.

77. Gratz, "Landmarks: A Rating after Ten Years."

78. Wood, "Taking the Long View," 35, 41; and MAS Minutes, February 24, 1965.

79. Anthony Wood, "Preservation's Scholarly Roots: Talbot Hamlin and the Avery Library," *Village Views* 2 (Summer 1985): 3–37.

80. "News Notes," *AIA Journal* (December 1965): 23.

81. Ada Louise Huxtable, *Goodbye History*, 18–20.

82. Wood, "Geoffrey Platt," 20.

83. Thomas W. Ennis, "Director of Landmarks Panel Quits on Advice of Physician," *Times*. Undated clipping in MAS Archives.

84. MAS Minutes, April 24, 1967, and May 24, 1965.

85. "Summary of the First Meeting of the Landmarks Preservation Commission—September 21, 1965." MAS Archives.

86. Ellen Perry Berkley, "The Public Theater," *Architectural Forum* 134 (March 1971): 48–51.

87. "Dramatic Rescue," *Architectural Forum* 128 (April 1968): 64–67.

88. Harmon Goldstone, interview by author.

89. Paul Byard, interview by author.

90. Quoted in Brown, "Preservation, Private Property and the Law," 31.

91. Harmon Goldstone, interview by author.

CHAPTER 19

1. Margot Gayle and Harmon Goldstone, interviews by author.

2. David Prager and Otis Pratt Pearsall, interviews by author.

3. Ruth McAneny Loud, interview by author.

4. David Prager, interview by author.

5. Otis Pratt Pearsall, interview by author.

6. Kent Barwick, quoted in Ira Wolfman, "Skyline: Preservationist Kent Barwick Speaks Softly and Carries a Very Big Stick," *Daily News Magazine*, January 3, 1988, pp. 10–12.

7. Kent Barwick and Joan Davidson, interviews by author.

8. Kent Barwick and Brendan Gill, interviews by author.

9. "New Roots for the City," *New York Times*, May 20, 1968. Clipping in MAS Archives.

10. Harmon Goldstone, interview by author.

11. "A Friend of the Parks: Newbold Morris," *Times*, March 27, 1964. Clipping in MAS Archives.

12. Quoted in Roy Rosenzweig and Elizabeth Blackmar, *The Park and the People: A History of Central Park* (Ithaca, N.Y.: Cornell University Press, 1992), 483.

13. Henry Hope Reed and Sophia Duckworth, *Central Park: A History and a Guide* (New York: Clarkson N. Potter, 1967), 88.

14. Letter, Robert Alpern to the Honorable Paul O'Dwyer, filed with MAS Minutes, November 30, 1964.

15. *Times*: "Oldsters' Center to Be Built in City," May 30, 1955, p. 15; "For the Older People," June 1, 1955, p. 32; "Plan for Ramble Upheld by Moses," September 5, 1955, p. 13; "Bird-lovers Balk at Moses Project," October 2, 1955, p. 54; "Jack to Inspect Ramble," November 25, 1955, p. 29; "Compromise for the Ramble Is Pressed on Park Tour," November 27, 1955, p. 1; and "Arts Group Fights Ramble Building," November 29, 1955.

16. Lisa Rebecca Gubernick, *Squandered Fortune: The Life and Times of Huntington Hartford* (New York: Putnam, 1991).

17. August Heckscher, *Alive in the City: Memoir of an Ex-Commissioner* (New York: Scribner's, 1974), 275.

18. Harmon Goldstone, interview by author.

19. "Park Café Dispute Reaches N.Y. Court," *Architectural Forum* (July 1963): 7–8.

20. Clippings in MAS Archives.

21. Kent Barwick, interview by author.

22. Heckscher, *Alive in the City*, 255.

23. Ibid., 72.

24. Kent Barwick, interview by author.

25. Robert Makla, Letter to the Editor, "Against Museum Expansion Into Park," *Times*, November 23, 1967. Clipping in MAS Archives.

26. "Dendur-in-New York," *Times*, November 23, 1967. Clipping in MAS Archives.

27. Heckscher, *Alive in the City*, 267.

28. Brendan Gill, interview by author.

29. See Ada Louise Huxtable, *Goodbye History, Hello Hamburger* (Washington, D.C.: Preservation Press, 1986), 183–86.

30. MAS Minutes, November 16, 1971.

31. Ibid.

32. Otis Pratt Pearsall, interview by author.

33. Harmon Goldstone, interview by author; and Jane Jacobs, *The Death and Life of Great American Cities* (New York: Random House, 1961), 232.

34. Anthony Wood, "An Interview with the Late Geoffrey Platt, the First Chairman of the Landmarks Commission," *Village Views* 4 (Winter 1987): 28.

35. Quoted in Rebecca Read Shanor, *The City That Never Was* (New York: Viking, 1988), 30.

36. Ibid.

37. James R. Hudson, *The Unanticipated City: Loft Conversions in Lower Manhattan* (Amherst: University of Massachusetts Press, 1987).

38. Ada Louise Huxtable, *Goodbye History*, 96.

39. Margot Gayle, interview by author. Also see Margot Gayle and Edward Gillow, Jr., *Cast-Iron Architecture in New York* (New York: Dover, 1974).

40. MAS press release, June 15, 1970, and miscellaneous correspondence, SoHo Historic District File, MAS Archives.

41. Margot Gayle, interview by author.

42. MAS Minutes, October 28, 1957, November 22, 1965, and June 10, 1968.

43. Charles Platt and Harmon Goldstone, interviews by author.

44. Harmon Goldstone, interview by author.

45. Roberta B. Gratz, "Saving the Ansonia: An Uphill Battle," *New York Post*, January 11, 1973. Clipping in MAS Archives.

46. Ibid.

47. Roberta B. Gratz, "Landmarks: A Rating of Ten Years," *New York Post*, January 12, 1973. Clipping in MAS Archives.

48. Charles Platt, Harmon Goldstone, and Kent Barwick, interviews by author.

49. Letter, Harmon Goldstone to Brendan Gill, January 24, 1972. MAS Archives.

50. MAS Minutes, January 16 and March 5, 1973.

51. Harmon Goldstone, interview by author.

52. Brendan Gill and Kent Barwick, interviews by author.

53. Harmon Goldstone, interview by author.

54. MAS Minutes, November 22, 1954.

55. Cristopher Gray, "Restoration for a Despised, but Hardy, Landmark," *Times*, March 11, 1990, sec. 10, p. 6.

56. Roberta B. Gratz, "Old Tweed Courthouse Could Haunt Mayor," *New York Post*, June 22, 1974. Clipping in the Giorgio Cavaglieri archives.

57. Margot Gayle, interview by author.

58. MAS Minutes, March 10, 1975.

59. "Is Landmark Designation Finished?" *Village Views* 4 (Winter 1987): 29–34.

60. Carl W. Condit, *The Port of New York: A History of the Rail and Terminal System from the Grand Central Electrification to the Present* (Chicago: University of Chicago Press, 1981), 234.

61. Letter, Giorgio Cavaglieri to John V. Bennett, February 23, 1955. Copy in the Cavaglieri archives.

62. Harmon Goldstone, interview by author.

63. Wood, "Taking the Long View," 31–32.

64. Quoted in Goldstone and Dalrymple, *History Preserved*, 225.

65. William H. Waggoner, "Impressive Battery of Legal Talent Joins the Battle to Save Grand Central Terminal from Demolition," *Times*, July 30, 1972. Clipping in MAS Archives.

66. Ibid.

67. Anthony Wood, "An Interview . . . with Geoffrey Platt," 31.

68. Kent Barwick, interview by author.

69. Laurie Beckelman, interview by author.

70. William H. Whyte, *City: Rediscovering the Center* (New York: Anchor Books, 1988), 50.

71. MAS Minutes, January 20, 1976, and January 11, 1977.

72. Quoted in Geoffrey Brown, "Preservation, Private Property and the Law," *Village Views* 4 (Spring 1987): 33–34.

73. Laurie Beckelman, Margot Wellington, Harmon Goldstone, and Kent Barwick, interviews by author.

74. David Prager and Margot Wellington, interviews by author.

75. Kent Barwick, Brendan Gill, Margot Wellington, and David Prager, interviews by author.

76. Margot Wellington, interview by author.

77. MAS Minutes, January 16, 1935.

78. MAS Minutes, September 28, 1967, and December 30, 1968; and Giorgio Cavaglieri, interview by author.

79. Brendan Gill and Frederick Papert, interviews by author.

80. Margot Wellington, interview by author.

81. Brendan Gill and Margot Wellington, interviews by author. Also see Brooke Astor, "Dinner at Eight—White Tie," *Architectural Digest*, February 1985, pp. 34–40.

82. Fred Papert, Margot Wellington, and Tim Prentice, interviews by author.

83. Fred Papert, interview by author.

84. William C. Shopsin and Mosette Glaser Broderick, *The Villard Houses: Life Story of a Landmark* (New York: Viking Press, 1980).

85. Giorgio Cavaglieri, interview by author.

86. MAS Minutes, February 17 and March 21, 1983; and Anthony Wood, interview by author.

87. Anthony Wood, interview by author.

88. "Is Landmark Designation Finished?" *Village Views*: 39.

89. Robert A. M. Stern, Gregory Gilmartin, and John Montague Massengale, *New York 1900* (New York: Rizzoli, 1983), 240, 242.

90. Anthony Wood, interview by author.

91. Paul Byard, interview by author.

92. Robert A. M. Stern, Gregory Gilmartin, and Thomas Mellins, *New York 1930* (New York: Rizzoli, 1987), 147–155.

93. Anthony Wood, interview by author.

94. MAS Minutes, September 22, 1983.

95. Anthony Wood, interview by author.

CHAPTER 20

1. Giorgio Cavaglieri, "Thoughts on Zoning and the New Proposed Zoning Resolutions for New York City," address at the Tilden Democratic Club, May 28, 1959. Typescript in Mr. Cavaglieri's files.

2. Ada Louise Huxtable, *Goodbye History, Hello Hamburger: An Anthology of Architectural Delights and Disasters* (Washington, D.C.: Preservation Press, 1986), 17–18.

3. Ely Jacques Kahn, "Needed: Oases in the Asphalt Desert," *New York Times*, May 26, 1963, c. 6, p. 54.

4. Robert Zion, "Midtown Parks for Busy Cities." Clipping in MAS Archives.

5. William H. Whyte, *City: Rediscovering the Center* (New York: Anchor Books, 1988), 89.

6. Rebecca Read Shannor, *The City That Never Was* (New York: Viking, 1988), 30–34.

7. Peter Blake, "Slaughter on Sixth Avenue," *Architectural Forum* 122 (June 1965): 16.

8. Huxtable, *Goodbye History*, 18.

9. "News Report: GM on the Plaza," *Progressive Architecture* 46 (January 1965): 39–40.

10. MAS Minutes, November 30, 1964.

11. Harmon Goldstone, interview by author.

12. MAS Minutes, February 28, 1972.

13. Mary Perot Nichols, "The Greening of New York," *Village Voice*, January 25, 1973. Clipping MAS Archives.

14. Brendan Gill, *A New York Life: Of Friends and Others* (New York: Poseidon Press, 1990), 266.

15. William H. Whyte, *City: Rediscovering the Center* (New York: Anchor Books, 1988), 233.

16. Ibid., 107.

17. Ibid., 124.

18. Laurie Beckelman, interview by author.

19. Thomas J. Lueck, "Are Plazas Public Boons, or Nuisances?" *Times*, October 7, 1990, c. 10, p. 1.

CHAPTER 21

1. For contrasting views of New York's fiscal crisis, see Jack Newfield and Paul Du Bruhl, *The House of Power: The Permanent Government and the Fall of New York* (New York: Viking Press, 1977); and Ken Auletta, *The Streets Were Paved with Gold: The Decline of New York, An American Tragedy* (New York: Random House, 1979).

2. MAS Minutes, May 27, 1976; November 17, 1976; and July 6, 1977.

3. Ada Louise Huxtable, *Architecture, Anyone? Cautionary Tales of the Building Art* (New York: Random House, 1986), 142–46.

4. Margot Wellington, interview by author.

5. Ibid.

6. MAS Minutes, March 25, 1979.

7. MAS Minutes, January 13, 1983.

8. Margot Wellington, interview by author.

9. Robert Fitch, *The Assassination of New York* (New York: Verso, 1993), 222.

10. Margot Wellington, interview by author.

11. William H. Whyte, *City: Rediscovering the Center* (New York: Anchor Books, 1988), 245–55.

12. H. V. Savitch, *Post Industrial Cities: Politics and Planning in New York, Paris and London* (Princeton, N.J.: Princeton University Press, 1988), 53–56.

13. Margot Wellington, interview by author.

14. Susan S. Fainstein, *The City Builders: Property, Politics and Planning in London and New York* (Cambridge, Mass.: Blackwell, 1994), 49.

CHAPTER 22

1. William R. Taylor, ed., *Inventing Times Square: Commerce and Culture at the Crossroads of the World* (New York: Russell Sage Foundation, 1991).

2. "Half a Million Dollars in Broadway's Flashing Signs," *New York Times*, February 25, 1912, sec. 5, p. 13.

3. Quoted in Josh Alan Friedman, *Tales of Times Square* (New York: Delacorte Press, 1986), 4●

4. Brooks Atkinson, *Broadway* (New York: Macmillan, 1970), 415.

5. Quoted in Roberta Brandes Gratz, *The Living City* (New York: Touchstone, 1989), 346.

6. Stanley Tankel, Boris Pushkarev, and William B. Shore, eds., *Urban Design Manhattan* (London: Studio Vista, 1969), 86.

7. Gail Sheehy, "Cleaning up Hell's Bedroom," and "The Landlords of Hell's Bedroom," *New York* (November 13 and 20, 1972); and Friedman, *Tales of Times Square*, 145.

8. Fred Papert, interview by author.

9. Margot Wellington, interview by author.

10. The most complete account of the Portman Hotel can be found in Gratz, *The Living City*, 337–79.

11. Margot Wellington, interview by author.

12. Quoted in Friedman, *Tales of Times Square*, 196.

13. Gratz, *The Living City*, 349–51.

14. Margot Wellington, interview by author.

15. Joan Davidson and Margot Wellington, interviews by author.

16. Margot Wellington and Fred Papert, interviews by author.

17. Margot Wellington, Carole Rifkind, and Tim Prentice, interviews by author.

18. Joan Davidson, interview by author.

19. Friedman, *Tales of Times Square*, 147–48.

20. Ibid., 148.

21. Brendan Gill, interview by author.

22. MAS Minutes, May 14, 1980.

23. Fred Papert, interview by author.

24. Friedman, *Tales of Times Square*, 143, 149.

25. Fred Papert, interview by author. Also see New York City Planning Commission, *Forty-second Street Study* (January 1978).

26. H. V. Savitch, *Post Industrial Cities: Politics and Planning in New York, Paris and London* (Princeton N.J.: Princeton University Press, 1988), 72.

27. Ibid.

28. Kent Barwick, interview by author.

29. Savitch, *Post Industrial Cities*, 73.

30. Halina Rosenthal, interview by author. Also see Paul Goldberger, "Four New Towers for Times Square," *Times*, December 21, 1983, sec. 2, p. 1.

31. Ada Louise Huxtable, *Goodbye History, Hello Hamburger* (Washington, D.C.: Preservation Press 1986), 23–25; and Huxtable, *Architecture, Anyone? Cautionary Tales of the Building Art* (New York: Random House, 1986), 136–42.

32. Charlotte Curtis, "An Honor for Philip Johnson," *Times*, December 6, 1983. Clipping in MAS Archives.

33. Beverly Russell, "Philip Johnson's Shape of Third Avenue to Come," *New York Post*, December 19, 1983. Clipping in MAS Archives.

34. Curtis, "An Honor."

35. Margot Wellington, interview by author.

36. Quoted in Michael Sorkin, "Why Goldberger's So Bad," *Village Voice*, April 2, 1985, pp. 90–91.

37. Margot Wellington, interview by author.

38. MAS Minutes, October 18, 1984.

39. Fred Papert and Kent Barwick, interviews by author.

. Margot Wellington, Carole Rifkind, Tim Prentice, Fred Papert, and Kent Barwick, interviews by author.

. MAS Minutes, March 21, 1985; Kent Barwick and Fred Papert, interviews by author.

. MAS Minutes, March 21, 1985.

. Paul Goldberger, "Will Times Square Become a Grand Canyon?" *Times*, October 6, 1985. Clipping in MAS Archives.

. Maureen Dowd, "Tales and Legends of All-Night Clubs," *Times*, April 23, 1986, sec. 2, 1.

. Paul Goldberger, "A Darkened Canyon of Towering Offices," *Times*, April 23, 1986, sec. 2, 1.

. Hugh Hardy, interview by author; and MAS Minutes, May 30, 1985.

. Margot Wellington and Kent Barwick, interviews by author.

. Reprinted in Tony Hiss, *The Experience of Place* (New York: Knopf, 1990), 230–31.

. Kent Barwick, interview by author.

. Kent Barwick and Philip Howard, interviews by author.

. MAS Minutes, November 15, 1984; and "Protest Darkens Times Square," clipping in MAS Archives.

. Hugh Hardy, Kent Barwick, and a source who requested confidentiality, interviews by author.

. Hugh Hardy, interview by author; and zoning studies in Times Square file, MAS Archives.

. MAS Minutes, September 5, 1985.

. Anthony Wood, interview by author.

. MAS Minutes, October 17, 1985.

. MAS Minutes, January 23 and May 22, 1986; and letter, Times Square Advisory Committee to Herbert Sturz, June 20, 1986. MAS Archives.

. MAS Minutes, December 4, 1986.

. MAS Minutes, February 26, 1987.

. Hugh Hardy and Carole Rifkind, interviews by author.

. Quoted in Ada Louise Huxtable, "Re-inventing Times Square: 1990," in Taylor, ed., *Inventing Times Square*, 366.

. Hugh Hardy, interview by author.

. Huxtable, "Re-inventing Times Square: 1990," 369.

. Hugh Hardy and Carole Rifkind, interviews by author.

. Kent Barwick, interview by author.

CHAPTER 23

1. Henry Hope Reed, *The Golden City* (1959; reprint, New York: Norton, 1970), 108.
2. MAS Minutes, January 28–October 26, 1953.
3. MAS Minutes, November 23 and December 31, 1953, and March 22, 1954.
4. Quoted in Carter Wiseman, "Cashing In on the Coliseum," *New York*, July 29, 1985, p. 44.
5. Paul Byard, interview by author.
6. Philip Howard and Margot Wellington, interviews by author.
7. Philip Howard, interview by author.
8. Joan Davidson, Paul Byard, and Kent Barwick, interviews by author.
9. Paul Byard, interview by author.
0. Philip Howard, interview by author.
1. Wiseman, "Cashing In on the Coliseum."
2. MAS Minutes, May 7, 1987, and January 7, 1988.
3. "The Nay-Sayers Never Give Up," *New York Post*, June 7, 1988. Clipping in MAS Archives.

14. "Coliseum Site," *Amsterdam News*, July 9, 1988. Clipping in MAS Archives.

15. Paul Byard, Anthony Wood, and Philip Howard, interviews by author; and clippings in Coliseum file, MAS Archives.

16. Kent Barwick, interview by author.

17. Jack Newfield and Wayne Barrett, *City for Sale: Ed Koch and the Betrayal of New York* (New York: Harper & Row, 1988), 157; and Wayne Barrett, *Trump: The Deals and the Downfall* (New York: HarperCollins, 1992), 118–34, 139–77.

18. For a history of Trump's involvement in the Penn Yards site, see Barrett, *Trump*, 106–16, 391–404, and 462–63.

19. Philip Howard, interview by author.

20. Kent Barwick, interview by author.

21. Brendan Gill, interview by author.

22. Quoted in Newfield and Barrett, *City for Sale*, 83.

23. Quoted in Charles V. Bagli, "Case of Trump City Shows City Fiddled As Others Planned *New York Observer*, March 11, 1991, p. 1.

24. Kent Barwick, interview by author.

25. *New York Times:* "New York City Is Urged to Buy Big Trump Site," July 12, 1990; David W. Dunlap, "Civic Groups to Sue, Urging Alternative to West Side Highway Plan," December 11, 1990, sec. 2, p. 1.

26. Kent Barwick, interview by author.

27. Philip Howard, interview by author.

28. Brendan Gill, "The Sky Line: Hazards of Bigness," *New Yorker*, August 31, 1992, pp. 69–75.

29. Paul Byard, interview by author.

30. Gill, "Hazards of Bigness," 73.

ILLUSTRATION CREDITS

Justice, by Edward E. Simmons, Criminal Court: Photograph, before 1941. Exhibition File #1323, Archives of the Art Commission of the City of New York.

Richard Morris Hunt, 1900. Prints and Photographic Division Biographical File. Courtesy The Library of Congress.

Appelate Court House. Detroit Publishing Company Collection. Courtesy The Library of Congress. LC D4 16365.

The Hunt Memorial. Detroit Publishing Company Collection. Courtesy The Library of Congress. LC D4 33380, Negative Still #17283.

Bryant Park, statue of Dr. J. Marion Sims. Museum of the City of New York. Gift of Marion Sims Wyeth.

Criminal Courts Building, part of the reexamination of the building, unidentified photographer, n.d., negative number 69849. Collection of The New-York Historical Society.

The Plaza, undated. The Wurts Collection. Museum of the City of New York.

New York and the Nations. Municipal Archives, Department of Records and Information Services, City of New York.

Columbus Circle. Courtesy New York Bound Bookshop.

The Dewey Arch. Courtesy Con Edison Archives. Photo by H. N. Tiemann.

Map Showing the Proposed Area of Greater New York with Index to the Ward Maps, New York, W. & C. B. Colton & Co., 1896. Map Division, The New York Public Library. Astor, Lenox and Tilden Foundations.

Electrolier, 23rd Street and Fifth Avenue, Manhattan: Photographer of model, 1902. Exhibition File #51, Archives of the Art Commission of the City of New York.

Hall of Records, 1906. Courtesy The Library of Congress. Lot 12481.

"For Beauty and Utility in New York City," November 29, 1908. Courtesy of The New York Times Company. Reprinted by Permission.

Hall of Records, 1906. Lot 12481, Box 1 of 2. Courtesy The Library of Congress.

House and Garden, Vol. III, no. 6, June 1903, p. 301, "Improvements in City Plan" (MSA+). General Research Division, The New York Public Library. Astor, Lenox and Tilden Foundations.

MAS's 1905 scheme for new subway lines. Courtesy of the Municipal Society. Photograph: Steven Tucker.

The Report of the New York City Improvement Commission, 1907, plate XIV: "Connection Between Fifth Avenue and Blackwell's Island Bridge" (IRH). United States History, Local History & Genealogy Division, The New York Public Library. Astor, Lenox and Tilden Foundations.

MAS's 1905 scheme for new subway lines, Courtesy of the Municipal Society. Photograph: Steven Tucker.

The Report of the New York City Improvement Commission, 1907, plate II: "General Bird's Eye View Looking North" (IRH). United States History, Local History & Genealogy Division, The New York Public Library. Astor, Lenox and Tilden Foundations.

"Project for Brooklyn Bridge Terminal and Civic Center," *Architects and Builders*, Vol 4, August 1903. Avery Architectural and Fine Arts Library, Columbia University in the City of New York.

"Court of Honor," from the Charles Lamb Collection, Division of Drawings and Archives, Avery Architectural and Fine Arts Library, Columbia University in the City of New York.

"The New Fifth Avenue," June 27, 1909 (Front Page, Part Five Mag. Sect.). Courtesy of The New York Times Company. Reprinted by permission.

Bronx County Courthouse. © The Bronx County Historical Society.

Manhattan Bridge. Unidentified photographer, n.d., negative number 69847. Collection of The New-York Historical Society.

Flatiron Building. Photo by Fowler, 1903, negative number 43502. Collection of The New-York Historical Society.

Broadway, north on the east side from #104 adjoining Pine Street. Unidentified photographer, ca. 1888, negative number 69848. Collection of The New-York Historical Society.

View of Woolworth Building with lone man standing on catwalk. Photo by Cass Gilbert, n.d., negative number 53453. Collection of The New-York Historical Society.

Plan for setback skyscrapers. From the Charles Lamb Collection, Division of Drawings and Archives, Avery Architectural and Fine Arts Library, Columbia University in the City of New York.

"Saving the Sunshine." From the Charles Lamb Collection, Division of Drawings and Archives, Avery Architectural and Fine Arts Library, Columbia University in the City of New York.

"Planning Great Boulevards for New York City," August 9, 1908 (Front Page, Part Five Mag. Sect.). Courtesy of The New York Times Company. Reprinted by permission.

The Singer Building, 149 Broadway. Photo by George P. Hall, n.d., negative number 69043. Collection of The New-York Historical Society.

"King's Dream of New York," from *King's New York Views*, 1908–09, drawn by Harry M. Pettit, negative number 55742. Collection of The New-York Historical Society.

Equitable Building, 1929. Irving Underhill Collection. Courtesy The Library of Congress. Lot 124.

"Double-Decked Streets for Lower New York," August 6, 1911. Courtesy of The New York Times Company. Reprinted by permission.

"DeWitt Clinton High School Interior," photograph of DeWitt Clinton High School auditorium. Exhibition File #154, Archives of the Art Commission of the City of New York.

"View of piers 55–61 on West Street, N.Y.C.," unidentified photographer, ca. 1910, negative number 58798. Collection of The New-York Historical Society.

Bulletin of the Municipal Art Society, number 23, February 1923. Courtesy of the Municipal Art Society. Photograph: Steven Tucker.

"If Improvement Plans Had Gobbled Central Park," March 31, 1918. Courtesy of The New York Times Company. Reprinted by permission.

War Memorial by Thomas Hastings, Central Park: Photograph of rendering. Exhibition File #1244, Archives of the Art Commission of the City of New York.

"Park Row Looking North," ca. 1917. The Underhill Collection. Museum of the City of New York.

"Plan for Development of the Lower Reservoir Site." Reprinted with permission from Regional Plan Association and Avery Architectural and Fine Arts Library, Columbia University in the City of New York.

"Squatters' Shacks in Central Park," ca. 1930, photograph by Nat Norman. Museum of the City of New York.

Statue of Balto, Central Park: Photograph, ca. 1930. Photographic Collection of the Art Commission of the City of New York.

Scheme for the Christie-Forsyth Parkway. Reprinted with permission from Regional Plan Association and Avery Architectural and Fine Arts Library, Columbia University in the City of New York.

"West Side of Fifth Avenue, 52nd–53rd Streets," (Vanderbilt Houses). Museum of the City of New York. The Byron Collection.

"St. John's Park (Hudson Square)," unidentified photographer, ca. 1866–67, negative number 4578. Collection of The New-York Historical Society.

Jefferson Market Courthouse. Courtesy of the Municipal Art Society.

Colonnade Row. Courtesy of Constance M. Jacobs.

Brooklyn Battery Bridge Rendering G29A. Courtesy Triborough Bridge and Tunnel Authority Special Archive.

Washington Square North. Courtesy New York City Municipal Archives. Seagram Building. Ezra Stoller © Esto.

2 Fifth Avenue. Courtesy Emery Roth & Sons.

Pennsylvania Station waiting room. Photograph by A. F. Sozio, courtesy of The Pennsylvania Railroad Company.

"Pennsylvania Station," ca. 1900 (nearing completion). Museum of the City of New York.

AGBANY protest. Photo by Peter Samton.

Pennsylvania Station column hoisted. Courtesy of the New York City Landmarks Preservation Commission. Photograph by John Barrington Bayley.

Pennsylvania Station rubble in the Hackensack Meadow. Edward Hausner/New York Times Pictures.

The Public Theater exterior. Courtesy of the Municipal Art Society.

Brokaw Mansion, The Underhill Collection, Museum of the City of New York.

Newman Auditorium, The Public Theater. Photograph by George Cserna, courtesy Giorgio Cavalieri.

Kent Barwick at landmarks rally. Courtesy of the Municipal Art Society. Photograph: Steven Tucker.

Mayor Robert F. Wagner signing the Landmarks Law of 1965. Courtesy of Margot Gayle.

Haughwout Building. Historic American Buildings Survey, detail of Broome Street facade. Cervin Robinson, MAS Collection. Courtesy The Library of Congress.

Grand Central Terminal. Courtesy of the Municipal Art Society. Photograph: Steven Tucker.

Exterior of Grand Central Terminal, 1976. © Thorney Lieberman.

Breuer scheme for Grand Central. Courtesy of the Municipal Art Society.

Grand Central Terminal concourse. NYC Municipal Archives.

Villard houses courtyard. Photograph © Steven Zane.

Urban Center entrance. Stephen L. Senigo/Architectural Photography.

"St. Bartholomew's Scrapbook," two collages. © Tim Prentice. Courtesy Tim Prentice. Photographs: Steven Tucker.

Candlelight vigil at St. Bartholomew's. Courtesy of the Municipal Art Society.

The old Times Tower. Courtesy of the Municipal Art Society.

Times Square at night. Courtesy of the Municipal Art Society.

Times Square Construction. © David W. Dunlap. All Rights Reserved.

Times Square celebration. © 1994 Andrew Garn.

Coliseum Center, Edward Safdie design. Courtesy of the Municipal Art Society.

Coliseum Center, David Childs designs. Courtesy Skidmore, Owings & Merrill.

Central Park photomontage. Courtesy of the Municipal Art Society.

Upper West Side view. © Jeff Perkell. Courtesy of Jeff Perkell.

"Introducing the Midstreet," © 1994 by Roz Chast, reprinted with the permission of Wylie, Aitken & Stone, Inc.

Model of Television City. Courtesy of Westpride.

Model (May 1992) of Riverside South final project. Design: SOM/Willen. Photograph © Wolfgang Hoyt.

Drawing of Riverside South. Design Paul Willen F.A.I.A. Rendering © Paul Willen/Steve Evanusa.

INDEX